AF817317

Toward Effective Counseling and Psychotherapy

Toward Effective Counseling and Psychotherapy

Training and Practice

Charles B. Truax &
Robert Carkhuff

Routledge
Taylor & Francis Group
LONDON AND NEW YORK

First published 1976 by Transaction Publishers

Published 2017 by Routledge
2 Park Square, Milton Park, Abingdon, Oxon OX14 4RN
711 Third Avenue, New York, NY 10017, USA

First issued in hardback 2017

Routledge is an imprint of the Taylor & Francis Group, an informa business

Copyright © 1976 by Taylor & Francis

All rights reserved. No part of this book may be reprinted or reproduced or utilised in any form or by any electronic, mechanical, or other means, now known or hereafter invented, including photocopying and recording, or in any information storage or retrieval system, without permission in writing from the publishers.

Notice:
Product or corporate names may be trademarks or registered trademarks, and are used only for identification and explanation without intent to infringe.

Library of Congress Catalog Number: 2007026388

Library of Congress Cataloging-in-Publication Data

Truax, Charles B.
Toward effective counseling and psychotherapy : training and practice / Charles B. Truax and Robert Carkhuff.
p. ; cm.
Originally published: Chicago: Aldine, 1967.
Includes bibliographical references and index.
ISBN 978-0-202-30988-0 (alk. paper)
1. Psychotherapy. 2. Counseling. I. Carkhuff, Robert R. II. Title.
[DNLM: 1. Counseling. 2. Psychotherapy. WM 420 T865td 1967a]

RC480.T7 2008
616.89'14--dc22

2007026388

ISBN 13: 978-1-138-53978-5 (hbk)
ISBN 13: 978-0-202-30988-0 (pbk)

To our wives
Janie and Bernice,
who have given us understanding
and genuine warmth.

CONTENTS

FOREWORD

THE field of counseling and psychotherapy has for years presented the puzzling spectacle of unabating enthusiasm for forms of treatment whose effectiveness could not be objectively demonstrated. With few exceptions, statistical studies have consistently failed to show that any form of psychotherapy is followed by significantly more improvement than would be caused by the mere passage of an equivalent period of time. Despite this, practitioners of various psychotherapeutic schools have remained firmly convinced that their methods are effective. The growing demand for psychotherapy is evidence that many recipients of these forms of treatment also believe that they are being helped.

The series of investigations reported in this impressive book have succeeded in resolving this paradoxical state of affairs, and the consequences may be far-reaching. The investigators have overcome two major obstacles to progress in the past—lack of agreement on measures of improvement, and difficulty of measuring active ingredients of the psychotherapy relationship. The inability of therapists of different theoretical persuasions to agree on criteria of improvement has made comparison of the results of different forms of treatment nearly impossible. The authors have cut this Gordian knot by using a wide range of improvement measures and showing that, regardless of measures used in different studies, a significantly higher proportion of results favor their hypothesis than contravene it.

It has long been recognized that the beneficial effects of any human interchange are enhanced by such qualities as accurate and sensitive awareness of the other person's feelings, deep concern for his welfare without attempts to dominate him, and openness about one's own reactions to him. Because these attributes are in part inherent in the participants and in part emergent from their interaction, they have proved difficult to objectify. The central methodological achievement of the studies reported here is the development of reliable scales, rated from short excerpts of tape recordings of interviews, for measuring three important aspects of the psychotherapeutic relationship: accurate empathy, nonpossessive warmth, and therapist's self-congruence.

Results of research based on these methodological advances convincingly demonstrate, at long last, that psychotherapy really does work. Studies of many different types of help-seekers, including college underachievers, delinquent girls, and hospitalized schizophrenics, show that all respond favorably to therapeutic encounters in which the qualities mentioned above are strongly present and, more significantly, that they react unfavorably to the absence of these qualities. The latter finding is particularly important since it clarifies why research findings have previously failed to confirm clinical enthusiasm. By re-analyzing the data from other studies of psychotherapy in the light of their own findings, the authors have shown that the reason that average improvement rates of treated populations did not differ from those of untreated control groups was often that the number of patients who became worse counterbalanced those who had improved.

It has been customary to report results of psychotherapy in terms of whether patients were improved or unimproved, implying that they could not possibly have been harmed by the treatment. In retrospect, this assumption that psychotherapy could make people better but could not hurt them is a strange one. Any other remedy that is powerful enough to do good, from aspirin to pencillin, will do harm if misused. The fact that a relationship offered by a therapist to a patient can be harmful is disquieting. It raises the uncomfortable question of how much harm "noxious" psychotherapy may have done in the past.

Fortunately, the authors are able to show that the helpful or harmful aspects of therapeutic encounters depend primarily on the therapists, not the patients, and that the former can be quickly trained to offer a higher level of the beneficial qualities than they initially displayed. The authors describe a brief training program for this purpose which is as suitable for nonprofessionals as for trainees in psychology, psychiatric social work, or psychiatry. This greatly increases the prospects for coping with one of the major problems confronting psychotherapy in America today—how to train therapists in sufficient numbers to meet the ever-growing demand.

In view of the magnitude of their achievements, the authors may be pardoned for choosing to focus almost exclusively on the psychotherapeutic relationship. Since the training program will probably be widely emulated, however, it should be pointed out that it apparently pays inadequate attention to such matters as diagnosis, collaboration with community agencies, and the use of psychopharmacological agents. Psychoactive drugs are dismissed with the comment that they are useful when psychotherapy is contraindicated or to facilitate psychotherapy in grossly disturbed patients. This is too restrictive a view of their value. They can aid psychotherapy with a wide range of patients, and nonmedical psychotherapists should know enough about their modes of action to obtain prescriptions from a physician when indicated.

The value of this book is enhanced by its abundant documentation. The findings are placed in the perspective of a comprehensive and detailed critical review of the literature; scales are amply illustrated by brief segments of tape recordings of interviews; and research results are presented fully. Possible implications of the various findings are explored, and abundant suggestions for future research, practice and training are offered.

The authors have, moreover, succeeded remarkably well in tempering their justified enthusiasm with scientific objectivity. They recognize, for example, that the therapeutic conditions they have identified account for only part of a therapist's effectiveness, and give due attention to possible alternative explanations for their findings.

All in all, this book represents a major advance—one that deserves the overworked term "breakthrough." The research findings resolve some of the most stubborn research problems in psychotherapy, and the training program based on them points the way toward overcoming the shortage of psychotherapists. The impact of these achievements may well be revolutionary.

JEROME D. FRANK, M.D.

PREFACE

THIS book is intended to discuss an approach to counseling and psychotherapy—its training and practice—that is based on the growing body of research evidence specifying some known effective ingredients in the therapeutic process. In its attempt to focus on what has been verified by research evidence, this book is incomplete, just as our scientific knowledge of effective therapeutic encounters is incomplete. Our knowledge and evaluation of the evidence must inevitably suffer from errors of omission and commission that grow out of our current understanding—and lack of understanding—of the phenomena of counseling and psychotherapy. As our own understanding grows we will wish to change this book and to improve upon it. Our current biases are reflected throughout the book in both what is said and what is not said.

Used as a textbook for introductory courses preparing students for the professional practice of counseling or psychotherapy, or for courses designed to acquaint other persons (such as nurses, clergymen, educators, etc.) with the fundamentals of effective therapeutic encounters, the book must be supplemented with readings from other sources. In our own attempts to train beginning psychotherapists and counselors, extensive reading lists of other books and articles have been an integral part of the trainees' learning experience. This emphasis on the necessity for reading widely about divergent theories and practices is based on the assumption, as Donald Hebb (1959) states it, that:

> . . . theory is not an affirmation but a method of analysis and can't produce any belief. Knowledge progresses by stages, so the theory one holds today must be provisional, as much a formulation of one's ignorance as anything else, to be used as long as it is useful and then discarded. Its function is to organize the available evidence and guide the search for better evidence. It is really only a working assumption which the user may actively disbelieve. (p. 270)

Although this book relies heavily on research knowledge, even this knowledge is subject to change, as the early scientist Karl Pearson (1898) noted so well:

> No scientific investigation is final; it merely represents the most probable conclusion which can be drawn from the data at the disposal of the writer. A wider range of facts, or more refined analysis, experiment, and observation will lead to new formulae and new theories. This is the essence of scientific progress.

It is our hope that what is offered here for the reader does indeed represent the most probable conclusions that can be drawn from the wide range of evidence currently available dealing with effective therapeutic encounters.

The Arkansas Rehabilitation Research and Training Center faculty and staff have focused their efforts on producing new knowledge of ingredients of effective counseling and psychotherapy that translate into client or patient benefit. The training programs of the Center are aimed at transforming research knowledge into effective practice. As a part of this effort, training films and tapes illustrating the present approach to training are available for professional use. The Center also invites other persons or organizations with similar research or training goals to collaborate in joint research and training programs. Tentative reports of current research and theory are available from the Center in its *Discussion Papers* publication.

The ideas presented here are not at all original: they have their roots in the antiquity of man. Both the direction and impetus for our current view of counseling and psychotherapy have been greatly influenced by the thinking and example of Carl Rogers and the other leaders of the client-centered viewpoint. At the same time we have also been greatly influenced by such psychoanalytic writers as Frieda Fromm-Reichmann, Harry Stack Sullivan, Franz Alexander, and Rollo May; more learning-oriented writers including Albert Bandura, Joseph Wolpe, Hans Eysenck, B. F. Skinner, and Clark Hull; and the more eclectic writings of Edward Bordin, Frank Robinson, Norman Cameron, Frederick Thorne, and Jerome Frank. Most of all we are indebted to our clients, patients, and students, who have provided us with our most meaningful learning experiences.

For the support of much of our research efforts we are indebted to the Vocational Rehabilitation Administration and to a lesser extent by grants from the National Institute of Mental Health, both part of the United States Department of Health, Education, and Welfare.

In the preparation of this book we owe special thanks to Joseph D. Matarazzo, Phillip Trapp, David Aspy, Bernard Berenson, John Douds, Gerald Fisher, G. Robert Leslie, and Fay Smith for their helpful comments. In the initial development of the research and the present approach to training we are especially thankful for the support and help of Milton Miller, Frank A. Pattie, Carl Tatum, Donald G. Wargo, Robert DeBurger, Leon Silber, John Corcella, Logan Gragg, and Frank Kodman. A special debt is owed to Edward P. Williams for his contributions to the research and for the preparation and checking of the tables and data.

Finally, we are grateful to Fran Pape, Janet Ramsey, Ladonna Spann, Bonnie Edington, Sally Jackinowski, and Leta Duckworth for devoted clerical assistance.

CHARLES B. TRUAX
ROBERT R. CARKHUFF

TOWARD EFFECTIVE COUNSELING AND PSYCHOTHERAPY

SECTION I THEORETIC AND RESEARCH BASES FOR TRAINING AND PRACTICE IN PSYCHOTHERAPY AND COUNSELING

IN this first section we have tried to review the body of research evidence and theoretical convergence that forms the foundation for the current approach to training and practice. The focus is on the question: "What are the effective ingredients of successful therapeutic efforts?"

Chapter 1 sets the stage for the remainder of the book by asking the basic question "Are counseling and psychotherapy indeed effective ways of helping the client or patient toward constructive personality and behavioral change?" After evaluating the current available research evidence pro and con, the chapter comes to four conclusions: (1) the therapeutic endeavor is, on the average, ineffective; (2) *therapy itself is a non-unitary phenomenon;* (3) some counselors and therapists are significantly helpful while others are significantly harmful, with a resulting *average* helpfulness not demonstrably better than the effect of having no professional treatment; and (4) through research it is possible to identify the major ingredients of helpful and harmful therapy, and thus markedly increase the average effectiveness of counseling and psychotherapy.

Chapter 2 attempts to identify the elements of effective therapeutic encounters as specified by widely divergent theorists. The search is for *common elements* cutting across divergent theories (which, in their own expositions, focus heavily on their major differences.) The chapter also focuses on what these theories, whether psychoanalytic, client-centered, behavioristic, or eclectic, have to say about the person and the characteristics of an effective therapist.

Although most theorists concern themselves in their writings with discussing the client, three characteristics of an effective counselor emerge from the divergent viewpoints:

(1) An effective therapist is integrated, nondefensive, and authentic or *genuine* in his therapeutic encounters.

(2) An effective therapist can provide a non-threatening, safe, trusting or secure atmosphere by his acceptance, unconditional positive regard, love, or *nonpossessive warmth* for the client.

(3) An effective therapist is able to "be with," "grasp the meaning of," or *accurately and emphathically* understand the client on a moment-by-moment basis.

The theoretical convergence of widely divergent theorists is illustrated by direct quotations from their writings. From their own statements and in their own language it can be seen that the major representatives of existing "schools" of psychotherapy and counseling recognize the central therapeutic importance of these three basic ingredients; each adds his own emphasis to the developing clinical and theoretical meanings of the concepts of *accurate empathy, nonpossessive warmth,* and *genuineness.* Finally, the chapter includes research scales that have attempted to capture and quantify the essential meaning of these three concepts. The scales are presented both because of their potential value in specifying the concepts more concretely and because most of the research findings in the succeeding chapter were based upon them, and they are central to the present approach to training discussed in Section II.

Chapter 3 reviews the mounting research evidence that confirmed the importance of these three central therapeutic ingredients. The research reviewed also tends to confirm the conclusions reached in Chapter 1: that counseling and psychotherapy as currently practiced are both for better and for worse, but on the average are ineffective. The findings go further (and confirm the conclusions of Chapters 1 and 2) by indicating that counselors and therapists who offer high levels of empathy, warmth and genuineness produce positive changes in their clients, while therapists who offer low lovels of these "therapeutic conditions" produce deterioration or no change in their clients.

Chapter 4 discusses the implications of recent research conducted by learning-oriented experimentalists and therapists. Although the evidence reviewed suggests that "behavior therapy" is not demonstrably more therapeutically effective than any other approach, this chapter suggests that many of its specific basic principles, if carried out within the context of high levels of the central therapeutic ingredients discussed in Chapters 2 and 3, can markedly enhance the effectiveness of traditional or interpersonal approaches to counseling or therapy. The viewpoint that a behavioristic approach (except for the language) need not be antagonistic, and may even be complementary, to a more humanistic approach is presented with evidence suggesting its applicability to psychotherapy in general and client-centered counseling in particular.

Chapter 5 views the person who comes for psychotherapeutic help. Research evidence concerning characteristics of successful and unsuccessful clients or patients is reviewed. The conclusions drawn are that, although some of the evidence is conflicting, the client most likely to benefit is the one who (1) has a high degree of inner or "felt" disturbance but a low degree of behavioral or "overt" disturbance; (2) has a high degree of readiness, positive expectancy, or hope for personal improvement; and (3) engages in deep and extensive self-exploration.

Since the available research evidence and major theoretical views discussed converge in indicating that the client's level of self-exploration is due in part to the influence of the therapist and can therefore be changed, *depth of self-exploration* is viewed as a fourth major ingredient of effective therapeutic encounters.

The Depth of Self-Exploration Scale, on which much of the research has been based, is presented. This scale, along with scales for accurate empathy, nonpossessive warmth and genuineness presented in Chapter 2, is an integral part of the present approach to training discussed in Section II. It provides a crude but convenient moment-by-moment method of evaluating the client's response to therapy and the therapist's or trainee's skill in engaging the client in the therapeutic process.

Chapter 6 reviews existing approaches and viewpoints in the training of counselors and therapists and thus sets the stage for the succeeding chapters on training. The heavy emphasis in existing viewpoints toward either a didactic or an experiential approach is discussed in the context of the goal of training—producing a technician skilled in the use of techniques but, above all, an open and flexible person who has self-awareness and yet is sensitively attuned to the client both in receiving and communicating vital personal messages.

CHAPTER 1 COUNSELING AND PSYCHOTHERAPY: DIFFERENTIAL ANTECEDENTS WITH DIFFERENTIAL CONSEQUENCES?

AN INTRODUCTORY NOTE

LIKE any presentation of existing literature, the present book is to some degree selective and biased in content and viewpoint, since it has grown out of the human, and therefore selective, readings of literally thousands of articles and countless books and chapters. In attempting to cite the relevant evidence for a particular conclusion, rarely does space allow for more than the briefest description of the evidence. This seems to be one unfortunate but necessary part of writing a book, and in many ways is grossly unfair, since some of the evidence cited in a sentence or paragraph has been presented by the original authors in a book which is itself a condensation of years of thought and research involving dozens of people. Then, too, a small study of 14 or 29 clients may be given more space here than a better study involving hundreds of patients because it is better known, because it seems to require more comment, or because the findings are simply more complex. Finally, the reader should bear in mind that no single presentation can hope to include all of the available evidence; this is an aim but not an actuality. In the course of preparing this book we, like all authors, have had the experience of finding studies that were important or even central to an issue during a chance rereading of old and new journals or books—after we had finished that portion of the writing. Books, unlike research and practice, are not continuing evolving and changing processes—and to that extent they fail to reflect reality.

Although we have endeavored to be "objective," in a very real sense this ideal cannot be met in practice: we are left with the simple fact that what follows throughout both this chapter and this book reflect the evidence and the most probable conclusions *as we see them.*

TOWARD EVALUATING THE OVERALL EFFECTS OF COUNSELING AND PSYCHOTHERAPY

Counseling or psychotherapy is aimed at producing constructive behavioral and personality change. Its rapid growth over recent decades implies that the procedures involved are indeed highly effective; certainly the client, or patient, as well as the professional counselor or psychotherapist, seems convinced of its value. It has become a principal part of clinical psychology, psychiatry, social work, school counseling, marriage counseling, rehabilitation counseling, and vocational counseling; and is a principal activity of parole officers, group workers, recreation and playground counselors, anti-poverty workers, welfare workers, clergymen, educators, family physicians, and nurses.

This book, which focuses on training and practice, obviously implies that at least some kinds of counseling and psychotherapy are of significant value, and that some significant aspects of the process are now known and can be learned.

However, a considerable amount of evidence also seems to suggest that counseling or psychotherapy is not superior to "no treatment." Eysenck (1960) went so far as to suggest that it could be described like the "wondrous cure" developed by Galen, the father of modern medicine. Galen promoted *his* remedy as follows: "All who drink this remedy recover in a short time, except for those whom it does not help, who all die and have no relief from any other medicine. Therefore, it is obvious that it fails only in incurable cases."

This assertion that psychotherapeutic approaches were ineffective in helping either the disturbed child or the neurotic or disabled adult raised a considerable controversy (Eysenck, 1952, 1955, 1961; DeSharmes, Levy, and Wertheimer, 1954; Luborsky, 1954; Meehl, 1955; Rosenzweig, 1954; Sanford; 1954; Shoben, 1956; Strupp, 1963; Teuber and Powers, 1953).

However, after a careful review of the relevant research literature, it now appears that Eysenck was essentially correct in saying that *average* counseling and psychotherapy as it is currently practiced does not result in average client improvement greater than that observed in clients who receive no special counseling or psychotherapeutic treatment. (This is in spite of Eysenck's inclusion of questionable data and indiscriminate pooling of data from reports with divergent criteria for treatment and outcome.) Frank (1961) and others have noted that statistical studies consistently report that about two-thirds of neurotic patients improve immediately after treatment regardless of the type of psychotherapy received, but that the same improvement rate has been found for comparable clients who have not received psychotherapy. However, some other relatively well-controlled studies show that certain counselors or therapists do produce beneficial effects beyond that observed in equivalent control groups.

Putting together these two bodies of evidence, it logically follows that if psychotherapy has no overall average effect, but that there are valid specific instances where it is indeed effective, then there must also be specific instances in which it is harmful. That is, to achieve this average, if some clients have been helped, then other clients must have been harmed. This suggestion *that psychotherapy and counseling can be for better or for worse* is the major starting point for the present approach to practice and training. Much of the recent research evidence supporting the "for better or for worse" hypothesis will be reviewed in Chapter 3, in the context of specific aspects of the therapeutic relationships that lead to constructive or deteriorative personality and behavioral changes in the client. This chapter, though, will attempt to review the literature suggesting that, as currently practiced, *average counseling and psychotherapy is ineffective,* but *some is indeed effective.* This implies that differences in effectiveness *between* therapists are much larger than differences between therapy or counseling and no treatment.

EVIDENCE FOR AVERAGE INEFFECTIVENESS OF COUNSELING AND PSYCHOTHERAPY

The single largest controlled study of the effects of counseling, guidance, or psychotherapy was one of more than 600 delinquency-prone boys, reported by Teuber and Powers (1953). The initial 650 boys were individually matched in pairs on such variables as age, intelligence, school grades, delinquency ratings and socioeconomic background. One member of the pair was assigned randomly to the treatment group, the other to the control group. Although there was some turnover in counselors and therapists during the eight years of treatment, much of the treatment was supportive therapy in which the individual counselor attempted to develop a friendly and supportive relationship with the boys. Both psychoanalytically oriented and client-centered counselors participated in the treatment program. As expected, the treatment group looked quite successful, but analysis of the data also indicated that the control group showed equivalent positive changes. In fact, the evidence suggested a slight difference in outcome favoring the control group. This negative finding occurred despite the facts that a majority of the boys in the treatment group personally reported their belief in the value of the counseling, guidance, and psychotherapy, and that the counselors themselves considered their therapeutic relationships highly effective.

A second major report attempted to analyze statistically the results of treatment of war neuroses that occurred during World War II. That study by Brill and Beebe (1955) made highly sophisicated comparisons between large numbers of neurotic soldiers receiving individual therapy and similar large groups of neurotic soldiers receiving routine hospital care, rest and sedation, or no treatment. Their findings in general indicated that the percentage of patients who improved was slightly higher for the nontreated group. The only positive findings related to improvement were sociological factors: the unskilled and poorly educated soldier was less likely to improve and more likely to become worse. It should also be noted that there was an overall tendency for both control and treated patients to show improvement over time. With most measures of outcome utilized by Brill and Beebe, the patients receiving only rest and sedation appeared to show slightly greater improvement than those receiving either individual therapy or no treatment.

A third major study of psychotherapy was reported by Barron and Leary (1955). Of 150 neurotic patients who had applied and been accepted for treatment in a psychiatric clinic, 23 were placed on a waiting list and thus served as a control during a six-month period of observation. Eighty-five were assigned to group therapy and 42 were assigned to individual therapy. All patients in treatment received a minimum of three months of therapy; they all were tested on the MMPI (Minnesota Multiphasic Personality Inventory) initially and after treatment. The Barron and Leary study is of particular importance since it is one of the few studies utilizing fully qualified therapists: the psychiatrists, psychologists, and social workers had at least three years of postdoctoral or postgraduate training and experience. The therapy could be described as being dynamically oriented and neopsychoanalytic.

Comparisons between the experimental and control groups at the outset indicated close comparability in diagnosis, prognosis, severity of initial illness, and such demographic characteristics as age, sex, and educational level. The interval between initial and terminal outcome measures slightly favored the treatment groups, since the control group was posttested at seven months, while the individual and group therapy patients were tested after slightly more than eight months. As expected, there was a reduction in major pathology in both of the treatment groups, particularly on the neurotic scales of the MMPI. However, patients in the control group who had received no treatment showed similar reductions in neurotic pathology. The overall findings indicated no significant [1] differences on any of the measures between the control group, the group psychotherapy group, or the individual psychotherapy group.

A much smaller study of 29 patients receiving client-centered counseling at the University of Chicago was reported in a book edited by Rogers and Dymond (1954). Although they lacked an adequate control group (they used a group of normals as a so-called "control" group), they did provide a contrast group by having half of their original 29 patients defer treatment for two months. Unfortunately, the time interval of the waiting period was not equal to the treatment period, and so there was not equal opportunity for spontaneous improvement. Thus the control group did not control for improvement over time. Further, some clients who were to serve in the group with the two-month waiting period were felt to be in immediate need of therapy and so were given counseling. Since this was decided on the basis of their "apparent need" rather than on a random basis, the adequacy of this control group is open to further serious question.

1. Throughout this book, "significant" is used to mean that there is statistical reason to believe that differences are large enough so that there are less than 5 chances out of 100 that "chance alone" could explain the differences ($p < .05$).

Rogers and Dymond's data indicated that the primary changes occurring during client-centered psychotherapy consisted of changes in self concept rather than change in behavior. Thus, observations and reports by friends of the clients in treatment indicated no significant difference between behavior before and after therapy for the treatment group as a whole. Some patients in the study decided, after waiting for psychotherapy, that they no longer felt in need of treatment. In one analysis of data on self concepts, Dymond compared them with successful psychotherapy patients. The changes in self concept of these "spontaneous remitters" were equivalent in degree to those of the successful psychotherapy patients.

The Cartwright and Vogel (1960) study at the Chicago Counseling Center perhaps throws light on the report by Rogers and Dymond. There, essentially similar client-centered therapy was used on a different population with a more adequate control group. In that study, the findings indicated no overall greater improvement in the therapy group than in the control group.

Again, in a study of 100 junior high school students assigned to counseling and control conditions, Mink and Isaacson (1959) reported no overall differences in outcome between the counseled and control clients.

In a study comparing symptom reduction in psychoneurotic patients, Gliedman, Nash, Imber, Stone, and Frank (1958) compared the effectiveness of short-term psychotherapy with the administration of a placebo. Their findings indicated that symptom reduction occurred to a significant degree in both groups, but the administration of a simple placebo was as effective as short-term psychotherapy. Thus, again, with carefully controlled evaluation of outcome, psychotherapy proved ineffective.

A similar failure to obtain extra-treatment effects of counseling was reported by Broedel, Ohlsen, Proff and Southard (1960) in a study of group counseling with gifted underachieving adolescents.

A study by James (1962) focused upon the effects of counseling on superior college students. In terms of grade-point averages, those who received counseling were not significantly different from those who received none. Another study that dealt with brief counseling (Searles, 1962) also attempted to assess its effects on the performance of superior college students. The students were selected on the basis of high grades in high school and placement in the upper third on college entrance examinations. The 62 selected students were assigned randomly to either counseling or control conditions. No significant differences occurred between the counseled and control groups in terms of grade-point average, grades received in two courses taken by all freshman students, or number of students placed on academic probation.

In an attempt to evaluate the effects of counseling on poorer students, Richardson (1960) compared counseled and noncounseled students in the lower one-third of their classes. Again, the findings indicated that the counseled students were no better academically than noncounseled students.

Similarly, Goodstein and Crites (1961) studied the effects of counseling on academic achievement of poorer college students. They selected 82 subjects who were from the lower 30 per cent of all students taking the Iowa College Scholarship Placement Test. These 82 students were notified that they would not be admitted to college unless they completed at least six semester hours of college work during the summer session. Of these 82, 33 actually started and completed a summer session. They were divided into three groups: one group received counseling, a second group was contacted but did not apply for couseling, and a third group was not contacted and so served as the base control group. The findings of Goodstein and Crites offered no support for the belief that vocational-educational counseling was effective in improving academic achievement. On the contrary, they indicated a significant difference in academic achievement favoring the control group.

Psychotherapy as a treatment for alcoholism also appears to be quite ineffective. Thus, Gerard, Saenger, and Wile (1962) studied the long-term effectiveness of clinical services for alcoholic patients. The authors chose a random sample of 400 patients from state-supported alcoholism clinics. The patients were randomly interviewed at either two, five, or eight years following intake. Of the 299 patients reached in the follow-up, only 18 per cent remained abstinent for at least one year during this follow-up period. Of the others, 41 per cent were unchanged, while 10 per cent had deteriorated to the point where they were institutionalized, and an additional 17 per cent were dead. Quite significantly, among the 18 per cent who actually remained abstinent for at least a year, more than half continued to manifest gross overt symptoms of psychologic impairment. Of this same 18 per cent, only 10 per cent sustained their improvement independently, while the rest relied on Alcoholics Anonymous, etc. Quite surprisingly, the drinker who finally abstains rarely quits drinking during psychotherapy. The most common reasons given for abstinence were fear of death or severe liver damage or arrest. Those few who were relatively sustained in their abstinence most commonly gave as their reason, "people like me better sober."

In a relatively well-designed study of the effectiveness of group therapy as opposed to drama group-activity, Anker and Walsh (1961) studied improvement with groups of hospitalized patients. The findings clearly indicated consistently greater improvement for the control group engaged in a drama-activity than for those in group psychotherapy.

Studies by Frank, Gliedman, Imber, Stone and Nash (1959) of 54 neurotic patients bear directly on the question of the effects of psychotherapy. They randomly assigned patients to group or individual therapy on a once-a-week basis, or to individual therapy on a once-every-two-weeks basis. The effects of differences between therapists were controlled by having three psychiatrists conduct all three types of treatment, with six patients in each type of treatment with each psychiatrist. Sixty-eight per cent of these patients remained in therapy for at least six months. A comparison was then made with an additional 23 patients who had dropped out of therapy before the fourth interview. In that comparison, 70 per cent of the patients who had received treatment for six months and 74 per cent of the dropouts showed a decrease in symptoms—improvement actually favored the dropouts. Further, on the discomfort scale measure, there were no differences between minimal-contact therapy and regular group or individual treatment.

The only positive finding for psychotherapy was obtained with the measure of "change in rated social ineffectiveness": of those for whom measures were available over a five-year period, the 11 patients who received minimal treatment showed less change than either the 11 patients in individual therapy or the 8 patients in group therapy. Unfortunately, the three groups had also differed significantly prior to treatment, raising a question about the meaning of the positive findings in degree of change. That the reduction in symptoms was not due to psychotherapy is indicated by a further study in which Frank and his associates located 12 patients from the original research some two to three years later. These patients' symptoms had reappeared and they again wished help. Instead of psychotherapy, however, they were given placebos (an inert medication) for a two-week period. Analysis showed a significant decrease in symptoms which was as great as that which had followed six months of psychotherapy when they had been treated earlier.

In still another, but less well-controlled study, Walker and Kelley (1960) studied the effects of short-term psychotherapy with hospitalized schizophrenic patients. One group of newly admitted patients was given psychotherapy while another group was not. Again, no differences in improvement between the two groups were reported.

In a controlled study of children treated in a child guidance clinic, Levitt, Beiser, and Robertson (1959) found no significant differences on follow-up between treated children and defaulters from treatment. In fact, the defaulters had made slightly better adjustment than the treated children.

Barendregt (1961) compared outcome in sizable groups of neurotic patients receiving traditional psychotherapy, psychoanalysis, and no treatment. The findings were mixed and inconclusive, with no strong evidence favoring any of the three groups.

A smaller study aimed at determining the effects of psychotherapy or counseling with 16 matched pairs of hospitalized schizophrenics was reported by Rogers (1962), Truax (1963), and Truax and Carkhuff (1965). Sixteen patients received individual psychotherapy lasting from six months to four and one-half years; they were compared on a variety of measures to 16 control patients receiving only routine hospital treatment. The overall results indicated that the therapy and control patients were essentially equal in outcome. The reports by Truax (1963) and Truax and Carkhuff (1963), found no differences in outcome and reported that, in the measure of hospitalization during the three and one-half year period of study, the control population and the therapy population spent approximately equivalent periods of time out of the hospital, with a slight difference in favor of the control patients. Further, there were no differential advantages for either therapy or control patients on outcome assessments made by experienced diagnosticians using pre- and post-therapy data obtained from the MMPI, ward behavior ratings, the Rorschach, self-concept measures, or measures of anxiety.

(A report of reruns of studies on those 16 patients by Kiesler, Mathieu and Klein is in preparation [Rogers, Gendlin, Kiesler and Truax, 1966]. It appears that these findings may differ to a major or minor degree from the original studies. However, since this report is not yet in final form it cannot be critically commented upon. Should it report differences in, say, hospitalization rates favoring the treated patients, our present statements of the findings would not be altered, since therapy was discontinued on most patients in 1962 and on all patients in 1963. Any such differences, moreover, can be corrected by checking the Mendota State Hospital records of hospitalization dates for the patients involved. Since the 14 to 16 therapy patients involved do not weigh heavily in the total evidence, we have decided to mention this possibly controversial piece of evidence here.)

May and Tuma (1964) studied 80 hospitalized patients in a carefully designed study involving random assignments of patients to a control group, a psychotherapy group, a chemotherapy group, and a psychotherapy-plus-chemotherapy group. Their findings indicated no significant superiority of psychotherapy over the control group, but instead found chemotherapy to be, in general, more effective than psychotherapy.

Poser (1966) studied therapeutic outcome in 343 hospitalized male schizophrenics by comparing the effects of experienced psychiatrists and psychiatric social workers to a control group who were seen by totally untrained college students and a control group receiving no new attention. The findings favored significantly better outcomes for the control group treated by untrained college students.

Another line of evidence suggesting the ineffectiveness of counseling and psychotherapy was reviewed by Eysenck (1960) and by Levitt (1957) who summarized reported improvement rates in patients receiving psychotherapy and counseling. Eysenck's table combines the reports on 19 evaluations covering more than 7,000 cases treated by eclectic or psychoanalytic approaches to psychotherapy. His tables indicate that 64 per cent of the 7,293 patients seen in treatment showed improvement. As Eysenck points out, this 64 per cent improvement rate tends to be somewhat poorer than the estimates of spontaneous recovery rates in nontreated neurotics—an average improvement of 66 to 72 per cent. The percentage improvement rate for counseling and psychotherapy with children as reported by Levitt indicated that psychotherapy resulted in a 67 per cent improvement rate at termination of therapy in 3,399 reported cases, and in 78 per cent improvement at a five-year follow-up on 4,219 cases. Since the five-year follow-up for spontaneous recovery rates suggests that at least 80 per cent show remissions of symptoms, these data also suggest an *average ineffectiveness* of counseling and psychotherapy.

Further review of more recently published reports dealing with percentage improvement of patients in counseling or psychotherapy would in no way tend to contradict this implication about the average effects of psychotherapy. In fact, a re-review of the reports tabulated by Eysenck and by Levitt would tend to indicate that these reviews were biased *in favor* of psychotherapy. For example, the report by Morris, Soroker, and Burress (1954) is included to show 97 per cent improvement as a result of treatment. Actually, Morris' report states that the 97 per cent improvement was for essentially nontreated (control) cases. Morris says, "Most of these cases were classified as diagnostic or consultation cases. Recommendations and advice were given but there was no continuous treatment by the clinic staff."

Thus the weight of the evidence, involving very large numbers of clients or therapists, suggests that the average effects of therapeutic intervention (with the average therapist or counselor) are approximately equivalent to the random effects of normal living without treatment (control groups, or what has been traditionally labeled "spontaneous" improvement).

This evidence (and there are other supporting studies one could cite) has been very difficult for the profession to accept. Because we have wished so hard that it were faulty, it is not surprising that many writers among us have attempted to ignore or argue away this large and growing mass of evidence. As the arguments are well known, they deserve comment.

The various apologist arguments that have been used most often against the evidence and conclusion that counseling and psychotherapy on the average have no effect boil down to four main ones: (1) that measurements of improvement are crude and hence do not capture the subtle changes produced, *i.e.*, that the failure of research to amass positive evidence for the effects of therapy does not actually show a lack of effect; (2) that one cannot compare or average the results of different studies because they use different outcome measures, different therapists, different patients, etc.; (3) that the base rate of improvement or change occurring in the absence of therapist or counselor (traditionally labeled "spontaneous improvement" or "spontaneous remission of symptoms") should not be used as a base line to evaluate therapeutic effectiveness, *i.e.*, that when therapy and control groups both show equivalent improvement it does not show that therapy is ineffective but that *both* therapy and "control groups" are effective; and, (4) that the presentation of the evidence itself is selective, biased and distorted, and that there is really more solid evidence for than against average therapeutic effectiveness.

Several comments on these arguments should be made. The first line of argument in effect claims that the average results of therapy are either so small or so socially unimportant that current measurement cannot detect them, *i.e.*, that neither patients nor observers can notice them enough for them to be reflected in measures of personality functioning, anxiety, social functioning, etc., etc. It would be difficult indeed to justify the massive use of treatment procedures with effects so small that no one notices them! Certainly the average patient or client seeking help would refuse it if he were told that the hoped-for results of the effort would not be noticed by himself, his friends, the therapist or anyone else! The client who comes to us for help is seeking at least noticeable change. Those of us who have chosen to become professional counselors or therapists would be the first to claim that successful therapy results in *large* and *noticeable* improvement—otherwise we would not choose to be therapists or counselors!

The second line of argument in effect *concedes that counseling and psychotherapy is not on the average effective.* It *assumes* instead that it must have some effects on some patients or with some therapists. Thus, this argument is simply an affirmation of faith that counseling and therapy must do some good, sometimes, under some unknown conditions with some kind of therapists and some kind of clients.

The third line of argument (that against the phenomena traditionally labeled "spontaneous improvement") is, in effect, that the therapeutic effectiveness of professional help is obscured by the fact that the normally existing "nonprofession help" of friends, acquaintances, clergymen, bartenders, etc., is *also* (equally) therapeutically effective. Such an argument, of course, implicitly concedes that the professional counselor or therapist is no more effective than the nonprofessional "help" a client would ordinarily seek and find if he did not first see a professional!

In short, the first three main lines of argument against the evidence and conclusion that counseling and psychotherapy have no average detectable beneficial effects are not argument at all. They all concede the main point, and then go on to argue that, even so, there may be some benefit that is obscured by this overall finding.

The fourth line of apologist argument against the evidence, particularly the evidence as presented by Eysenck, is that the presentation itself is biased. This line of argument questions the exhaustiveness of any presentation and the adequacy of any single study. Indeed, the present authors would be among the first to say that the presentation of the evidence in this chapter is not exhaustive—it is very likely that there are other relevant studies which we have not cited. However, no responsible writer has ever reviewed the evidence of outcome studies and concluded that counseling and psychotherapy as usually practiced have an average benefit beyond that seen in comparable control groups. Further, the studies with the best methodological controls and the largest samples of clients are those that failed to detect positive therapeutic effects, even though the studies themselves were openly biased toward showing positive results: they were initiated and carried out by investigators who publicly hoped to show that their average counseling or psychotherapy was indeed effective! Most of the few studies that do show positive effects have dealt with small samples of therapists who were specifically selected because the investigator thought them particularly effective. All of these few studies used only a very small sample of clients. Moreover, many of them found positive effects on only a minority of the outcome measures used. In short, any bias in the evidence concerning average therapeutic outcome is *in favor of,* rather than against, therapeutic effectiveness.

If all the studies on outcome were to be averaged on the basis of the number of clients involved, it is clear that the overall result would be close to zero effect beyond that observed in comparable clients not receiving counseling or psychotherapy.

Inasmuch as the available evidence indicates that the average ineffectiveness of psychotherapy and counseling, as currently practiced, is due to the presence of large numbers of practitioners who have negative effects offsetting the equally large number of those who have positive effects, it would seem sensible for professional organizations, clinics, schools, hospitals and other interested agencies to attempt to identify the effectiveness of individual practitioners. In that way, and in that way only, can the patient's welfare and the public good be best served. Unfortunately, this has almost never been done. Almost never do individuals or agencies keep even crude outcome measures of a given therapist's effectiveness! In the licensing or certification or the employment of an individual practitioner, he is almost never asked to give evidence of his average effect on patients. Whether he has a long history of helping or harming clients seems to have no bearing; in most cases, no one even asks or bothers to keep records. It is perhaps time that schools, clinics, hospitals, counseling centers and above all, universities and professional organizations began to evaluate the average effects on clients of given individual practitioners. While such evaluations are fraught with difficulty (but no greater than that in the current approach of defining competence in terms of theoretic knowledge), the public and professional benefit would be enormous. As things stand today, a counselor or therapist receives his doctorate from a university, becomes licensed by his state, employed or enters private practice, and even passes specialty board examinations in his profession without anyone making a systematic evaluation of his actual effects (for better *or* for worse) on his all-too-human clients! We have been, in this respect, negligent. Both our public and moral responsibilities require that we bend our efforts toward continuing evaluation of average client response to individual practitioners; there seems to be no surer way of improving the effectiveness of a clinic, a hospital, a counseling service, a community agency or the field as a whole.

EVIDENCE FOR THE EFFECTIVENESS OF SOME COUNSELING AND PSYCHOTHERAPY

In spite of the seemingly overwhelming evidence that the average counselor or psychotherapist is not significantly helpful in producing improvement beyond that observed in patients receiving no treatment, specific studies involving specific therapists do demonstrate positive effects of counseling or psychotherapy.

Thus in a study of time-limited, client-centered and Adlerian psychotherapy, Shlien, Mosak, and Dreikurs (1962) showed statistically significant positive changes in self-concept for patients receiving counseling or psychotherapy, but no changes in a contrast group of untreated neurotics.

Using a matched treatment and control population, Williamson and Bordin (1940) studied the effects of counseling on achievement levels in college students. Their findings indicated that the counseled students showed slightly superior college achievement. As a group they had a grade-point average of 2.18, which was significantly above the grade-point average of 1.97 for the control students. A recently reported follow-up by Campbell (1965) of the groups used by Williamson and Bordin examined the functioning of individuals in both the therapy and the control groups 25 years after counseling. An analysis of the 123 pairs of males indicated that in a measure of "contribution to society" the counseled group showed a statistically significant superiority over the control group. While most differences would not prove significant, the fact that *any* difference could be detected 25 years later is in itself rather striking evidence.

Spielberger, Weitz, and Denny (1962) studied the effects of brief group counseling on academic achievement in anxious college freshmen. The 28 counseled and 28 control students were carefully matched on such factors as entrance exam scores, major field of study, and type of high school attended. Their findings showed greater gain in the counseled students' grade-point averages at the end of counseling than in the control students' averages during the same time. Further, when the data were analyzed by subdividing the counseled students into those who attended more than seven sessions and those who attended fewer than seven sessions, those who attended the most counseling sessions showed the greatest gain in college grades.

The findings of Baymurr and Patterson (1960) also dealt with underachievement, but used high school students as clients. Thirty-three underachieving high school students were assigned to four matched groups: individual counseling, group counseling, noncounseled controls, and controls who were contacted but not counseled. The findings indicated significant superiority for the counseled students in grade-point averages and in *Q*-sort measures of self-concepts, but no differential change in study habits in either group.

Graham (1960) focused his study on the effects of psychoanalytic psychotherapy upon sexual activity and sexual satisfaction. Although he lacked a control group, his findings indicated that both frequency and enjoyment of sexual activity increased with the length of psychoanalytic treatment.

A further report suggesting the efficacy of psychotherapy is that by Draspa (1959) which focused upon patients suffering from presumed psychosomatic muscular pains. One hundred and twelve patients were assigned to psychotherapy and 112 to routine medical treatment. Reduction in muscular pains significantly favored the patients receiving psychotherapy; thus, the average recovery from pain required 25 days for the experimental group and 59 days for the control group. Further, at the end of the study the group receiving psychotherapy had almost twice as many patients who were completely free of pain as did the control group. Another study dealing with psychosomatic patients which also reports positive results utilized psychotherapy and psychoanalysis on patients with ulcerative colitis. The report by O'Connor et al. (1964) dealt with 57 patients treated by psychotherapy and matched patients who had routine medical care. This was a subsample of a larger population, including only those for whom follow-up could be maintained for five years or more. The findings indicated that patients receiving psychotherapy showed on the average marked and sustained improvement, while the control group remained relatively unchanged.

Shouksmith and Taylor (1964) studied the effectiveness of nondirective counseling for a group of underachieving twelve- and thirteen-year-old students having high ability, using two comparable control groups. The 12 students in each group were matched for I. Q., age, and previous achievement. After six months there was significantly greater improvement on four out of six achievement tests for the group receiving counseling as compared to the control groups. Of the 12 students receiving counseling, 8 could not be classified as underachievers after treatment (66%), while all but 2 of the other 24 students were still classed as underachievers (8%). Additionally, sociogram ratings indicated greater improvement in peer acceptance and in teacher ratings for those receiving counseling, as compared to either of the control groups.

In a report of a study by Lazarus (1961), in which he served as the therapist, he found that his patients responded better to desensitization than to his group interpretation procedure or to his group interpretation procedure with relaxation instructions. That desensitization aspects of behavioral approaches to counseling or psychotherapy do have positive effects is indicated by other studies.

Thus Paul, and Paul and Shannon, studied desensitization procedures in small samples of individual (1965) and group treatment (1966), with results suggesting moderate positive benefit. Similar findings have also been reported by Lang (1965), using equally good control procedures in studying reduction in fear of snakes among mild snake-phobic college students. These studies tend to confirm the clinical reports of positive effects reported earlier by Wolpe (1958).

In a report of the effects of group psychotherapy, Ends and Page (1957) compared remission rates for patients assigned to client-centered and analytic group therapy with those in control groups of leaderless discussion and didactic learning. The findings indicated that patients in client-centered and analytic group psychotherapy had remission/nonremission ratios of 1 to 2 while both control groups showed ratios of 1 to 5.

Three studies reported mixed findings generally indicating little effect of counseling or therapy; the few differences that were obtained do provide modest evidence of some effects attributable to treatment. Seeman, Barry and Ellinwood (1964) made a carefully controlled study of eight children receiving play therapy and eight under control conditions. The children were tested initially and posttherapy at the end of one school year, and for follow-up 19 months later. On all measures there were no significant changes from before therapy to after it. On one of the measures there was a significant change on a special test between the pretherapy status and the follow-up. However, teachers were unable to notice any reliable changes at any point. Another study that reported positive results was that by Ricks, Umbarger, and Mack (1964). They studied temporal or time perspective in "successfully treated adolescent delinquent boys." There they found some measures (most measures) to show no difference between the treatment group and the control group, but did find one measure of "prospective time spans" which increased greatest in the treatment group. In a study of 82 patients seen in clinics, McNair, Lorr, Young, Roth, and Boyd (1964) lacked a control group, but reported findings suggesting that the number of interviews during psychotherapy relates significantly to certain measures of social, psychological, and symptom-reduction changes.

Several laboratory studies have also produced evidence suggesting beneficial effects of counseling or psychotherapy. A study by Thetford (1948) compared laboratory-induced frustration before and after client-centered counseling (observing a control group for a comparable time period). Thetford's data showed a reduction in the counseled group's emotional response to frustration, as measured by GSR's respiratory rate and heart rate, but no change in the control group's reaction.

Using a different approach to therapy, Weiner (1955) studied the effects of rest, catharsis, and brief psychotherapy on the response to laboratory-induced stress. The evidence indicated that brief psychotherapy was more effective in reducing laboratory-induced stress than either rest or catharsis.

In addition, not all clinical literature suggesting the effectiveness of psychotherapy can be disregarded as mere wishful thinking or distorted reporting on the part of the therapist involved. An example in clinical literature of evidence for the effectiveness of counseling and psychotherapy is the report by Gottschalk (1953) of marked changes in seizure frequencies and electroencephalogram patterns in three epileptic cases treated by psychoanalytic therapy. The recordings indicated that these marked reductions in seizure frequency were maintained over a long period of time. Since reduction of seizure frequency occurred in all three patients as a result of psychotherapy, and since seizure frequencies are relatively stable, such findings provide further evidence that at least some kinds of psychotherapy under some circumstances are indeed effective.

Finally, a number of studies (to be reviewed in Chapter 3) now exist which point to specific therapist characteristics as being significantly related to patient improvement; the same body of evidence suggests that when certain therapist characteristics are present, positive patient outcome occurs, while deterioration occurs in their absence.

TOWARD AN ASSESSMENT OF THE EVIDENCE

The assertion (and the supporting evidence) that psychotherapy produces no reliable effect seems to fly in the face of the whole body of science and knowledge of human behavior: a prolonged series of dramatic and emotion-laden antecedents without any ensuing consequences? The laboratory behavioral scientist, who observes reliable and statistically significant performance and personality changes that accompany anxiety induction by very brief "failure instructions" and then sees these changes reversed by instructions for "failure disabusal," must be deeply puzzled by evidence suggesting that psychotherapy has no effects. The nullifying evidence would at first seem to sound the death knell of a science of human behavior; even a casual reading of physiological recordings of patients in psychotherapeutic interviews would suggest the intensity of the stimulus complex called "psychotherapy." Filmed psychotherapeutic interviews where the patient shows intense anger, anxiety, anguish, tears, and even panic, emphasize the seeming paradox of psychotherapy that confronts the behavioral scientist: powerful clinical phenomena lacking measurable consequences.

The answer to this seeming paradox, of course, lies in the inappropriateness of comparisons between "psychotherapy" and "control" conditions of "no psychotherapy." Both the behavioral scientist and the practicing counselor or psychotherapist can agree that "psychotherapy" or "counseling" is hardly a unitary phenomenon. As practiced, it contains a variety of conditions involving both positive and negative experiences. Thus, to ask whether psychotherapy is indeed therapeutic, and to attempt to answer that question by comparing behavioral or personality change in counseled and "control" groups, is very much like a pharmacologist asking, "Is chemotherapy therapeutic?" and then conducting his research by randomly giving unknown kinds and quantities of drugs to one group of patients with various complaints, and no drugs to a similar "control" group. In effect, the evidence concerning the outcome of counseling or psychotherapy has all too often been obtained in precisely this way: one group of patients has been given random unknown amounts of various psychological "conditions" collectively labeled "psychotherapy," while another group has received "no psychotherapy."

If studies of chemotherapy were indeed conducted as just outlined, we would not be surprised to find no mean differences in the effects on treated vs. control groups. Would this mean that chemotherapy produced no effects? Most pharmacologists would reject the assertion that such data supported this null hypothesis. The pharmacologist might also suggest that even if there were no average differences between randomly applied "chemotherapy" and "control," there would still probably be differences in variances, with the patients who received unknown drugs in unknown quantities showing greater variation (more extreme positive and negative changes) than control patients. He would certainly suggest that to study chemotherapy appropriately would require first the isolation of particular "drugs," then the measurement of their amounts, and *only then* the study of their relationship to outcomes.

What of the parallel with research in counseling and psychotherapy?

In the reported research comparing "psychotherapy" to "no psychotherapy," differences in variability of outcome have usually not been investigated. However, Bergin (1963), in a careful reevaluation of the effects of psychotherapy, notes that in the results of the Barron and Leary (1955), the Cartwright and Vogel (1960), and the Truax (1963) reports, which showed no overall mean differences between therapy and control groups, the expected critical finding does emerge: the patients receiving psychotherapy show significantly greater *variability* in personality change indices at the conclusion of psychotherapy than do the controls. Also, an analysis by Barendregt in Holland has found increased variability in treatment groups when compared to controls. Eysenck [2] had noted in preparing his chapter (1960) on the effects of psychotherapy that several people had reported greater variability in the treated groups than in the untreated, and that this seemed to suggest a two-way effect of psychotherapy.

It is particularly pertinent that Cartwright and Vogel went further in their analyses to demonstrate that the patients of experienced therapists tended to show more improvement than those seen by inexperienced therapists, which suggests that the generic experience of "psychotherapy" must have been different for the two groups of patients, since the outcomes of the experience were different.

Another pertinent report comes from the Cambridge-Somerville youth study involving a ten-year study of a comparison between 325 potentially delinquent boys who received supportive counseling or psychotherapy, and 325 untreated boys in a control group. Although the reports (Teuber and Powers, 1953) indicated no overall average differences favoring the treated group, they indicated not only the variability in the treatment, but also considerable variability in outcome. Perhaps more significantly, the more

2. Personal communication (1963) from Eysenck, which continued ". . . and this seemed to suggest a two-way effect of psychotherapy, I was very much tempted to put this into the chapter as a hypothesis but as Barendregt had not then published his paper I decided the evidence was too tenuous, and the implication that psychotherapy might do harm too serious to make it advisable for me to say so."

complete report indicated that certain specific counselors or case workers tended to form poor relationships with the youths and generally had poor outcomes; other case workers very seldom had either poor relationships or poor outcomes.

It is of some significance that Allport, in the introduction to the book which presented in detail the findings of the study, specifically mentions that some counselors or therapists were quite ineffective while others were noticeably effective. In particular he points to the most effective therapist, a social worker, who had had only a minimal amount of professional training in therapy but who was a "warm," mature and understanding person.

A similar pattern emerges in the work of Mink and Isaacson (1959). In their study of 100 junior high school students forming groups of counseled and control clients, there were no overall differences in outcomes, but the variability of outcome on the change indices was significantly greater for the counseled group than for the noncounseled group (more extreme positive *and* negative changes).

It should also be pointed out that even in the surveys of effectiveness of counseling and psychotherapeutic treatment reported by Eysenck (1960) and Levitt (1957), the specific improvement rates, which were combined to give an average, again showed considerable variability in outcome among different therapist groups. For instance, one study (Ross, 1936) reported an improvement rate of 77 per cent for 1,089 patients, while another (Matz, 1929) gave an improvement rate of only 41 per cent in 775 cases. These two widely different reports are both from eclectically oriented therapists.

Even more striking variability in the estimated effects of counseling and psychotherapy occurs in the tables presented by Levitt. There, improvement rates of 91 per cent on 70 cases (Irgens, 1936) and 91 per cent on 78 cases (Healy et al., 1929) are averaged together with reports as low as 42 per cent improvement on 191 cases (Maas, 1955). Clearly, the 91 per cent improvement rates from some studies differ significantly from the 42 per cent improvement rate of another. On the basis of a base rate expectancy of 70 per cent, some reports seem to suggest that psychotherapy is helpful (over 70 per cent) while others report that it is harmful (less than 70 per cent). Thus, reports by different therapists and by different treatment clinics or institutions suggest not only that some are much more effective than others but also that, on the basis of expected improvement, some therapists or clinics are helpful while others are harmful.

The notion that psychotherapy can be and is harmful as well as helpful is often difficult for the practicing counselor or therapist to accept. It raises a host of profoundly distressing ethical questions concerning both training and practice. Counselors and therapists have most often assumed implicitly that although they could be helpful, they would rarely prove harmful or "psychonoxious." [3] *The evidence now available suggests that,*

3. A term coined by Hiam Ginott to describe effects of harmful therapists, in contrast with *psychotherapeutic*.

on the average, psychotherapy may be harmful as often as helpful, with an average effect comparable to receiving no help.

Even findings from research with clients of counseling centers suggest frequent harmful effects from what passes for acceptable counseling. Thus, when Cartwright (1961) analyzed the data from a group of unsuccessful cases, she found clear deterioration in interpersonal relationships. Similarly, Butler (1960) analyzed *Q*-sort data measuring the adequacy of clients' self concepts; and found, as early as the eighth interview, evidence of nonrandom *positive and negative* changes resulting from counseling.

What accounts for this large variability in outcome? How do the helpful counselors and therapists differ from the harmful ones? These are the critical new directions for research, theory, training, and practice. These are the questions that give impetus and direction to the present viewpoint in counseling and psychotherapy.

To summarize, the evidence reviewed thus far concerning the effectiveness of "counseling" or "psychotherapy" suggests that: (1) certain relatively unspecified kinds are indeed effective (Chapter 3 will review the evidence for the effectiveness of specific therapeutic ingredients offered by the therapist or counselor); (2) under certain unspecified conditions, therapy and control patients show equivalent average outcomes, but those treated by psychotherapy show greater variability in outcome than those in control conditions; and, (3) what is called "psychotherapy" or "counseling" is a heterogeneous collection of ingredients or psychological conditions that produce varying degrees of both positive and deteriorative personality change in patients.

This latter point is the critical one. It suggests that psychotherapy research should concern itself primarily with identifying, isolating, measuring, and relating to client outcome the specific ingredients or dimensions of the psychotherapeutic process. We would thus be following the model of the pharmacologist who investigates the effectiveness of chemotherapy by identifying specific drugs and evaluating their effectiveness alone and in combination with other drugs. The analogy between psychotherapy research and drug research seems close in another important respect: unlike physics or chemistry (often the model for the behavioral scientist), pharmacology deals not with the effects of basic elements and their interactions, but with specifiable chemical compounds and mixtures such as caffeine, diamphetamine, nembutal and the barbiturates. The pharmacologist studies the effects of such compounds or mixtures separately and in interaction. Moreover, he knows that the physical properties of drugs (such as weight, volume, specific gravity, etc.) have no direct relationship to their functional effects on human physiological or behavioral response. It seems likely that a similar state of affairs exists for psychotherapy research: we are not likely to find direct relationships between the physical dimensions of the psychotherapy interview and its functional effect on the physiology and behavioral system of the human organism.

It might be noted that the pharmacologist proceeds in four major ways: (1) he isolates, in the laboratory, specific effects of drugs that are commonly used; (2) he modifies known drugs in an attempt to produce new drugs, maximizing desired effects and minimizing unwanted side effects; (3) he studies, statistically and by naturalistic observation, the relationship between specific compounds or mixtures and physiological or behavioral changes in an organism; and, (4) he engages in trial-and-error screening of compounds in an attempt to isolate drugs with specific desired effects. Pharmacologists, like psychotherapists, have theories (even some of structure-function relationships), although they fit the facts and predict new facts about as poorly as psychological theories do in psychotherapy.

Pursuing the analogy of the pharmacologist, the psychotherapy researcher and practitioner should be asking, in effect, "*What* dosage level of *what* drug produces which therapeutic effects?" The suggestion is that the scientific study of psychotherapy should focus upon relating the antecedents and ingredients of the therapeutic relationship to the outcome; rather than concentrating its energy and talents on studies of momentary processes that may or may not be related to therapeutic outcome, or naively asking such questions as "Is counseling or psychotherapy effective?" without regard to the nonunitary nature of the counseling process.

For psychotherapy research to focus on outcome would quickly bring it into greater intimacy with the mainstream of psychotherapy practice. Psychotherapy research can converge on the goal of practice by directing its efforts toward discovering and isolating the effective elements in the psychotherapeutic process that lead to constructive change in the patient. That is, we can attempt to discover which elements, among all those present, contribute to the patients' constructive change. Further, if counseling or psychotherapy is to be a universally effective tool in the remediation of human malfunctioning, researchers and practitioners alike must attempt to discern the elements of psychotherapy that inhibit such constructive changes in patients. It has been clear to the clinician, as it is now becoming clear from the research evidence, that not everything that happens in psychotherapy is indeed beneficial or even relevant to constructive change in the client.

The present book is an initial attempt to specify and give evidence for the ingredients in counseling or psychotherapy that lead to positive or deteriorative client changes, and to suggest application of these dimensions to training and practice.

CHAPTER 2 CENTRAL THERAPEUTIC INGREDIENTS: THEORETIC CONVERGENCE

THE existence of many alternate theories in any field of endeavor implies that none of them is adequate to the task at hand—the explanation and organization of the stable body of phenomena involved (if indeed there is such). The great proliferation of theories of counseling and psychotherapy reflects more and more clearly the inability of any one existing theory to prove itself universally correct and useful in prediction and practice. However, as greater research knowledge is gained, it tends to eliminate parochial theories and "schools" of psychotherapy and counseling. Even now we are fast witnessing the demise of "schools" or "cults" in psychotherapy or counseling that have held sway for more than a generation.

Indeed, the more we learn from research, the more we become acutely aware of the limitations and inadequacies of current theoretic formulations. Perhaps this is as it should be, since our knowledge is so limited and the average level of practice so ineffective. The unfortunate fact is that there is no good evidence that the beginning therapists trained today are demonstrably more effective than those trained ten or even twenty years ago. And if this is true, then it must also be true that either the theories developed in the past ten or twenty years are grossly inaccurate; or that training institutions are teaching the theories but not their implementation.

Part of the difficulty in translating even partially correct theories into effective practice clearly lies with the training institutions themselves. More often than not they choose training and supervisory therapists on the basis of their academic, research, and theoretic contribution, ignoring to a large extent the effective professional therapist. With such a selection procedure, universities and other training institutions are likely to reward and retain training and supervisory therapists who are probably, as a group, only average in therapeutic effectiveness; that is, they produce average effects in patients, comparable to no-therapy control conditions. Since such faculty members have made their greatest contributions in research, theory and purely academic areas, they are likely to stress in their training programs areas that are unrelated or minimally related to actual effective therapeutic practice.

Another source of difficulty in producing effective counselors and therapists may derive from the fact that much of current theory emphasizes the dynamics of personality and psychopathology rather than antecedents to effective therapeutic outcome. Too often, the result is a focus on theoretical statements about the patient, and too little focus on the therapist. But in a very clear sense, the patient is a "given"—and we have no choice but to deal with him as he actually exists. The therapist, however, is relatively free to vary "for better or for worse" in terms of his effect on clients. To the extent that existing theories are correct concerning the role of the therapist, then, we can make significant gains in the effectiveness of average treatment only by focusing our training and theoretic effort on the therapist.

The central question to be asked in counseling and psychotherapy is "What are the essential characteristics or behaviors of the therapist or counselor that lead to constructive behavioral change in the client?" This question admits that not everything a therapist or counselor does in the therapeutic relationship is effective or even relevant for constructive change in the client. What, then, are the common elements in effective counseling in psychotherapy?

In a critique of existing theoretic viewpoints, Thorne (1950) cogently notes:

> It must be emphasized that in psychodiagnosis and psychotherapy, unproven theories and unvalidated practices are in current use far more widely than in any other clinical field. In the field of psychotherapy we find a large number of competing theoretical systems and schools all being widely applied in the almost complete absence of validation and standardization.

He adds:

> . . . the attempt to validate theories *logically* by constructing supposedly comprehensive and consistent systems is obsolete in an area where experimental-statistical validation is possible. It is regrettable that so much time is being currently spent in the attempt to secure respectability for unvalidated clinical methods by relating them to theories which have some systematic prestige.

Thorne concludes:

> . . . the fact that many methods (of treatment) appear to produce results can only have two possible explanations. Either similar dynamic factors are operating in diverse methods, or there is more than one method for achieving the same specific goals. (pp. 234-244)

A careful review of the available evidence suggests that both explanations are valid to some degree. Finding the common elements in diverse methods should throw light upon the central therapeutic skills necessary for effective counseling or psychotherapy. Over the years, most attempts to specify the commonalities of diverse approaches to treatment have attempted to identify the characteristics of those therapists who are able to provide an effective interpersonal relationship. In short, the search has most often been for what can be regarded as the central therapeutic ingredients: the interpersonal skills of the counselor-therapist. As Black

(1952) noted: ". . . our lack of progress in understanding the process of therapy and in developing a systematic methodology may lie partly in our preoccupation with specific techniques and 'schools' to the neglect of what may well account for the most significant share of the behavioral changes produced by psychotherapy—the interpersonal relationship itself."

Despite the bewildering array of divergent theories and the difficulty in translating concepts from the language of one theory to that of another, several common threads weave their way through almost every major theory of psychotherapy and counseling, including the psychoanalytic, the client-centered, the behavioristic, and many of the more eclectic and derivative theories. In one way or another, all have emphasized the importance of the therapist's ability to be integrated, mature, genuine, authentic or congruent in his relationship to the patient. They have all stressed also the importance of the therapist's ability to provide a nonthreatening, trusting, safe or secure atmosphere by his acceptance, nonpossessive warmth, unconditional positive regard, or love. Finally, virtually all theories of psychotherapy emphasize that for the therapist to be helpful he must be accurately empathic, be "with" the client, be understanding, or grasp the patient's meaning.

These three sets of characteristics can, for lack of better words, be termed *accurate empathy, nonpossessive warmth,* and *genuineness.* The discovery of the therapeutic effectiveness of these three interpersonal skills grew out of Freud's historic development of the "talking cure." They are, however, aspects of the therapist's behavior that cut across virtually all theories of psychotherapy and appear to be common elements in a wide variety of approaches to psychotherapy and counseling. Their occurrence and recurrence in theoretical orientations derived from different patient populations, from different periods in time, and from effective therapists who have widely differing personalities, suggest that they are indeed central ingredients in effective psychotherapy. In more recent years they have been given more specific attention and have grown in their central importance. Thus, Rogers (1957a) specifies that the therapist's ability to communicate empathic understanding and unconditional positive regard for the patient, and his being a congruent or genuine person in the relationship, are both "necessary and sufficient" conditions for patient therapeutic change.

Rogers deserved enormous credit for his 1957 statement, since it served to bring client-centered theory into closer alignment with other positions. More important, it focused renewed interest on these interpersonal therapeutic skills and served as an impetus to further thought and research. Rogers' position was, of course, the basic impetus for the present authors' research and current thinking. While many other theorists had stressed these same factors at an earlier date, Rogers was one of the first leading theorists to give them a special preeminence as *the* effective ingredients for successful therapy. Although it is unlikely that *any* therapeutic ingredients will ever prove either ncessary or sufficient, Rogers' concise theoretic statement served to emphasize the role of these three central skills. His development of this recent position was, of course, within the *zeitgeist* of the increasing emphasis (Bordin 1955) upon these factors within the mainstream of psychotherapeutic theory. Indeed, the early Freudian discoveries provided the origin and central direction for the development of client-centered theory. Thus, Nicholas Hobbs (1955), in commenting on the origin of client-centered therapy, notes that it evolved directly from the influence of Frederick Allen (the distinguished Philadelphia child psychiatrist) and Jesse Taft, who in turn were students of Otto Rank, an early student and associate of Sigmund Freud.

Rank's emphasis on the therapeutic effectiveness of the therapist's warmth, empathy and genuineness as a real person shows marked similarity to the current client-centered view, even though the language used is far different. Thus, according to Ruth Munroe (1955), Rank:

> . . . relies for cure (the Rankian word is "helping") on the direct relationship between himself and the patient . . . what he needs is *the acceptance of his will by another so as to justify himself*. . . . It is in therapy that the patient can encounter an "other" who accepts his will problem as entirely valid and requires that he face it directly; *who throws back the essential will conflict into the patient's own ego*. . . . The course of Rankian therapy is aimed at the encouragement of a more *realistic partialization through constant discussion of the actual life situation,* past and present. It is essential to the growth of the patient's will that the relationship with the therapist be in close connection with his everyday reality problems. (pp. 590-592)

For Munroe, the stress in Rankian therapy is towards a "warmly supportive attitude" where ". . . the therapist becomes himself a reality figure in a manner new to the patient: *accepting* but limited. While the therapist does not offer direct advice on the conduct of the patient's affairs, *it is understood that he is a real person,* helping on a real problem . . ." and, "because the therapist is *unconditional in this basic acceptance,* but deliberately realistic and 'partial' in his concrete relationship to the patient, he can help the patient towards creative, constructively integrated partialization instead of the blind, totalistic reaction to separation fear characteristic of the neurotic" (p. 592).

The interchange between the Adlerian and client-centered approaches through students and faculty at Chicago also led to further emphasis upon the role of empathy and warmth. Warmth, in particular, was stressed by Adler as most central to his therapeutic approach. Munroe notes that in the Adlerian view:

> The therapist must temper his *warmth and encouragement* with understanding of the special problems of the patient, and must bring the patient to the same understanding. . . . I use this example to show that Adler's emphasis on warmth and encouragement was no namby-pamby "bucking up" treatment. . . . but Adler did not expect cure to follow merely as a result of new insight. Equally important was the positive experience of love in the relationship with

the therapist, and the positive appreciation the patient obtained for any advance toward a more realistic evaluation of himself and toward more genuine social feelings. (p. 509)

She summarizes:

In summary, although Adler emphasized the importance of understanding in therapy, he also emphasized the importance of love, appreciation, and *collaboration* in the therapeutic situation. The therapist loves and appreciates the patient for what he is, not for his neurotic strivings, and so reassures him during the difficult period of transition from the faulty life style to a life style in which social feelings and common sense hold sway. (pp. 509-510)

Since much of Freudian theory has become cloaked in its own peculiar jargon, the outsider might at first see psychoanalysis itself as an artificial and non-genuine relationship in which the patient receives didactic instruction and aloofness rather than warmth, empathy and genuineness. Indeed, some recent theorists have attempted to build up such a straw man. Nothing, however, could be further from the truth. Again, in the words of Ruth Munroe:

. . . the "Freudian" does not often interpret the patient's problems *to the patient* as orality, anal sadism, etc.; however, he thinks of them, and however he reports his thinking to colleagues. He is fully aware of the therapeutic assignment of talking to the patient in terms the patient can understand and accept. "Freudian" interpretations mostly follow a common-sense vocabulary hardly different from that of other schools. He often uses the same materials and draws much the same conclusions. (p. 512)

She continues:

. . . Probably one may say the more the psychoanalytic approach emphasizes examination of the reaction patterns of the patient in the current life situation, the more important it becomes that the analyst be able to understand very directly the patient's value systems, the cultural background and his attitudes, his modes of verbal expression, even his personality makeup. Although the analyst must always be on guard against over identification with the patient, there can be little doubt that the analytic work proceeds better when the analyst as a person is well equipped to understand the special problems of the patient. (p. 514)

In speaking of the relationship of patient and therapist Munroe further observes:

As regards the analyst as a "real" person, I have remarked that the non-libido schools seem to encourage a greater informality and positive friendliness toward the patient, although the difference between the "Freudians" in this respect has probably been exaggerated. The "Freudians" are friendlier than their non-libido critics imply; the "objectivity" recommended by Freud comes close to the "neutrality" urged by Fromm-Reichmann. At most, there are technical variations in executing what Freud presented as a major *therapeutic* function of the analyst as a person. (p. 521)

The basic similarity between seemingly divergent approaches is further underlined by Cameron (1963) who notes that such divergent methods as the psychobiologic approach of Meyers, the neo-Rankian client-centered approach developed by Rogers and his followers, the existential approach, psychoanalytically oriented psychotherapy, psychodrama and most group therapies can be considered together as subvarieties of "expressive psychotherapy."

This essential common agreement among leading therapists of diverse orientation was neatly reflected in the research carried out by Fiedler (1950, 1951), which indicated that skilled or experienced therapists of divergent schools of psychotherapy agreed on the elements of an ideal therapeutic relationship, which they characterized as being warm, accepting and understanding. Fiedler's research suggested that experienced therapists of different orientations agreed with each other more closely than they did with beginning therapists from their own orientation.

Indeed, even learning theorists such as Shoben (1953) focused upon the importance of empathic understanding and warmth in attempting to formulate psychotherapy as a learning process. Thus, Shoben, in specifying the ideal therapeutic relationship says:

> The attributes of the relationship are, first, friendliness, warmth, and a comfortable emotional closeness. . . . this implies a second characteristic, permissiveness. . . . warmth and permissiveness, so described, shade into a third aspect of the therapeutic relationship; its "safety." This is sometimes spoken of as "acceptance," a term which is a little troublesome because it has connotations of approval. Fourth, the therapist seems to be constantly attempting to clarify his own understanding of the patient and to communicate that understanding within the therapeutic context. . . .

Shoben continues:

> If warmth, permissiveness, safety and understanding seem to be prerequisites of any desirable human relationship rather than being peculiar properties of the psychotherapeutic interaction, this is precisely the case.

Shoben sums up his view of psychotherapy:

> From the standpoint of what the psychotherapist does, then, psychotherapy may be defined as a warm, permissive, safe, understanding, but limited social relationship within which therapist and patient discuss the affective behavior of the latter, including his ways of dealing with his emotionally toned needs and the situations that give rise to them. (p. 126)

In the field of counseling, Bordin (1955) heavily stressed the role of the therapeutic triad of empathy, warmth, and genuineness as central attributes of an effective counselor. In considering the intertwining nature of empathy, genuineness, and warmth, he noted:

> The counselor or therapist who mechanically applies the formulas of therapy

will probably not be of much help to his clients. His reactions must be relatively spontaneous manifestations of his understanding of the client and his current needs, both overt and latent. . . .

The dominant ideology in both counseling and psychotherapy forbids the counselor's thrusting of himself or his problems upon his clients . . . however, some forms of involvement seem to be necessary prerequisites to really effective objective observation. . . . One of the things he is trying to understand is the inner life and experience of another person. In order to fully understand what it means to be helpless or to be in a rage, and how it feels when some other person turns away from you when you feel helpless or when you feel another person tells you to calm down when you feel in a rage, the observer must draw upon his own experience. Doing this seems to be a central part of the idea that it is the role of empathy to assist us in understanding other people. It would appear that the conditions for understanding observation are most fully achieved when an observer is sufficiently involved to be able to make full use of his own emotional experience and, at the same time, sufficiently detached to be able to differentiate his own experiences from those of the other person. . . . There is another quality that the therapist brings to the relationship which we will call warmth. Warmth is related both to objectivity and to involvement. Warmth refers to involvement insofar as the latter term used to include an ability to empathize and to give one's self the freedom to express feeling. Warmth refers to objectivity to the extent to which it includes the maintenance of a clear differentiation from the client. But warmth goes beyond objectivity and involvement. It refers to a kind of spontaneity in interpersonal relationships which makes the relationship "real" for the patient or client. The "warmly" interacting therapist cannot be a "blank screen" or an "echoing" machine. . . . Although the emotional tone (warmth) of the therapist's reactions may not be natural if always under his calculated control, yet through his empathy for the mood of the client, it can be brought easily and naturally under a form of indirect control. . . .

That there may even be times when the most secure and well integrated therapist becomes irritated or angry, and it may contribute to therapy if the therapist admits having become angry and thereby eschews omnipotence and admits his error. One need not burden the client unnecessarily with a masochistic denunciation of one's own faults. Yet, when the occasion demands it, a client can profit from noting that it is possible to own up to one's mistakes without loss of self-respect. (pp. 170, 173, 175)

The essential agreement on these three therapeutic ingredients is further illustrated by the eclectic view of Brammer and Shostrom (1964), in speaking of the requirements for an effective therapist or counselor:

What was said about spontaneity as a characteristic of the mature personality applies doubly to the counselor. It has been mentioned several times that counseling is not a rigid mechanical application of formulas for producing behavior changes. The counselor's responses to clients' statements and feelings must be a spontaneous outgrowth of his understanding of that client. . . .

It is well established in counseling theory that attitudes are changed very little by advice, persuasion, or threats. The client's attitudes appear to change most effectively in the presence of other attitudes, for example, positive, tolerant attitudes on the part of the counselor. The client experiences acceptance as a feeling of being unconditionally understood, liked, and respected. Sometimes this positive attitude described is a basic form of altruistic love. The counselor, too, must open his defenses to make the relationship effective.

The risk element involves the possibility of failure or rejection by the client, and, if he does so, the counselor may lose part of himself. (p. 155)

In discussing the role of empathic understanding, Brammer and Shostrom suggest:

Porter made a useful distinction between understanding diagnostically and understanding therapeutically . . . an attitude of therapeutic understanding emphasizes seeing the client as he sees himself. Closely related to therapeutic understanding and acceptance attitudes is the often heard term "warmth" to describe an aspect of the relationship. Warmth appears to encompass the sensitive, friendly, considerate, and responsive elements of the counselor personality. And the counselor above all must be honest and sincere in his attitudes. Counseling cannot be a masquerade. (p. 165)

A similar description of the effective qualities of the therapist is given by Wyatt (1948):

The therapeutic situation is an unusual one in that the patient comes for help and talks about matters otherwise not disclosed. He is met by an attitude of unconditional acceptance, a point common to all systems of psychotherapy. The feeling of confidence fostered under these circumstances, a composite of trust, respect and liking of the therapist, is rapport. . . . Rapport, let alone transference, can only develop when the therapist has succeeded in showing that he understands the patient more effectively than the patient does himself. . . . Psychotherapy is not a cast of behavior, something that has to be put on, but a delicate interaction which has to be appropriate to its avowed purpose, but otherwise leaves the therapist as natural and spontaneous as he can be. It is actually a sign of professional maturity when the therapist begins to drop role and gesture and undertakes to be himself, and . . . therapeutic understanding of others will be effective only if the therapist maintains a constant scrutiny of his own self. (p. 83)

Even in the psychoanalytic treatment of schizophrenics, the requirements for an effective therapist show the same general qualities. Thus Arieti (1961) talks of the specifics in the patient-therapist relationship:

It is hard to teach, hard to learn, and at times seems to consist largely of "intuitional improvisations." . . . In speaking of the therapeutic attitude, there must be an *immediate* attempt on the part of the therapist to remove the fear which is automatically aroused by the fact that a human being (the therapist) wants to establish contact. There must be a general attitude of reassurance. . . . and, a sixth activity, which actually includes the previous five, consists in the establishment of *basic trust*. . . . different therapists convey this feeling of trust in different ways. . . . now that we have described the positive qualities necessary for the establishment of relatedness, we must mention the two main negative characteristics to be avoided. First, anxiety, at least to a great degree, must be avoided. . . . Second, clinical detachment. If the patient feels he is just a medical specimen or a "case," no effective relatedness can be established. (pp. 69, 77)

Arieti adds:

I do not want to give the impression I assume an artificially therapeutic attitude of relaxation and non-intellectuality, because to the best of my knowledge I do not. But my roles are different in different situations. I stress this point to indicate that although spontaneous and sincere, the therapeutic attitude cannot be the therapist's usual attitude toward life, it requires the acquisition of a special role. When I am with my wife, the accumulated tensions of the problems of the day may find easy manifestations. With my friends I am a peer, and since intellectuality is a part of me, it soon comes to the surface. With the patient, except at an advanced stage of treatment, I am not a peer. Although there is an exchange between the patient and myself, I want to give more than I take. I do not burden him with my own anxiety if I can help it, and intellectuality does not enter into the immediacy of our relatedness. (p. 78)

Similarly, Noyes and Kolb (1964), from an eclectic psychiatric orientation, note:

Although many different psychological techniques may be employed in an effort to relieve problems and disorders and make the patient a mature, satisfied and independent person, an important therapeutic factor common to them all is the therapist-patient relationship, with its interpersonal experiences. Through this relationship, the patient comes to know that he can share his feelings, attitudes, and experiences with the physician and that the latter, with his warmth, understanding, empathy, acceptance, and support, will not depreciate, censure, or judge him no matter what he may reveal but will respect his dignity and worth. This desired, positive patient-therapist relationship with its psychotherapeutic value, is often known as *transference.*

They continue:

The therapist, regardless of the type of therapy he employs, must have certain qualities. He should have a liking for people, possess a warm capacity for projecting himself into the situations and feelings of others, and be able to understand human motivation. He should not possess too many personality characteristics that are defensive in nature. (p. 504)

TOWARD THE EXPERIENCE AND MEANING OF THE CENTRAL THERAPEUTIC INGREDIENTS

The theories of practitioners who represent a variety of therapeutic and counseling approaches converge upon the central therapeutic ingredients of a "helping relationship." To be sure, their emphases vary, and there are large and small differences in the exact meaning of the constructs involved. Further, they diverge in many ways on *other* issues. It is perhaps worthwhile to repeat that these central ingredients of empathy, warmth, and genuineness do not merely represent "techniques" of psychotherapy or counseling, but are interpersonal skills that the counselor or therapist employs in *applying* his "techniques" or "expert knowledge," whether he be a psychotherapist, a vocational rehabilitation counselor, or a personnel counselor.

Having labeled the central therapeutic ingredients, there is the further crucial question of their operational meaning and practice.

As Rogers and Truax (1966) have suggested, the order in which these three therapeutic conditions are considered is especially significant because of their interlocking nature. To be facilitative toward another human being requires that we be deeply sensitive to his moment-to-moment experience, grasping both the core meaning and significance and the content of his experiences and feelings. Such deep empathic understanding requires first that we have at least a degree of warmth and respect for the other person. Thus, empathic understanding can scarcely exist without a prior or concomitant feeling of nonpossessive warmth. In turn, neither the empathy nor the warmth could be constructively meaningful in any human encounter unless it were "real." Unless the counselor or therapist is "genuine" in relating to the client, his warmth and empathy may even have a potentially threatening meaning. To be understood deeply by a potential enemy or by an unpredictable "phony" can be deeply threatening rather than facilitative.

In essence, then, the suggestion by Rogers and Truax was that the element of genuineness or authenticity is most basic to a relationship. Once this reality of the person of the therapist is established, the warmth and respect communicated to the patient becomes the second central ingredient in an effective relationship. Finally, given a relationship characterized by *warmth* and *genuineness,* the "work" of therapy or counseling proceeds through the therapist's moment-by-moment *empathic grasp* of the meaning and significance of the client's world.

These three therapeutic ingredients, as Shoben (1953) has noted, are not at all unique to psychotherapy or counseling. Instead, they are qualities of universal human experience that are present or absent in varying degrees in virtually all human relationships.

TOWARD THE EXPERIENCE AND MEANING OF GENUINENESS

In every person's experience are relationships with people who are not what they seem, who hide behind a conventional facade, who say things because they sound appropriate rather than because they mean them—who, in a word, are artificial. They contrast sharply with those about us who do say what they mean, who are spontaneously themselves, who are "real." As in the therapeutic relationship, we tend in everyday life to distrust and be wary of the artificial and to relate more securely and deeply to the genuine. Genuineness implies most basically a direct personal encounter, a meeting on a person-to-person basis without defensiveness or a retreat into facades or roles, and so in this sense an openness to experience.

This lack of defensiveness on the part of an effective therapist is stressed by Frieda Fromm-Reichmann (1952) in saying:

> It has been stated that the psychotherapist is expected to be stable and secure enough to be consistently aware of and in control of that which he conveys to his patients in words, and mindful of that which he may convey by empathy; that his need for operations aimed at his own security and satisfaction should not interfere with his ability to listen consistently to patients, with full alertness to their communications *per se* and, if possible, to the unworded implications of their verbalized communications; that he should never feel called upon to be anything more or less than the participant-observer of the emotional experiences which are conveyed to him by his patients. (p. 86)

> Nowadays many psychoanalysts no longer think of the psychotherapist as being unresponsive to and only a mirror of the patient's utterances. We consider him a participant-observer in the psychotherapeutic process. Also, we do not believe that it is necessary or desirable for the psychiatrist to bar responsive reactions of spontaneity from the psychotherapeutic scene, as long as his responses cannot be used by patients as a means of orientation inadvertently guiding their productions and behavior. Also they must, of course, be *genuine* responses to the patient's communications and not colored by his private collateral experiences. (p. 69)

> . . . He may feel called upon to hide his insecurity by displaying professional pompousness. Such an endeavor is highly undesirable; in fact, it may doom the psychotherapeutic procedure to failure. (p. 70)

In many ways, a lack of genuineness is at the core of what psychoanalytic theorists have called countertransference, in the sense that there may be serious distortions in the therapist's own personality. In speaking of countertransference, Noyes and Kolb (1964) say:

> This consists of such negative attitudes of physician to patient as anger, impatience, or resentment. These and similar attitudes are almost certain to interfere with the therapeutic effectiveness of the physician. For the most part, the countertransference reactions arise in the therapist as a result of the patient's influence on the physician's unconscious feelings and have their origin in the latter's irrational projections and identifications. The therapist must not permit his own unconscious feelings and attitudes aroused during phases of treatment to intrude in his relation toward the patient. (p. 505)

The kind of incongruence that arises from the counselor's or therapist's own psychological disturbance is emphasized as highly detrimental by virtually every therapeutic approach since Freud's early discovery and delineation of countertransference. Thus, in summarizing the commonalities between divergent approaches to treatment, Rotter (1964) finds:

> In fact, there is general agreement on many points; that the therapist should be accepting, sympathetic and interested in his patients; that the therapist should be either free from serious distortions of his own personality, or at

least thoroughly understand his own problems and be on his guard against projecting them onto his patients. . . . (p. 86)

Whitaker and Malone (1953) have strikingly described the harmful effects of the artificiality that arises from the counselor's or therapist's insecurity and his consequent retreat into the "therapist role." They have gone further than anyone else in suggesting that such attempts by the therapist served no real defensive purpose, since the patient was not fooled: "Patients can always see beneath the therapist's technical skill, and if this is artificial, it becomes another barrier placed between the patient and the person of the therapist."

There is no real alternative to genuineness in the psychotherapeutic relationship. Even if he were a skilled, polished actor, it is doubtful that a therapist could hide his real feelings from the client. When the therapist pretends to care, pretends to respect, or pretends to understand, he is fooling only himself. The patient may not know why the therapist is "phony," but he can easily detect true warmth from phony and insincere "professional warmth."

The importance of the genuineness of the human encounter itself has been greatly stressed by the existential approach to psychotherapy and has thus influenced therapists of various other orientations. In speaking of psychotherapeutic treatment of children, Moustakas (1959) describes this aspect of genuineness in his own personal therapeutic encounters with children:

> I saw that I must stop playing the role of the professional therapist and allow my potentials, talents, and skills, my total experience as a human being to blend naturally into the relationship with the child and whenever humanly possible to meet him as a whole person. Thus, I came to realize that one person, a direct, human-loving person, a unified personal and professional self, meets another person, a loving or potentially loving child and through a series of deep human encounters, waits for, and enables the child to come to his own self fulfillment. (p. 201)

Since the best operational definitions of genuineness revolve around describing its absence, it is clearly not easy to describe or to achieve. It involves the very difficult task of being quite intimately acquainted with ourselves, and of being able to recognize and accept, as well as respect, ourselves as a whole, containing both good and bad.

TOWARD THE EXPERIENCE AND MEANING OF WARMTH

Although warmth is of central importance to any trusting relationship, it is even more crucial for the therapeutic relationship, which centers on the inadequacies, the life failures, and the guilt-ridden feelings and acts of the client. As English (1945) puts it:

Most people, however, have what they call—a sense of importance and of their own completeness—and when the doctor makes any implication that they are childish, that they are reacting to life in an immature way, that they are emotionally weak, that they ought to do better in some way, the medicine is not easy to take. In applying it the doctor has to do so with a great deal of tact, understanding and kindness. (p. 402)

As early as 1912, Freud spoke of the curative effects of "warmth or positive affect." In a discussion of the transference phenomenon and the therapeutic relationship, he specifically advocated the therapist's use of warmth and its role in suggesting:

So the answer to the riddle is that the transference to the physician is only suited for resistance insofar as it consists in "negative" feelings or in the repressed "erotic" elements of positive feeling. As we "raise" the transference by making it conscious we detach only these two components of the emotional relationship from the person of the physician; the conscious and unobjectionable component of it remains, and brings about the successful result in psychoanalysis as in all other remedial methods. (p. 319)

The warm and permissive aspect of the therapeutic relationship was stressed in 1927 by Ferenczi, according to Thompson (1950). His use of a warm and permissive relationship was based upon his developing belief that the neurotic patient was essentially one who had received an insufficiency of love and acceptance as a child.

This view of warmth as curative and involving the essence of love has been given greater and greater prominence by analytic theorists. Thus Rosen (1947), who relied heavily on the transference mechanism in treatment, stated: "He [the therapist] must make up for the tremendous deficit of love experienced in the patient's life." Menninger (1958), in turn, speaks of warmth as: ". . . the example of the psychoanalyst himself—his poise, his patience, his fairness, his consistency, his rationality, his kindliness, in short—his *real* love for the patient."

Nunberg (1955) suggests:

Contact between patient and analyst is established through the transference, which is facilitated by the fact that every human being feels the need for a companion. The majority of neurotics, perhaps all of them, in spite of their disturbed social relations, are anxious for contact with another person. (p. 339)

The interrelationship between the genuineness and self-acceptance of the therapist and his ability to feel and communicate warmth for the patient is discussed by Frieda Fromm-Reichmann (1949) as follows:

One of the important principles of intensive psychotherapy is that the psychiatrist endeavor not to hurt the patient's self-respect unnecessarily. (p. 68)

There is one more reason why the psychiatrist's self-respect is of paramount significance for the therapeutic procedure. If it is true that one's ability to respect others is dependent upon the development of one's self-respect, then it follows that only a self-respecting psychotherapist is capable of respecting his patients and of meeting them on the basis of mutual human equality. . . . The psychiatrist's respect for his patients will also help to safeguard against the previously mentioned mistake of assuming an attitude of personal "irrational authority" instead of listening and conducting therapy in the spirit of collaborative guidance. (pp. 72-73)

The nonpossessive, or unconditional, aspect of this warmth has been heavily underscored by Rogers et al. (1951, 1957a, 1966) in speaking of the warmth and prizing for the client being without "if's, and's, or but's." This nonpossessive aspect of therapeutic warmth has also long been central to the psychoanalytic view. The nonjudgmental nature of the therapist or psychoanalyst's role was heavily underscored by Freud as early as 1912, and has now been accepted by virtually all approaches to relationship and expressive psychotherapy. In considering the vital role of an accepting, warm and expressive therapist-patient relationship, Cameron (1963) suggests:

[Psychotherapy] may begin, as does supportive psychotherapy, merely with sincere accepting attitudes, with genuine respect for human beings, and with a mature understanding of the difficulties inherent in human life. The relationship psychotherapist provides a warm, friendly, wholesome adult in the therapeutic situation, who not only tolerates disagreement and opposition in his patient but expects tolerance from the patient when he expresses opposition or refuses to agree. . . . He is neither praised for defiance and opposition nor condemned for expressing his dependency needs. (p. 769)

Cameron comments upon some commonalities in all forms of psychotherapy:

The patient must feel free to establish psychological closeness with the therapist, or to put psychological distance between himself and his therapist, without fear of arousing personal affection or personal offense. The therapist, for his part, remains always friendly, warm, firm and accepting, but he avoids anything that approaches a personal *entanglement* with his patient. The competent psychotherapist is not offended by a patient's coolness, criticism, hostility or provocation. (p. 769)

That nonpossessive warmth does not mean unwarranted optimism or mere reassurance is suggested strongly by psychoanalytic writings and by such experienced counselors as Robinson (1955), who offers:

This continuum varies from unintentional rejection (e.g., incorrect use of assurance presenting a "silver lining" in response to a client's problem statement, pursuing the counselor's line of thought rather than the client's, etc.) through differing degrees of acceptance (i.e., differing degrees of warmth and approval indicated in response to different client ideas). (p. 166)

Other counselors, such as McGowan and Schmidt (1962), suggest that it is the warmth of the relationship that allows the patient to overlook the mistakes and errors that the counselor must inevitably make:

> If the counselor is able to convey to the person he is working with the impression that he is sincerely interested in him, and wants to help him, then the counselor can use different responses and techniques, and even make certain technical "errors" within the relationship without seriously impairing the process. And . . . what we say as counselors is not as important as how we say it. (p. 322)

That the warmth must be genuine, with the aspect of a personal encounter, has been reemphasized by White (1948) in his attempt to describe commonalities of the therapeutic relationship in all forms of psychotherapy. He notes:

> The therapist is an expert . . . the therapist is permissive, the therapist is *interested* and *friendly,* communicating in this way a certain *warmth* that makes the relationship more personal than is ordinarily the case . . . the therapist is a source of encouragement. (p. 45)

Even the behavior therapist who describes his work in a mechanistic rather than humanistic form and relies on Pavlovian psychology finds it necessary to stress the role of warmth. Thus Wolpe (1958) asserts the following:

> All that the patient says is accepted without question or criticism. He is given the feeling that the therapist is unreservedly at his side. This happens not because the therapist is expressly trying to appear sympathetic, but as a natural outcome of a completely non-moralizing objective approach to the behavior of human organisms. (p. 106)

Rotter (1964) also notes the crucial role of warmth even in a social learning approach to psychotherapy:

> [The therapist is] more active in making interpretations to the patient and directly reinforcing or rewarding particular kinds of optimal behavior, and in helping the patient find new alternatives to deal with problems. In order to do this successfully, it is necessary that the patient *trust* him and accept his objectivity in the situation. Consequently, the good therapist is "warm" and communicates to his patients his concern and interest in them. (p. 86)

Warmth, of course, can be communicated in a variety of ways. Most importantly it can be active and challenging, as described by Harry Stack Sullivan (1954):

> For instance, sometimes the interviewer may ask a question which leads the interviewee to make what he feels is a most damaging admission so that he then becomes intensely anxious—although he may cover the anxiety by equally intense feelings of anger or another emotion. The remedy lies in the interviewer's then asking a question about the "damaging admission"; for

example, he may ask, "Well, am I supposed to think badly of you because of that?" Now this may seem like a strange kind of operation, but its value is that it puts into words the content of the interviewee's signs of anxiety. The answer is ordinarily "Yes," and the next step is to ask, "Well, how come? What's so lamentable about such a thing?" (p. 225)

In recent years some theorists of particular schools of psychotherapy have attempted to convince themselves and perhaps others that warmth and empathy were new and even revolutionary concepts. Cameron (1963) notes:

It was Freud who developed and openly advocated these procedures. It was he who practiced them with his patients from the beginning of the century, and for more than thirty years thereafter. They have always been, and still are, essential components in all intensive psychotherapy.

Ever since Freud, it has been established practice among competent psychotherapists to treat patients and their complaints with respect, warmth and understanding, to meet the emotional aspects of their behavior with empathy, that is with thorough emotional understanding. (p. 770)

Nonpossessive warmth has also been emphasized as basic to almost all forms of group therapy. Slavson (1956) stresses the role of warmth between group members as an analogue to the mother-child relationship:

The ego debilities that result from the feeling of being unique and isolated are overcome through group relationships. Instead of relying solely upon himself in bearing the stresses of life, the individual shares his burdens with others who support and guide him. His capacity for relationship, trust and faith in people is thus increased through fellow group members whose basic intent is one of helpfulness and support rather than hostility and destructiveness. (p. 8)

It is safe to hypothesize that the therapist, whether male or female, symbolizes in groups the father figure, while the group as an entity represents the mother image. It is from the group that patients expect and demand protection, kindliness, understanding and support, as they did from their mothers. (p. 13)

TOWARD THE EXPERIENCE AND MEANING OF EMPATHY

That an empathic understanding of another human being grows out of the warmth, respect, and even love for that human being is underscored by Buber in his translation of a Hasidic parable:

[He] sat among peasants in a village inn and listened to their conversation. Then he heard how one asked the other, "Do you love me?" And the latter answered, "Now, of course, I love you very much." But the first regarded him sadly and reproached him for such words: "How can you say you love me? Do you know, then, my faults?" And then the other fell silent, and silent they sat facing each other, for there was nothing more to say. He who truly loves knows, from the depths of his identity with the other, from the root ground of the other's being he knows where his friend is wanting. This alone is love. (p. 248)

For Buber (1953), accurate empathy is indeed the working force of any helping relationship. The growth of the self (whether of client, patient, or the plain unlabeled human being) takes place primarily in empathic relationships:

For the inmost growth of the self is not accomplished, as people like to suppose today, in man's relation to himself, but in the relations between the one and the other, between me, that is, preeminently in the mutuality of the making present—in the making present of another self and in the knowledge that one is made present in his own self by the other—together with the mutuality of acceptance, affirmation and confirmation. (p. 249)

In psychoanalysis proper, Cameron (1963) points out:

The myth of the analyst as a blank screen, however, belongs to the history of psychoanalysis, not to its current practice. When the psychoanalyst does speak, it's to encourage the free flow of verbalized thought, and emotion, to comment upon something that needs comment, sometimes to repeat a fragment that seems promising, to confront the patient with what he is expressing, and once in a while to make an interpretation. The competent psychoanalyst is exceedingly sparing with his interpretations . . . when the psychoanalyst makes an interpretation, it is usually to *reformulate* what the patient is expressing, and to relate it to unconscious material which has neared the surface. (p. 771)

Actually, empathy has long been a central tool in psychoanalysis—not a diagnostic and external understanding, but a truly empathic understanding as described by Fliess (1942):

[It depends] essentially on his ability to put himself in the latter's place, to step into his shoes, and to obtain in this way inside knowledge that is almost first-hand. The common name for such a procedure is "empathy"; and we, as a suitable name for it in our own nomenclature, should like to suggest calling it trial identification. (p. 212)

Indeed, White (1948) notes that even the procedure of "interpretation," the cornerstone of psychoanalytic procedure, does not sharply differ from the client-centered procedure of "recognition of feelings." For White:

Interpretation may be regarded as a more active form of recognition. Instead of recognizing the patient's feelings as they are expressed, the therapist recognizes feelings before they are expressed or when they are still being expressed in disguised ways—at all events, before the patient himself has recognized them. When suitably timed, this procedure also results in corrective emotional experience. (p. 346)

For psychoanalytic theorists, as well as client-centered and many eclectic ones, the tentative nature of the therapist's empathic responses are central. In this respect, Cameron (1963) adds:

Every psychoanalyst knows that some of his interpretations will be incorrect, that some will be half-correct, and that some will be correct but ill-timed. What seemed ready to emerge was not actually ready. It may have been near the surface, but too laden with anxiety to be released into conscious awareness. It should be abundantly clear that psychoanalysis today does not haul things from the unconscious into consciousness, as many of its critics seem to assume. The psychoanalyst makes use of everything and anything that appears in the patient's behavior. He notices how the patient comes in and how he leaves, what he says, how he looks, his mannerisms, his movements, and his postures. A sign, a blush, a change in breathing or in the speed of talk, a stammer, a flooding of free associations, the patient's restlessness, or his very want of appropriate feelings, may any one of them be much more important than what the patient happens to be saying. (p. 772)

When viewed in terms of actual *behavior* rather than differences in jargon, the analytic and client-centered approaches to empathic understanding seem to converge. In describing the main technique of client-centered therapy, Shlien (1961) offers:

That technique is "reflection"—particularly reflection of feeling rather than content. At most points in communication where others would interpret, probe, advise, encourage, we reflect. . . . Reflection can be, in the hands of an imitating novice, a dull, wooden mockery. On paper it often looks particularly so. Yet it can also be a profound, intimate, empathically understanding response, requiring great skill and sensitivity and intense involvement. (p. 302)

Further similarity in the actual therapy behavior of divergent therapists is shown by their use of everyday words in the actual therapeutic encounter. Cameron (1963) highlights this in speaking of psychoanalytic and all forms of expressive psychotherapy:

True expressive psychotherapy is carried out by both patient and therapist alike in ordinary everyday terms. The good psychotherapist always adopts some of the patient's own terms in their communication, always being sure he does this without artificiality, condescension, or facetiousness. When a patient says approvingly, "you speak my language," this may well be a sign that the therapist is reaching the patient at a commonsense, personal level. (p. 769)

That empathic understanding is not a passive phenomenon in which the therapist somehow mystically comes to know the patient and his inner world is suggested by Burnham (1961) in his description of his own approach to therapy with schizophrenics. He describes his own attempts to understand:

In his effort to facilitate communication the therapist strives to understand the patient's behavior by observing how he behaves and by formulating ideas as to why he behaves in that particular way. This requires that he gain some idea of how the world looks to the patient. Therefore, the therapist tries by observation, inference, and guess work to gain a reasonably accurate picture of the flow of thoughts and feelings across the stage of the patient's consciousness, and to grasp the representation of reality which the patient organizes from this flow of conscious experience. . . . To the extent that the observer is unable to grasp or imagine the patient's personal frame of reference, the latter's behavior may seem senseless, purposeless, unaccountable, strange, or bizarre. (pp. 209-210)

The effects of shared empathy are described from a phenomonological point of view by van Kaam (1959):

. . . experience of "really feeling understood" is a perceptual-emotional Gestalt. A subject, perceiving that a person coexperiences what things mean to the subject and accepts him, feels initially, relief from experiential loneliness, and, gradually, safe experiential communion with that person and with that which the subject perceives this person to represent. (p. 69)

From still a different point of view, which has grown out of a Slavsonian approach to group treatment of disturbed children, Ginott (1965) has underlined the importance of accurate empathic understanding for the parent-child relationship (and indeed any human relationship). He says:

How can we help a child to know his feelings? We can do so by serving as a mirror to his emotions. A child learns about his physical likeness by seeing his image in a mirror. He learns about his emotional likeness by hearing his feelings reflected by us.

The function of a mirror is to reflect an image as it is, without adding flattery or faults. We do not want a mirror to tell us, "You look terrible. Your eyes are bloodshot and your face is puffy. Altogether you are a mess. You'd better do something about yourself." After a few exposures to such a magic mirror, we would avoid it like the plague. From a mirror we want an image, not a sermon. We may not like the image we see; still, we would rather decide for ourselves our next cosmetic move.

The function of an emotional mirror is to reflect feelings as they are, without distortion:

"It looks as though you are very angry."
"It sounds like you hate him very much."
"It seems that you are disgusted with the whole set-up."

To a child who has such feelings, these statements are most helpful. They show him clearly what his feelings are. Clarity of image, whether in a looking glass or in an emotional mirror, provides opportunity for self-initiated grooming and change. (pp. 35-36)

Further, there is considerable agreement among therapists of varied orientations that an effective empathic response does not merely reflect the client's current state of awareness, but expands that awareness by going beyond his current verbalizations. Speaking as a counselor, Robinson (1955) says: ". . . all agree that the degree to which a counselor's remarks tend to go beyond what the client has said represents a sensitive means of adjusting to moment-by-moment changes in client characteristics. . . ." From a psychiatric and psychoanalytic point of view, Cameron (1963) is in close agreement in saying:

> The good therapist does not, of course, coerce his patient to move too rapidly into sensitive areas. As French has often expressed it, the good therapist, like the good gardener, waits until he recognizes something which is struggling to emerge, and then makes it easier for it to emerge. He never tries to drag anything up from the unconscious or deep preconscious into awareness. (p. 769)

Although it may seem from these views that the effectiveness of accurate empathy and understanding in producing patient personality and behavioral change depends on warmth and genuineness, this does not imply that the therapist will first be genuine, then develop a feeling of warmth for the client, and finally be better able to empathically grasp the client's meaning. It seems that in practice quite the reverse is true. Most often we come to value, prize, respect and like a patient or client as we listen and discover the nature of his inner world. In addition, with increasing understanding we can be ourselves more easily and freely in the relationship with the client.

As we come to know some of his wants, some of his needs, some of his achievements and some of his failures, we find ourselves as therapists "living" with the patient much as we do with the central figure of a novel. In this crucial sense, the psychoanalytic view of empathy as "trial identification" has great meaning in the practice of therapy. Just as with the character in the novel, we come to know the person from his own internal frame of reference, gaining some flavor of his moment-by-moment experience. We see events and significant people in his life as they appear to him—not as they "objectively are" but as he experiences them. As we come to know him from his personal vantage point we automatically come to value and like him. Perhaps precisely because we are concentrating on *his* experience, we are much freer from everyday threat and insecurity and so can be in those moments more genuine and authentic. This trial identification has the "as if" quality that Rogers (1957b) speaks of in describing empathy. We begin to perceive the events and experiences of his life "as if" they were parts of our own life. It is through this process that we come to feel warmth, respect and liking for a person who in everyday life is unlikable, weak, cowardly, treacherous, vile, or despicable.

As with the hero of outstanding novels, we come to know and value and respect the client not because he is good, exemplary, or what we ourselves would like to be, but because we understand him and his life experiences from his own internal frame of reference rather than from an external "objective" viewpoint. This, it seems to us, is the central essence of Rogers' (1951) client-centered approach to therapy, which differs more in print than in practice from others.

TOWARD A TENTATIVE MEASUREMENT OF THE CENTRAL THERAPEUTIC INGREDIENTS

When accurate empathy, nonpossessive warmth and genuineness are thought of as dimensions of the psychotherapeutic process, then some attempt to specify degrees of these three factors is a necessary prior step to research and training. Building on the work of prior researchers, attempts were made in 1957 to specify rating scales measuring accurate empathy, nonpossessive warmth and genuineness. These global scales made heavy use of the raters, who were asked to draw upon their own abundant experience of being understood and misunderstood, warmly and coldly received, and met with an artificial and a genuine human being. At first the scales were quite closely tied to Rogers' statements and grew out of a seminar with him during the early part of 1957. Since that time the evidence has suggested that "empathy" is not so related to client improvement as "accurate empathy," which contains elements of the psychoanalytic view of moment-to-moment diagnostic accuracy. The evidence has also suggested that "unconditionality" of positive regard does not greatly contribute to outcome, and that what seems most related to outcome is the communication of a "nonpossessive" warmth in the sense specified by Alexander (1948).

Also, what seemed most related to client improvement was not simply a congruence between the therapist's organismic self and his behavior or self concept, but rather the absence of defensiveness or phoniness—his seeming genuineness. Thus the identifying labels for the three therapeutic interpersonal skills discussed in this chapter (and at greater length in later chapters) have changed. The three rating scales to be presented shortly have not changed since 1962. Most certainly they will be changed and greatly improved upon. It has been a constant temptation to modify the scales in the hope of improving them—a temptation resisted in order to allow more direct comparisons to be made between studies and training efforts based on them. Although the present measurement scales are highly inferential and crude in construction, they represent a beginning attempt to specify the operational meaning of the concepts.[4] The scales were

4. The Accurate Empathy Scale was developed in 1961 and the Unconditional Positive Regard and Genuineness Scales in 1962 by Charles B. Truax with the support of NIMH Grant No. M3496 and Grant No. RD906 from the Vocational Rehabilitation Administration. The author is deeply indebted to Carl R. Rogers, Shirley Epstein, Edward Williams, Eugene T. Gendlin, Ferdinand van der Veen, and to a number of colleagues and students who served as raters, for suggestions, criticism and advice.

designed primarily for use with live observations or tape recordings of counseling or therapy interviews. They have been used with only a slight loss in reliability on typescripts of psychotherapeutic interaction. The authors and others have applied the scales to samples of psychotherapeutic interaction varying from as short as two minutes to as long as sixteen minutes of continuous therapy transactions. The scales have been used in both individual and group psychotherapy or counseling, although they were originally designed for the study of individual counseling and psychotherapy.

The research scales which follow serve to provide more concrete specifications, along quantified dimensions, of the three seemingly common central ingredients of effective therapeutic encounters, on which this book focuses. They provide a crude but beginning operational definition of accurate empathy, nonpossessive warmth, and genuineness.

Before turning directly to the scales themselves some evidence of their value should be indicated. In general, the value of any instrument is assessed in terms of its reliability and its validity.

The reliability of the scales is easy to assess. The question is, simply, can you get repeated measures that are closely alike? A way of answering that question is to correlate different raters' ratings on the scales for the same samples of therapeutic transactions. Such correlations for twenty-eight studies involving a variety of therapist and patient populations is presented in Table 1. The answer in general, then, seems to be that most often a moderate to high degree of reliability is obtained with the scales whether measurement is of counseling or therapy, group or individual.

Establishing validity raises the question: Do the scales measure what they purport to measure? Does the Accurate Empathy Scale measure accurate empathy or something else? That kind of question is more difficult to answer in any clear fashion. The reader can assess the face validity of the scales themselves as he reads them. Beyond that, we know from the evidence cited in the next chapter (Chapter 3) that these scales are significantly related to a variety of client therapeutic outcomes. From this we might say that *whatever* they are measuring is what we believe the theory should say constitutes central therapeutic ingredients. Moreover, what the scales do indeed measure is what the fields of counseling and therapy should make central aspects of training and practice. In fact, the reader should become quite familiar with the scales themselves, for when theory or clinical description enlarges upon them, then we move to that degree toward supposition and belief and away from the hard evidence. It is for this precise reason that the scales themselves are used as an essential and integral part of training.

The three scales shown here define the meaning of the findings to be reported in Chapter 3, since the bulk of the research reviewed there was based upon use of them. They were the basis for the ratings, and thus the findings, in a growing number of research studies. Moreover, the Accurate Empathy Scale, the Nonpossessive Warmth (or Unconditional

Table 1
Reliabilities of Rating Scales for Accurate Empathy, Nonpossessive Warmth, and Genuineness from Specific Studies

Study		N Samples	N Patients	N Therapists	Group or Individual		Accurate Empathy	Nonpossessive Warmth	Genuineness
Truax (1961		384	8	7	Individual		.87		
Truax & Carkhuff (1963)		297	14	10	Individual		.89	.50[a]	.40[a]
Truax & Carkhuff (1963)		112	28	24	Individual		.69[a]	.55[a]	
Truax (1962)		448	14	10	Individual		.69[a]		
Bergin & Solomon (1963)		28	28	18	Individual		.79[a]		
Melloh (1964)		56	28	28	Individual		.62[a]		
Truax, Wargo, Frank, Imber, Battle, Hoehn-Saric, Nash, & Stone (1966a)		182	40	4	Individual		.63	.59	.60
Truax, Carkhuff & Kodman (1965)		192	40	4	Group		.87	.91	.72
Truax & Wargo (1966c)		698	160	15	Group		.81	.76	.80
Truax & Wargo (1966b)		366	80	6	Group		.95	.90	.95
Truax, Wargo & Carkhuff (1966)		89	80	8	Group		.88	.77	.41
Wargo (1962)		297	14	10	Individual		.89	.50[a]	
Di.kenson & Truax (1966)		72	48	1	Group		.83	.75	.25
Truax, Wargo & Silber (1966)		192	40	2	Group		.93	.81	.56
Truax & Carkhuff (1963)		64	8	8	Individual		.57[a]	.62[a]	.45[a]
Truax (1962e)		104	26	1	Individual		.69[a]	.55[a]	.40[a]
Truax, Wargo, Frank, Imber, Battle, Hoehn-Saric, Nash, & Stone (1966b)	(Screening Interviews)	80	40	2	Individual	(Screening Interviews)	.75[a]	.57[a]	.55[a]
	(Therapy Interviews)	182		4		(Therapy Interviews)	.63	.59	.60
Truax (1966b)	(Edited)	50	5	5	Individual	(Edited)	.66[a]	.84[a]	
	(Non-Edited)	50				(Non-Edited)	.76[a]	.81[a]	
Truax (1966a)	(TPT)	283	63			(TPT)	.84	.86	.81
	(PTP)	305	65	8	Group	(PTP)	.89	.85	.73
	(Time)	384	80			(Time)	.92	.95	.95
Truax & Carkhuff (1965a)		45	3	1	Individual		.78	.70	.83
Carkhuff & Truax (1965)		151	70	28	Individual		.43[a]	.48[a]	.62[a]
Truax & Silber (1966)		144	48	16	Individual		.54	.52	.46
Truax, Silber & Carkhuff (1965)		342	80	5	Group		.50	.71	.48
Truax (1966)		161	30	4	Group		.59	.84	.85

a. Average Pearson correlations. All others are Ebel intraclass reliabilities for the pooled data used in analysis of findings.

Positive Regard) Scale, and the Therapist Genuineness (or Self-Congruence) Scale which follow were central to the present approach to training that is discussed in Section II.

A Tentative Scale For The Measurement Of Accurate Empathy

GENERAL DEFINITION

Accurate empathy involves more than just the ability of the therapist to sense the client or patient's "private world" as if it were his own. It also involves more than just his ability to know what the patient means. Accurate empathy involves both the therapist's *sensitivity to current feelings* and his *verbal facility to communicate this understanding* in a language attuned to the client's current feelings.

It is not necessary—indeed it would seem undesirable—for the therapist to *share* the client's feelings in any sense that would require him to feel the same emotions. It is instead an appreciation and a sensitive awareness of those feelings. At deeper levels of empathy, it also involves enough understanding of patterns of human feelings and experience to sense feelings that the client only partially reveals. With such experience and knowledge, the therapist can communicate what the client clearly knows as well as meanings in the client's experience of which he is scarcely aware.

At a *high* level of accurate empathy the message "I am *with* you" is unmistakably clear—the therapist's remarks fit perfectly with the client's mood and content. His responses not only indicate his sensitive understanding of the obvious feelings, but also serve to clarify and expand the client's awareness of his own felings or experiences. Such empathy is communicated by both the language used and all the voice qualities, which unerringly reflect the therapist's seriousness and depth of feeling. The therapist's intent concentration upon the client keeps him continuously aware of the client's shifting emotional content so that he can shift his own responses to correct for language or content errors when he temporarily loses touch and is not "with" the client.

At a *low* level of accurate empathy the therapist may go off on a tangent of his own or may misinterpret what the patient is feeling. At a very low level he may be so preoccupied and interested in his own intellectual interpretations that he is scarcely aware of the client's "being." The therapist at this low level of accurate empathy may even be uninterested in the client, or may be concentrating on the intellectual content of what the client says rather than what he "is" at the moment, and so may ignore or misunderstand the client's current feelings and experiences. At this low level of empathy the therapist is doing something other than "listening," "understanding," or "being sensitive"; he may be evaluating the client, giving advice, sermonizing, or simply reflecting upon his own feelings or experiences. Indeed, he may be accurately describing psychodynamics to the patient—but in the wrong language for the client, or at the wrong time, when these dynamics are far removed from the client's current feelings, so that the interaction takes on the flavor of "teacher-pupil."

STAGE 1

Therapist seems completely unaware of even the most conspicuous of the client's feelings; his responses are not appropriate to the mood and content of the client's statements. There is no determinable quality of empathy, and hence no accuracy whatsoever. The therapist may be bored and disinterested or actively offering advice, but he is not communicating an awareness of the client's current feelings.

Example A:

C: Sir, are you ready? (Earnestly)

T: (Mumbled) What about?

C: I want one thing to know—us—is it or is it not normal for a woman to feel like that, like I felt—degraded—one thing right after the other from Sunday on—or is it a lesson? (Sadly, dramatically) Is it immature to feel like this? Is really maturity—what it says in the books, that one has to understand the other person—is a woman supposed to give constantly and—be actually humiliated?

T: (Casually) If she asks for it.

C: (Registering surprise) If she asks for it. Did I ask for it? (Testily)

T: Well, I don't know. I doubt—I don't think you did. (Mechanically)

Example B:

C: I wonder if it's my educational background or if it's me.

T: Mhm.

C: You know what I mean.

T: Yeah.

C: (Pause) I guess if I could just solve that I'd know just about where to hit, huh?

T: Mhm, mhm. Now that you know, a way, if you knew for sure, that your, your lack, if that's what it is—I can't be sure of that yet.

(C: No)

T: (Continuing) . . . is really so, that it, it might even feel as though it's something that you just couldn't receive, that it, if, that would be it?

C: Well—I—I didn't, uh, I don't quite follow you—clearly.

T: Well (pause), I guess, I was, I was thinking that—that you perhaps thought that, that if you could be sure that, the, uh, that there were tools that, that you didn't have, that, perhaps that could mean that these—uh—tools that you had lacked—way back there in, um, high school

(C: *Yah*)

T: (Continuing) . . . and perhaps just couldn't perceive now and, ah . . .

C: Eh, yes, or I might put it this way, um (pause). If I knew that it was, um, let's just take it this way. If I knew that it was my educational background, there would be a possibility of going back.

T: Oh, so, I missed that now, I mean now, and, uh . . .

C: . . . and really getting myself equipped.

T: I see, I was—uh—I thought you were saying in some ways that, um, um, you thought that, if, if that was so, you were just kind of doomed.

C: No, I mean . . .

C: I see.

C: Uh, *not doomed.* Well let's take it this way, um, as I said, if, uh, it's my educational background, then I could go *back* and, catch myself up.

T: I see.

C: And come up.

T: Um.

STAGE 2

Therapist shows an almost negligible degree of accuracy in his responses, and that only toward the client's most obvious feelings. Any emotions which are not clearly defined he tends to ignore altogether. He may be correctly sensitive to obvious feelings and yet misunderstand much of what the client is really trying to say. By his response he may block off or may misdirect the patient. Stage 2 is distinguishable from Stage 3 in that the therapist ignores feelings rather than displaying an inability to understand them.

Example A:

C: You've got to explain so she can understand . . .

T: Mhm, mhm (in bored tone)

C: Without—uh—giving her the impression that she can get away with it, too. (Excitedly)

T: Well, you've got a job satisfying all the things that—seem important, for instance being consistent, and yet keeping her—somewhat disciplined and telling her it's good for her. (Conversationally)

C: There's where the practical application of what we have just mentioned comes into being. (Laughs)

T: Mhm, mhm. (Sounding bored)

C: And when it's a theoretical plan—

T: Mhm.

C: It's beautiful! (Shrilly)

T: Mhm—mhm.

C: But . . .

T: (Interrupting) Something else about it that I feel *really* dubious about (banteringly)—what you can really do on the practical level (inquiringly)—I sometimes say that's what—we're most encouraged about, too. (Mumbling)

C: (Chiming in loudly) Yes—uh—there are many—uh problems in our lives in the practical application of—trying to be consistent. (Informatively)

STAGE 3

Therapist often responds accurately to client's more exposed feelings. He also displays concern for the deeper, more hidden feelings, which he seems to sense must be present, though he does not understand their nature or sense their meaning to the patient.

Example A:

C: I'm here, an' uh—I guess that maybe I'll go through with it, and—(nervous laugh)—I'll have to—there's no use—

T: (Interrupting) You mean you're here—you mean you're right here—I wasn't sure when you said that . . .

C: Well . . .

T: . . . Whether you meant you were—I guess you mean you were in—this is your situation. (Stumbling)

C: (Interjecting) I'm in—I'm in—I'm in the stage of suffering—well, yes, I'm here too because of that. An'—uh—(sighs audibly)—but, I can see where—uh . . . (T: murmurs "Mhm" after every other word or so.)

T:(Filling in) You feel it's—you feel it's a pretty tough situation to be in? (Inquiringly)

C: Sometimes I do, sometimes I don't. (Casually)

Example B:

C: Now that you're . . . know the difference between girls; I think they were about 9 to 8 years old and, uh, they were just like dolls, you know, and (laughs) uh, I used to spend a lot of time with 'em. I used to go over there and would spend more time with these kinds than what would with . . .

T: Mhm, hm.

C: But nobody ever told me why I was dragged in here. And I own my own place, I have my, my . . . and my farm, I think I still own them. Because that, there was a little mortgage on it. And, uh, (pause) my ex-wife but I don't see how in the world they could change that.

T: Mhm, hm.

C: But they sold my livestock and, uh, I, I worked with horses, and they sold them all, and ah . . .

T: I think probably, should I cross this microphone? (Noises)

C: And then I had a bunch of sheep.

T: Mhm, hm.

C: And they sold that stuff off, and the social worker, Mrs. L., says to me, she says that, uh, she says I was ill when I was brought in here.

T: Mhm, hm.

C: And that, which I know that I was not ill. Now, I'll tell you what she might've meant in what way I was ill. Now I'll tell 'ya, I batched it out there on the farm and I maybe just didn't get such too good food at the time. Now, whether she wanted to call that ill, or whether she wanted to call it mentally ill, that she didn't say.

T: Mhm, hm.

C: But she says I was ill, well, they could put that I was sick that I didn't have the right kind of food because I gained quite a bit of weight after I was brought in here.

T: Mhm, hm.

C: Yeah, but she didn't say which way she meant or how she meant that.

T: Uh, huh.

C: And she wouldn't give me any explanation and then I got mad at her . . .

T: Mhm, hm.

C: . . . and of course I told her off. Then I asked her if she, they kept from me for a long time that my stock was sold and I thought quietly, anyhow, I says, I won't give my work . . .

STAGE 4

Therapist usually responds accurately to the client's more obvious feelings and occasionally recognizes some that are less apparent. In the process of this tentative probing, however, he may misinterpret some present feelings and anticipate some which are not current. Sensitivity and awareness do exist in the therapist, but he is not entirely "with" the patient in the *current* situation or experience. The desire and effort to understand are both present, but his accuracy is low. This stage is distinguishable from Stage 3 in that the therapist does occasionally recognize less apparent feelings. He also may seem to have a theory about the patient and may even know how or why the patient feels a particular way, but he is definitely not "with" the patient. In short, the therapist may be diagnostically accurate, but not emphatically accurate in his sensitivity to the patient's current feelings.

Example A:

C: If—if—they kicked me out, I—I don't know what I'd do—because . . .
T: Mhm.
C: I—I—I *am* really dependent on it. (Stammering)
T: Even though you hate this part—you—say, "MY GOD, I—I don't think I could—possibly exist without it either."
(C: Mhm)
T: And that's even the—that's the worst part of it. (Gently)
C: (Following lengthy pause) Seems that—(catches breath)—sometimes I—uh—the only thing I want out of the hospital—s' tuh have everyone agree with me . . .
T: Mhm, hm.
C: . . . that's—I—I—I guess that if (catches breath)—everybody agreed with me—that everybody'd be in the same shape I was. (Seriously, but ending with nervous laughter)
T: Mhm, well, this is sort of like—uh—feeling about the friend who—didn't want to do what I wanted to do; that—even here—if you agreed with me—this is what I want because if you don't agree with me, it means you don't like me or something. (Reflectively)
C: Mmmmm (thoughtfully)—it means that I'm wrong! (Emphatically, quick breathless laugh)

Example B:

C: You know, I'll bet you tell that to all the girls. And when we would have oh, go out for department, frequently had parties and picnics and that sort of thing, and I knew his wife and, and, children and, uh there, there was no affair. It was, and, as a matter of fact, I, that was at the time that I had an affair with A. I didn't need a man because I had one. Now I, I don't think when I was living in that city and working for the welfare department that even though I *hadn't* been having an affair with A, I don't think that I would at that tme have had an affair with B. I really don't. (T. says "Mhm" after every sentence.)

T: One of the impressions I have (name) is that you, ah, your guilt feelings are *way* out of proportion—to what uh, they should be. In some ways you've got some really, ah, ah, Victorian attitudes that you apply to yourself . . .

C: (Interrupting therapist) Well, I had an *affair* with a man and had an illegitimate baby and then go right ahead and have an affair with another married . . .

T: (Interrupting client) I'm not talking about that here. That's, that's serious. I mean, maybe you were indiscreet. Maybe uh, you were uh, you took chances that you shouldn't have taken, uh, what I'm saying is, uh, you have sexual feelings, you're going to have sexual feelings. It's a part of you because you're a person and, an . . .

C: (Interrupting) But I didn't used to have them, doctor!

T: (Going right on) You want to, and you're going to want to find expression for them. And ah, and most people in your circumstance would find expression for them. And wouldn't have to feel so terribly guilty about it, as you do—they wouldn't have to go around hating themselves afterwards like you do. You've got built into yourself a good whip somewhere, (name), you whip yourself (pause). I'm saying that compared to what most people in your circumstance, uh, what their feelings are like . . .

STAGE 5

Therapist accurately responds to all of the client's more readily discernible feelings. He also shows awareness of many less evident feelings and experiences, but he tends to be somewhat inaccurate in his understanding of these. However, when he does not understand completely, this lack of complete understanding is communicated without an anticipatory or jarring note. His misunderstandings are not disruptive by their tentative nature. Sometimes in Stage 5 the therapist simply communicates his awareness of the problem of understanding another person's inner world. This stage is the midpoint of the continuum of accurate empathy.

Example A:

C: I gave her her opportunity . . .

T: Mhm.

C: . . . and she kicked it over. (Heatedly)

T: Mhm—first time you ever gave her that chance, and—she didn't take it? (Inquiring gently)

C: No! She came back and stayed less than two weeks—a little more than a week—and went right straight back to it. (Shrilly) So that within itself is indicative that she didn't want it. (Excitedly) (T answers "Mhm" after each sentence.)

T: Mhm, mhm—it feels like it's sort of thrown—right up in your face. (Gently)

C: Yah—and now I would really be—crawling . . .

T: Mhm.

C: . . . if I didn't demand some kind of assurances—that, that things was over with. (Firmly)

T: Mhm, mhm, it would be—pretty stupid to—put yourself in that—same position where it could be sort of—done to you all over again. (Warmly)

C: Well, it could be—yes! I would be *very* stupid! (Shrilly)

T: Mhm.

C: . . . because if it's not him—it might be someone else. (Emphatically)

Example B:

C: Uh, it's really a store window there, uh, in M—(city).

T: Uh, huh. But this had been your idea, and you'd suggested it and then, lo and behold it comes out as . . .

C: Well, uh, you see, I have to investigate the contract I signed with the company, you know, these companies have to have a contract whereby they have rights to all patients and, and, copyrights us, for uh, for so—so long a time after you leave the company, you know . . .

T: Yeah.

C: . . . and uh, in other words, uh (both talk at once here).

T: So you might have been all right in doing this but you're not really sure about that. You'd have to investigate that.

C: I'd have to investigate that and some other ideas I'd given them.

T: Uh, huh. And I know too, that, that this is another sign of how, another indication of how many things there were—that you need to track down. The drug was just one, this is just another, the movie camera, and

C: Mhm.

T: . . . and there are probably a number of others too.

C: Well, all those other ideas (T talks simultaneously with client here, adding "Mhm" frequently.) Even before they . . . when the, when the rocket uh, was fired by a balloon the first time; I remember, uh, that, right after, uh, this time, that I had gotten into that trouble, I started a little office over in P— and, and, uh, I submitted to the department of uh, well, the National Inventors Council, *that* one particular idea. Well then, I just wrote in, an, asking uh, for a little recognition on it. And of course, it was one of those ideas, like most of mine that any, anybody will think of and not many people will do anything about, you know and uh . . .

T: Not that hard an idea to think of but you were at least the one who did something about it and who tested it or something, but then didn't get recognition for it.

C: Well, they uh, they wrote me back and said they had nothing like that in their files.

T: Mhm.

C: Well, also, uh, well, I had figured out a few, uh, affairs that, that, uh, amounted to sort of a gyroscope, uh, affair that I had submitted too, and, uh, they also didn't know anything about that. So, uh, I—I was pretty sick at that time, I, uh . . .

STAGE 6

Therapist recognizes most of the client's present feelings, including those which are not readily apparent. Although he understands their content, he sometimes tends to misjudge the intensity of these veiled feelings, so that his responses are not always accurately suited to the exact mood of the client. The therapist does deal directly with feelings the patient is currently experiencing although he may misjudge the intensity of those less apparent. Although sensing the feelings, he often is unable to communicate meaning to them. In contrast to Stage 7, the therapist's statements contain an almost static quality in the sense that he handles those feelings that the patient offers but does not bring new elements to life. He is "with" the client but doesn't encourage exploration. His manner of communicating his understanding is such that he makes of it a finished thing.

Example A:

T: You're sort of—comparing—things you do do, things you have done—with what it would take to be a priest—is that sort of—the feeling? (Very gently)

C: (Following long pause) I don't know. (Meekly, then a lengthy pause)

T: Suppose we mean right now feeling real guilty? (Softly)

C: (Sighs audibly) Real small. (Very softly—protracted silence)—I can't see how I could feel any different—other than—feeling small or bad . . .

T: Mhm.

C: . . . guilty (Softly)

T: Things you've done just—so totally wrong to you—totally bad—you can't help sort of—hating yourself for it? (Assuming client's tone)—is that the sort of quality? (Very gently, almost inaudibly)

C:(Following pause)—And yet right now I feel as though I want to laugh—be gay.

T: Mhm.

C: I don't feel anything else. (Monotonously)

T: (Speaking with client) Right at this—at this moment?

C: Mhm.

T: So—it's too much to really—feel—very miserable and show it? (Inquiringly)

C: Yeah, yeah (urgently). I—I—don't want to show it anyway. (Haltingly)

Example B:

C: . . . gained a lot of weight, I'm way overweight, just the last couple of years, the more I, put on a lot of weight—I, well I *did* weigh around 160-165, now I weigh a little over 200, about 208 pounds or so. I really am overweight.

T: Mhm. You feel like . . .

C: Yeah.

T: . . . you've got 40 pounds too much and you don't feel too good.

C: That's right. I washed medicine glasses for a little over three months this last summer so I, I feel like it right now, but some job, like *that,* that was —wasn't too hard, I could do it.

T: Mhm.

C: I done that four times a day and it'd take me about—oh, half an hour, three-quarters of an hour each time I done it, to wash, see, to wash the medicine glasses first. All the different ones that take medicine. They give out medicine four times a day. I done that from, oh, the middle of May until the last part of August—the last day of August.

T: So you're saying, well, you're well enough to, to do some work.

C: Yeah, I went off—they wanted me to go on lawn detail last year but

I didn't, I hardly feel that—I went out and shoveled snow last winter, just a day or two. If the work isn't too hard, I think I could do it all right. Now that really, that was really a nice good job for me, that washing glasses—I should've kept with that but uh, but, oh, I made the beds sometimes, about twelve, or something like that—sometimes I mop the floor.

T: Mhm. Then you do feel well enough to, to do that sort of work

C: Yeah.

T: . . . around here in your saying . . . You don't feel well enough or you don't really want to . . .

C: Well, I don't really know, I wouldn't really be well enough to. I have to take medicine all the time and everything, to keep my nerves calmed, and uh . . .

STAGE 7

Therapist responds accurately to most of the client's present feelings and shows awareness of the precise intensity of most of the underlying emotions. However, his responses move only slightly beyond the client's own awareness, so that feelings may be present which neither the client nor therapist recognizes. The therapist initiates moves toward more emotionally laden material, and may communicate simply that he and the patient are moving towards more emotionally significant material. Stage 7 is distinguishable from Stage 6 in that often the therapist's response is a kind of precise pointing of the finger toward emotionally significant material.

Example A:

C: Th—the last—several years—it's been the other way around—I mean he'll say, "Well let's—go do this or that," and—and I—sometimes I actually wanted to, but I'd never go because—I feel like I'm getting my little bit of revenge or something. (Voice fades at end)

T: By God, he owed it to you, and—if he didn't come through, you'll just punish him now . . .

C: Yah.

T: . . . now it's too late or—something. (Very softly)

C: (Laughingly) *Yah*—that's-uh—that's just the way I—uh—*now it's too late*—It's your turn to take your medicine now. (Assuming therapist's tone)

T:Mhm—I'm gonna treat you like—you've treated me. (Pause)—Uh . . .

C: Mhm . . . it's pretty—that's a—pretty childish way to think, but—I know uh—if I went home tomorrow, I'd do it tomorrow—if I had the chance. (Defiantly) If . . .

T: (Interrupting and overtalking client) One part of you could say, "Well, this is stupid and childish 'cause I—I *want* to be with him,"—and yet—another part says, "No, you gotta make him pay for it—you want *him* dangling there now." (Gently)

Example B:

T: (After long silence) Are you interested in knowing any more about that or any more about your dreams or about anything else that has seemed important to you here in the hospital?

C: Oh no, the last few months I haven't felt like having any recreation at all. I don't know why—it just doesn't appeal to me. And last night I almost had to force myself to go on a talent show.

T: Mm, Mhm. Just feel as though something like this, you just feel, oh, gosh, I'm not interested.

C: Mhm. I used to go to all the dances when I first came here, but now I don't care to now.

T: You sort of feel that even with things that at first you were quite interested in, now they seem less and less interesting.

C: Mhm.

T: I guess you're saying you don't quite know why that is but, uh, it seems that way.

C: Mhm.

STAGE 8

Therapist accurately interprets all the client's present, acknowledged feelings. He also uncovers the most deeply shrouded of the client's feelings, voicing meanings in the client's experience of which the client is scarcely aware. Since the therapist must necessarily utilize a method of trial and error in the new uncharted areas, there are minor flaws in the accuracy of his understanding, but these inaccuracies are held tentatively. With sensitivity and accuracy he moves into feelings and experiences that the client has only hinted at. The therapist offers specific explanations or additions to the patient's understanding so that underlying emotions are both pointed out and specifically talked about. The content that comes to life may be new but it is not alien.

Although the therapist in Stage 8 makes mistakes, these mistakes are not jarring, because they are covered by the tentative character of the response. Also, this therapist is sensitive to his mistakes and quickly changes his response in midstream, indicating that he has recognized what is being talked about and what the patient is seeking in his own explorations. The therapist reflects a togetherness with the patient in tentative trial and error exploration. His voice tone reflects the seriousness and depth of his empathic grasp.

Example A:

C: I'm getting *real* worried—be-because—I don't know just what I'm gonna have to face. (Insistently; raising voice to overtalk therapist who attempts to interject comment)—I mean I can't even find—find what I'm gonna have to—uh—fight. (Last word barely audible)

T: It must be something—pretty—Godawful terrible—and yet you don't even know what it is. (Gently)

C: No—uh—I mean—someone could tell me that—I don't have enough confidence—uh—mmm-and I know I've—uh—I've always been afraid of—uh—*physical violence*—and-uh . . .

T: (Interjects) That you've always been afraid of—*being hurt*—and I sort of sense, too, it's—being hurt by people—uh—that—physical violence like a—uh—*train* crashing in isn't frightening with you. (Gently)

C: No-uh . . . (Reflectively)

T: That a fight with people is upsetting? (Softly)

C: *Yah!* (Forcefully and registering surprise) I—I think I'm—uh—afraid—uh, uh—I'm afraid of ever losing—uh, I think—not so much because of—uh the physical pain—but—the idea that—I lost and uh, everybody knows it. (Haltingly)

T: The idea that someone beat you . . .

C: Mhm.

T: . . . that you were weak or something. (Very gently)

Example B:

T: The way she wanted me and I was always terribly afraid that she wouldn't put up with me, or would put me out, out (C: Yeah) I guess I can get something else there, too, now I was always afraid that she didn't really care.

C: I still think that though. (T: Mhm) 'Cause I don't know for sure.

T: Mhm. And don't really know for sure whether she cares or not.

C: (Pause) She's got so many other, uh, littler kids to think about.

T: Mhm.

C: That's why . . .

T: Maybe she likes them better or . . .

C: No, it's not that, I think she likes us all. (Pause) I think seein' that I'm the black sheep but, uh, the only one that served time and, that—'n got in the most trouble. Seein' that I hurt her so much, that's why I think she's starting ta—she just don't care for me anymore. (T interjects "Mhm" after most completed thoughts.)

T: You believe, maybe "because I have hurt her so much, maybe she's fed up with me, maybe she's gotten to the point where she just doesn't care." (Long pause)

STAGE 9

The therapist in this stage unerringly responds to the client's full range of feelings in their exact intensity. Without hesitation, he recognizes each emotional nuance and communicates an understanding of every deepest feeling. He is completely attuned to the client's shifting emotional content; he senses each of the client's feelings and reflects them in his words and *voice*. With sensitive accuracy, he expands the client's hints into a full-scale (though tentative) elaboration of feeling or experience. He shows precision both in understanding and in communication of this understanding, and expresses and experiences them without hesitancy.

Example A:

C: . . . uh—I've always been—so afraid—uh—show just how I—how I felt—(T: Mhm)—and I—and I—I think . . .

T: (Interrupting) Showing feelings is—weak or—something. (Gently, fading to near inaudibility)

C: Yeah—that's how it seems to me. (Lengthy pause) I know I—I've been in the TV room—and I—all of a sudden—had the feeling that—I was going to start crying. (Almost tearfully)

T: Mhm.

C: . . . and—uh—I knew then I'd have to leave and go somewhere . . .

T: Mhm.

C: . . . where nobody was, so in case I did start crying that nobody'd see me. (Bashfully)

T: Mhm—it'd just be—terrible to stand if you—if you ever did show this much feeling. (Sorrowfully) (Long pause)

C: The thing is—that—I'm—I'm afraid of—well, I'd be so embarrassed afterwards. (Ashamedly)

T: Mhm—this would be—just—terrible—uh—a man wouldn't cry, a grown-up wouldn't cry. (Almost tearfully)

C: Yeah.

T: . . . or at least . . . (Leaves thought suspended)

C: (Filling in for T) At least without an apparent reason.

T: Mhm.

C: (Long pause) An'—uh—'an—I—I don't have—an apparent reason. (Emphatically)

T: . . . it wouldn't only be weak, but—be crazy or something. (Very gently)

C: (Chiming in) Yeah! (Very positively)

Example B:

T: . . . I s'pose, one of the things you were saying there was, I may seem pretty hard on the outside to other people but I do have feelings.

C: Yeah, I've got feelings. But most of 'em I don't let 'em off.

T: Mhm. Kinda hide them.

C: (Faintly) Yeah. (Long pause) I guess the only reason that I try to hide 'em, is, seein' that I'm small, I guess I got to be a tough guy or somethin'.

T: Mhm.

C: That's the way I, think I people might think about me.

T: Mm. Little afraid to show my feelings. They might think I was weak, 'n take advantage of me or something. They might hurt me if they—knew I could be hurt.

C: I think they'd try, anyway.

T: If they really knew I had feelings, they, they really might try and hurt me.

(Long pause)

C: I guess I don't want 'em to know that I got 'em.

T: Mhm.

C: 'Cause then they couldn't if they wanted to.

T: So I'd be safe if I, if I seem like a, as though I was real hard on the outside. If they thought I was real hard, I'd be safe.

The following brief revision of the Accurate Empathy Scale by Bergin and Solomon was found useful by them in dealing with tapes taken from trainees in clinical psychology. As the reader will notice, their revision involved the addition of a new stage at the lower end of the scale, which allows for greater differentiation when rating tapes from relatively unempathic therapists.

This revised version was used in a study of "Personality and Performance Correlates of Emphatic Understanding in Psychotherapy" by Allen E. Bergin and Sandra Solomon at Columbia University.

The materials reproduced below are merely guidelines derived from the original scales which were used by the raters in evaluating recorded therapist responses.

Truax Scale Points	*Bergin-Solomon Points*	
1	1	Inaccurate responses to obvious feelings.
2	2	Slight accuracy toward obvious feelings. Ignores the deeper feelings.
—	3	Slight accuracy toward obvious feelings. Concern with deeper feelings but inaccurate with regard to them.
3	4	Often accurate toward obvious feelings. Concern with deeper feelings and occasionally accurate with regard to them.
4	5	Often accurate toward obvious feelings. Concern with deeper feelings and fairly often accurate with regard to them although spotted by inaccurate probing.
5	6	Always accurate toward obvious feelings. Frequently accurate toward deeper feelings although occasionally misinterpreting them.
6	7	Always accurate toward obvious feelings. Frequently accurate toward the content but not the intensity of deeper feelings.
7	8	Always accurate toward obvious feelings. Frequently accurate toward deeper feelings with regard to both content and intensity, but occasionally misses the mark of depth of intensity. May go too far in direction of depth.
8	9	Always accurate toward obvious feelings. Almost always accurate toward deeper feelings with respect to both content and intensity. May occasionally hesitate or err but correct quickly and accurately.
9	10	Always accurate toward obvious feelings and unerringly accurate and unhesitant toward deep feelings with regard to both content and intensity.

A Tentative Scale for the Measurement of Nonpossessive Warmth

GENERAL DEFINITION

The dimension of *nonpossessive warmth* or unconditional positive regard, ranges from a high level where the therapist warmly accepts the patient's experience as part of that person, without imposing conditions; to a low level where the therapist evaluates a patient or his feelings, expresses dislike or disapproval, or expresses warmth in a selective and evaluative way.

Thus, a warm positive feeling toward the client may still rate quite low in this scale if it is given conditionally. Nonpossessive warmth for the client means accepting him as a person with human potentialities. It involves a nonpossessive caring for him as a separate person and, thus, a willingness to share equally his joys and aspirations or his depressions and failures. It involves valuing the patient as a person, separate from any evaluation of his behavior or thoughts. Thus, a therapist can evaluate the patient's behavior or his thoughts but still rate high on warmth if it is quite clear that his valuing of the individual as a person is uncontaminated and unconditional. At its highest level this unconditional warmth involves a nonpossessive caring for the patient as a separate person who is allowed

Table A
A Schematic Presentation of
A Scale for the Measurement of Accurate Empathy[a]

DEGREES OF THERAPIST ACCURACY IN THE PERCEPTION OF CLIENT FEELINGS AT THE STAGES OF THE ACCURATE EMPATHY SCALE

LEVEL OF CLIENT FEELINGS PERCEIVED AND REFLECTED BY THE THERAPIST	Stage 1	Stage 2	Stage 3	Stage 4	Stage 5	Stage 6	Stage 7	Stage 8	Stage 9
Present obvious feelings	ignores	understands poorly	often accurate	usually accurate	accurate	accurate	accurate	accurate	unhesitating flawless accuracy
Veiled feelings		ignores	senses but under-stands poorly	accuracy very low but trying	sensitive but somewhat inaccurate tentative interpre-tation	accurate toward content but not intensity	accurate	accurate	
Preconscious feelings						ignores	a precise "pointing toward"	sensitive trial-and-error exploration	

a. This schematic presentation of levels of accurate empathy, developed by Richard A. Melloh, University of Florida, has been found useful for both research raters and therapist trainees. It provides a brief summary of the table scale, and is intended to facilitate the training of raters in the use of the scale.

to have his own feelings and experiences; a prizing of the patient for himself regardless of his behavior.

It is not necessary—indeed, it would seem undesirable—for the therapist to be nonselective in reinforcing, or to sanction or approve thoughts and behaviors that are disapproved by society. Nonpossessive warmth is present when the therapist appreciates such feelings or behaviors and their meaning to the client, but shows a nonpossessive caring for the person and not for his behavior. The therapist's response to the patient's thoughts or behaviors is a search for their meaning or value within the patient rather than disapproval or approval.

STAGE 1

The therapist is actively offering advice or giving clear negative regard. He may be telling the patient what would be "best for him," or in other ways actively approving or disapproving of his behavior. The therapist's actions make himself the locus of evaluation; he sees himself as *responsible for* the patient.

Example A:

C: . . . and I don't, I don't know what sort of a job will be offered me, but—eh . . .

T: It might not be the best in the world.

C: I'm sure it won't.

T: And, uh . . .

C: . . . but . . .

T: But if you can make up your mind to stomach some of the unpleasantness of things

C: Um hm.

T: . . . you have to go through—you'll get *through* it.

C: Yeah, I know I will.

T: And, ah, you'll get out of here.

C: I certainly, uh, I just, I just *know* that I have to do it, so I'm going to do it but—it's awfully easy for me, Doctor, to—(sighs) well, more than pull in my shell, I-I just hibernate. I just, uh, well, just don't do a darn—thing.

T: It's your own fault. (Severely)

C: Sure it is. I know it is. (Pause) But it seems like whenever I—here—here's the thing. Whenever I get to the stage where I'm making active plans for myself, then they say I'm high. An . . .

T: In other words they criticize you that . . .

C: Yeah.

T: So tender little lady is gonna really crawl into her shell.

C: Well, I-I'll say "okay."

T: If they're gonna throw, if they're gonna shoot arrows at me, I'll just crawl behind my shield and *I* won't come *out* of it. (Forcefully)

C: That's right. (Sadly)

T: And that's worse. (Quickly)

C: (pause) But why don't they let me *be* a little bit high? Why—right now I'm taking . . .

T: (Interrupting) Because some people . . .

C: (Talking with him) . . . 600 milligrams of malorin, whatever that is, malorin

T: . . . because a lot of people here don't know you very well at all. And because people in general, at times, you have to allow that they could be stupid. You too. I mean you're stupid sometimes, so why can't other people . . .

C: So *much* of the time.

T: Why can't other people? I mean, you're an intelligent person and are stupid. Why, why can't you allow that other intelligent people can also be stupid? When it comes to you they don't *know* very much.

C: Mmm. (Muttering)

Example B:

T: . . . another part here too, that is, if they haven't got a lot of schooling, there may be a good argument, that, that they—are better judges, you know.

C: Yeah . . .

T: Now, I'm not saying that, that's necessarily true, I'm—just saying that's *reality*.

C: Yeah.

T: And you're in a *position* that you can't argue with them. Why is it that these people burn you up so much?

C: They *get by with* too many things . . .

T: Why should that bother you?

C: 'Cause I never got by with anything.

T: They're papa figures, aren't they?

C: (Noise) Yeah—(pause) I told the aides last night, I said, "You're making me—I *want to forget* the past and—you're making me think of my father again."—They don't *understand*.

T: (Breaking in) But you're bringing it into the present, I don't want to keep dragging up the past; the present seems to me—uh, the same thing you've been going through all your life . . .

C: Mhm.

T: . . . this fighting against this father.

C: (Pause with sigh) So what will it take to straighten it out?

T: You're the only guy that can straighten it out.

C: But, how?

T: You've got to understand—

C: (Breaking in) I mean between me and the aides?

T: How could your dad straighten that out?

C: Tell 'm!

T: *Nah!* (Scornfully)

C: He *would* do it.

T: It is up to you to change.

C: If them aides would listen to me, if the doctors knew what was going on. I was fighting my dad, I wasn't fighting the aides, because . . .

T: Yeah, but everybody realizes you're fighting like this, they are not going to know it's your dad that you're fighting for. They are going to look at it and say, "My God, this kid is sick. Look at this, we—we tell him something and he gets *real* angry, or the doctor won't allow fighting, who . . ."

C: (Breaking in) . . . they are not going to do that on the outside. They do it in here.

T: Now look at this Doctor G——, Now look . . .

C: At —— Hospital. I didn't get upset until I ran into G——.

T: I'm sure this is going to come up again. Now look at Dr. M——, whew, you-uh, *tell* her that she's *not competent,* and you *rebel* against her, she's not thinking to herself, "Well, this kid, he's had problems with his dad, and he's carrying them over now," she's just gonna sit back and say, "My God, that's sick behavior!" And, uh, she's gonna prescribe the medicine . . .

C: Did you tell Doctor P—— this?

T: No, I didn't tell Doctor P—— this!

C: No, but today, well, I'll bring it up.

T: Without even bringing it up, it's still up to you to handle this. People can't make allowances for your times, I mean, we can *understand it,* but it's up to you to understand it and *change your behavior,* so . . .

C: Why do they bring it up?

T: Why does who bring it up?

C: *The aides!*

T: What have they done, now?

C: They act too much like my daddy does.

T: Well, there's going to be a lot of people act like your dad—does—throughout life . . .

C: (Interjecting) How do you think I can learn to live with that?

T: You've gotta learn how to, to respond to it, to handle it in a way it doesn't lead you to be *more* unhappy. Now you were very unhappy when they acted like your *dad*—but my guess is that you're a lot more unhappy *now*—because you responded the way you did.

C: I am.

T: So, uh—you've got to learn to live with it; you've got to learn some other way of handling—people like this . . .

C: (Yawns agreement)

STAGE 2

The therapist responds mechanically to the client, indicating little positive regard and hence little nonpossessive warmth. He may ignore the patient or his feelings or display a lack of concern or interest. The therapist ignores client at times when a nonpossessively warm response would be expected; he shows a complete passivity that communicates almost unconditional lack of regard.

Example A:

C: (Speaking throughout in a woebegone voice) You don't have to sit down and, and, and write like that but I thought he'd answer my letter. I thought, I didn't think he'd answer the letter, I thought he'd *come up.*

T: Um, hm.

C: . . . and, and visit me; it's only 50, he hasn't been to visit me yet. It's only been about, uh, it's only about 50, 60 miles from here.

T: Um, hm.

C: And I kind of expected him last Sunday but he didn't . . .

T: You were just sort of looking for him but he . . .

C: (Interrupting insistently) Well, I wasn't, I wasn't, I was looking for him, I wasn't looking for him. I had a kind of a half-the-way feeling that he wouldn't be up here. I know him pretty well and he's—walks around, you know, and thinks and thinks and thinks and—maybe it'll take him two or three weeks 'an all of a sudden he—he'll walk in the house (laughs)—"Let's go see—so and so." (Nervous laughter) He's a—he's a lot like I am—we're all the same, I guess. He probably—read the letter and—probably never said very much, walked out, forgot about it (laughing nervously) then all of a sudden it dawned on 'im (nervous laughter) and, ah, that's, ah, that's about, about the size of it, as far as that goes. And, uh, uh, so as I say, I—I wouldn't be, I wasn't—too overly disappointed when he, when he didn't, ah, ah, ah, ah, *answer* it or come to see me. He probably will yet. (Laughs) I'm an optimist, I always have been, he'll probably come and visit me some day. Maybe he'll come and let me go down there 'n live. Maybe he won't, won't make much difference (laughs) one way or another.

T: Hmmm. You can sort of . . .

C: Yeah.

T: . . . take things as they come. (Brightly)

Example B:

C: (At point of near hysteria throughout) (Sighs) Sometimes I get pressure in my head, and that's when I—*just*—lost control of myself—I can't . . .

T: You don't hardly know what you're doing at those times, is that it?

C: *No,* I don't!

T: It isn't your fault, is that the way it feels, what you're doing (pause)—when you're like that?

C: (With exasperation) *Yes,* that's the way it is, it—it's been that way ever since I was a kid, I don't know why—I wanted to be normal like other kids, and I *tried* hard but—(silence)—I went down to my sister's and it was a regular nut house there, I couldn't work. I had good jobs working at the hotel—as a hostess—and I might just as well have been here, it was such a nut house. And my brother made us—(Silence) But, I've been *threatened* with this place, ever since I was a kid. They come to take me once but my dad wouldn't let 'em. (Silence) I mean it was such an upsetting home all of the time, and my brother said he'd go to the judge, and when I was 29, they'd take me. *I lived in fear all the time!* (Pause) I *went to church,* and I *tried to read the Bible,* and to—*pray* and—I took care of children. And a—and my dad would always say mean things to my mother and I tried to help and do what I could but . . . (Silence) (Sighs)

STAGE 3

The therapist indicates a positive caring for the patient or client, but it is a *semipossessive* caring in the sense that he communicates to the client that his behavior matters to him. That is, the therapist communicates such things as "It is not all right if you act immorally," "I want you to get along at work," or "It's important to me that you get along with the ward staff." The therapist sees himself as *responsible for* the client.

Example A:

C: I still, you sorta hate to give up something that you know that you've—made something out of, and, and, uh, in fact, it amounts to, uh, at least, uh, what you would, uh, earn working for somebody else, so . . .

T: (Enthusiastically) O.K. What, well, eh, why don't—why don't we do it this way? That, uh, I'll kind of give you some homework to do. (Laughs) And when you're going home these weekends, um, really talk to your wife, and, ah, think yourself about *pretty specific possibilities* for you, considering the location and considering what time of year it is and, what you can do and things like this, and, eh, then we can talk it out *here* and really do some some working on this in earnest, and not just talk plans . . . (C answers "Yeah" after every phrase or so.)

C: (Interrupting) Well, I actually, I'd almost feel gettin' out right away but I, somethin' sort of holds me back, yet the season isn't—there (T: Uh, huh) and I don't know if it's good for me or not (T: Uh, huh) but I, ah . . .

T: O.K., but at least this next couple of months we can use in—*trying* at least to set something up or, or . . .

C: Cuz I feel that I, I don't know, I—feel I just want to do things again. (T: Um, hm) Uh, 'cuz the longer you stay away from work, I was just reading about that psychologist James here the other day, an' it seems like if once you get into things and work, you feel better. (T: Sure) . . . and you don't, uh, it seems like, uh, the further you stay away from things, eh, you, well, ah, you sort'a think about it, put it that way.

T: Um, hm. O.K. So, ah—in our thinking about it, though, that next few weeks, let's get closer to the doing of them. O.K.? (Warmly)

C: Well, yes, that's—what . . .

T: Sound okay to you,

C: Yes, It sounds okay to me.

T: Good enough. (Amiably)

Example B:

C: It's gettin' so I can't even—can't even sleep at night anymore—roll and toss all, toss all night long . . .

T: Pretty upset?

C: Oh, well, just lay there and think of everything—and some of the guys that come in after I did. There, there's some of them guys what of gone home, 'n' I'm still in here.

T: It's sort of up to you when you, as to when you go.

C: You can't do anything?

T: Well, I said, I sort of feel you have been—ah—you've been holding down that job—you still work in the kitchen, don't ya?

C: Yeah. (Mumbles)

T: Okay, but you—you been holding that job, and you have your card, well, okay. You fouled up somewhere, but you'll have your card again. And, well, you, in a sense showed the staff that you can handle these things, without getting into difficulties, *you* are on your way *home.*

C: That doggone kitchen detail, detail—seven cents a day—just ta scribble a bunch of junk. (Mumbled)

T: Well, you're sure as hell not gonna get rich on it.—What about this trouble, talking about money—what about this trouble you were raising the last time? About borrowing some money from this gal, have you come to any decision on that?

C: Well (pause) I'd rather not say, I ain't gonna say nothin' as long as that tape recorder's on.

T: Want me to turn it off for a while?—It's a part of the project. That's why I sort of feel it's your responsibility to—to record these things.

STAGE 4

The therapist clearly communicates a very deep interest and concern for the welfare of the patient, showing a nonevaluative and unconditional warmth in almost all areas of his functioning. Although there remains some conditionality in the more personal and private areas, the patient is given freedom to be himself and to be liked as himself. There is little evaluation of thoughts and behaviors. In deeply personal areas, however, the therapist may be conditional and communicate the idea that the client may act in any way he wishes—*except* that it is important to the therapist that he be more mature or not regress in therapy or accept and like the therapist. In all other areas, however, nonpossessive warmth is communicated. The therapist sees himself as *responsible to* the client.

Example A:

T: By—showing you that or trying to show you that—it isn't lack of things to talk about but it's, uh (pause) as far as I'm concerned your being unable to find something to talk about (pause) is only, uh, a part of your inability to see me as a person—that you want to see—that, uh . . .

C: You think it's wrong for me to see you as a doctor rather than a person?

T: Oh, no, no, I didn't mean that. Uh (pause) no, uh—no, what I meant was—that your inability, the fact there's nothing for you to talk about as far as you can judge. (Coughs) All this means is you don't want to get close to me.

C: No, it doesn't mean that. No, you're mistaken about it.—It only means just what it says. (Curtly)

T: Well, let me ask you, ah—would you object getting close to me? Becoming, ah, friendly with me? Have *me* interested in *you?*

C: Why should I *object* to that?

T: I don't know. Would you?

C: No. (Pause) But, how am *I* supposed to know, uh, what to say or what we should talk about that would accomplish that end?

T: Well, I don't know. Do you have trouble meeting friends, making friends on the, uh, outside?

C: What?

T: Do you have trouble making friends on the outside?

C: Trouble making friends? Is that what you're assuming about me?

T: I'm asking you, do you?

C: (Coughs) No, I don't believe so. (Pause) I have no trouble making friends.

T: Okay. Well, then, I expect you'd know what to say to someone, and how to talk to someone with whom you wanted to make friends, with whom you wanted to become close.

C: Well, of course the obvious thing is that we should—ask each other about—well, probably—*personal* matters.

T: Okay—well, ask me about a personal matter. (Quietly)

C: That and there again I question what good that does—There again, I'm I'm apparently, you, you see me as—well, apparently you must think I'm (pause) somehow unable to see what, what to you m-must be more obvious.

That, that *can* do some kind of good, but that I can't, but I just can't see it. I don't, I don't see how it can be used.

T: Um, hm—Yeah, I know that. That's the kind of *damning* thing about this whole—attempt, as I see it. (Pause) Because I—I just—uh, kinda get that feeling . . .

C: (Inhales and expels breath noisily)

T: For you it's a dead certainty that there's just no *point* in—getting friendly or trying to talk about anything 'cause there's nothing I can do for you. (Warmly)

Example B:

T: One thing that occurs to me is I'm so glad you came. I was afraid you wouldn't come. I had everything prepared, but I was afraid you wouldn't come. (Pause)

C: What—would you have thought of me then? I guess maybe I shouldn't have, but I did anyway (Rapidly)

T: Is that—like saying, "Why or what?" But, partly you feel—maybe you shouldn't have come—or don't *know* if you shouldn't or "not should." There's something about—feeling bad that could make you—not want to come. I don't know if I got that right, but—because if you feel *very* bad then—then, I don't know. Is there anything in that?

C: Well—I've told you before, I mean, you know, two things that, when I feel bad. I mean one that always—I feel that there's a possibility, I suppose, that, you know, that they might put me back in the hospital for getting that bad.

T: Oh, I'd completely forgotten about that, yeah—yet, and that's one thing—But there is *another?*

C: Yeah, I already told you that, too.

T: Oh, yeah, you sure did—I'd forgotten about it—and the other you've already said, too?

C: I'm sure I *did* tell it. (Pause)

T: It doesn't come. All I have when I try to think of it is just the general sense that if you feel—very bad, then it's hard or unpleasant to—but, I don't know—so I may have forgotten something—must have. (Pause)

C: You talk—you always, hear what I'm saying now, are so good at evading me, you always end up making me talk anyway . . .

T: You're right.

C: You always comment on the question or something, and it just doesn't tell me.

T: (Interjecting) Right, I just instinctively came back—to you when I wondered—what I, well like saying, because—that's what I felt like saying. You mean to—you mean to say that a few minutes ago we had decided that *I* would talk . . .

C: Well, you—you mentioned it, but (T: Right.) that's as far as it got.

T: You're right—and I just—was thinking of what you're asking—I'm more interested in you right now than anything else.

STAGE 5

At stage 5, the therapist communicates warmth without restriction. There is a deep respect for the patient's worth as a person and his rights as a free individual. At this level the patient is free to be himself even if this means that he is regressing, being defensive, or even disliking or rejecting the therapist himself. At this stage the therapist cares deeply for the patient as a person, but it does not matter to him how the patient chooses to behave. He genuinely cares for and deeply prizes the patient for his human potentials, apart from evaluations of his behavior or his thoughts. He is willing to share equally the patient's joys and aspirations or depressions and failures. The only channeling by the therapist may be the demand that the patient communicate personally relevant material.

Example A:

C: . . . ever recovering to the extent where I could become self-supporting and live alone. I thought that I was doomed to hospitalization for the rest of my life and seeing some of the people over in, in the main building, some of those old people who are, who need a lot of attention and all that sort of thing, is the only picture I could see of my own future. Just one of (T: Mhm.) complete hopelessness, that there was any—

T: (Interrupting) You didn't see any hope at all, did you?

C. Not, not in the least. I thought no one *really* cared and I didn't care myself, and I seriously—uh—thought of suicide; if there'd been any way that I could end it all *completely* and not become just a burden or an extra care, I would have committed suicide, I was that low. I didn't want to live. In fact, I hope that I—I would go to sleep at night and not wake up, because I, I really felt there was nothing to live for (T: Uh, huh. [very softly]) Now I, I truly believe that this drug they are giving me helps me a lot, I think, I think it is one drug that really does me *good.* (T: Uh, hm.)

T: But you say that, that during that time you, you felt as though no one at all cared, as to what (C: That's right.) . . . what happened to you.

C: And, not only that, but I hated *myself* so that I didn't, I, I felt that I didn't *deserve* to have anyone care for me. I hated myself so that I, I, I not only felt that no one did, but I didn't see any reason why they *should.*

T: I guess that makes some sense to me now. I was wondering why it was that you were shutting other people off. You weren't *letting* anyone else care.

C: I didn't think I was *worth* caring for.

T: So you didn't ev—maybe you not only thought you were—hopeless, but you wouldn't allow people . . . (Therapist statement is drowned out by client)

C: (Interrupting and very loud) I closed the door on everyone. Yah, I closed the door on everyone because I thought I just wasn't worth *bothering* with. I didn't think it was worthwhile for *you* to bother with me. "Just let me alone and—and let me rot that's all I'm worth." I mean, that was my thought. And I, I, uh, will frankly admit that when the doctors were making the rounds on the ward, I mean the *routine* rounds, I tried to be where they wouldn't see me. The doctor often goes there on the ward and asks how everyone is and when she'd get about to me, I'd move to a spot that she's already covered . . .

T: You really avoided people.

C: So that, so that she wouldn't, uh, *talk* with me (T: Uh, hm.) and when—the few times that I refused to see you, it was for the same reason. I didn't think I was worth bothering with, so why waste your time—let's just . . .

T: Let me ask you, ask you something about that. Do you think it would have been, uh, better if I had insisted that, uh, uh, you come and talk with me?

C: No I don't believe so, doctor. (They speak simultaneously)

T: I wondered about that; I wasn't sure. (Softly)
C: I don't—I, I, I . . .

Example B:

T: And I can sort of sense—and when you want to, when you feel like it, I'd be glad if you shared some of those . . .
C: *What?* (Abruptly)
T: I said, when you want to, and when you feel like it, I'd be glad if you shared some of those feelings with me . . .
C: (Breaking in and speaking with therapist) Why, why—whoa, whoa, whoa . . .
T: (Continuing) I'd like to just sort of see'm . . .
C: Why, you gettin' rich off this silent character or somep'n or what? (Raucous laugh) Ten, fifteen, twenty dollars an hour? (Loudly) Then he just sits here—an' that's it, huh? Oh, I know. (Mumbling)
T: I'd say that—that's a good point—what'ya mean? (Softly)
C: Oh, I don't know. (Pause)
T: Well, that-uh, makes me say something stupid-uh. (Laughs)—I sometimes get paid fifteen, twenty dollars an hour, but that, I'm not getting paid . . .
C: (Interjecting loudly, overtalking therapist) Why, the state's paying ya' that now, ain't they?
T: Not for you, no. I thought you might think that.
C: Who is, then? (Insistently)
T: No, I get a salary from the University for doing research. (Calmly)
C: Oh—*research!* (Incredulously)
T: Mhm. (Pause)
C: I think that's just a—roundabout way to put it—th-that's what, that's what I think.
T: Well, let's put it this way; I get it, but—I get exactly the same salary whether—I see you or not. (Gently)
C: Oh, there, there probably is a—there probably is a—that type doctors there, but-uh, but I wouldn't call it *research!* (Scornfully) I, I, I, I, I, I, I, I don't know, I don't know. I don' care—I don'—I . . . (Ending in angry confusion)
T: (Speaking with conviction) Well, I'd like you to know—that, that's not *research.*"

A Tentative Scale for the Measurement of Therapist Genuineness or Self-Congruence

GENERAL DEFINITION

Perhaps the most difficult scale to develop has been that of therapist *genuineness.* However, though there are notable points of inconsistency in the research evidence, there is also here an extensive body of literature supporting the efficacy of this construct in counseling and therapeutic processes.

This scale is an attempt to define five degrees of therapist genuineness, beginning at a very low level where the therapist presents a facade or defends and denies feelings; and continuing to a high level of self-congruence where the therapist is freely and deeply himself. A high level of self-congruence does not mean that the therapist must overtly express his feelings but only that he does not deny them. Thus, the therapist may be actively reflecting, interpreting, analyzing, or in other ways functioning as a therapist; but this functioning must be self-congruent, so that he is being himself in the moment rather than presenting a professional facade. Thus the therapist's response must be sincere rather than phony; it must express his real feelings or being rather than defensiveness.

"Being himself" simply means that at the moment the therapist is really whatever his response denotes. It does not mean that the therapist must disclose his total self, but only that whatever he does show is a real aspect of himself, not a response growing out of defensiveness or a merely "professional" response that has been learned and repeated.

STAGE 1

The therapist is clearly defensive in the interaction, and there is explicit evidence of a very considerable discrepancy between what he says and what he experiences. There may be striking contradictions in the therapist's statements, the content of his verbalization may contradict the voice qualities or nonverbal cues (i.e., the upset therapist stating in a strained voice that he is "not bothered at all" by the patient's anger).

Example:

C: He seemed pleased that I was going *back*. And when I got to the bus station, when he took me *by* the bus station in C—— he had the bus driver arrange it there where I had lost my ticket, and they fixed me up a ticket all the way to M——, *all the way through,* with the excuse that I had lost my ticket. So that's how I got back home from C——. I was kind of lucky.

T: Yeah, that is, that's quite a story. (Long pause)

C: Can I ask you a question? (Pause)

T: Yeah. I guess so.

C: Do you think I'm crazy?

T: Oh no—not in the sense that *some* of the patients you see out on the ward, perhaps.

C: I don't mean *mentally,* not—where I don't know anything, but I mean, am I out of my head? Do I do things that are foolish for people to do?

T: Well, I'd say you do things that you might say are—foolish, in a *sense.* You do things that aren't . . . (Pause)

C: (Filling in for therapist) *Normal.*

T: Yeah, well, they aren't usual by any means, of course.

STAGE 2

The therapist responds appropriately but in a professional rather than a personal manner, giving the impression that his responses are said because they sound good from a distance but do not express what he really feels or means. There is a somewhat contrived or rehearsed quality or air of professionalism present.

Example:

T: Does it seem like it will be a long time to you?

C: Yeah, it does to me, yes, because I've been through some *rough* times, but I try to forget it sometimes. Somehow I get the idea I'll be just like this the rest of my life.

T: It seems that way now. Like it's going to go on and on . . .

C: Yeah.

T: . . . and like you'll never be relieved.

C: Well, I—I—well, you go ahead and analyze it now.

T: No, go ahead.

C: Well, last week, I—went home and I only had two pills, these pills I get every afternoon about 4:00. So Monday I came back and I just felt worse, *lousy*, again. It seems like, if I were to hit you in the arm it would hurt you more now than it would tomorrow, wouldn't it?

T: Mhm.

C: Well, that's the way my system is. If somebody hit me now it wouldn't bother me now.

T: But tomorrow.

C: But the next day it would bother me. Do you see what that is? That's the same way I am. If I was to go out and play ball now, I'd be stiffer than—all get-out. Not by tonight, but by tomorrow.

T: Tomorrow.

C: And that's the way my system runs as far as my nerves are concerned. I go through a strain or stress and I don't show it until the next day.

T: You say you went home this weekend?

C: I went home last weekend, just over Sunday. I left home at 8:00—from about 9:30 till 8:00 in the evening.

T: And then you felt badly when you came back?

C: Well, I had a few cigars. I guess I smoked too much. That's the only time I'll smoke anything is when I go home.

T: You felt all tired?

C: I felt pretty bad Monday—but that's the way I am, though. See, actually, taking them two pills didn't affect me that day, but it affected me again the next day.

T: Uhuh. Are these pills that the doctor gave you to take on the way home?

C: No. Well, the nurses give me my medications now.

T: The nurses give them?

C: But they wouldn't give me any to take home, I mean.

T: They gave them to you before you left?

C: Two before I left and one when I got back here. I missed two pills that day and that made me more, made me feel *worse*, actually.

T: You missed them. Was it the—you're saying it's the *missing* of the pills when you didn't have any?

C: Yes, the missing of the pills didn't bother me too much Sunday, but *Monday* they did.

STAGE 3.

The therapist is implicitly either defensive or professional, although there is no explicit evidence. (Two patients are present in the sample given.)

Example:

T: Is this a common concern to everyone in here?

1: I believe so, doctor, the—you come in and you expect help right away. Now, take for example my case. I've been here three weeks and I've yet to talk to a doctor. They make their morning rounds; all the ladies are in the room, and they stop and ask, "How are you?" and everything. And I asked the doctor, I told him I only had a leave of absence from work, would I be able to see him. He said according to my tests I need my work—my personal attention. So I'm leaving Saturday. I was a volunteer patient and I asked. So I'm being discharged Saturday. But—uh—the ones that helped me, it's like this lady here—and a few of us would have our own small group therapy and talk out our problems.

T: Mhm, mhm— . . .

C1: And I think I'm happier now than I've ever been in my life.

T: (To second patient) Do you feel the same way about—this situation?

C2: Well, I only—need help with the business of checking my medicine.

T: When, then?

C2: About a couple of months.

T: A couple of months. I see.

STAGE 4.

There is neither implicit nor explicit evidence of defensiveness or the presence of a facade. The therapist shows no self-incongruence.

Example:

C: What I have always wanted since we have been married, more than anything else, was to be able—for us to move somewhere away from our town where everybody knows me.

T: Mhm . . .

C: All of us to move together, my husband, my two children and myself. Maybe go to L ——, or not L ——, but F ——. He has a cousin up there. I went with his cousin twice before I went with him; they picked us up one day while we were going to school. And, too, he could get him a butcher's job up there like he has now, not work *half* as hard and make *twice* as much money! I could be a *hundred* percent happier, and we could still have somebody that we knew, that we could be around, that we could visit and play cards with, to go places with, to talk to . . .

T: Mhm . . .

C: . . . and then, if we had to, we could come back to A —— and visit Dad and his dad, and if anybody got sick we could always come back home.

T: Well, I really think that's a very good idea!

C: But *he won't go!* I've tried and tried and tried to talk him into leaving and he will *not go*.

T: Do you think he's sort of tied down to his family, or is he a pretty dependent sort of person, do you think?

C: Well, yes, he is. But by dependent do you mean—on his own?

T: Does he *not like* to be on his own; does he like to have someone to look out for him?

C: No, no—he likes to be completely "let —— do it," that's my husband's name. He wants to do it *himself,* but when anything doesn't work out he goes straight back to daddy!

T: Well, that's what I was sort of thinking. Does he need, well, somebody you know you can *turn to* . . .

C: Uh, yes.

T: . . . when things go wrong, sort of *lean* on? He's pretty—dependent on his father then. But, as you say, you wouldn't be so far away.

STAGE 5.

The therapist is freely and deeply himself in the relationship. He is open to experiences and feelings of all types—both pleasant and hurtful—without traces of defensiveness or retreat into professionalism. Although there may be contradictory feelings, these are accepted or recognized. The therapist is clearly being himself in all of his responses, whether they are personally meaningful or trite. At stage 5 the therapist need not express personal feelings, but whether he is giving advice, reflecting, interpreting, or sharing experiences, it is clear that he is being very much himself, so that his verbalizations match his inner experiences.

Example:

C: I guess you realize that, too, don't you? Or do you? (Laughs)

T: Do I realize that? You *bet* I do! Sure, yeah—I always wanted somebody to take *care of me,* you know, but I also wanted them to let me do what I wanted to do! Well, if you have somebody taking care of you, then you've got to do what *they* want you to do.

C: That's right. (Pause)

T: So, I never could kind of get it so that I'd have both, you know, *both* things at once: either I'm doing what *I* want to do and taking care of myself or, you know, I used to have somebody taking care of me and then I'd do what *they* wanted to do. And I'd think, "Aw, hell!" It just—never works out, you know.

C: Always somebody there, isn't there? (Laughs)

T: Yeah, just somebody goofing up the works all the time. (Pause) Yeah, if you're dependent on somebody else, you're under their control, sort of.

C: To a certain extent . . .

T: Yeah, that's what I was going to say—yeah, you're right. (Pause) So, you just sit around the ward and you read a little bit, and then you go out and play horseshoes and—boy, that sounds like a *drag!*

TOWARD MEASUREMENT OF THE CENTRAL THERAPEUTIC INGREDIENTS AS PERCEIVED BY THE CLIENT OR PATIENT

Another approach to measuring the central therapeutic ingredients involves a questionnaire to determine levels of offered therapeutic conditions. The use of a questionnaire to measure the patient's perception of psychological conditions offered by his therapist was first tried in outcome research by Barrett-Lennard (1962). The available evidence suggests that measuring the level of therapeutic conditions with questionnaires filled out by clients is a significantly less valid procedure than the rating of objective tape recordings (Truax, 1966a). Moreover, as the evidence to be reviewed in the next chapter indicates, the questionnaire approach seems of little value in assessing empathy, warmth, and genuineness with severely disturbed or psychotic individuals. However, since it is extremely economical and has proved valuable with juvenile delinquents, outpatient neurotics, and a wide variety of vocational rehabilitation clients, the relationship questionnaire is being reproduced here for the reader's use. It should also provide a further definition of the central concepts of empathy, warmth, and genuineness. (The relationship questionnaire, as well as the preceding scales for accurate empathy, nonpossessive warmth, and genuineness or self-congruence, may be used and reproduced by the reader without permission.)

The measures of therapeutic conditions derived from the relationship questionnaire correlate between .53 and .56 with the ratings made from objective tape recordings on less disturbed clients, such as juvenile delinquents. However, there is virtually no correlation when the relationship questionnaire is used with hospitalized mental patients (correlations of .10 to .20). In general, the available data suggest that the severely disturbed patient is unable to report or perceive adequately the level of therapeutic conditions offered by his therapist. Where reported measurements have been made with psychotic patients, a given patient would describe his therapist as a "saint" on one day and a "devil" on another; so that measurements of conditions perceived by severely disturbed patients appeared almost totally unreliable.

On the scale, the scoring for accurate empathy, nonpossessive warmth, genuineness, and overall therapeutic conditions is indicated to the right of the items.

Additionally, subscale scoring keys have also been developed for measuring the intensity and intimacy of the therapeutic contact and the concreteness or specificity of the therapist's responses. These two latter characteristics of the counselor or therapist are not considered to be central to therapeutic outcome. However, evidence presented in later chapters does indicate significant relationships between both of them and patient outcome.

Relationship Questionnaire (and Scoring Key)[1]

People feel differently about some people than they do about others. There are a number of statements below that describe a variety of ways that one person may feel about another person, or ways that one person may act toward another person. Consider each statement carefully and decide whether it is true or false when applied to your present relationship with your instructor. If the statement seems to be mostly true, then mark it true; if it is mostly not true, then mark it false.

	Accurate Empathy	*Nonpossessive Warmth*	*Genuineness*	*Overall Therapeutic Relationship*	*Intensity and Intimacy of Interpersonal Contact*	*Concreteness*
1. He seems to hold things back, rather than tell me what he really thinks.			F	F	F	F
2. He understands my words but does not know I *feel.*	F			F		F
3. He understands me.	T			T		
4. He understands exactly how I see things.	T			T	T	T
5. He is often disappointed in me.		F	T	F		
6. He seems to like me no matter what I say to him.		T	T	T	T	
7. He is impatient with me.		F	T	F		
8. He may understand me but he does not know how I feel.	F			F		F
9. Sometimes he seems interested in me while other times he doesn't seem to care about me.		F		F	F	
10. He often misunderstands what I am trying to say.	F			F		F
11. He almost always seems very concerned about me.		T		T	T	
12. Sometimes I feel that what he says to me is very different from the way he really feels.			F	F		
13. He is a person you can really trust.		T	T	T		
14. Sometimes he will argue with me just to prove he is right.	F	F	F	F		
15. Sometimes he seems to be uncomfortable with me, but we go on and pay no attention to it.		F	F	F		F
16. Some things I say seem to upset him.		F	T	F		
17. He can read me like a book.	T			T		T
18. He usually is not very interested in what I have to say.		F		F	F	
19. He feels indifferent about me.		F		F	F	
20. He acts too professional.			F	F	F	
21. I am just another student to him.			F	F	F	
22. I feel that I can trust him to be honest with me.		T	T	T		T
23. He ignores some of my feelings.	F	F		F	F	F
24. He likes to see me.		T		T		
25. He knows more about me than I do about myself.	T			T		T

1. Scale developed by Charles B. Truax during 1963. It is an attempt to translate the previous scales used for ratings objective tape recordings into a questionnaire form that can be answered by the client. In this respect it follows closely the thinking and earlier work of Barrett-Lennard in his development of the relationship inventory.

Relationship Questionnaire (and Scoring Key) (Cont.)

	Accurate Empathy	*Nonpossessive Warmth*	*Genuineness*	*Overall Therapeutic Relationship*	*Intensity and Intimacy of Interpersonal Contact*	*Concreteness*
26. Sometimes he is so much "with me," in my feelings, that I am not at all distracted by his presence.	T	T	T	T	T	T
27. I can usually count on him to tell me what he really thinks or feels.			T	T		T
28. He appreciates me.		T		T	T	
29. He sure makes me think hard about myself.				T		T
30. I feel that he is being genuine with me.			T	T		
31. Even when I cannot say quite what I mean, he knows how I feel.	T			T	T	
32. He usually helps me to know how I am feeling by putting my feelings into words for me.	T			T	T	T
33. He seems like a very cold person.		F	F	F	F	
34. He must understand me, but I often think he is wrong.	F			F		F
35. I feel that he really thinks I am worthwhile.		T		T	T	
36. Even if I were to criticize him, he would still like me.		T	T	T	T	
37. He likes me better when I agree with him.		F	T	F		
38. He seems to follow almost every feeling I have while I am with him.	T			T	T	T
39. He usually uses just the right words when he tries to understand how I am feeling.	T			T		T
40. If it were not for him I would probably never be forced to think about some of the things that trouble me.				T		T
41. He pretends that he likes me more than he really does.			F	F		
42. He really listens to everything I say.		T		T	T	
43. Sometimes he seems to be putting up a professional front.			F	F	F	
44. Sometimes he is so much "with me" that with only the slightest hint he is able to accurately sense some of my deepest feelings.	T	T		T	T	T
45. I feel safer with him than I do with almost any other person.		T	T	T		
46. His voice usually sounds very serious.				T	T	
47. I often cannot understand what he is trying to tell me.	F			F		F
48. Sometimes he sort of "pulls back" and examines me.			F	F	F	
49. I am afraid of him.		F		F		
50. He seems to pressure me to talk about things that are important to me.				T		T
51. Whatever he says usually fits right in with what I am feeling.	T			T	T	T
52. He sometimes seems more interested in what he himself says than in what I say.	F	F	T	F	F	F

Relationship Questionnaire (and Scoring Key) (Cont.)

	Accurate Empathy	*Nonpossessive Warmth*	*Genuineness*	*Overall Therapeutic Relationship*	*Intensity and Intimacy of Interpersonal Contact*	*Concreteness*
53. He tells me things that he does not mean.			F	F		
54. He often does not seem to be genuinely himself.			F	F		
55. He is a very sincere person.			T	T		
56. With him I feel more free to really be myself than with almost anyone else I know.		T		T		
57. He sometimes pretends to understand me, when he really does not.	F		F	F		F
58. He usually knows exactly what I mean, sometimes even before I finish saying it.	T			T	T	T
59. He accepts me the way I am even though he wants me to be better.		T	T	T		T
60. Whether I am talking about "good" or "bad" feelings seems to make no real difference in the way he feels toward me.		T		T		
61. In many of our talks I feel that he pushes me to talk about things that are upsetting.				T		T
62. He often leads me into talking about some of my deepest feelings.	T			T	T	T
63. He usually makes me work hard at knowing myself.				T	T	T
64. Sometimes I feel like going to sleep while I am talking with him.				F	F	
65. He is curious about what makes me act like I do, but he is not really interested in me.		F		F	F	
66. He sometimes completely understands me so that he knows what I am feeling even when I am hiding my feelings.	T			T	T	
67. I sometimes feel safe enough with him to really say how I feel.		T	T	T		
68. I feel I can trust him more than anyone else I know.		T	T	T		
69. Whatever I talk about is okay with him.		T		T		
70. He helps me know myself better by sometimes pointing to feelings within me that I had been unaware of	T			T	T	T
71. He seems like a real person, instead of just a teacher.			T	T		
72. I can learn a lot about myself from talking with him.	T			T		T
73. In spite of all he knows about me, he seems to trust my feelings about what is right and wrong for me.		T		T	T	
74. Sometimes he is upset when I see him but he tries to hide it.			F	F		
75. He would never knowingly hurt me.		T		T		
76. He is a phony.			F	F		
77. He is the kind of person who might lie to me if he thought it would help me.		F	F	F		

Relationship Questionnaire (and Scoring Key) (Cont.)

	Accurate Empathy	*Nonpossessive Warmth*	*Genuineness*	*Overall Therapeutic Relationship*	*Intensity and Intimacy of Interpersonal Contact*	*Concreteness*
78. When he sees me he seems to be "just doing a job."	F	F	F	F	F	
79. In spite of the bad things that he knows about me, he seems to still like me.		T	T			
80. I sometimes get the feeling that for him the most important thing is that I should really like him.		F		F	F	F
81. There is something about the way he reacts to what I tell him that makes me uncertain whether he can keep my confidences to himself.			F	F		
82. He gives me so much advice I sometimes think he's trying to live my life for me.		F		F		
83. He never knows when to stop talking about something which is not very meaningful to me.	F	F		F	F	
84. He sometimes cuts me off abruptly just when I am leading up to something very important to me.	F	F		F	F	
85. He frequently acts so restless that I get the feeling he can hardly wait for the day to end.		F		F	F	
86. There are lots of things I could tell him, but I am not sure how he would react to them, so I keep them to myself.	F	F		F		
87. He constantly reminds me that we are friends though I have a feeling that he drags this into the conversation.	F	F		F		
88. He sometimes tries to make a joke out of something I feel really upset about.	F	F				F
89. He is sometimes so rude I only accept it because he is supposed to be helping me.		F		F	F	
90. Sometimes he seems to be playing "cat and mouse" with me.		F	F	F	F	
91. He often points out what a lot of help he is giving me even though it doesn't feel like it to me.	F	F		F	F	
92. It is hard to feel comfortable with him because he sometimes seems to be trying out some new theory on me.		F	F	F		
93. He's got a job to do and does it. That's the only reason he doesn't tell me off.		F	F	F		
94. If I had a chance to study under a different instructor, I would.	F			F		F
95. He is always relaxed, I don't think anything could get him excited.			F	F	F	
96. I don't think he has ever smiled.		F			F	
97. He is always the same.		F		T		
98. I would like to be like him.		T		T		
99. He makes me feel like a guinea pig or some kind of animal.			F	F		
100. He uses the same words over and over again, till I'm bored.	F			F		

Relationship Questionnaire (and Scoring Key) (Cont.)

	Accurate Empathy	Nonpossessive Warmth	Genuineness	Overall Therapeutic Relationship	Intensity and Intimacy of Interpersonal Contact	Concreteness
101. Usually I can lie to him and he never knows the difference.	F			F		
102. He may like me, but he doesn't like the things I talk about.		F		F		
103. I don't think he really cares if I live or die.		F	F	F	F	
104. He doesn't like me as a person, but continues to see me as a student anyway.		F	F		F	
105. I think he is dumb.	F			F		
106. He never says anything that makes him sound like a real person.			F	F	F	F
107. He is all right, but I really don't trust him.			F	F		
108. If I make mistakes or miss a class, he really gives me trouble about it.		F		F		
109. He lets me talk about anything.		T		T		
110. He probably laughs about the things that I have said to him.	F		F	F		
111. I don't think he knows what is the matter with me.	F			F		F
112. He sometimes looks as worried as I feel.			T	T		
113. He is really a cold fish.		F	F	F	F	
114. There are times when I don't have to speak, he knows how I feel.	T			T		
115. If I am happy or if I am sad, it makes no difference, he is always the same.		T		T		
116. He really wants to understand me, I can tell by the way he acts.				T	T	
117. He knows what it feels like to be ill.	T			T		
118. He must think he is God, the way he talks about things.		F	F	F		
119. He really wants to understand me, I can tell by the way he asks questions.				T	T	
120. He must think that he is God, the way he treats me.		F		F		
121. He rarely makes me talk about anything that would be uncomfortable				F		F
122. He interrupts me whenever I am talking about something that really means a lot to me.	F			F		
123. When I'm talking about things that mean a great deal to me, he acts like they don't mean a thing.		F		F		
124. I can tell by his expressions sometimes that he says things that he does not mean			F	F		
125. He really wants me to act a certain way, and says so.						
127. There are a lot of things that I would like to talk about, but he won't let me.		F		F		
127. He really likes me and shows it.		T	T	T	T	
128. I think he could like someone, but I don't think he could love anybody.		F		F		

Relationship Questionnaire (and Scoring Key) (Cont.)

	Accurate Empathy	Nonpossessive Warmth	Genuineness	Overall Therapeutic Relationship	Intensity and Intimacy of Interpersonal Contact	Concreteness
129. There are times when he is silent for long periods, and then says things that don't have much to do with what we have been talking about.	F	F		F	F	F
130. When he is wrong he doesn't try to hide it.			T	T		
131. He acts like he knows it all.		F		F		
132. If he had his way, he wouldn't walk across the street to see me.		F	F	F		
133. Often he makes me feel stupid the way he uses strange or big words.	F		F	F		
134. He must think life is easy the way he talks about my problems.	F					
135. You can never tell how he feels about things.			F	F		F
136. He treats me like a person.		T		T	T	
137. He seems to be bored by a good deal of what I talk about.		F			F	
138. He will talk to me, but otherwise he seems pretty far away from me.	F	F		F	F	F
139. Even though he pays attention to me, he seems to be just another person to talk with, an outsider.	F	F		F	F	F
140. His concern about me is very obvious.			T	T	T	
141. I get the feeling that he is all wrapped up in what I tell him about myself.				T	T	

CHAPTER 3 CENTRAL THERAPEUTIC INGREDIENTS: RESEARCH EVIDENCE

THE research evidence briefly cited in this chapter, which seems to confirm the importance of the therapeutic triad discussed in the preceding chapter, grew out of Carl Rogers' leadership. Although it has also incorporated aspects of other schools of thought, the original efforts grew out of the client-centered orientation. This was due in part to Rogers' early advocacy of research as a means of more fully understanding the intricacies and complexities of the therapeutic transaction; in part to his pioneering in the use of the tape recorder as a means of objectively capturing significant aspects of the therapeutic process; in part to his own openness to new evidence in modifying his existing theoretic stance; but his major contribution was the theoretic specification (1957b) of empathy, warmth, and genuineness (empathic understanding, unconditional positive regard and congruence) as both *necessary and sufficient conditions* for therapeutic outcome. In this he went further than his predecessors, who had specified these therapist qualities as important but not all-important. For Rogers (1957b) they became not just important and essential, but *the only therapist qualities* that contributed to patient outcome: they were both necessary and sufficient to account for the therapist's role in the therapeutic transaction. While few researchers believed that any three therapist characteristics would in fact be either necessary or sufficient to account for the therapist's contribution to patient outcome, Rogers' recent theoretical formulation proved to be the major stimulus for research in this area.

In this chapter we shall briefly review the major evidence. Since space limitations will not permit a critical evaluation of similarities or differences in therapist and patient samples, methodological intricacies, or the many problems of measurement involved in the studies listed, the reader is urged to read carefully the studies cited for a more detailed understanding of the evidence.

Research into the effective role of the therapist in therapeutic outcome grew out of the pioneering work of Whitehorn and Betz at the Johns Hopkins Hospital (Betz, 1963a, 1963b; Whitehorn, 1964; Whitehorn and Betz, 1954). Their now-classic contribution was a retrospective study of seven psychiatrists whose schizophrenic patients had an improvement rate of 75 per cent, as contrasted with seven other psychiatrists of similar training who had an improvement rate of only 27 per cent. Their evidence indicated that the patients seen by the two sets of therapists did not differ in any systematic way that favored one group over the other, and yet they showed this striking contrast in success rates. Further analysis of the two groups of psychiatrists showed that the success of the patients appeared greatly dependent on the type of therapist seen for help. We note that if the two groups of patients were combined, they would yield an overall success rate of 46 per cent. However, when they are divided according to the characteristics of the therapist, it is clear that one group of therapists was indeed helpful, since a 75 per cent success rate is somewhat above the improvement rate seen in comparable control populations. By contrast, the other group of therapists was, in fact, quite clearly damaging to their patients, since a 27 per cent success rate is considerably below the average improvement rates of comparable control populations. Thus, if carefully examined, the data given by Whitehorn and Betz is in strong agreement with the recently emerging evidence that suggests that psychotherapy can indeed be "for better or for worse"; therapists and counselors can indeed be helpful, but many are also harmful (Truax, 1963).

The work of Whitehorn and Betz was an attempt to discover, in retrospect, some significant differences between the successful and unsuccessful therapists. The differences related to their therapeutic effectiveness suggested that the usual ways in which people differ were not important; both groups of therapists worked with talkative and quiet, passive and active, extroverted and introverted clients. The therapists themselves included both bright and dull conversationalists. The differences appeared to lie in their attitudinal approach to the helping relationship. The successful therapists were warm and attempted to understand the patient in a personal, immediate and idiosyncratic way; by contrast, the less successful therapists tended to relate to the patient in a more impersonal manner, focusing upon psychopathology and a more external kind of understanding. In Betz's further delineation of successful and unsuccessful therapists (1963) the descriptions were consistent, although not identical, with the three recurring themes that run through almost all major theoretical formulations designed to describe effective counseling or psychotherapy: empathic understanding of the patient; nonpossessive warmth for the patient; and therapist genuineness or authenticity.

Although Betz (1963a, 1963b) has continued to find support for the early research, other investigators have suggested limitations of their findings, particularly when the simple scale from the Strong Vocational Interest Blank Test is used to define therapist types. Thus, McNair, Callahan and Lorr (1962) suggest that similarity of patient and therapist types may be critical, since the reverse of the original findings was found for a sample of neurotic patients.

As McNair, Callahan and Lorr note, Whitehorn and Betz had originally differentiated the effective and harmful therapists on the basis of clinical notes and observations rather than on the 20 items in the Strong Vocational Interest Blank. The relationship of therapist qualities to those

20 items may be idiosyncratic to a particular social class and cultural style of therapists and may not hold at all for the general population of therapists. (It *is* very hard to imagine what preferences for "making a radio set," or being a "photoengraver" or a "building contractor" have to do with the personal qualities described by Whitehorn and Betz.) It may be, as McNair, Callahan and Lorr suggest, that the items simply happened to tap a set of common interests in this particular subsample of therapists and patients that were related to therapeutically important factors "such as ease of communication."

Although a number of people, most notably Strupp (1960a), have developed procedures to measure empathic ability of therapists, only quite recently has the focus of research been centered upon the relationship between all three central therapeutic ingredients and *constructive changes* in the patient or client. The growing body of research evidence suggesting the critical importance of these three ingredients to human encounters intended to change human behavior can be grouped into four broad categories: (1) studies of client or patient outcome in cases receiving relatively high levels of these therapeutic conditions, contrasted with those receiving relatively low levels: (2) studies of the three conditions themselves, utilizing control groups for comparisons of client or patient change; (3) studies focusing upon the role of the therapeutic conditions in the question of causation; and (4) converging evidence from laboratory and classroom studies of learning, and from studies of parental effects upon children.

STUDIES OF THERAPEUTIC CONDITIONS AND OUTCOME

One of the first studies attempting to relate the therapist's level of the therapeutic triad to patient outcome was by Halkides (1958), who selected brief samples from early and late therapy interviews from ten most successful and ten least successful therapy cases. Ratings were made, using a very brief scale based upon Rogers' writings (1957a), for the therapist levels of empathic understanding, unconditional positive regard, and self-congruence. Her report indicated that the most successful cases showed significantly higher levels of these three conditions than did the least successful ones. However, a replication of that study by Hart (1960), using the same data and similar procedures but different judges, failed to confirm those findings. It could be suggested that this discrepancy in findings on the same data might be due to the scales used by Halkides and Hart, which were primarily global and implicitly defined, relying heavily on the raters' knowledge of what constitutes empathy, warmth, and therapist congruence. In this connection it might be noted that the ratings in Halkides' study were made by experienced client-centered therapists (including Halkides herself), while Hart used raters less experienced within the client-centered orientation.

In a study of group psychotherapy with hospitalized patients (Truax, 1961a), accurate empathy, warmth (or unconditional positive regard), and genuineness were all found to be significantly associated with the patients' engagement in the process of therapy, self-revelation, and self-exploration. Using analysis of variance of multiple regression, the findings suggested that of the three, the therapist's accurate empathy and genuineness (or self-congruence) were by far the most important for patient behavior.

From the Chicago group, Barrett-Lennard (1962) studied the client's reported perception of the level of these three therapeutic conditions in relation to his personality change. Barrett-Lennard's findings on 42 clients seen by different therapists indicated that experienced therapists were perceived as offering significantly higher levels of empathy, warmth and congruence than less experienced therapists. Further, among the more disturbed patients in his sample there was a positive relationship to therapeutic outcome.

The Wisconsin Schizophrenic Project

A number of studies have come from the study of psychotherapy with 16 hospitalized schizophrenic patients begun in 1958 at the University of Wisconsin under the leadership of Rogers. The majority of these studies have not been published in full detail because of an agreement to forego such publication until after the appearance of the joint book, but many of the findings have been reported. The report by Truax and Carkhuff (1963) is the most detailed to date, and thus expands on the earlier published reports of Rogers (1963) and Truax (1963). It would now appear that the findings to be reported by Kiesler, Mathieu and Klein which will appear in the book by Rogers, Gendlin, Kiesler, and Truax (1966) differ in varying degrees from the other earlier reports. Since these later reports of findings are not based on new data (all patients terminated therapy by 1963, a majority of them in 1962), the discrepancies do not appear to be due to changes in the 14 to 16 patients themselves. Since the report to be made in book form has changed from time to time over the past three years, any critical analysis of discrepancies between the reports of the findings will have to await publication of the book and then of the research and studies. Thus, the findings cited here may or may not appear in the joint book. In any event, they are the findings that seem most valid to the present authors. Should any of the reports now to be reviewed turn out to be in error, the authors would, of course, change their views to that extent. However, a growing number of studies conducted over the past four years, with larger samples of therapists and patients, appear to cross-validate the essential findings that were originally reported, as well as a majority of the research reports from the Wisconsin program completed in 1962 and 1963.

It may seem that an undue amount of attention is being given to a series of studies based on only 16 patients receiving therapy (only 14 of whom had pre- and posttherapy outcome data), but it is important both as a report of findings and as a predecessor for a series of more recent studies.

One of the first studies (Truax, 1961b) compared the levels of accurate empathy in four hospitalized patients who showed clear improvement on a variety of personality tests and four who showed clear deterioration after six months of intensive psychotherapy. A total of 384 two-minute samples was selected from the middle third of the therapy sessions, then randomly assigned code numbers and submitted to judges for rating on the accurate empathy scale. The findings indicated that the psychotherapists whose patients improved on the tests rated consistently higher on accurate empathy than those with test-deteriorated cases ($p < .01$). Further, the therapists' level of accurate empathy did not tend to vary throughout the six months of intensive psychotherapy.

Figure 1 shows the trends of accurate empathy across time during the first six months of treatment for the two groups of patients.

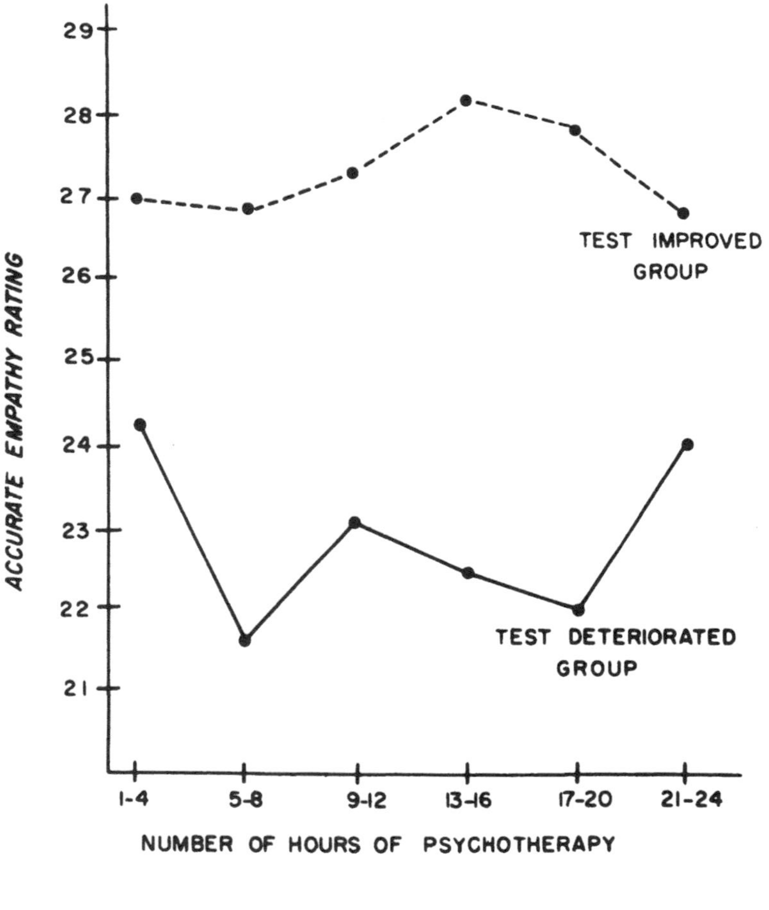

This initial finding relating one of the three therapeutic conditions to case outcome (success versus deterioration) was clarified and extended by later studies (Truax, 1963) involving 14 schizophrenic patients, who had been seen in intensive psychotherapy for periods ranging from six months to four and one-half years. A four-minute, tape-recorded sample was selected from every fifth interview throughout the course of treatment. In an effort to obtain "objective" ratings uncontaminated by the theoretic bias of the rater, undergraduate students who were naive with respect to the theory and practice of psychotherapy were trained separately in the use of the three scales. The raters themselves were trained on other data to minimum rate-rerate and inter-rater reliabilities of .50.

The five raters who were employed on the accurate empathy scale had no knowledge of the therapists, the patients, the case outcomes, or the order in which the samples given to them for rating were arranged. A comparison was made between (1) the mean level of accurate empathy offered by the therapist in each case and (2) personality and behavioral change in the patient. The correlation between accurate empathy and case outcome, as measured by the Final Outcome Criterion (which included psychological test change data, diagnostic evaluations of personality change, and a measure of time actually spent in the hospital since initiation of therapy), was .77 ($p < .01$). A second outcome criterion was based upon blind evaluations by two experienced psychologists, of degree of change in personality functioning, based primarily on the Rorschach and MMPI, given before therapy and late in therapy. The correlation between these diagnostic evaluations of constructive personality change and the level of accurate empathy offered by the therapist was .48 ($p < .05$). Also, both the high and minimal levels of accurate empathy in each case were significantly related to outcome. An analysis of the distribution of actual ratings on the Accurate Empathy scale for the most improved vs. the most deteriorated patients is shown in Figure 2.

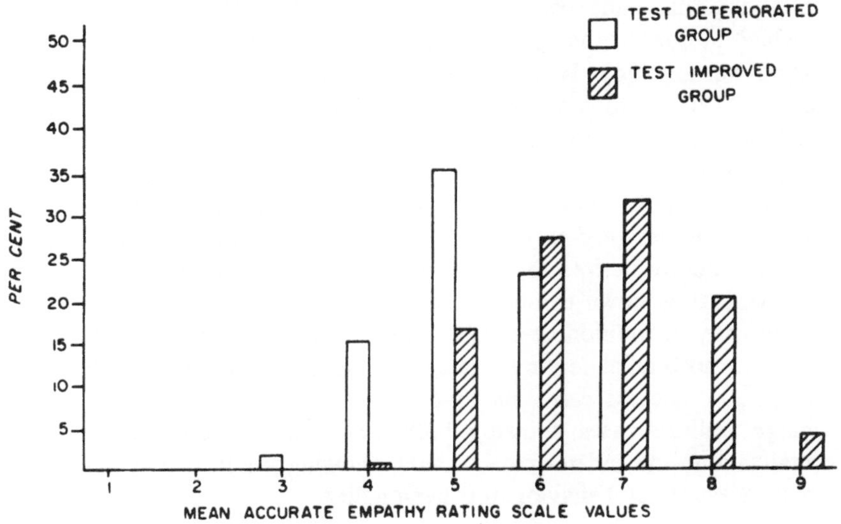

The analysis of the distribution indicated highly significant differences ($p < .01$) between the two groups of patients. As can be seen in Figure 2, there was a rather strong tendency for the therapists of improved patients to be rated at consistently high values of accurate empathy throughout the course of treatment, while the therapists of patients who showed deterioration had a relatively large frequency of lower levels of accurate empathy throughout the course of treatment. Thus, the patients who showed deterioration received virtually no deeply empathic responses from their therapists, while the patients who showed improvement rarely received even a trace of merely superficial understanding (reflection of words and obvious feelings).

Using identical procedures, but with a different set of four raters trained on the Unconditional Positive Regard or Nonpossessive Warmth scale, the correlation between the level of nonpossessive warmth offered by the therapist for each case and the Final Outcome Criterion was .73 ($p < .01$). The relationship using the case outcome criteria of diagnostic evaluations of test change was .47 ($p < .05$).

When three more raters were trained with the Therapist Genuineness or Self-Congruence scale, the same data were analyzed for the relationship of case outcome and level of therapist genuineness offered throughout the course of therapy. The obtained correlation with the Final Outcome Criterion was .66 ($p < .01$), while the correlation with the diagnostic evaluation of change was .45 ($p < .05$).

The three therapeutic conditions tended to show similar relationships such that one might predict a relatively high intercorrelation between measures of the conditions themselves. Accurate empathy measures correlated .54 with nonpossessive warmth measures, and .49 with measures of therapist genuineness. Warmth and genuineness correlated .25, indicating that between 6 and 30 per cent of the variation in one measure is common to another.

Studying this same patient population, Spotts (1962) obtained findings which suggested that positive regard or warmth, regardless of conditionality, was significantly associated with constructive personality change. Wharton (1962) studied the effect of therapist-communicated level of positive regard during the first 30 interviews upon patient outcome measures obtained two and one-half years after the beginning of the therapy research. The Spotts-Wharton scale of Positive Regard (1962) was used. That scale was designed to measure a continuum of therapist warmth, interest and attentiveness to the client extending from deep prizing and nonpossessive caring, down through mere diagnostic or intellectual interest, to mere curiosity or indifference. Using pre- and posttests such as the MMPI, *Q*-sort and hospitalization rate data, the therapy cases were divided into three groups: success cases showing both test improvement and hospital discharge; failure cases showing both test deterioration and continued hospitalization; and indeterminant cases, showing a mixed outcome on the various measures of behavior and personality.

Spotts' data indicated that approximately one-third of the therapy cases showed clear improvement after therapy, one-third clear deterioration, and one-third indeterminant or mixed results. The substantive findings indicated that successful cases in therapy had received significantly higher levels of positive regard throughout the first 30 sessions of therapy as compared to both the failure and indeterminant cases. The deteriorated and mixed-outcome patients had received approximately equivalent levels of positive regard from their therapists.

In another report from the Wisconsin program, Gendlin and Geist (1962), using procedures similar to Wharton (1962) and Truax, Liccione and Rosenberg (1962), divided the therapy patients into those showing constructive change, those showing deteriorative change, and those essentially unchanged or mixed. They then compared these case outcomes with levels of therapist congruence communicated to the patient throughout the total course of psychotherapy. They used the "Congruence G" scale, which was related to the Therapist-Self Congruence scale. Their findings indicated that the minimal level of therapist self-congruence was positively related to outcome in the predicted direction. Mean level of congruence, however, was not significantly related to outcome, although the mean levels for both the improved and mixed-outcome patients were higher than that for the deteriorated patients. The researchers conclude that instances of extremely low genuineness in the therapist may invalidate the effects of higher levels of other conditions offered by him. Thus, in effect, the measurement of genuineness alone may serve only to indicate the deleterious effects when its level is low.

In an effort to extend to an outpatient population the findings obtained with hospitalized schizophrenics, Truax (1963) obtained an additional 14 cases (seven relative successes and seven relative failures) from Stanford University and the University of Chicago. Using samples obtained from early and late interviews with the 14 hospitalized and 14 outpatient cases, he found that the level of accurate empathy offered in therapy was significantly higher for successful cases than for failures ($p < .01$). This positive relationship between accurate empathy and outcome of therapy held for both hospitalized schizophrenics and outpatients seen in counseling. An analysis of the distribution of the ratings of accurate empathy indicated that the failure cases were typified by frequent low and moderate levels of accurate empathy. In particular, the failure cases had a high frequency of therapist responses characterized by *inaccuracy* in responding to "preconscious" material ($p < .05$). This data is shown in Figure 3. Although a direct comparison cannot be made with the earlier analysis of the distribution of accurate empathy for hospitalized patients alone, since the absolute values for accurate empathy vary from one set of raters to another, the same pattern holds: successful cases received fewer moments of superficial understanding from their therapists, while failure cases received far fewer moments of deeply empathic understanding.

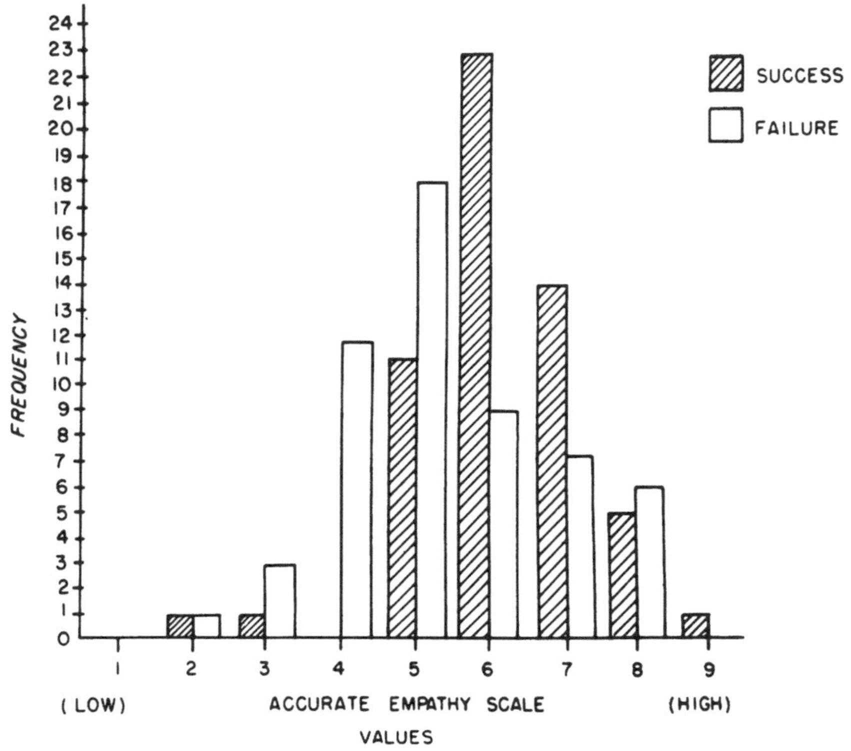

To further clarify the relationship between empathy and outcome, a study of complete interviews from early and late therapy in 14 schizophrenic cases was completed. In that study, consecutive five-minute samples were made throughout the 28 interviews, thus covering every single moment of therapeutic interaction during those sessions. Since therapists vary in their level of accurate empathy from moment to moment, an analysis could be made on that data of both high and low moments of accurate empathy, and mean or average levels of accurate empathy. Thus, the question became, "Is the average level of accurate empathy the important factor, or does the patient respond most to those rarer moments of *high* accurate empathy?" A further question was, "Do occasionally quite low levels of accurate empathy impede the process of therapy?"

The analysis of that data (Truax, 1962a) indicated that although patients who received average higher levels of empathy were those who showed improvement ($p < .05$), the highest moments of accurate empathy obtained throughout the interviews were more predictive of outcome ($p < .01$) compared to cases with relatively lower "highest" moments. By contrast, there was no relationship between the level of the lowest moments of accurate empathy and case outcome. That study was of particular practical and theoretic significance, since it indicated that a therapist would be more helpful by striving for deeper understanding, even at the risk of occasional misunderstanding; that the occasional low moments of accurate empathy had no relationship to outcome; and that outcome was significantly affected by both the average levels and the very highest moments of accurate empathy.

More Recent Studies

Continuing the line of investigation using the Accurate Empathy scale, Bergin and Solomon (1963) presented evidence indicating that the level of accurate empathy as measured from tape-recorded therapy conducted by fourth-year clinical psychology graduate students, was significantly related to the student-therapist's ability to produce outcome as judged by his supervisors.

Several studies have now indicated that the therapist's level of empathy does not tend to vary systematically across time in therapy with patients (Truax and Carkhuff, 1963; Melloh, 1964). However, the recent Cartwright and Lerner study (1963), using a different measure of empathic understanding, reported results indicating that the therapist's final, but not his initial, level of empathic understanding of the patient was related to improvement in therapy.

The work of Strupp, Wallach, Wogan, and Jenkins (1963) further extended the available data on therapist warmth. Studying a population of therapists who were analytically oriented, they found substantial correlations between the therapists' ratings of outcome of therapy and the patients' own ratings of specific emotional attitudinal variables, particularly the therapist's feeling of warmth and liking for the patient.

Some converging evidence for the importance of empathy and warmth is available in a study by Combs and Soper (1963), who obtained significant correlations between supervisors' judgments of effectiveness of counselors and aspects of the counselors' attitudinal orientation. Effective counselors tended to assume the internal rather than the external frame of reference with others; to be oriented toward people rather than things; and to see people as able, dependable and friendly, rather than unable, undependable and unfriendly.

A further report by Strupp, Wallach, and Wogan (1964) of a questionnaire survey of therapists and patients indicated strong consensus about the essential aspects and outcome of psychotherapy. Their findings converged on both warmth and genuineness. They summarize their findings on clientele who are essentially comparable to those of the average psychiatrist or psychoanalyst as follows:

> The emergence of a large general "warmth" factor deserves emphasis. There was additional evidence to suggest that overshadowing this attitudinal-emotional factor is the patients' conviction that he has the therapist's respect. This faith in the integrity of the therapist as a person may be called the capstone of a successful therapeutic relationship subsuming other characteristics. Technical skill on the part of the therapist may go a long way to capitalize on such a relationship, although the present data do not specifically inform us how such

a relationship comes into being, is deepened, and turned to maximum therapeutic advantage. However, there is little doubt that a relationship having these qualities represents the most basic ingredient of beneficial therapeutic influence irrespective of the formal aspects of the setting. (pp. 36-37)

Another piece of converging evidence is discussed by Lorr and McNair (1966). In a correlational study of 523 male neurotic, psychotic and other patients from 43 veterans' clinics, they attempted a crude dimensionalizing of therapist behaviors by asking patients to fill out questionnaires describing some selected aspects of their perceptions of their therapists. Concomitantly, they asked for patient and therapist ratings of client outcome. Their factor of therapist understanding correlated .31 with patient rating of improvement, .19 with therapist rating of improvement, and .30 with the patient's judged satisfaction with therapy. For the factor of therapist acceptance (warmth) the correlations were .24, .16, and .24 respectively (all $p < .01$). For their factors of "authoritarian therapist" and "critical-hostile" (specific types of low empathy and warmth), they obtained negative correlations with the judgments of therapeutic outcome. Although the relationships obtained were quite low and may have been due simply to response sets rather than true reflections of either the therapist's behavior or the patient's outcome, the fact that they are consistent with more objective evidence suggests their validity.

Board (1959) had earlier done a retrospective study of patient and therapist judgments of success in therapy with outpatients. There, patients tended to equate "successful therapy" with being able to express their feelings and gain insights in the presence of interested and understanding therapists. By contrast, "unsuccessful therapy" was related mainly to disinterested therapists and to the use of multiple therapists (which might be thought to lower the therapist's understanding and interest).

Lesser (1961) reported findings suggesting that the therapist's ability to predict accurately the degree of similarity between his own and his patient's *Q* sort was significantly and positively related to the patient's progress. This, too, seemed to suggest that the sensitive, empathic therapist who is able to assess accurately the patient as well as himself is perhaps most effective.

A recently completed study on 40 outpatients treated by resident psychiatrists at the Phipps Psychiatric Clinic at Johns Hopkins (Truax, Wargo, Frank, Imber, Battle, Hoehn-Soric, Nash and Stone, 1966a) was an attempt to cross-validate the findings from the studies on individual psychotherapy with hospitalized schizophrenics with data from a very different patient and therapist population. Analysis of that data indicated greater improvement for patients of therapists offering high levels of accurate empathy, nonpossessive warmth and genuineness combined than for patients receiving relatively lower levels of these combined conditions. The differences proved statistically significant on the two overall measures of patient improvement.

On the three more specific measures of outcome available, two of the differences favored patients receiving high conditions while the third measure favored patients receiving low conditions. Analysis of convariance was used to control for any possible differences in initial patient status that could have differentially affected outcome. On the question of improvement versus deterioration (the direction rather than the extent of change), the findings suggested that patients receiving high conditions tended to show positive change, while a higher percentage of patients receiving low conditions tended to show negative change. On the measure of improvement that was available for all 40 patients, there was an overall improvement rate of 70 per cent, which roughly approximates the average improvement rate reported by Eysenck (1960) as characteristic for both control and treated populations. However, the therapists who provided high levels of conditions in the present study produced a *90 per cent* improvement rate, while those who offered relatively low levels of conditions produced a rate of only 50 per cent.

The Hopkins data thus suggested psychotherapy can indeed be for better or for worse depending upon the level of therapeutic conditions actually offered by the therapists. When the specific conditions of accurate empathy, nonpossessive warmth, and genuineness were analyzed separately, the data indicated identical findings for empathy and genuineness, but a reversed tendency for nonpossessive warmth. That is, patients receiving high levels of warmth tended to show less positive change than patients receiving low levels of warmth. This puzzling finding seems to be explained by the interrelationships between the three conditions themselves in that sample of therapists: the ranking of therapists on empathy and genuineness was identical (*Rho* = 1.00), while nonpossessive warmth was negatively related to both the other conditions (*Rho* = — .40). The Hopkins data, then, suggests that *when one of the three conditions is negatively related to the other two* in any given sample of therapists, then patient outcome is best predicted by whichever two conditions are most closely related to each other. In general form, this idea suggests that when any two of the three therapeutic conditions are sufficiently high, positive patient or client change will occur. Since the same measures of therapeutic conditions in this study of the Johns Hopkins data gave essentially identical findings when used in prior studies with hospitalized patients and outpatients seen in college counseling centers, it now seems that the same therapeutic conditions are therapeutic for a wide variety of human beings regardless of the specific type of emotional disturbance or psychopathology.

A study by Truax, Carkhuff and Kodman (1965) attempted to evaluate the generality of these three therapeutic ingredients by studying their relationships to outcome in group psychotherapy. That study involved 40 hospitalized mental patients, all relatively chronic, who were given group therapy sessions twice weekly over a three-month, time-limited period. The MMPI was administered before and after therapy. When the patients were divided into those in groups receiving relatively high levels of accurate empathy and those in groups receiving relatively low levels, those receiving high levels of accurate empthy showed improvement on all the MMPI subscales equal to, or greater than, that of the patients receiving relatively low levels. Statistically significant differences occurred on the *Pt* scale, the *Sc* scale, and the Welsch Anxiety Index obtained from the MMPI.

The data on the therapist's genuineness was, surprisingly, in direct opposition to the prediction. There was a uniform tendency on all subscales for the patients who had received relatively *low* levels of therapist genuineness to show greater improvement than those receiving high levels. Statistically significant differences favoring *low* genuineness occurred on the *Pd* scale, the *Pt* scale, the *Sc* scale, the *Si* scale, and the sum of clinical scales.

The data on nonpossessive warmth came out much like that for communicated accurate empathy. Significant differences favoring greater improvement in patients receiving the highest levels of communicated therapist warmth were obtained on the *Pt* scale, the *Sc* scale, and the Welsh Anxiety Index from the MMPI, although differences in improvement on all clinical scales favored the high group.

Thus, the findings give support to the generality of the therapist-offered ingredients of accurate empathy and nonpossessive warmth. These findings parallel nicely those obtained in individual psychotherapy, although the magnitude of the association between those two ingredients and patient change in group psychotherapy was somewhat less than that obtained in individual psychotherapy. However, the findings on the therapist's genuineness are in sharp contrast to the previous findings in individual psychotherapy.

It is of considerable interest to note that in the Truax, Carkhuff and Kodman group therapy study, there was a strong positive correlation between empathy and warmth, but genuineness was negatively related to both empathy and warmth. Thus, as in the Hopkins data on individual psychotherapy, the findings in group therapy suggest that when two conditions of the therapeutic triad are highly related but the third is negatively related, the prediction of outcome should be based on the two that are most highly related. In both cases (nonpossessive warmth for the Hopkins data and genuineness for the group therapy data) the therapeutic condition that was negatively related to the other two was not itself absolutely low for any group of patients. It may very well be as Gendlin and Geist (1962) suggest, that when any one of the therapeutic conditions is sufficiently low, it will interfere with therapy regardless of the level of the remaining two therapeutic conditions. That the contrary finding with respect to therapist genuineness does not hold in general is indicated by a more recent study using a larger population of patients and therapists.

Studying an initial population of 160 hospitalized patients receiving time-limited group psychotherapy, where pre- and post-treatment personality and behavioral measures were used, Truax and Wargo (1966c) extended the earlier group therapy findings to a much more heterogeneous patient and therapist population. Analysis of covariance was used to control for any possible differences in initial patient status that could have differentially affected outcome. The data analysis indicated that the levels of accurate empathy, nonpossessive warmth, and therapist genuineness were associated with measures of positive patient outcome.

On the critically important measure of the amout of time spent in the hospital by patients during their one-year followup, the findings indicated a tendency for patients receiving high levels of the three conditions to spend more time out of the hospital (average of 112 days) than did patients receiving low levels (average of 72 days). In general, these findings are consistent with those on individual psychotherapy, in indicating that high levels of therapeutic conditions are associated with positive patient changes on a number of personality and behavioral measures, while low conditions are associated with less positive and even negative changes in patients. On the 28 specific measures of therapeutic outcome available for analysis, those receiving high levels on all conditions showed above-average improvement on 21 measures and below-average improvement on only 7 measures; while, by contrast, patients receiving low levels of conditions during group therapy showed above-average improvement on only 7 measures, and below-average improvement on 21 measures ($p < .001$). Significant differences in improvement favoring patients receiving relatively high levels of empathy, warmth and genuineness combined was obtained on *Q*-sort measures of self concept, the Welsch Anxiety Index, the MMPI subscales of *Mf* and *Sc,* time spent out of the hospital during one-year followup, and the Final Outcome Criterion, which includes several measures of psychological test change as well as the hospitalization rate data.

Moreover, patients who received relatively low levels of conditions, as a group tended to show greater negative or deteriorative change in contrast to the patients receiving high levels of conditions. On the *Sc* (Schizophrenia) scale, which is particularly critical with the hospitalized patients, patients receiving high levels of conditions showed an average positive change, while patients receiving low conditions showed an average negative or deteriorative change. Such findings suggest that low conditions during group psychotherapy do indeed tend to facilitate negative or deteriorative change in patient personality functioning. The same general pattern of findings held individually for levels of accurate empathy, nonpossessive warmth, and genuineness. The degree of positive and negative changes observed in the 160 hospitalized patients was less marked than that observed in the study of individual therapy; in part, this might seem at first glance to be due to the group therapy experience. However, those patients in time-limited group therapy were seen for a total period of three months involving 24 sessions. That differences in degree and direction of personality change were associated with the level ol therapeutic conditions offered over such a brief period suggests that gıoup psychotherapy might be equally effective if continued over a time span equivalent to that in the studies of individual therapy. Considering that the patient population as a whole consisted of chronic long-term hospitalized patients, an even more striking finding was that the level of conditions offered during only three months of twice-weekly group therapy tended to have differential effects on the patients' ability to get out and stay out of the hospital during the one-year followup. It is particularly important to note that in that study the therapists varied greatly in theoretic orientation, professional discipline (including psychiatrists, psychologists and social workers), and amount of training. Moreover, the patient population itself was quite diverse, including patients from one Veterans Administration Hospital, a state hospital serving the Appalachian depressed area, and a state hospital serving a northern rural and suburban area.

In a study of an original population of 80 institutionalized juvenile delinquents receiving three months of group counseling, Truax and Wargo (1966b) reported findings that again indicated significant association between the levels of empathy, warmth and genuineness offered by the group counselor and the degree of behavioral and personality change occurring in the juvenile delinquents. Analysis of covariance was used to control for any possible differences in initial patient status that could have differentially affected outcome. With the juvenile delinquent population, the outcome measures indicated that high conditions in group therapy were associated with positive changes, while low conditions were associated with negative or deteriorative changes. On the 19 specific measures of therapeutic outcome available, those juvenile delinquents receiving high levels on all conditions showed above-average improvement on 18 measures and below-average improvement on only one measure: by contrast, those delinquents receiving low levels of conditions showed above-average improvement on only one measure and below-average improvement on 18 ($p < .001$). Further, in terms of improvement vs. deterioration, the juvenile delinquents receiving high conditions showed average improvement on 18 measures and deterioration on only one, whereas the delinquents receiving low conditions in group therapy showed absolute deterioration on 17 measures and nonsignificant improvement on the other 2 ($p < .001$). The differences favoring the juvenile delinquents receiving high conditions proved statistically significant on 14 of the 19 specific measures (including 5 of the subscales of the Minnesota Counseling Inventory, the measures of self concepts and ideal concepts, the Palo Alto Group Therapy Scale and, most importantly, the measures of institutionalization during the 12-month followup).

Replicating the same basic design and study on an original population of 80 outpatients receiving group psychotherapy, Truax, Wargo and Carkhuff (1966) obtained essentially similar findings for all conditions combined. Analysis of covariance was used to control for any possible differences in initial patient status that could have *differentially* affected outcome. On the 23 individual measures of therapeutic outcome available, outpatients receiving high levels on all conditions showed above-average improvement on 21 measures and below-average improvement on 2 measures, while the reverse was true of patients receiving relatively low conditions ($p < .001$).

When accurate empathy, nonpossessive warmth and genuineness were analyzed separately, the data suggested that nonpossessive warmth in particular was critical for outpatients in group therapy. Thus, patients receiving high levels of nonpossessive warmth showed above-average improvement on 21 of the 23 measures while those receiving low levels of warmth showed above-average improvement on only two measures ($p < .001$). Patients receiving high levels of genuineness showed above-average improvement on 18 measures, while those with low levels of genuineness during group therapy showed above-average improvement on only 5 measures ($p < .001$). On separate analysis of accurate empathy, the majority of measures came out in the opposite direction. Thus only 6 of the specific measures favored better outcome for high levels of empathy while 17 favored better outcome for low empathy ($p < .01$). However, the differences for the most part were small and nonsignificant. On the two specific measures on which significant differences occurred (the Welsch Internalized Anxiety Scale and the Palo Alto Scale), both differences favored significantly better outcome for those patients who received high levels of accurate empathy than for those with low empathy ($p \leq .05$, $p \leq .05$).

Thus in analyzing the effects of the three conditions with outpatients, the data suggest that warmth is most important, genuineness less important, and empathy least important.

Of particular importance for an outpatient population, significantly greater gains for patients receiving high levels of all conditions occurred from pre- to post-therapy testing on the MMPI subscales of *Hs, D, Hy, Pd, Pa, Pt, Sc, Si,* and the sum of clinical scales. With the outpatient population the effects of warmth alone were more pronounced than either of the other two therapeutic conditions, so that the differences favoring high conditions reached statistical significance in more than half of the 23 specific measures. In contrast to the earlier reported findings concerning deteriorative effects of low therapeutic conditions, the findings from the group therapy study with outpatients suggested very little evidence of absolute deterioration from before therapy to after it. However, since spontaneous improvement is relatively frequent with outpatients, low conditions might be expected to reduce such spontaneouse improvement rather than result in actual absolute deterioration.

STUDIES OF CONDITIONS AND OUTCOME UTILIZING CONTROL GROUPS

The above studies, taken together, support the theoretical view that the levels of therapist accurate empathy, nonpossessive warmth and genuineness are related to constructive change in patients. Still, the research reported above deals with cases that were relatively successful or unsuccessful, rather than with comparisons to control groups receiving no psychotherapy. Eysenck (1952), for one, has insisted on the value of comparisons to control groups by suggesting that even under the best conditions, psychotherapy may not be significantly superior to no treatment. A few studies have now been completed utilizing control groups.

The Wisconsin Schizophrenic Project

In a study involving 14 schizophrenics receiving individual psychotherapy and 14 carefully matched control patients (Truax, 1963), analyses were carried out to evaluate the effects of high and low conditions upon outcome. Patients had been randomly assigned to either therapy or control conditions within the matched pairs, and a complete battery of psychological tests was given initially and later. The therapy patients received a minimum of 30 individual therapy sessions and a maximum of 280 sessions throughout a three and one-half year period. Using procedures described earlier, samples of tape-recorded psychotherapy were independently rated for therapist accurate empathy, nonpossessive warmth, and genuineness. The mean value for each case was examined, and the therapy patients divided at the closest significant gap in level of conditions, so as to divide the treated group into halves. Six patients had received relatively high levels of conditions while eight had received relatively low levels. Using the clinician's "blind" analysis of pre- and posttest battery information to establish levels of overall psychological functioning, the findings indicated that patients receiving high levels of the three conditions showed an overall gain in psychological functioning; but those patients who received rather low levels showed a *loss* in psychological functioning. Control patients showed moderate gains.

An overall test of the differences proved statistically significant. In terms of the number of patients at or above the median change in psychological functioning, the control group had a rough 50-50 split, while *all* patients in the group receiving low levels of conditions were below the median. The six (of the fourteen) patients receiving high conditions showed positive change. Looking more closely at individual psychological test measures, the following findings emerged. On measures of anxiety level, patients receiving low conditions showed a significant increase, the controls showed almost no change, and patients receiving high conditions showed a significant drop in anxiety level. Using the *Q*-sort measure of change in self concepts, *both* the control group and the patients receiving high conditions in therapy showed a slight positive gain, while the patients receiving low conditions showed a significant change toward poorer adjustment and self concepts. On the MMPI, significant differences between the three groups occurred in the predicted direction on the sum of clinical scales, the Depression scale, the Psychopathic deviate scale, the Schizophrenia scale, and the Social Introversion scale. No differences, however, were observed on any of the subscales of the Wittenborn Psychiatric Rating Scale as filled out by ward attendants. In terms of the hospitalization experience of the three groups during a three and one-half year period after the initiation of psychotherapy, the findings indicated that patients receiving high conditions in psychotherapy spent significantly more time out of the hospital than either the control group or patients receiving low conditions; patients who received low conditions in psychotherapy did not differ from the control population.

In a related study from the Wisconsin project, Wargo (1962) studied the effects of accurate empathy, positive regard and unconditional positive regard upon the Barron Ego Strength Scale (Barron, 1953), developed to predict psychotherapeutic outcome, and the LH^4 scale developed by Meeker (1958) to predict length of hospitalization. Wargo's findings indicated that change in ego strength was significantly greater in a positive direction for patients receiving high conditions for all three measures. Differences were in the same direction for the LH^4 scale, but reached statistical significance only with the unconditional positive regard scale. When all therapy cases (both high and low conditions) were compared with control cases, there were no significant differences in change on either scale. Thus, Wargo says "They [the findings] would indicate that the therapists who present to the client low degrees of unconditional positive regard, accurate empathy, and positive regard may be facilitating loss of ego strength. . . . It may well be, then, that no therapy is better than low conditions therapy, but that high conditions constitute the essential ingredient in constructive personality change during therapy."

More Recent Studies

Working with a quite different population—emotionally disturbed college underachievers—Dickenson and Truax (1966) investigated the effects of time-limited group counseling upon college academic achievement. In a *matched* therapy and control population of 48 patients, those receiving group counseling showed significant improvement over the control patients. Thus, during the semester postcounseling, 17 of the 24 students receiving group counseling obtained a passing grade point average, while only 11 of the 24 control students obtained passing grades. Similarly, 19 of the 24 underachievers receiving group counseling had a higher grade point average after therapy than before; only 11 of the 24 underachievers in the control group had a higher grade point average in the same period ($p < .005$).

When those students receiving relatively high and only moderate levels of therapeutic conditions in group therapy were compared with the control population, the data indicated that those with high conditions showed the greatest positive gain (2.45 out of a possible 4.0 grade point average after therapy). Those receiving only moderate levels did not differ (grade point average of 1.92 after counseling) from the control population (grade point average of 1.95). One of the more striking findings from that study was that the total group of patients receiving therapy functioned after therapy at the level predicted by their college entrance exam scores, and so were no longer "underachievers," while the control population continued to achieve college grades at a level significantly below the predicted one.

When those receiving counseling were divided according to the levels of therapeutic conditions they were offered during therapy, the findings indicated that only those receiving relatively high levels of empathy, warmth and genuineness showed improvement over the controls. Those receiving only moderate levels showed grade-point averages and changes approximating those in the control group. These findings are shown in tables 2 and 3.

A recent study (Truax, Wargo and Silber, 1966) aimed at evaluating the effects of high levels of accurate empathy, nonpossessive warmth and genuineness in group counseling with female juvenile delinquents. That study is of particular significance, since only therapists who (on the basis of prior research) were known to provide high levels of accurate empathy and nonpossessive warmth worked with the group. A total of 70 institutionalized delinquents were assigned on a random basis to a control population of 30 girls and a therapy population of 40. The treatment population received 24 sessions of group psychotherapy, but otherwise were given the same institutional treatment as the control population. Analysis of covariance was used to control for any possible differences in initial patient status that could have differentially affected outcome. On all 12 measures obtained before and after therapy, the delinquents receiving high conditions in group psychotherapy showed improvement beyond that seen in the control group. In particular, they showed significant gains over the control group toward more adequate self concepts and toward perceiving parents and other authority figures as more reasonable and less threatening. Most importantly, the therapy group showed significant superiority over the girls receiving control conditions on a psychological test measure specifically designed to differentiate between delinquents and nondelinquents.

Since the aim of treatment with juvenile delinquents is to change them in the direction of nondelinquency, their ability to stay out of institutions during a one-year follow-up was evaluated. The findings are presented in

Table 2
Outcome for Underachievers Receiving Control or Counseling Treatments

	Number of Subjects	Number Post with Passing Grades	Number Post with Higher Grades	Mean GPA Pre	Mean GPA Post	Mean Change Pre To Post In Under-achievement Score	Mean Under-achievement Score Post
Control Underachievers	24	11 (46%)	11 (46%)	1.73	1.95	+.22	—.39
Counseled Underachievers	24	17 (71%)	19 (79%)	1.73	2.29	+.57	—.08
High Conditions	16	13 (81%)	15 (94%)	1.72	2.45	+.74	+.04
Moderate Conditions	8	4 (50%)	4 (50%)	1.75	1.92	+.19	—.37

Table 3
Tests of Significance on Outcome Between Control, All Counseling Combined and High and Moderate Levels of Therapeutic Conditions Separately

	X^2 Number Post with Passing Grades	X^2 Number Post with Higher Grades	t Test Mean GPA Post	t Test Mean Change in Under-achievement	t Test Mean Under-achievement
All Counseling vs. Control	4.20 *	7.20 **	1.98 *	2.78 **	1.71 +
High vs. Moderate Conditions	4.26 *	9.13 **	1.71 +	1.90 *	1.40 +
High vs. Control	6.60 *	11.91 ***	2.17 *	4.33 ***	1.96 *
Moderate vs. Control	0.38	0.38	0.10	0.73	0.07

*** $p < .001$
** $p < .01$
* $p < .05$
+ $p < .10$

Figure 4 where percentage of time out of institution is plotted for the complete one-year follow-up. Not only did the overall differences in the amount of time spent out of an institution significantly favor the delinquents who had received high conditions in group therapy but, as can be seen in Figure 4, the superiority over the controls extends throughout the total follow-up.

A fourth series of studies (Carkhuff and Truax, 1965a, 1965b) utilized a control group to evaluate the effects of high conditions therapy with hospitalized patients, but since it also deals with training, a discussion of its findings will be presented in a later section of this chapter.

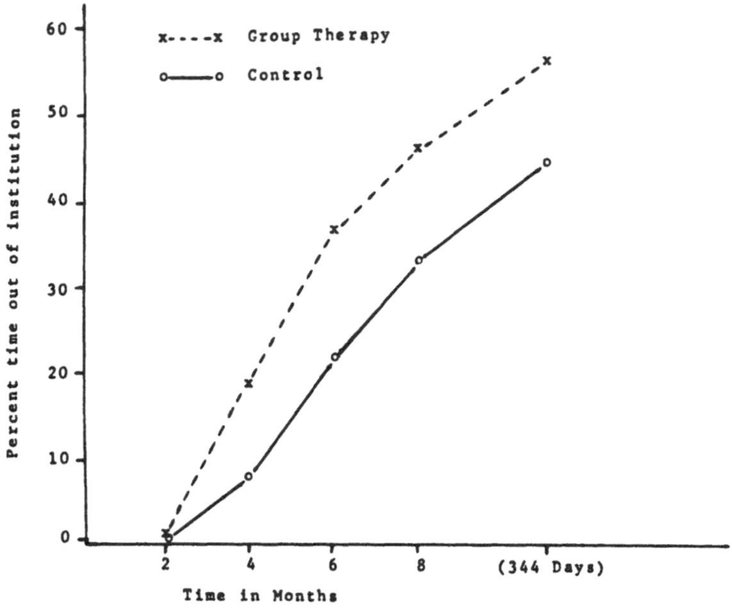

TOWARD RESOLVING THE QUESTION OF CAUSATION

These studies taken together suggest that therapists or counselors who are accurately empathic, nonpossessively warm in attitude, and genuine are indeed effective; the greater the degree to which these elements were present in the therapeutic encounter, the greater was the resulting constructive personality change in the patient. These findings seem to hold for a wide variety of therapists and counselors, *regardless of their training or theoretic orientation;* and for a wide variety of clients or patients, including college underachievers, juvenile delinquents, hospitalized schizophrenics, college counselees, mild to severe outpatient neurotics, and the mixed variety of hospitalized patients. Further, the evidence suggests that these findings hold in a variety of therapeutic contexts and in both individual and group psychotherapy or counseling.

These findings lead to questions of causation. First, there is the question of *who* is causing the therapist to be accurately empathic, nonpossessively warm, and genuine. Is it the therapist or the patient who determines the level of, say, accurate empathy that will occur in a given psychotherapy relationship? The second question concerns the relationship between therapist behavior and patient engagement in the process of self-exploration. Do the therapist-offered conditions determine the depth of patient engagement in the process of self-exploration?

In our research to date, several approaches have been made to the first question of causation: "Who is causing conditions in therapy to be be high or low?"

One study was aimed at clarifying this relationship in the case of accurate empathy. A possible way of answering the question of causation is to have a group of therapists see each member of a group of patients and, in turn, have each patient see all therapists. If the level of conditions is different for different therapists, even when seeing the same patients, then this would show that therapists control the level of conditions. A study has been completed using data from 24 patients living on one continuing treatment ward at Mendota State Hospital, where eight different therapists offered psychotherapy to all patients on a demand basis. From the tape recordings of all interviews, samples were selected in which the same eight therapists saw the same eight patients in a balanced incomplete block design. This research design allowed us to find out if the therapist has an effect on the level of accurate empathy and, separately, if the patient affects the level of accurate empathy. Analysis of the accurate empathy ratings indicated that different therapists indeed produced different levels of accurate empathy, even when interacting with the same set of patients ($p < .01$). The therapist-offered level of accurate empathy appeared independently of the client's. The ability to empathize seemed to be part of the therapist's makeup and not contingent upon the client's makeup. In sharp contrast, different patients did not receive significantly different levels of accurate empathy when interacting with the same therapists.

Analysis of the same data on measures of nonpossessive warmth and therapist genuineness yielded quite similar findings: different therapists produced different levels of both nonpossessive warmth ($p < .01$) and genuineness ($p < .05$), but *different patients did not tend to evoke* different levels of either nonpossessive warmth ($p < .40$) or genuineness ($p < .50$) when they were being seen by the same set of therapists. That is, patients seemed to elicit each individual therapist's own level of these three conditions, independent of the patient; and to elicit a different level from each therapist (thus allowing for individual differences in these ingredients among therapists).

A recent report by van der Veen (1965), using only three patients from the same population as the study just described, indicated that patients had significant effects on the level of accurate empathy and congruence. However, when van der Veen's data was reanalyzed using a more appropriate statistical test (Truax and Wargo, 1966d) the patients did not tend to affect significantly the levels of accurate empathy and congruence.

Another line of evidence suggesting that the therapist, not the patient, determines the level of conditions occurring in psychotherapy was derived from analysis of sampling interviews carried out in studies of individual psychotherapy with hospitalized schizophrenics (Truax, 1962f). In an attempt to provide a standard sampling of the in-therapy patient behavior of all patients, a single standard interviewer saw each patient every three months throughout the course of therapy. With such data, if the level of conditions occurring in therapy were to any large degree influenced by the patient, then we would have significant correlations between the level of conditions occurring in a patient's therapy and the level of conditions occurring in his interview with the standard sampling interviewer. Thus, if some patients were easier to empathize with than others, they should have high levels of empathy occurring in both their therapy and in their standard interview, while others would have low levels of empathy in both situations. The findings indicated no significant correlation between the level of accurate empathy and genuineness offered throughout therapy and the levels occurring in the sampling interview, thus indicating that neither accurate empathy nor genuineness was significantly affected by differences between patients. On the measures of nonpossessive warmth, however, there was a moderate positive relationship ($p < .05$) suggesting that to some extent patients did indeed affect the level of nonpossessive warmth offered by the therapist and the sampling interviewer. Evidently, to a moderate degree some patients do tend to elicit more warmth from therapists than others.

A further evidence on this vital question of whether the patient or the therapist determines the level of conditions provided in psychotherapy or counseling, is available from a study by Truax, Wargo, Frank, Imber, Battle, Hoehn-Saric, Nash and Stone (1966b). In that study the 40 patients were initially seen by two different psychiatrists for screening interviews. Tape recordings from both the screening interviews and the therapy interviews were analyzed to determine the extent of the patient's effect. Twenty of the patients were assigned randomly to each of the two screening interviewers. Analysis indicated that the two interviewers differed from each other significantly on both accurate empathy ($p < .001$) and therapist self-congruence ($p < .01$), but not on nonpossessive warmth. Since the variation between therapists was evaluated by the variation in conditions within therapists in interviewing patients, the findings clearly indicated that it was the interviewer who determined the levels of empathy and congruence. The nonsignificant findings with warmth may mean either that the patients as well as the therapists affected the level of warmth or that these two interviewers happened to provide equal levels of warmth.

A similar analysis was carried out on the average levels of therapeutic conditions offered to the patients throughout the course of psychotherapy. Since patients were assigned randomly to the four different therapists who participated in that research, the comparison was made of the level of conditions offered between and within the four therapists. The findings indicated that the different therapists offered different levels of accurate empathy ($p < .001$), nonpossessive warmth ($p < .05$), and genuineness ($p < .001$) to their patients even though the patients themselves had been randomly assigned.

Several quite recent studies also confirm the original findings suggesting that the levels of therapeutic conditions offered throughout counseling are due to the counselor rather than the client. This was confirmed in a study by Hirshberg, Carkhuff, and Berenson (1966) of out-patient counselors and in-patient therapists, each treating both schizophrenic patients and college student clients. Similarly, in a study of professional counselors versus non-professional friends, the levels of conditions were associated with the "helper" rather than the "helped." Finally, the study of counseling with Negro clients (which also showed that level of empathy, warmth, and genuineness was critical for Negro clients' acceptance of white counselors) carried out by Banks, Berenson, and Carkhuff (1966) also indicated that counselors rather than clients determined the degree to which these therapeutic conditions occurred in the realtionship.

Putting together these several studies that focus on the question of *who* is causing the levels of conditions in interviewing, counseling, or psychotherapy, the evidence is both uniform and strong in indicating that it is the interviewer, not the patient, who determines what the level of accurate empathy and genuineness shall be. The findings from both interviews and therapy sessions are consistent. In considering nonpossessive warmth, however, the findings from therapeutic interviews indicate that different therapists offer different levels of warmth, and that patients in general have little effect on the level of warmth offered. However, the data from *nontherapeutic* interviews (that is, the standard sampling interviews in one study, and the screening interviews in the other) suggest that patients do indeed have a significant effect upon the level of nonpossessive warmth offered by the interviewer.

The overall evidence, then, is not nearly so clear about non-possessive warmth. It may be that in nontherapeutic interviews the interviewer has not made a personal commitment to the patient or client's welfare, and is thus more susceptible to the likable and dislikable characteristics of the client as symptoms of the patient. We might speculate, then, that in the therapeutic relationship, where the therapist or counselor has already made a personal commitment to the patient, he regards dislikable characteristics as symptoms or transient qualities that both he and the client are committed to change as one of the goals of therapy.

A further question deriving from the question of causation arises from a methodological question about the actual measurement of the therapist's levels of conditions. The vast majority of the studies thus far cited measured these levels by having trained raters use research scales (designed to measure the three therapeutic conditions) on randomly coded samples of tape-recorded psychotherapy. Thus, in the measurement process itself, the ratings of the therapist statements were made with full knowledge of the patients' statements. Attempting to measure the level of therapist conditions by such a procedure involves, of course, the possibility of contaminating the measurement of one with the measurement of the other. The raters who judged levels of therapist conditions also *heard* the response of the patient. Might they have been substantially influenced in their rating of therapist conditions by their knowledge of what the patient was doing and how well he responded to the therapist's statements? Might the measures of therapist conditions thus obtained really reflect measures of "good therapeutic interaction" rather than just the therapist's behavior?

The other evidence just reviewed, which indicates that the patient has no detectable effect on the level of therapeutic conditions occurring in psychotherapy, would argue against this possibility. Moreover, in a study aimed specifically at answering this question, Truax (1966b) provides direct evidence. In that study 50 samples of tape-recorded therapeutic transactions obtained throughout the course of therapy with five different patients and therapists provided the basic data for analysis. Using stereophonic recordings with tightly focused "gun" microphones and careful editing, it was possible to obtain only the therapist statement portion of the same 50 samples (the patient's statements had been completely edited out). Ratings were then made on both the set of complete samples (therapist and patient transactions) and separately on the edited samples (containing only the therapist statements). Analysis of those ratings indicated no significant differences between the measurements of accurate empathy and nonpossessive warmth, in the edited and unedited samples for the different therapy cases, for the different sessions from which the samples were drawn, or for different raters. Further, the correlation across the samples between the measures obtained for these conditions in the edited and unedited samples approximated quite closely the reliabilities of the scales themselves. Thus, the direct evidence from that study indicates that measurement of the therapist's levels of therapeutic conditions is in general not contaminated by the patient's responses.

Two kinds of further questions were dealt with in a study (Truax, 1966a) of 40 juvenile delinquents and 40 hospitalized patients in group psychotherapy. The first deals with the role of the patient or client's *perception* of the level of therapeutic conditions offered during psychotherapy. Rogers (1957a) has suggested that for therapeutic conditions to be effective they must be first perceived by the client himself. The evidence that the measures of conditions taken from objective tape recordings of psychotherapy are predictive of outcome suggests that either patients do readily and accurately perceive the conditions offered, or, that such perceptions are irrelevant to how the therapeutic conditions operate in producing outcome.

Since one quite common characteristic of nearly all emotional upset or disturbance is distortion or inaccuracy in interpersonal perceptions, Rogers' assumption concerning the necessity of the patients' accurately perceiving the level of conditions should be examined. The Truax (1966a) study compared the relationship between conditions and outcome in juvenile delinquents and hospitalized patients, using an inventory to assess the level of perceived conditions with measures taken from the objective tape recordings. The findings indicated that the measures of the patients' perceptions of conditions were significantly less associated with outcome ($p < .05$) than were the measures obtained from the tape recordings; suggesting that the effects of accurate empathy, non-possessive warmth, and genuineness operate in producing constructive therapeutic outcome relatively independently of the patients' perceptions of them.

The second question, specific to group psychotherapy, dealt with the question of whether it is the level of conditions offered the group therapy group as a whole that is of significance in producing outcome, or whether it is instead the specific level of conditions offered to each individual patient. A number of group therapists have noted that the level of conditions in group psychotherapy varies not only between groups but also within them, so that a therapist might be more empathic to one patient than another even in the same group therapy group. To study this question, two kinds of samples (patient-therapist-patient and therapist-patient-therapist) were taken for each patient in eight different groups throughout the course of group therapy. Time samples of therapeutic interaction were also taken from the same groups. Measures of the three therapeutic conditions were then made on the time samples, yielding measures of the levels of therapeutic conditions offered the group as a whole; they were compared with measures obtained from the two types of patient-therapist samples, yielding measures of the levels of conditions provided individual patients. Those measures were then compared in terms of their value in predicting individual patient outcome.

The findings indicated that both types of measures had a significant relation to outcome; and that the levels of conditions offered to the group as a whole were as predictive of the outcome for an individual patient as the particular level of conditions offered a given patient. Although the differences in predictive power were not significant, the measure of the level of conditions offered to the group as a whole yielded the highest relationships to outcome. Thus, the findings suggested that in group psychotherapy the levels of accurate empathy, nonpossessive warmth, and genuineness offered to the group as a whole are relatively stronger and may overshadow the level of conditions offered to the individual group member.

Since there is a considerable body of evidence (see Chapter 5) indicating that successful cases differ from nonsuccessful or failure cases in the extent to which clients or patients engage in self-exploration, and since there is also evidence that the level of therapeutic conditions offered by the therapist is significantly related to the degree of patient self-exploration (Truax and Carkhuff, 1964b; Tomlinson, 1962), one aspect of the role of therapeutic conditions in causing patient change could be directly studied: the effect of therapeutic conditions on the patient's level of self-exploration. An experimental study (Truax and Carkhuff, 1965b) has provided direct evidence of the causal relationship between the therapist level of accurate empathy and nonpossessive warmth and the degree of patient self-exploration.

The procedure was quite simple. After a level of patient self-exploration was established during the first 20 minutes of an initial interview, where relatively high conditions of accurate empathy and warmth were present, the experimental variable of lowered conditions was introduced and maintained for the next 20 minutes. Then the experimental procedure of lowered conditions was withdrawn, and relatively high conditions of accurate empathy and warmth were re-established. One would expect patient self-exploration to be high when conditions were high but to drop when lowered conditions were introduced, and then return to a relatively high level when the higher conditions were re-established. The test of the causal hypothesis was simply an evaluation of the levels of patient depth of intrapersonal exploration, to determine whether or not the lowered conditions do indeed produce lowered levels of self-exploration. The experiment was replicated on three schizophrenic patients who had recently been admitted to an acute treatment ward. It should be noted that the conditions were not dropped precipitously; the therapist was neither grossly nonempathic nor showing negative regard toward the patient during the experimental operation of lowered conditions. This was done to maintain the integrity of the therapist and not present a direct "about face" to the patient. Also, therapist genuineness was maintained throughout the course of study; since it was felt that a lack of therapist integrity or genuineness would distort and totally mar the therapeutic encounter.

The experimental operation of reducing levels of accurate empathy and nonpossessive warmth was checked by determining the levels of these conditions throughout each of the interviews. The three periods for each patient were subdivided into fifths, and the resulting samples were drawn, randomly assigned code numbers, and given "blind" to raters trained in the use of the scales.

The data indicate that the attempted experimental lowering of conditions during the middle portion of the therapeutic encounter was indeed successful. That is, conditions were moderately high during the initial and terminal periods and relatively low during the middle period of each session. Further, communicated therapist genuineness remained relatively high (and, in fact, there seemed to be some overcompensation in this variable during the period of lowered conditions).

Finally, the test indicated that with all three patients there occurred the predicted consequent drop in depth of intrapersonal exploration during the period when the conditions were experimentally lowered. Where there is an experimentally induced drop in accurate empathy and warmth, a clear effect is produced in the form of a consequent drop in the level of patient self-exploration.

The learning of empathy, warmth and genuineness: Further evidence of causation

Direct evidence concerning the causal role of the therapeutic conditions in producing patient or client personality change might easily be gained by deliberately subjecting a number of patients in long-term psychotherapy to a number of months of low conditions followed by a number of months of high conditions. If such a procedure were followed, we would expect to see improvement in the client or patient followed by deteriora-

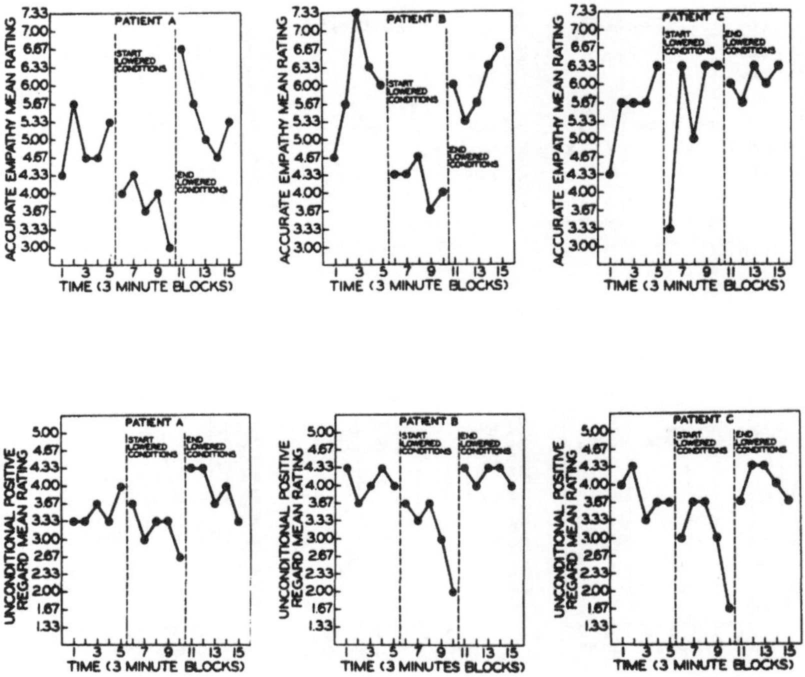

EXPERIMENTAL MANIPULATION OF THERAPIST LEVELS OF EMPATHY AND WARMTH (*Discussed on Pages 105-106 of Text*)

tion which would in turn be followed by improvement. Although such a procedure would be useful for scientific purposes, it would be ethically difficult, if not impossible, to justify, since it would entail the possibility of irreversible damage to a client during the period of low conditions.

One way of directly attacking the central question of causation would be to train 'prospective therapists specifically to provide high levels of accurate empathy, nonpossessive warmth and genuineness, and then see if they were indeed effective in producing constructive change in patients or clients.

The degree to which these three ingredients of effective psychotherapy can be learned is also of central importance to the aim of enhancing human relationships that change people. A large number of training supervisors have been convinced over the years that good therapists are born, not made. Many educators have felt that the same holds true for good teachers. To some degree, the nature of accurate empathy, nonpossessive warmth, and genuineness fits nicely with this belief, since these ingredients are in part a description of the attitudes and personality of the therapist rather than merely effective techniques. However, it also

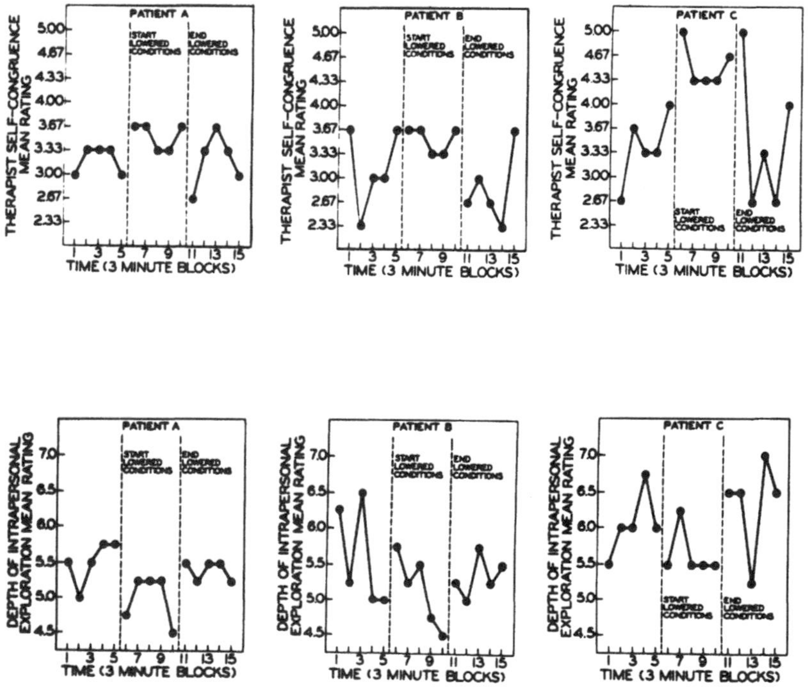

Effects of Experimental Manipulation of Therapist Levels of Empathy and Warmth upon Level of Patient Depth of Self-Exploration and upon Therapist Level of Genuineness (*Discussed on Pages 105-106 of Text*)

seems possible that even potential therapists who, in their usual human encounters, are nonempathic, hostile and defensive could learn to communicate these ingredients in the specific encounter of the therapy hour.

A program for applying the research instruments designed to measure these three ingredients to the training of professional and lay persons has been described by Truax, Carkhuff and Douds (1964). Evidence from this didactic and experientially-based program suggests that specific training can lead to relatively effective communication of accurate empathy, non-possessive warmth and genuineness. A report by Carkhuff and Truax (1965a) compared the levels of these three ingredients in postgraduate clinical psychology trainees and lay persons (mainly psychiatric aides in a hospital setting) with the levels in a group of relatively effective and highly skilled therapists. The contrast group of experienced therapists included such therapists as Drs. Carl Rogers, Albert Ellis, Rollo May, Julius Seeman, and Carl Whitaker. After slightly less than 100 hours of training, extending over a four-month period, the levels of accurate empathy communicated to patients were not significantly different between the three groups, although the ordering of the groups was in the expected direction. The lay trainees averaged a level of 4.6, the graduate psychology trainees a level of 5.1, and the experienced therapists a level of 5.2. Similarly, there were no significant differences between the three groups in terms of the level of nonpossessive warmth communicated to the patient: lay trainees averaged scale values of 2.8, graduate psychology trainees 3.0, and experienced therapists 3.1. With respect to therapist's genuineness, however, the experienced therapists showed a significantly higher level of genuineness or self-congruence than did the lay trainees, while the psychology trainees had an intermediate level. Experienced therapists averaged 5.5, psychology trainees 5.2, and lay trainees 4.8. Also, and perhaps of greatest interest, the level of patient depth of self-exploration achieved in therapy did not differ significantly between the three groups. The average scale value was 4.8 for the experienced therapists, 4.6 for the lay trainees, and 4.5 for the psychology trainees. These data suggest that these ingredients can be learned, by both professional and nonprofessional persons.

In a cross-validation on a new group of 16 graduate student trainees (Truax and Silber, 1966) essentially similar findings were obtained. Further, the evaluation of the effectiveness of training was extended by randomly assigning patients to the trainees for a "one-shot therapeutic interview" early in the training program, and repeating this with different patients late in the program. Before the early interview the trainees had received 14 class hours of training and had spent an average of 11 hours listening to experienced therapists, so that they could provide moderately high levels of therapeutic conditions, insuring that the patients for the "one-shot" interviews would not be harmed. The late "one-shot" interviews were made after an additional 34 to 36 hours of training, so that an evaluation of the trainees' change in level of conditions could be made. The analysis indicated significant gains in the level of accurate empathy ($p < .05$) and genuineness ($p < .05$), but a nonsignificant gain in nonpossessive warmth, over the nine-week period of additional training.

Still another training process study (Berenson, Carkhuff, and Myrus, 1966) with prospective undergraduate dormitory counselors has yielded similar results. The trainees, in relatively brief periods of time, demonstrated significant improvement and high levels of functioning on the therapeutic dimensions of empathy, positive warmth, genuineness, concreteness and the level of client self-exploration elicited. This counselor training study is worth noting since it is the first one to incorporate a "training-control" group (in effect, a placebo group) in addition to a regular control group. Thus, 36 student volunteers were randomly assigned to three groups, (1) the training group proper, (2) the "training-control" group (which spent exactly the same number of hours doing everything that the training group proper did, except employing the research scales and incorporating the group therapy experience), and (3) the control group proper. All groups had standardized interview experiences both before and after training.

The following change indices were employed: (1) the tapes were rated on all counselor and client proces variables; (2) the standard interviewee filled out an inventory concerning his experience of the counselor's functioning on the therapeutic dimensions; (3) the counselor himself filled out a similar inventory concerning his own functioning; and (4) the dormitory roommates of the counselors filled out the same inventory as the standard interviewee. Overall, the trends were consistent: the training group proper demonstrated the greatest change; the "training-control" group demonstrated positive change, but never as great as the training group proper; the control group demonstrated minimal practice or temporal effects. Overall on all indices, Group I demonstrated significantly greater change ($p < .05$) than Group III; only on the "interviewee" and the "self" inventories did Group II demonstrate significantly greater change ($p < .05$) than Group III. In addition, Group I demonstrated significantly greater overall change than Group II on the reports of interviewees and significant others.

It still could very well be that these three ingredients are effective only within the context of an expert knowledge of personality dynamics and psychopathology. It might be that the therapists who were relatively unable to communicate high levels of these three ingredients might also be the therapists who have poor ability and knowledge in the area of personality dynamics and psychopathology. However, the data from the Bergin and Solomon study (1963) indicated no significant relationship (even though a slightly negative one) between the level of accurate empathy actually communicated by the therapist in the therapeutic relationship and his graduate school grades in clinical psychology.

One convenient way of attempting to get further information about this question was to observe the effects on patient outcome of the lay persons who had had the four-month training program, and who were communicating, on the average, a relatively high level of accurate empathy, nonpossessive warmth and therapist genuineness. In a research evaluation (Carkhuff and Truax, 1965b) five volunteer, but otherwise unselected, trainees (three psychiatric aides, a volunteer worker and an industrial therapist) were assigned as group therapists to eight different groups of hospitalized mental patients. Seventy patients also served as a control group, with a total of 150 patients randomly assigned to the two populations. The patients themselves were by and large an old, chronic, relatively uneducated population with a long history of hospitalization and extremely poor prognosis. The average patient in the treatment group was fifty years old and had a seventh grade education, with an average of two hospital admissions, the last admission averaging 13½ years. The control group was essentially identical, with an average age of 47 years, a little over a seventh grade education, and an average of two admissions, with the last hospitalization averaging ten years. Less than one-third of the patients were testable by any of the usual psychometric techniques, so that evaluations of patient improvement were based upon ratings of ward behavior filled out by the ward staff. Statistically significant differences were obtained in favor of the patients who received group psychotherapy on the overall measure of degree of general improvement and on all three of the sub-scales: degree of psychological disturbance, degree of constructive intrapersonal concern; and degree of constructive interpersonal behavior.

Since the lay group counseling sessions with the hospitalized patients were recorded for supervision purposes, a further report of the lay training program (Truax, Silber and Carkhuff, 1966) evaluated the level of conditions that lay therapists provided throughout the group counseling sessions and related these conditions to therapeutic outcome. It is of interest to have some idea of the relative levels of conditions offered by the lay therapists and by experienced professional therapists. Since levels of conditions offered by the 16 experienced therapists in the study of group psychotherapy with hospitalized patients referred to earlier (Truax and Wargo, 1966a) were available, some comparison could be made with the lay therapists. Precise comparison is not possible since the patients seen by the lay therapists were markedly more chronic, less verbal, and in general poor group therapy candidates. Under these conditions, the average levels of accurate empathy and nonpossessive warmth for the lay therapists were lower than for the experienced professional therapists. Although the experienced professional therapists as a group provided higher levels of conditions, 31% of the sample of experienced professional therapists provided levels of accurate empathy and nonpossessive warmth *at or below the level* provided by the beginning lay therapists. Examination of the levels of conditions provided by the lay group therapists indicated that of the 74 patients receiving group counseling, 32 had received relatively high conditions, 16 had received moderate levels, and 26 had received relatively low levels. Comparisons were then made of the number of patients showing improvement, no change, and deteriorative changes among these three levels of therapeutic conditions and in comparison with the patients receiving control conditions. As anticipated, patients in group counseling who received low levels of therapeutic conditions showed no benefit from group counseling, with outcomes on all four measures approximating the control group. By contrast, patients who received relatively high and moderate levels of conditions in group counseling showed significant improvement over control patients on all four measures of patient outcome. Further, there were no differences in outcome between the patients receiving high and moderate levels of therapeutic conditions; both groups tended to show improvement superior to the patients receiving low conditions.

The currently available evidence, then, suggests that these ingredients of accurate empathy, nonpossessive warmth and therapist genuineness are "teachable"; and that even nonprofessional persons lacking expert knowledge of psychopathology and personality dynamics can, under supervision, produce positive changes in chronic hospitalized patient populations after specific training in the communication of accurate empathy, nonpossessive warmth and therapist genuineness. This latter finding not only indicates that the effective therapeutic ingredients can indeed be learned, but also suggests the possibility that they have a causative relationship to outcome that is independent of expert knowledge of psychopathology and personality theory.

INCIDENCE OF THERAPEUTIC CONDITIONS IN PRACTICE

Since virtually all theoretic views of psychotherapy converge in suggesting the importance of the therapist's communicating to the patient his accurate empathic understanding and nonpossessive warmth in the context of a relationship characterized by his authenticity or genuineness as a person, we might expect that relatively few therapists would themselves be unempathic, "cold," "rejecting," or insincere in their relationships with patients. That such is not at all the case is indicated both by the outcome research just reviewed and by the results of studies conducted by Strupp and his co-workers (1960b). In a study of 126 psychiatrists, Strupp's data (based on ratings of responses to standardized sound films of patient-therapist interviews) indicated that of 2,474 analyzed responses, only 4.6 per cent could be classified as communicating any degree of warmth and acceptance. That is, more than 95 per cent of the responses were either neutral or communicated coldness and rejection. Even more striking, on their measure of therapeutic attitude toward a patient, less than one-third (39) of the therapists could be rated overall as having positive or warm attitude; while more than one-third (51) were rated overall as having clear negative, cold, or rejecting attitudes. When comparisons were later made between 55 psychiatrists and 55 psychologists, matched on the basis of length of experience, the psychologists did not differ overall in their attitudes toward the patient from the sample of psychiatrists. Strupp's questionnaire data, dealing with an overall sample of 237 therapists representing psychiatric social workers, psychologists, psychiatrists, and psychoanalysts, yielded similar data on the prevalence of positive, negative, and neutral or ambivalent attitudes toward patients: less than one-third had positive attitudes, while more than one-third had negative ones.

On the basis of the many studies completed by himself and his co-workers, Strupp finds that current therapists can be categorized into two broadly defined groups: "Group I therapists appear to be more tolerant, more humane, more premissive, more "democratic" and more "therapeutic." "Group II therapists emerge as more directive, disciplinarian, moralistic, and harsh" (p. 99). In discussing these two broad groups of practicing therapists, the one "therapeutic" and the other perhaps "anti-therapeutic," Strupp characterizes them in a manner essentially consistent with the present view of "high conditions therapist vs. low conditions therapists."

What is meant by this distinction? On the one hand, it is a basic attitude of understanding, respect, and compassion—what Albert Schweitzer calls "reverence for life." It is the ability to listen without preconception, prejudgment, or condemnation. It is the ability to pierce the neurotic distortions, the socially unacceptable attitudes and acts, the more unsavory aspects of the personality, and to see behind it a confused, bewildered, and helpless individual trying to shape his destiny, hampered and hindered by his neurotic conflicts and maladaptations. On the other hand, it is an attitude of coldness, calculation, "clinical evaluation," distance, "objectivity," aloofness, moral judgment, and condemnation. It is a readiness to take the neurotic defenses and the patient's character structure at face value and to react to them with irritation, impatience, annoyance, and anger. It is also an attitude of forming a moral judgment about the patient's illness from the beginning of the interview.

On another level, we seem to be dealing with groups of therapists whose philosophical orientation differs about determinism and free will. The prevalent view of emotional disturbances in contemporary Western culture—certainly since the time of Freud—lays heavy emphasis upon man's impotence in coming to terms with unconscious forces by which he lived, and for whose existence and influence he bears no greater personal responsibility than for the rising of the sun. On the other hand, the data reveal another group of therapists who seem to be more deeply imbued with the traditional, moralistic position which identifies neurotic conflicts and resulting attitudes and actions with a "weakness of character," lack of moral fiber, laziness, and laxity. Accordingly, the way to "improve" is by an act of will, not through self-understanding and insight. It is astonishing to encounter the moralistic view with such frequency among professional therapists, unless one is willing to assume that this particular patient's seeming unreasonableness, demandingness, and hostility led to a momentary abandonment of the "therapeutic" position.

Thus we see that some therapists are willing and even eager to help the patient through long-term intensive psychotherapy, realizing that the acceptance of a patient for therapy constitutes an important decision to invest significant amounts of one's time, energy, and emotional resources, whereas others disclosed a marked distaste for this possibility. It seemed that occasionally this "avoidance" reaction was couched in such phraseology as: the patient is not going to get better anyway; certainly he will not get worse without treatment; he is a chronic complainer, he is generally "no good"; his motivation for therapy is poor. (pp. 99-100)

These findings should be viewed in light of the evidence given in this chapter to indicate that patients seen by therapists who communicate high levels of accurate empathic understanding, nonpossessive warmth and genuineness tend to show constructive personality change, while patients seen by therapists communicating low levels of empathy, warmth and genuineness tend to show deteriorative personality change. Seen this way, they provide an explanation for the mass of findings reviewed in Chapter I indicating that average psychotherapy or counseling is no better than no psychotherapy or counseling: Strupp's data suggest that less than one-third of practicing psychiatrists and psychologists may provide positive therapeutic conditions, while more than one-third may actually provide negative therapeutic conditions. Thus there seems to be a close parallel between the prevalence of positive, negative, and neutral levels of therapeutic conditions and the prevalence of positive, negative, and neutral patient outcome.

OTHER THERAPIST-RELATED CHARACTERISTICS CONTRIBUTING TO OUTCOME

In four recent studies the research design has allowed for evaluating the effects on patient outcome of individual differences between therapists within levels of conditions. That is, even among therapists who offer similar levels of empathy, warmth and genuineness, do different therapists tend to get reliably different therapeutic results? In all four studies (Truax, Wargo, Frank, Imber, Battle, Hoehn-Saric, Nash and Stone, 1966b; Truax and Wargo, 1966c, 1966d; and Truax, Wargo and Carkhuff, 1966) the findings indicated that even with the same levels of therapeutic conditions, some therapists tend to get better (or poorer) outcome than others, on various measures of client outcome. These findings clearly indicate that accurate empathy, nonpossessive warmth and genuineness (at least as they are currently measured) do not account for nearly all the important therapeutic characteristics of counselors and therapists. Thus, although the therapeutic conditions are perhaps critically important for client outcome, other therapist attributes, perhaps equally important, contribute significantly to therapeutic outcome. Thus the evidence suggests that the therapeutic triad may or may not be "necessary" but it is clearly not "sufficient."

These "other therapist attributes" are as yet completely unidentified by research. They may involve differential "reinforcement" of client behaviors by the therapist, the extent of his "expert knowledge," other personal or attitudinal characteristics, his ability to "handle the transference neurosis," or his ability to systematically desensitize the client's fears. We do not know. We know only that other individual differences between therapists significantly affect the degree of patient personality or behavior change. This is a "negative" but important piece of knowledge. We know that *some* "expert" or "human" differences between therapists will later prove to be of major therapeutic importance.

OTHER FIELDS OF HUMAN BEHAVIOR

Although psychotherapy can be thought of as a unique phenomenon, it can also be viewed as specific example of the broader class of phenomena labeled as "learning," and also of that labeled "interpersonal relations."

We would expect, therefore, that some converging evidence of the effectiveness of accurate empathy, nonpossessive warmth, and even therapist genuinenes should be available in the fields of laboratory studies of learning, classroom studies of learning, and parent-child studies.

Studies of Learning: Teacher Effects

In a laboratory study of verbal conditioning, Weiss, Krasner and Ullman (1960) reported data showing that a hostile experimenter (unempathic and not warm) decreased the number of verbal responses (lowered the verbal operant level); while an experimenter who showered assent and attention upon college student subjects (the warm, supportive therapist) produced an increase in the frequency of self-references. One very intriguing aspect of that study was the finding of greater emotional disturbance in the subjects during extinction (a period of non-reward for performance) with the experimenter who had previously showered attention and agreement on them. One cannot help wondering whether perhaps the extinction period under those conditions seemed to the subject an incongruence or artifice in the therapist who had previously been attentive and agreeable and then suddenly became aloof.

Another study of verbal conditioning by Sapolsky (1960) reported that when the experimenter had an incompatible relationship with the subject, there was virtually no response acquisition or learning; however, when the relationship was compatible, there was significant response acquisition.

There are some research studies dealing with teacher-child classroom interactions that also provide relevant evidence. Working at the preschool level, Truax and Tatum (1966) reported a study attempting to relate the level of empathy, warmth and genuineness communicated to the preschool child by his teachers to his preschool performance and social adjustment. Using both time sampling procedures (with observers making ratings) and relationship inventories as basic measures of these "effective ingredients," the findings indicated that the degree of warmth and the degree of empathy was significantly related to positive changes in the child's preschool performance and social adjustment. However, there seemed to be no relation to the teacher's genuinenesss. Thus, even in the very brief encounters of the preschool teacher-child relationships (modal interactions last less than one minute) the findings indicated significant positive effects of warmth and empathy.

In a study reported by Christensen (1960) the relationship between school learning achievement and degree of teacher warmth was investigated. The findings indicated significant relationships between the teacher's warmth and the student's levels of learning or achievement on measures of vocabulary and arithmetic. Students showed higher vocabulary and arithmetic scores when taught by teachers who showed high levels of warmth than by those teachers with relatively little warmth. Then, too, in a study by Hawkes and Egbert (1954) of teaching success, empathy was found to be a significant factor in students' ratings of teacher competence. Additional converging evidence comes from the Isaacson, McKeachie and Milholland report (1963) relating the teacher's personality to student ratings. There is also considerable anecdotal literature, such as Willis' book *The Guinea Pigs Ater Twenty Years* (1961), which is consistent with the research evidence.

Diskin (1956) also felt that empathy may function as a basic factor in teacher effectiveness. In a study of student-teacher trainees that studied specifically the trainees' ability to develop harmonious interpersonal relations in the classroom, he reported findings indicating that student-teachers who are high in individual empathy are best able to maintain harmonious interpersonal relations in the classroom.

A quite recent study by Aspy (1965) studied the relationship between the level of therapeutic conditions offered by teachers of third-grade reading classes and the consequent gains in children's reading achievement levels. Using tape recordings of the teacher's classroom instruction, measures of the levels of therapeutic conditions offered in the classroom were made (using the same scale for accurate empathy, nonpossessive warmth and genuineness presented in Chapter 2 that had been developed and used for studies of psychotherapy and counseling). This sample included eight teachers and 120 students in a nicely balanced design; half the students in each class had tested relatively high and half relatively low in IQ, and the classes were half girls and half boys. Controlling for any possible differences in initial level of achievement, his findings indicated that students receiving relatively high levels of accurate empathy, nonpossessive warmth and genuineness from their teacher in third-grade reading classes showed significantly greater gains in achievement (measured by the Stanford Reading Achievement Test) than students receiving relatively lower levels of these therapeutic conditions ($p < .01$). As expected, the levels of conditions were noticeably lower than in therapeutic settings. Still, the findings from Aspy's study strongly indicated that the teachers who were warm, empathic and genuine were able to produce greater behavioral change in terms of reading achievement than those who were less warm, empathic and genuine. In that data, in fact, the effect of high versus low conditions was as great as the effect of high versus low intelligence levels in the normal classroom.

In a study just completed by Aspy and Hadlock (1966), the findings obtained in a further study of gains in third to fifth grade reading achievement confirmed and extended previous findings. Students taught by teachers high in accurate empathy, non-possessive warmth, and genuineness showed a reading achievement gain of 2.5 years during a five-month period while pupils taught by low conditions teachers gained only 0.7 years. Even more striking, the truancy rate in classes with low conditions was twice that occuring in high-conditions classrooms.

These findings suggest that the person (whether a counselor, therapist or teacher) who is better able to communicate warmth, genuineness, and accurate empathy is more effective in interpersonal relationships no matter what the goal of the interaction (better grades for college students, better interpersonal relations for the counseling center outpatient, adequate personality functioning and integration for the seriously disturbed mental patient, socially acceptable behavior for the juvenile delinquent, or greater reading ability for the third-grade reading instruction student).

A study by Hollenbeck (1965) used the questionnaire method developed by Barrett-Lennard in attempting to measure the level of conditions perceived by college students from their parents in relation to measures of adjustment and college achievement level. The findings seemed relatively consistent in indicating that the more a college student perceives his parents as offering him relatively high levels of empathic understanding, nonpossessive warmth and genuineness, the better his adjustment as measured by the correlation between his self concept and his ideal concept. The findings were stronger for conditions offered from the father than from the mother and still stronger when measured for the perceived conditions coming from both parents together. Relationship between college achievement levels and the level of conditions from the parents, however, was modest, with statistically significant relationships holding only for men, not women. Interestingly, for both personality adjustment and academic achievement, there was no relationship to the degree of unconditionality of the warmth offered by parents.

Studies of Parent-Child Relationships: Effects of Parents

The growing body of literature studying the parent-child relationship also produces evidence consistent with the idea that empathy, warmth and genuineness are characteristic of human encounters that change people for the better.

The general line of evidence initiated by Spitz (1945, 1946) and the work of Skeels and Dye (1939) strongly suggests that a lack of interpersonal relationships in infants and young children leads to a complexity of interpersonal and emotional problems grossly defined as "intellectual and emotional immaturity." Although the early studies left much to be desired methodologically, later studies tend to confirm the trend of the finding. Thus the conclusion of Goldfarb (1944) that the impersonal care and coldness of an institutional program leaves permanent marks on the children in terms of a greater frequency of temper tantrums, stealing, kicking and hitting other children, distractability, inordinate demands for attention, and hyperactivity, seems to be at least reasonably accurate.

An inordinate degree of intrapersonal, conflict (lack of warmth, for example) has been found in the homes of schizophrenic patients by Frazee (1953) and by Lidz, Cornelison, Fleck and Terry (1957). The parent-child relationship is characterized as "ingenuine, distant, stereotyped, or defensive," and has been associated with the development of emotional disturbance in the child by a number of persons (including among others, Baxter, Becker and Hooks, 1963; Bowen, 1960, Lidz and Lidz, 1949; and Wynne et al., 1958). Current theory as exemplified by Bateson, Jackson and Weakland (1956) holds that family styles of communication which are unempathic and artificial are the major sources for the development of disturbed children.

We might note that Chorost's (1962) data indicated that warm parental attitudes were positively related to less hostility in their children. Similarly, Montalto's (1952) study indicated a positive correspondence between the adjustment level of six-year-old children and the warm attitudes of their mothers. In a study of delinquent children, Cass (1952) reported evidence suggesting that although parents of delinquents may not differ from parents of carefully matched normal children in degree of control, strictness, or even neglect and indifference, they show less empathy, awareness, or understanding of the child.

Typical of the findings was a study of 41 boys, ages 8 through 12, and their parents, reported by Schulman et al., (1962). Analysis of data based on observations during an experimental period indicated that parents of children with conduct problems were more hostile and rejecting toward their children than were the parents of the control group. Again, the study by Read (1945) reported findings indicating that children of mothers who expressed warmth and approval for them had significantly more favorable social behaviors than the contrast group.

That even the degree of possessiveness or nonpossessiveness of warmth is related to child development is suggested by the Freeman and Grayson (1955) study of maternal attitudes as factors in the development of schizophrenia. In their study, it was found that mothers of schizophrenics tended to be significantly more possessive in their attitudes toward their children.

Indeed, many of the findings concerning parental control and child development bear directly on warmth and nonpossessive warmth as a central factor in parent-child studies. Thus the experimental study by Bishop (1951) studied 34 mothers and their children in a "play" situation. Frequency counts from observers indicated that either possessiveness or lack of warmth, as indicated by such maternal behaviors as directing, interfering, and criticizing the child's play behavior, was significantly related (correlations from .45 to .71) to a high frequency of noncooperative, reluctant, and inhibited behaviors on the part of the child.

That a lack of authenticity or genuineness in the parents also plays a role in the development or maldevelopment of children is suggested by a variety of studies focusing on the ambivalence of feelings communicated by the parent to the child. Thus Mark (1953) in his study of mothers of schizophrenics reported that mothers of schizophrenics exhibited attitudes of both excessive warmth and cool detachment—either objective aloofness or highly possessive warmth. Indeed, in the review of early infantile autism (Eisenberg and Kanner, 1956), the main conclusion was that the typical autistic family does not provide a warm, flexible, growth-promoting emotional atmosphere. Rarely, they claimed, does one find warmth expressed by the parent to the autistic child. The parents' inauthenticity and lack of genuineness were suggested by their frequent references to "observing" their children, as though they were clinical subjects. In treatment, such parents are apt to apply literally any mechanistic rules rather than deal with the child as a person.

In an extensive analysis of TAT stories told by mothers of schizophrenic and mothers of so-called normal children, Mitchell (1965) was able to differentiate significantly between the two groups of mothers ($p. < 001$). The basic distinction seemed to be that mothers of schizophrenic children were often unempathic, even oblivious, to the demands of interpersonal relationships. Indeed, Mitchell saw that the schizophrenic's fundamental difficulty was the parent's possessive insistence that he "act out" their view of the world instead of organizing his own perceptions.

Studies of Mass Communications and Public Opinions

Gompertz (1960), in reviewing the literature, concludes that "the process of empathy seems to be the *sine qua non* for effective communication" and indicates the finding of a high positive correlation between empathic responsiveness and ability to communicate effectively.

That even communication via radio, television, and printed material is more effective when characterized by "high therapeutic conditions" is indicated by a number of studies. The more warm and personal the communications, the higher they are rated by the recipient as being responsible and calm (Sargent, 1965). Similarly, Zimbardo (1960) obtained findings indicating that the higher the level of personal involvement between the communicator and the recipient, even in mass communications, the greater the degree of opinion change in the recipient. This finding held even when the recipient in mass communications changed to a position he had already previously described as unreasonable and indefensible. The study emphasized the facilitation that occurs in opinion changes if warmth or friendship exists between communicator and recipient. This positive relationship between opinion change and feelings of warmth or liking was also reported in an earlier study by Winthrop (1958).

Studies of Small Group Processes

The considerable body of evidence dealing with group processes and the concept of cohesiveness is perhaps quite relevant to empathy, warmth, and genuineness. Since other evidence indicates that those who communicate high levels of these therapeutic conditions are better liked than those who communicate low levels, and since the basic operational definition of cohesiveness is the degree of interpersonal attraction or liking, much of the evidence on the functioning of cohesiveness may hold for the therapeutic triad. The bulk of the available evidence provides strong support for the assertion that members of groups high in cohesiveness or liking have considerably more power over each other than those low in cohesiveness (liking). Such studies as those by Schachter, Ellertson, and McBride (1951) and by Berkowitz (1954), for example, indicate that predictable behavioral consequences occur with experimental changes in the level of a group's cohesiveness (interpersonal liking): highly cohesive groups can exert more power over their members in inducing desired behavior changes. In general the evidence suggests that the level of cohesiveness is positively related to satisfaction in a wide variety of group settings. Thus, van Zelst (1951) reports such findings with actual work-teams of construction workers, and Darley et al. (1951) find the same relationship in a university housing community. Similarly, the general relationship between the level of cohesiveness and the amount of influence exerted on group members is shown in studies of output such as that by Schachter, Ellertson, and Gregory (1951), who in a laboratory study demonstrated that high levels of cohesiveness (liking) heightened the influence of the group over its members, and that this influence could either increase or decrease a member's output, depending on his own relationship to the group norm.

That cohesiveness or liking in groups holds for individuals as well is suggested by French and Snyder (1959) who focused their study of army personnel groups on the relationship between liking and interpersonal influence. The findings clearly indicated that the person who was highly liked was significantly more influential in influencing attitudes and behavior than those persons who were less liked.

We might not expect all the levels of facilitative dimensions to be as intense in other, more general instances of interpersonal process as we do in the experiences of counseling and psychotherapy. Martin, Carkhuff and Berenson (1965) studied the counselor and client process variables in a study of counseling and friendship. In a counterbalanced design employing both experienced therapists and "the best available friends," the 16 subjects were given a "mental set" to discuss anything that was troubling them, and both the counselor and the "best friends" were given the "set" to be as helpful as possible. The following findings emerged: the therapist provided significantly higher levels of *all* therapeutic conditions (empathy, positive regard, genuineness, concreteness and client self-exploration) than did the best friends, as indicated by tape ratings ($p < .01$) and inventories ($p < .01$). The implications are important, with the principal suggestion being that counseling and psychotherapy provide a "heightened" experience of the same dimensions present in friendship and have a more significantly constructive impact than the other sources of nourishment in our environment.

THE INTERACTION OF PATIENT AND THERAPIST IN PRODUCING THE LEVEL OF THERAPIST-OFFERED CONDITIONS

In discussing the question of causation, evidence was presented to indicate that the therapist was the primary or most significant determinant of the levels of accurate empathy, nonpossessive warmth and therapist genuineness. That data, however, dealt with *groups* of patients seen by therapists and thus simply means that although therapists do respond differently to different patients, the differences between therapists are greatly more important in affecting the therapeutic triad than differences between patients. Still, one would expect that some kind of interaction between individual therapist and patient would affect the level of conditions offered by the therapist. One might also expect that certain categories of patients would generally tend to receive higher or lower levels of conditions from almost any therapist. Certainly one might expect the principle of reciprocal affect to impinge in some way on the behavior of both the therapist and the patient. There is considerable evidence to suggest that certain types of patients are more likely than others to show improvement in psychotherapy. The central and crucial question is, of course, *why* this is so. We might also question whether this is *necessarily* so, or merely *often* so. Some tentative answers can be suggested.

An ideal therapist under ideal circumstances would provide high therapeutic conditions to all patients at all times. But the therapist, after all, is human. His own personal prejudices will inevitably operate to some degree —he will provide lower levels of conditions (say, warmth) to patients who are more personally irritating or unpleasant. (The present senior author, for example, finds patients usually labeled "hysteric" unpleasant to be with, and so inevitably offers them less warmth and empathy—and is therefore a less effective therapist.) The work of Fiedler and Senior (1952) early provided evidence that the therapist's feeling toward patients significantly affect the process of psychotherapy. In a study of the amount and quality of the feelings which the patient expresses during therapy sessions, the findings were clear-cut in indicating that patients who expressed themselves freely were seen by therapists with favorable feeling toward them, while patients who showed little expression of feeling in therapy had therapists who had unfavorable feelings toward them.

Similarly, an investigation by Goldstein and Shipman (1961) studied therapists' initial interview attitudes, using senior medical students as therapists. Their findings indicated that the reduction of disturbance symptoms in patients following an interview was significantly related to the favorableness or unfavorableness of the interviewer's attitudes: the greatest patient symptom reduction occurred with interviewers who had favorable attitudes. These findings are quite consistent with those presented earlier on the effects of warmth on patient outcome.

That the therapist's expectations for favorable or unfavorable outcome markedly affect his offering of therapeutic conditions is clearly indicated by the research work of Strupp and his associates (1958). A sound motion-picture technique in which therapists watch an initial interview and periodically make "vicarious" responses was used in a study of 55 psychiatrists and 55 psychologists. Therapists who regarded the patient's outcome as likely to be unfavorable gave more than four times as many "cold" responses than those who regarded the patient's outcome as likely to be favorable. That is, when the therapist expected a poor outcome, his responses to the patient were likely to be cold and nontherapeutic.

Beyond personal prejudices, there are general prejudices operative throughout the profession of psychotherapy. For instance, the average therapist has generally been taught that prognosis is poor for schizophrenic and psychopathic patients. It seems almost inevitable that he will communicate pessimism to such patients, as well as providing lower conditions to these people he believes he cannot help. The lowered level of therapeutic conditions would lead predictably to poor outcome, and thereby confirm his original pessimism. We would suggest that if the therapist could overcome such prejudices, both personal and professional, then his offering of high conditions would lead to positive outcomes for the low I.Q. patient, the schizophrenic, and even the psychopath.

The present viewpoint, in essence, is that in those moments when he is his most ideal self, the therapist can overcome the effects of his own prejudices, and even the effects of an obnoxious patient (who through the principle of reciprocal affect tends to elicit negative affect or low warmth), and can offer high levels of therapeutic conditions to all patients. From such a viewpoint it would be true to say that patients do determine in part the level of conditions provided in therapy; but that the patient's effect is not necessary, but often due to a human inadequacy of the therapist or counselor.

Beyond these considerations, however, it is still quite likely that even a given level of therapeutic conditions will have differential effectiveness depending upon the patient's current level of functioning and self concepts. Some of the research evidence dealing with initial patient characteristics and degree of constructive personality change will be discussed in Chapter 5.

THE DIRECTION AND CONSISTENCY OF THE EVIDENCE FOR THE ROLE OF ACCURATE EMPATHY, NON-POSSESSIVE WARMTH AND GENUINENESS

In looking closely at the research evidence suggesting that accurate empathy, non-possessive warmth and genuineness are perhaps critically important for effective counseling and psychotherapy, the specific findings vary from one study to another; just as each investigation varies in the therapists involved, the orientation, duration and type of therapy, the type of client, and the specific measures used to evaluate therapeutic outcome. In most of the studies reviewed here, multiple measures of client improvement or constructive behavioral change were used. Rarely were differences favoring better outcome with high conditions therapy found on all measures; in some, differences on only a few of the available measures reached statistical significance (*i.e.,* were greater than would be expected by chance in 5 out of 100 times). Since in some studies the number of improvement measures was large, we might ask whether positive results might possibly have been due to chance. Further, what is the pattern and direction of the findings? Has the evidence become stronger or weaker as time has passed? Is there a pattern to the kinds of outcome measures that successfully reflect psychotherapeutic change in the client? Do the same kinds of psychotherapeutic changes occur with individual and group treatment and with different types of patient populations? These and many more questions should be seriously raised and studied if we are to develop a systematic knowledge of the process and outcome of counseling and psychotherapy.

While complete answers are not yet known and must await further research, some brief answers can be gained from our current data.

Since in reviewing any research findings there is a natural tendency to spend more time and space discussing positive results than ambiguous ones, it is useful to attempt to summarize both positive and negative findings in tabular form. An attempt to provide such overall information is presented in Tables 4 through 7, where the results from all studies known to the authors—published and unpublished—are tabulated. The studies in these tables have only one thing in common: they all used the research scales presented in Chapter 2 to measure levels of accurate empathy, nonpossessive warmth and genuineness. Further, the studies themselves are arranged in order of their chronological sequence, with the earliest completed study at the top of the table and the most recent study toward the bottom.

Before attempting to interpret the pattern of findings, some comments about the specific outcome measures themselves should be made. In any study of personality change, and particularly studies of therapeutic change, it must be recognized, as Rogers (1951) and others have noted, that positive findings on any given outcome measure are as much a validation of the measure as of the hypothesis; and, conversely, a lack of positive findings may be as likely to suggest that the measure is invalid as that the hypothesis is wrong. In many of the studies a large number of outcome measures were used to provide a varied sample of the patient's personality and behavioral functioning without any expectation by the investigators that all such measures would reflect even major therapeutic change. Thus, in the early research on individual therapy with schizophrenics, the members of the research group did not expect positive findings on, for example, the Information Subscale of the Wechsler Adult Intelligence

Table 4
An Overview of Findings on the Therapeutic Effectiveness of Accurate Empathy, Nonpossessive Warmth and Genuineness: All Measures of Outcome

Study	Type of treatment (group or individual)	Type of client	Number of clients	Specific outcome measures favoring hypothesis	Specific outcome measures against hypothesis	Specific outcome measures significantly favoring hypothesis ($p < .05$)	Specific outcome measures significantly against hypothesis ($p < .05$)	Overall combined outcome measures favoring hypothesis	Overall combined outcome measures against hypothesis	Overall combined outcome measures significantly favoring hypothesis ($p < .05$)	Overall combined outcome measures significantly against hypothesis ($p < .05$)
Truax (1963)	Ind	Hospital	28	35	10	16	0	2	0	2	0
Truax, Wargo, Frank, Imber, Battle, Hoehn-Saric, Nash & Stone (1966a)	Ind	Outpatient	40	2	1	0	0	2	0	2	0
Truax & Wargo (1966c)	Grp	Hospital	160	20	7	6	0	1	0	1	0
Truax & Wargo (1966b)	Grp	Delinquent	80	18	1	13	0	1	0	1	0
Truax, Wargo & Carkhuff (1966)	Grp	Outpatient	80	21	2	12	0				
Dickenson & Truax (1966)	Grp	College counselees	48	5	0	5	0				
Truax, Wargo & Silber (1966)	Grp	Delinquent	70	13	0	7	0	1	0	1	0
Carkhuff & Truax (1965b)	Grp	Hospital	150	3	0	3	0	1	0	1	0
Truax, Silber & Wargo (1966b)	Grp	Hospital	74	3	0	3	0	1	0	1	0
Aspy (1965)		Elementary students	120					1	0	1	0
Totals			850	120	21	65	0	10	0	10	0

Note: All studies used the Accurate Empathy Scale, the Nonpossessive Warmth or Unconditional Positive Regard Scale, and the Genuineness or Self-Congruence Scale (given in Chapter 2).

Table 5
Findings on the Therapeutic Effectiveness of Accurate Empathy

Study	*Type of treatment (group or individual)*	*Type of client*	*Number of clients*	*Specific outcome measures favoring hypothesis*	*Specific outcome measures against hypothesis*	*Specific outcome measures significantly favoring hypothesis ($p < .05$)*	*Specific outcome measures significantly against hypothesis ($p < .05$)*	*Overall combined outcome measures favoring hypothesis*	*Overall combined outcome measures against hypothesis*	*Overall combined outcome measures significantly favoring hypothesis ($p < .05$)*	*Overall combined outcome measures significantly against hypothesis ($p < .05$)*
Truax (1961a)	Ind	Hospital	8					1	0	1	0
Truax (1963)	Ind	Hospital	14					2	0	2	0
Truax (1963)	Ind	Outpatient	14					1	0	1	0
Truax (1962a)	Ind	Hospital	14					1	0	1	0
Truax, Wargo, Frank, Imber, Batrle, Hoehn-Saric, Nash & Stone (1966a)	Ind	Outpatient	40	2	1	0	0	2	0	2	0
Truax, Carkhuff & Kodman (1965)	Grp	Hospital	40	16	0	3	0				
Truax & Wargo (1966c)	Grp	Hospital	160	18	9	3	0	1	0	1	0
Truax & Wargo (1966b)	Grp	Delinquent	80	18	1	13	0	1	0	1	0
Truax, Wargo, & Carkhuff (1966)	Grp	Outpatient	80	6	17	2	0				
Truax (1966a)	Grp	Hospital Delinquent	40 40					1	0	1	0
Totals			530	60	28	21	0	10	0	10	0

Table 6
Findings on the Therapeutic Effectiveness of Genuineness

Study	*Type of treatment*	*Type of client*	*Number of clients*	*Specific outcome measures favoring hypothesis*	*Specific outcome measures against hypothesis*	*Specific outcome measures significantly favoring hypothesis ($p < .05$)*	*Specific outcome measures significantly against hypothesis ($p < .05$)*	*Overall combined outcome measures favoring hypothesis*	*Overall combined outcome measures against hypothesis*	*Overall combined outcome measures significantly favoring hypothesis ($p < .05$)*	*Overall combined outcome measures significantly against hypothesis ($p < .05$)*
Truax (1963)	Ind	Hospital	14					2	0	2	0
Truax, Wargo, Frank, Imber, Battle, Hoehn-Saric, Nash, & Stone (1966a)	Ind	Outpatient	40	2	1	0	0	2	0	2	0
Truax, Carkhuff & Kodman (1965)	Grp	Hospital	40	0	16	0	5				
Truax & Wargo (1966c)	Grp	Hospital	160	16	11	4	0	1	0	0	0
Truax & Wargo (1966b)	Grp	Delinquent	80	17	1	13	0	1	0	1	0
Truax, Wargo & Carkhuff (1966)	Grp	Outpatient	80	18	5	2	1				
Truax (1966a)	Grp	Hospital Delinquent	40 40					1	0	1	0
Totals			494	53	34	19	6	7	0	6	0

Table 7
Findings on the Therapeutic Effectiveness of Nonpossessive Warmth

Study	Type of treatment	Type of client	Number of client	Specific outcome measures favoring hypothesis	Specific outcome measures against hypothesis	Specific outcome measures significantly favoring hypothesis ($p < .05$)	Specific outcome measures significantly against hypothesis ($p < .05$)	Overall combined outcome measures favoring hypothesis	Overall combined outcome measures against hypothesis	Overall combined outcome measures significantly favoring hypothesis ($p < .05$)	Overall combined outcome measures significantly against hypothesis ($p < .05$)
Truax (1963)	Ind	Hospital	14					2	0	2	0
Truax (1963)	Ind	Outpatient	14					1	0	1	0
Truax, Wargo, Frank, Imber, Battle, Hoehn-Saric, Nash, and Stone (1966a)	Ind	Outpatient	40	3	0	0	0	0	2	0	1
Truax, Carkhuff & Kodman (1965)	Grp	Hospital	40	16	0	3	0				
Truax & Wargo (1966c)	Grp	Hospital	160	17	10	3	0	1	0	0	0
Truax & Wargo (1966b)	Grp	Delinquent	80	17	1	13	0	1	0	1	0
Truax, Wargo & Carkhuff (1966)	Grp	Outpatient	80	21	2	12	0				
Truax (1966a)	Grp	Hospital Delinquent	40 40					1	0	1	0
Totals			508	74	13	31	0	6	2	5	1

Scale; such measures were included in an effort to sample an important area of human functioning (as noted earlier, no significant positive findings were obtained with any of the eleven subscales of this test).

Despite this, and despite both the problems involved in determining *relevant* measures of outcome and those introduced by the fact that therapists (and patients) differ among themselves in values and goals in counseling, certain a priori expectations can be thought of as common. Most counselors and therapists would tend to agree, for example, on these points: that successful outcome in *hospitalized psychotics* will, on the average, be reflected in positive change on the "psychotic" subscales of the MMPI, and by an increased ability to *remain* out of the hospital during a follow-up period; that successful outcome in *neurotic outpatients* will (on the average) be reflected in positive change on the "neurotic" subscales of the MMPI, and by self-reports of greater freedom from distress or unhappiness; that successful outcome in *college underachievers* will (on the average) be reflected in better college grades; and that successful outcome in *institutionalized juvenile delinquents* will (on the average) be reflected in positive changes on a psychological test designed to differentiate juvenile delinquents from nondelinquents and in an increased ability to remain out of an institution during a follow-up period of observation. Counselors and therapists, however, might tend to disagree strongly on the meaning for different patients of changes in anxiety levels, desires to conform, self concepts, ideal concepts, etc.

With these considerations in mind, Tables 4 through 7 present a frequency count of the findings on all measures in all studies—both the most relevant and the least relevant measures—so that, for example, all subscales of the MMPI are given equal weight regardless of the patient population studied. As can be seen, the number of measures favoring the therapeutic effectiveness of empathy, warmth, and genuineness generally far outweigh the number of measures where the findings were against the hypothesis. Further, with only the minor exceptions discussed earlier in this chapter, *virtually all differences that reached statistical significance showed the superiority of high therapeutic conditions over low (or control) conditions*. Clearly, then, the overall findings could not have been due to chance.

The tables also indicate that the direction of the mounting evidence tends, if anything, to get stronger as time goes on; later studies cross-validating and testing the generality of the earliest studies show stronger rather than weaker support for the therapeutic importance of empathy, warmth and genuineness. This latter point seems true in spite of the fact that later studies (except for those by Dickenson and Truax, and by Truax, Wargo and Silber) involved a majority of therapists who did not themselves believe in any crucial therapeutic importance of these conditions while the first study was primarily a study of client-centered therapists.

Since several of the studies used the MMPI before and after therapy as a measure of patient improvement, the findings on those studies can also be directly compared. Such a summary is presented in Table 8. As can be seen, the Schizophrenic Scale seems to be the MMPI subscale most sensitive to therapeutic change. As expected, differences on the "neurotic" scales are most frequent with positive findings for the neurotic population, while differences on the "psychotic" scales are most frequent with positive findings for the hospitalized mental patients (primarily schizophrenic reactions).

Finally, for all studies with institutionalized patients, Table 9 presents the summary of findings with measures of "time out of institution" during a follow-up observation period (1 to 3½ years, depending on the study). The findings are much stronger and more consistent than could be expected by chance—all differences favor high therapeutic conditions.

That the obtained findings are not due simply to chance or to techniques of measurement seems clear. What, however, of the possibility that they might be due to biases on the part of the investigators, the therapists, or the patients?

The variety of patient populations in different studies were sampled from the South, Midwest, and Northeastern United States and included a variety of socioeconomic, personality, age, sex, and even culture differences. To date, no pattern has emerged, and the findings seem not to change radically from one sample of patients or clients to the next.

Similarly, the findings for the importance of empathy, warmth, and genuineness do not seem to vary radically with the nature of the therapist sample—regardless of theoretic orientation, discipline, age, experience level, geographic location, or even beliefs.

In all studies, but especially those involving ratings, the possible biasing influence of the investigators should be carefully considered. In the research reviewed here it is clear that most of the investigators strongly believed in the importance of the therapeutic conditions being studied. (Actually, almost all scientists, despite their attempts at objectivity, are human enough to believe in the hypothesis they are studying and, consciously or unconsciously, *want* it to be confirmed in their research—biases of researchers are not peculiar to counseling and psychotherapy research.) Although a number of procedures used in the research were designed to prevent any biasing influence of the investigators (including the use of college students naive to psychotherapy theory and practice as raters, and procedures to prevent the raters from knowing the therapist, the patient or the case outcome), several of the findings could not have been biased by the investigators even if they had tried.

(1) In the last six studies completed, the ratings of the levels of therapeutic conditions based on the tape recordings were completed or nearly completed and tabulated *before* the posttherapy measures were obtained or scored. In the study of the Johns Hopkins data, the ratings were completed by some of the investigators at a site geographically separate from where the outcome data was collected; and only after the ratings were tabulated and exchanged were the outcome measures ex-

Table 8
Summary of Pattern of Findings in Studies Using the MMPI as a Measure of Outcome

Study	*Number of patients*	*Type of treatment*	*Sum of Clinical scales Deviations*	*Hs*	*D*	*Hy*	*Pd*	*Mf*	*Pa*	*Pt*	*Sc*	*Ma*	*Si*	*Truax's CPC*	*Barron's ES*	*Edwards' SD*	*Welsch's AI*	*Welsch's IR*	*Meeker's LH4*
Combined Conditions																			
Truax (1963	28	Ind.	+*	+	+	+	+	+	+	+	+	+	+	+	+	+	+	+	
Truax & Wargo (1966c)	160	Grp.	+	+	—	—	—	+*	—	+	+	—*	+	+	+	+	+*	+	
Truax, Wargo, & Carkhuff (1966)	80	Grp.	+*	+*	+*	+*	+*	—	+*	+*	+*	—	+*	+	+	+	+	+	
Accurate Empathy																			
Truax & Wargo (1966c)	160	Grp.	+	—	—	—	—	+	—	—	+	+	+	+	+	+	+	—	
Truax & Wargo & Carkhuff (1966)	80	Grp.	—	+	+	+	—	—	—	—	—	—	—	—	—	—	—	+*	
Truax, Carkhuff & Kodman (1965)	40	Grp.	+	+	+	+	+	+	+	+*	+*	+	+	+	+	+	+*	+	
Wargo (1962)	24	Ind.													+*				+

Nonpossessive Warmth																			
Truax & Wargo (1966c)	160	Grp.	+	+*	—	+	—	+*	—	—	+	+	—	+	—	—	+	—	
Truax, Wargo, & Carkhuff (1966)	80	Grp.	+*	+*	+*	+*	+*	—	+*	+	+*	—	+*	+	+	+	+	+	
Truax, Carkhuff & Kodman (1965)	40	Grp.	+	+	+	+	+	+	+	+*	+*	+	+	+	+	+	+*	+	
Wargo (1962)	24	Ind.													+*				+*
Genuineness																			
Truax & Wargo (1966c)	160	Grp.	—	+	+	—	+	—	—	+	+	—	+*	—	—	—	+*	+*	
Truax, Wargo & Carkhuff (1966)	80	Grp.	+	—	+	+	+	+	+	+	+	—	+	+*	+	—	+	+	
Truax, Carkhuff & Kodman (1965)	40	Grp.	—*	—	—	—	—*	—	—	—*	—*	—	—*	—	—	—	—	—	
Total in favor			9	9	8	8	7	7	6	8	10	5	9	9	10	7	10	9	2
Total against			3	3	4	4	5	5	6	4	2	7	3	3	4	5	2	3	0
Total significantly in favor			3	3	3	2	3	3	2	3	6	0	4	2	2	1	5	2	1
Total significantly against			1	0	0	0	1	0	0	1	1	0	1	0	0	0	0	0	0

Total measures, all studies combined, favoring high conditions—133

Total measures, all studies combined, against high conditions—63

Total measures, all studies combined, significantly favoring high conditions—45

Total measures, all studies combined, significantly against high conditions—5

Note: Results of studies tabulated as + if favoring the greater outcome with high conditions, — if against greater outcome with high conditions.

* $p < .05$

changed. (2) In almost all the studies, a different investigator from the one collecting the outcome data supervised the raters who rated levels of empathy, warmth, and genuineness. (3) In only two of the studies of institutionalized patients could the institutionalization rate be biased through indirect action by an investigator or by a therapist who believed in the hypothesis—in the other studies, the investigators had no contact with the institution, and a majority of the therapists had voiced their personal disbelief in the hypothesis. (4) Finally, in the study of underachievers, the investigators simply obtained the grade-point averages from the University Registrar's Office and did not consult with the students' professors; it seems unlikely that they could have consciously or unconsciously influenced the students' university grades.

Table 9

An Overview of the Findings on the Therapeutic Effectiveness of Accurate Empathy, Nonpossessive Warmth and Genuineness: Institutionalization Rates for All Institutionalized Patients

Study	Type of patient	Type of treatment	Number of patients	Favoring hypothesis	Against hypothesis	Significantly favoring	Significantly against
Combined Conditions							
Truax (1963)	Hospitalized	Individual	28	yes	no	yes	no
Truax & Wargo (1966c)	Hospitalized	Group	160	yes	no	yes	no
Truax & Wargo (1966b)	Delinquent	Group	80	yes	no	yes	no
Truax, Wargo & Silber (1965)	Delinquent	Group	70	yes	no	yes	no
Accurate Empathy							
Truax & Wargo (1966c)	Hospitalized	Group	160	yes	no	yes	no
Truax & Wargo (1966b)	Delinquent	Group	80	yes	no	yes	no
Nonpossessive Warmth							
Truax & Wargo (1966c)	Hospitalized	Group	160	yes	no	yes	no
Truax & Wargo (1966b)	Delinquent	Group	80	yes	no	yes	no
Genuineness							
Truax & Wargo (1966c)	Hospitalized	Group	160	yes	no	yes	no
Truax & Wargo (1966b)	Delinquent	Group	80	yes	no	yes	no
Totals				10	0	10	0

THE INTERRELATIONSHIPS BETWEEN THE THREE CENTRAL THERAPEUTIC INGREDIENTS

Since some of the early studies have obtained moderately high intercorrelations between the measures of accurate empathy, nonpossessive warmth, and genuineness, it is natural to suspect that there may be one underlying dimension—a sort of "good therapy relationship" dimension.

The evidence just reviewed in this chapter, however, clearly indicates the functional independence of these three therapeutic conditions. In most of the studies cited there were strong positive intercorrelations, but in others there were no relationships; and in the one group therapy study and the Johns Hopkins study of individual therapy, substantial *negative* correlations between the three therapeutic ingredients were obtained. Further, in the study of the experimental manipulation of empathy and warmth, the data clearly demonstrated that there was a compensatory rise in genuineness when empathy and warmth were experimentally lowered. There is an important lesson in this for psychotherapy research in general (indeed for much of psychological research): if we had looked only at the interrelationships obtained on a very large sample of therapists we would have easily concluded that we were dealing with one underlying factor (since they were on the average positively intercorrelated). If we were to factor analyze results from a large sample of therapists, we could most likely obtain one general factor. However, that would have completely obscured the facts that the three therapeutic ingredients are functionally independent, and that in particular therapists (or subsamples of therapists) these three ingredients sometimes vary independently and sometimes are even characteristically negatively related!

When measures of the levels of perceived therapeutic conditions (discussed below) are used, then the three ingredients appear even more highly intercorrelated—for the very simple reason that "halo" effects and other biases of the client lead him to give a global rather than specific view of the therapist's qualities.

PERCEIVED THERAPEUTIC CONDITIONS AND CLIENT OUTCOME

As noted earlier, the first study of perceived conditions was that reported by Barrett-Lennard (1962). In that study of 35 cases, the findings indicated that the 16 clients who showed the greatest change throughout therapy perceived significantly higher levels of therapeutic conditions from their therapist than did the 19 clients who showed the least change. The measure of change used was obtained from a two-fold index of change estimated by therapist ratings. When the *Q* sort for self-concept adjustment, the Taylor Manifest Anxiety Scale, and the Depression Scale from the MMPI were used as measures of outcome, a positive relationship was obtained only on a combined index of change using all three adjustment measures and the levels of perceived therapeutic conditions for the most disturbed half of the original 36 clients. In short, the findings provided only modest evidence that could be interpreted as supporting the importance of perceived therapeutic conditions. As noted earlier in this chapter, a study of group psychotherapy with 40 juvenile delinquents and 40 hospitalized mental patients (Truax 1966a) compared the relationship of the therapeutic conditions to outcome when outcome was measured in terms of ratings of the objective tape recordings and questionnaire method. The findings clearly indicated that the perceived conditions were less predictive of client outcome than the ratings using the scales presented in Chapter 2. A second series of analyses using the relationship inventory developed by Barrett-Lennard was carried out on 27 schizophrenic patients (Truax,

Table 10
Means and F Ratios Between Schizophrenic Control Patients, Individual Therapy Patients Perceiving High Conditions, and Individual Therapy Patients Perceiving Low Conditions

CHANGE SCORES MEAN VALUES

	Control (N = 14)	High (N = 8)	Low (N = 5)	F Ratios
Percentage of Time in Hospital Since Entry into Research Design	+.16	−.36	−.14	
FOC	+.05	−.08	−.08	
Clinical Estimates of Test Change	+.07	+.23	−.33	
MMPI				
Hs	−1.38	−2.33	−.75	
D	−5.23	−.78	−2.75	
Hy	−.31	−1.89	−2.00	
Pd	−4.00	0	+2.00	2.37
Mf	+1.00	−2.67	−3.00	1.51
Pa	−1.77	−.89	−.50	
Pt	−4.85	−3.22	−2.50	
Sc	−7.15	−8.67	−4.75	2.99
Ma	−2.08	−1.89	−.50	
Si	−2.46	−3.33	−4.00	
Σ Clinical Scales	−23.08	−16.89	−9.50	
CPC	+.15	−.03	+.30	
Welsch's Anxiety Index	−.77	−.11	−6.50	
Welsch's Internalization Ratio	−.06	−.03	−.09	
Barron's Ego Strength	+5.15	+3.00	−2.75	1.24
Edward's Social Desirability	+3.08	+1.56	+1.00	
Q Sort				
Self-Adjustment Score	+6.14	−5.00	+6.75	2.28
Self-Expert Correlation	+.217	−.252	−.071	3.51 *
Anxiety Reaction Scale				
Factor of Social Self-consciousness	−3.08	−3.56	−.67	
Factor of Internalized Anxiety	+3.15	−.33	+6.67	
Factor of General Anxiety	−3.15	−5.22	+1.67	
WAIS				
Verbal IQ	+2.70	−2.50	−5.00	1.54
Performance IQ	+.27	−2.63	−1.50	
Full Scale IQ	+1.64	−1.25	−3.75	
Wittenborn Psychiatric Rating Scales				
Sc Sub-Scale	−.08	−4.14	−2.50	
Sum of Items	+.08	−4.57	−9.25	
Stroop Interference Test	+33.43	+33.75	+15.00	2.75
F Authoritarian Scale	+4.93	−.56	−.25	

* $p < .05$

Mean Initial Relationship Inventory Scores and t Values for Test Improved and Test Deteriorated Schizophrenic Patients, Based on Overall Criterion of Change From Early to Late in Therapy

Relationship Inventory Scale	MEAN VALUE Test improved (N = 5)	Test deteriorated (N = 5)	t
Empathic Understanding	15.0	23.8	3.04 **
Positive Regard	29.8	17.8	3.60 **
Unconditionality	16.4	15.2	.40
Congruence	22.8	21.4	.06
Total Relationship	84.0	78.2	.18

** $p < .01$

1962p, 1962q). In that study, eight patients in long-term psychotherapy who perceived high levels of therapeutic conditions in their therapist and five patients who perceived low lovels were compared with 14 control patients on a variety of outcome measures. Also, five of the patients who were most improved on psychological tests and five who showed greatest deterioration during psychotherapy were compared to see if they differed on their initial relationship inventory scores. The results of those analyses are presented in Table 10.

As can be seen, there appears to be little relationship between the level of perceived conditions and therapeutic outcome as measure by a wide variety of instruments. Only three statistical tests proved significant, one opposite to its predicted direction. Since 36 tests were made, it seems likely that the significance of these three might be due to chance. This seems particularly likely since two of the three were on restricted subsamples.

Using the relationship questionnaire presented in Chapter 2, further studies of perceived therapeutic conditions and outcome have now been completed and have thrown further light on the previous conflicting findings.

The first study, by Truax, Tunnell and Wargo (1966), involved 63 hospitalized mental patients from the larger group therapy study who had filled out the relationship questionnaire. The earlier groups were not involved in this study since work with them was completed prior to the development of the scale. The relationship between perceived therapeutic conditions and outcome was determined by computing correlations between the level of perceived conditions, as measured by the relationship questionnaire, and change from before to after therapy on a variety of outcome measures. These findings are presented in Table 11.

The data was scored so that correlations in the positive direction indicate greater improvement for patients perceiving higher therapeutic conditions. In addition to accurate empathy, nonpossessive warmth, genuineness, and overall therapeutic relationship, scales were also scored for intensity and intimacy of interpersonal contact by the therapist, and for therapist con-

Table 11
Correlations Between Relationship Questionnaire and Measures of Outcome for Mental Hospital Patients

	Accurate empathy	*Nonpossessive warmth*	*Genuineness*	*Intensity and intimacy of interpersonal contact*	*Concreteness*	*Overall therapeutic relationship*
Number of Days Hospitalized During One-Year Follow-Up (N = 63)	.18	—.01	.06	.01	.18	.08
FOC (N = 63)	.04	—.15	—.13	—.19	.04	—.08
MMPI (N = 55)						
HS	.02	.15	.14	—.15	.01	—.05
D	.15	.08	.00	.06	.20	.17
Hy	—.05	—.14	—.13	—.16	.01	—.07
Pd	—.04	—.08	—.01	—.14	.09	—.02
Mf	.09	—.04	—.04	.01	.09	.04
Pa	—.01	—.05	—.04	—.05	.05	.00
Pt	.11	—.04	—.10	—.13	.09	.04
Sc	—.04	—.19	—.21	—.25 *	—.05	—.13
Ma	—.01	—.09	.04	—.04	—.02	—.10
Si	.24 *	.08	.07	.12	.30 **	.15
Σ Clinical Scales	—.01	—.18	—.18	—.23 *	.03	—.10
CPC	.05	—.08	—.09	—.11	—.01	—.06
Welsch Anxiety Index	.20	.15	—.02	.09	.19	.21
Welsch Internatalization Ratio	.21	.14	—.07	.09	.20	.23 *
Barron's Ego Strength	.11	—.07	—11	—.11	.02	—.04
Edwards' Social Desirability	.03	—.13	—.11	—.07	.00	—.12
Σ Deviations of Validity Scales	—.03	.04	.08	.01	—.02	.04
Q sort						
Self-Adjustment Score (N = 55)	.26 *	.14	.12	.20	.24 *	.22
Self-Expert Correlation (55)	.20	.10	.12	.17	.16	.18
Ideal Adjustment Score (N = 34)	.02	—.03	.01	—.17	—.03	—.03
Self-Ideal Correlation (34)	.16	.12	.11	.10	.10	.11
Ideal-Expert Correlation (34)	.13	.02	.03	—.10	.07	.03
Anxiety Reaction Scales (N = 53)						
Factor of Social Self-consciousness	.10	.09	.08	.10	.10	.04
Factor of Internalized Anxiety	—.02	—.11	—.12	—.13	—.01	—.11
Factor of General Anxiety	.00	—.01	—.08	—.05	.03	—.06
Palo Alto Group Therapy Scales (N = 59)	.00	—.02	.03	—.07	—.05	—.07

* $p < .05$, One-tailed test.
** $p < .05$, Two-tailed test.

creteness or specificity of response (discussed in later chapters). The correlations presented in Table 11 clearly offer no support for the relationship between perceived therapeutic conditions and outcome. Of the very large number of tests made, only six proved significant (four supporting the hypothesis and two contrary).

Clearly, the level of perceived therapeutic conditions does not seem relevant for outcome with hospitalized mental patients or severely disturbed schizophrenics.

Quite different findings were obtained in a study utilizing similar procedures on an original population of 80 male and female juvenile delinquents. In that study, relationship questionnaires were filled out on 75 of the 80 delinquents. The findings (Truax, Wargo, Carkhuff, Tunnell and Glenn, 1966) indicated extremely strong relationships in the predicted direction. All of the 114 computed correlations were in the predicted direction, and the overwhelming majority reached statistical significance. Also, as can be seen in Table 12, the changes related to perceived conditions were primarily obtained on psychological measures of improvement rather than on ability to stay out of an institution during a one-year follow-up (although the Final Outcome Criterion included the institutionalization measure).

In a further study of 52 outpatients receiving time-limited group psychotherapy, who had completed the relationship questionnaire, Truax, Wargo, Tunnell and Glenn (1966) used procedures essentially similar to those in the prior studies, and obtained findings presented in Table 13.

As can be seen, of the 138 relationships computed, 117 were in the predicted direction and 28 reached levels of statistical significance. Thus, with outpatients the evidence tends to suggest some relationship between the client's reported perceptions of the adequacy of the therapeutic relationship and the degree of client improvement. A final study which has just been completed is reported by Truax, Leslie, Smith, Glenn, and Fisher (1966). That study dealt with a population of 219 vocational rehabilitation clients served at the Hot Springs Rehabilitation Center. The clients are extremely heterogeneous with respect to type of disability, education, current vocational training, etc. An incomplete tabulation (some information was missing on a few patients) of the client characteristics is presented in Table 14.

The findings relating the level of perceived therapeutic conditions, as reported by clients, and degree of improvement, as measured by progress evaluations in the rehabilitation program, are presented in Table 15.

As can be seen, all 48 computed relationships are in the predicted direction, and 36 of them proved statistically significant. Thus the evidence seems relatively clear in suggesting a positive relationship between improvement and perceived therapeutic conditions in a heterogeneous population of vocational rehabilitation clients.

In summary, the evidence with respect to perceived therapeutic conditions seems to suggest that measures such as the relationship questionnaire

Table 12
Correlations Between Relationship Questionnaire and Measures of Outcome for Juvenile Delinquents

	Accurate Empathy	*Nonpossessive Warmth*	*Genuineness*	*Intensity and Intimacy of Interpersonal Contact*	*Concreteness*	*Overall Therapeutic Relationship*
Number of Days Institutionalized During One-Year Follow-up (N = 74)	.06	.07	.08	.10	.08	.08
FOC (N = 75)	.38 ***	.43 ***	.40 ***	.42 ***	.39 ***	.43 ***
MCI (N = 72)						
FR	.12	.16	.14	.11	.09	.16
SR	.34 ***	.37 ***	.34 ***	.37 ***	.37 ***	.37 ***
ES	.35 ***	.36 ***	.34 ***	.37 ***	.35 ***	.38 ***
C	.11	.15	.08	.07	.06	.14
R	.37 ***	.41 ***	.41 ***	.39 ***	.40 ***	.42 ***
M	.17	.24 **	.20 *	.20 *	.21 *	.22 *
L	.24 **	.29 **	.28 **	.28 **	.29 **	.30 ***
CPC	.42 ***	.44 ***	.41 ***	.43 ***	.44 ***	.45 ***
Q Sort (N = 72)						
Self-Adjustment Score	.28 **	.36 ***	.36 ***	.32 ***	.25 **	.33 ***
Self-Expert Correlation	.23 **	.29 **	.29 **	.27 **	.20 *	.27 **
Ideal Adjustment Score	.24 **	.26 **	.28 **	.23 **	.25 **	.25 **
Self-Ideal Correlation	.35 ***	.36 ***	.38 ***	.34 ***	.32 ***	.36 ***
Ideal-Expert Correlation	.22 *	.28 **	.26 **	.20 *	.21 *	.25 **
Anxiety Reaction Scale (N = 72)						
Factor of Social Self-consciousness	.19	.23 **	.15	.21 *	.19	.21 *
Factor of Internalized Anxiety	.16	.19	.13	.19	.17	.16
Factor of General Anxiety	.21 *	.27 **	.19	.25 **	.22 *	.23 **
Palo Alto Group Therapy Scales (N = 74)	.07	.07	.09	.12	.14	.10

* $p < .05$, One-tailed test.
** $p < .05$, Two-tailed test.
*** $p < .01$, Two-tailed test.

presented in Chapter 2 are indeed useful when used with patients who are not seriously disturbed in their ability to accurately perceive and report. Such positive findings have been obtained with juvenile delinquents, outpatients, and a heterogeneous population of vocational rehabilitation clients. By contrast, in schizophrenic or psychotic patients who have severe distortions in perception, such measures as the relationship questionnaire appear to be less useful as measures of the therapist-offered therapeutic conditions.

Table 13
Correlations Between Relationship Questionnaire and Measures of Outcome for Outpatients

	Accurate Empathy	Nonpossessive Warmth	Genuineness	Intensity and Intimacy of Interpersonal Contact	Concreteness	Overall Therapeutic Relationship
MMPI (N = 52)						
Hs	.18	.11	.20	.23 *	.19	.21
D	.15	.16	.21	.20	.17	.10
Hy	—.02	.04	.14	.06	.04	.08
Pd	.01	—.07	.10	.12	.01	.01
Mf	.23 *	.22	.28 **	.26 *	.21	.13
Pa	.09	—.07	.06	.12	.07	.02
Pt	.21	.18	.20	.28 **	.23 *	.21
Sc	.17	.06	.14	.18	.22	.19
Ma	—.03	—.01	.05	.02	.06	.12
Si	.31 **	.24 *	.24 *	.31 **	.32 **	.19
Σ Clinical Scales	.17	.06	.22	.22	.22	.15
CPC	.18	.08	.15	.22	.19	.08
Welsch's Anxiety Index	.25 *	.20	.20	.32 **	.25 *	.16
Welsch's Internalization Ratio	.29 **	.26 *	.13	.26 *	.25 *	.15
Barron's Ego Strength	.15	.13	.15	.26 *	.25 *	.10
Edwards' Social Desirability	.13	—.06	.06	.11	.08	—.05
Σ Deviations of Validity Scales	.05	—.03	.12	.10	.10	.10
Q Sort (N = 47)						
Self-Adjustment Score	.27 *	.27 *	.23	.29 **	.41 ***	.28 *
Self-Expert Correlation	.23	.20	.17	.20	.30 **	.19
Ideal Adjustment Score	—.16	—.18	—.05	—.14	—.30 **	—.13
Self-Ideal Correlation	.23	.22	.13	.21	.31 **	.18
Ideal-Expert Correlation	—.10	—.12	—.07	—.09	—.16	—.16
Palo Alto Group Therapy Scales (N = 57)	.04	.01	—.06	.04	.08	—.02

* $p < .05$, One-tailed test.
** $p < .05$, Two-tailed test.
*** $p < .01$, Two-tailed test.

Table 14
Client Characteristics of Students at the Hot Springs Rehabilitation Center

Sex	
Male	162
Female	60
Race	
White	187
Negro	35
Marital Status	
Married	172
Divorced	27
Widowed	23
Major Disability	
Personality-Behavioral-Emotional	49
Speech and Hearing	24
Mental Retardation	20
Spinal Cord Injury	15
Orthopedic (other)	14
Anterior Poliomyelitis	13
Visual Defect	12
Arthritis	8
Epilepsy	8
Neurological Conditions	8
Orthopedic (congenital)	8
Other	8
Orthopedic (post-fracture)	8
Cardiovascular Condition	7
Amputee—single	6
Orthopedic (intervertebral disc syndrome)	6
Cerebral Palsy	3
Tuberculosis	3
Endocrine Disorders	1
Hemiplegia	1
Cause	
Metabolic, Growth, or Nutrition Disturbance	104
Complications from Medicine and/or Surgery	59
Congenital or Birth Injury	29
Disease or Infectious Process	18
All Other Accidents	7
New Growths (neoplasms)	5

Secondary Disability	
Visual Defect	10
Personality-Behavioral-Emotional	6
Other	6
Epilepsy	5
Mental Retardation	5
Speech and Hearing	4
Orthopedic (post-fracture)	3
Endocrine Disorders	2
Anterior Poliomyelitis	2
Cardiovascular Condition	1
Hemiplegia	1
Neurological Conditions (other)	1
Orthopedic (congenital)	1
Tuberculosis	1
Orthopedic (intervertebral disc syndrome)	1
Orthopedic (other)	1
Amputee—multiple	1
Total with secondary disabilities	51
Education	
Grades 10-12	134
Grades 7-9	61
Some College—No Degree	13
Grades 1-6	11
Special Education	2
College Graduate	1
Training Courses	
Secretarial	36
Accounting	26
General Clerical	20
Stenographic	16
General Mechanics	12
Custodial	10
Woodworking	10
Cosmetology	9
Drafting	9
Painting	9
Upholstering and Furniture Repair	9
Food Service	8
Printing	8
Nurse Aide	7
Laundry, Dry Cleaning and Pressing	7
Body and Fender	4
Office Machine Repair	4
Auto Mechanics	3
Watch Repair	3
Shoe Repair	3
Appliance Repair	2
Radio Communications	2
Sewing and Tailoring	2
Radio-TV Repair	2

Table 15
Correlations Between Level of Perceived Therapeutic Conditions Offered by Vocational Instructor and Rehabilitation Client Functioning During Training

	Accurate Empathy	Nonpossessive Warmth	Genuineness	Intensity and Intimacy of Interpersonal Contact	Concreteness	Overall Therapeutic Relationship
Grades in Course (N = 219)	.14 **	.08	.13 *	.11 *	.10	.13 *
Progress Prior 30 Days (N = 219)	.17 **	.12 *	.01	.14 **	.23 ***	.14 **
Overall Progress in Course (N = 165)	.18 **	.11	.04	.16 **	.23 ***	.15 *
Work Production (N = 165)	.05	.06	.01	.03	.01	.04
Work Quality (N = 165)	.26 ***	.23 ***	.20 ***	.23 ***	.19 **	.23 ***
Work Attitude (N = 165)	.17 **	.16 **	.08	.18 **	.16 **	.18 **
Dependability (N = 165)	.24 ***	.26 ***	.17 **	.25 ***	.19 **	.24 ***
Cooperativeness (N = 165)	.16 **	.18 **	.09	.18 **	.13 *	.19 **

* $p < .05$, One-tailed test.
** $p < .05$, Two-tailed test.
*** $p < .01$, Two-tailed test.

SUMMARY AND IMPLICATIONS

The present research evidence, while in reality only a beginning step toward specifying the nature of the antecedents to constructive or deteriorative personality and behavior change, does represent a significant movement toward understanding, and thus toward predicting and influencing, behavior or personality development and change. Research seems consistently to find empathy, warmth, and genuineness characteristic of human encounters that change people—for the better. Future research must be aimed not only at developing further evidence to define more solidly the contexts within which these three conditions are indeed ingredients in effective psychotherapy, learning, education and human development, but also toward further specifying the exact behaviors and characteristics relevant to change. For example, since empathy seems to be of significance, it becomes important to know which specific behaviors among those now labeled as "empathic" or "warm" are doing the actual work; *e.g.*, is the tonal quality of the voice a significant factor, or only the understanding? At one point, parametric studies specifying exact functions must be carried out.

The finding that most human encounters can indeed be for better or for worse suggests promising leads for research into the prevention rather than just the treatment of psychological disturbance and upset, of underachievement, and of the symptoms of psychological poverty. The implications hold not only for the training and functioning of psychotherapists, but also for the training of teachers and educators, marriage partners, employers and supervisors, and parents.

Certainly it seems likely that if we can identify effective ingredients in the psychotherapeutic relationship, then using the same approach and tools we can identify the same elements in the husband-wife relationships, the employee-employer relationship, or indeed, in any other human encounter.

If the functional relationship between empathy, warmth, and genuineness and positive and negative personality change is a reversible one, as current research strongly suggests, it would be possible to teach husband and wife to offer each other and their children facilitative conditions, and to identify the presence of destructive conditions.

In essence, this is simply to say that the more we learn about how to *help* people, the more we also know about how *not to hurt* people.

In part, one of the implications of the research just reviewed is that the various related professions should take an active hand in weeding out or retraining therapists, educators, counselors, etc., who are unable to provide high levels of effective ingredients, and who therefore are likely to provide human encounters that change people *for the worse.*

The growing body of converging evidence has important implications for our own personal conduct in human encounters whether we are functioning as a therapist, an educator, a parent or, more generally, as a person.

To be facilitative toward another human being requires us to be deeply sensitive to the moment-to-moment "being" of the other person and to grasp both the meaning and significance and the content of his experiences and feelings. To do this, requires that we, at least to certain high degree, accept and nonpossessively prize this other person. Moreover, neither of these two facilitative conditions can be constructively meaningful in a human encounter unless it is "real." Unless the parent or teacher is genuine in relating to a child, his warmth, caring and understanding have no meaning, or may even have a potentially threatening meaning. To be understood deeply or to receive a communication in a "warm" voice can be deeply threatening if it comes from an unpredictable 'phony" or a potential enemy.

These findings might mean that we should aim at being *what we are* in our human encounters—that we would openly *be* the feelings and attitudes that we are experiencing. Most basically, this might mean coming into a direct personal encounter with a child or a patient or a spouse—a meeting on a person-to-person basis, which is often too rare.

These findings might also mean that to be therapeutic we should aim toward communicating in personal encounters an outgoing, positive warmth, communicated in a total, rather than a conditional, manner.

These research findings might also mean that we would move toward becoming listeners as well as talkers; we might aim toward developing both an ability to perceive sensitively and accurately the feelings and experiences and their meanings to another person, and an ability to communicate a greater degree of this understanding *in a language consistent with his language.* This means that we would be completely at home in the universe of our child, our patient, our student, our parent, or our spouse.

Finally, these converging research findings suggest that the human encounter itself, even when intended to be facilitative or helpful, can be *for better or for worse*—whether we are focusing on changes in personality functioning, changes in verbal conditioning, changes in social development, changes in the learning of arithmetic, or changes in college academic achievement.

CHAPTER 4 THE IMPLICATIONS OF LEARNING THEORY AND BEHAVIOR THERAPY FOR EFFECTIVE THERAPEUTIC ENCOUNTERS [5]

PIONEERING attempts aimed at interpreting the process of psychotherapy from a learning theory viewpoint were for the most part simply a translation of traditional psychotherapeutic practices into a different language system (Dollard and Miller, 1950; Shoben, 1948, 1949). Although the application of learning theory did have specifiable implications for the practice of psychotherapy, these implications were largely ignored by practitioners and theorists alike. The recent emergence of behavior therapy was not based on a reinterpretation of the more experiential and traditional psychotherapy, but on implementation of a learning theory based upon a didactic or interventionist approach. These behavioristic approaches to counseling and psychotherapy (Bandura, 1965a; Eysenck, 1960; Krasner, 1962; Wolpe, 1965) have emphasized the indisputable fact that the therapist himself is a potent influencer of the patient's thinking and behavior, and so have helped to put primary research focus upon the personality, role and functioning of the therapist himself. Also, by their claims of quick cures and by their more objective and scientific criticism of existing evidence concerning the efficacy of traditional counseling and psychotherapy, they have forced the traditional psychotherapists to examine their current practice more closely and to seek more relevant and effective antecedents to constructive behavioral or personality change. Further, these approaches have focused attention on the concrete diagnosis of the patient's current functioning because of their concern with the specific "symptoms" and their immediately present correlates, both internal and external to the patient. The focus upon diagnosis of the patient's current dysfunctioning seems to serve a useful corrective to the more prevalent approach which required either historical or nonspecific theoretical diagnosis or rejection of diagnostic attempts.

5. The present chapter includes material from a paper by Charles B. Truax, published separately as "Some Implications of Behavior Therapy for Psychotherapy," *Journal of Counseling Psychology*, 1966, *13*(2), 160-170.

THE EVIDENCE FOR BEHAVIOR THERAPY

A number of leading behavior therapists have asserted that their method is vastly superior in outcome and economy to existing forms of therapeutic treatment. Surprisingly, a large number of academic psychologists, particularly those with a learning or experimental orientation, have readily accepted this view, and have been uncommonly uncritical of "evidence" purporting to support this assertion. Actually, solid evidence concerning the relative efficacy and economy of current behavior therapy in comparison with traditional counseling and therapy has not yet been presented.

The most frequently cited evidence for asserting the marked efficacy of behavior therapy is the data presented by Wolpe (1960), which was comprised of cases treated by him in which he claimed that 44 per cent were "apparently cured," 46 per cent "much improved," 7 per cent "slightly or moderately improved," and 3 per cent "unimproved." It is noteworthy that in his evaluation not a single patient regressed during this therapy. The overall success rate was 90 per cent "apparently cured or much improved," which he compared with the Berlin Psychoanalytic Institute report (Knight, 1941) showing only a 62 per cent success rate. Several comments about Wolpe's comparisons should be made.

Better results than those reported by Knight are available (and presented in Chapters 1 and 3 of this book) for comparison purposes: the evidence is that a two-thirds improvement rate is actually characteristic of an untreated population. To suggest that the patients reported by Knight and those seen by Wolpe were at all comparable is to totally ignore rather wide divergences in patient and cultural populations. Further, the 90 per cent improvement rate reported by Wolpe was taken from a population from which a number of "unsuccessfully treated" cases had been removed. This is a point made by Stevenson (1964) and agreed to by Wolpe (1964). It appears that reported data was taken from a list of 295 patients who had initial interviews; when the excluded patients are actually included, Wolpe's "apparently cured or much improved" category accounts for only 65% of the total cases. Thus, on the total data dealing for the most part with phobic patients, the actual success rate of 65 per cent is comparable to "no treatment," and not superior to other uncontrolled reports of success rates, such as the 90 per cent success reported by Ellis (1957). Behavior therapy's effectiveness, then, is not proved at all by this data. It might be noted also that the success rate is clearly not superior to that reported from the Chicago Counseling Center (Rogers and Dymond, 1954; Shlien, Mosak and Dreikurs, 1960).

Wolpe (1964) goes on to say, "I must emphasize again that the greater speed and economy of conditioning therapy are much more important than its higher percentage of recoveries. One should also remember its other merits—its experimental basis, its clearly defined methods and the usual complete absence of unpleasant reactions during therapy" (p. 18). However, his data indicate that with "complex cases" (that is, more than a single, simple, clearly defined phobic reaction to a specific stimulus), the number of interviews averages between 50 and 60 sessions. It should be pointed out that the time involved in 50 to 60 sessions on a twice-weekly basis is not markedly different from the average length for a "complex case" seen at the Chicago Counseling Center or almost any other clinic or counseling center, nor, indeed, from many cases seen in private practice. In terms of comparisons with other forms of traditional psychotherapy, then, its economy falls far short of being striking.

The claim of having clearly defined methods and experimental basis is somewhat overstated. Breger and McGaugh (1965) note that in actuality the behavior therapists themselves behave in a way very inconsistent with their theoretical position. They quote from one of Wolpe's own case descriptions (1960) to substantiate this:

> Case 5. An attractive woman of 28 came for treatment because she was in acute distress as a result of her lover's casual treatment of her. Every one of her very numerous love affairs had followed a similar pattern—first she would attract the man, then she would offer herself on a platter. He would soon treat her with contempt and after a time leave her. In general she lacked assurance, was very dependent, and was practically never free from feelings of tension and anxiety. (Breger and McGaugh, 1965, p. 349)

Quoting further from Wolpe (1960), it is noted that treatment is quite reminiscent of usual psychotherapeutic procedures:

> Case 4. The patient had 65 therapeutic interviews, unevenly distributed over 27 months. The greater part of the time was devoted to discussions of how to gain control of her interpersonal relationships and stand up for herself. She had considerable difficulty with this at first, even though it had early become emotionally important to her to please the therapist. But she gradually mastered the assertive behavior required of her, overcame her anxieties and became exceedingly self-reliant in all interpersonal dealings, including those with her mother-in-law. (Breger and McGaugh, 1965, p. 353)

That traditional interviewing procedures occur in almost any form of behavior therapy is further indicated by their quotation from Rachman (1959):

> Interview no. 12. The patient having received a jolt in her love relationship, this session was restricted to the sort of nondirective, cathartic discussion. No desensitizing was undertaken because of a.g.'s depressed mood and obvious desire to "just talk." (Breger and McGaugh, 1965, p. 353)

Breger and McGaugh (1965) also add:

> As can be seen, the number and variety of activities that go on during these treatment sessions is great, including these few examples of discussion, ex-

planations of techniques and principles, explanations of the unadaptiveness of anxiety and symptoms, hypnosis of various sorts, relaxation practice and training with and without hypnosis, non-directive cathartic discussions, obtaining an understanding of the patient's personality and background, and the unearthing of a 17-year old memory of an illicit affair . . . what should be abundantly clear from these examples is that there is no attempt to restrict what goes on to learning techniques. Since it seems clear that a great variety of things do go on, any attribution of behavior change to specific learning techniques is entirely unwarranted. (p. 353)

In the reviews of effectiveness of behavior therapy (Bandura, 1961a, 1965b; Grossberg, 1964) it is clear that the large body of reports cited are mainly case reports in which the therapist claims that he is indeed effective. (We might note that there are very few reports from *any* approach to treatment where therapists claim that on the average they are unsuccessful or damaging.)

Despite the undisputed facts that behavior therapists do engage in many aspects of "conversation" therapy that does not seem to differ from much of traditional counseling or psychotherapy, and that much of the claim for the superiority of behavior therapy over traditional therapy is based on relatively uncontrolled reports, recent research findings do unequivocally show that certain specific techniques unique to their approach are indeed effective. In particular, the procedure of *desensitization* has been shown in several research studies to reduce anxiety significantly and to improve client adjustment, as compared with control or untreated clients.

This is not always so. In a series of very well-controlled studies of behavior therapy relying heavily on desensitization procedures, Marks and Gelder (1966) reported findings that indicated matched control patients suffering from agraphobia showed essentially equivalent overall improvement to those receiving behavior therapy. In one specific study with mild phobic out-patients, desensitization therapy produced greatest effects on improvement in phobic symptoms while group and individual therapy had greatest effects on improvement in social adjustment and personal relationships.

The work of Lazovik and Lang (1960), Lang and Lazovik (1963), Lang, Lazovik and Reynolds (1965), and Lang (1965) have been reports of an ongoing study to which additional patients and treatment contrast groups have been added over the years.

The most complete report by Lang (1965), is of quite considerable theoretic interest since he had an untreated control, a desensitization group, and a special control group involving a therapist-client relationship in which the therapist specifically avoided any discussion of snakes, fear of snakelike objects, etc. The special control group termed "pseudotherapy" we might consider as a control group receiving average levels of nonpossessive warmth, average levels of genuineness, and deliberately low levels of accurate empathic understanding. Lang (1965) says of the pseudotherapy control group:

It was explained that phobic individuals had higher levels of general autonomic tonus than non-phobics. Relaxation would be used in the subsequent sessions to lower this high level of tonus, thus paving the way for a reduction of specific fears. To further enhance this process, the hypnotized subject would visualize pleasant and relaxing scenes. The subsequent non-directive conversations were explained by a rationale vaguely reminiscent of uncovering therapies: "As you probably know, fears such as yours are often related to situations which seem unimportant . . ." It was explained that a number of areas of living would be explored and that a reduction in fear could be expected as the subject obtains a better understanding of himself. (p. 8)

Lang reports positive effects of desensitization and no effects of psuedotherapy. However, from the data he presented, it should be noted that on every one of the four measures used, the pseudotherapy groups (traditional therapy but with specific avoidance of "snake" topics) yielded results superior to those obtained by the desensitization group that had completed 14 or less items in the hierarchy. The general ordering of effective reduction in snake fear was as follows: 15 or more items of desensitization; pseudotherapy; no treatment controls; and desensitization of less than 15 items. Thus from Lang's data it would appear that pseudotherapy, having average levels of nonpossessive warmth and genuineness and decidedly low levels of accurate empathy, was somewhat better than either densensitization when fewer than 15 items were completed, or nontreatment control. On the other hand, subjects who had completed 15 or more items (success cases?) were significantly superior to controls or pseudotherapy clients. It may be that the number of items completed in the hierarchy is a good way of differentiating success cases from failures. If such is the case, we need to know what would have been the result if the pseudotherapy group, too, had been divided into success and failure cases.

The studies of Lang and his associates, however, do tend to suggest that the procedure of desensitization adds something to client improvement beyond that accounted for by the therapeutic context, and that systematic desensitization of a specific fear generalizes positively to other fears.

The work of Paul (1965) and Paul and Shannon (1966) adds further evidence showing the efficacy of desensitization procedures. They focused more clearly on generalized socially induced anxiety, and made a direct comparison between group desensitization, individual densensitization, insight-oriented psychotherapy, and an attention-placebo control group. Their findings of improvement on measures of anxiety, emotionality and introversion, and in public speaking and even grade-point average in college, suggested significant positive effects of systematic densensitization. Since five different experienced therapists participated in the study, serving as therapists for those receiving insight psychotherapy, their evidence confirms the earlier report by Lazarus (1961) but with better controls. Since there is no way of determining from their reports the general level of effectiveness of the traditional therapists involved in that study (or their average levels of accurate empathy, etc.), it might be assumed that they, like the average therapist or counselor, have no average positive effect.

Still, though these studies do not unequivocally show the *superiority* of desensitization procedures over traditional therapy, they do confirm that Wolpe (1948) has made a unique contribution to knowledge of therapeutic effectiveness by his development of systematic desensitization procedures.

The assertion that conditioning, like desensitization, is more efficacious and more economical than psychotherapy has frequently been made by such writers as Bandura (1965a) and Krasner (1962). The work of Ayllon and his associates (1959, 1960, 1962) has often been cited as an exemplary use of reinforcement or conditioning technique applied to one of the more serious behavior reactions, that of the chronic schizophrenic. However, Lindsley (1965) in reviewing his own work (1960) and that of Ayllon, as well as other operant conditioning studies dealing with behavior disorders, has made the candid statement that the improvement seen in patient populations as a result of reinforcement techniques is transitory: when the research is over *there is immediate recurrence of symptoms with no overall long-term gain.* Others such as Baumeister (1965), who have used conditioning procedures in producing significant positive changes, have also noted that symptom recurrence follows termination of the reinforcement program and that no long-term gains are obtained. If this indeed is the state of affairs, then the reported results using reinforcement techniques may only indicate that all people, even patients, respond differently to different environments. Therapists have long known this but have found it feasible to reshape the environment only in the case of children, and even there they have often been unsuccessful in modifying the parent's manner of relating to the child. If the effects are transient and cease when therapy ceases, then the value of such therapy may lie in institutional management of psychotics, delinquents, etc., rather than in treatment aimed at producing constructive changes in the patient that will allow him to function in the normal everyday environment.

There are, however, some reports of more lasting beneficial change that suggest that reinforcement or reward procedures will become more important in psychotherapy as we understand more clearly (1) what kinds of reinforcers are most effective, and (2) what kinds of client behaviors can be reinforced to produce the greatest and longest-lasting improvements.

To summarize, the present evidence does not suggest that behavior therapy is indeed superior to psychotherapy. On the other hand, the evidence is far from complete: it *may* be that behavior therapy or conditioning therapy is more effective or more economical with certain kinds of patients. The case history material certainly does suggest that in its present state of development *it is, on the average, equivalent in effectiveness to other commonly used therapeutic approaches.* Certain research studies also suggest that it has contributed unique therapeutic procedures that indeed produce positive client change.

It seems likely, moreover, that behavior therapy, reinforcement therapy, and basic learning theory may significantly contribute to a more effective traditional psychotherapy. The potential fruitfulness of a dialogue between behavior therapy and more traditional forms of psychotherapy comes from the viewpoint that man is at once both a whole being and a collection of habits and behaviors; that man's total being can be seen as a product of the interplay between the molar self and the specific acts and habits that fill in the mosaic of daily living. The research evidence reviewed in Chapter 3 was derived mainly from the molar approach, and pointed to the conclusion that therapists who provide relatively high levels of accurate empathic understanding, nonpossessive warmth and genuineness do indeed induce greater constructive behavioral and personality change in patients than do therapists who provide low levels of such conditions. Perhaps also as important, the available evidence suggests that when these same factors are present to a low degree in psychotherapy, then they lead predictably to negative or deteriorative changes in functioning. It should, however, be noted that the evidence itself clearly suggests that other factors are operative; there is still considerable variation in the degree of patient outcome among both "very high conditions" and "very low conditions" therapists.

A tentative view borrowed from behavior therapy theory and from learning theory and experimental research suggests that this variability would in part be accounted for by the particular patterns of reinforcement, modeling, desensitization, etc., provided by the therapist *within the context of his level of "therapist-offered conditions."*

There is the possibility that counselors or therapists high in empathy, warmth, and genuineness are more effective in psychotherapy because they are personally more potent positive reinforcers and thus elicit a high degree of positive affect in the patient, which increases the level of the patient's positive self-reinforcement, decreases his anxiety, and increases the level of positive affect in the patient (which, in turn, increases the level of the patient's positive self-reinforcement, decreases anxiety, and increases the level of positive affect and positive reinforcement received from others). It is also possible that therapists who are low in communicated accurate empathy, nonpossessive warmth, and genuineness are themselves ineffective and produce negative or deteriorating change in the patient because they are noxious stimuli who serve primarily as aversive reinforcers; thus, they elicit negative affect in the patient (which increases the level of his negative self-reinforcement, increases the level of negative affect communicated to others, and thus increases the negative affect and negative reinforcement received from others).

It might be tentatively proposed that these three "therapeutic conditions" have their direct and indirect effects upon patient change in the following four modalities: (1) they serve to reinforce positive aspects of the patient's self concept, modifying the existing self concept and thus leading to changes in the patient's own self-reinforcement system; (2) they serve to reinforce self-exploratory behavior, thus eliciting self concepts and anxiety-laden material which can potentially be modified; (3) they serve to extinguish anxiety or fear responses associated with specific cues, both those elicited by the relationship with the therapist and those elicited by patient self-exploration; and (4) they serve to reinforce human relating, encountering, or interacting, and to extinguish fear or avoidance learning associated with human relating.

Accurate empathy, nonpossessive warmth and genuineness are conceived of as having both direct and indirect effects in these four modalities: a direct effect through their introduction into the relationship by the therapist, and an indirect effect by eliciting positive affect (warmth, "comfort responses, " "positive feelings," etc.) through the principle of reciprocal affect. Briefly, the "principle of reciprocal affect" simply states that in any interpersonal situation the affect elicited in one person is in kind and proportion to the affect communicated by the other. In S-R terminology, an *affective stimulus* serves as an unconditioned stimulus in automatically eliciting an affect response which is in kind and proportion to the stimulus. In the therapy situation, when the counselor communicates warmth, he thereby tends to elicit warmth in response from the client. By contrast, if the therapist communicates negative affect, then he elicits negative affect in the patient. Assuming the presence of the therapeutic triad to a high degree, then, the stimulus is positive affect and the patient's consequent response is also positive. This positive affect in the patient tends to have the same effect as the positive affect communicated by the therapist and, since it varies with the therapist's degree of warmth throughout the process of therapy, tends to be under the direct influence of the therapist.

THE FOUR BEHAVIORAL AREAS OF EFFECT

The four basic channels through which the therapeutic triad operates can be thought of in a hierarchy of priority which is useful both in theory and as a guideline for the practicing psychotherapist in specifying priority when a choice between subgoals in psychotherapy must be made. The *reinforcement of approach responses to human relating* is of highest priority; not only because fear or avoidance of interpersonal relationships is a potent symptom in almost all patients, but because psychotherapy, or even behavior therapy, is not profitable without the presence of the patient himself.

Second in priority is the *reinforcement of self-exploratory behavior* by the patient. Client self-exploration is necessary to identify the sources of anxiety, and to elicit anxiety cues so that they can be extinguished. Further, patient self-exploration is necessary to identify and modify the elements of the self concept and the self-reinforcement system.

The third priority is the *elimination of specific anxieties or fears.*

Although the elimination of such anxiety is itself a major goal, it also reinforces or rewards approach responses to human relating and self-exploratory behavior, and tends to eliminate negative self concepts.

Last in priority is the *reinforcement of positive self concepts and self-valuations.* This serves as a continuing, though less critically immediate goal of the therapist in the psychotherapeutic process.

The next section is intended to explicate the role of the therapeutic conditions in effecting the patient's movement toward greater *human relating.* For the most part, similar analyses can be applied to the other three modalities of effect (self-exploratory behavior, anxiety extinction and self-concept modification), and so are not specifically presented here.

TOWARD EFFECTIVE REINFORCEMENT OF "HUMAN RELATING"

The typical patient's inability to relate well to other human beings can be thought of as deriving at least in part from a deficit in learning or experience. His inability also stems from attempts at relating which are associated with noxious or painful experiences and so have led to his being conditioned to fear the cues associated with interpersonal closeness, which in turn has led to avoidance responses to interpersonal relationships. Although there are certainly other antecedents to his inability to relate effectively, these two are common to a wide variety of patient populations and can be directly modified by the therapist.

The therapeutic triad serves as a potent reinforcer throughout the process of therapy. For the therapist to use this therapeutic triad successfully in aiding the patient to develop effective modes of human relating, the relative intensity of the offering of therapeutic conditions must be made contingent upon the patient's responses in the therapy situation. It might be suggested that the most effective therapist would tend to offer relatively high levels of warmth and empathy to any and all verbalizations by the patient (random reinforcement) and also, on a selective basis, provide higher levels of warmth and empathy more frequently to the patient's attempts toward human relating. Thus the effective therapist might respond with empathy and warmth 40 per cent of the time to any verbalizations by the patient, but 90 per cent of the time to definite attempts at human relating. As in all learning situations, for "shaping" to be effective, the reinforcement must begin with the responses currently available in the patient. Thus, responses with even the slightest resemblance to attempts at human relating would immediately be followed by a relative increase in empathy and warmth. With some patients this would particularly mean that even negative or hostile reaction to the therapist would be met by heightened expressions of warmth and accurate empathy. Over time, as the patient consequently begins to relate more frequently, more closely and more effectively, the therapist should become more selective in his offering of warmth and empathy. The criterion for reinforcement is gradually raised as the patient is better able to relate. This suggests that the therapist, to be more effective, would offer high levels of warmth and empathy more and more selectively across time in therapy.

Another important source of the client's change toward more effective human relating would derive from his observation and imitation of the therapist. The work of Bandura (1962, 1965a, 1965b) and Bandura and McDonald (1963) as well as the work of Berkowitz (1964) indicate that "modeling processes" are effective in behavior change. The therapist himself serves as a model to be imitated as an example of effective human relating. By observing the therapist, the patient is able to learn for himself positive and negative consequences of different ways of relating. As Bandura and Kupers (1964) have shown, modeling processes are in fact extremely important in their effect on a person's pattern for self-reinforcement. One would expect the patient to modify his own self-reinforcement system in the direction of increasing the congruency between it and the reinforcement system provided by the therapist. This in turn could be expected to lead to greater self-reinforcement for the patient's attempts at positive human relating. The modeling process itself might be expected to be more potent in the group therapy situation. As the relationship between patient and therapist becomes more intense and intimate, the more likely it is that the therapist will be used as a model, which is consistent with research findings indicating that intensity and intimacy of the relationship are significantly associated with outcome (Truax and Carkhuff, 1964a).

Recent research (Truax and Carkhuff, 1965a) has indicated positive benefit of the use in group psychotherapy of vicarious therapy pretraining tapes; these allow the patient to experience aspects of good therapeutic interaction vicariously, by listening to recorded segments of actual therapy. This seems to be an extratherapy use of modeling processes in an effort to modify self-reinforcement patterns relevant to "good" and "bad" ways of relating in therapy.

Another example of successful therapeutic use of modeling processes is given by Dickenson's (1965) study of therapist self-disclosure,, which indicated positive effects of such self-disclosure in group psychotherapy.

As Goodstein (1965) has noted, the value of a reinforcement or reward—in this case, empathy and warmth—is greatly enhanced by shortening the time interval between the termination of a patient's response and the delivery of the reward or reinforcement. In the therapeutic process, this would suggest that more frequent therapist responses of empathy and warmth, when they are selectively used, are more efficacious than less frequent responses. The learning research data suggest that the therapist would be more effective if he more frequently expressed empathy and nonpossessive warmth, even if with the same intensity. It should be noted that this communication need not be lengthy nor even verbal, since the therapist can use facial, postural and gestural modes of communicating warmth, as well as brief verbal expressions.

The presence of the therapeutic triad at a high level tends to reduce the perception of threat and threat potential in interpersonal relating, and would be expected to generalize. Minimizing threat is critical—the presence of threat induces anxiety which militates against the patient's continuing in therapy, and against his becoming deeply involved in relating to the therapist. This is in addition to the frequently demonstrated deleterious effects that anxiety has on complex performance and learning, problem-solving, creativity, and the general verbal interchange of conversation therapy itself. Behavior theorists such as Bandura (1965a) have pointed out that permissiveness often leads to extinction of conditioned emotionality or anxiety in traditional psychotherapy, as evidenced by the studies of Dittes (1957a, 1957b). This suggests that minimally high levels of the therapeutic conditions must be present *at all times*.

Assuming that the patient has learned either conditioned responses of anxiety or fear and/or conditioned avoidance responses to human relating or intimate human involvement, one of the central aims of the therapist would be to extinguish the conditioned anxiety or fear as well as any conditioned avoidance responses.

Many years ago Guthrie (1938) noted the three major modes of extinction, which should apply both to the learned fear and the learned avoidance of intimate human relating: (1) desensitization or adaptation; (2) reactive inhibition or internal inhibition; and (3) counterconditioning.

In studies of reactive inhibition, the massing of extinction trials with brief intertrial intervals has yielded the best results. In terms of the traditional psychotherapy procedure, this might suggest that longer therapeutic sessions (more than the 50-minute hour) might potentially prove most effective early in the therapeutic relationship in extinguishing fear associated with human relating.

Studies of desensitization suggest that extinction is most rapid when the therapist provides relatively weak anxiety cues that initially elicit very little fear or anxiety, and then gradually increases either the intensity or the number of anxiety cues as the patient becomes adapted to each level of fearful stimuli. The suggestion is that therapists should not become too deeply empathic and thus elicit high anxiety intensity too early in therapy. Research findings (Truax and Carkhuff, 1963), have indicated that, with hospitalized patients, deep empathic responses in the first session *were* significantly associated with premature termination of therapy.

The development of *systematic desensitization* as a therapeutic method (Lang, 1965; Wolpe, 1958) has significance for the practice of traditional counseling or psychotherapy, since it can be directly applied by helping the patient to explore systematically, along an ascending hierarchy of anxiety cues, his own anxiety-laden or unconscious material.

One major source of failure in traditional psychotherapy may stem from an "overdose" of anxiety cues given by the therapist's relentless probing of "unconscious" material that is heavily laden with anxiety-eliciting cues. For such probing to be effective, using the model of reactive inhibition, the therapist would first have to eliminate the defense mechanism of repression, and second, somehow get control of the patient's inner mind so that he could not escape the massing of anxiety. This seems unlikely.

Using the model of systematic desensitization, the traditional therapist would aim at empathic responses that would move the client's self-exploration of anxiety-laden material *gradually* along an ascending hierarchy of anxiety cues, at a pace which would allow for desensitization of cues *before* moving on to new material (or more anxiety-arousing cues). The traditional therapist would be using the human "relationship" as the source for counterconditioning.

It is essential that the therapist constantly concentrate on the patient's being and, in particular on the moment-to-moment change in anxiety level or upsetness. In his close attentiveness he must discriminate between those anxiety changes evoked by the patient's self-exploration and those evoked by his own threatening or inept attempts at interpretation or empathic responses. If the therapist fails to make this discrimination it is unlikely that he will prove helpful. It may be best to assume that whenever the patient shows an increase in anxiety *and withdrawal,* the therapist's response (or lack of response) is the source of anxiety arousal; by contrast, adept therapist responses always lead to closer or continued "relating" even when the patient moves into deeper contact with the anxious and disturbed aspects of the self.

As Shoben (1948, 1949) has noted, the counterconditioning model is most appropriate to the therapeutic triad in extinguishing the patient's fear, anxiety, and learned avoidance connected with human interpersonal relating. The therapeutic triad, and particularly nonpossessive warmth, tends to automatically elicit warmth and comfort responses in the patient through the principle of reciprocal affect. Where the therapeutic triad is present to a high degree, the response is incompatible with an anxiety response. Thus the patient tends to become conditioned to the new response of elicited warmth or comfort, which competes with anxiety cues and fear associated with interpersonal relating. It seems probable that eliciting warmth and comfort as responses incompatible with anxiety or fear and avoidance produces more potent and adaptive counterconditioning than deep muscle relaxation or candy bars.

Many clients are likely to have developed conditioned anxiety responses to "human warmth" communicated from other significant people in their pasts. This suggests that the intensity of the relationship should be increased over time by the therapist rather than being offered full-blown at the outset.

It is perhaps worth remarking that phobic reactions, or intense learned or conditioned avoidance behaviors, are among the simplest to treat by behavior therapy. If this is so, then the traditional counselor psychotherapist should profit from the example of the behavior therapist. The patient's fearfulness of the psychotherapy relationship and his general fearfulness of any intense human relationship can be thought of as a mild phobia, consisting at least in part of learned avoidance behavior. When traditional conversation psychotherapy fails in the treatment of learned avoidance responses, the explanation seems likely to be the failure of the therapist to either (1) elicit the actual anxiety cues, or (2) extinguish them either by systematic desensitization, counterconditioning, or both. In behavior therapy, the cues are specifically evoked in a systematic manner along an ascending hierarchy of anxiety cue intensity (Wolpe, 1965). If similar anxiety hierarchy were used in traditional conversation therapy where a high level of the therapeutic triad is present, traditional psychotherapy might very well prove more effective. Again, this suggests that while the therapist should proceed *gradually* in establishing the relationship when the fear of human relating is prominent in the patient, he must be equally careful to continue offering a relationship with gradually increasing levels of intensity. This suggests that the therapist who is initially permissive but gradually presses for an intimate relationship would be most effective.

The role of reciprocal affect should, perhaps, again be stressed as multiplying or enhancing the effectiveness of the therapist-offered triad of conditions. The automatic evocation of positive affect in the patient that occurs through the therapist communication of positive affect, and their moment-to-moment relative covariation means that the patient's own variations in positive affect would tend to reinforce and extinguish the same feelings, thoughts, and behaviors reinforced and extinguished by the therapist's selective use of accurate empathic understanding, nonpossessive warmth, and genuineness or authenticity.

Although the concept of insight as such has received relatively little attention from behavior therapists, experimental studies of verbal mediation of learning would indicate its importance. Even though Bandura (1965c) notes that awareness of response-reinforcement contingencies influence overt performance, he tends to devalue the role of insight. Although awareness of the historical or etiological genesis of one's current behavior may have no significant impact on current behavior, the laboratory research of Dulaney (1961), Erickson (1962), and Farber (1963) does suggest that empathic responses that promote recognition and identification of "response-reinforcement" contingencies should prove effective. In psychotherapy this may mean that the therapist should attempt to focus empathic responses specifically on the acts, thoughts, or feelings in the patient which, on the one hand, are followed by fear, guilt, or aversive reinforcement and, on the other, are associated with positive consequences.

Closely related to the development of insight is the process of labeling. Either self-labeling by the patient or therapist labeling, as Mowrer (1939), Dollard and Miller (1950), and Farber (1963) have noted, facilitates generalization and discrimination of learning. In psychotherapy, empathic responses can perhaps be made more effective by focusing on the patient's own labeling of his experiences, feelings, and behaviors. Thus, empathic responses may aid in eliminating fear responses to all human relating by helping the patient discriminate between those human relationships that lead to painful experiences and those that lead to pleasant and fulfilling ones.

Research indicating the positive effects of therapist concreteness and specificity and the negative effects of therapist ambiguity (Truax and Carkhuff, 1964a) reflects the role of labeling. In a sense, the facilitation, through empathic responses to the patient's self-labeling, is akin to the patient's own development of insight into "what leads to what" in his current existence because it aids his discrimination of precisely "what leads to what."

The patient's self-concept system has strong indirect effects on the extent to which he engages in human relationships, as well as his modes of relating. The crucial importance of the patient's self-concept system lies in its controlling effect upon his self-reinforcement system, which in turn markedly affects his behavior. As Marston (1965) has suggested, the self-reinforcement system links overt behavior to self concepts. The patient's self-concept system can be viewed as a superstructure which subsumes his positive and negative self-evaluations, and hence his system of self-reinforcement. In the present context, it is assumed that changes in self concepts relevant to engagement in human relations would lead to changes in self-reinforcement for both the extent and manner of human relating. Laboratory research suggests that direct external reinforcement of the self-reinforcement responses (i.e., the things people say to themselves) can indeed be effective (Kanfer and Marston, 1963a). The general experimental research (Farber, 1963; Kanfer and Marston, 1963b; Marston, 1964a, 1964b, 1964c) implies that an effective therapist would be one who selectively reinforces self-concepts that have a positive value for interpersonal relating (by offering greater intensities of nonpossessive warmth, etc.).

TOWARD A BEGINNING EVALUATION

The evidence suggests that extinction of anxiety in the therapy setting generalizes to extratherapy contexts. A question has been raised, however, about the generalization to extratherapy behavior of other changes in verbal behavior that occur in the therapy situation. That such verbal reinforcement in therapy does generalize to real life behavior is indicated by a study (Krumboltz, 1963; Krumboltz and Thoreson, 1964) in which the counselor gave verbal approval statements to vocational counselees whenever they indicated a verbal intention to seek information. Compared with a contrast group, the patients who had been verbally reinforced during counseling actually engaged in significantly greater information-seeking behavior in real life. Thus reinforcement of verbal behavior was shown to affect real life behavior directly.

The principle of "reciprocal affect" and the feasibility of the application of conditioning or reinforcement to traditional psychotherapy loom as central to the present viewpoint.

Reciprocal affect has been noted in clinical writings (Rogers, 1951) and in research (Fey, 1955) in terms of a strong positive relationship between acceptance of self and acceptance of others. It has also been observed in laboratory analogue studies (Kanfer and Marston, 1963a) in terms of the correlation between externally induced changes in the rate of self-reinforcement and the consequent change in the rate of reinforcement given to others. A recent study by Heller, Myers, and Kline (1963) demonstrates the operation of reciprocal affect in psychotherapy. Using actors to simulate patients for unsuspecting real therapists, they studied the effects upon the therapists of "patients" who were essentially friendly versus "patients" who were essentially hostile. Their results indicated that reciprocal affect was generated in the real therapists; therapists responded in a more friendly fashion to friendly "patients" and in a more hostile manner to hostile "patients." Converging evidence is also available from the Schizophrenic Research Project using real patients and real therapists (Truax, 1962e).

The very notion of selective responding or the selective offering of high intensities or frequencies of such human qualities as empathy and warmth has been frequently decried by many dynamically oriented traditional therapists. Rogers (1951, 1957a) has consistently been a strong exponent of the view that selective responding is damaging rather than helpful. In particular, Rogers has argued that empathy and warmth are primarily attitudinal in nature and that, to be effective, they must be offered in a nonselective fashion to the patient; he specifies that they are not to be contingent upon the patient's in-therapy verbalizations or behaviors.

A recent report (Truax, 1966a) deals specifically with the feasibility of the reinforcement aspect of the present viewpoint. A single, long-term, successful case handled by Carl Rogers was used as the basic raw data. Therapist-patient-therapist interaction units were selected randomly from the middle one-third of therapy hours throughout the 85 interviews.

To analyze these data, some nine separate classes of patient behavior which might theoretically be expected to be significant for behavioral change were separately rated by five experienced psychotherapists. Additionally, three "reinforcers" were also measured: (1) empathy; (2) non-possessive warmth or acceptance; and, (3) directiveness. The expectation was simply that the therapist, in this case Rogers, would systematically or non-randomly vary the level of his "reinforcers" with levels of patient verbal behavior.

If there were no systematic selective use of empathy, warmth or directiveness, then correlations between these variables and the patient categories would approach zero. The data, however, indicated strong relationships with certain patient behavior classes. The therapist significantly tended to respond selectively with differential levels of empathy, warmth, or directiveness to high and low levels of five of the nine classes of patient behavior. He did not systematically vary his level of empathy, etc., with four classes of patient behavior. Thus the data indicated a clear and significant pattern of selective responding.

Now, since the basic property of a "reinforcer" is that it leads to change in behaviors, it was predicted that, other things being equal, the five classes of patient behavior that were selectively "reinforced" would show increases over time in therapy, while the four classes of patient behavior not "reinforced" would show no such increase. Of the classes of patient behavior to which the therapist selectively responded or "reinforced," four out of five showed significant changes in the predicted direction over time. By contrast, of the four classes of patient behavior to which the therapist did not selectively respond (those not selectively "reinforced"), three did not show increase or decrease over time in therapy. Thus in seven out of the nine classes of patient behavior the data were consistent with the predictions from a reinforcement view (78 per cent correct prediction).

Considering the likelihood that the therapist also used other types of reinforcers, as well as reinforcing other related classes of patient behavior in unknown intensities and frequencies; considering also the unknown differential difficulty level of the discriminanda of patient response classes, changes in levels and types of motivation, etc.; and, finally, considering the crudity of measurement, the findings strongly suggest the appropriateness of a "reinforcement" interpretation as an explanation, at least in part, of the process of psychotherapy.

A study just being completed (Truax, 1966d) bears more sharply and directly on this question of the importance of reinforcement for therapeutic outcome itself. Using basic raw data of tape recordings, with outcome measures obtained from pre- and posttherapy personality inventories and the measure of time out of hospital during the one-year follow-up, reinforcement analyses were made on 30 hospitalized mental patients seen by four different group therapists.

As in the previous study, therapist-patient-therapist (TPT) interaction unit samples were taken for each of the 30 patients in group therapy by selecting a TPT unit on a random basis from each of six blocks of four sessions each across 24 sessions of therapy. Elaborate procedures were used to be certain of identification of a given patient by the voice qualities. Again, separate groups of raters were used for the accurate empathy scale, the nonpossessive warmth scale and the genuineness scale. A separate set of raters also rated each sample, as it was randomly assigned, on the depth of self-exploration scale.

Thus the study focused on the degree of reinforcement (using empathy, warmth, and genuineness as reinforcers) of the level of depth of self-exploration by the patient, and on any consequent effect on outcome.

To determine the degree of reinforcement, correlations were computed (for each of the 30 patients across the six samples) between the level of conditions offered by the therapist and the level of patient self-exploration. The actual correlations ranged between +.97, indicating extremely high reinforcement and —.95, indicating extreme negative reinforcement. That is, in the former case (+.97) the therapist responded with high levels of empathy or warmth or genuineness whenever the patient engaged in high levels of self-exploration, and with low levels when the patient engaged in low levels of self-exploration. In the latter case (—.95) the therapist responded with high levels of therapeutic conditions when the patient showed the least self-exploration and offered the lowest levels of conditions whenever the patient engaged in the highest levels of self-exploration.

In this sample, the patients receiving the highest levels of reinforcement for self-exploration were compared with those receiving the lowest. If reinforcement were indeed effective, of course, one would expect greater self-exploration in the highly reinforced group. This expectation was confirmed by the analysis of variance, which indicated a higher level of self-exploration for those patients who were receiving the highest level of reinforcement for self-exploration. Interestingly enough, this finding held whether the data was analyzed in terms of high and low reinforcement of the therapy group as a whole, or of the reinforcement given an individual patient (in an individual relationship with the therapist, regardless of the level of reinforcement given to the group as a whole).

The most critical expectation was that patients receiving high levels of reinforcement would show more favorable therapeutic outcome. To assess this, a final outcome criterion was computed by transforming the eight separate measures of outcome to standard scores and then obtaining an average outcome score for each patient. When these data were analyzed, the findings indicated that patients in groups receiving high levels of reinforcement for self-exploration showed significantly better outcome than patients in groups receiving low or negative reinforcement. Although the data were in the same direction, there was no significant difference when individual patient-therapist patterns of reinforcement were analyzed. This latter finding suggests that the level of reinforcement offered in group therapy to the group as a whole is more potent in its effect on outcome than that offered to individual patients. This seems quite consistent with previous findings on group therapy, which indicate that the general level of conditions offered to the group is somewhat more predictive of outcome than the level offered to individual patients within a group (Truax, 1966a). Another finding from that study was that the level of reinforcement of patient self-exploration offered to each patient was unrelated to the absolute level of therapeutic conditions offered to that same patient. In fact, the correlations between the level of reinforcement of self-exploration and the absolute levels of therapeutic conditions amounted to correlations ranging between .01 and .15, all nonsignificant. As a further check of these data, the two patients receiving the highest level of reinforcement and the two receiving the lowest were selected for each of the four therapists, giving a total of 16 patients. In that analysis, it was expected that a greater differentiation between high and low reinforcement could be obtained, since two of the therapists tended to reinforce their groups as a whole more highly than the other two. This procedure, then, allowed comparisons among the eight patients who themselves received high levels of reinforcement and who were also members of group therapy groups that received high levels of reinforcement for self-exploration. Thus, they might be expected to show even greater differences in outcome. That expectation was confirmed by the findings.

Thus, it would appear that one of the suggested modes for therapeutic effectiveness—reinforcement of client self-exploration—is supported by direct research findings.

SUMMARY

The present chapter is offered as a tentative step toward a constructive encounter between the emerging behavior therapy and traditional conversation psychotherapy. Many traditionally oriented therapists will be repelled by some aspects and some implications of behavior therapy for traditional psychotherapy, and yet we can profit from their achievements. As training supervisors, we are intrigued with the possibility of making the "art" of psychotherapy more specific and therefore more teachable. To researchers, the behavioristic models offer potentially fruitful avenues for specifying and explicating the general findings that the very humanistic qualities of accurate empathic understanding, nonpossessive warmth, and therapist authenticity or genuineness lead in some fashion to constructive behavioral and personality change in a wide variety of patient populations. For researchers the task is only to find out how the world works, and we are free to actively disbelieve any theory.

The major implication of the present tentative analysis is that the therapists or counselors who are high in empathy, warmth, and genuineness are more effective in psychotherapy because they themselves are personally more potent positive reinforcers; *and* also because they elicit through reciprocal affect a high degree of positive affect in the patient, which increases the level of the patient's positive self-reinforcement, decreases anxiety, and increases the level of positive affect communicated to others, thereby reciprocally increasing the positive affect and positive reinforcement received from others. By contrast, counselors or therapists who are low in communicated accurate empathy, nonpossessive warmth and genuineness are ineffective and produce negative or deteriorative change in the patient because they are noxious stimuli who serve primarily as aversive reinforcers *and* also because they elicit negative affect in the patient (which increases the level of the patient's negative self-reinforcement, increases the level of negative affect communicated to others, and thus increases reciprocally the negative affect and negative reinforcement *received* from others).

Further, the findings have confirmed the importance for client outcome of the therapists' selective offering of the therapeutic conditions so as to reinforce or reward patient self-exploration.

CHAPTER 5 THE FOCUS OF THE THERAPEUTIC ENCOUNTER: THE PERSON BEING HELPED

MOST major contributions in the literature of psychotherapy and counseling have focused their attention on the dynamics of the emotional disturbance operating within the patient. The client, in coming to see the professional psychotherapist, the vocational counselor, the personal counselor, or the rehabilitation counselor, can indeed be viewed as a person with emotional disturbance. However, a fairly sizable percentage of people seeking help require help not just because of emotional disturbance, but also because of motivational or learning deficit. That is, they may not only suffer from irrational anxiety, misperceive their world, and engage in self-defeating interpersonal relationships, but many of them also have never learned or even been motivated to learn to achieve: they do not know how to please employers, how to relate in a manner that will allow them to earn the love and respect of others, or, in short, how to get at least the minimum, if not the maximum, from everyday living.

As May (1953) has observed, one of the principal immediate problems for psychotherapy and counseling comes from the fact that we have, through historical accident, incorporated almost totally the vocabulary of medicine in our attempts to explain and define the process of psychotherapy or counseling. This is most striking when we think of the person coming for psychotherapy or counseling. Most often this person is referred to as the "patient," which creates the image of a person being acted upon by the doctor, a person who is passive and can help himself only by taking his medicine and following the doctor's prescriptions. In this sense, the term "patient" is an inappropriate one and likely to prove a barrier to the kind of help that the therapist has to offer. The Rogerian therapist's term "client" is an improvement. It suggests what seems to be the case, that the person being helped still fundamentally has direction over his own future and is free to accept or reject the offering of the therapist. Unfortunately, the term "client" also implies the purchasing of services, and thus lacks the essential interpersonal meaning inherent in the therapeutic relationship. Until a better word comes along, it seems closer to an accurate description than the alternatives. (If it were not so confusing in writing and speaking, it would perhaps be best to follow May's lead and use the term "person" as the label for the patient or client.)

Matarazzo (1965a) puts it well when he discusses his own use of terms to describe the person being helped:

> . . . the question of "patient" versus "client" . . . seems to be, from the many journal references to it, a perennial problem for clinical psychology. Yet in actual professional practice it rarely has seemed a problem to me and, I suspect, to other professional psychologists. If I see an individual in a hospital, I call him what he, himself, and everyone else calls him: namely, a patient. If instead I see him in my office (after referral by an attorney, industrial firm, high school principal, a judge, or by self-referral) I refer to him as a client. If he is referred to my office by a physician who is continuing to see him medically, and my role is that of a collaborating consultant, I call him a patient. Thus, the *context* of the individual referral determines patient versus client status—not partisan professional considerations. In like manner, when I am called in consultation to see a person in jail and awaiting trial I refer to him as "prisoner" or by his given name, and not patient or client. A school child seen in school is referred to as "the student," and an executive in industry as, for example, "the Vice President for Marketing." This *same* executive, when sent to me by his physician for a serious depression, with its multitude of medical signs and symptoms, is a patient. If he consults me for a nonmedically related marital difficulty, he is a client (pp. 437-438)

The basis for the use of the terms "client" or "patient" is often the same one used for the terms "counselor" and "psychotherapist": at one time it was clear that counseling and psychotherapy were separate disciplines using different approaches. Today, however, the distinctions used to differentiate a counselor from a therapist have become more fuzzy and at times unreal. Since the overlap between the roles of counselor and therapist has grown and the differences diminished over recent years, for our present purposes we have chosen to use the terms more or less interchangeably. However, like Matarazzo, we suspect that it may be best to use the terms according to the setting in which the professional person works: the therapeutic person would be called a psychotherapist if working with patients, and a counselor if working with clients.

Who is this person labeled *patient* or *client?* The answer seems to be that he is very close to a randomly selected member of our society. He may be a person with a lifelong series of failures but, on the other hand, is often a person with a great many achievements and accomplishments. Sometimes he is a physically handicapped person. Sometimes he is a highly creative and talented artist, novelist, or scientist. He is often a person of middle age, but sometimes he is a child who has yet to meet life head-on, or an older person in retirement facing death and asking for the meaning of life. In short, the individual person, labeled as *client* or *patient,* covers the full range of human types and thus the full range of human experience. Even if we attempt to pinpoint his personality we will find a wide range on any given dimension. He may be passive and subservient, or he may be a leader of men. Except for the old and quite sensible rule that leads counselors and therapists to accept only strangers as clients or patients, he might be an acquaintance, a neighbor, a friend, or a loved one. In other circumstances or at other times, he may even be one of us.

He differs from nonpatients in one respect: he is currently seeking a therapist or a counselor. That is, he has a long-term or short-term problem that he thinks he can resolve or learn to live with better if he has the help of an expert on human relationships with specialized knowledge. Sometimes, of course, he does *not* believe that a therapist or counselor can help.

Too often, it seems, therapists and counselors are apt to think of the patient as a person who is weak, helpless, incapable, sick, or just plain inadequate. In part, he is. But although he will spend his time with the therapist talking of the confused and unsatisfying aspects of his existence, there are other parts to his life. Even the therapist working with severely disturbed schizophrenics living in state mental hospitals is likely to encounter patients who are, or have been, more capable than he is in many aspects of living. What is perhaps most remarkable about the patient is that he seems to be able, at least to a degree, to overcome his difficulties under his own steam: in studies of psychotherapy and counseling with widely varying types of clients, the control groups often show a significant average improvement.

THE MATCHING OF CLIENT TYPE AND THERAPIST TYPE

A perennial hope in the search for more effective counseling and therapy is that we may someday be able to define therapist and patient characteristics in such a way as to effectively match the therapist best-suited to the needs of an individual patient. In clinical practice we often assign a patient on the basis of his presumed need for an adequate "mother figure," "father figure" etc. However, research evidence is mostly lacking. The few studies thus far completed have not yet systematically explored enough of the area to arrive at solid conclusions. Since the goal is so plausible we might hope for more research in this potentially fruitful area.

The major studies with sizable groups of clients have been those with positive findings. The findings, however, may not apply to professionally trained counselors and therapists, and so their implications for practice must be viewed with caution.

Grant and Grant (1959) reported intriguing findings on young offenders (probably comparable to older juvenile delinquents). The subjects were 335 Marines, all undergoing group therapy and living in essentially closed-group conditions. The supervisors themselves were divided into those who were defined as "mature and flexible" versus those defined as "rigid and aloof," while the patients were divided into high and low levels of interpersonal maturity based on ratings from an interview. Using the men's return to active service for six months without further offense as the outcome criterion, the findings indicated that the high maturity subjects responded with better outcome to the mature and flexible supervisors and showed very poor outcome when seen in group therapy by rigid and aloof supervisors. On the other hand, just the opposite pattern was found with patients defined as having low interpersonal maturity. One cannot help but suspect that the actual psychological conditions provided during group psychotherapy differed markedly for high and low maturity patients. This suspicion is especially strong in this case since the study involved Marine Corps noncommissioned officers as "therapists."

A similar study reported by Adams (1961) focused on older juvenile delinquents in the California Department of Correction who were treated by probation officers. Again, the patients were divided into those defined as "relatively amenable" to their therapist and those who were defined as "non-amenable." One hundred of each were assigned to treatment and to no treatment control conditions. On a variety of outcome measures, including a 36-month follow-up of recidivism it was found that those who were amenable to treatment responded with better outcome than any other group. However, those who were non-amenable and were treated anyway performed somewhat worse than either of the control groups. As in the Grant and Grant study, it seems likely that those defined as non-amenable were likely to receive poor therapeutic conditions from other people, particularly from probation officers (acting as therapists), who anticipated poor results.

In one of the largest studies on the matching of types of juvenile delinquent probation officers to types of delinquents, Palmer (1965) reported another study from the California system. The report suggests that the important element in matching is that the probation officer and juvenile delinquent share common values, goals and concerns—so that communication can actually occur. They found that the probation officers defined as "relationship-self-expressive," who were concerned with personal accomplishment, independence versus dependence, etc., were most effective with delinquents who were defined as communicative-alert, impulsive-anxious, and verbally hostile-defensive—and who were also concerned with personal accomplishment, independence versus dependence, etc. By contrast, the probation officers defined as "surveillance-self-control" in orientation, whose focus was upon conformity and control, tended to have their best results with anxious and dependent juvenile delinquents. As the author notes, these delinquents as probationers shared the probation officer's concern with conformity and the control of behavior. Although differences occurred on matching, the overall results strongly favored the greater effectiveness of the "relationship-expressive" officers. As the author also states, the problem of matching delinquents with probation officers essentially comes down to putting together an officer and a delinquent so that the officer can offer understanding, warmth, respect, and thus communicate with that delinquent.

To generalize, it would seem likely that matching of patient and therapist types plays a critical role in cases where the therapist is quite restricted in his ability to show understanding, warmth, or genuineness to all but a narrow range of human beings.

PERSONAL CHARACTERISTICS OF CLIENTS WHO CHANGE FOR THE BETTER

One question which has become a focus for much writing and research is "What kinds of clients or patients are most likely to be helped by counseling or psychotherapy?" In view of the fact that the demand for professional services far exceeds the supply, it would seem to make sense to concentrate therapeutic efforts where they will do the most good. What, then, is the evidence?

The Prediction of Therapeutic Benefit

In some ways it would seem that the energy invested in studies attempting to identify the kinds of clients who show the greatest therapeutic gains has been misdirected. Such energy would likely have been more profitably spent in identifying the kinds of therapists that are maximally helpful. The kind of therapist who enters the therapeutic transaction can be changed, through both training and selection, to maximize patient benefit. The kind of client who enters into the therapeutic equation, however, is always a given: he exists and needs help. Moreover, the studies to date (even if their findings were always consistent) point only to the kinds of clients who are likely to improve or deteriorate, not those who respond best to therapy. Thus, in the studies where the same predictors were used in control groups not receiving therapy, the results were the same. That is, the existing data (even where the findings are reasonably consistent from study to study) merely identify the kinds of clients who are likely to improve (or deteriorate or show no change) regardless of the treatment they receive. It is likely that the same factors in the patient that contribute to his readiness to improve operate whether he receives psychotherapy, chemotherapy, recreational therapy, etc., or no treatment.

It is a very different question to ask "To what extent will effective therapy add to (or subtract from) the degree of improvement that a given type of client would otherwise show?" Research on this latter question, which is the appropriate one to ask in order to predict which patients will *profit* most from counseling or psychotherapy, has not yet been done! The available evidence, then, may not even be appropriate since it does not deal with *therapeutic response* but with likelihood of improvement (regardless of treatment).

The person who will profit most from therapy may improve the least or the most: the degree of absolute *improvement* may or may not be related to the degree of *benefit* that a patient receives from counseling or therapy.

To approximate an answer to the question "What kinds of patients will profit most (and least) from therapy?" we would have to estimate the degree of "predicted" improvement (or deterioration) and subtract that from the "observed" change with (and without) therapeutic intervention. Such research has not yet been done, so there is no evidence at all on this theoretically and practically important question.

The evidence that does exist deals with predicting the degree of positive or negative change during therapy, not with the prediction of therapeutic benefit or profit. Even that evidence is difficult to evaluate since the studies give no indication of whether the counseling or therapy used was on the average helpful, harmful, or without effect. If we assume that the treatment corresponds to the average for the field as a whole in each study, we assume that the therapy had no average effect but did increase the variance (the extent of positive and negative changes). This situation makes the existing evidence (which, as already indicated, has nothing to do with "therapeutic benefit" or "therapeutic response") not even an adequate reflection of "predicted improvement" (degree of positive or negative change) since it is contaminated by the "random" positive and negative effects of the therapies that were used in the studies.

With these rather severe limitations clearly in mind, let us turn to the kinds of evidence that do exist, with the hope that future research will address itself to the prediction of therapeutic *benefit*. We will not attempt an exhaustive listing of this evidence, but simply indicate the major areas of research interest and cite several studies in each area to indicate the trend or lack of trend of the findings relating to outcome.

A number of studies have suggested that the client's "readiness" is a moderately good predictor of degree of improvement. Lipkin (1954) studied closely the relationship between client attitudes and degree of personality change. His data indicated that clients who had high expectations and positive attitudes toward the counselor showed the greatest immediate change. Other studies have shown similar findings. Cartwright and Lerner (1963) found that the patient's own pretherapy need to change not only related significantly to outcome, but also interacted with the therapist's level of empathy in producing outcome. That is, the Cartwright and Lerner data indicated that patients who had a highly empathic therapist as well as a felt need for change showed the most rapid improvement; when both empathy and need for change were low, the clients not only did not improve but also tended to terminate the therapy relationship quickly.

Isaacs and Haggard (1966), in several careful studies of patients' "relatability," report that in general the patient's capacity for interpersonal and object relationships is significantly predictive of therapeutic outcome. The therapeutically successful patient is able to be empathic, is objective about himself, and has a sense of individuality of self and others.

Heine and Trosman (1960) have obtained findings indicating that when therapist and patient do not agree on the aims or methods of help, then the patient tends to discontinue treatment quickly. This type of finding, which has also been reported by others, may reflect the inadequacy of therapists who are unable to understand their client or shift their approach to meet his needs.

Unfortunately, such factors as readiness for therapy or counseling seems to be in large part an indirect measure of adjustment. For a large number of male and female potential clients, Hielbrun (1961) found strong and significant negative relationships between personality measures of adjustment and counseling readiness. His finding fits well with several studies suggesting that clients or patients who are relatively well-adjusted show the greatest improvement while the more disturbed clients show the least improvement.

If this evidence dealt with prediction of therapeutic benefit (which it may not, as explained earlier) then one could say that it simply means that therapy works best with those who need it least and worst with those who need it most. However, it can also be interpreted to mean that the better-adjusted client or patient is more likely to disregard harmful therapeutic relationships and profit from helpful ones.

The evidence concerning the characteristics of patients who are likely to show positive change during therapy is to some degree inconsistent and unclear. Crider (1946) reported data indicating that those who had the greatest intellectual capabilities and were psychologically more sophisticated showed the greatest improvement. Wood, Rakusin, Morse and Singer (1962a) and Wood, Rakusin, Morse and Singer (1962b) studied closely both the degree of illness and the diagnosis or personality pattern in relation to improvement in mental patients. The findings indicated that *neither* the degree of illness nor the diagnostic category was related to outcome. Similarly, in studying formal group and adjunctive therapies with male sex offenders, Cabeen and Coleman (1962) found that intelligence, age, recidivism, etc., were unrelated to outcome. In the study of psychotherapy with hospitalized schizophrenics, Truax and Carkhuff (1964a) reported findings indicating no relationship between outcome and age, sex, socioeconomic class, initial degree of disturbance (the Health-Sickness Scale), or premorbid adjustment (Phillips Scale), in either therapy or control patients. In further analysis of initial status on a number of personality instruments and ratings of ward behavior, their findings did indicate significant associations between initial status and outcome. In general, the data indicated that the patient with *the greatest "felt disturbance"* (measured by self-report items on the Q sort and MMPI) and *the least overt disturbance* (better adjustment on the Wittenborn Psychiatric Rating Scales) were those *showing the greatest improvement.*

At Johns Hopkins, the work of Stone, Frank, Nash and Imber (1961), reporting the data from a five-year follow-up of 30 outpatients, suggested that those showing greatest change were the most disturbed to begin with.

It is important to note, however, that the Johns Hopkins measures of degree of disturbance were based primarily upon "felt disturbance," and that in actuality these patients might have been judged relatively well-adjusted by experts. Similarly, the Stephens and Astrup (1965) study at Johns Hopkins showed that low "overt" disturbance (as measured by length of hospitalization) was related to positive change regardless of the type of psychotherapeutic treatment. This again points to the need for studies of "therapeutic benefit" (as noted earlier) rather than merely of prediction of degree of improvement. The two may be unrelated!

From a study just being completed, Truax, Tunnell, Fine and Wargo (1966) obtained additional information to add to the sometimes puzzling mass of evidence aimed at predicting from initial status the kinds of patients likely to improve. Correlations were computed between various measures of initial status and several specific measures of both *overt disturbance* (hospitalization during a one-year follow-up, and the Palo Alto Scale) and *felt disturbance* (the MMPI measures of the sum of all deviations on the clinical scales, and the Constructive Personality Change Scale) as well as a combined final outcome measure obtained by converting improvement (change) scores to standard scores and then averaging them.

The findings for a population of mental hospital patients is presented in Table 16. On the overt or behavioral measure of past hospitalization the results were in agreement with several past studies: the more disturbed patients were initially, the less they improved. However, the Palo Alto Scale, which measures level of socialization, is in line with the measures of felt or inner disturbance and the combined final outcome criterion: the more disturbed they were initially, the *more* they improved.

When a similar analysis was completed on a population of institutionalized juvenile delinquents, which is presented in Table 17, the findings were in relatively close agreement with those obtained from the mental hospital patients. Thus, length of prior institutionalization predicted positively: the poorer the initial status, the poorer the outcome. The other psychological test measures tended to predict in the negative direction: the poorer the intial status, the better the outcome.

When data from a population of outpatients were analyzed in a similar fashion (except that there was no measure of hospitalization or of combined measure), the findings presented in Table 18 were obtained. There, the trend was in a comparable direction: on psychological test measures the more disturbed the patient was initially, the more he was likely to change. With outpatients, exceptions to this generalization occurred on the Palo Alto Scale and on the measure of the patient's "Ideal Self" concept, where the reverse was true.

Since these later findings in sizable and diverse patient populations fit reasonably well with prior findings, the tentative conclusion we shall draw about the relationship between degree of initial disturbance and subsequent degree of improvement is this: *the greater the initial psychological disturbance* (measured by self-report psychological test, etc.) but *the lesser*

Table 16
Prediction of Outcome from Initial Client or Patient Status[1] (Mental Hospital Patients)

Initial Status Measures		*Number of days out of the hospital in one-year follow-up (N = 141)*	*Palo Alto Group Therapy Scale, Change (N = 131)*	*MMPI Σ Clinical Scales Deviations, Change (N = 118)*	*CPC Scale from the MMPI, Change (N = 118)*	*FOC Change (N = 138)*
Number of Days in Hospital, Pretherapy	(N = 141)	+.47 ***	+.08	+.06	+.18 **	+.29 ***
Palo Alto Group Therapy Scale	(N = 131)	—.03	—.69 ***	+.04	+.02	+.04
MMPI Σ Clinical Scales' Deviations	(N = 118)	+.03	+.11	—.38 ***	—.21 **	—.14
Σ z Scores for Measures used in FOC	(N = 138)	+.27 ***	+.05	—.29 ***	—.27 ***	—.22 ***
CPC Scale	(N = 118)	+.09	+.11	—.27 ***	—.38 ***	—.23 **
MMPI						
Hs	(N = 118)	+.27 ***	—.01	—.17 *	—.04	+.02
D	(N = 118)	+.35 ***	+.04	—.12	—.11	+.00
Hy	(N = 118)	+.13	+0.3	—.14	—.02	—.02
Pd	(N = 118)	+.38 ***	+.01	—.25 ***	—.06	—.08
Mf	(N = 118)	—.32 ***	—.06	—.05	—.15 *	—.20 **
Pa	(N = 118)	+.06	+.10	—.31 ***	—.31 ***	—.28 ***
Pt	(N = 118)	+.24 ***	+.06	—.28 ***	—.19 **	—.12
Sc	(N = 118)	+.23 **	+.07	—.39 ***	—.24 ***	—.19 **
Ma	(N = 118)	+.02	+.07	—.20 **	—.21 **	—.21 **
Si	(N = 118)	+.19 **	+.10	—.17 *	—.17 *	—.10
Barron's Ego Strength	(N = 118)	+.10	+.05	—.13	—.30 ***	—.19 **
Edwards' Social Desirability	(N = 118)	+.16 *	+.08	—.29 ***	—.38 ***	—.26 ***
Σ Validity Scales Deviations	(N = 118)	+.09	—.03	—.24 ***	—.09	—.04
Welsch's Anxiety Index	(N = 118)	+.20 **	+.05	—.17 *	—.16 *	—.07
Internalization of Anxiety Ratio	(N = 118)	+.36 ***	—.01	+.02	—.01	+.10
Q Sort						
Self-Adjustment Score	(N = 114)	—.01	+.05	—.17	—.24 ***	—.32 ***
Self-Expert Correlation	(N = 114)	—.00	+.05	—.22 **	—.26 ***	—.32 ***
Ideal-Self Adjustment Score	(N = 92)	—.11	+.01	—.03	—.04	—.09
Ideal-Expert Correlation	(N = 92)	—.10	—.12	—.02	—.04	—.11
Self vs. Ideal Self-Correlation	(N = 89)	—.10	—.14	—.11	—.14	—.15
Truax Anxiety Reaction Scale:	(N = 118)					
Factor of General Anxiety		+.02	+.11	—.13	—.21 **	—.27 ***
Factor of Social Self-Consciousness		+.02	+.13	—.17 *	—.24 ***	—.25 ***
Factor of Internalized Anxiety		+.05	+.07	—.13	—.17 *	—.21 ***

* $p < .10$
** $p < .05$
*** $p < .01$

1. Scored so that "+" means that the more disturbed the patients are on the initial status measure, the *less* they improve, and "—" means that the more disturbed they are on the initial status, the more they improve.

Table 17
Prediction of Outcome from Initial Client or Patient Status[1]
(Institutionalized Juvenile Delinquents)

Initial Status Measures		Number of days out of the institution in one-year follow-up (N = 80)	Palo Alto Group Therapy Scale Change (N = 74)	CPC Scale from the MCI Change (N = 75)	FOC Change (N = 78)
Number Days in Institution, Pretherapy	(N = 80)	+.30 ***	+.04	+.20 *	+.14
Palo Alto Group Therapy Scale	(N = 74)	+.04	—.77 ***	+.04	—.08
CPC Scale, MCI	(N = 75)	+.06	—.26 **	—.50 ***	—.42 ***
Sum of z Scores for Measures Used in FOC	(N = 78)	+.10	—.34 ***	—.25 **	—.39 ***
MCI					
Family Relationship	(N = 75)	+.05	—.07	—.05	—.15
Social Relationship	(N = 75)	+.03	—.18	—.43 ***	—.33 ***
Emotional Stability	(N = 75)	+.01	—.29 **	—.43 ***	—.47 ***
Conformity	(N = 75)	—.16	—.12	—.15	—.19 *
Adjustment to Reality	(N = 75)	—.02	—.27 **	—.40 ***	—.41 ***
Mood	(N = 75)	+.17	—.25 **	—.37 ***	—.26 **
Leadership	(N = 75)	—.01	—.21 *	—.37 ***	—.34 ***
Q Sort					
Self-Adjustment Score	(N = 74)	+.01	—.07	—.20 *	—.40 ***
Self-Expert Correlation	(N = 74)	+.05	—.06	—.18	—.38 ***
Ideal-Self, Adjustment Score	(N = 74)	+.16	—.32 ***	—.15	—.16
Ideal-Expert Correlation	(N = 74)	+.23 **	—.30 ***	—.20 *	—.20 *
Self vs. Ideal-Self Correlation	(N = 74)	+.04	—.08	—.15	—.29 **
Truax Anxiety Reaction Scale:	(N — 75)				
Factor of General Anxiety		—.02	—.24 **	—.21 *	—.32 ***
Factor of Social Self-Consciousness		—.08	—.15	—.26 **	—.39 ***
Factor of Internalized Anxiety		—.05	—.22 *	—.27 **	—.29 **

* $p < .10$
** $p < .05$
*** $p < .01$

1. Scored so that "+" means that the more disturbed the patients are on the initial status measure, the *less* they improve, and "—" means the more disturbed they are on the initial status, the more they improve.

the initial behavioral disturbance (measured by prior length of institutionalization, etc.), the greater the predicted improvement.

Again, this tentative generalization has to do with prediction of client *improvement* during therapy, and it does not necessarily follow that the same will hold for predicting therapeutic *benefit* (how much more he will improve with therapy beyond what he would be expected to improve anyway).

Table 18

Prediction of Outcome from Initial Client or Patient Status[1] (Outpatients)

Initial Status Measures		*Palo Alto Group Therapy Scale, Change (N = 64)*	*MMPI Σ Clinical Scales Deviations, Change (N = 56)*	*CPC Scale from MMPI, Change (N = 56)*
Palo Alto Group Therapy Scale	(N = 64)	−.76 ***	+.42 ***	+.38 ***
MMPI				
Σ Clinical Scales' Deviations	(N = 56)	−.09	−.40 ***	−.22 *
CPC Scale	(N = 56)	−.15	−.28 **	−.32 **
Hs	(N = 56)	−.15	−.38 ***	−.05
D	(N = 56)	−.12	−.36 ***	−.23 *
Hy	(N = 56)	−.05	−.34 ***	+.03
Pd	(N = 56)	−.21	−.25 *	−.07
Mf	(N = 56)	−.03	−.21	+.07
Pa	(N = 56)	−.17	−.21	−.06
Pt	(N = 56)	−.02	−.36 ***	−.26 **
Sc	(N = 56)	−.23 *	−.25 *	−.21
Ma	(N = 56)	+.07	−.11	−.02
Si	(N = 56)	−.11	−.20	−.27 **
Barron's Ego Strength	(N = 56)	−.24 *	−.32 **	−.20
Edwards' Social Desirability	(N = 56)	−.09	−.20	−.29 **
Σ Validity Scales' Deviations	(N = 56)	−.45 ***	−.10	−.13
Welsch's Anxiety Index	(N = 56)	−.04	−.26 **	−.30 **
Internalization of Anxiety Ratio	(N = 56)	−.06	−.23 *	−.23 *
Q Sort				
Self-Adjustment Score	(N = 51)	−.06	−.26 *	−.22
Self-Expert Correlation	(N = 51)	−.08	−.27 *	−.23
Ideal-Self Adjustment Score	(N = 52)	−.61 ***	+.07	+.24 *
Ideal-Expert Correlation	(N = 52)	−.59 ***	+11	+.22
Self vs. Ideal-Self Correlation	(N = 50)	+.02	−.28 **	−.30 **

* $p < .10$
** $p < .05$
*** $p < .01$

1. Scored so that "+" means that the more disturbed the patients are on the initial status measure, the *less* they improve, and "−" means the more disturbed they are on the initial status, the more they improve.

It may very well be that the diagnostic type of patient with the best prognosis varies from therapeutic setting to therapeutic setting, depending to some degree upon the biases and expectations of the counselors or therapists themselves. Since certain types of patients are more likely than others to show improvement during psychotherapy in specific settings, the crucial question becomes "Why is this so?" It seems probable that the expectations of the therapist for therapeutic outcome will markedly affect his therapeutic behavior. That is, he will offer higher levels of therapeutic conditions for those patients whom he rightly or wrongly believes to be good prospects, and relatively lower conditions for poorer prospects.

The earlier research chapter discussed the evidence dealing with whether the therapist or the patient caused the level of conditions to differ in therapy; the general findings were that the therapist was primarily the determining influence. Still, with research on a wider range of patients, we would also expect some kind of interaction between the individual therapist and the individual patient in producing the level of conditions offered in psychotherapy. Under ideal circumstances, the ideal counselor or therapist would indeed provide high levels of accurate empathy, nonpossessive warmth and genuineness to all clients at all times. But the therapist, after all, is human. His own personal prejudices will inevitably operate to some degree. The findings about the level of warmth offered in therapy indeed suggest that more likable patients receive greater warmth. The findings by Stoler (1963) also indicated that the likability of a client was significantly related to improvement and to the degree of patient involvement in the process of therapy: the more likable clients, as measured independently by raters listening to tape recorded samples, showed greatest improvement and greatest engagement in the process of therapy.

Some of the therapist biases that seem to be operative in psychotherapy are idiosyncratic to the individual therapist. Thus some therapists react negatively to passive-dependent patients and therefore provide lower levels of conditions for such patients, which in turn produce poorer outcome with such patients. Other therapists may have similar prejudices against clients with hysteric behavior, against clients with regional accents, etc.

Beyond personal prejudices, however, there are general prejudices operative throughout the professions of counseling and psychotherapy. Although there is no solid evidence, certain prejudices still seem almost universally institutionalized. Thus, most counselors and therapists believe that prognosis is poor for clients with low intellectual capacity. It seems almost inevitable that a counselor would communicate pessimism to such patients as well as lower conditions, *because* he believed he could not help them. His lower level of therapeutic conditions, in turn, would lead to poorer outcome and thereby confirm his original pessimism.

It is suggested that when the therapist overcomes such prejudices, both personal and professional, and offers high levels of conditions, he then obtains positive outcome for the patient of low intellectual capacity, the chronic schizophrenic, and even the psychopath.

It should be remembered, however, that even under the best conditions the patient's initial personality and behavioral status will be a major determinant of the degree of patient improvement. To repeat, it seems likely that a *high level of "felt" disturbance* (as measured by self-report questionnaires of felt anxiety, etc.) and *a low level of "overt" disturbance* (as measured by ward behavior ratings, length of institutionalization, current college grades, etc.) *are most predictive of positive outcome.*

Since some theorists and therapists have tended to consider diagnosis as of relatively little value, it should be stressed that the present viewpoint is not meant to minimize the usefulness of diagnosis. On the contrary, adequate diagnosis is crucial for effective empathic understanding: the more we know about the client we seek to help, the more able we will be to correctly understand his moment-to-moment communications. Beyond this consideration, lack of adequate diagnosis may allow a counselor or therapist to do the patient irreparable harm. Without a careful diagnostic evaluation he may not be able to know adequately whether a patient is suicidal, is on the edge of a psychotic panic, or has brain disease.

The present viewpoint, in essence, holds that the therapist, at his ideal best, can overcome his personal and professional prejudices so as to provide relatively high levels of therapeutic conditions to virtually all clients, and can therefore be effectively helpful *even* to patients who are generally regarded as poor therapy candidates. From such a viewpoint it would still be true to say that certain types of patients in certain settings do have better outcome than others, but that this differential outcome is *partly* dependent upon the outlook of the therapist.

That the prediction of patient behavior is markedly affected by the therapist himself is indicated by a recent study reported by White, Fichtenbaum and Dollard (1964). They attempted to predict dropouts in psychotherapy by analyzing initial interviews. Their data indicated that while they could attain 83 per cent overall correct prediction, *the accuracy of prediction varied from therapist to therapist.* Thus, 50 per cent of one therapist's patients were incorrectly predicted but only 12 per cent of another's.

That the patient's social status or social class is not the important variable it was once thought to be is suggested by a study by Albronda, Dean and Starkweather (1964). They found no differences attributable to social class affecting the tendency to remain or to drop out of therapy, nor in measures of improvement. The lower class client was just as likely to improve or to remain in therapy.

The Stieper and Wiener (1965) study of hospitalized patients looked closely at a range of socioeconomic and other variables (occupational level, educational level, intelligence) and found no relationship to therapeutic outcome. Some biographical correlates of improvement were obtained in one sample but did not replicate in another, so conclusions are difficult to draw.

As more evidence is amassed it becomes more apparent that the findings relating social class variables to type and duration of treatment offered simply reflect general prejudices common to the field, but *do not necessarily reflect client response to treatment.*

A second major aspect of the client's "readiness" involves his initial expectations toward psychotherapy. Frank (1965) has conceptualized this in terms of the role of *hope*. His view, which is quite consistent with the other related evidence on client readiness, is that the patient's initial hope for improvement is a major factor contributing to the likelihood of its actually occurring. Also, expectation or hope for improvement is closely linked to the client's attitude toward the therapist. It may very well be, as Frank suggests, that the effectiveness of empathy, warmth, and genuineness is due in part to its role in inspiring the client's hopes.

Although Frank recognizes that positive expectations of improvement may have temporary rather than permanent effects upon patient adjustment, he also recognizes that being able to shorten episodes of emotional disturbance is perhaps a fundamental goal of counseling and psychotherapy: "Psychotherapy may enable the patient to conduct his personal relationships in such a way as to decrease the likelihood of being exposed to certain stresses in the future, but the chances of finding psychotherapeutic methods that will confer permanent and total immunity to life stresses is remote."

Frank's stress on the role of hope in counseling and psychotherapy has grown out of work aimed at studying the "placebo response." In a very intriguing study, Frank, Nash, Stone, and Imber (1963) studied placebo effects in 109 psychiatric outpatients. Their findings indicated significant overall improvement in patients receiving a placebo. Further, the greatest improvement in symptomatic discomfort was in terms of relief from anxiety and depression, with the most improvement occurring immediately (within the hour) although it remained over a two-week period. When the scales were readministered to the same patients three years later, the average symptomatic discomfort was still considerably below the amount they had reported initially, prior to the placebo. At that point the researchers readministered the placebo to some patients who had initially improved but then relapsed. Even on the second time around, improvement in anxiety and depression occurred. Their evidence further suggested that the degree of improvement was unrelated to the personalities of the patients and that there was no correlation between the patients who responded to the placebo the first time and those who responded on the second occasion. Thus the data seemed to indicate clearly that measurable improvement in a psychiatric outpatient setting occurred even with the placebo method of arousing the patient's positive expectations.

The role of hope in psychotherapy is yet to be thoroughly studied but, as it affects motivation, it should contribute greatly not only by its immediate and transient effect on depression and anxiety, but also by its effect upon motivation for the learning and relearning involved in the total psychotherapeutic process.

THE EFFECTIVENESS OF ACCURATE EMPATHY, NONPOSSESSIVE WARMTH, AND GENUINENESS WITH HIGH AND LOW PROGNOSIS CLIENTS

From the research reviewed in Chapter 3, which involved a wide variety of patient or client populations, it would appear that the same kinds of therapeutic conditions offered by therapists tend to be effective regardless of the type of client involved. As yet, however, there is no clear evidence suggesting that the same levels of therapeutic conditions lead to the same *degree* of client change when clients differ in degree of initial disturbance (or in other prognostic personal characteristics). In analysis of data currently underway, the present tentative findings suggest that the degree of client change in counseling or psychotherapy is independently influenced both by the level of therapeutic conditions the therapist provides and by the initial degree and type of personal disturbance of the client.

When the client comes to a therapist for help, his current status can be thought of as *fixed* at that moment and time—it is a "given" with which the therapeutic process begins. If his prognosis is poor, the therapist or counselor may wish that it were good, but the therapeutic encounter still must begin with his current level and style of functioning. In spite of a lack of evidence, most theorists and practitioners strongly believe that different techniques should be used with different types of patients. In part, we would agree with this belief on purely common-sense grounds, even though there is no available evidence to suggest its validity. Since the interpersonal skills of accurate empathy, nonpossessive warmth, and genuineness tend to cut across all techniques of psychotherapy, a critical test of the generality and necessity of these therapeutic skills is whether or not they are equally effective with high and low prognosis clients. It is conceivable that the overall results reviewed in Chapter 3 were due primarily to "good prognosis" clients. That is, empathy, warmth and genuineness may be effective with clients who are ready to be helped but ineffective with the poor prognosis client. If this were true it would greatly alter our understanding of the role of therapeutic conditions in producing outcome.

There is now some beginning evidence available which bears directly on this question. In group psychotherapy, whether the patient population be composed of hospitalized mental patients, institutionalized juvenile delinquents, or the usual outpatients in a clinic and counseling service population, two sets of factors have long been considered important as prognostic indicators: (1) the degree to which the client is verbal or silent; and (2) the degree of personality and behavioral adjustment. As a beginning attempt to study the potential differential effectiveness of therapeutic conditions with high and low prognosis clients, two studies have been completed focusing upon outcomes in group psychotherapy.

The first study (Truax, Tunnell, and Glenn, 1966a) made use of the data collected to study the relationship between the level of therapeutic conditions and patient outcome in an original population of 160 hospitalized mental patients, 80 institutionalized juvenile delinquents, and 80 outpatients. On the basis of specific items (from the Palo Alto scale) dealing with amount of verbal participation during the first four sessions of group therapy, each therapy group in each of the three basic populations was divided into the most silent half and the most verbal half. Using this procedure, the level of conditions offered by each therapist, other therapist characteristics, and environmental and situational factors were all relatively constant for the silent and verbal group members. The overall findings on all measures with all patients are summarized in Tables 19 through 23. Tables 19 through 22 deal with the overall results of analysis on all measures combined; Table 23 deals specifically with the findings from a one-year follow-up on time out of institution for the mental patient and juvenile delinquent populations.

Although high levels of accurate empathy, nonpossessive warmth and genuineness combined tend to have slightly more effect upon outcome for the nonverbal hospitalized mental patients and for the more verbal outpatients, the general trend of the findings would suggest that the therapeutic conditions combined are in general almost equally as effective with the nonverbal as the verbal client. In looking more closely at the effects of the individual therapeutic conditions on outcome with relatively silent and relatively verbal clients, several findings emerge. First, contrary to expectation, accurate empathic understanding seems to be more critical for outcome with nonverbal patients, whether they are mental patients, juvenile delinquents, or outpatients. Since accurate empathy is considered to be the most heavily verbal of the three therapeutic conditions, this is an intriguing finding. By contrast, nonpossessive warmth and genuineness overall tend to be equally effective in producing outcome with both the verbal and nonverbal clients.

Table 23 shows that when this question is examined in terms of the time out of institution during a one-year follow-up, the three therapeutic conditions, both combined and separately, tend to be effective with both the nonverbal and verbal patient.

In the second available study (Truax, Tunnell, and Glenn, 1966b) the focus was upon any differential effectiveness of therapeutic conditions with most and least adjusted patients. As in the study on comparisons with verbal and nonverbal clients, the study focusing on differential initial levels of adjustment or disturbance was able to control for other therapist characteristics and situational factors by splitting each group in each of the basic subpopulations into halves. The level of adjustment was measured by the initial FOC combined measures of personality and behavior disturbance (described in Chapter 3). The overall findings from the analysis of the data are presented in Tables 24 through 28. In terms of the combined effectiveness of accurate empathy, nonpossessive warmth, and genuineness, the findings suggest that these therapeutic conditions are of equal importance in producing positive personality change in the most disturbed and least disturbed (or most or least adjusted) clients. There is a slight nonsignificant tendency for the therapeutic conditions to be more important with the most disturbed (least adjusted) clients.

Table 19

An Overview of the Findings on the Therapeutic Effectiveness of Accurate Empathy, Nonpossessive Warmth and Genuineness: All Measures of Outcome with Most Verbal and Most Silent Patients in Group Psychotherapy

Study	Type of treatment	Type of client	Number of clients	Specific outcome measures favoring hypothesis	Specific outcome measures against hypothesis	Specific outcome measures significantly favoring hypothesis ($p < .05$)	Specific outcome measures significantly against hypothesis ($p < .05$)	Overall combined outcome measures favoring hypothesis	Overall combined outcome measures against hypothesis	Overall combined outcome measures significantly favoring hypothesis ($p < .05$)	Overall combined outcome measures significantly against hypothesis ($p < .05$)
Most silent											
Truax & Wargo (1966c)	Grp	Hospital	80	23	4	5	0	1	0	0	0
Truax & Wargo (1966b)	Grp	Delinquent	40	17	1	12	1	1	0	1	0
Truax, Wargo & Carkhuff (1966)	Grp	Outpatient	40	19	4	4	0				
Totals			160	59	9	21	1	2	0	1	0
Most Verbal											
Truax & Wargo (1966c)	Grp	Hospital	80	14	13	0	0	1	0	0	0
Truax & Wargo (1966b)	Grp	Delinquent	40	18	0	6	0	1	0	1	0
Truax, Wargo & Carkhuff (1966)	Grp	Outpatient	40	19	4	9	0				
Totals			160	51	17	15	0	2	0	1	0

Table 20

Findings on the Therapeutic Effects of Accurate Empathy: Most Verbal and Most Silent Patients in Group Psychotherapy

Study	Type of treatment	Type of client	Number of clients	Specific outcome measures favoring hypothesis	Specific outcome measures against hypothesis	Specific outcome measures significantly favoring hypothesis ($p < .05$)	Specific outcome measures significantly against hypothesis ($p < .05$)	Overall combined outcome measures favoring hypothesis	Overall combined outcome measures against hypothesis	Overall combined outcome measures significantly favoring hypothesis ($p < .05$)	Overall combined outcome measures significantly against hypothesis ($p < .05$)
Most silent											
Truax & Wargo (1966c)	Grp	Hospital	80	23	4	4	0	1	0	1	0
Truax & Wargo (1966b)	Grp	Delinquent	40	17	1	12	1	1	0	1	0
Truax, Wargo & Carkhuff (1966)	Grp	Outpatient	40	11	12	3	2				
Totals			160	51	17	19	3	2	0	2	0
Most Verbal											
Truax & Wargo (1966c)	Grp	Hospital	80	9	18	0	2	1	0	0	0
Truax & Wargo (1966b)	Grp	Delinquent	40	18	0	6	0	1	0	1	0
Truax, Wargo & Carkhuff (1966)	Grp	Outpatient	40	5	18	1	2				
Totals			160	32	36	7	4	2	0	1	0

Table 21
Findings on the Therapeutic Effects of Nonpossessive Warmth: Most Verbal and Most Silent Patients in Group Psychotherapy

Study	Type of treatment	Type of client	Number of clients	Specific outcome measures favoring hypothesis	Specific outcome measures against hypothesis	Specific outcome measures significantly favoring hypothesis ($p < .05$)	Specific outcome measures significantly against hypothesis ($p < .05$)	Overall combined outcome measures favoring hypothesis	Overall combined outcome measures against hypothesis	Overall combined outcome measures significantly favoring hypothesis ($p < .05$)	Overall combined outcome measures significantly against hypothesis ($p < .05$)
Most silent											
Truax & Wargo (1966c)	Grp	Hospital	80	20	7	2	2	1	0	0	0
Truax & Wargo (1966b)	Grp	Delinquent	40	17	1	12	1	1	0	1	0
Truax, Wargo & Carkhuff (1966)	Grp	Outpatient	40	19	4	4	0				
Totals			—	—	—	—	—	—	—	—	—
Most Verbal			160	56	12	18	3	2	0	1	0
Truax & Wargo (1966c)	Grp	Hospital	80	17	10	1	1	1	0	0	0
Truax & Wargo (1966b)	Grp	Delinquent	40	18	0	6	0	1	0	1	0
Truax, Wargo & Carkhuff (1966)	Grp	Outpatient	40	19	4	9	0				
			—	—	—	—	—	—	—	—	—
Totals			160	54	14	16	1	2	0	1	0

Table 22

Findings on the Therapeutic Effects of Genuineness: Most Verbal and Most Silent Patients in Group Psychotherapy

Study	Type of treatment	Type of client	Number of clients	Specific outcome measures favoring hypothesis	Specific outcome measures against hypothesis	Specific outcome measures significantly favoring hypothesis ($p < .05$)	Specific outcome measures significantly against hypothesis ($p < .05$)	Overall combined outcome measures favoring hypothesis	Overall combined outcome measures against hypothesis	Overall combined outcome measures significantly favoring hypothesis ($p < .05$)	Overall combined outcome measures significantly against hypothesis ($p < .05$)
Most silent											
Truax & Wargo (1966c)	Grp	Hospital	80	16	11	1	2	1	0	0	0
Truax & Wargo (1966b)	Grp	Delinquent	40	17	1	12	1	1	0	1	0
Truax, Wargo & Carkhuff (1966)	Grp	Outpatient	40	15	8	1	3				
Totals			160	48	20	14	6	2	0	1	0
Most Verbal											
Truax & Wargo (1966c)	Grp	Hospital	80	17	10	1	0	1	0	0	0
Truax & Wargo (1966b)	Grp	Delinquent	40	18	0	6	0	1	0	1	0
Truax, Wargo & Carkhuff (1966)	Grp	Outpatient	40	17	6	5	1				
Totals			160	52	16	12	1	2	0	1	0

Table 23

An Overview of the Findings on the Therapeutic Effectiveness of Accurate Empathy, Nonpossessive Warmth, and Genuineness, with Most Verbal and Most Silent Patients in Group Psychotherapy: Institutionalization Rates for All Institutionalized Patients during One-year Follow-up

Study	Type of patient	Type of treatment	Number of patients	Favoring hypothesis	Against hypothesis
Most silent					
Combined conditions					
Truax & Wargo (1966c)	Hospital	Group	80	yes	no
Truax & Wargo (1966b)	Delinquent	Group	40	yes	no
Accurate Empathy					
Truax & Wargo (1966c)	Hospital	Group	80	yes	no
Truax & Wargo (1966b)	Delinquent	Group	40	yes	no
Nonpossessive Warmth					
Truax & Wargo (1966c)	Hospital	Group	80	yes	no
Truax & Wargo (1966b)	Delinquent	Group	40	yes	no
Genuineness					
Truax & Wargo (1966c)	Hospital	Group	80	yes	no
Truax & Wargo (1966b)	Delinquent	Group	40	yes	no
			Totals	8 yes	0 no
Most Verbal					
Combined conditions					
Truax & Wargo (1966c)	Hospital	Group	80	yes	no
Truax & Wargo (1966b)	Delinquent	Group	40	yes	no
Accurate Empathy					
Truax & Wargo (1966c)	Hospital	Group	80	yes	no
Truax & Wargo (1966b)	Delinquent	Group	40	yes	no
Nonpossessive Warmth					
Truax & Wargo (1966c)	Hospital	Group	80	yes	no
Truax & Wargo (1966b)	Delinquent	Group	40	yes	no
Genuineness					
Truax & Wargo (1966c)	Hospital	Group	80	yes	no
Truax & Wargo (1966b)	Delinquent	Group	40	yes	no
			Totals	8 yes	0 no

When the differential effectiveness of each of the three conditions for the least and most disturbed or adjusted clients is analyzed separately, additional findings emerge. Empathy appears to be more critical for outcome in the least adjusted or most disturbed clients; nonpossessive warmth and genuineness appear to be equally critical for outcome no matter what the patient's degree of adjustment. Finally, as in the analysis of verbal-nonverbal clients, the effects of therapeutic conditions upon the client's ability to stay out of an institution during a one-year follow-up show no differences between least and most adjusted clients.

Table 24
An Overview of the Findings on the Therapeutic Effectiveness of Accurate Empathy, Nonpossessive Warmth, and Genuineness: All Measures of Outcome with Most and Least Adjusted Clients in Group Psychotherapy

Study	Type of treatment	Type of client	Number of clients	Specific outcome measures favoring hypothesis	Specific outcome measures against hypothesis	Specific outcome measures significantly favoring hypothesis ($p < .05$)	Specific outcome measures significantly against hypothesis ($p < .05$)	Overall combined outcome measures favoring hypothesis	Overall combined outcome measures against hypothesis	Overall combined outcome measures significantly favoring hypothesis ($p < .05$)	Overall combined outcome measures significantly against hypothesis ($p < .05$)
Least adjusted											
Truax & Wargo (1966c)	Grp	Hospital	80	18	9	5	0	1	0	1	0
Truax & Wargo (1966b)	Grp	Delinquent	40	18	0	6	0	1	0	0	0
Truax, Wargo & Carkhuff (1966)	Grp	Outpatient	40	20	3	3	0				
Totals			160	56	12	14	0	2	0	1	0
Most adjusted											
Truax & Wargo (1966c)	Grp	Hospital	80	12	15	1	1	1	0	1	0
Truax & Wargo (1966b)	Grp	Delinquent	40	18	0	7	0	1	0	0	0
Truax, Wargo & Carkhuff (1966)	Grp	Outpatient	40	19	4	4	1				
Totals			160	49	19	12	2	2	0	1	0

Table 25

Findings on the Therapeutic Effectiveness of Accurate Empathy: Most and Least Adjusted Clients in Group Psychotherapy

Study	Type of treatment	*Type of client*	Number of clients	Specific outcome measures favoring hypothesis	Specific outcome measures against hypothesis	Specific outcome measures significantly favoring hypothesis ($p < .05$)	Specific outcome measures significantly against hypothesis ($p < .05$)	Overall combined outcome measures favoring hypothesis	Overall combined outcome measures against hypothesis	Overall combined outcome measures significantly favoring hypothesis ($p < .05$)	Overall combined outcome measures significantly against hypothesis ($p < .05$)
Least adjusted											
Truax & Wargo (1966c)	Grp	Hospital	80	17	10	2	0	1	0	1	0
Truax & Wargo (1966b)	Grp	Delinquent	40	18	0	6	0	1	0	0	0
Truax, Wargo & Carkhuff (1966)	Grp	Outpatient	40	15	8	3	1				
Totals			160	50	18	11	1	2	0	1	0
Most adjusted											
Truax & Wargo (1966c)	Grp	Hospital	80	16	11	1	1	1	0	1	0
Truax & Wargo (1966b)	Grp	Delinquent	40	18	0	7	0	1	0	0	0
Truax, Wargo & Carkhuff (1966)	Grp	Outpatient	40	3	20	1	1				
Totals			160	37	31	9	2	2	0	1	0

Table 26

Findings on the Therapeutic Effectiveness of Nonpossessive Warmth: Most and Least Adjusted Clients in Group Psychotherapy

Study	Type of treatment	Type of client	Number of clients	Specific outcome measures favoring hypothesis	Specific outcome measures against hypothesis	Specific outcome measures significantly favoring hypothesis ($p < .05$)	Specific outcome measures significantly against hypothesis ($p < .05$)	Overall combined outcome measures favoring hypothesis	Overall combined outcome measures against hypothesis	Overall combined outcome measures significantly favoring hypothesis ($p < .05$)	Overall combined outcome measures significantly against hypothesis ($p < .05$)
Least adjusted											
Truax & Wargo (1966c)	Grp	Hospital	80	15	12	2	4	1	0	0	0
Truax & Wargo (1966b)	Grp	Delinquent	40	18	0	6	0	1	0	0	0
Truax, Wargo & Carkhuff (1966)	Grp	Outpatient	40	20	3	3	0				
Totals			160	53	15	11	4	2	0	0	0
Most adjusted											
Truax & Wargo (1966c)	Grp	Hospital	80	14	13	1	0	1	0	1	0
Truax & Wargo (1966b)	Grp	Delinquent	40	18	0	7	0	1	0	0	0
Truax, Wargo & Carkhuff (1966)	Grp	Outpatient	40	19	4	4	1				
Totals			160	51	17	12	1	2	0	1	0

Table 27

Findings on the Therapeutic Effectiveness of Genuineness: Most and Least Adjusted Clients in Group Psychotherapy

Study	*Type of treatment*	*Type of client*	Number of clients	Specific outcome measures favoring hypothesis	Specific outcome measures against hypothesis	Specific outcome measures significantly favoring hypothesis ($p < .05$)	Specific outcome measures significantly against hypothesis ($p < .05$)	Overall combined outcome measures favoring hypothesis	Overall combined outcome measures against hypothesis	Overall combined outcome measures significantly favoring hypothesis ($p < .05$)	Overall combined outcome measures significantly against hypothesis ($p < .05$)
Least adjusted											
Truax & Wargo (1966c)	Grp	Hospital	80	22	5	5	0	1	0	0	0
Truax & Wargo (1966b)	Grp	Delinquent	40	18	0	6	0	1	0	0	0
Truax, Wargo & Carkhuff (1966)	Grp	Outpatient	40	12	11	2	4				
Totals			160	52	16	13	4	2	0	0	0
Most adjusted											
Truax & Wargo (1966c)	Grp	Hospital	80	14	13	2	1	1	0	0	0
Truax & Wargo (1966b)	Grp	Delinquent	40	18	0	7	0	1	0	0	0
Truax, Wargo & Carkhuff (1966)	Grp	Outpatient	40	20	3	5	0				
Totals			160	52	16	14	1	2	0	0	0

Table 28

An Overview of the Findings on the Therapeutic Effectiveness of Accurate Empathy, Nonpossessive Warmth, and Genuineness, with Most and Least Adjusted Clients in Group Psychotherapy: Institutionalization Rates for All Institutionalized Patients during One-year Follow-up

Study	Type of patient	Type of treatment	Number of patients	Favoring hypothesis	Against hypothesis
Least adjusted					
Combined conditions					
Truax & Wargo (1966c)	Hospital	Group	80	yes	no
Truax & Wargo (1966b)	Delinquent	Group	40	yes	no
Accurate Empathy					
Truax & Wargo (1966c)	Hospital	Group	80	yes	no
Truax & Wargo (1966b)	Delinquent	Group	40	yes	no
Nonpossessive Warmth					
Truax & Wargo (1966c)	Hospital	Group	80	yes	no
Truax & Wargo (1966b)	Delinquent	Group	40	yes	no
Genuineness					
Truax & Wargo (1966c)	Hospital	Group	80	yes	no
Truax & Wargo (1966b)	Delinquent	Group	40	yes	no
			Totals	8 yes	0 no
Most adjusted					
Combined conditions					
Truax & Wargo (1966c)	Hospital	Group	80	yes	no
Truax & Wargo (1966b)	Delinquent	Group	40	yes	no
Accurate Empathy					
Truax & Wargo (1966c)	Hospital	Group	80	yes	no
Truax & Wargo (1966b)	Delinquent	Group	40	yes	no
Nonpossessive Warmth					
Truax & Wargo (1966c)	Hospital	Group	80	yes	no
Truax & Wargo (1966b)	Delinquent	Group	40	yes	no
Genuineness					
Truax & Wargo (1966c)	Hospital	Group	80	yes	no
Truax & Wargo (1966b)	Delinquent	Group	40	yes	no
			Totals	8 yes	0 no

Putting these two studies together as evidence dealing with high and low prognosis clients, the currently available evidence suggests that *in general* the therapeutic conditions are equally important for both types. Further, accurate empathy appears to be individually more important with some clients than with others—it is most critical for therapeutic outcome with the low prognosis client who is most in need of help. The suggestion is, then, that accurate empathy is most critical with clients who are least ready for change, while nonpossessive warmth and genuineness are equally important for the client who is ready to change and the one who is not ready.

CHARACTERISTICS OF THE THERAPY BEHAVIOR OF SUCCESSFUL CLIENTS

For the practice of psychotherapy, perhaps the most crucial question to ask about the patient is "What do successful patients do *in* psychotherapy that is different from unsuccessful patients?" In the moment-to-moment encounter with the client, the therapist takes some clues from the patient's moment-by-moment behavior as guidelines for evaluating his own effectiveness. Perhaps the most useful guideline would be an increase in the kind of client behavior that is typical of successful cases and untypical of failure cases.

In successful psychotherapy, both individual and group, the patient spends much of his time in self-exploration—attempting to understand and define his own beliefs, values, motives, and actions—while the therapist, by reason of his training and knowledge, is attempting to facilitate this process. This is the essence of the "talking cure" pioneered by Freud and his associates. In the terminology of psychoanalytic theory, this process of self-exploration is described as the patient's becoming aware of and exploring unconscious material and distortion effects of that unconscious material upon perception of reality (Munroe, 1955). Even those psychoanalytic theorists, such as Otto Rank, who largely rejected the desirability and necessity of dealing with unconscious material and chose to work at the ego level, placed great emphasis on self-exploration. In what can be termed the "ego psychology" tradition, therapeutic change is viewed as occurring through the client's ability to solve his problems himself as he sees more deeply into them as a result of the facilitative interaction with the therapist. This central role of the client's self-exploration and verbal revelation, although more structured, is seen in virtually all forms of psychotherapy, including behavior therapy.

Rogers in particular has stressed the role of patient self-exploration. In attempting to describe this in the client, Rogers (1955b) describes in a different language the basic phenomena dealt with by Freud: "Optimal therapy has meant an exploration of increasingly strange and unknown and dangerous feelings in himself. . . . Thus he becomes acquainted with elements of his experiences which have in the past been denied to awareness as too threatening, too damaging to the structure of the self."

Regardless of one's theoretic viewpoint about the significance of different areas of content and different manners of relating, the "talking cure" of counseling, or psychotherapy, obviously relies upon some degree of verbal interchange. A mass of research evidence has been accumulating which in broad form tends to verify the significance for outcome of the client's degree of self-exploration. Much of this research has been stimulated by the work of Rogers (1951). One of the early studies by Peres (1947) investigated differences between benefited and unbenefited patients in client-centered group counseling. Using tape recordings of the actual sessions, she developed a classification of patient statements based upon whether or not the statements referred to personal problems. Her findings indicated that early in group counseling both the benefited and unbenefited patients made equal numbers of references to personal problems. However, during the last half of group counseling, the successful clients made significantly more references to personal problems than did unsuccessful clients. This finding is perhaps related to Cartwright's finding concerning the critical significance of the therapist's final rather than initial level of understanding. Even considering all sessions combined, the successful clients in group counseling made almost twice as many references to personal problems as the unsuccessful ones.

Focusing on the degree of exploration of problems in individual counseling using a client-centered approach, Steele (1948) did a comparative study of more and less successful cases. The findings indicated that more successful clients increasingly explored their problems as therapy proceeded, while the less successful ones tended to explore their problems less. Quite similar results were reported by Wolfson (1949), while corroborating evidence dealing with client-centered counseling is available in the reports of research by Seeman (1949) and Blau (1953).

Again using data from individual psychotherapy carried out from a client-centered orientation, Braaten (1958) attempted to determine the amount of *change* in self-references for successful and unsuccessful cases. Findings for the more emotionally disturbed part of his sample indicated a *greater increase in the amount of self-references for the more successful than for the less successful cases,* particularly, those self-references involving expressions of the private self (awareness of being and functioning, internal communication).

Tomlinson and Hart (1962) used the Process Scale developed by Rogers, Walker and Rablen (1960) in comparing successful and unsuccessful counseling cases. Their data indicated that the successful cases tended to score higher on the Process Scale, which essentially measures the degree of self-exploration, the rigidity of concepts, and the degree of immediate experiencing. Similarly, Wagstaff, Rice and Butler (1960) reported data from a study of client-centered counseling indicating that patients with successful outcomes tended to explore themselves more in the course of psychotherapy, whereas patients who could be classified as therapeutic failures showed little self-exploration and emotional involvement.

The research on individual psychotherapy with schizophrenics (Truax and Carkhuff, 1964a) involved use of the Depth of Intrapersonal Exploration Scale applied to the tape recordings of psychotherapy. The overall findings indicated that patients who were high in self-exploration showed significantly greater personality change than patients who were relatively low in degree of self-exploration. This finding held both with the final outcome criterion, which was based on a number of psychological tests including a blind analysis of the Rorschach and percentage of time hospitalized, and with a number of specific measures. The overall analysis indicated that the patients engaging in a high level of self-exploration showed an average improvement one standard deviation beyond that of patients low in self-exploration. In specific subanalysis, the data suggested that the basal level of self-exploration (the average of the three lowest samples of self-exploration per patient) was most highly related to outcome, but that the altitude (highest levels) of self-exploration was not significantly related.

Of particular interest, serial analyses of the first 30 interviews, covering a period of up to three and one-half years, indicated that for the most part this positive relationship between the level of self-exploration and outcome held whether measurement was taken early or late in the process of therapy. There was one significant exception to this, a clear reversal of the pattern at approximately the fifth interview of therapy: successful cases who started off significantly higher in self-exploration appeared to show a sharp drop in level of self-exploration at about the fifth interview and then returned to a high level by the tenth interview and thereafter; cases who were later to show deterioration or no change showed a relatively constant lower level of self-exploration. Analyses using the Problem Expression Scale developed by van der Veen and the Experiencing Scale developed by Gendlin yielded quite similar findings. The relationships to outcome were somewhat less and in some cases nonsignificant, and there was an even sharper reversal at around the fifth interview.

Although the available data could not yield conclusive findings, an analysis by Rogers and Truax (1962) obtained findings suggesting that the Depth of Intrapersonal Exploration Scale, the Experiencing Scale, and the Problem Expression Scale measured something quite akin to readiness for help. That is, the data, while not totally conclusive, favor the hypothesis that low levels on the scales describe clients who are relatively rigid and unready for help, and high levels describe clients with a readiness to change, who are already exhibiting some "changingness" by their self-exploratory behavior.

One intriguing finding from those studies was the indication that successful cases, as a group, showed significantly more self-exploration as early as the second interview. The correlation between the level of self-exploration in the second interview and the final case outcome was .70, even though some cases were continued for more than three and one-half years. When comparisons were made using a control group, the data indicated that patients who engaged in a relatively high level of self-exploration showed improvement significantly greater than the control patients, but those showing low levels of self-exploration showed less improvement (even deterioration) than the controls. Significant differences, favoring greater improvement for those high in self-exploration, also showed in the time patients spent hospitalized during a three and one-half year period; here, improvement was measured by psychological tests: the sum of the clinical scales of the MMPI as well as the Pd, Mf, Pt, and Ma subscales.

Analyses were also made relating the levels of accurate empathy, nonpossessive warmth and genuineness offered by the therapist throughout the course of therapy to the levels of patient self-exploration. Although the relationship was not strong, there was a significant relationship between the levels of accurate empathy and nonpossessive warmth offered by the therapist and the average level of self-exploration engaged in by the patient. The level of congruence tended to show a similar pattern.

Using the same data that had been used for analysis of the therapeutic conditions, an attempt was made to determine the relative contribution of therapist and patient to the patient's level of self-exploration. With data from the study in which hospitalized patients had each seen a different therapist in the Youden Square design, the findings indicated that both patient and therapist significantly affected the level of patient self-exploration. That is, different therapists, when seeing the same set of patients, tended to *evoke* different levels of patient self-exploration; and different patients, when seeing the same set of therapists, tended to engage in different levels of self-exploration.

That the patient, however, plays the major role in determining his own level of self-exploration is further indicated by an analysis making use of the sampling interviews in the schizophrenic research study. For each case, the level of self-exploration occurring in the periodic sampling interviews with a constant standard interviewer was computed. Then the average level of self-exploration occurring for each case in actual therapy was computed separately. With such data, the degree to which self-exploration was solely a product of the patient (and not the therapist) could be examined more closely. The obtained correlation of .67 between the level of self-exploration occurring in therapy per case and the corresponding level in the sampling interviews strongly suggests that although the therapist may indeed *influence* the patient's self-exploration by offering certain levels of therapeutic conditions, the patient himself is the one who primarily *determines* his level of self-exploration.

In recent attempts to extend the findings on self-exploration to group therapy, Truax and Wargo (1966b) studied the relationship between level of patient self-exploration and outcome on an initial population of 80 juvenile delinquents. The findings themselves were quite equivocal. On a few specific measures the differences favoring those who were in groups where high levels of self-exploration occurred reached statistical significance; however, on some of the other submeasures the exact reverse was found. Self-exploration, then, did not seem critical for delinquents.

In a study of 80 outpatients receiving time-limited group therapy (Truax, Wargo, and Carkhuff, 1966) the findings suggested that successful outpatients in group therapy engage in greater self-exploration than outpatients who show poorer outcome in group therapy ($p < .05$).

In the related study by Truax and Wargo (1966c) of 160 hospitalized patients, the evidence for the importance of patient self-exploration in group therapy was stronger. On 21 of the 28 specific measures of outcome available for analysis, patients in groups with high levels of self-exploration showed greater improvement than patients in groups low in self-exploration ($p < .001$).

Finally, in the study reviewed in Chapter 4 dealing with the therapist's reinforcement of patient self-exploration (Truax, 1966d), those patients who were rewarded or reinforced by higher momentary levels of therapeutic conditions when they self-explored were also those who showed the overall highest levels of self-exploration and the greatest improvement following therapy.

IMPLICATIONS FOR TRAINING AND PRACTICE

Taken together, the available research evidence tends to confirm clinical and theoretic writings that point to the significance for outcome of the client's engagement in the process of self-exploration. However, there is far from a one-to-one relationship between the various measures of self-exploration and therapeutic outcome. This, in turn, suggests that a large part of psychotherapeutic outcome is not mediated by the patient's verbal or even emotional self-exploration throughout the course of counseling or psychotherapy. It may be that our current and crude measurement of the client's behavior is insensitive to many of the significant emotional and cognitive happenings. It may also be that much of the change in the patient comes about *between* therapy sessions as he is trying out new modes of living in a tentative fashion and risking himself in new ways of relating to the world. We suspect that both these possibilities are true.

Even with the current crude measurement, levels of patient self-exploration can provide some guideline for the beginning therapist just as they do for the experienced practitioner. The experienced counselor or therapist uses the patient's behavior as a guideline by which to judge his own moment-by-moment effectiveness. The current tentative research scale defining levels of client self-exploration can be used in a similar fashion. That is, as a general guideline for practice, the counselor might aim toward facilitating the highest possible levels of self-exploration, regardless of the specific technique, verbalization or approach he finds most effective with any given client or patient.

A Tentative Scale for the Measurement of Depth of Self-Exploration[6]

The present scale (which was used in much of the research just cited) was based upon the theoretic and clinical conception of self-exploration as an antecedent to psychotherapeutic outcome. Aspects of the present scale were derived from the original Process Scale developed by Rogers, Walker and Rablen (1960) and the specific subscales developed by Gendlin, Tomlinson, and van der Veen (1962). It is an attempt to measure the extent of patient self-exploration with additional weightings or corrections given for "personally private" and "personally damning" material. An earlier version of the present scale included factors of relationship quality, personal constructs, relationship to problem elements of the self, immediacy of feeling, and defensiveness. Research using that scale, however, indicated that those additional factors showed no relationship to outcome; and for that reason they are omitted in the current version (Truax, 1962j; 1962k; 1962l; 1962m; 1962n).

The scale of self-exploration is presented here not only to give the reader a more precise understanding of the research findings already reviewed in this chapter but, more importantly, for use as a moment-to-moment guideline of therapist effectiveness, as a way of evaluating the patient's response to the therapist in both training and practice. This scale (just as those presented in Chapter 2) was an integral part of the present approach to training discussed throughout the remainder of the book. Its value for training and practice of counseling lies in its crude but quantitative specification of the kinds of client behaviors that the effective counselor seeks to elicit during the therapeutic session. The trainee, the supervisor, and the experienced practitioner alike should question the effectiveness of their therapeutic approach whenever the client responds in a manner typified by the lower ranges of the following scale.

The reliabilities obtained in various studies with the present scale are presented in Table 29.

In general, then, the scale can be considered to be reasonably reliable, particularly in view of the inherent ambiguity of tape-recorded samples of the therapeutic process.

The validity of the measure, however, cannot be so easily assessed. As with the conditions scales of therapeutic conditions presented in Chapter 2, one must depend on the face validity and the research evidence showing predictable relationships to therapeutic outcome. Beyond this, the finding that experimental manipulation of levels of conditions produces pre-

6. The Depth of Self Exploration Scale was developed in 1963 by Charles B. Truax with the support of NIMH Grant No. N3496 and Grant No. RD906 from the Vocational Rehabilitation Administration. The author is deeply indebted to Carl R. Rogers, Shirley Epstein, Edward Williams, Eugene T. Gendlin and Ferdinand van der Veen, and to a number of colleagues and students who served as raters, for suggestions, criticisms and advice.

Table 29
Reliability of Rating Scale for Depth of Intrapersonal Exploration from Specific Studies

Study	N *Samples*	N *Patients*	N *Therapists*	Group or *Individual*	*Correlation*
Truax & Carkhuff (1963)	297	14	10	Individual	.68[a]
Truax & Carkhuff (1963	64	8	8	Individual	.59[a]
Truax, (1962e)	104	26	1	Individual	.68[a]
Truax & Wargo (1966b)	366	80	6	Group	.79
Truax, Wargo & Carkhuff (1966)	89	80	8	Group	.74
Truax & Wargo (1966c)	698	160	15	Group	.80
Truax (1962 j,k,l,m,n)	420	14	10	Individual	.68[a]
Truax & Carkhuff (1965a)	45	3	1	Individual	.78
Carkhuff & Truax (1965a)	151	70	28	Individual	.59[a]
Truax & Silber (1966)	144	48	16	Individual	.77
Truax, Silber & Carkhuff (1965)	342	80	5	Group	.88
Truax (1966d)	161	30	4	Group	.68

a. Average Pearson Correlations. All others are Ebel's intraclass reliabilities for the pooled data used in analysis of findings.

dictable changes in the measure of self-exploration, and the finding that differential reinforcement of self-exploration produces consequent differential levels of self-exploration and outcome, add further evidence for the validity and utility of the following measure of self-exploration.

Basic Scale of Depth of Self-Exploration[5]

The following is a 9-point scale attempting to define the extent to which patients engage in self-exploration, ranging from no demonstrable intrapersonal exploration to a very high level of self-probing and exploration. Although this basic scale is intended to be a continuum, corrections should be added to determine the final assigned scale value.

STAGE 0.

No *personally relevant* material and no opportunity for it to be discussed. Personally relevant material refers to emotionally tinged experiences or feelings, or to feelings or experiences of significance to the self. This would include self-descriptions that are intended to reveal the self to the therapist, and communications of personal values, perceptions of one's relationships to others, one's personal role and self-worth in life, as well as communications indicating upsetness, emotional turmoil, or expressions of more specific feelings of anger, affection, etc.)

Example A:

T: So you'll see Mrs. Smith about taking those tests? Have you got your slip?
C: Yeah.
T: As I mentioned earlier, I have to leave a little early today. (Phone rings) Hello, yes, this is Dr. Jones. Right, right, okay, right away. Goodbye. (Hangs up) So then I'll see you next Tuesday?
C: At ten?
T: Yes, or a little bit after. Okay, I'll see you next week.

Example B:

T: I am sorry that I'll be gone for . . . several weeks now or . . .
C: Mmm . . . Oh!
T: Maybe over two weeks.
C: Mmm.
T: 'Cause here I just—we just start, and then . . .
C: Mmm.
T: I go away and . . .
C: Well, it's the holidays coming up—I mean that . . . are you . . . from here?
T: No, I'm from Utah.
C: Oh, uh huh . . .
T: So that's why I'm going on this trip . . .
C: Mmm . . . (Pause)
T: And I'll be back on January 3rd . . .
C: Mmm . . . mmm . . .
T: I'll be—I can make up the time for you.
C: Mmm . . . You know . . . it certainly couldn't make any difference to me if it's in the morning at . . . ah . . . couple morning periods.
T: You don't smoke, do you?
C: No, I don't.
T: You don't mind if I smoke, do you?
C: No, I don't . . . (Laughs)

STAGE 1.

The patient actively evades personally relevant material (by changing the subject, for instance, refusing to respond at all, etc.). Thus, personally relevant material is not discussed. The patient does not respond to personally relevant material *even* when the therapist speaks of it.

Example A:

T: As though you're just feeling kind of down about these things . . .
C: Tired.
T: What?
C: Tired.
T: Tired . . . kind of worn out?
C: Couldn't sleep last night. (Pause)
T: You're just feeling kind of worn out.
(Client does not respond—silence to end of tape.)

Example B:

C: Dining room?
T: Hmm?
C: You're dialing room? (Pause) That's why the operator always answers when I dial half around.
T: Is this your dialing room?
C: Sometimes when I'm in the kitchen. Umm, whenever I make a dial, dialed numbers, it reminds of dinner. What are we having today, do you know? (Pause)
T: Something good? (30-second pause—dialing of telephone—another long pause) It's kind of interesting to make phone calls even when they're not real?
C: (Dialing telephone and talking at the same time) It seems like fun.
T: Not so much fun. (Telephone is dialed 18 times)
C: Could I go back now? I don't want to do anything 'til they make me dress . . .
T: I think you can. Umm, I guess you feel this isn't very interesting, is it? I'm sorry I couldn't do a better job of playing a brother-in-law, but I didn't know what kind of guy he is.
C: (Mumbles) You did quite good.
T: Did I? (Silence to end)

STAGE 2.

The patient does not volunteer personally relevant material but he does not actually evade responding to it when the therapist introduces it to the interpersonal situation.

Example A:

T: I gather it is rather tiresome for you to wait because unless somebody else says something you don't know when it'll be, you'll be out.
C: Uh huh. I hope someone does something for me pretty soon. (Long silence)
T: There's such a feeling about all this as if—me, I'm powerless. I can't do a thing.
C: You wait until your doctor tells you . . . can do something but . . . (Silence)

Example B:

Five minutes of silence have preceded this interchange.
T: Our time is nearly up. I guess you just feel kind of somber?
C: Yeah, hopeless.
T: Hopeless . . .
C: Everything . . .
T: Everything's a mess, nothing can . . . nothing can work out. (Pause) It's just hopeless (pause) . . . feeling might be going into it or talking about it. It's hopeless anyway.
C: Yeah, I . . . nothing makes sense anymore. (Laughs)
T: Hmm?

C: Nothing makes sense anymore.
T: Nothing makes sense.
C: Just don't know . . .
T: Messy, hopeless . . . (Mumble) . . .

STAGE 3.

The patient does not himself volunteer to share personally relevant material with the therapist, but he responds to personally relevant material introduced by the therapist. He may agree or disagree with the therapist's remarks and may freely make brief remarks, but he does not add significant new material.

Example A:

T: And I guess you don't need to, uh, see that doctor at all. But I'll see him and ask him—if you'd like me to?

C: Yes, I would.

T: Okay, I wanted to ask him also about your staffing because it was scheduled for this Monday and they must have had some kind of mix-up again. They didn't have it, did they?

C: No. Uh uh. They didn't call on it. (Silence)

C: There are a few new patients over there now.

T: Oh, . . . a few new faces in the building?

C: Oh, no. They're from . . . well, we have one there, two, is, but there's a couple from over here I know.

T: Um hmm.

C: I got, you know, she came over there.

Example B:

T: What did you do during those couple of years?
C: Nothing. Just stayed home.
T: Stayed home?
C: Right.
T: That's when you stayed home and looked after your little sister?
C: Yes. Except one year I did have a summer job.
T: How did that go?
C: Okay. But it was dirty.
T: Your sister . . . how did that go?
C: Not too good.
T: Not too good? You didn't like her?
C: That's right. (Yawns)
T: Did you always resent her? Or did it start at a particular time?
C: Right when she came . . .
T: When she was born?
C: I think so.
T: Do you have any ideas about that?
(Silence to end)

STAGE 4.

Personally relevant material is discussed (volunteered in part or in whole). Such volunteer discussion is done (1) *in a mechanical manner* (noticeably lacking in spontaneity or as a "reporter" or "observer"); and (2) *without demonstration of emotional feeling*. In addition, there is simply discussion without movement by the patient toward further exploring the significance of meaning of the material or feeling in an effort to uncover related feelings or material. Both the emotional remoteness and the mechanical manner of the patient make his discussion often sound rehearsed.

Example A:

C: (Talks in a flat, monotone voice) . . . It was hot, too.

T: It was a kind of hectic and not too satisfying experience, I take it?

C: I mean the whole day was a flop. (Nervous laugh) It started out we were just goin' to take a ride. A trip. Take a ride up north. I . . . 'cause I knew all the places would be busy, you know, and with the children it isn't too nice . . . and . . . so I . . . Nobody seemed to know where they . . . where they wanted to go . . . I mean it wasn't too well planned in the first place. Thought we'd just get out for a while and drive and stop off if we saw something we would like to see. And then he said the night before we weren't going to go, 'cause they were acting up some . . . and they were crying over that. Because one was trying to boss the other. (Laughs nervously) And then on the way up, we stopped every few miles and looked at a map. (Said slowly, with a tired and resigned tone of voice) It was . . . I don't know . . . it was . . . It wasn't nice.

T: Is it kind of discouraging to see the same darned old pattern of . . . ?

C: It was the same all over again . . . (Long pause) . . . it certainly was . . . Got a good start anyway.

T: You had a good start.

C: I say it had a good start. (Following told in a dry monotone voice) I did quite a bit of work Monday night. And Sunday night I made a dinner and was doing the dishes at 9:30 that night so we could go and get a good start and all. It was hot that night and the kids didn't want to settle down. I tried to get them to settle down and maybe I got kind of nasty to them. Then he told me, "Well, we're not going to go tomorrow. We're going to stay home or get up late. . . ." I didn't know what it was all about and just didn't do much. I stayed in the bedroom. I couldn't quiet them down. And they were so excited. It was late enough. It was 10 o'clock or something like that. Ten-thirty, I think it was. He had worked from about 4 o'clock, no, 5 o'clock, to about 9 o'clock. No 8 o'clock. We didn't get there until quarter to nine.

Example B:

C: Yeah . . . and let's see, what else did we do last weekend? We went to look at some new houses. The landlord said that we may not have to move. But my husband is going to talk to him again this week and then we'll know more . . .

T: Um hum.

C: S . . .

T: You may not have to go through that, huh?

C: Yes, may not have to go through that.

T: Yes, um hum.

C: When we go through some houses that you can buy without a down payment—just closing costs. But they're so expensive, but at least it's something and my husband sort of would like to buy one of those.

T: Hmm, at least that's possible.

C: Yes.

T: And when you could have your own stuff in it without . . .

C: Yes.

T: That situation doesn't seem as much of a problem as it did recently.

C: No, not as much of a problem. (Voices flat and trailing off)

T: Still unsettled but . . .

C: (Pause) If we have to move we just have to move that's all. We, we might buy a place without a down payment . . .

T: If you have to . . .

C: Yes, My husband wants to anyway, so we might . . . I don't know yet. (Pause)

T: I can't get how that feels to you . . . would that be fun or are you a little concerned?

C: What?

T: Buying a house.

C: Well, in a way that'd be nice. You know it would be a new house . . .

T: Yes.

C: But the trouble is they want so much money for them.

T: Hmm.

C: I think you would pay a little bit more that way than it was actually worth if you were to get it . . .

T: Yes, you do. Yes you do . . .

C: Without a down payment. (Long pause)

T: Our time is up?

C: Is it up? Well, I'd better go now.

T: I'll see you . . . ?

C: Tuesday.

STAGE 5.

This stage is similar to Stage 4 except that the material is discussed either *with feeling* indicating emotional proximity or *with spontaneity,* but not both. (Voice quality is the main cue.)

Example A:

C: He's the only close relative I have. But he's wrapped up in his own family up there . . . and he doesn't seem to . . . to realize that this house is the type . . . it's dear to me . . . I don't want to sell it, it . . . I *really* don't.

T: But he wants to sell it.

C: . . . He wants to sell it. He's eager to get rid of it because it's not worth keeping . . . to him, because he has his own home. But this is all the home that I have. (Pause) But of course, he is perfectly willing to sell it for as much money as he can get, and on that score he doesn't give me any trouble. He doesn't want a sacrifice sale as my guardian seems to want . . .

T: That's one of the few things that you have to look forward to . . . and going back to it . . .

C: . . . Going back there is one of the . . . I know I can't live there alone . . . one of the few things I have to look forward to. I know I can't live there alone as soon as I leave the hospital because I don't have the money to keep it up. But given a few years, I could. And I was hopeful that, if I could get a job, then perhaps I could get a mortgage on the house and pay off my hospital bill because. . . . You see that's the whole catch, is the what do they call it . . . the collections board or what is that? Bureau or board or something of Collections and Deportations.

T: I don't know . . .

C: . . . Here is Footville, wants the house sold so I can pay my hospital bill. But if they sell it for the ridiculously low price that it's listed at, it won't even pay my hospital bill.

T: Yes.

C: That, to me, seems stupid. I mean it, it would seem to me . . . that since they can't get the full amount of my hospital bill out of it, by selling it at the list price they would be . . . it would be better not to force sale of it and apply the rent that we get on my hospital bill. Or, at least my share of the rent . . . But they don't seem to—figure that that's . . . oh. I don't know. I give up.

T: Yes . . . it's a rather narrow way that they look at it . . . very cold and inhuman-like.

C: I don't know.

T: I think it would make me pretty darn mad if they tried to take my house away from me. Especially one that . . . I lived in for a long time and was really a part of me.

C: (Groans softly)

Example B:

T: Part of what it says to me is, "Boy, I had a wonderful time this weekend, and I found that my home was getting put together again, that I don't have to worry about my mother taking my son. My husband is doing something good, and when I do get out of here, at least I have something to look forward to now."

C: That's right. I mean, no matter what, what you said now, I mean I didn't let it, let it bother me, it being that like my sister was quite ill and expecting another baby. I think she has about five or six children now, I mean, my mother said, well, she had a seven or eight hundred dollar doctor bill. She was just . . . just, it's just the insinuation that . . . the . . . uh . . . they could afford it, and I couldn't and I belonged here is . . . and didn't have the money financially to do, uh, to do what, what uh . . . the rest of my family, with their big homes and that, can do. 'Cause we're in no position and never did have our, our own home, and . . . uh . . . but it didn't bother me, being that my husband was home now and able to take some responsibility. And, if he wouldn't have went and taken this job, coast-to-coast on the road there, I know I never would have been back in here again.

T: Mmm.

C: 'Cause, uh, then my son was out there more than he was home and my, my mother wanted me to go back already. I mean, I wasn't home a month, and she said, "I think you ought to, uh . . . take her back in there again." And uh, in . . . back to, again. So. uh . . . that's just . . . so now I, it doesn't, it doesn't bother me though, because I know now she wouldn't be able to take them and, and to keep them out there. I mean and, that they couldn't commit me now, if my husband doesn't, uh . . . knows, uh . . . that . . . uh . . . there's nothing wrong with me.

T: Mmm . . . before you had a feeling everybody was working to get you in here.

C: They *were*. My relatives, I mean, they, they, they seemed to think all the while there was something wrong with me.

T: And now you have kind of proof that, at least your husband and probably your children, are on your side.

C: Hmm . . . (Pause) . . . Well, I was . . . there was never enough money . . . my husband worked in a quarry at that time, too, and Billy was a baby, and I never was in the hospital to have either one of them, and I had to depend on my mother for that. Now, I went home to have both of them, the second time he was in the army. And, uh . . . and then, well, he left me, and he went to join the army. And it was fifteen, fifteen years ago. And, uh . . . it seemed he always . . . when they had to, someone does something like that for you, you always have to be under obligation to someone. And I mean, they want to do something then like they . . . she wanted my son in there then . . . the youngest one, because she took care of him from the time he was a baby and spoiled him. And, uh . . . I was always afraid someday that when he would grow up, that . . . well that's just what did happen. And I guess I worried a little bit too much about it. And now, well, now I have the feeling that it . . . that, uh . . . things'll be, be different. 'Cause he's first anyway, my husband . . . to, to, to . . . take the responsibility that no one else could have, because the one that's nineteen, well, he's on his own with his own job and that, and nobody would bother him anymore. So, he doesn't get into any trouble. Sometimes too much money isn't good either, for boys of that age.

T: So, almost as long as you've had Billy, you've always been afraid that somebody would want to take him away from you? Your mother?

C: Yeah . . . the youngest one . . . not the oldest one. The youngest one.

T: Yeah.

C: Well, I had, I had to go home that time because I . . . he left me already and, early in winter, and he was born first in September, and I had to depend on my relatives that whole summer for something to eat. And, uh . . . then, then I had to go to my mother's . . . there was no place . . . I live in a small apartment. And, uh . . . there . . .

STAGE 6.

In Stage 6 the level of Stage 4 is achieved again, with the additional fact that the personally relevant material is discussed with both *spontaneity and feeling*. There is clear indication that the patient is speaking with feeling, and his communication is laden with emotion.

Example A:

C: (Speaks with trembling voice throughout interview, almost always on the verge of sobbing, and in instances, does weep.) Do you have a match, or don't you use them?

T: Yes, I have one . . .

C: (Lights cigarette) Thank you.

T: You're welcome.

C: (Pause) . . . Like I said, you can't go back to living like that. (Pause) I've said, and even if he said he wouldn't do those things again, I'd still . . . I mean I just can't trust him anymore. (Voice becomes very thin) I know it'd be that way. Not because I want to go back again. It'd be on account of the children. I don't want to come home. (Long pause) So there he's again using it. Now it's my fault. I don't want to go home so they think I don't want to come to them, back to them. (Crying) *See?*

T: Yes.

C: And since . . .

T: (Very quietly) Seems like everything gets twisted the wrong way so that you come out the goat.

C: I really felt bad last week. I've been taking the kids up to my folks. See? And I said, I told them, why I can't go back with him and like that. I said, "He'd do the same things all over again." And they said, "Oh, you don't want to come home with us. You don't love us. You don't want to be with us." You know? Like that. I try to explain to them. (Very upset) It's so hard and you hate to get them upset again. I mean, they've been upset so much already. (Long pause) I don't know what to do.

T: At times it must seem impossible that you could be so completely misunderstood, doesn't it, as if no one can see this thing the way it looks to you?

C: (Weeping) . . . So there again he's using it.

Example B:

C: Dr. Smith showed me exactly how they do this. I was working at . . . at that time.

T: Um hmm.

C: But it sure . . . God! I never saw a fella, I never saw a child, change so much from a . . . well, I had a picture of him before and after. I just never saw . . . he was just . . . (Pause, groping for words)

T: Very striking, I guess.

C: Huh?

T: It must have been very striking.

C: Oh boy! (Nervous laughter) It was, uh, it was, uh, well . . . I just . . . never you just don't believe it. That's all, because people just don't . . . well you saw pictures of malnutrition and . . .

T: Um hmm, yes.

C: He was just bone. And his stomach all puffed and the shoulder . . . that's just exactly the way he looked. His legs was about, uh, as that (demonstrates how large) that big around. He walked around and never said hardly anything. Course you couldn't blame him, poor kid. Sittin' up here with gas pressing on his diaphragm. It's a wonder he could breathe. And just like that (snaps fingers) you see a person get an operation . . . and then all of a sudden he's straight as well, just as tall and straight as you or I. (Voice cracks with emotion) Can't help but appreciate the people who develop those things, take the time to develop those things. And that, that, that, well, that . . . that was. . . . well, I'll tell you, I'm kind of a calloused individual but I sure was grateful for that. There's no getting around that. I used to worry about that little fella. I guess I worried more about him than his mother.

T: Uh hmm, hum.

C: He'll go along now. He's strong. Boy, he's strong. Before he wasn't very strong, but now . . . just as strong as they come now. The other, I got a girl, she's got a crossed eye. She wears glasses. That'll straighten itself out. Outside of that, they haven't any ailments outside of childhood meanness.

STAGE 7.

Tentative probing toward intrapersonal exploration. There is an inward probing to discover feelings or experiences anew. The patient is searching for discovery of new feelings which he struggles to reach and hold on to. The individual may speak with many private distinctions or with "personal" meanings to common words. He may recognize the value of this self-exploration but it must be clear that he is trying to explore himself and his world actively even though at the moment he does so perhaps fearfully and tentatively.

Example A:

C: What . . . do you think this about, what would anybody get out of this?

T: Hmm. Not quite sure what you're asking.

C: This kind of therapy?

T: Hmm. You mean, "What is there in it for me?"

C: What could, could anybody get out of it?

T: Uh hmm. Well, saying, "Right now, I don't really feel I am getting anything."

C: Well, I guess I haven't been in it long enough.

T: Uh hmm. Well, anyway, is it uh, "Few times we have talked, I don't really feel I've gotten much out of it?"

C: Umm, I ain't got nothing.

T: Uh hmm. "Am I just going to go on this way or when do you, gonna get anything. It's just pretty useless, pretty hopeless."

C: Seem to be hopeless.

T: Uh hmm. Doesn't seem to, do anything or help really at all.

C: And I don't think this hospital ever done me any good yet. 'Cause I think I got worse since I been here.

T: "I felt really worse. I guess especially since I had read last night about this other fellow."

C: Oh, I've always thought that.

T: Um hmm.

C: Guess that was a couple of weeks ago. I haven't gotten any better.

T: Hmm.

C: I'm . . . I just don't care for anything now.

T: Not much interested in anything. Don't care what happens or . . . doesn't happen.

C: Don't care if I live today or die tomorrow.

T: Nothing really has any meaning or purpose. (Pause)

C: Seems funny that . . . the whole world seems all funny.

T: Sort of distant or . . .

C: Don't even seem like it's real.

T: Uh hmm. Sort of like seeing a movie or what?

C: No, it ain't like seeing a movie. You know it's real but you don't feel it.

T: Umhmm. "I know this is all there is, that this is, this is really real, but it don't seem that way."

C: Seems so crazy. (Laughs)

T: Umm. Logically it doesn't make sense but it sure seems that way.

C: Don't make no sense to me. I don't feel like, like one person's got, uh, like he should say, "You get in here and spend the rest of your life in prison." I don't see how he can judge another person like that.

T: Uh hmm. How can one person make this decision?

Example B:

C: (Coughs) There are a lot of things that, that hurt. Yet I know I shouldn't . . . let them bother me because some way they seem foolish, but in other ways they carry a great deal of weight. (Pause)

T: Um hmm. You know that there's an irrational part of it, but knowing that doesn't prevent you from feeling that.

C: No. Nor does it stop me from undergoing the compulsions. (Pause)

T: That was an example, and even talking about it . . .

C: It just makes my heart beat fast. I just feel myself going up.

T: Were you ever afraid that you might do something like that? Try and recall . . .

C: Well, just the thought of it frightens me . . . so much. It's like the, I think I told you one time, it's like playing a game, only you don't want to play it. That every thought would come into your mind . . . successively each time. Then there's a counterpart. I mean you can, you can't have any good feelings without having bad . . .

T: . . . without having bad feelings.

C: And then . . .

T: . . . then have the reverse of that, is if you have a bad feeling. You try to think something good, or you try to do something that gets rid of the bad.

C: Well, I, I never get that far. About the best I get is the bad feeling and then I have to undergo my washing, or (Pause) . . .

T: Um hmm.

C: Dr. Smith told me one time . . . I don't believe it . . . that it was due to the . . . the church . . . the ceremonies, involved the Catholic Church. Now I, I . . .

T: Who's Dr. Smith?

C: He was down to the County.

T: Umm.

C: And, uh, that seems kind of (Pause) . . . I think he was a little bit queer, I don't know.

T: It doesn't seem to make sense to you that part of it, or whatever it was that he meant by that.

C: Oh, he told me another one too. That people (clears throat), that unconsciously try to keep from giving out to a doctor, you know, that sounds like a psychiatrist, generally have constipation, and those people that, uh, give out pretty freely, have good running bowels or loose bowels. Now that, hah, does that make any sense to you? Is there . . .

T: The important thing is that it didn't make any sense to you.

C: No it didn't. Just the same as . . .

T: Or at least that didn't give you an answer or clue for ah, what going on around here, impulse.

C: That's right. But he, as I say, said it was again the church, the, the ceremonies, and all that, ah, you know how a Catholic Church operates.

T: Umm. (Pause)

C: Oh there's been some lulus. Dr. Jones said he thought it due . . . to my marrying against my father's wishes. That didn't strike a responding cord either.

T: Yes, a lot of people have suggested a lot of different things, but you've never hit upon anything yourself that makes sense to you.

C: No, I haven't . . . except for the last couple times in here talkin' to you, I don't know if it's helped, maybe some.

T: Yah, I certainly get this feeling, that you're getting close to some things.

C: Well, I sure hope so.

T: You're kind of ah, grasping at some things, You haven't quite got them yet, but you're close.

C: If I could get the beginning of it, I think it would help a great deal.

T: It's though that there's something there that's been forgotten, or . . .

STAGE 8.

Active intrapersonal exploration. The patient is following a "connected" chain of thoughts in focusing upon himself and actively exploring himself. He may be discovering new feelings, new aspects of himself. He is actively exploring his feelings, his values, his perceptions of others, his relationships, his fears, his turmoil, and his life-choices.

Example A:

C: (She is relating experiences in Germany during World War II) I don't want to exaggerate but, why, you could have killed for some things! And the pendulum was always swinging. You never knew. You'd steal carrots to eat because you were always so dreadfully hungry. There was no clothing, no fuel . . . and the cold . . . (Voice soft, reflects a great deal of concentration) They had . . . they always announced the dead, those who had been killed in the war. And one always went and read the lists. I don't recall exactly where they were . . . (Pause) It was conducive to think that life was . . .

T: Unendurable, and getting used to the, that way of living.

C: Yes, yes, uh hum, I had no . . . I was not . . . I have a very close girlfriend who shared my things but I was not kind and tender with my brothers. I remember one thing that really shames me still. I was to watch out for them, and my younger brother fell and bruised his head one day, and I just pulled his cap over that. Really, really, but . . . but my excuse I think I can say was that nobody ever treated me lovingly. At least I think that.

T: It was a hard life and you have to be hard. This is what you knew.

C: I think I was harder than I really had to be but I was just, ah, hard . . .

T: Because you hadn't been taught to be soft and loving.

C: Yes, ah, yes. I don't know whether you teach somebody to be, to be . . . do you?

T: Well, you haven't experienced it?

C: I feel that way now, toward my family, my husband and children . . . I can . . . love them.

Example B:

C: I think, ah, ah, I think you are probably right and, and, and, I wouldn't believe it. But I have the results and I owe the results to you. (Pauses, makes a series of tentative starts, then continues) Sometimes it may, must be a process of getting better that you make out of something that you hear, like—like an attack that galvanizes you into action, because in the end this is what I must do myself and I, and ah, ah . . . I know the tender subtleties that are involved and I know the immense vulnerability of any person. I didn't think I could hurt as much and I didn't think that could be, ah . . . take the bite of others as well as their bark. I talked to my husband yesterday about mother's death. It was very lonely and very stupid in a poorly run hospital on a Sunday afternoon where they just sort of gave her no care at all and I, I said to my husband how terrible, how terrible that was and he pointed out rather patiently to me; he said, "Well, your brother brought her there in the afternoon and then she died four or five hours later." And that nobody was there was unfortunate but basically somebody was there, and, and, and my brother and my sister-in-law were as concerned as you would have been, only they were told there was no . . . danger at all, and so, in the meantime, my mother had died. And I found myself so gratefully holding on to this explanation. Why I am unable to find the positive explanation, I don't know, but I am constantly unable to look at the positive side. Yet I think I can learn it . . . (pause) certainly if meaninglessness doesn't do it then I think willingness will do it. And, and, I thought, I thought now here he knows I have a problem and we not only talk about . . .

T: I think I was trying to say to you something about this . . .

C: And don't you think I can find out? I mean beyond the words are . . . is . . . this universe where . . .

T: Yes, . . .

STAGE 9.

Stage 9 is an extension of the scale to be used in those rare moments when the patient is deeply exploring and being himself, or in those rare moments when he achieves a significant new perceptual base for his view of himself or the world. A rating at this stage is to be used at the judge's discretion.

CORRECTIONS

The following corrections should be applied to each basic rating where appropriate.

A. If a therapist is doing the talking but is speaking for the patient (i.e., depth reflection) and the patient is "with" him, then give the segment the rating based on the way the therapist is talking and subtract one full stage.

B. If a segment fits a given stage but does not clearly include all elements of the preceding lower stages (for example, Stage 7 lacking spontaneity), then subtract one-half stage for each missing element.

C. Add one-half stage for "personally private" material. "Personally private" material is any communication which thereby makes the individual more vulnerable. It may be information given that could be thrown back at the patient by a hostile person in a very hurtful way. It thus has the potential of being personally damaging material.

D. Add one full stage for discussion of "personally damning" material. This is material that would be revealed only in a safe, accepting, and nonthreatening close relationship. Said in any other context it would hold the threat that the other person could "throw it in his face," which might be catastrophically damaging. It would almost invariably involve the patient's making a "damaging admission" about personal weaknesses, failures, or "terrible" things that he has thought, felt, said, or done.

CHAPTER 6 TRAINING IN COUNSELING AND PSYCHOTHERAPY: AN INTRODUCTION

THE field of counseling and psychotherapy has too often seemed reluctant to make systematic inquiries into the process and outcome of training. Indeed, very few researchers have made even an attempt to assess dimensions of training that are related to the patient's therapeutic outcome. In the instances where rigorous attempts have been made to assess traditional training programs and their relation to client outcomes, the results have sometimes been equivocal if not negative.

Let us again consider briefly one recent project, a case in point. Bergin and Solomon (1963) sought to assess the therapeutic level of functioning of final-year, post-internship graduate students in a traditional program. They found the students' levels of empathic understanding in this well-established and traditional program to be positively correlated with the outcome assessments of the students' patients. These levels, were, to be sure, remarkably low, suggesting perhaps the benign or possibly even deteriorative consequences of traditional graduate training. Their study is another in a long and growing list of studies substantiating the efficacy of dimensions such as empathy. However, Bergin and Solomon also found their ratings of empathy to be slightly negatively correlated with both (1) the students' grade-point averages and, more important, (2) the students' practicum grade averages.

In the following pages the authors will attempt to explore the processes of counseling and psychotherapy and their training programs in order to demonstrate what it is that we know with some degree of certitude concerning efficacious treatment and training.

A few quick passages may give us an historical perspective on therapeutic practice and set the stage for the rest of this book:

> This history approach is based upon the assumption that the task of psychotherapy is to explore with the patient those of his life experiences which have contributed to the development of symptoms, and to help him achieve insight into the meaning of these symptoms. In general, insight is considered to be the intellectual comprehension of unconscious attitudes, fantasies and drives, and it is therefore considered important to dig out a good deal of repressed content of the patient's thinking. It is interesting that many psychiatrists who have had no training in psychoanalysis accept so completely the analytic doctrine of the therapeutic value of bringing the unconscious to consciousness. What is of more interest, of course, is the appropriate application of the doctrine to the problem of psychotherapy. The practical consequences of this theory of method is that it creates in the patient's mind the prejudice that he

will get well only if he can obtain this kind of insight. It commits the therapist to active probing and interpreting until both therapist and patient become discouraged. If the patient has obtained any benefit in the process, it will not have been the result of the psychiatrist's theory, but of the sustaining relationship which common work on the problem has afforded the patient. . . . The successful practice of psychotherapy implies an attitude toward the patient which might greatly enrich the art of medical practice. It implies an acceptance of the patient as a person—his interests, desires, strivings, and feelings; a recognition of his right to find his own solution of problems; a respect for emotionally determined attitudes toward his illness and toward the physician; and a willingness to work with the patient in terms of his own way of looking at the world and at other people. (Coleman, 1947, pp. 622-624)

Concerning training for psychotherapy specifically, Whitaker (1949) prescribed the following:

Teaching psychotherapy differs specifically from every other type of medical teaching. One teaches attitudes rather than facts and that which is intuitive, abstract and personal becomes more significant than the factual or historical. Part of the confusion in the present day teaching of psychiatry arises from the effort to teach psychopathology and dynamics concurrently with teaching the process of a therapeutic doctor-patient relationship. (p. 899)

One of many significant passages from the 1965 *Annual Review of Psychology* chapter on psychotherapy will prove meaningful in relation to the quotes from Coleman and Whitaker.

Feifel and Eells (1963) found that therapists and patients differ in their perception of both process and outcome. Following successful therapy, therapists perceived *behavioral* changes in the relief of patients' symptoms and improvement in social relationships; whereas patients reported changes (subjective) in insight, self-understanding, and self-confidence. Regarding therapy process, patients underlined, as helpful, the opportunity to *talk over* problems and the human (warmth) characteristics of the psychotherapist, whereas therapists highlighted therapeutic *technique* and support to the patient as most beneficial. Congruent with these reported differences in patient-therapist perceptions and responses is the report by Kamin and Caughlan (1963). These authors interviewed 64 clinic patients in their homes one to two years after termination of therapy. The patients' comments make it clear that patients construe psychotherapy differently than do therapists. Patients want a friend, in Schofield's sense. Therapists tend to be stiff, formal, and technique-oriented. Those who are human and natural are rated the best therapists and, interestingly, obtained the best outcome ratings from their patients. This finding appears consistent with the findings reported by Truax (1963) for the Rogers group. (Matarazzo, 1965, pp. 199-200)

Let us briefly quote a few more conclusions from Matarazzo's *Annual Review* chapter on psychotherapy:

. . . Freudian psychoanalysis clearly is no longer the most dominant theme in psychotherapy theory, practice, or research. (p. 217)

> Those psychotherapists who heretofore have seemed to make a fetish of such concepts as the process of psychotherapy, or who exalted the *transference* relationship to a position of almost religious pre-eminence will learn, to their surprise I believe, that such mystical phenomena are probably little more than what occurs in most, if not all, social interactions; and that the same *general* laws and principles which are relevant to the study of other behavior also apply to the study of psychotherapy. (p. 218)

> I end this chapter with a strong personal conviction that research in psychotherapy soon again will become attractive to young investigators. Now that the mystery and aura are being removed the psychotherapy relationship is being looked on again by varieties of researchers as fruitful a phenomenon for investigation as are the parent-child, peer-peer, teacher-student, experimenter-subject, and other important human relationships. Also, importantly, it is being seen in its true perspective; i.e., no more important than any of these other relationships. (p. 219)

The first two articles (Coleman's and Whitaker's) pre-date the third (Matarazzo) by nearly 20 years. The significance of the messages of Coleman and Whitaker, the medical emphasis of which has been placed in historical perspective by the efforts of a generation of nonmedical practitioners, has not been diminished by the proliferation of therapeutic and training practices which have followed it in time but not necessarily in direction. Its significance is underscored by Matarazzo's concluding sentence to the review paragraph: "One wonders when psychotherapy theorists, teachers, and researchers will acknowledge the full implications of these findings."

We shall begin our chapter where Matarazzo ends his review of the literature in psychotherapy—with an exploration of those current studies relating to therapeutic training and outcome.

SOURCES OF LEARNING IN TRAINING

The detailed report by Ekstein and Wallerstein (1958) was an important contribution since it gave an excellent description of training at an important psychoanalytic center. The teaching method is closely tied to psychoanalytic theory, with the therapist's primary use of personal analysis and controlled observation of himself while attempting analysis of a patient. The approach to training is well described, but no effort has thus far been made to substantiate the value of any aspects of the training approach by research findings.

Rogers (1957a) has presented a very explicit approach to training, involving (1) listening to tape recordings of experienced therapists, (2) role-playing between trainees; (3) observation of live demonstrations of technique and approach by the supervisor; (4) participation in personal therapy, and (5) recording of interviews conducted by the trainees. Above all, Rogers has stressed the need for a teaching atmosphere where the supervisor offers facilitative therapeutic conditions. The approach to training suggested in this book (Chapter 7) draws heavily upon Rogers' early formulations, but attempts to add elements of a didactic approach without doing violence to the more experiential aspects stressed by such theorists as Rogers.

A number of naturalistic studies have attempted to determine what it is that instructors tend to emphasize in their activities with therapists in training. Adams, Ham, Mawardi, Scali and Weisman (1964) have presented a most interesting training process breakdown which, though medical in emphasis, might well serve as a basis for the definition and assessment of clinic or training objectives. Among the activities stressed were (1) an expressed concern for the learning environment, including especially the potential value of positive faculty-student relationships, and (2) recognizing and dealing with the student's strengths and needs, particularly in regard to his evaluation. In casting light on the teaching of psychoanalysis, Fleming and Benedek (1964) offer illumination for the highly complex supervisory process of therapeutic practices in general: ". . . the learning tasks for the student are highly personal and individualized. Success depends on the student's ability to develop and use his own personality as an instrument in the treatment process" (p. 71). From an an analysis of the material from their own supervisory processes, Fleming and Benedek identified and classified the activities which might occur in the supervisory session. Acknowledging that "the supervisory focus changes depending upon the needs of the patient, the competence of the student analyst, and on the pedagogical choices of the supervisor," the authors developed a model chart centering around (1) the teacher-supervisor's overall teaching aims to develop the student as a therapeutic instrument, (2) the supervisor's pedagogical diagnosis calculated to cultivate self-observation, insight and awareness in the student, and (3) the teaching targets toward which the supervisor directs his teaching maneuvers in relation to the motivation for the trainee's behavior and its effect on the patient and the supervisor.

Educators who have been active in the teaching of counseling and psychotherapy have become involved in the controversial issue of *teaching* versus *treating* the student. Perhaps as a reflection of their more dominant and assertive role in the system of things, "medical educators apparently still prefer focus on the doctor-patient relationship and to avoid unnecessary involvement with the student-doctor as a patient" (Lester, Gussen, Yamamoto and West, 1962, p. 29). The medical profession has focused principally upon the didactic aspects of the treatment process. Schwartz and Abel (1955) agree with Wolberg (1954) that supervision is a teacher-student relationship and not in any way analagous to that of therapist and patient. Romano (1961a, 1961b), although acknowledging the likelihood of unrest and discomfort in his students, has made clear his mandate that the "ethos of teaching program should fundamentally be pedagogic and not therapeutic in design" (1961a, p. 95). For Romano, the fundamental emphasis in training should be upon "rational understanding." Lester and his co-workers (1962) are perhaps more open in pointing up the teaching-treating conflict that nevertheless points in the same direction: "During the coming years an attempt should be made to structure the student's attitude concerning himself, his patients and their progress. Without some systematic attempt to evaluate and reverse teaching methods, little progress can be made in our efforts to help future physicians to understand the vicissitudes of the doctor-patient relationship" (p. 31).

On the other hand, perhaps because of its less dominant and more passive role, social work has tended to place greater emphasis upon the supervisor-supervisee relationship. Boehm (1961), Towles (1961) and Wessel (1961) have focused upon facilitating in the student an openness to his own experiences. The focus is upon the student's own personal development in the context of a therapeutic atmosphere calculated to cultivate the essential self-knowledge which frees the student to become his most facilitative self.

Clinical and counseling psychology and education, especially in the counseling aspect, have found themselves in conflict, perhaps reflecting their own role conflicts so promenent in practice and concern. On the one hand, Korner and Brown (1952) offer direct control, while on the other, the views of Rogers (1957b) emphasize the experiential base of learning as do those of Boehm, Towles and Wessel. Arbuckle (1963) and Patterson (1964) prominently display the conflicts underlying their training orientations. Arbuckle first distinguishes the role of teacher, as one involving ideas and products, from the role of the counselor, which involves people and "change" and "process." He then proceeds to make a case for the necessary consistency in counselor and educator and then makes a further jump to the necessity for a nonevaluative relationship, finally concluding that the counselor-educator's primary concern is to help the student-counselor to learn about himself. Patterson does us a service in pointing up the implicit behavioral change that is being asked for in the "influencing situation" of therapeutic training, but confuses us by concluding that the supervision is neither counseling nor teaching but is "closer to counseling."

Strauss (1950) has recommended having the student sit in while the instructor conducts short-term therapeutic sessions with patients. Lott (1952, 1957) and Adams (1958) have emphasized the learning virtues of multiple psychotherapy in which both supervisor and trainee work directly and actively with the patient. Korner and Brown (1952) and Ward (1961, 1962) have conducted "three-cornered therapy" by means of electronic preceptors, during which the supervisor was "judiciously" present for the trainee alone through the "mechanical third ear." All have offered anecdotal evidence sufficient to warrant further and systematic investigation.

Fleming and Hamburg (1958) have not gone quite to the length of full and direct participation but have instead developed the classroom training technique which they call the "dynaminetic interview," during which the instructor plays the patient and the trainee the therapist. They believe that such an approach fulfills the following critical aspects of learning in training without jeopardizing the therapist-patient relationship: (1) there is firsthand information available to the students; (2) the thinking of therapist and patient are available; (3) there is maximum participation by the class; (4) the impact of the therapist's interventions are directly known; (5) the modifications in the therapist's approach are directly known; (6) there is economy of time; and (7) there is avoidance of harm to the patient. Flint and Rioch (1963), in the context of the lay therapist training program of Rioch *et al.* (1963), have similarly carried off an experiment in teaching family dynamics using the vicarious experience of tape recordings along with observation of interviews and therapy and more traditional and cognitive kinds of learning.

Herzberg, Inkley and Adams (1960), struggling to develop an evaluation approach that would allow the trainee to experience "the necessity of approaching the patient as a total person, with empathy but without emotional exploitation of the patient" (p. 666), conducted systematic observations of what the trainee does in an open-ended "critical incident" study. The authors describe a procedure in which they request clinic supervisors to describe the last time they observed a student behave or perform "in such a manner that you felt he deserved to be praised (criticized) for what he did." This evaluation procedure encouraged on-the-spot specifics of student performance rather than the more traditional total recall global assessments. Salzman and Romano (1963) have developed a systematic method of evaluating performance which involves a 9-point rating scale assessing the trainee's level of responsibility, knowledge, psychological perceptiveness, relations with the patient, relatives and staff, quality of write-up, and personal growth.

SOME INTEGRATIVE APPROACHES

More specifically integrative programs have been evident in the literature. Enelow, Adler and Manning (1964) and Adams (1958) have focused on at least two sources of learning: (1) the direct work of student and supervisor in three-cornered therapy with client; (2) the facilitative contextual atmosphere in which this teaching takes place. Fleming and her associates (1953, 1958, 1964) have attempted to describe the sources of learning in training to include not simply "corrective learning" and "creative learning," but also "imitative learning." In addition, the naturalistic studies cited above by Adams, et al. (1964) and Fleming and Benedek (1964) offer illumination for the highly complex supervisory process.

Consistent with Fleming's conceptual breakdown of the sources of learning in training, but employing different terminology, is the work carried on at Kentucky, Arkansas, and Massachusetts (Berenson, Carkhuff and Myrus, 1965; Carkhuff and Truax, 1965a, 1965b; Truax, Carkhuff and Douds, 1964; Truax and Silber, 1966). This work is a logical extension of the extensive research support for the therapeutic dimensions of empathy, warmth and genuineness (and concreteness or specificity of expression), using both professional and nonprofessional trainees. The research scales assessing these conditions in conjunction with the additional "cross-cult" process variables, such as client depth of self-exploration, are didactically taught in the context of a relationship offering high levels of these facilitative conditions in order to encourage student self-exploration and experimentation. Concurrent with the program, quasi-group therapy sessions are held to cope with students' difficulties in implementing the constructs involved. Thus, three sources of learning are operating at once, and the necessary consistency of the teaching, the experiential base, and the role-model is established.

Thus far we have dealt primarily with the training practices, *i.e.,* the training processes per se, for the very good reason that very little of the training literature incorporates assessments even approaching meaningful process or outcome criteria. The pioneering research study in the field of training grew out of a counseling course at the Chicago Counseling Center in 1946, Blocksma and Porter (1947) assessed counselor behavior before and after the six-week training course for 37 trainees. The intensive training lasted at least eight hours a day and involved (1) lectures, (2) group discussion and quasi-group therapy, (3) practice in counseling, (4) listening to tape recordings of experienced therapists, (5) informal discussion, and (6) opportunity for personal therapy. Marked and significant changes in their therapy behavior before and after training led toward their becoming more nondirective, more able to allow the client to evaluate himself, and more able to think *with* rather than *about* the client. Those who showed the most change tended to have fewer dropouts among their clients during the first year after training.

Thus it seemed clear that at least some of the six major training activities, if not all, were effective to a measurable and significant degree.

A quite recent study of changes in medical students taking clerkships in psychiatry has been reported by R. G. Matarazzo, Phillips, Wiens and Saslow (1965). The students were closely supervised in a practicum arrangement and were asked to read Rogers (1942), Wolberg (1954) and other texts. After training, the trainees showed significant changes in their interview behavior, tending to make fewer errors (defined in terms of the readings) such as interruptions, asking of yes-no questions, etc.; and to talk less and allow the patient to talk more. Also of importance in their studies was the finding that improvement in interview method occurred primarily within the first month of training. Basically, the changes had to do with minimizing the trainee as an *obstacle* to the patients' telling about himself. These changes, however, did not measurably translate into changes in patient behavior.

The impact of a number of shorter-term programs has been important. Beginning with the inception of six- to eight-week (National Defense Education Act) guidance institutes (Dugan, 1960; Fossett, 1960) a number of meaningful quasi-outcome studies have been made possible (Demos, 1964; Demos and Zuwaylif, 1963; Hansen and Barker, 1964; Jones, 1963; Munger and Johnson, 1960; Webb and Harris, 1963). The change indices have been primarily attitudinal in nature, with the most consistent finding being the increased tendency for trainees to make more "understanding" and less evaluative responses. The efforts of Demos and of Hansen and Barker are perhaps most noteworthy because they attempt to assess therapeutic or facilitative dimensions which have been related to the client's improved functioning in previous and extensive research. Demos found that excerpts from the short-term vocational-educational counseling tapes of the ten NDEA Institute counselors who were regarded as most successful on a variety of criteria were rated significantly higher on empathy, positive regard, and respect than tapes from the ten counselors rated least successful. In a variation of this research involving the conditions of empathy, warmth, and genuineness assessed by different measures, Hansen and Barker found "that when conditions are perceived as 'therapeutic' by the trainee, he will allow himself to participate more deeply in intrapersonal exploration, i.e., higher experiencing, less being defensive."

Although most professional training programs are reluctant to investigate their outcomes, a number of lay-counselor training programs, in addition to those of Kentucky, Arkansas, and Massachusetts, have concerned themselves with their pragmatic consequences. Because of various limitations on obtaining professional help in Australia, lay persons with a full experience of life, including especially successful marital and other relationships, who appear to have a sincere regard and acceptance for others and themselves, and who appear intelligent, warm and empathic as judged by interviews complemented by testing, have been trained to become marital counselors (Harvey, 1964). With training two evenings per week for between 15 months to two years, these lay counselors have brought about marital-counseling case outcomes that are outstanding when compared with those of their professional counterparts.

In addition, two other lay-training programs involving related conditions were conducted by Mendel and Rapport (1963) and Appleby (1963), following on the foosteps of the earlier work by Tudor (1952) and Freeman, Cameron, and McGhie (1958). Although the characteristics of lay therapists were not measured by Appleby, he found significant improvement in experimental groups of chronic schizophrenic patients who were treated by hospital aides functioning as models to provide the "psychological conditions for stable structure, identification and intense involvement." Perhaps even more striking, Mendel and Rapport presented data from a group of 166 chronically disturbed female patients. Their findings indicated that 70 per cent of the women were maintained outside the hospital at a minimally adequate level of functioning during a 51-month period of observation by being provided with monthly contacts with nonprofessional persons focusing upon activities and perceptions "in specific and *concrete action terms.*" The treatment results of the non-professionals compared very favorably with those of their supervising psychiatrists.

Still on the topic of lay-therapist training programs, we should mention the work of Rioch et al. (1963) whose well-known training program clearly demonstrated that specially selected, bright, sophisticated and educated housewives could learn from very intensive and long-term psychoanalytic training (similar to that involved in graduate schools with good practicum programs) and could be as well regarded by supervisors and other "experts" as those trained in regular graduate school. Again we have the traditional assessment of a program traditional in selection and orientation, on which the work of Bergin and Solomon and of Weiss and others have cast doubt. Although its replicability, generalizability and efficacy may be questioned, those concerned with the ever-growing mental health needs should become acquainted with this important demonstration project.

THE PRODUCTS

A variety of attempts have been made to characterize the kind of a person the therapist should be. In a very real sense the description of this person might well constitute a statement of the goals of therapeutic training. Notable, as well as representative, among these attempts to describe the effective therapist is the description given by Schwartz and Abel (1955):

> . . . The school, teachers and supervisors must allow for individual styles in psychotherapy. Acceptance of differences in therapist as well as in patients is to be expected. The psychotherapist, then, must learn to tolerate individual life-styles in patients and in others. He has a broad cultural background and is not rigidly culture-bound. He is not shocked by any behavior of patients or their families which is characteristic of their but not the therapist's background. He must be able to see his patients as people capable of learning, growing and changing.
>
> The psychotherapist should have sufficiently overcome his personal anxieties so that they do not interfere with his spontaneity in the therapeutic interaction. Being warm and friendly is his central personality trait. His anxieties may have been resolved in his personal analysis or by interaction

and self-correction in the course of his own life and therapeutic work. Although he may become involved, he does not become defensive and block independent movements of his patients. The psychotherapist is not compelled to take the lead and restrict the patient's freedom, or to solve his own problems and seek fulfillment through the patient. The patient is permitted to try to solve his own problems in his own way, to gratify his own needs without having to satisfy those of the therapist.

The . . . therapist understands the patient's communication and does not respond only to their manifest content. He can accept and understand unconscious processes and help make them conscious. [He] can see connections in the patient's presentation, life history, fantasy, and patterns of behavior in life and in therapy.

The therapist should have the ability to learn from his own mistakes. He must have self-critical capacity. He is not rigid nor does he think he knows everything. On the other hand, his functioning is not chaotic or lacking in surety. He is able to relate to his patients without becoming over-anxious. If patients tend to become dependent upon him, he does not infantilize them by being over-protective. Hostility and other feelings of the patient can be tolerated. The therapist needs to have the humility not to be compelled to treat the patients outside his competence. Not every therapist can help every patient. The analyst must be willing to let patients go elsewhere, when he is convinced that he is no longer able to help.

The psychotherapist must be able to handle his own hostility and his problems with authority. He does have to struggle with authority for power. He has overcome his resistance to criticism and accepts it, when it is constructive. At the same time, he does not give up his critical judgment and accept all criticism by authority, as if it were a dictum . . . (pp. 259-260)

It is interesting to note the consistency of some of these themes throughout *all* treatment processes. For example, Aring (1961), in defining his nine critical precepts of neurology, suggests above all: "Know thyself. The stage of 'knowing' where one is able to examine oneself entirely without fear or favor, perhaps is not achievable; but there is no better guarantee of becoming more useful to patients than the continuing attempt to do so" (p. 589).

It can be readily seen that the hoped-for product of our training programs is not simply a technician skilled in the employment of a variety of techniques—although he certainly must be that. He is more, much more. He is, not unlike the hoped-for client products of our sessions of counseling and psychotherapy, an open and flexible person possessed with a great amount of self-awareness and self-knowledge, sensitive and attuned to receiving and communicating vital messages with other persons. To pursue the analogy with clients further, the description of our trainee products is quite congruent with the goals for our counseling clients and therapy patients. Our goals *in training as well as therapy* are geared toward providing the kind of complex which will allow our cultural concept of the healthy person to emerge: a person who lives effectively both with himself and others.

Although there is a great consistency in the development of the goals in training, it has become apparent that there is at the same time a proliferation of orientations and techniques, some quite confusing, calculated to complement, operationalize and actualize these goals. One is forced to wonder about the effect of the biases concerning these sources and techniques of learning. A rational theory does not always dictate a predictable source. For example, the authoritarian teacher-supervisor whom we have all known, or will come to know, may have a well-developed and systematic theoretical stance underlying his pedagogy. However, the model that he provides of the more "knowing" person in interpersonal learning processes may be a better predictor of the modes of treatment of his supervisees and, indeed, their very effectiveness. The student's very experience—and often it is a retarding one—may have a great deal of effect on his effectiveness or ineffectiveness in his therapeutic encounters.

Educators and supervisors concerned with counseling and psychotherapy have traditionally focused upon one of two principle approaches to training. In the first, the *didactic-intellectual,* or pedagogic, approach, the emphasis is upon the direct teaching, structuring, or shaping of the thinking and responding of the trainee in accord with the teacher's belief system concerning what dimensions of the therapeutic process are most conducive to constructive change. The second approach is *relationship-oriented,* or experientially based, in the sense that the trainer provides a free, safe and secure atmosphere in which the trainee can come to experience and know himself more fully, can experiment with different approaches, and finally can evolve into the most effective practitioner that he can be. Traditionally, these approaches have operated to the exclusion of one another. However, recent developments in training practices have led to the emphasis upon more realistic and meaningfully integrative programs in which the teacher actively "shapes" trainee behavior in accordance with the best available evidence on effective practices *in the context* of a free and open relationship. The trainee-products, then, have an opportunity to come to know themselves more fully in interaction with the learning practices which are currently most effective. In addition, the trainees have a model of a genuine human who shares his own belief system in a therapeutic context.

SECTION II TOWARD AN INTEGRATED DIDACTIC AND EXPERIENTIAL APPROACH TO TRAINING

EVEN with fully adequate research and theoretic bases for effective therapeutic practice, how can we translate these learnings into practice? What constitutes a minimally adequate training approach for learning the effective practice of counseling or psychotherapy?

We believe we have at least a beginning answer. The approach to training presented in this section is closely tied to the research findings and theoretical views presented in the preceding chapters of this book. This approach is an attempt to translate research and theory into effective practice by focusing on the experiential and didactic elements concurrently. The didactic elements lean heavily on the research scales (from Chapter 2 and in Chapter 5)—thus we have tried to turn the research tools directly into the training tools.

The critical question is "To what extent does the approach detailed throughout the following chapters succeed in producing more effective therapists?" Although we wish we had more complete evidence available, several studies reviewed here indicate a significant degree of success, both in the training of graduate students in clinical and counseling psychology and in the training of nonprofessional "lay counselors." It is on the basis of these beginning research findings that we recommend the present training approach for potential use with both professional and subprofessional trainees. Indeed, we believe it to be of potentially significant value for the training of people engaged in any form of helping relationships, as a method of learning the therapeutic interpersonal skills involved in communicating high levels of accurate empathy, nonpossessive warmth and genuineness.

Chapter 7 is intended to specify the ingredients of effective training for therapeutic practice. The research evidence and theory pointing to essential ingredients in training is reviewed, as are the current research findings which suggest the utility of the present training approach. This chapter goes further to present in capsule form the outline of an approach to training aimed at integrating didactic and experiential elements. This chapter, then, serves as a contextual base for the following chapters (Chapters 8 through 13), which discuss in greater detail aspects of training to develop the interpersonal skills of accurate empathy, nonpossessive warmth and genuineness.

Chapter 8 presents an overview of how this theoretic view is translated into actual training practice. The focus is on the operational specifics and sequencing of training, and the attempts to provide a classroom atmosphere or experiential base in which high therapeutic conditions are offered to the trainees themselves.

Chapter 9 focuses upon the structured experiential component of training—the quasi-group therapy sessions. Transcripts from two such actual quasi-group therapy groups are presented in an effort to describe the clinical phenomena of group therapy for trainees and illustrate common themes and areas of self-exploration typical of many such groups.

Chapter 10 explores more fully the clinical and theoretic meaning of the concept of accurate empathic understanding as it occurs in therapeutic practice, what it is and what it is not. An attempt is made to specify attitudinal and behavioral correlates and preconditions of the highly empathic therapist. The concept of "resistance" and the role of anxiety in the therapeutic process are discussed as providing cues for empathic understanding. Finally, empathy training proper and its implementation, based on the research scales presented in Chapter 2, is discussed in detail.

Chapter 11 specifies more fully the theoretic and clinical meaning of nonpossessive warmth, and discusses the interaction of the phenomena of transference and repression with adequate communication of warmth to the client. The use of "warmth training" and the application of the research scale presented in Chapter 2 to the training program is discussed and illustrated.

Chapter 12 focuses upon a further exploration of the meanings of genuineness or authenticity as applied to the counselor or therapist. Aspects of attempts at "genuineness training" are discussed and illustrated.

Chapter 13 presents an application of the training program: Dr. Dickenson, who was a trainee in the program, gives a clinical case report of group counseling focused on a single client and the extent to which his attempts to provide effective therapeutic conditions succeed and fail. This chapter thus provides a transition from beginning training to movement toward becoming a mature counselor or therapist. Dickenson gives a clinical example of a trainee's beginning attempt to apply both the didactic and experiential aspects of the training to actual practice—to his own process of becoming an effective counselor.

CHAPTER 7 TOWARD EFFECTIVE TRAINING: A THEORETIC VIEW [7]

SUPERVISION for training programs in the fields of counseling and psychotherapy has traditionally been formulated in terms of either a didactic-intellectual approach with emphasis upon theoretic learning, or an experiential-accepting approach with emphasis upon the trainee's personal growth and development through his own experiences. The present effort attempts to develop an approach to supervision or training that integrates both basic approaches into a program whose focus is on the implementation of the therapeutic conditions of accurate empathy, nonpossessive warmth and genuineness. This approach concentrates on shaping of the trainee's behavior so that he will communicate to patients and clients higher levels of these three basic therapeutic ingredients. However, making the communication of these ingredients a genuine communication of real aspects of the therapist himself requires an equally important experiential development. If the approach were purely theoretic and didactic, even under the best circumstances we would probably produce therapists and counselors who provided "canned" empathy rather than a deep personal knowing of the client. It is this sense that the training process is a learning process that takes place within the context of a growth-producing interpersonal relationship that is free of threat and that facilitates self-exploration.

Although it seems certain that a highly effective therapist must have some specific knowledge of the client population with which he intends to work, some grasp of social phenomena, community organization, human growth and development, norms and their predictive deviations, inhibition and creativity, the likely antecedents of psychopathology and their consequences, and in general a large storehouse of "expert" knowledge, *he is first and foremost an expert in interpersonal relationships*. He is the person who can induce trust, facilitate the client's self-revelations, self-discovery, and self-integration, and thus the difficult process of decision-making and acting in the real world.

Although many theorists have recognized for some time that a prospective therapist must first learn the skill of effective interpersonal relationships (i.e., become highly skilled in accurate empathic understanding and

7. The present chapter includes material from a paper by Charles B. Truax, Robert R. Carkhuff and John Douds published separately as "Toward an integration of the didactic and experiential approaches to training in counseling and psychotherapy." *Journal of Counseling Psychology*, 1964, 11, *3*, pp. 240-247.

the communication of nonpossessive warmth and genuineness), this has often not been translated into a focused training program. It may well be that the lack of efficacy of most counseling and psychotherapy training programs lies not in the method of training (didactic or experiential) but in what is emphasized. Most training programs parallel closely most books on psychotherapy: the interest and attention is upon the patient, his psychodynamics and his unconscious, preconscious, and conscious thoughts and feelings. Such a program would well equip a student for being a patient. It is not at all clear how it would prepare him for being a therapist. Too often, after such training, the beginning therapist still wonders what kind of things to say, how to say them, what voice qualities to use—in short: *how to relate when he encounters the real person,* not the textbook client or patient.

Although a number of views of how to train effective counselors and therapists were considered, evidence for the efficacy of existing training procedures is virtually nonexistent. Surely, since accurate empathy, nonpossessive warmth and genuineness appear to be central ingredients (common to a wide variety of theories and even more central to effective practice in counseling and psychotherapy), training programs should at least initially focus most of their attention on the understanding and implementation of these therapeutic conditions.

Three recent studies throw some light on the question of the relationship between existing training programs and the ability to communicate high levels of accurate empathic understanding to a patient or client. The first, a study by Bergin and Solomon (1963), studied the level of communicated accurate empathy in tape-recorded psychotherapy sessions from 18 post-internship students at one of the major training institutions in clinical psychology. It should be mentioned that the authors did find a correlation between rated empathy and client outcome: the clients of those trainees rated highest demonstrated the most constructive change. The scale measuring the level of empathy was a slight modification (inserting an additional stage between Stages 2 and 3) of the Accurate Empathy scale used in the majority of research studies reviewed earlier. Even so, in their data comparing six supervisory groups, the actual range in accurate empathy was from 1.91 to 3.84. Although absolute comparisons cannot be made because of the tendency for some groups of raters to rate high, while others rate low, these data suggest that the existing training program produced therapists who were below the intermediate levels of the Accurate Empathy scale. A large percentage of "trained" therapists respond at best to only the most conspicuous of the patient's feelings and contents. That the program was not itself highly focused on teaching effective communication of accurate empathy is suggested by the finding that the actual level of accurate empathy of the trainee correlated —.17 and —.16 respectively with practicum and academic grades given the students. Even more surprising, those findings indicated that the supervisors could, to a moderate degree, sense differential levels of empathic ability in their students, and that they took this into account in evaluating their therapeutic effectiveness. That is, the obtained correlation between the supervisor's rating of the students' effectiveness and their actual level of accurate empathy in therapy was positive and significant (.41, $p < .01$).

Another aspect of the Bergin and Solomon findings, which is highly important to the extent that it is typical of all major training institutions, was the finding that even the supervisor's evaluation of a student's therapeutic effectiveness correlated negatively with academic grades (—.14) and practicum grades (—.22). Since grades have a large effect in determining which trainees receive degrees and, therefore, professional status, those findings are highly sobering. They empirically confirm the suspicion that training institutions tend to reward and, therefore, produce only average or below-average therapeutic ability. One other aspect of the Bergin-Solomon study should be mentioned in this respect: although all six supervisors from diverse orientations evaluated empathic ability in trainees, the students who were supervised by a faculty member who explicitly attempted to teach them specific empathic behaviors were substantially more highly empathic than those from other supervisory groups (an average on the Accurate Empathy scale of 3.8, compared with an average of 2.1 for all other supervisory groups combined).

A second study by Melloh (1964) focused on accurate empathy in 28 post-practicum counselor trainees being trained in one of the major training institutions for counselors. Again, using the research scale for evaluating tape-recorded sessions, he obtained an average level on accurate empathy of 2.46 (against 2.50 for the Bergin and Solomon study), suggesting that the counselors being produced were mostly low or average in the communication of empathy. In this study of counselor training, and in the Bergin and Solomon study (1963), there was no relationship between the level of accurate empathy that the trainees actually provided in their counseling relationships and their grades received in practicum ($r = -.008$).

Both studies together offer strong support for the suspicion that major training programs in counseling and psychotherapy reward students selectively and grant them degrees on bases that appear not to be relevant to their capability for functioning therapeutically. These training programs also seem to provide students with little specific training in how to effectively implement conditions that seem both theoretically and empirically central to virtually any helping relationship. The main concern is not with encouraging graduate programs to offer degrees only to students who are rated as good therapists. Rather, it is with erasing the artificial distinction between research training and therapy training. In conducting studies in the helping professions we cannot separate theory and research from practice. Rather we are continually researching the therapeutic process and its outcome in order to explicate its effective ingredients, training persons to provide higher levels of these ingredients, and then researching the resultant process and outcome to determine if indeed there is a significant improvement.

The third study evaluating accurate empathy in relation to training began as an evaluation of a teaching machine program presumably designed for training in effective interpersonal relationships (Berlin and Wyckoff, 1964). In that study, Baldwin and Lee (1965) compared the use of the programed teaching machine instructions with an informal, didactic group-therapy experience in undergraduate college students. Again they used the Accurate Empathy scale to evaluate tape-recorded, two-person interactions of the students before and after training. Their findings indicated that students who had participated in the teaching machine approach to training in interpersonal relationships showed no change in measured empathic ability (2.7 pretherapy and 2.7 posttherapy); but the students who received informal, didactic group therapy showed significant improvement in empathic ability (2.4 pretraining against 3.2 posttraining).

The lack of any measurable effect from the teaching-machine approach is significant, but even more significant was the finding that informal, didactic group therapy (which they had actually used as a supposed "control" group) had a constructive effect upon the trainees' level of therapeutic functioning. First, it should be noted that the initial level of empathic skill of these undergraduate college students approximates the level of the empathic skill of the advanced trainees in counseling reported by Melloh (1964) and in those in clinical psychology reported by Bergin and Solomon (1963). The suggestion is, of course, that the training programs in counseling and psychotherapy are aimed at theory rather than implementation, and at psychodynamics rather than psychotherapy. More importantly, the suggestion is that an *experiential and didactic* approach focusing on interpersonal relating can produce significant increments in empathic skill. The Baldwin and Lee results fit with both the previous findings and the present approach to training, suggesting that good counselors and good therapists can indeed be *trained* as well as selected.

It is perhaps worthwhile at this point, before detailing this approach to training, to look more closely at the research evidence suggesting its actual effectiveness in producing "therapeutic counselors" or "therapeutic psychotherapists." This would seem particularly appropriate since the overwhelming evidence reviewed in Chapter 1 indicates that the majority of existing approaches to training tend to produce, on the average, ineffective practitioners.

A RESEARCH VIEW OF THE EFFECTIVENESS OF THE PRESENT APPROACH TO TRAINING

One of the first studies aimed at evaluating the approach to training, presented in this book evaluated the levels of accurate empathy, nonpossessive warmth, and genuineness, and the level of patient self-exploration occurring at the end of 100 hours of training (Carkhuff and Truax, 1965a). The study involved twelve trainees who were graduate students in clinical and counseling psychology and five lay counselors; this group was then compared with fifteen highly experienced counselors and psychotherapists. In that study, each trainee conducted an interview with each of three hospitalized patients. From these three tapes for each trainee, four-minute excerpts were randomly selected from each interview. These excerpts were then rated using the usual procedures described in Chapter 2 for much of the research findings. The comparison population of experienced therapists included leaders in client-centered therapy, psychoanalytic psychotherapy, rational-emotive therapy, and eclectic therapy, and involved both psychologists and psychiatrists. Using the scales for therapeutic conditions, presented in Chapter 2, and the scale in Chapter 5 defining levels of self-exploration, analysis of the data suggested that graduate students being trained in the present approach for 100 hours closely approximated the level of therapeutic conditions communicated by experienced psychotherapists. Further, the findings suggested that even the lay therapists (primarily hospital attendants) did not differ from the experienced therapists in the level of accurate empathy or of nonpossessive warmth. These findings are presented in Tables 30 and 31. It can also be noted that, in comparison with the data on accurate empathy from the Melloh (1964) and the Bergin and Solomon (1963) studies, the present approach to training appears to be superior in results to the usual existing training program. Both of these studies obtained findings suggesting that the average level of accurate empathy for graduate students after training

Table 30
Mean Scale Values of Therapy Process Variables for Groups of Trainees and Experienced Therapists

Scale	*No. of Points*	*Lay* [a] *(N = 5)*	*SD*	*Students* [a] *(N = 12)*	*SD*	*Experienced (N = 15)*	*SD*
AE	(9)	4.58	.30	5.14	.69	5.22	.84
NPW	(5)	2.82	.62	3.05	.32	3.16	.40
GEN	(7)	4.86	.35	5.23	.48	5.51	.45
DX	(9)	4.66	.30	4.56	.60	4.86	.56

a. Personnel involved in training program.

Source: From Carkhuff, R. R. and Truax, C. B. Training in counseling and psychotherapy: an evaluation of an integrated didactic and experiential approach. *J. consult. Psychol.*, 1965(a), *29*, 333-336.

Table 31
t tests for Significant Differences of Therapy Process Variables for Groups of Trainees and Experienced Therapists

Scale	*Students vs. Lay*	*Students vs. Experienced*	*Lay vs. Experienced*
AE	1.750	.267	1.641
NPW	1.045	.786	1.417
GEN	.487	1.556	2.955 *
DX	.357	1.340	.741

* Significant at the .01 level.
Source: From Carkhuff, R. R. and Truax, C. B. Training in counseling and psychotherapy: an evaluation of an integrated didactic and experiential approach. *J. consult. Psychol.*, 1965(a), *29*, 333-336.

was 2.50, considerably below the 5.14 level obtained with the present sample.

The results suggest that in a relatively short training period, *i.e.*, approximately 100 hours, both graduate students and lay hospital personnel can be brought to function at levels of therapy nearly commensurate with those of experienced therapists.

It is notable that on the empathy dimension all the groups functioned near Stage 5, which is characterized by the ". . . therapist accurately respond(ing) to all of the client's more readily discernible feelings. . . ." All groups hovered around Stage 3 of the unconditional positive regard scale, where ". . . the therapist indicates a positive caring for the patient or client but it is a semi-possessive caring. . . . " On the therapist self-congruence scale all groups functioned near Stage 5, where ". . . there are no negative cues suggesting any discrepancy between what he says and what he feels, and there are some positive cues indicating genuine response to the patient. . . ." The patients of all the groups of therapists were engaged in the therapeutic process of self-exploration at levels 4 and 5 where ". . . personally relevant material is discussed . . ." and frequently, ". . . either with feeling indicating emotional proximity, or with spontaneity. . . ." Summing up these results, it may be said that the trainees, both students and lay personnel, succeeded almost as well as the more experienced therapists in giving what would commonly be characterized as *effective psychotherapy*.

The significant difference obtained on the level of genuineness, with the ordering from highest to lowest of experienced therapists, graduate students, and lay personnel, suggest that perhaps greater experience in the role of being a therapist allows the therapist himself to become less defensive and be more freely and deeply himself within the therapeutic encounter.

A second study aimed at evaluating the effectiveness of the present approach to training evaluated the effectiveness of the lay trainees in producing behavioral and personality change in hospitalized mental patients. For that study (Carkhuff and Truax, 1965b) Eastern State Hospital in Lexington, Kentucky, made available 144 hospitalized patients who were randomly assigned, with 74 patients in treatment and 70 in control groups.

Criteria for patient selection included the following: patients who were not expected to be discharged within a three-month period; who were not currently being seen in any form of psychotherapeutic treatment; who were not diagnosed to be mentally retarded or to have organic diseases. The patient population involved the typical multiplicity of diagnostic categories, both among various patients and within the clinical histories of the individual patients. The variety of current diagnoses included manic-depressive reactions of both manic and depressive types, psychotic depressive reactions and schizophrenic reactions, simple catatonic and schizo-affective types, with the great majority of all patients diagnosed as hebephrenic, paranoid or chronic undifferentiated types. One patient fell into all of the following categories: psychoneurotic anxiety reactions; sociopathic personality disturbance; passive-aggressive personality trait disturbance; transient adult situational personality disturbance.

The treatment group ranged in age from 24 to 64 years, with a mean of 50.03 years (*SD,* 11.14). These patients had an average of 7.44 (*SD,* 3.65) years of education, with some patients having had no schooling and some having college degrees. The number of hospital admissions, including their present stay, ran from one admission to four, and averaged 1.96 (*SD,* .92); the length of stay during the present hospitalization ranged from 1 to 36 years, with a mean of 13.62 years (*SD,* 11.23).

The control group members varied in age from 20 to 66 (mean, 46.96; *SD,* 11.47); and in schooling from none to 16 grades, or college (mean, 7.51; *SD,* 3.36). The average number of hospital admissions was 2.09 (*SD,* 1.04), ranging again from one to four, while the years of the present hospitalization varied from 1 to 34 with a mean of 10.03 (*SD,* 8.19).

In summary, the population was essentially an older chronic group, with an average of two hospital admissions. Although the sample was a severely disabled one, it represented the great bulk of the hospital population which is usually not serviced by the professional staff, and thus provided a testing ground for the usefulness of lay treatment.

The patients were seen twice a week over a period of approximately three months for a total of 24 sessions in time-limited group counseling by the lay trainees. There was no problem-oriented or personnel-oriented basis for group assignment. Patients were simply randomly assigned to individual treatment or control groups. The sessions were recorded for the purposes of supervision and any subsequent analyses. The lay counselors continued to meet as a group for supervision twice a week for an hour.

In the treatment process, the lay counselors were oriented only toward providing high levels of therapeutic conditions. They had no other cognitive map. The therapist's role was to communicate a warm and genuine concern and depth of understanding. There was no special focus for discussion; no topics were forbidden, and as the sessions evolved, they generally included discussions of the usual range of emotion-laden or intellectualized topics, from sexual material to concerns for the practical business of "getting out" and "making a go of life."

All the patients were rated before and after treatment on the short form "gross ratings of patient behavior" (Carkhuff and DeBurger, 1964), a series of four 9-point scales where "nine" represents the highest positive value and "one" represents the lowest value in the negative direction. The scales assessed four critical areas: (1) "degree of psychological disturbance," (2) degree of constructive interpersonal concern," (3) "degree of constructive intrapersonal concern," and, perhaps most important, (4) "degree of overall improvement over the past three months" (for which ratings were obtained only after treatment). The post-treatment ratings were available for all treatment and control group members. Twenty of the pretreatment ratings necessary to assess the first three indices of ward behavior of the control group were, however, lost or misplaced. Analysis of the post-treatment "overall improvement" ratings indicates that these 20 patients tended to be rated slightly worse than the control group in general, thus suggesting that the differences between treatment and control groups on the three other scales are conservative. Five of the 20 were rated improved, five deteriorated, and ten, no change. As can be seen from Table 32, all scale differences between treatment and control groups were statistically significant. It is notable that only one of the treatment group patients was rated as deteriorated in his overall behavior over the previous three months, while 28 were judged improved. Twelve of the control group members were rated as deteriorated, while 19 were rated improved. Furthermore, it is clear from the other scale values that control group members tended to remain unchanged, but the treatment group showed greater variability.

It is significant that the patient population used in this evaluation was nonselective, involving a preponderance of chronic hospitalized patients. A recent study by Spitzer, Lee, Carnahan and Fleiss (1964) has indicated that this particular Kentucky hospital population is significantly more pathological and less communicative, perhaps because of lower socioeducational status, than patient populations in similar institutions in more urbanized northern states. So in this case, lay group counseling produced significant improvement in patients who, on the average, had spent an average of 13½ years in their current hospitalization, had had one previous hospitalization, had a seventh grade education, and who were already 50 years of age.

Since ratings of ward behavior before and after treatment were used as the basic measure of change, the possibility of biased reports from

Table 32
Direction of Changes of Gross Ratings of Patient Behavior by Ward Personnel

	PATIENT GROUPS		
	Treatment		*Control*
Overall improvement	(N = 74)		(N = 70)
(Posttherapy ratings only)			
Improved	38		19
Deteriorated	1	$X^2 = 21.47$ ***	12
Unchanged	35		39
Psychological disturbance	(N = 74)		(N = 50)
(Pre- and posttherapy ratings)			
Improved	28		8
Deteriorated	19	$X^2 = 17.28$ ***	5
Unchanged	27		37
Interpersonal concerns	(N = 74)		(N = 50)
(Pre- and posttherapy ratings)			
Improved	33		16
Deteriorated	14	$X^2 = 11.23$ **	2
Unchanged	27		32
Intrapersonal concerns	(N = 74)		(N = 50)
(Pre- and posttherapy ratings)			
Improved	28		15
Deteriorated	16	$X^2 = 6.79$ *	4
Unchanged	30		31

* Significant at the .05 level.
** Significant at the .01 level.
*** Significant at the .001 level.
Source: Carkhuff, R. R. and Truax, C. B. Lay mental health counseling: the effects of lay group counseling. *J. consult. Psychol.*, 1965(b), 29, 426431.

the ward staff should be considered. We have long been somewhat suspicious of reported improvement when the ward doctor treated patients and asked the ward staff to evaluate his effectiveness. These lay counselors had no direct connection with any of the wards involved; it should be noted also that the ward staff and the hospital personnel in general were initially resistant to the idea that hospital attendants should even be allowed to conduct group counseling. The lay therapists did not initially enjoy high status. The admitted and outspoken bias of the ward personnel involved in the behavioral ratings was against lay group counseling; the initial expectation of the ward personnel was that the lay group counseling would upset the patients and that "therapy" with nonprofessional therapists would be harmful rather than helpful.

Another factor that should be considered is the "attention factor" in relation to the patients themselves. Most of the patients had received no special treatment, especially no psychotherapeutic treatment, during their many years of hospitalization. There was, in fact, great difficulty at first in getting patients to attend the group sessions, although most attended regularly after the first few weeks, many looking forward to this special form of attention which they were receiving. Although resources did not allow for such a control in this study, future replication should incorporate a second control group of patients attending "sessions" conducted by untrained lay personnel.

The evidence that the treatment group produced comparatively greater variability in outcome than the control group parallels equivalent findings in psychotherapy (Barron and Leary, 1955; Cartwright and Vogel, 1960; Shlien, Mosak and Dreikurs, 1960). It is perhaps of some significance that only one treated patient was judged deteriorated in overall behavior. This compared most favorably with reported effects of professional group psychotherapy with less chronic hospitalized patients.

A third study analyzed the lay group counseling data from a different viewpoint. Since all lay group counseling sessions were tape-recorded for purposes of supervision, an analysis of the level of conditions actually provided in group counseling by the lay trainees could be made and compared to the degree of patient outcome. That study (Truax, Silber, and Carkhuff, 1966) obtained findings comparing the control group with the counseling on measures of high, medium and low levels of accurate empathy, nonpossessive warmth and genuineness. The findings indicated quite clearly that patients in lay group counseling who received low levels of therapeutic conditions showed no benefit beyond that seen in the control group on any of the four measures of outcome. By contrast, both moderate and high levels of therapeutic conditions offered by the lay group counselors resulted in significant improvement over the control group on all four measures ($p < .05$).

This second study, relating levels of conditions offered by lay group counseling trainees to therapeutic outcome in hospitalized patients, tends to argue strongly for the validity of the findings obtained in the first study (using ward ratings). That is, since the ward personnel themselves could not possibly know the level of conditions actually provided by the different lay group counselors, the consistent and statistically significant findings linking level of conditions to outcome suggest a lack of bias in the ratings of patient behavior.

A fourth study, by Berenson, Carkhuff, and Myrus (1966), studied the effects of this approach to training on undergraduate dormitory counselors. In that study, 36 student volunteers were randomly assigned to three groups: (1) the training group proper; (2) a control group which spent the same total number of hours in training with a program that involved neither the research scales as didactic instruments nor the quasi-group therapy as an experiential aspect of training; and (3) a control group who had no specific training in therapeutic practice. The findings from that study indicated significantly greater change ($p < .05$) on each of the therapeutic conditions for the trainees receiving the total training program, as measured by one inventory filled out by a standard "client" who was interviewed by all trainees and by another measuring the counselor's perceptions. Furthermore, the trainees receiving the total training program showed the same significant superiority over both control groups ($p < .05$) when the measure of the level of therapeutic conditions was obtained from their dormitory roommates.

In a further study of 16 graduate students in clinical and counseling psychology, Truax and Silber (1966) cross-validated the earlier findings and extended the study of the effects of this approach to training by taking "in therapy" measures early and late in the training program. Before the early interview, the trainees had received 14 class hours of instruction and had spent an average of 11 hours listening to tape recordings of psychotherapy, so that at that point they were able to provide moderately high levels of therapeutic conditions. (Because real patients were used for the interviews, it was felt necessary that the trainees have some minimal training to lessen the chances of their actually harming the client). The "late" interviews with real clients were made after an additional 34 hours of training. The level of accurate empathy obtained in the "late" interview averaged 4.50 for the 16 trainees; the level of nonpossessive warmth averaged 3.87; and the level of genuineness averaged 3.74. Thus the data tended to confirm the earlier findings. It should also be noted that, in that replication, different instructors or supervisors were used in applying the present approach to training.[8] More importantly, that study evaluated the amount of change from early to late in the training program. The obtained findings indicated a significant increase in the level of accurate empathy ($p < .05$) and in the level of genuineness ($p < .01$), but a nonsignificant improvement in the level of nonpossessive warmth.

A further study on the same 16 trainees (Truax, Silber and Wargo, 1966) will be discussed in the next section; it also indicated a significant degree of positive personality change in the graduate students undergoing the present training program.

Taken together, then, the available evidence, while more meager than we might hope for, strongly suggests positive benefit for this new approach to training. In light of the Bergin and Solomon (1963) and the Melloh (1964) data, indicating little positive effects of existing training programs, the available evidence just reviewed seems even stronger.

SELECTION OF TRAINEES

Although both the available evidence and the viewpoint of this approach to training agree in suggesting that essential therapeutic skills can be learned, it must also be clear that one way of producing more effective therapists is to be more selective in reviewing prospective trainees.

8. Appreciation extended to Donald G. Wargo for his participation as a supervisor.

Ordinarily, supervisors in counseling and psychotherapy tend to select potential trainees on the same bases that they select patients or clients: intelligent, verbal, well-motivated, high socioeconomic status, high ego-strength, etc. In part, current selection procedures derive from the fact that solid evidence for selection has been largely nonexistent. A supervisor does not know a "good prospective therapist" from a poor one, except in terms of very private norms and experience.

Some studies, such as that by Combs and Soper (1963), attempted to discriminate between attitudes held by good and poor counselors. Their findings indicated that better counselors were those who tended to assume an internal rather than external frame of reference in understanding others, who were people-oriented rather than thing-oriented, and who had an optimistic view of man, but solid criteria of counselor effectiveness were lacking. In their data, as in most cases, the definition of counselors' effectiveness was based upon their supervisor's ratings. The Bergin and Solomon (1963) study, however, did investigate a number of correlates of empathic ability, which seem to have relevance to selection. Their data indicated that within the restricted range of intelligence occurring in graduate school students, there was a nonsignificant *negative* correlation with verbal intelligence (—.30) and, equally surprising, a nonsignificant negative correlation (—.18) with the "psychologist" subscale of the graduate record exam. Their findings also indicated that personality was significantly associated with empathic ability: they found negative relationships with test indicators of personality disturbance (such as the Psychasthenia and Depression scales of the MMPI), and positive relationships with measures of personal strength (the Dominance and Change scales of the Edwards Personal Preference Schedule). Also of importance, empathic ability seemed to be negatively related to a cognitive orientation, as measured by *n* Order and even Intraception on the Edwards Scale.

The study (Truax, Silber, and Wargo, 1966) of the 16 students receiving the present approach to training also yielded some information of suggestive value for the selection of potential trainees. Personality inventories were administered to that group of students before and after training, and were then compared with their learning achievement. That is, using the measures of their actual ability to communicate accurate empathic understanding, nonpossessive warmth, and genuineness early and late in the training program, those students who showed the most gain in ability were compared on a number of personality variables with those students who showed the least improvement in therapeutic skills. Here, then, the questions posed were, "What kind of trainee benefits the most from the training program?" and, "What personality changes occur in trainees who change the most, compared to those who show little gain in therapeutic skill?"

Some of the findings fit well with the Bergin and Solomon (1963) findings. Bergin and Solomon found a negative relationship between Need for Order (on the Edwards scale) and empathic ability; among the students in the present training program, those who showed the greatest gains in the therapeutic conditions were initially slightly lower on Need for Order than those who showed little or no gain, and they showed a significant drop in post-training. Those who showed the least improvement in therapeutic skill showed no change in Need for Order. The Bergin and Solomon data showed significant positive association between the Change Scale and empathic ability; in the present training program, those students who showed the greatest gain in the therapeutic conditions were significantly higher on the Change Scale both before and after training than those who showed least gain, and there was a nonsignificant tendency during training for the most improved to increase on the Change Scale and for the least improved to decrease.

The Bergin and Solomon data indicated a nonsignificant negative association between empathic ability and Abasement on the Edwards; those who gained most and least from the present training program were equivalent on the Abasement Scale before therapy, but the most improved students showed a significant decline during training, while the students who showed least gain in therapeutic skill showed an increase in the Abasement scale. The Bergin and Solomon data indicated a positive correlation between the Autonomy scale and empathic skill; students who showed greatest gain in the present training program started off significantly higher and showed large and significant gains in Autonomy, while those who showed the least gain started off significantly lower in Autonomy and showed negative change. Finally, the Bergin and Solomon data indicated nonsignificant negative association between the Defensiveness scale on the Edwards and empathic ability; in the analysis of students in the present training program, the findings indicated that those students who showed the greatest gain in therapeutic skill were initially significantly lower on Defensiveness, while both groups of students showed a decline in Defensiveness during training. A summary of the findings are presented in Table 33.

These findings dealing with initial personality measures for "successful versus unsuccessful trainees" are only suggestive for trainee selection, since both the Bergin and Solomon (1963) and the Truax, Silber and Wargo (1966) data are based on small samples. However, the agreement between these two studies made with widely different student populations and training approaches is at least encouraging. More importantly, the Truax, Silber and Wargo data dealing with *personality change* of students during training in psychotherapy provide evidence that the changes in ability to communicate therapeutic conditions made during the present training program were not "only skin-deep." Those students who showed significant gains in therapeutic (or interpersonal) skills also showed relevant positive personality change.

Before outlining the present approach to training, it would perhaps be well to have firmly in mind the essential characteristics of traditional didactic and experiential approaches.

Table 33
Summary of Findings on Personality Correlates of Therapeutic Conditions for Therapists

	BERGIN AND SOLOMON 1963	TRUAX, SILBER, AND WARGO 1966b	
	Initial	*Initial*	*Direction of Change with Training*
MMPI			
Pt scale	low *	low	lower *
D scale	low *	low *	lower *
Mf scale	low	curvilinear average best *	higher *
Ma scale	low	curvilinear average best *	higher *
Si scale	low	low *	lower *
Welsch's A.I. Index	not scored	low *	lower *
Welsch's I.R. Index	not scored	low *	lower *
Constructive Personality Change Scale	not scored	high *	higher *
Edwards Personal Preference Schedule			
N Defensiveness	low	low *	lower
N Dominance	high *	high	lower
N Change	high *	high *	higher
N Order	low *	low	lower *
N Intraception	low *	low	lower
N Abasement	low	no relationship	lower *
N Autonomy	high	high *	higher *
N Conformity	low *	low	lower

THE DIDACTIC AND THE EXPERIENTIAL APPROACH

The didactic approach is supported by theorists who hold that supervision represents the conscious effort of a profession to "program" future therapists with the proper "sets" and repertoires of correct responses (Krasner, 1961, 1962). The approach, as typified by Wolberg (1954) and Thorne (1950), includes supervisors who emphasize the more didactic aspects of shaping therapist behaviors. It is natural that learning principles be applied, to the extent that they are currently known, to the acquisition and performance of therapeutic behavior. Unfortunately, such a view has led to the assumption that traditional educational procedures alone are effective means of shaping desired therapist behaviors.

In supervision, the teacher-supervisor brings to bear his accumulated store of knowledge, born perhaps of his own experience and the experiences of others, which may themselves have been passed on to him in didactic formulations. Often, then, the supervisory process may be seen as involving overt reinforcement to produce performance of desired therapist behaviors, and lack of reinforcement or even punishment to produce extinction of undesirable therapist behaviors. Winokur (1955) has gone so far as to characterize this kind of supervision or training for therapists as a forced modification of both behavior and thinking to conform to that of the teacher-supervisor; he likens it to "brainwashing."

The implicit paradox involved in didactic supervision for therapy and counseling is that often the conditions, techniques, or attitudes that the future therapist is "taught" to employ are precisely *not* the conditions and attitudes offered by the supervisor. In fact, they are often antithetical. To be sure, many of the more didactic supervisors find repugnant the thought of "forced modification" or even of "programing" the trainee's behavior. Still, by the nature of a didactic approach, the trainee does not receive the conditions conducive to his own freedom and openness to self-exploration; he is not facilitated in the self-exploration that, together with the opportunity to tap prior knowledge in the field, might be expected to produce an effective therapist. The trainee does not experience an analogue of therapy; he does not get from his supervisor a chance to experience a therapist role-model that he might imitate in psychotherapy or counseling.

Perhaps even worse, the trainee caught in the implicit "double-bind" of the paradox may re-enact in therapy the contradictions between what the supervisor *tells* him to do as a therapist in therapy and what the supervisor himself *does* to him as a trainee in training.

With a healthy aversion for the doctrinaire "technicianship" which the didactic approach is accused of fostering, many (Boehm, 1961; Towles, 1961; Wessel, 1961) emphasize the importance of genuine acceptance and respect for individuality. These supervisor-offered conditions are calculated to give the trainee feelings of safety and freedom that will promote openness to experiences and a willingness to experiment. Here, the focus is upon the experiential aspect which is illustrated by the client-centered orientation (Rogers, 1957b):

> . . . The student should develop his own orientation to psychotherapy out of his own experience. In my estimation every effective therapist has built his own orientation to therapy within himself and out of his own experience with his clients or patients. It is quite true that this orientation as finally developed may be such that it closely resembles that of others, or closely resembles the orientation to which he was exposed. Nevertheless, the responses made by the effective therapist in his interviews are not made in a certain way because that is the psychoanalytic way, or the client-centered way, or the Adlerian way, they are made because the therapist has found that type of response effective in his own experience. Likewise, he does not put on certain attitudes because those are the attitudes expected of an analyst or client-centered therapist or an Adlerian. He discovers and uses certain attitudes in himself which have developed because they have been rewarded by the effective outcome of earlier experiences in carrying on therapy. Thus the aim of a training program in therapy should be to turn out individuals who have an independent and open attitude toward their own therapy and continually formulate and reformulate and revise their own approach to the

individuals with whom they are working in such a way that their approach results in more constructive and effective help. (p. 87)

While the experiential group shuns thoughts of control in therapy supervervision or in therapy (Rogers and Skinner, 1956), they should perhaps admit, even reluctantly, that they are deeply engaged in the influencing of trainee behavior. They influence therapist behavior subtly by exposure and initiation of the social-imitation process. They influence behavior by instituting certain attitudinal conditions in which, protestations to the contrary, the trainee has no more voice than he does in a didactic supervision and from which certain behavioral consequences are anticipated and even predicted (Frank, 1961) Perhaps, unlike the didactic approach's conscious efforts to "program," the experiential approach represents the *unconscious* efforts of a profession to "program" future therapists.

Both the didactic and the experiential orientation in essence provide the trainee with a stimulus complex of conditions that determine the probability of his responding to one kind of behavior in therapy rather than another; thus these conditions greatly determine his effectiveness (Ashby, Ford, Guerney, and Guerney, 1957; Dinoff, Rickard, Salzberg, and Sipprelle, 1960; Fey, 1958; Fiedler, 1950, 1951; Holt and Luborsky, 1958; Krasner, 1962; Lakin and Lebovits, 1958; Strupp, 1955a, 1955b, 1960a). The impact of the therapist's early supervision and training is undoubtedly modified by the kind and patterning of reinforcement received from real patients as he practices the art of psychotherapy, but it is still present. Perhaps this openness to feedback from patients results in the learning, relearning, and unlearning that, rather than most training, produces effective psychotherapists. This openness to feedback is probably an essential quality of any effective therapist; through it he comes to trust his own experience.

The didactic orientation emphasizes passing down an accumulated store of knowledge in the traditional learning setting: the flow is downward. For the student the experience is one of accepting and incorporating a set of "established" premises, from which he may deduce certain modes of doing things in therapy. In contrast, the experiential approach nurtures, elicits, and even predicts behavioral change on the part of the supervisee, but it focuses mainly on instituting certain attitudinal conditions. The belief is that growth, born of the trainee's own experience, will follow: in generalizing from experiencing, the flow is upward. Thus, the didactic orientation is largely deductive, and the experiential orientation largely inductive.

These two orientations need not be mutually exclusive in psychotherapy training; they often are not in practice. For both supervisor and trainee the process of learning in supervision is not unlike the seesaw process of theory-building in general—the interactional process of inductive generalizations from experience which qualify and modify the deductions of earlier experiences which, in turn, are qualified and modified in deductive testing. The present approach incorporates both the didactic and the experiential approach; the therapist-supervisor brings to bear a knowledge of therapy accumulated from his own experience and the experiences and work of others *in the context of a therapeutic relationship* that gives the trainee the conditions which research and clinical learning suggest are essential for psychotherapeutic personality change. Training in counseling or psychotherapy can be viewed as a special form of learning akin to psychotherapy itself: a learning process that takes place in the context of a particular kind of deep and meaningful relationship which facilitates positive change. This deep and meaningful relationship is a product of a stimulus complex of therapist-offered conditions that develop the "something more" which has been attributed to the therapeutic relationship itself. This specific complex elicits certain trainee responses that seem to be critical to his learning and growth. Thus it seems reasonable to believe that most training approaches, including even the most didactic approaches attempting to "shape" behavior, will be most effective when high levels of empathy, warmth, and genuineness are present.

Since the research evidence (presented in Chapter 3) indicated that these therapeutic conditions are indeed important for positive change in such varied groups as third grade students learning to read, college students attaining passing grades, psychotics attempting to cope with an estranged world, etc., it seems tragic when a skilled therapist or counselor fails to integrate his therapeutic skills in training the new generation of therapists and counselors.

Assuming an analogy between the personality and behavior changes seen in therapy and the goal of behavior change in therapy training, it would follow that those trainees who are able to explore themselves are those who would show greatest positive change in therapeutic skills. The trainee's self-exploration, is then, posited as one of the critical elements in supervision, whether that supervision is aimed at producing analytic, client-centered, behavioral, or eclectic therapists.

The therapeutic relationship is seen as an essential part of any training program. It provides the conditions for a trainee's self-exploration of his own feelings, values and attitudes and thus, the discovery of his effective therapeutic self. Self-exploration directly affects how the trainee is able to put into use intellectual learnings of "how to be a good therapist," regardless of the orientation used. In an integrated training program the supervisor, in his contacts with the trainee, would continuously attempt to provide the therapeutic conditions that lead to this trainee self-exploration. The trainee's growing awareness of intellectual content and learnings in psychotherapy (in the context of a relationship which nurtures his own self-exploration) leads to his genuine growth as a therapist, not merely "canned" empathy or professional warmth.

The present view suggests that supervisors of the experiential orientation would become more effective as they became more aware of their role as a direct influencer and even controller, however subtle, of behavior. Their awareness of the controlling nature of the experiential approach would lead to a more open attitude toward the potential application and understanding offered by learning theory principles. On the other hand, supervisors of the didactic school of thought might be more effective if they came to recognize the capacity of supervisor-offered conditions (or, if you will, the therapeutic relationship) to elicit from the trainee greater depth of self-exploration and personal involvement, and thus to contribute to the personality and behavioral change necessary for him to become a genuine counselor or therapist.

The integrated approach combining both didactic and experiential viewpoints should provide a training approach where the past (in the form of accumulated knowledge) can tentatively be brought to bear in a relationship that elicits the value of a potentially therapeutic present (in the form of the client's current experiencing).

TOWARD IMPLEMENTATION

Since the training of a therapist involves constructive changes in the trainee's interpersonal skills, the supervisor should provide him with empathic understanding and nonpossessive warmth in a relationship characterized by transparency and genuineness. But training can offer more than just the conditions and a "role-model." The trainee can learn to implement accurate empathic understanding, nonpossessive warmth and genuineness in much the same way that people learn to drive a car or play bridge. It may be more demanding, much more complicated, and involve more of himself, but the process of learning is similar. He can be told concretely and specifically some things to do or try; he can be told some things not to do. He can be given practice in role-playing, just as the beginning motorist makes a "dry run" with the engine turned off or the beginning bridge player is dealt a trial hand with the cards face up. He can observe experienced therapists and build up a storehouse of things *he* might do or say, just as the beginning motorist sits next to the driver and watches, or the beginning bridge player observes and asks questions. The trainee's role-playing can be interrupted moment-by-moment to tell him what he is doing right and wrong. Fnally, he can learn from his own experience of success and failure and develop his own *unique style*, so that his skill becomes truly a part of himself and no longer a mere mechanical technique. As is frequently the case in other skills, he can often surpass the teacher.

In the case of psychotherapy or counseling, the beginner imitating the experienced therapist will feel unnatural, artificial, and self-conscious. (This is also true of the beginning motorist, who has to think about where to move his arm and his foot and how to coordinate speed and steering.)

As the therapist trainee succeeds in his new skill, his self-conscious concentration on technique disappears and his undivided focus is upon the therapeutic transaction. It is then that the technique of communicating warmth becomes a genuine human caring or love relationship, and the technique of empathic understanding takes on the quality of "being-in-the-world-together." It is then also that the communication of his own authenticity or genuineness as a person is no longer just a technique of receptivity and openness, but a profoundly human acceptance of himself and others, with a respect for "what is" as well as for "what can be." To be sure, the ultimate incorporation and integration of these skills depends mainly on the ultimate reinforcement he receives from his environment—how effective his acquired approach is.

In training, the beginning therapist or counselor can be exposed to tape-recorded samples in which experienced therapists are providing very high levels of therapeutic conditions (Truax, 1963; Truax and Carkhuff, 1963)—not just any tapes of good therapists, but selected samples of therapeutic conditions at their best. From such tapes he can learn from positive examples of what should be done in therapy. In addition, these recorded samples provide a storehouse of knowledge and awareness of typical patient problem areas and conflicts, as well as conflicts and problem areas involved in transference and countertransference, effective handling of such problems, and a host of patient-therapist transactions that, though not rare, are specific to therapy and so are often baffling and embarrassing to the beginning trainee (Carkhuff, Feldman, and Truax, 1964; Feldman and Carkhuff, 1963). The value of these learnings from the past lies in their concreteness or specific form, just as specificity seems important in psychotherapy (Truax and Carkhuff, 1964a). This is not at all the kind of "tape-listening" usually provided in training. Ordinarily a tape is played for 20 minutes (or even an hour), and then the supervisor and trainees join in speculation about the case "dynamics," the personality of the patient, or other quite general remarks about the therapist. But to be of value, the samples must be brief and to the point, or the point itself and the learning will be lost. Even in some of the best recorded examples of complete psychotherapy sessions, there are perhaps only 20 minutes of highly empathic, warm and authentic transactions, and those are often interspersed with what are really examples of what not to do. Few therapists or counselors, even without objective measurements, would believe that they had ever had a therapeutic session so perfect that it contained no good examples of what *not* to do. Since the research literature on learning is overwhelming in showing that people in the beginning stages of any learning task, learn best from positive examples rather than negative ones, great care should be taken to provide only positive instances of high therapeutic skill. Usually, this means listening to samples of therapeutic interaction of less than five minutes. Although such brief samples do not give the trainee (or the supervisor) a grasp of the patient's dynamics, or even the larger picture of the dynamics of therapy itself, this is actually an advantage: it focuses attention on the moment-by-moment therapeutic skill.

In psychotherapy the trial run "with the engine turned off" can be carried out by playing a tape recording of a few moments of client talk and requiring the trainee to make a therapeutic response. Just as in any other trial run, the experienced therapist or counselor need not sit idly back and make occasional general comments; he can immediately correct the trainee for content, for voice quality, for posture, for failure to listen, etc. In supervising a group of trainees, he can have them respond successively to the same patient statements, letting them compete in trying to be the most accurately empathic, the warmest, and most genuinely "real" in their responses.

In an attempt to teach beginning counselors or therapists, the supervisor can mimic the "advanced dry run" (the beginning driver going down an empty residential street) by designating someone to role-play a patient and then asking the trainees to become therapists, successively, for brief periods of a few minutes. Again, the supervisor need not sit idly back. He can, and should, interrupt; he can illustrate responses that would be more empathic, warmer, or more genuine. In short, he can teach.

Finally, he can ask the trainee to engage in a large number of single "one-shot" therapeutic interviews, first with other trainees who role-play a patient and then with actual clients or patients. If these are tape recorded, then in the very next class period or supervisory session, the supervisor and other trainees (providing they have learned to use the research rating scales) can rate the degree of accurate empathy, nonpossessive warmth and genuineness on randomly selected samples from these tapes (three to five minutes). Such rating would not only provide specific feedback about when the trainee is warm, when he is communicating rejection, etc., but it would also bring to bear the potent shaping effects of peer pressures. A trainee who may not inwardly respond to the supervisor's saying "It sounds sort of rehearsed and mechanical," usually will react if his fellow trainees say, "Frank, you may feel that was a genuine response on your part, but to me it sounded more like Dr. Truax than Frank."

Another central aspect of the present training approach involves the experience of being the "patient" or "client" in a "quasi-group therapy experience." Here the beginning counselor or therapist comes to know what it means and feels like to be "helped": what accurate empathic understanding (or the lack of it), nonpossessive warmth (or the lack of it), and a genuine human encounter (or the lack of it) mean to those whom he will dedicate his life to helping. It is only "quasi" therapy, but even so, it sometimes involves deeply personal revelations, tears, intense emotional experiences, and times that are "intellectual sessions": it at least approximates the therapeutic encounter. In such sessions the trainees also focus upon their feelings, conflicts, and problems which arise from their own initial attempts to be helpful in therapeutic relationships with patients. The trainee can explore his own feelings that his attempts to be helpful are to him "phony," that even when he tries he can't help being somehow cut off and aloof from the patient, that at some moments of therapy he wants to be a god or a mother or a lover instead of a therapist.

During these quasi-group therapy sessions, the trainee also has the opportunity to explore his own life values, his feelings of adequacy and inadequacy, his life choices, etc. Thus, trainees may explore their own inhibitions in expressing warmth and caring for patients, their own irrational feelings of hostility or anger at certain patients, or their need to play the role of a therapist, rather than *be* the person of a therapist.

The three elements central to the present training approach, then, can be summarized: (1) a therapeutic context in which the supervisor himself provides high levels of therapeutic conditions; (2) a highly specific didactic training in the implementation of the therapeutic conditions; and, (3) a quasi-group therapy experience where the trainee can explore his own existence, and his own individual therapeutic self can emerge.

CHAPTER 8 THE PRESENT APPROACH TO TRAINING: AN OPERATIONAL AND EXPERIENTIAL OVERVIEW

THE theoretical view of an approach toward effective training in counseling and psychotherapy presented in the preceding chapter can be implemented in a variety of settings with a variety of trainees. Available research evidence makes the basic didactic and experiential components appear to be essential for successful training; but the specifics of application will vary with the goals and nature of the supervisor, the trainees, and the total training setting. In particular, the list of supplementary required readings will differ greatly, depending upon whether training is for practice in pastoral counseling, rehabilitation counseling, guidance counseling, clinical psychology, psychiatry, social work, nursing, or education.

The training course used here to illustrate the application of the present viewpoint was a beginning course in psychotherapy for clinical and counseling psychology graduate students. They had already completed courses in personality theory and psychodiagnostics. We feel that such prior training is useful as a prerequisite for training in counseling or psychotherapy, but our experience with hospital aides, nurses and others suggests that the present approach can be used independently of such prior learnings.

Samples of the classroom interaction of this group of graduate student trainees are given throughout to illustrate the operational meanings of training as it occurred when the present approach was first introduced into a total program which had been more traditionally oriented. Dialogue transcripts were chosen as a major mode of communicating to the reader the "experience" or flavor of the actual training with some reservations. But although transcripts of the "stuff" of training—of the human interaction—are but a pale and sometimes boring reflection of the reality, they still seem more accurate and less distorted than well-organized and predigested theoretic descriptions of what we think might have happened.

With these considerations in mind, let us turn to the training program in operation.

THE TRAINING PROGRAM IN OPERATION

At the outset the trainees were provided with an extensive reading list of selections from a wide variety of leading theorists and therapists. Since this list was so lengthy, the trainees collaborated and provided each other with abstracts of some of the books and articles. All trainees, however, were responsible for learning the content in order to pass a "theory" examination. They were also required to listen to some 25 hours of individual and group psychotherapy from the tape library. This listening experience was to be completed in the first six weeks of the training and a sign-up sheet was maintained to ascertain this. The purpose of both the reading list and the tape recordings was to provide a large general catalog and storehouse of therapeutic responses, tactics, and approaches which the trainees might imitate. The tape listening, especially, was expected to increase the response repertoire of the beginning therapist or counselor.

Also at the outset, the trainees were given copies (Chapter 2) of the Accurate Empathy scale, the Nonpossessive Warmth scale, and the Genuineness scale and were asked to attempt to rate specific excerpts as they were listening to the experienced therapists on tapes from the tape library. Thus, while listening to experienced therapists, they were forced to focus their attention on the specific therapeutic conditions. Further, they had practice in discriminating different levels of therapeutic conditions. They were also asked to rate specific brief samples of psychotherapy that had already been rated by experienced raters, and so gained intensive experience in becoming raters themselves. After this preliminary experience, the trainees had at least to some degree learned to recognize and discriminate different levels of accurate empathic understanding, nonpossessive warmth and genuineness. A considerable portion of the training hours was spent on "dry runs" of making individual responses to tape-recorded client or patient statements. Probably the most significant of these was what we have termed "empathy training."

In this procedure the trainees were presented as a group with a series of tape recorded statements from a variety of patients; they had to listen to the statements and then reformulate verbally the essential communication made by the patient, in terms of both the feeling and the content of that communication. After a few "round-robin" series of this empathy training, the trainees were asked to respond whenever the supervisor pointed to them (which he did randomly), so that each trainee had to listen intently. Thus, they learned to concentrate on listening to the *meaning* of the patient's communication and developing *facility in verbalizing this meaning*. The procedure was aimed at sharpening the beginning counselor or therapist's sensitivity and skills in both *understanding and communicating* the patient's essential meaning. The rapid, public, competitive, and random nature of the situation was aimed at sharpening empathic skills. Perhaps because of its competitive nature and the immediate feedback, "shaping" of responses occurred rapidly.

As the empathy training proceded to the point where trainees could grasp and communicate the meaning of the patient's communications, the training moved on to "warmth training." The trainees were now asked to concentrate on not just *what* they were saying in their responses, but *how* they were saying it. The emphasis was upon low-pitched, full vocal tones in a slowed rate of speech, communicating the intentness and seriousness of the therapist's response (if these were the appropriate qualities). The training in vocal qualities thus moved the tone as well as the content of their responses toward a more studied attempt to communicate "warmth."

At this point, the responses clearly sounded mechanical, rehearsed, or "canned"—which they were. Now the trainees were encouraged to somehow "put more of themselves" into the brief responses and make them less rehearsed and mechanical.

After spending several sessions in this "therapeutic responding" type of role-playing, the trainees were asked to pair off between the supervisor sessions and record role-playing tapes. The two members of a pair would alternate role-playing "therapist" or "patient" to develop experience in being a therapist for larger units of time. These role-playing attempts were themselves tape-recorded and brought to the supervisory sessions; random samples were selected to be rated on the therapeutic conditions scales by the supervisor and the trainees as a group. This provided an opportunity for the trainee, his peers, and his supervisor to provide critical feedback about his own beginning attempts to offer understanding, warmth, and genuineness.

Only after the trainee had attained minimally high levels of therapeutic conditions in his role-playing was he given appointments with a number of all-too-real patients for single (one-shot) therapeutic interviews. His goal in such interviews was to facilitate deep self-exploration by the patient and to establish "a good therapeutic relationship." Although the relationship in true therapy or counseling develops gradually over time, even first interviews can be deeply involving for both client and therapist. The trainee, of course, attempted to provide high levels of therapeutic conditions.

These single interviews, again, were tape-recorded so that selected samples could be played in the supervisory sessions and rated by the trainee himself, his peers, and the supervisor. The aim was to provide concrete feedback with a number of patients (rather than a single case continued over time) so that the trainee could learn more specifically which elements of his own behavior contributed to a therapeutic relationship and which ones impeded or detracted from that relationship.

When the trainee had developed his therapeutic skills to the point where he could provide minimally high levels of therapeutic conditions in single interviews, and was able to facilitate moderately high levels of the patient's own self-exploration, he was ready to begin to see clients or patients on a continuing therapeutic basis. He would still continue to tape-record all sessions; periodically, samples would be selected randomly for evaluation in the supervisory sessions.

Somehow, when outlined in this form, the training program sounds cold, mechanical, and inhuman—like a gigantic teaching machine. To add that the quasi-group therapy sessions were begun during the sixth week of the program and continued to meet once weekly for a two-hour session, does not make it sound any less "bloodless" on paper.

Actually, of course, a great deal more went on during the supervisory sessions. A considerable amount of time was spent in theoretic and clinical discussions of the meaning and implication of the therapeutic conditions; of a variety of "techniques" of analytic therapy, behavior therapy, client-centered therapy, rational-emotive therapy; and of the behavioristic and existential views of human nature. Questions were asked such as "How can that work with an obsessive patient?" or "What do you do with a hostile schizophrenic who doesn't want to see you?" At these times the supervisor would momentarily "role-play" the therapist while the trainee role-played the problem patient. There were moments of defensiveness and deeper human encounter for both the supervisors and the trainees throughout the training sessions. In attempting to put these perhaps crucial happenings on paper, communication might easily break down, since they happen in no step-by-step fashion and vary with the *person* of the supervisor and the trainee. Perhaps, for that reason, the best way of communicating the *flavor* of the training experience is to introduce transcriptions of the verbal interchanges.

The trainees' initial reaction to the first attempt to implement the training program, was, "This isn't how you become a counselor or a therapist —you're using us as research guinea pigs." In the first session, the trainees looked disillusioned, dismayed, aghast—in short, they had very low therapeutic conditions to offer the supervisors. The supervisors in turn felt totally frustrated, angry and dismayed because, from their point of view, they were offering a unique opportunity that would be so helpful it would be beyond value—not valueless. By the third session, however, the trainees had become thoroughly involved in the experience. The second group of beginning trainees, since they had been informed or propagandized by the first group of trainees, began the first session both committed and involved.

Perhaps some flavor of the first group's initial reaction can be gained from the transcription dealing with the question of graduate school grades to be given at the end of the semester. At first, the trainees had very mixed feelings about the supervisor's asking them to establish their own criteria for grading. They seemed to feel that they would certainly be untrustworthy on such a question, and weren't even convinced that they themselves could have any real voice in the selection of criteria; one student commented after the supervisor had offered an opinion, "This sounds like a communist election."

As might have been anticipated, there was considerable disagreement among the trainees about criteria for grading: some felt that written exams were the best basis; others felt that performance with patients would be best; still others felt that oral exams or even the supervisor's subjective judgments would provide the best basis for grading. In all, almost an hour and a half of course time was spent on the question of grading. In terms of the importance of the grading question, that was an undue and exorbitant waste of time. At the time, though, and looking back from the present perspective, neither of the supervisors would want to shorten it or cut off the discussion. Perhaps for the first time in their graduate careers, the trainees were asked to participate actively in setting up the basis for their own evaluations. In grappling with the question of criteria for grading they were facing the crucial question of why they were there and, more precisely, what they hoped to gain from the training experience. In their own fashion, they had to puzzle out for themselves the questions of whether they should "know about" counseling and therapy, and in what sense this "knowledge" was quite different from "being" an effective counselor or therapist. In a very real sense, this set the tone for the rest of the training program by providing the trainees with an opportunity—or even gently forcing this opportunity on them—to explore their academic and professional goals and the ultimate relationship between their training, their immediate goals, and their life goals. It also provided a way for the supervisors to take the role of facilitators rather than evaluators. The responsibility for learning, growth, or change in the trainee—as with the client or patient—was squarely on his own shoulders. The role of the supervisors had been clarified as that of "teachers as resource persons."

AN INITIAL DISCUSSION OF CRITERIA FOR GRADES

The following transcript, taken from the latter part of the discussion on grading and examination (which took place with this group of trainees in two different class sections) perhaps serves to illustrate the quality of the interaction.[9]

Dr. T: How many people are interested in taking the written exam? Remember that this is going to be optional.

Ben: Tell us some more about it.

Dr. T: I'm not sure what you mean.

Ben: Well, essentially how long an exam would it be?

9. The initials for Dr. T and Dr. C are those of the authors; the student names have been changed to ensure anonymity.

Dr. T: Oh, I think that a two-hour exam would probably give people more of a chance to say things that they know. I was going to ask how many people would be interested in this. What I had thought of was an essay exam with some short answer identifications.

Al: I think I'd be interested in it.

Dr. T: Who else would be? Two. Is anybody else?

Bill: I'd be interested in seeing the exam. (Laughter)

Dr. T: Well . . .

Sam: This is a feedback exam, right?

Dr. T: Yeah. Yes, it's a non-penalty exam. People can't do badly on it.

Jane: Yeah. I would be willing to . . .

Sam: Oh yeah? (Laughs)

Dr. T: Would you be willing, the two of you, be willing to let people see your answers?

Al: Oh, I don't know—not very.

Sam: Yeah, okay.

Dr. T: You could answer on dittoes.

Sam: I reserve the right to disagree. I think it would just be appropriate that if the others wanted to see something, to just see the question, because the others of us who chicken out shouldn't see the answers.

Dr. T: Well, it's not a penalty thing.

Al: Well, no, I don't care.

Dr. T: When would you like to have the oral? Any special preferences?

Ben: First of all, are you planning on giving us the oral during the final week or before the final week—or is that what you want to ask us?

Dr. T: Yes, I don't care.

Bill: Our last class meeting is on a Thursday. Why don't we start them on the following Friday?

Dr. T: Okay.

Bill: Then we'd just schedule whenever someone could.

The topic of conversation, unresolved in the first discussion, meaningfully extended itself into a second class session:

Dr. T: While we're waiting, I wanted to refresh my memory and everybody else's on what we had thought was the most sensible way of determining grades. (Laughter) I suppose this is an appropriate time to ask that.

Sam: I think we said we left it up to you. I think that's what we ended up by saying. It's up to you.

Ben: Isn't that what the oral is for?

Dr. T: Right. I just wanted to get it clear, so that we all have the same expectation.

Al: I would think that the oral should be one of the more important determinants of our grade.

Dr. T: Why?

Al: Because it allows you to get an idea of just how much we do know of the overall field of psychotherapy.

Dot: I didn't think that was the main objective.

Al: What about the tapes, doing it with the tapes?

Dr. T: Yeah. Let me try to restate the way I felt. My conception of the course experience was both intellectual and practical, and that we will discuss, I suppose, what we would call formally a lot of theory or at least about certain theories, about certain concepts, and there is the reading list —outside readings. People presumably spend some time getting a feel for a number of other points of view and in listening to other tapes, getting some clinical feel for a variety of other individual approaches. I guess my feeling was that the oral would be more important for people who had real difficulty operationally. I think we talked about this at the beginning, and we didn't want people whose main probable contribution to the field would be intellectual rather than operational to be penalized. So that both the practical and theoretical knowledge would be going into grades for people who would be particularly strong in one or the other. As with anything else, the strengths would be more important than lacks. Someone who is quite strong in one area probably would make a real contribution to the field, whereas someone who is quite mediocre in all areas, and has no strengths but no weaknesses, probably just wouldn't be as useful in the field. Does this sound like what we had agreed on or not?

Sam: If you think it's reasonable. It's hard to say, for me. It's hard to say what we really expect as far as what a grade . . . I mean, I can't see how the hell we can even be graded.

Bill: No?

Al: That's sort of partly given with the patients you have to see.

John: I felt, when you said that, to you, it felt like you were saying it like you heard it for the first time because I have some memory of us having worked it through to at least this level before. If we are functioning at some kind of minimal level . . .

Ben: Oh no, I've heard it before.

Sam: I think this is the same thing that was said before. I think . . .

Dr. C: Oh, okay.

Ben: It's reasonable. I think it's about the only way, well, it's not the only way, but I think it's as good as any other way.

THE POSSIBILITY OF QUASI-GROUP THERAPY IS DISCUSSED AND EXPERIENCED

The quasi-group therapy experience can be introduced to the training program as either a requirement for the course experience, or a "possibility" that the trainees can themselves consider. In this case the opportunity for quasi-group therapy experience was presented to the trainees as something they might use. A thorough discussion of the advantages and disadvantages of a quasi-group therapy experience is not just a decision-making process; it is in itself a valuable experience in self-exploration for the trainee. Any thorough discussion must inevitably focus on the way the trainee values or devalues the psychotherapeutic experience itself, and on the way in which he perceives patients or clients, particularly in relationship to himself, as a future therapist or counselor. Necessarily, such a discussion must touch upon the trainees' own feelings of adequacy and inadequacy. It becomes, in a sense, an experiencing of quasi-group therapy. The following three excerpts from the session dealing with the decision to enter into quasi-group therapy are perhaps typical:

Dr. T: Let's hear everybody, everybody's feelings before we discuss the quasi-group therapy experience.

Ben: Well, originally I guess I was for it because, well, I've had some quasi experience with such a thing, but talking to Sam and a few others considering this matter I happened to think about the code of ethics—this section where conducting research where it will hinder your social life if you participate in something like that and so on, and this is the question which I guess concerns me: actually whether this will hinder social relationships.

Dr. T: Whether having some kind of relationship in quasi-group therapy experience would make people less socially desirable to you or you less socially desirable to them?

Ben: Well, I don't know. Just the point of whether it will hinder, or you know whether it will affect the social relationships . . . even with students or with the professors.

Dr. T: Um hmm. I get that as originally feeling positive but really having some serious doubts about whether or not this might have some real harmful effects.

Ben: Well, I guess my main concern is what the code of ethics states, not necessarily what the . . .

Dr. T: I think clearly the code of ethics has nothing negative to say about the experience because there are a number of schools where it has been done, where it's routine and even some schools require it, obviously somebody would have objected to it . . . along the way.

Ben: Well . . .

Dr. T: I guess what I respond to is the question of whether or not it would be harmful . . .

Ben: Yeah, well, this is the important thing.

Dr. C: Even at the school where it's done I think there is one major difference here, and that is that we, as class leaders, are offering to get involved in the group and I think this is usually done with some external people, some people external to the class itself. That is, in terms of group leaders.

Ben: Yeah, that's what . . .

Al: Well, stop fussing about that.

John: This would in a way . . .

Hank: I don't know if it's even possible for us to go to the hospital and sit in on group therapy sessions with people that probably need more help than we do, this sort of thing. But if this is possible, I'd like to see this happen.

Jim: How about time arrangements?

Dr. T: Well, I'd really like to get everybody's response before . . .

Tod: This is not our main consideration.

Dr. T: Yeah, to me that's a structural thing. I would tend to want to play it by ear. I would think that people would bring up reactions and feelings about their initial interviews with patients and that would take up more time, and it's impossible to know whether the group experience would focus perhaps exclusively on reactions to patients, feelings about patients. It would depend upon, to me, how it developed, that whether this was two hours a week or one hour a week in therapy would really depend on how we wound up using it, because I think each of us would probably use it in a somewhat different way.

Ben: Flexible.

Dr. T: Yeah. (Pause)

Al: Yeah, well, I think I agree with the question of Jack's position, I think really that this could be a very valuable experience for all of us.

Bill: I'm a little bit surprised . . . at the resistance that has come up to it. I think that therapists really should have some, you know, goals, and know as much about themselves as possible before going into therapy, to know what their own stimulus value is, to know how they feel about different things, and this is as close to me, this therapy, to get to a really deep experience in a group of people. It is a little threatening as far as the social aspects are concerned. I think I really, there may be some voices to the contrary, but I think if we're serious about our graduate program we really ought to want to better ourselves as therapists more. I think that ought to be more meaningful than the social relationships keeping adjusted to the part they are now. I feel pretty seriously about it. I think, definitely, that I have been in favor of it all along.

Dr. T: Um hmm. You spoke, Sam?

Sam: Well, I'm caught in a three-way bind here. One, I do have the same feeling that, first I agree with Jack that it'd probably be a valuable experience and we'd probably gain a hell of a lot from it but I also think that it may *not* be the same experience and things can come from this that we're just not capable of handling or dealing with and maybe something bad coming from it. Too, I again agree with Ben about this learning about ourselves, but I feel more the role is of our individual, well, psychotherapist, not of group therapy among the graduate students. I just don't like the basic idea. I also have the feeling that, well, if I would give in a little bit it's one thing, but I also have to be consistent with the thought in mind here that I would like to do it but I'm afraid of the things that may happen to the contrary . . . the good for it. I'm caught in a consistency bind here.

Dr. T: So that, partly you want to be consistent . . .

Sam: And partly, I want to try it. I'm in favor of it.

Dr. T: Partly . . . "it could be a valuable experience but suppose it weren't?"

Sam: The key here, I think is the control of the group; who is in charge; how far the group will go; where it will go; and I think just to express hostility among members of the group, I think, this is damaging.

Dr. T: Right.

Sam: I think the therapist has to be very forceful and very well adapted at doing this.

Dr. T: I guess, I don't know whether you feel like responding to this, Dr. C., but I do, in that . . . I suppose, myself, not just as a therapist, but as a person in the group. My feeling is that it would be important for me to have it be a constructive experience partly for my own feelings because I don't like to experience anxiety, and . . . partly, too, that it's very important for me in any kind of group experience to make sure that other people don't get hurt. I think I wouldn't be at all alone in those feelings in the group. I think I would feel very much that at least half of the people and probably all of the people would be as much concerned with that as I, and if, say, two people were being destructive to one another in a group setting. I have the feeling that I could rely on at least several other people saying, "Hey, aren't you really hurting each other? Are you really being helpful or are you just sort of cutting each other?" . . . Last night was a very meaningful experience for me, the process of terminating an outpatient group. These were people, a much sicker group than you ordinarily see in an outpatient group. Oh, there were some people who weren't so disturbed but the thing that was very striking to me was that, as one of the outcomes of the group experience, you can almost plot the liking for each other that developed. Not just disembodied liking but a real personal liking, so that at least at this point, these people have concern for the welfare of each other, and they're concerned now that the group is ending. They want, not only for themselves, but they want other people's lives to go well. They're concerned about what's going to happen to this other person. This kind of concern, I think, and the opening up to this kind of concern, well, it made me feel very much that people just couldn't be just venting hostility toward each other; that most of the people in the group would see this and say, "Hey, you don't really want to do this. Can't you see you're really hurting each other?" . . . this kind of thing.

Ben: I was wondering where all this hostility is going to come from. (Laugh) We're so concerned about our social relationships? Really, we must be somewhat fond of each other . . . I see his point.

Sam: I can see this is a possibility. I don't say this is what will happen but there's a possibility of it.

Dr. C: I can see that, you know, just the fact that it is destructive doesn't distract from the feelings of other people at that moment. That to point out that they're being destructive to each other and not constructive—I don't know what positive value this has of necessity. I think it may in some groups.

Dr. T: I think it almost always does if it's pointed to rather than insultingly *thrown* at somebody. You know, if it's done like "Look here, you rat, you're . . ."

Dr. C: (Interrupts) That would shut off feelings.

Dr. T: Well, I think it opens up feelings. I think that anger and hostility; I think they're the nicest defense against feelings that man has ever invented; it prevents exploration and involves just the extra-punitive.

Dr. C: I think there's a full range of feelings. Don't eliminate the hostile and the negative feelings. They're very real and I would hope that the group would be one place for them to come out. That's my own viewpoint; not just hostile feelings for each other but maybe toward us. Maybe this does really underscore that question of who should be the therapist.

Sam: Who should be in which group. This to me, these two are problems for us: who is controlling the group and the individual people in the group.

Dr. C: That's my idea, that there would be two groups.

Dr. T: Yeah, we've still got a couple of more people to consult before we get really into a discussion. Ray?

Ray: What if we want to abstain? I share Sam's feelings. I think that these sessions could be quite beneficial for us but on the other hand they could possibly be damaging. However, I think that the last statements of Dr. T. have somewhat reassured me, the fact that he will be on guard.

Dr. T: Thank you, Ray. (Laughter)

Ray: I feel I have a couple of protectors over there, so I would like for us to draw up some kind of rules of the game, you might say. For example, if anyone should at any point feel so threatened that he does not want to go on with his problem that he's concentrating on at the moment, I think that he should feel free . . .

Dr. T: Um hmm.

Ray: . . . with saying, "Okay, let's . . . I don't feel like talking about this anymore, maybe tomorrow, and . . ."

Dr. T: Let me respond to that. How would people feel about it? Suppose I were exploring myself and I came to something that I didn't want to share; I might just have gone far enough. Maybe too far. What would you feel?

Ben: This seems implicit in the idea of group therapy. A person goes as far as he wants to. Good grief, we're not there to push.

Dr. C: It's your privilege.

Dr. T: I sort of sense that we're, I don't know, to me respect of the individual's rights and decisions are fundamental and basic. . . . I would think even the most directive therapist that I can think of, if he's really capable, if he's really able, would not be drawing things out of people whether they wanted to let loose of them or not. To have something yanked out of you, I can't think of as therapeutic.

Al: After all, as adults, we'd be able to say, "If you don't like it, go to hell!" (Laughter)

Dr. T: Even if one person at that moment, for whatever reasons, wanted to keep that exploration going I think the rest of the group would say, "Hey, why are you doing this? What need is this in you to get this person to open up, that prevents you from respecting his decisions?"

Dr. C: I think that is the point, that you don't have to make up these rules beforehand, and I would hate to see a guy have his hands tied so that he doesn't feel that he can't push at anytime. If he does push, he's on his own and he can be corrected by the group . . . I feel pretty strongly that the freedom . . . to the full range, to the pusher as well as the person being pushed must be there, that this be a group experince and not all structured beforehand in any way.

Tod: You mean it shouldn't be pollyanna-ish.

Dr. C: That's right.

Dr. T: I can see what you're leading to, Dr. C. I think, just as clearly, when you say the full range you do mean something different than what that can communicate because I guess you wouldn't be in favor if people were acting destructively toward each other. I'm sure you'd be one of the first people to say, "Hey, don't you know that hurts?" This kind of thing.

Dr. C: Yeah, I think that a lot of meaningful things come out of it and to restrict it beforehand, I think, is really kind of delimiting a lot of the efficacy in this process. The point that I would like to emphasize, though, is I think there are a couple of real critical questions that have been missed so far, but maybe we ought to hear her first.

Dot: I'm in favor of it. It seems to me that it would make the therapist more congruent.

Dr. T: I was sort of trying to take in the whole range of feelings here. One thing that seems to be very striking is, and it's darn well worth mentioning, that it's damn hard to believe that talking will help, that it's damn hard to believe that therapy will not be a terribly disintegrative thing! In a sense we're committing years of our lives to be able to become therapists and yet even we have real reservations—sort of like saying, "Yeah, if you're really in a mess, then what do you have to lose?" But unless you're really in a mess, maybe talking about things will make them worse. I don't know, "can we trust another human being, can we trust another human being in group therapy?" Maybe we can't, maybe a therapist isn't therapeutic. I guess patients of any type must experience it even more acutely. Because when we're not so acutely disturbed, maybe we have less to lose. We can hold ourselves in, and we're more under control; whereas if we're more upset, maybe we'd be more afraid of such an experience. I don't know. I sort of think, with the reservations I have at this point, I wonder if they wouldn't be multiplied if I felt less sure of my ability to withdraw.

The session continued:

Tod: Oh, I was agreeing with him in saying, we're sort of waiting to get on with it, a lot of us are, I am.

Ben: I'd say that there are three or four people involved, but I'd say that for most of us that's decided.

Dr. T: I guess part of my feeling about it being sort of quasi-group therapy today is, yeah, I sense this and I have this sort of feeling in myself. I, at this point, feel that, really, I have come to closure and so has the group as a whole. I would agree with you that "Yeah, we're probably going to have this experience." On the other hand, I really do have some kind of concern about people's ambivalences and skepticism and negative feelings, too. I wonder if this isn't a great deal like group therapy where people have some respect for each other's feelings and also want to say, "Yeah, but let's go on," or have this impatience.

Tod: That is a good point both of you are making: this is a sort of an introduction to group therapy, the first session.

Dr. T: Maybe even more like the second session where you then—in the first session some people sort of say a lot of things, tell their story—where in the second session, people are wondering, "well, really should I be here? What am I really getting into here? Does it really make sense?" I guess even though I feel some closure, I also feel I would particularly hate to have a group experience, not just without some members because they would be more cut off, but I would particularly feel a loss with Ray and Sam. I feel that there's a certain amount of spontaneous honesty, this joking bit, that really is very meaningful to me.

Tod: This is something I was wondering about. I'd hate to see the group split in this way—I hate to miss the other group experience. It would be nice in a way if we could work all together except for . . .

Dr. T: I think that's what we've been saying. (Laughter) We don't want the group to be split.

Al: I had the same feeling, I don't want to miss the other. Somehow, I feel a little like this is just too big—it's kind of hard to be spontaneous with this size. As much as I would think something would fit in, I'm not going to say it.

Ben: Yeah.

Al: You're a little bit inhibited about imposing yourself when there's so many others. You say well, they haven't talked at all, then you've maybe talked a couple of times before, and you think, "Well, we could always tape and listen to the other group."

Tod: I think this is a real problem.

Al: No, I'd rather keep it in one group, but there are these bad aspects of it.

Sam: There isn't enough time for just one big group really. Just two different levels here—the people who are really verbal, opposed to the ones who don't talk, and if we get the ones who don't verbalize, freely verbalize, they're dead. They don't stand a chance.

Al: No.

Sam: That's why I was thinking of the two groups.

Bill: At least it's been my experience from being in one of these things before. One guy shuts up and doesn't say anything, it isn't long before the whole attention of the group is brought to getting him to say something, like "dah!" (Laughter) At any rate it focuses on, at different times, on different people. Just because he doesn't say much the whole group will respond to one person and try to draw him out. Not to pry or anything, but just to get him to participate. If one guy says something and one person sitting over there hasn't said anything, usually someone will say, "well what do you think about that, what he's just said?"

Tod: I don't think that would be particularly true of a smaller group, yet, it would become more readily apparent in a large group. In a large group a couple of people could sit back for maybe half an hour or 45 minutes before anybody realized that they hadn't said anything. Then, in a smaller group, where you have maybe half a dozen or eight people, it would show itself up pretty fast.

Ben: How are these two groups going to be selected?

Sam: How about just random selection.

Al: Wait a minute, have we decided to split? (Laughter) I wasn't aware that the decison was made.

Dr. T: From the response, I guess people do feel that one group is too large. How many people would like to, would be in favor of a small group—how many people would be in favor of having small groups even if they got in the small group they would least prefer, with people they would least prefer?

The session finally concluded:

Dr. T: Some of us are sort of curious as to what closure we're at now. How about you, Ray? you haven't said much?

Ray: That we will have the sessions, has been decided, and I think it's more or less set. We will have this combination, of one, and two group sessions. I think that's the general feeling.

Ben: We'll meet as whole group first hour . . .

Dr. T: I don't know, what do you think? One thought I had now was that we could meet in small groups next time . . . start off that way.

Al: I think the other way around would be best, that is to meet in a large group first. The various problems and issues can come out.

Dr. T: Yeah.

Al: And then they could be more closely focused upon in small groups.

Ben: Too, you have the other perspective. You develop problems in smaller groups and want to share them with the rest.

Dr. T: Well, how many people would like to meet in a large group first? How many people would like to meet in a small group first? I suppose the next order is to sort of decide which people will be in which group.

Ben: Just randomly assigned. (Several voices agreeing)

Dr. T: Well, okay, we'll have A and B. Let's just see what happens. We can do it randomly—just go around the room and say who wants to be an A and who a B. (Voting by group: A, B, A, B, B, etc.) All right. Everybody in A raise your hand. How many are in B? The rest of the people don't care either way? I don't know, would you rather have your friends in the same group or a different group?

Sam: It makes it easier this way.

Dr. T: I suppose the sensible way of deciding about group leaders would be to just flip a coin if we're going to switch later.

Ben: I would prefer you'd make a selection and begin, myself. I have one vote.

Dr. T: I'll tell you what. Why don't Dr. C. and I leave and you can decide the formation of the group and which will be the initial group leader. I'd like to get closure so that we could get started next period.

Sam: We can verbalize everything. Why can't you just stay?

Ben: I'd prefer to stay myself.

Dr. T: Okay.

Bill: I have a preliminary suggestion. I would suggest that, first of all, we vote on the issue of whether we are going to vote on who we want to have or whether we want to do it by flip of the coin.

Dr. T: Okay. All those in favor of coin—all those in favor of choice. Four to five, is that it?

Bill: Four people who were, who voted for the selection are in one group. I personally have no qualms about just letting them go ahead and take whichever one they want because obviously they must have a preference.

Dr. T: They may not have the same preference.

Sam: Let's find out. Let's find out. Jack?

Jack: I would prefer to start with Dr. C.

Ben: I second.

Sam: I agree too.

Dr. T: Is that agreed then?

Sam: Um hmm.

Dr. C: Group A is the hostile group. (Laughter)

With these early encounters the training program was off the ground. Lines of communication had been established. The students had come to some realization that they were to be a very real part of the decision-making process in the program. For most purposes this problem-solving was to involve a level of self-exploration in both trainees and teachers. At the same time the teachers were attempting to bring to bear things that had proved valuable in their own experience and learning, with the implicit hope that the students would come to feel free enough both to experience for themselves and to let their own experiences interact with those of their supervisors. This interaction process can often be productive of a new direction in learning for both student and teacher. In this sense, the teacher as well as the student remains open to new experiences. Both the teacher and the student are involved in a continual learning process.

THE EXPERIENTIAL CONTEXT OF THE TRAINING PROGRAM

Nonpossessive warmth and genuineness appear to be basic conditions in a relationship facilitating the personality and behavioral changes necessary to produce effective counselors and therapists. These two conditions are the critical bases for the trusting relationship assumed necessary to allow trainees the freedom both to be their present selves and to move toward the more mature aspects of themselves. Psychotherapy training is not merely the memorization of a list of do's and don't's. To be effective it must give the trainee an opportunity to examine his own values, his goals, and the potentially useful aspects of his current self as therapeutic tools.

Throughout the classroom sessions and the entire training program, the supervisors attempted to provide at least minimal levels of these conditions, in the expectation of fostering feelings of safety and freedom in the trainees. They also hoped to promote in the trainees an openness to their own experience and a consequent willingness to experiment; a willingness on the part of the trainee to risk himself both by exposing new aspects of the self and by trying new modes of communicating and behaving. At times in the actual classroom, the learning experience moved toward an essentially group therapy experience, in which students and teachers alike became involved in an interactional process of self-exploration and experiencing. This occurred even during essentially intellectual discussions of the meaning of empathy, warmth and genuineness. In fact, the classroom sessions, while sometimes resembling the format of university seminars, rarely involved formal lecturing. Instead, the students were expected to read on their own material that otherwise might have been given in lecture form. Some flavor of this kind of classroom interaction can be gained from the first group of students.

Ben: I'd like to make a contribution, saying how I, one of the ways I see the situation. I think it's obvious to all of us that there has been much more hostility and negativism expressed in this class toward the professors than in any other class that most of us have been in, in this university. Part of it has to do with the fact that many people are afraid that they are being indoctrinated—they are being brainwashed—as they have been brainwashed in other classes. They've been indoctrinated in psychoanalytic theory, indoctrinated in rat-running and so forth and so on. Now people have the feeling that . . . these two professors, these two men are trying to shove nondirective therapy down our throats—they are being a little bit overly enthusiastic about selling their form . . . and the reason that this hostility is explicit in this class where it's not expressed in the other classes in which we are being, shall I say "brainwashed" is because of the attitude that the teachers have assumed. They have been much less authoritarian, they are young men not much older than ourselves, they have adopted a friendly-type relationship with us. They have been congruent, I'd say. They have not been, oh, so ultraprofessional—I won't use the word phony there (laughter)—as some of the other professors I have taken. Perhaps, to a certain extent, this is a . . . displacement mechanism: we are displacing all our hostility upon them. Upon our two teachers here, hostility which was built up in all the other classes.

Al: (To the supervisors) You make a good target. (Laughter) Because you make targets of yourselves for antagonisms or what in a normal situation would be antagonistic. I would react antagonistically to some things you say, and so I would get mad.

Dr. T: Um hmm.

Al: If you'd said, as I said at the beginning, if you'd said to me what you said to him I would be mad and nobody else lets themselves open for it and so I think there's much truth to this.

Dr. C: I guess my feeling is, would you ever be able to say the things that Sam has—been able to open it up, if we hadn't?

Al: Well, I think in this kind of class it's wonderful. But I'm saying in relation to his conversation . . .

Dr. T: (Jokingly) You gotta say we're pretty good. (Laughter)

Al: No . . .

Dr. T: (Jokingly) Underneath it all . . . (Laughter)

Al: What he's saying in essence is you're targets and you have opened yourselves up to be targets.

Ben: Perhaps some of us are taking advantage of the situation. Maybe that's too strong of a term, but . . .

Dr. T: But I think the nature of this experience is more threatening in the sense that the usual structure isn't there to hold on to. It's a different kind of experience. You know, anything unknown, unpredictable, is always anxiety arousing, more threatening . . .

Bill: I had the reaction when this little exchange was going on that, "Dammit, can't you say anything without being a therapist, sounding like a therapist?" And, if I were in this situation I think I would probably have gotten pretty mad because to me it would seem like, well this is taking unfair advantage. I'm trying to argue with you, I don't want to be a patient of yours at this particular moment, and it just seemed like at that moment you were sounding like a therapist.

Dr. T: About a second ago? The response that was welling up in me was, "Don't treat me like a damn patient!" That was what I wanted to say to you. Then I caught myself, and I'm not sure I should have caught myself.

Bill: Um hmm.

Dr. T: I caught myself because you were just then saying, "Don't do this." (Laughter) On the other hand I really felt maybe it would have been better if I had let myself say that.

Tod: You have more of a capacity to roll with the punches than we do because, after all, you've got more power. If you had punched back at Al right then he probably wouldn't have . . .

Dr. T: But would that have been a punch?

Al: I don't think so because I wasn't attacking you. I was trying to argue with you.

Dr. T: I guess part of my feeling is, what do you really want to argue about?

Al: Well I thought that Tod wanted to argue about the merits of the therapy tape recording we just heard.

Dr. T: I didn't really feel that's what he was arguing about. It would have been dishonest for me to pretend as if I really thought that's what he was arguing about. I didn't.

Tod: The fact that there was this tape business underneath . . . very critical reaction to that tape, I think. I think you're right . . . because it's not that bad a tape. I . . . (laughter) because whenever I hear my tapes, God, they sound terrible!

Dr. T: Partly I felt, well, . . . nobody responded that way to Dr. S.'s tape the other day when we played part of Dr. K.'s tape, and that was not something that would be a real good example of therapy and yet nobody bothered to knock it. And yet it seemed you really had the set that you were determined to knock it, and if I argued with you, I would have been pulled into your need system in the first place and pulled the whole class into it. More than that, if I had at that moment played that role, I would have been dishonest because I didn't really feel that was the issue. If I don't feel that's the issue, why should I argue about it? . . . My feeling was, no matter what I said, and I have a barrage—I have, I could be quoting authority figures to buttress what he did and I could, maybe, even name two authority figures *for*, for everyone you could name *against*. (Laughs) But that would have been, I think, phony, because I didn't really feel that was the issue. I thought no matter what I said, you would just shift over to new ground and argue.

Tod: Yeah, I notice a big difference in the way I feel about the tape now. I think it's because you pointed out the underlying motivation underneath it, or maybe just getting it out in the open.

This kind of classroom interaction suggests a greater degree of individual "freedom" but greater self-responsibility. It also involves a kind of straightforward genuineness or even candor which is more typical of therapy than of the usual graduate training program. The early part of the training experience involved a shift from the teacher's taking responsibility for the student to a more equal sharing of responsibility for the learning experience. Both the supervisors and the trainees are involved in a process of testing this "sharing" of responsibility, the kinds of freedom it implies, and the responsibilities required. The students become more free to examine both what they are getting from the supervisor and what they are giving; they can confront themselves and the teachers with both their negative and positive feelings. As indicated by the laughter, the interchange is anxiety-arousing for both the students and the teachers; and yet they still tend to attempt to be genuine and not retreat into the traditional role of teacher and student. This results in movement toward some self-exploration and more immediate experiencing by both students and supervisors.

Discussion of critical encounters in counseling and psychotherapy often developed from the trainee's readings and from his listening to the tape library of experienced therapists. In the context of the interpersonal atmosphere and the consequent attempts toward more candor for both supervisors and trainees, this frequently evolved toward self-disclosures not always expressed in academic programs. Again, such interactions reflect a blend of the classroom with the therapeutic encounter. The following excerpt from the class discussion grew out of a comment about a tape recording by a particular therapist who uses "swear words" in the privacy of his relationship with the patient.

Sam: Is this person being real? Does a "real" therapist swear maybe, or is it not real . . . or maybe one shouldn't. How does this affect the therapy?

Dr. C: To me it seemed valuable. I would like in a client who's made progress . . . I would like him to be open to my way of doing things, just as well as I would feel that I would want to be open to his way of doing things. That is, one way that Dr. L. characterizes this is that the therapist can grow from this therapeutic relationship just as well as the client. But I would also like to expose the client to my pathology if you want to look at it as pathology . . . but why change your behavior? You know, maybe they live in a dichotomized world of right and wrong, and this is wrong. Well, you know in the world I come from, it's not wrong, but maybe, some of the artificial ways are wrong. Maybe I can grow in that relationship too.

Sam: What I had in mind, for instance, therapists who are somewhat restricted in environment . . . enter therapy armed with warmth, accurate empathy and congruence. A real quiet-type therapist enters therapy and then the patient assails him with the whole verbal language, abuse, and everything else. How does he react to this? In other words, right away, if the person starts giving him a whole mess of crap, this immediately might set him off. How does this affect therapy? I'm dealing with the personality of the therapist here.

Dr. C: Maybe he would. You mean, are you aiming at whether the therapist is going to react aggressively?

Sam: That's right.

Dr. C: Maybe his way of doing it would be to say, "I get a very strong feeling like, sounds like you're taking advantage of me. You've come in here and give me all this stuff . . ."

Sam: In other words, what I'm also saying is, it bothers the hell out of you to see a naive therapist, for instance, me, walk into therapy armed only with warmth, and a patient attacks me like crazy.

Dr. C: But what does it do in you; what does it evoke in you?

Sam: It scares the hell out of me. First of all, when he starts to attack I don't know what to do, both from ignorance and *not;* well, mostly from ignorance, not knowing what to do. It sort of evokes a defensive reaction in me. But I think, this is what I'm getting—are these three things . . .

Dr. C: What's a defensive reaction—to fight back?

Sam: Fight back, you might say. Or, and not knowing how to fight back. You have you own feelings of what you'd like to do. They may not be proper and they may not be right, so you just don't do anything.

Dr. C: I'm just thinking . . . right at the beginning, when you are at the "being scared" level . . . a lot of things to think about there. One is that he may be testing you, for one thing. But even more than that, these are your very real feelings.

Al: That's right.

Dr. C: That he shakes you up when he does this. I wonder if you couldn't make this known to him, would it be too much of a risk to take?

Sam: Well, I just don't know. In other words, this happened real early in a couple of therapy relationships with me and I didn't know what to do. I sort of retreated and more or less avoided issues . . .

Dr. C: Um hmm.

Sam: Taking out his hostility, maybe his anxiety, maybe his aggression on me . . .

Dr. C: When you do this to other people, I mean, you can accept this kind of behavior in yourself . . .

Sam: Sure.

Dr. C: When you attack other people?

Sam: Sure, I do.

Dr. C: But somehow it's hard to accept in him when he lets you have it.

Sam: Well, I don't know if it's hard to accept—it's that I don't know how to combat it. What does one *do* when this happens?

Dr. C: What I think I'm driving at is a more direct dealing with it . . . and . . . that's not necessarily fighting back.

Tod: That's right. It seems like if Sam knew what to do, he wouldn't feel, he wouldn't be scared, he'd be doing that which he should be doing. Like for example, if he would say something, like "You're very angry the way it sounds," like you'd be taking an active role and have a feeling of at least doing *something.*

Dr. C: This would be, this would be Dr. L.'s way, for example, "It's something about it that gets you really upset" or something like that, or he might even bring himself more into it; "It really shakes the hell out of me. Apparently something in me gets you upset and you let me have it and it gets me upset," which you know, just by its recognition means really that you're not afraid of dealing with it anymore. You see, you only go on the run when you can't deal with it. I'm not saying to say it the way I said it . . .

Bill: Um hmm.

Dr. C: But I have my own idiosyncratic way of responding, and we're not trying to give you a repertoire of responses to use in these situations, but I think if you deal more directly with it, with yourself and the client in this interaction . . . it might be worth trying.

Tod: The surprising thing is that it's actually the client who is much more anxious, you know . . .

Dr. C: Yeah.

Tod: And as long as you, when you pick up the anxiety underneath the attack . . .

Dr. C: Well, one way of structured leading here and I say, I'm not selling it, but one way of structured leading him might be to go beyond, say, what I said here and say, "I very often find myself attacking people when I'm in a situation that I don't understand." In other words, telling him that you understand him but you understand yourself also and that you respect this in both of you. But not with the sole purpose of shutting it off. Maybe you want to encourage this more. Maybe you want to bring it out more—not just combat it and shut it off you know, like, "Let's get this therapy organized so I can do therapy on you." You know, not that.

Sam: I think that I mean more than that. Throughout all the years that you do therapy, no matter how much you really get attacked . . . you know, somewhere along the line you always get attacked . . . maybe little things or the patient will hit you with things. There are difficult things to deal with.

Dr. C: You're sure right. Right here. Right here with my second session with a patient group, delinquents, and you know, after we got into the second session a girl sits there and says, "Phony, phony, phony, phony!" You know, and yeah, it shakes you up for a second. (Laughter) You don't want her to feel that your *group* is phony. If she was in another group before that was phony, you want to make it clear that yours is different and everything, but her experience is "phony" at that moment. It arouses feelings in me but also I want to understand more the feelings in her.

Al: What did you do then?

Dr. C: I took the nice, neat defensive way out (laughter) by concentrating on her feelings. No, but I think that I might have handled it much more openly. You might say I wasn't overwhelmed by it but I didn't open up either.

Ben: Perhaps, you know, you might have said, "Oh, you really hurt me by saying that . . ."

Dr. C: But then to go further, "You must feel like this group is a dead-end road, that we're not going to accomplish anything worthwhile." You know, I think I might have handled it better than I did. But the kind of impact it has on you at the moment shakes you up.

Al: This is right.

Dr. C: And you don't always (laughter), you don't always *do* what you know would be most effective.

Here the original question about whether "real" (or perhaps "ideal") therapists "swear" in therapy led directly into an exploration of the feelings of both patient and therapist when a patient verbally or physically assaults the therapist. Trainees and the supervisors explored the question together and arrived at tentative directions. In part the trainees learned from the supervisor's recounting of a moment when he was less therapeutic and more threatened than he would like. Such attempts at a more genuine relationship and more open candor between students and supervisors in each classroom session cannot be fully planned in advance. Varying modes of approaching questions and issues are tried. Experimentation and experience dominate, with the focus not on the method of teaching, but on the issues. When it seems that an issue can be handled best by discussion, there is discussion; when an issue seems best handled by therapeutic self-exploration, that is attempted.

In the following excerpt, the discussion centered on implementing empathic understanding with an extreme obsessive-compulsive patient. At the outset a trainee is concentrating on why empathic responses aren't possible with such patients. After a few moments of discussion, when it's obvious that the discussion is leading nowhere, spontaneous role-playing is tried. The student has begun by describing a patient who gives a "machine-gun-like" barrage of complaints that overwhelm the therapist.

Dr. T: All right, let's say you were the patient doing this to me (the therapist) right now.

Ray: Um hmm.

Dr. T: You were giving me this line, you would probably do it in a recital fashion, in a mechanical fashion, or something like that.

Ray. Um hmm. Um hmm.

Dr. T: And I might say, "I've been sitting here trying to puzzle through what meaning this has for you. I'm sure you mention all this because it's important to you in some way and yet I can't really grasp in what way."

Ray: Well, what if they felt that you should know this about them, so you just better understand them.

Dr. T: Well . . .

Ray: . . . Some situation about which they're bothered . . .

Dr. T: Yeah . . .

Ray: Mean, you take . . .

Dr. T: But then I might still respond . . .

Ray: Then it would take half a dozen sessions for them to tell you about it.

Dr. T: Oh, I doubt it would take that long.

Ray: No . . .

Dr. T: I would try to be cutting through that, because I might be saying, you know, like—let's role-play this for a second . . .

Ray: I couldn't make it up . . . (Laughter)

Dr. T: Yeah. Try . . . You're seeing me, I say "what meaning does it have," you know, trying to figure out what meaning it has to you and you say, "Well, I want you to really know my whole background" and you start going on again, to tell all of the details of your background so I could really understand you. Is that it? In other words, that would automatically tend to focus them on their current feelings.

Ray: Um hmm.

Dr. T: I think recital without feeling is probably a waste of therapy time. That's probably why I would tend to focus on that. I think I have become completely conditioned to respond to feeling, anxiety-laden material . . . height of feelings, and I'm real eager to hear depressive statements. All of these kinds of things I have been habituated to in therapy. I think that these are probably valid things to be conditioned to. And I think it's only in this way that the present and the past and the future make sense to each other.

Al: Are you implying that if the person does not express, the patient, client, does not express his feelings, little benefit can obtain from therapy? For example, if an obsessive-compulsive keeps on saying in a very flat manner, "Yes, I am bothered by my stomach hurting, I am bothered by my head hurting" and so forth and so on—feeling like . . . schizophrenic?

Dr. T: Um hmm. I think if he kept that up it would probably represent a real failure of the therapist to get through.

Ray: How would the therapist get through?

Dr. T: Well, let's try it. I think by responding to this. Try it; try to be such a patient. Can you make a good one?

Ray: I don't think it would take too much imagination. (Laughter) Okay, I'm the patient now. (Sounds of chairs shuffling) I was sent here by the internist who examined me in the clinic. My stomach bothers me, I feel, I go about three hours without eating and if I don't have a glass of milk my stomach feels pretty bad. I keep myself to a certain extent by taking an antacid tablet, and I just worry all the time about my stomach. I worry, I worry and I worry. And I'm unable to see how talking about this can do any, any good.

Dr. T: It seems to you you're really falling apart. That you're really going to pot and talking just won't help.

Ray: Well, I don't know if I'm going, falling apart but (laughs) my stomach's about ready to erupt.

Dr. T: Um hmm. It's getting pretty serious.

Ray: Yes, it's, I don' know how serious it is. I worry about it becoming serious but I don't know how serious it is.

Dr. T: It's darned serious to you.

Ray: Oh, sure, definitely . . . important.

Dr. T: And you're afraid that it's going to get worse and worse and worse.

Ray: That's right. I'm afraid my stomach might become cancerous.

Dr. T: That you might just get eaten up.

Ray: Well, yes.

Dr. T: You might just rot away.

Ray: Yes . . . so what are you going to do about it?

Dr. T: "Can't anything be done for me?"

Ray: That's right.

Dr. T: "Can I be saved at all?"

Ray: That's right. That's what I want to know.

Dr. T: "And I'm sure that talking won't help it."

Ray: I'm not sure of anything. I'm very indecisive . . .

Dr. T: Um hmm.

Ray: . . . doubting person . . . I'm not sure of anything. I cannot see how it can help me, but it might help . . .

Dr T: "Doesn't make sense, but it might."

Ray: That's right. I'm willing to say probably; small probability that it might help.

Dr. T: "I guess I'd be willing to give it a chance."

Ray: Oh, I don't know.

Dr. T: Would you?

Ray: Well, what do you think the probability is of its helping me?

Dr. T: Well, . . . more often than not, talking has helped things, strange as it seems.

Ray: Well, that is encouraging. I would be willing to talk with you then under these circumstances. Now tell me how I should go about, I mean what I should say, so that I can cure my ulcer by talking.

Dr. T: Um hmm. Let's start right there. It's clear you want to cure it.

Ray: I didn't hear what you said.

Dr. T: It's clear that you want to cure it.

Ray: Yes, that's right.

Dr. T: And yet you feel it's really very likely that you'll wind up rotting away inside.

Ray: Oh, I think that's pretty likely. Probable. Actually I don't really have any idea of the probability, it's something I'm afraid of. I worry all the time.

Dr. T: Um hmm.

Ray: About just my stomach rotting away so to speak. But I, really, when I think of things objectively, I know that my ulcer is probably in the duodenum, not in the stomach proper and that just from the statistical point of view, my ulcer will probably not become cancerous . . .

Dr. T: When you really look at it, it does seem unlikely but you really feel inside almost certain . . . almost certain.

Ray: Well, I wouldn't say that I feel inside almost certain but let's say the idea keeps on going around and around in my head. I'm . . .

Dr. T: And it doesn't make sense and the probabilities are way against it, and yet you just can't help but think about it and worry about it all the time.

Ray: I guess that's true, yes.

Dr. T: Even though it doesn't make sense, you sure spend your time worrying about it.

Ray: I guess that's true. And I can't see how just talking can stop me from worrying . . .

Dr. T: "What will stop me from worrying?"

Ray: Yes, that's right.

Dr. T: "Doesn't make sense and yet I spend most of my time worrying."

Ray: Yes, that's right.

Dr. T: And I guess the other aspect is, "It's darn scary."

Ray: Yes, I guess that's right. What, what should I say to cure my ulcer?

Dr. T: Guess that's almost a question you're always asking, what should I, what should I, what should I . . .

Ray: Yes, I would say so, say that I'm a person who, seems as though my cognitive processes are just continually active. I cannot slow them down even moderately. Thoughts just keep on going through my mind, what should I do, what am I doing that I should not be doing, what am I not doing, that should be doing and so forth and so on.

Dr. T: And, "I'm always worrying about right and wrong and what I should do and what I ought not to do . . ."

Ray: Well . . .

Dr. T: "I'm never sure about it . . ."

Ray: Not sure about anything. Course I still don't know how that's going to do any good. Just talking about the fact that I'm not sure of anything, just talking about my symptoms; I don't know how that will help my stomach; I don't know how that will ease my worry.

Dr. T: I guess the other bad side would be, that you're always afraid of being wrong.

Ray: Oh, not necessarily being wrong, but afraid of something happening.

Dr. T: Um hmm.

Ray: Afraid of some impending disaster, afraid of getting sick, afraid of being hit by a car, afraid of everything.

Dr. T: Something bad could happen just anytime.

Ray: Yes, that's right. I'd say that pretty well characterizes my . . .

Dr. T: I, I think this sort of . . . (Moves chair to end role-playing)

Ray: This is dangerous . . . I find myself getting involved. (Laughter)

I'm afraid, I'm afraid we, we chose a poor example (laughter) getting close to home. (Laughter)

Dr. T: I think when we do role-play we always have to give a little of ourselves. You know, that's like even some actors: any actor, very few actors can play all roles. They have to play something that feels like a part of them.

That might give a feel, for the emphasis is upon the momentary feeling and for the feeling state, not just the words that come out. Obviously I was making use of diagnostic kinds of impressions. Not in the classical sense, the dynamic sense, but I know that most everybody who is concerned about their stomach rotting away, that they really feel they're rotting away. I also suspect they think they're bad, they think they're wrong and they're always frightened. All these things that generally go together in such people, I can make use of. We can make use of all these pieces of information, and apply them. We can try to do it in a fairly tentative way so that the patient is free to say, "No, that doesn't fit me." But making use of the information in terms of feeling, not that people behave this way, as is the more traditional diagnostic information, but in terms of the diagnostics of feeling state—we know that obsessive-compulsives have certain kinds of feelings that are very typical of them—plus there are some feelings that are typical of everybody . . . and I think it is facilitating in a number of ways even if it's something quite obvious and some things you're quite aware of.

By expressing it, makes more of a bond between us; makes the client feel more comfortable in exploring further; makes him feel more like the therapist is really with him and concerned and interested. I think it does communicate that we value him. The therapist doesn't have to feel burdened by coming up with . . . marvelous insights to make a response. I certainly didn't make any marvelous insights there. The kinds of statements I made tended more to say "I'm with you, yeah, I sort of sense how that must feel," and invite you to explore it more. And the fact that I concentrate on the feelings invites and, to some degree, elicits from you exploration of feelings. You would start repeating, well, it doesn't help me . . . to talk and I would focus, instead, *quite deliberately* on the feeling you had expressed just before that, because of the conscious decision that that wasn't the important feeling to focus on at this point. So that, very clearly, part of my selectivity in responding to the range of feelings the patient provides is that I pick those that seem to have more emotional meaning and those also which the patient seems more willing to explore. So that, it's partly on the basis of how willing the patient is to explore feelings.

In this role-playing demonstration of possible responses to an obsessive-compulsive patient, the therapist responses seemed to lead quite readily into the real feelings of the person role-playing the patient—to the surprise and alarm of the student. The role-playing was broken off when it seemed that it was taking on the character of a real therapeutic process with the student's own feelings. Such encounters within the classroom have from the start a "to-be-filled-in" character. Such unplanned and spontaneous role-playing serves a useful function in communicating possible therapeutic behaviors in a specific and concrete manner. The spontaneous role-playing carries with it some risk for the supervisors since being a therapist to a momentary "patient" is often more demanding than counseling with a real client. It exposes the supervisor to inevitable moments of displaying gross ineptitude. Even then, he can use it as a very good example of what *not* to do. Often, transient and spontaneous role-playing effectively communicates by "pointing" to potential therapeutic behaviors. The following excerpt begins by dealing with defensive feelings in the therapist.

Dr. T: Well, if you kept being defensive, this would be an indication that you were missing the boat; that if you were defensive, one of the things that you would be communcating was that you felt uncomfortable or threatened, etc. This is a good avenue for pointing up the importance of the empathy being focused upon the momentary feeling state of the patient. That if we focus upon the momentary feeling state of the patient, we will eventually have covered everything of importance anyway. I really can't imagine a patient having areas that are deeply troubling to him and still find himself unable to bring them up if the context is there.

Sam: I was thinking, for example, you're being hostile about the patient's hostility.

Dr. T: Then what would you do?

Sam: I don't know.

Dr. T: Let's role-play. Let's role-play and see what happens. Be a hostile patient and I'll be a therapist and see how it goes. (Pause) It's a . . . little difficult this far away. (Chairs shuffling, mumbling—"we're somehow together," "I'm the hostile patient," etc.) We have to have some kind of context, I guess. Where are we; where would you like us to be? Out in the VA Hospital, and why are you seeing me? Have you seen me before?

Sam: Why don't you demand a change in the medicine, you're mad because you're taking too much medicine, just don't want to take it anymore.

Paul: I don't really want to be mad at him.

Sam: Well, it could be . . .

Tod: You're a patient that's taken down to role-playing sessions at the VA. You don't want to be role-playing. You're angry at them for trying to make you role-play.

Paul: That won't be hard to do. (Remarks and laughter)

Sam: Why don't you just be a graduate student in this course? (More laughter)

Paul: Okay. (Starts role-playing the client) . . . Well, look, I don't feel like we're doing any good here.

Dr. T: "We're just getting nowhere here."

Paul: Seems like a complete waste of my time.

Dr. T: You're getting nowhere. You're getting nothing out of it so why should you even come? (Pause)

Paul: Seems like we just come here and talk and talk and talk and it never does any good.

Dr. T: "What do you have to show for it?"

Paul: I don't know, I keep wandering back to, I don't know, I guess I expect maybe you will tell me what to do or something—give me some suggestions, make some suggestions about my problem.

Dr. T: You really want a lot more out of me than you're getting.

Paul: I think so. I guess you . . . kind of let me down.

Dr. T: Um hmm.

Paul: Mean, I've been coming here now for several weeks.

Dr. T: Sort of feeling, "Well, he doesn't really care?" Or, "He just doesn't know." (Pause)

Paul: Which do you think it is?

Dr. T: "Surely must be one of the two."

Paul: Can't you give me some suggestion—tell me what to do?

Dr. T: I suppose I could give you a list of things to do that might help . . . things that would work in my life. The real question is whether they would work in your life.

Paul: At least it'd be something to try. I feel now that I just don't know where to go.

Dr. T. Um hmm. As though there's nothing inside of you that could give direction. If only someone would tell you how to act.

Paul: Wish there'd be something . . . I don't really feel like I've got any idea of how, how to solve . . .

Dr. T: Um hmm. "There's nothing to try now." What should you do?

Paul: I, I just feel like, if you can't get any, some kind of suggestion, what good does it do to come?

Dr. T: Um hmm. You feel empty inside and no help coming from the outside.

Paul: That's the truth. Maybe I could talk to other people on the ward. See . . .

Dr. T: "They really help."

Paul: No, except they feel, they feel like they're getting help, though.

Dr. T: Umm.

Paul: And I don't feel like, feel like I'm . . .

Dr. T: Other people seem to get help but not you. (Pause)

Paul: Mean, I like to come, but . . . I like to feel I've got something to show for it.

Dr. T: Um hmm. Something really solid to prove it's worthwhile.

Paul: Well, not really, not necessarily to prove it's worthwhile . . .

Dr. T: That sort of felt better then when you dropped your arms, because you were holding yourself away.

Paul: I didn't know. (Pause) What about all these problems?

Dr. T: They're still there.

Paul: Yeah, I guess they'll always be there . . . unless you can tell me how to get rid of them.

Dr. T: "How can we do something about them?" (Pause)

Paul: I don't know. I come down here week after week. I tell you all these things. I try to explain my problems to you. I guess, you just can't understand them. You probably have never gone through anything like this.

Dr. T: I'd really like to try.

Paul: Well, we've gone over them several times . . .

Dr. T: I guess, I'm waiting today.

Paul: Waiting today? You mean, to go over them again?

Dr. T: I suppose more than just over them. I would really like to see us go *into* them.

Paul: Well, we talked about it several times, already.

Dr. T: (Turning the chair to break off the role-playing) This may give some flavor to focusing on the momentary state.

Paul: I had the feeling that I was too hostile to believe . . .

Dr. T: Well, I didn't feel you get too hostile. I feel it's pretty impossible. I think as you start to get hostile, I'm willing to bet almost anything that you felt more inappropriate.

Paul: (Laughter) Yeah.

Dr. T: It requires a stimulus to get hostile. One just can't get mad at me as a therapist you know, a poor little helpless . . . you just don't feel like going out and . . . (Laughter)

Dr. C: Well, why do you want to avoid hostility?

Dr. T: Well, I think there's a radical difference between avoiding hostility and provoking it.

Tod: Well . . .

Dr. T: Not that I'm wanting to avoid hostility , but I think I can really *not* see any great value in, as a therapist, *eliciting* hostility. Even less, can I see the value of then pretending as if I had no part in it, so that I deliberately, consciously or unconsciously, elicit hostility by my ambiguity, by my outward signs of rejection, by not responding, perhaps. I get the patient angry and then I suddenly say . . .

Tod: You're very angry.

Dr. T: You're inappropriate. The question is whether or not it really is inappropriate. It would be inappropriate here, but I didn't respond to you, if by my ambiguity or by my failure to respond I provoked further hostility, then I would have to say, yes, I was being a stimulus for hostility.

Dr. C: I think you're setting up a bit of straw man here. I think in a sense even by reflecting and getting at the feelings, underneath what he was saying, that you could have elicited more hostility except that you concentrated more on the other kind of feeling—in getting nowhere, the dead-end road where . . . you know actually this guy is pretty teed-off, too.

It's not just that he's concerned about getting nowhere, but he's teed-off about getting nowhere.

Dr. T: Well, if he were more this way, I might have responded.

Dr. C: Yeah.

Dr. T: But there are few situations where I as a therapist, elicit hostility and then I would really explore that.

Dr. C: Yeah, that's different though. I'm not . . . in other words, you may have elicited it in the past in the sense that this guy isn't getting anywhere and he's teed-off about that and he . . .

Dr. T: But I think that would be inappropriate, for me to focus on *me not getting him anywhere.* I could focus upon what a rat the therapist is for not getting him anywhere but I think that would be totally untrue. I mean, *he's* the one that's not getting anywhere. My life isn't unhappy. And this is an important thing for him to know. He's got to do something about it. It could be, for example, say if I were involved administratively with him and I said he couldn't have a home visit, or whatever, he would have legitimate anger. It could be that I had insulted him the session before or something of this nature which does happen from time to time in therapy. If I make a straw man out of his hostility toward the therapist, if he's really angry with himself or really angry and frustrated with the situation, what good does it do to try to pretend that he's really angry at the therapist.

Dr. C: I think a benevolent, understanding therapist can still be a stimulus for hostility.

Tod: To that point here, . . . you've got enough hostility right now as it is without provoking more.

Dr. C: I'm not saying about provoking it . . .

Tod: Now wait a minute . . .

Dr. T: I think this hypothetical man you suggest may exist . . .

Dr. C: No, I don't think that's hypothetical. I think it's in you and it's in me and the rest of us here . . . that . . . go ahead. What is your second point? (Laughter)

Tod: I'm saying there's no point in backing off and diverting him from expressing hostility if he feels it. It gives him a chance to get it off.

Dr. C: It's very interesting. I think Dr. T.'s point there was a real insight. The therapist in effect, in that kind of process which really focuses, I guess, more on empathy than, say, congruence, is not a stimulus for hostility . . . and he doesn't see himself as eliciting hostility in the client. And as a matter of fact, it's very clear that everybody feels that they don't deal with hostile feelings. This is what I was trying to get at. I admit, it's born of the formulation there, and I think maybe you have to say, here, that the therapist essentially sees himself as benevolent, and . . .

Tod. Loving . . .

Dr. C: Loving, and he's not a stimulus to hostility so he doesn't even look for the hostility which is there.

Dr. T: Some therapists see the nature of man and adjustment as a problem in controlling hostile, destructive drives.

Dr. C: Okay. That's the other extreme.

Dr. T: All right. I suspect the reality is that people are not born good or bad . . . not destructive or creative.

Dr. C: Right.

Dr. T: That these are learned phenomena and, as far as I can tell, the people who are seemingly destructive, aggressive and hostile are people who really don't have a hostility problem—they have a tenderness problem. They have been taught to believe that tenderness and kindness is a sign of weakness and something to be avoided because you open yourself up to destruction.

Tod: The huff and the puff is really defensive, to prevent this.

Dr. T: Yeah, very often you see this in the delinquents we're working with now. My God, they have this real tough exterior because they're afraid not to. They're really afraid not to, and in fact, often in their own situation they couldn't survive if they did. They can't see the potential of surviving without this hard exterior.

Tod: But there is a good point here, that the kind therapist would tend to inhibit the patient.

Dr. T: I don't think that always happened.

Dr. C: I think he may, I think this goes back into that triad, that he sees himself as kind and benevolent and doesn't really understand, or respect, or love the hostile side of himself, and he doesn't look for it in the client, or he doesn't even sense it. He just doesn't pick it up. Where I think for example, it's in this client here, I think that there's a degree . . .

Dr. T: Right. Right, he was hostile. (Laughter)

Dr. C: What I'm saying is that somehow when *I* become hostile, somehow it's inappropriate.

Dr. T: Well, it has to be appropriate, if you are very angry, because somebody has taken advantage of you, because life is frustrating, okay. But as a therapist, I should never pretend that this is appropriate to take this out on me. If it doesn't make sense, it doesn't make sense.

Tod: I don't agree with that.

Dr. T: Well, why?

Tod: The patient has to displace his hostility on the therapist and get him to understand its origins . . .

Dr. C: But for example, I think it would get irritating to me if all the therapist was, was my alter ego—if all he was doing was reflecting his understanding of me; if he wants a second party in the relationship. After a while that would get irritating, I'd get . . .

Dr. T: Try it. Try it—experience it and then see what you think. You're throwing up hypothetical straw men now. I don't think he's ever had that experience.

Dr. C: Oh yeah, I think I have, plenty of times.

Dr. T: Yah (laughs), who was your therapist?

Dr. C: I don't have to have a therapist.

Dr. T: The thing is this though . . . this doesn't automatically make one angry. It may be that at times when one has nothing else to do, and you're not working, you could say, "Hey, dammit, why don't we go out and have a drink? Do you think you're too good to go out and have a drink with me? That's probably what you think." That might occur.

Dr. C: I see that, kind of. Maybe more for me, I feel that's more my psychopathology, whereas I think more of just relating to the immediate situation between you as a therapist and me as a patient . . .

Dr. T: Well, what are you there in therapy for?

Dr. C: To get help.

Dr. T: What does that mean?

Dr. C: Direction facilitative to implement my hope for improvement and so on. But sometimes, as a matter of fact, I know that as a person, sooner or later, I'm going to have to test you and find out if I can get you hostile.

Dr. T: That's part of your psychopathology then.

Dr. C: Right. Well, no, I want to know if *you're* real.

Dr. T: That's a different question. That's a different question. If part of your psychopathology is that you want to try to make me hostile, it's important for me and you to explore this facet of yourself—not just for me to react. That would be just playing into your pathology. To explore why is it important for you that you can make me mad or that you can't make me mad.

Dr. C: See now, you're getting me teed-off . . . (Laughter)

Dr. T: I've attacked you.

Dr. C: No, you're backing down, you're not attacking me, but also the notion of having a guy there just understanding me and trying to help me explore my pathology all the time (laughter) gets me angry.

Dr. T: Sure, you're not pathological.

Dr. C: Well that's part of it (laughter), I think. But the real part of it is that I know you're pathological too.

Dr. T: "So, God dammit, get sick in front of me."

Dr. C: Well, God dammit, I don't want to see that aspect of your feelings.

Dr. T: That was a therapeutic response I just made, and it made sense to you, didn't it?

Dr. C: Yeah.

Dr. T: It didn't make you angry.

Dr. C: Right.

Dr. T: "All right, darn it!" (Laughter)

Dr. C: Yeah, but I think you reacted as much. You know, therapists and reactors, they converge . . . Now in a reactor like you were just then, I like that; that's real therapy for me which is different from what you were giving him in role-playing.

Dr. T: No, it's the same kind of thing except . . .

Dr. C: Naw . . .

Dr. T: . . . He didn't have any strong feelings. He didn't have any strong feelings. He was mostly hidden within himself.

Dr. C: That's probably right to some degree . . .

Dr. T: Here I have a choice of either interacting with you as a person . . . or staying with the role as therapist, and essentially in that moment, I was responding to what's in you, not what's in me.

Dr. C: Some of it's in you too. I think they're interwoven.

Dr. T: Yeah. Except that in that moment I would feel I was responding as an alter ego because I was responding in terms of what meaning it had for you, not what meaning it had for me. I may, at moments have responded at what meaning it had for me as for example when you opened your arms. You were like this (gesture) and then you opened up. I responded from within me, in a sense, to that, but . . . I think if a person gets angry and for example, wants to test you . . . what is really crucial is that you explore what the hell it is in him that makes him want to do this. Why does he have to do this?

Dr. C: You said . . . I agree with you. I think that was beautiful therapy right there and partially because I started getting teed-off and elicited some greater emotional response from you, too. You know at the same time you were interacting with me and giving me this greater emotional response, you were being therapeutic in what you said. You said, "So God dammit, why not show it," you know like that, and this I like.

In this interaction, the role-playing served as a stimulus for a heated interaction focusing on the meaning of hostility in patients and on sharply differing approaches to dealing with hostility. The interaction was deeply interpersonal and concerned a central problem in counseling and psychotherapy. From the interaction came a new experiential "learning" for both the supervisors and the students. By its occurrence, this situation reflects the atmosphere of mutual trust that fosters such openness.

These examples perhaps give some flavor of the contextual base of the learning situation. The blend of content with personal experience is evident.

Although the experiential context served as a background for the classroom interactions, the experiential qualities came to the foreground in the quasi-group therapy experience (as described in the following chapter), which provided a more concentrated therapeutic encounter.

In the context of an atmosphere intended to provide high levels of the three conditions, the research scales measuring them were employed in "shaping" trainee responses. The trainees learned first to identify and discriminate the various levels of the therapeutic dimensions; they then moved through various practice phases to the goal of training: *the communication of high levels of those conditions related to constructive client change.* Practice phases that helped shape trainee responses involved immediate and concrete feedback as the class rated these responses in person or on tape. Along with the class procedures, a formal quasi-group therapy experience was provided, dealing primarily with personal difficulties encountered by the trainees in their role as therapist. When the trainee had developed his therapeutic skills in role-playing to the point where he could provide minimally high levels of therapeutic conditions, he was allowed to see real clients on a continuing therapeutic basis. (The excerpts from discussions of criteria for grades and the possibility of quasi-group therapy have been provided for the reader's illumination and edification, but are not critical in this development.)

The experiential base of the training program constituted the essential starting point for all other activities. If the trainees could not experience high levels of warmth and regard, understanding and genuineness from the supervisor, then they could not be expected to function at high therapeutic levels themselves. If they could not trust the trainers' motives, they would ultimately meet conflicting "double-bind" messages, in which the trainers were saying one thing but the trainees were receiving very different messages. In a very real sense, this experiential context was the substratum of the training program. It must be emphasized that the intent was not *merely* to present high levels of warmth and understanding. With the recognition that a free atmosphere alone does not elicit expressivity at the highest level, highly interactive and spontaneous communications pushed the trainees into interpersonal reactions. Their responsiveness was elicited by the supervisors' spontaneous expressions of emotionality; their attempts to establish emotional contacts with others were greeted with reciprocity.

CHAPTER 9 THE QUASI-GROUP THERAPY EXPERIENCE

LEARNINGS from a large number of training programs developed by others, as well as the research by Baldwin and Lee (1965), have suggested the importance of some kind of therapeutic experience for effective training in psychotherapy and counseling, and so the quasi-group therapy experience is perhaps basic to the present training approach. Although intensive individual and group psychotherapy for trainees might be even more useful, not all institutions and communities have such resources readily available. Further, intensive didactic psychotherapy for trainees might well constrict their own development by "converting" them to the sole viewpoint of their training therapist or counselor. Personal growth and personality change relevant to the development of more effective interpersonal skills were, of course, goals of the total training approach, but the quasi-group therapy experience would not directly aim at correcting existing emotional, behavioral, or personality problems. Since the available evidence (see Chapter 7) suggests that therapists who themselves are anxious, upset, immature, or emotionally disturbed are less effective in practice, it seems wiser to train those prospective trainees who have no serious psychological problems than to aim at both treating and training prospective students with personal problems; they can, like any other person in our society, seek help from the traditional sources.

The aim of the quasi-group therapy experience was, first, to give trainees experiential meaning for the role of the therapist by their own participation as clients; and second, to provide an opportunity for self-exploration of their own goals, values, and experiences in relation to their emerging role as counselor or therapist. Such firsthand experience in the human encounter of counseling from the client's viewpoint would also allow them to move toward integrating their own personality, values, and goals with the didactic and cognitive learnings. Although some of the quasi-group therapy sessions developed into personal therapeutic experiences for the trainees, this was not the primary aim. Both the trainees and the supervisors understood at the outset that the experience was not aimed at uncovering deep emotional problems, although this still occurred in some instances.

In the two groups of postgraduate students who participated in the formal training, the classes were large enough to necessitate breaking the total class into smaller groups for the quasi-group therapy experience.[10]

10. Drs. Truax and Carkhuff served as quasi-therapists with the first class of trainees, and Drs. Truax and Wargo served with the second class.

Different therapists using different approaches produce different styles of interaction, but there are several commonalities which seem to occur by the fact that they are embedded in a training experience. Except for deeply personal self-explorations, the following transcriptions taken from the quasi-group therapy experience represent examples of recurrent content.

In this first brief excerpt a student reacts to her first contact with a hospitalized patient:

Dot: Well, I had my first interview yesterday.

Dr. T: Traumatic, or enjoyable or . . . ?

Dot: Well, it was an experience, to say the least. It was my first experience with a schizophrenic. I have wondered since . . . I would have carried it off better if I had known more about schizophrenics. This woman was shaking all over and perspiration was just pouring down her face and the least little thing you would touch on, she would break into tears.

Dr. T: I guess a number of people here worked with that kind of a population—what were others' reactions?

Dot: Well, I wondered.

Dr. T: Any response?

Tod: I'm just trying to think back . . . I don't recall hearing a patient quite like that, but . . . I'd say schizophrenics do cry more easily because they're just plain more fearful of themselves and the whole world.

Dot: I wondered if she was in the beginning . . . or if I said something that . . .

Dr. T: Well, it was pretty upsetting to deal with . . .

Dot: Well, I felt that if I penetrated very far she might just go to pieces. I . . . I was afraid I might go too far . . .

Dr. T: Um hmm. Sort of like walking on eggs.

Dot: Um hmm. I didn't think this was what she really . . . you know, you're supposed to talk about things that are troubling a patient but I needed to go someplace where she wouldn't fall apart. When she would break into tears I would generally try again to change the topic to something else.

Dr. T: Sort of become nonempathic . . . to stop it.

Dot: Um hmm.

Tod: Sometimes you have to.

Dot: She didn't seem unintelligent. She was a country woman, I imagine somewhere in her thirties. She had six children and she came from down in the South. She seemed to be completely in touch with reality as far as knowing . . . she was telling me all about her family. Things like that. She was terribly upset over her nervousness. It was just torturing her. My first feeling when I saw her shaking so much was . . . I almost felt like shaking with her. But I didn't feel that was going to help her any. (Laugh)

Dr. T: I gather, too, that you sort of wanted to calm her.

Dot: Um hmmm. I felt that she wanted calming.

Ray: There's something that bothers me when I see people apparently suffering from a feeling—it's the same thing you were stuck with—it's ah, something which makes me uncomfortable. It's okay . . . if I talk to someone who tells me in a matter-of-fact fashion about the people who are plotting against them, about having this "brain control" by radar and so forth, but they're not really . . . not so anxious about it as when I talk with somebody who says, "I just can't stand it." Your patient was shaking all over saying I'm so nervous, I'm just so miserable, and I know that there's not too much that I could hand them that would help, at least not in a short period of time and it really makes me uncomfortable.

Dr. T: Um hmmm.

Ray: "To see people suffer like that." Oftentimes people, people from outside of psychology, ah, say to me "it must be terrible to work and study in a mental hospital. I don't know how you can stand something like that." And I always tell them it doesn't bother me that much. But what *I* would not be able to stand is the physician who works in a let's say, surgical-medical hospital and see people moaning and groaning in pain—I would not be able to stand that. However, I haven't, I don't want to tell them this. I guess I hadn't thought of it like that—any kind of *real* suffering bothers me. I'm not saying it really shakes me up terribly, but it really makes me question whether I want to be a psychologist or not.

The discussion continued, moving toward a more meaningful exploration of what it means to be a therapist and sit through hours of each day attempting to share the very real suffering and pain endured by a troubled client; an exploration of the students' own human limitations and the natural temptation to want to "do something, do something right now that would really help, instead of just talk."

Part of becomnig an effective counselor or therapist involves a shift in perception in hearing about the agony, pain, and suffering experienced by others. In everyday life the reaction may be to want to stop them somehow—to prevent them from visibly experiencing or expressing their upsetness—but the role of the therapist or counselor is to encourage this visible suffering. He must shift to the reaction, "If it's upsetting, then talk about it here and now with me and suffer through it deeply now, and it will go away." It requires a major change at the visceral level for a therapist or counselor to find satisfaction in being able to facilitate the patient's expressing and exploring deep hurt, fear, and anguish.

The culturally imposed resistance to the expression of feelings may be good or bad for society in the normal world of casual social contacts, but it is clearly out of place in a consulting room. It is perhaps just as out of place for the therapist as for the patient. One of the meanings of *genuineness* includes an ability to express feelings and to communicate them adequately when that is appropriate. The beginning trainee, like the majority of human beings in our culture, has not developed high levels of skill in adequately expressing his own feelings. One of the values of the quasi-group therapy experience is to develop some beginning skill in self-exploration; a skill in accurately perceiving and communicating inner feelings. The following excerpt shows some of the problems surrounding the accurate perception and communication of emotions:

Tod: I get here that same message I got with Jane the other day down in the library: "I'm going to tell myself what I do feel regardless of what I really feel, what really comes out in the interaction." I don't think she ever acts like she feels anything. Not really.

Jane: I know that's what it seems, but that's not the way *I* feel, I still, I can't convince myself that that's what it is.

Tod: Well, you may be right.

Jane: You know when I was talking to you all about it. Well sometimes I have the same difficulty like now, of, of really getting across what I feel. Although I tell the people really, what I say . . . what I'm trying to get across, still they feel I'm a robot. Ah, Tod thinks that I don't feel well . . . I don't want to talk about my feelings. It's not that I can't express them or . . .

Dr. T: Somehow people wouldn't understand them.

Jane: Well, I think if I *could* get them across they could.

Joe: So let me try my type of response with you. (Laughs nervously) "You would rather not say anything about your feeling rather than say something wrong and give . . . so they'll misinterpret . . ."

Jane: Because then, you know, it could hurt. I could hurt that way.

Dr. T: Important to you that you don't hurt someone.

Tod: Well, that's true. What she said before is real true.

Dot: But doesn't listening have part of it too. Others are viewing or judging from some other sense of value.

Dr. T: Or I guess, from what you were reacting to. You're trying to say something and they apply some elaborate interpretation to what you wanted to say.

Tod: Dammit, he doesn't take it at face value!

Dr. T: Or, "He won't even let me say it, he has to give me his dumb interpretation."

Joe: Say, if I say I feel like crying or I'm mad. What does this convey to others about my bad feelings. This fellow isn't. If I say I'm mad, you know, you take it in, you have your own reference and you say well, he's feeling rough himself. But this may be entirely different from what I feel and what I'm trying to communicate.

Dr. T: Why?

Joe: Because, well, I guess because I'm mad may mean something to me that is different from what it means to you; that there are different connotations to it for me than for you. Perhaps I shouldn't worry about these . . . I don't think this, I don't think this would sound that way. I see it almost as a slam on everyone else's ability, but people don't usually understand what you're really feeling when you're "mad."

Paul: No, no, no, not at all. It's just that if I *can* say it better with words which have fewer meanings, and with the right inflections and things like this, then I can get across a crisper meaning and a more defined meaning and *I'll* know that *you'll* know what I'm talking about . . . more.

Joe: Well, if you are mad and you say you're mad . . . that is not enough; people won't understand *how* you're mad. Like if you're mad in a way that's different from anybody else's way of being mad, other people don't possess . . . you know, don't *like* to understand . . .

Dr. T: Um hmm.

Joe: To me it's almost a slam on other people's intelligence.

Dr. T: It's a slam not just to other people but to you.

Joe: I see this as kind of a, a superiority, and that's why I say I was disillusioned because I, of all the graduate students I know, I have . . .

Dr. T: Your feelings really came out before us, well dammit, you'd better . . .

Jane: I don't get that feeling at all. I get the feeling that he's placing the whole responsibility for the communication upon himself.

Dr. T: Yeah, but this seems to relate back to what Tod was talking about at the beginning of the hour. I guess I would feel, like you did, that this perception of Ted's slam grew out of Ted.

Joe: Is there anyone else?

Dr. T: I guess the message I get from you is, it's hard for me to say anything that I feel because if I say I'm mad at him, well that's only partly true because I may feel like shaking him but I feel like loving him and all kinds of other things too. It's not really as though I want to hurt him . . . and, if I do say the word "mad," maybe you think I want to hurt him and I don't.

Paul: Well, if you're saying . . . a feeling can't be in a capsule, in one word, I would disagree and feel, well, and what's so special about your "mad" that we can't understand it.

Dr. T: I guess it comes out to you, it's him, not you. That it's not as though you could really hear him saying that that would be true of you too. Well, I would really like you to ask him whether what he's just said would apply to *your* feelings or whether he really does think that you're. . . .

Joe: Don't you ever have trouble expressing how you feel or . . . anything really?

Paul: Sure I do, but I don't think that. . . .

Tod: . . . I found that I have the most trouble expressing what I feel when I don't really feel "that" at all. When I try to tell myself I feel "that." If I go with what I feel, it comes out, but I have to hold it in mostly.

Joe: Well, I don't know. I would say I have trouble expressing *any* kind of feelings. It relates back to what Tod said the first time . . . I see you as a person kind of living in a shell, not going to let anything in. You're not going to let people see what's really, *really* inside. I feel the same, the very same thing in myself.

Paul: I don't think I live in a shell in relation to other people. This, this may be quite true. . . .

The groups continued then, in a more personal vein, to explore the outer social "shell" that "protects" them in their career as graduate students. Judging from the group of lay trainees mentioned earlier, graduate students seem particularly unskilled in handling human emotions—both their own emotions and the emotions of others. In all likelihood this derives from the highly intellectual nature of graduate training and from the selection process for graduate training. As one student put it: "If you want to get through graduate school, you keep your feelings to yourself, and just stick to the facts . . . you don't come to a university to feel anything, you're just supposed to learn." This seems to be a central aspect of the paradox of many traditional training programs—the behaviors necessary for success as a trainee are sometimes precisely those leading to failure as a practitioner. The quasi-group therapy experience provides an opportunity to explore and perhaps overcome this paradoxical but necessary aspect of academic training for professional practice.

An important part of being able to experience a deep empathic understanding of an "other" in the therapeutic encounter is an openness to differing value systems. If the therapist himself cannot be open to differing value systems, he is unlikely to understand another's inner world correctly. To understand empathically means that in the process of "trial identification" the therapist must grasp the other's value system, and, use it to view the "other's" world. His openness to differing value systems also seems basic to experiencing unconditional warmth toward a client who differs in background, goals, and values. In the following excerpt the group is beginning to explore what it means to be "open" to the values of others, the risks and the seeming initial impossibility.

Dr. C: I think what we are talking about is not so much the values that you hold as a person but an openness to the experiences of other people . . . I think this is the difference. My values are going to remain different from yours, Ben . . . except that every time I expose myself to a new experience I expose myself to the possibility of changing my values. What just happened for me was, I was exposing myself to a new experience in you. I really was oblivious to it. This is my own shortcoming. I think I got some appreciation for it today. In exposing myself to your experience I think I'm also exposing myself to the possibility of shifting my values.

Ben: I had pretty much the same feeling for myself but even talking about it like this, bringing it out in the open like this to the whole group even made my own a little more subject to shifting.

Jim: I guess this is what we would hope would happen.

Dr. C: I think there is a very real . . . striving for openness. But sure the therapist is never going to get there. He's never going to be perfect, but he's striving to be open to as much of the experience of the client as possible, and when you do this you are exposing your whole life structure, your whole life style, your whole way of life, your values.

Sam: I guess what we're really saying is that we are told to accept all these things but, actually, do we, and can we or are we. And actually this is what it's boiling down to. We try and think: we find out we are just human beings and we just can't accept all these things. It's just unreal and we just can't do it.

Dr. C: But a very real feeling like . . . I feel like you're saying the same thing now that you said to him before, like, I can't do it and that's it, man.

Sam: Yea, I think this is real. This is real for me. Sometimes I just can't and no amount of forcing, no amount of wanting and no amount of desire, will . . . I just can't. This is one of the things I have to deal with.

Jim: I've had sort of the same feeling like so many times they're training you to just be a blob, to accept everything the patient feels and pretty soon what's your own feelings, and where do *I* fit in? Here's where I am, and I can't take back this part of me and I won't.

Sam: The desire to change a value system is not as quick and not as easy to attain as gaining the value system itself. I think values are very hard to have and to hold and to really get. I think it is very resistant to change . . . I would question the nature of your value system if it can be changed so readily.

Dr. C: When you get a hold of some good values, darn it, they're really worth holding. As hard as it may have been for me when Ben brought it up to me, I think I tried to be open to his experience and I was . . . it had some meaning for me when he said it. I had all kinds of mixed feelings, defensive feelings and negative feelings as well as feelings like "what a schnook I've been," but to be open to his feelings doesn't mean to me that I've got to change those good values that I have. At the same time just the very meaning to me in life doesn't change that much. In a way I hear you saying that you found the core in life and you simply don't want to change that. Even though one of the things that has meaning for you in life is to be open.

Sam: I think for me to live the way *I* live and to do what *I* want to do is fine for me. But if I were to incorporate a value like Ben's, well I just couldn't be the way I am . . . I just couldn't be Sam, because then I couldn't be me.

Jim: You know that he feels that way. You don't know *how* he feels that way.

Sam: O.K. But this borders on the huge question, "Is it ever possible to feel like another person feels?"

Inevitably, as the trainees explore their own professional goals and their current experiences, their feelings about the total academic program will enter the discussion. Even in the best universities or training centers all requirements, all rules and all procedures will not hold up well under close scrutiny. Beyond the historical anachronisms such as the nonfunctional language examinations for the Ph.D., there are many requirements or rules in any graduate training program that appear on inspection to be irrelevant or even unreasonable. Graduate training in and of itself is often a frustrating experience for the student. The resultant feelings of anger, resentment, or frustration are likely to present themselves as part of the group experience. When the supervisor also serves as the therapist, it makes for a difficult encounter. The following excerpt in which the supervisor feels "caught in the middle" illustrates the beginning exploration:

Dr. T: Yeah, I guess I too have the feeling that we started off with some things that were really important to the group and then we shifted to a "neutral" discussion which was just a defensive retreat. And I guess I felt, my perception was . . . I felt that people started bringing up real strong, angry feelings about the university department here and what it means to them, to their lives. And I felt really sort of caught because I felt in a way I was being asked, "Well, why don't you *do* something about this? Do something for us." (Laughter) "Agree with us or do something." And instead what I did was to say that I thought this was life; and in a way we had to grow up and either take it or leave it, either play the game or not play the game. This tended to close off the discussion . . . to totally close it off, as though I had said: "Look, all you're doing is complaining. I don't want you to express feeling on this." And in some ways I really didn't want you to express feelings on this because as a faculty member I felt very uncomfortable.

Dot: I had the feeling you were kind of caught in the middle. After all, you represent . . . something else.

Dr. T: Yes, I guess I felt, it's not just a matter of loyalty to the department or to members of the department, but more a feeling that I wouldn't want to do anything that would wind up hurting you. I think I would do everybody a terrible disservice if I somehow encouraged dissension and complaining because that might encourage people to not want to deal with reality. You know, sort of implying "you can get away with not dealing with the real world." I guess this is partly because I, I think this is the terrible thing about someone who I knew when I was in graduate school. I think he forever unintentionally harms students. He's supportive, he encourages them to be hostile toward restrictive department rules. And this leads them somehow to fight against it and therefore be less able to deal with it. They almost think, "Well, he's encouraging me, he's on my side, so I don't have to." So they don't get a degree. I'm personally afraid I might do that if I listened to complaints and gripes here.

Dot: Kind of like you can say, this far I understand how you feel, but *these are* the rules and facts that we have to deal with.

Dr. T: Yeah, I'm sure you know, in some ways I did want to cut off the discussion because of that. Because it made *me* uncomfortable. And clearly I did cut it off.

Jane: You were telling me too, that "you've already chosen to play the game so don't bitch." And I was saying, "Well, I've got to see the possibility of winning this game."

Joe: What about . . . you've committed yourself to play the game and you don't like it? Why can't you feel these feelings? Why not? Why not recognize it? Why play?

Tod: Yeah, but why not get rid of the feelings?

Dr. T: I guess for me, my fear was that somehow I might wind up encouraging people to believe that "yeah, they're unreasonable." Some rules don't make much sense and so make it much harder for you to deal with it. I suppose the question now is, so how do we resolve our feelings, it isn't fair but how do we play and win the game.

As often happens, personal problems mix with feelings about graduate training, life goals, and the total process of becoming a counselor or therapist. The following excerpt reflects a beginning attempt in an early session to explore more personally private material—the beginning of the point at which quasi-group therapy becomes a personal therapeutic experience for the trainees:

Dot: I had a reaction, too, last week after we left. I . . . you had spoken about relating with faculty and other people the same way you'd related to your father and I just wondered if you might be giving that more importance than maybe you should. Haven't you known many people who were very authoritarian to reinforce this other than your father?

Tod: Well, maybe, but I really see the roots in my relation with my father. I had very strong reactions, emotionally, after I left last session. After I left our little session, it was just overpowering. The image came back; the experience of when my father was saying, "You *will* cut that lawn" and I go out and I start pushing the lawnmower and every step got harder to take. And then he'd come home. And the lawn was a little higher, hadn't been cut yet. "Why isn't that cut?" And I'd try a little harder and I simply couldn't cut the lawn. And then I got the hell beat out of me. I'm very much remote from it when I'm talking about it here, right now. I was last time. I wasn't remote afterwards, after the session it was overpowering. In fact I dreamed about all this last night. My father came up very clearly. I woke up in a dream that's right at the core of my problems here in graduate school.

Joe: "At the core of my problems"—that I was wondering how you identified the core of your problems?

Tod: Well, there're certain things you know about yourself intellectually, you know, from what you read and put together. You piece it together and you can make inferences on that basis, but you don't know. You still have the feeling part.

Joe: I was wondering how much of the core was intellectual and how much was feeling.

Tod: Well, I sort of have a feeling of reticence in pouring forth feelings. I always think I would be the only one pouring forth feeling, that's why I tend to be reticent to relate that intensively.

Dr. T: I sort of have the feeling you're holding back right now.

Joe: Tod, I don't think you should talk about your feelings . . . I'm not sure who should answer this when you get down to it.

Dr. T: It's not worth trying?

Joe: I don't think so. It doesn't involve the rest of the group. I mean part of it is what we were talking about before, the theoretical structure which you, Tod, have worked out. I don't think really—too much has gone between he and I before, and to try to explain all this would take too much time.

Dr. T: Maybe we can just listen. We don't have to know everything. I don't know, how do other people feel . . . I get a little concerned about this groupiness, there are just us here, there's no group. I don't know that we have to talk about things that are necessarily meaningful for the whole group. If they're meaningful to us and other people can't draw any meaning out of it, it's their problem. I would hate to see us wind up with a lot of—if we would only talk about things that would be of interest to an audience. (Laughter)

Dot: Well, Tod's talking the other day helped me a great deal to understand my husband who has a similar problem with his father, and I felt *very* grateful for his bringing out some of his problems.

Paul: It had meaning for me. I still can't stand to be told "you have to," even here in graduate school.

In summary, then, having considered many of the dimensions of therapy in the classroom setting, the trainees now had an opportunity to glean from their learnings what had proved meaningful, and to integrate these learnings in a "real life" experience. Gone was the "canned" quality of the responses in empathy training. Gone was the intellectual awareness of the pseudo life of role-playing. In affording each trainee the opportunity to confront himself and others, the quasi-group therapy encounter enabled the trainees to try and test and incorporate the conditions of a therapeutically effective way of relating.

In the following excerpt, another student explores very personal material involving experiences which color his whole existence and influence all of his interpersonal relations. Insofar as he found these feelings influencing his therapeutic efforts, he felt it necessary to work them through.

Sam: . . . well, everybody looked at a Jewish kid and said that this is the way that I was. It's pretty rough to live against this . . . and feel this and hear this and have it said to you. There were times that it did make a difference . . . and it really did.

Dr. C: You want your own identity but you don't want to deny that you're Jewish.

Sam: I can never deny it . . . I just can never deny it . . . It's with me and it will always be with me . . . Well, let's put it this way, I did try to deny it once and I think everyone is pretty well aware of it. Things happened that I really found out that no matter what happens that I really am a Jew . . . this is the way I am and this is the way it will always be and then I think that the more important thing to realize is that it's not so bad after all . . . things just aren't so bad . . . and this has a certain amount of importance to me . . . and probably more so these last two years than ever before.

Dr. C: No matter what happens I will always be a Jew.

Sam: I am, I just am a Jew.

Dr. C: It's partially in me and partially in the rest of us.

Sam: This is part of what I was trying to answer Jim before . . . I really can't . . . at this time I really can't give you a specific answer either way. I know a hell of a lot of it is in me but I can't say specifically how much of it is in the rest of you . . . so this is . . . I just can't give any answer.

Jim: The way you talk, it's almost as if people were trying to take Judaism away from you.

Sam: Hm . . . I have to think that over . . . I think there are times that I do feel this way, yes.

Dr. C: They try to take it away but they won't let you be anything but.

Sam: I think this comes more close to it.

Dr. C: But maybe it's both . . . they don't really want you to be a Jew all the way but you are sure known to them as a Jew.

Sam: Uh huh . . .

Dr. C: They're never going to forget that.

Sam: Or I won't let them forget it . . .

Jack: . . . Sam gives the appearance of being brash and superficial. I feel I know Sam pretty well and I personally would like to see Sam change.

Dr. C: Change to what?

Jack: I just thought of that after you two thought of it . . . and uh . . .

Sam: I tried to . . . I'm a completely different person than when I got here, other than the basic compulsiveness and the way I take notes . . . the rest is changed.

Dr. C: Well, hell, that other stuff makes sense for a graduate student.

Sam: Everything else from the way of approaching grades to my complete outlook on life has changed.

Dr. C: You've been freed in lots of ways to release this other more warm side of yourself.

Jack: When Sam says he's changed, I think he means now he can accept himself.

Sam: I feel free to do what I want when I want.

(Whole group reacts immediately and simultaneously)

Dr. C: Now you're nudging him, boy . . . you're telling him off but good.

Jim: Perhaps . . . everything Jack has said has influenced the attempt to change you but this is an emotional reaction . . .

Dr. C: And not much different from what you were saying—they won't let him be anything but a Jew, and I goddamn well am going to be proud of being a Jew.

Jim: I think Sam and I are really reacting to similar kinds of things . . . Only yours is a very generalized reaction and mine is very specific to here . . . I don't know how satisfied you are with the way you are . . . that's neither here nor there, but the reaction is one of reacting to the kind of pressure to cheat, the pushing of others who are, perhaps, different than you are . . . and perhaps right now you don't want to be much different from what you are . . . the subtle cultural influence . . . it's more than just religion . . . it's a cultural kind of thing . . . the pressures to be . . . since you are not in the Lexington in-group, a pressure to change yourself and be that way . . . I think it is a reaction to this, possibly the same sort of pressure to be different from the way you are.

Sam: Well, maybe it is that I can sense a certain pressure although many people won't come out and say things . . . but there has always been a certain amount of this . . . which Jack says . . . I think it is obvious that I did get the feeling that you like to see certain changes . . . I mean my roommate . . . he briefly mentions but never pushes or says anything more than that . . . that . . .

Dr. C: Did you resent it?

Sam: Sure I did . . . fish on Friday nights and other things . . .

Jack: I tell you, but . . .

Sam: I've enjoyed change . . . you've told me many times.

Dr. C: You know, I had an image in my mind for a moment there of your yelling at us almost the way that girl in the first interview yelled, "Phony, phony, phony . . ." that's, ah . . .

Sam: Why don't you say what you mean.

Dr. C: Well, that all these pressures to change and at the same time they won't let you change, they really do put you in a double bind sometime.

Sam: I think it's more than that. It's the pressures to change and they won't let me change . . . I'm not sure I want to change . . . Do I want to change . . . I can't . . .

Dr. C: My image was like you almost got sucked into this phony world after awhile and . . .

Sam: That's the way I felt.

Dr. C: . . . Yea, but now you know. But you almost got sucked in by . . .

Sam: I did get sucked in . . . I did get sucked in.

Dr. C: . . . all these people want you to change but wouldn't let you change . . . they did suck you in.

Sam: Well . . .

Dr. C: That was the "phony" that I felt.

Sam: I did get sucked in but more than that I wanted to get sucked in . . . that goes above and beyond . . .

Dr. C: Uh huh.

Sam: Well, okay. I just did get sucked in.

Sam, who was initially the most resistant to the idea of exposing himself, has committed himself to a very early and personal involvement in the therapeutic process. Sensing free atmosphere and trusting his own motives and those of the others, in the group, Sam talked for the first time in this setting of some of those intimate experiences which influence his daily living in general and his therapeutic functioning specifically.

As can readily be seen, the group and individual discussions have run the gamut from areas which are related to classroom and training to areas of a very personal nature. The trainees were not pushed to open up in very personal areas, but the opportunities for such exploration were available. Under different circumstances and in a longer-term program, a more extensive and personal therapy experience, perhaps with leaders other than the classroom instructors, would be desirable, if not necessary. The therapist who is unable to experience, recognize and develop constructs and directions from his own experience will be severely limited in enabling others to do so. Aside from these considerations, it seems eminently critical that those who would dispense therapy must experience it.

A more concentrated therapeutic encounter takes place in the form of formal quasi-group therapy sessions held concurrently with the regular classroom sessions. These sessions are free of classroom cues and dedicated to problems and difficulties encountered by the trainees, at first in their attempts to implement the therapeutic conditions effectively in practice; and finally in their own actual therapeutic encounters. In a very real sense, the beginning point of all effective therapeutic encounters is the therapist himself. The degree to which he understands himself will be reflected in the degree to which his clients can come to understand themselves. In the quasi-group therapy experience, the therapist-trainee has an opportunity not simply to reconcile his own problem areas of functioning but also to come into contact with his own emotional resources. Not unlike the client in therapy, he has the chance to explore himself, others, and his surroundings in the hope of finding more constructive resources within himself and more rewarding relationships with others.

CHAPTER 10 TOWARD THE ACCURATELY EMPHATIC THERAPIST: THE PERCEPTIVE AND COMMUNICATIVE ASPECTS

THE central ingredient of the psychotherapeutic process appears to be the therapist's ability to *perceive and communicate,* accurately and with sensitivity, the feelings of the patient and the meaning of those feelings. By communicating "I am with you" and "I can accurately sense the world as you construe it," in a manner that fully acknowledges feelings and experiences, he facilitates the patient's movement toward a deeper self-awareness and knowledge of his own feelings and experiences and their import.

At the higher levels of accurate empathy, the therapist unerringly responds to the client's full range of feelings in their exact intensity, whether he communicates this in the form of "reflection of feeling," "depth reflections," or sensitive "interpretations." The therapist's sensitive matching of his own communication to the intensity of feelings experienced by the client means that his verbal response will often be more intense than the patient's, because the client may not be able immediately to verbalize the depth and intensity of his anger, despair, or aloneness. At the highest levels of accurate empathy, the therapist's response expands the patient's verbal, gestural and content hints into full-blown, sensitive, but still tentative verbalizations of feelings or experiences. The deeply empathic counselor or therapist is completely attuned to the client's shifting emotional content, and thus senses the major strands of the client's experiences, which he reflects in *both* his vocal tones and the content of what he communicates.

Such understanding means that the therapist has to a great degree successfully assumed the internal frame of reference of the patient. As described in an earlier chapter and in the words of Fliess, this "trial identification," where the therapist steps into the patient's shoes and views the world from this emotional and perceptual vantage point, allows him for the moment to experience the world, events, and significant people *as if* he were the client himself. To be "inside" the client, and yet to remain "outside," lets the therapist sense the meaning of the anger or the fear, its antecedents and its consequences, without being overwhelmed by the experiencing. Thus he can contribute to the expansion and clarification of the patient's own awareness of experiences and feelings. This is the essence of the fine balance between identification and objectivity that the therapist must achieve to become effective.

In the words of Rogers and Truax (1966), "To sense the client's bewilderment, anger, love or fear *as if* it were the therapist's (own) feeling is the critical perceptive aspect of empathic understanding. To communicate this perception in language attuned to the client that allows him more clearly to sense and formulate his feelings is the essence of the communicative aspect of accurate empathy." The psychoanalytic conception of accurate empathic understanding as a process of "trial identification" accurately formulates the "as if" aspect and points directly to the process. In being empathic, the therapist can be seen as assuming the role of the patient, and in that role initiating the process of self-exploration as if he were the patient himself.

It is in this sense that the therapist, through trial identification, becomes the "other self" or "alter ego" of the client; and through his example leads the patient into deeper self-exploration and experiencing of feelings and emotional content. As the patient moves tentatively toward feelings and experiences that he experiences as shameful, fearful, or even terrifying, the therapist steps into the patient's shoes and takes him one step further in self-exploration, doing so in a self-accepting and congruent manner that lessens the patient's own fears of coming to grips with the experiences or feelings. It is as if the therapist were providing a model for the patient to follow; as if he were saying by his example, "Even these fearful or terrifying experiences or feelings are not so terrible that they can't be touched and looked at." The therapist's example of self-acceptance and congruence is perhaps as crucial as his ability to sense or at least point to the next step in the patient's self-exploration.

In a book entitled *Between Parent & Child,* Ginott (1965) has presented guidelines for parental relationships with children which are not only useful for parents but also valuable reading for anyone attempting to form a helping relationship. Although Ginott's own work has grown out of the tradition of Slavson's approach to group therapy, this book offers an operational approach to defining accurate empathic understanding, nonpossessive warmth and genuineness. He sees two requirements as the bases for effective communication: (1) that all communications be aimed at preserving the self-respect of the person being helped as well as the helper; and (2) that the communication of understanding precede any suggestions of information or advice-giving. He also notes what is so true of almost every patient or client—that while he may desperately want understanding, he wants it without having to disclose fully what he is experiencing. Self-disclosure on a deep and intimate basis is risky, and so his internally motivated resistance leads him to reveal only a little of what is needed for us to understand.

Much of Ginott's contribution can be directly applied to the client-therapist relationship, as the following quotation illustrates:

When a child tells us, "The teacher spanked me," we do not have to ask him for more details. Nor do we need to say, "What did you do to deserve it? If your teacher spanked you, you must have done something. What did you do?" We don't even have to say, "Oh, I am so sorry." We need to show him that we understand his pain and embarrassment and feelings of revenge. How do we know what he feels? We look at him and listen to him, and we also draw on our own emotional experiences. We know what a child *must* feel when he is shamed in public in the presence of peers. We so phrase our words that the child knows we understand what he has gone through. Any of the following statements would serve well:

"It must have been terribly embarrassing."

"It must have made you furious."

"You must have hated the teacher at that moment."

"It must have hurt your feelings terribly."

"It was a bad day for you."

A child's strong feelings do not disappear when he is told, "It is not nice to feel that way," or when the parent tries to convince him that he "has no reason to feel that way." Strong feelings do not vanish by being banished; they do diminish in intensity and lose their sharp edges when the listener accepts them with sympathy and understanding.

This statement holds true not only for children but also for adults. (pp. 22-23)

In discussing principles of understanding, Ginott delineates the importance of responding not to the event that the client or the child asks about or speaks of, but to the relationships, feelings, and ambivalences implied by the communication; and of responding in a manner that is both concrete and specific.

Two characteristics of the therapist's responses which seem clinically important for empathic understanding and for which there is beginning confirmation in research findings (Truax, 1961a) are first, the responsiveness of the therapist, and, second, the specificity or concreteness of response. That is, within a modest range, the more frequently the therapist responds to the client, even if only with an "um-hmm," the greater the likelihood that a high level of accurate empathy will be perceived and communicated. The research findings suggest that, within the range studied, the therapist's responsiveness is positively related to both the level of accurate empathy he achieves and the level of process in which the patient engages. Responsiveness seems to ensure that any errors in empathy by the therapist will be corrected immediately rather than being allowed to stand and thus lead to wider misunderstandings. When the therapist responds only infrequently, it becomes more likely that he will get "out of touch" with the client and, having misunderstood one aspect of the client's current being, will build upon it and misunderstand the client even more as he goes deeper into the self. Research also indicates that the specificity or concreteness of the therapist's response is related to both the level of accurate empathy and the level of patient engagement in process.

In its dual role, specificity seems to lessen the chance of the therapist's response becoming abstract and intellectual and hence more emotionally remote from the patient's current feelings and experiences; and it also seems to force the therapist to be more precise in his understanding, so that even his small misperceptions or misunderstandings become clear and can be corrected immediately. Thus the specificity or concreteness of the therapist's response seems to function both to *ensure emotional proximity,* and to enhance empathic accuracy.

One key to the successful implementation of accurate empathy seems to lie in the therapist's concentration upon the client; such intense concentration on receiving the patient's communications, both verbal and nonverbal, automatically achieves several goals for the therapist. First, by concentrating his attention on what the patient is communicating, his "being," the therapist has neither the time nor the energy to reflect on how the patient's statement relates to his own personal ideal, values, norms, or codes of conduct; thus he tends to eliminate distracting evaluations and minimizes the possibility of feeling or communicating a "conditional" warmth. Although it has its limitations, the analogy of "trial identification" with the hero of a novel seems appropriate here. When the reader is thoroughly engrossed in the novel, he cannot at the same moment reflect upon how he himself would feel or act if he were the hero of the novel—to do so he must pull back from his "trial identification" and engrossment.

Similarly, if the therapist is intensely focused on the client, he cannot simultaneously introduce his own personal need system. If personal implications are not drawn, then the therapist is much less likely to become threatened in the relationship; he is more able to maintain his own self-congruence or genuineness within the relationship. The therapist himself is less likely to become bound up in the anxiety and emotions of the client, since his attention is upon "the other" rather than "the self."

Intense focusing on the client is, of course, central to the perceptive aspect of deep empathic understanding because it makes the therapist aware of subtle nonverbal communications—the minute facial, postural, and gestural clues that often contradict or multiply the meaning of the client's verbal communication.

Although many practitioners of psychotherapy have stressed the importance of nonlinguistic signs of emotion, this is one of the most difficult lessons to be learned by clinicians. It is relatively easy to point to the words spoken by the psychotherapy client as cues of one's responses, and the beginning clinician may quickly learn to rationalize his attempt at accurate empathy in these terms. Emotional cues are readily observed in nonlinguistic vocal qualities, however, and in facial and body position and movement. If the therapist can learn that he is responding to these kinds of signs, he will be more able to correct himself when supervision or later client behavior shows him to have been "unempathic."

Shapiro (1965) showed that individuals differ in the degree of congruence between their linguistic and non-linguistic behavior, indicating that therapists must respond to each client's idiosyncratic portrayal of himself as a word-using, voice-using, and facially communicative individual. Further he showed (1966) that in general one could not predict the verbally communicated degree of pleasantness by observing a subject's face or vice versa. Thus, the therapist who wishes to become more empathic must learn that he can be influenced by different channels of emotionality. He must choose a response at one or another level or one which is a response to cues from the whole person. Of course, the psychotherapist must remember that the client will be responding to the therapist's linguistic and nonlinguistic behavior as well.

Thus Shapiro (1965) found that the correspondence or congruence of verbal and nonverbal modes of communication varied from person to person. Further, Shapiro (1966) in a study of interviews found that the degree of verbal communicated pleasantness (warmth) did not predict facially communicated pleasantness (warmth). Clearly the therapist must be attuned to both modes if he is to understand the client *and* communicate effectively.

Finally, the therapist's intense concentration on the client tends to insure that errors in either the perceptive or communicative aspects of accurate empathy will be recognized. He will be able to sense from the client's often subtle response when his own responses do not fit exactly and, sometimes in mid-sentence, can shift his own response to correct for errors of language or content. In short, the intensity and intimacy of the relationship itself, because of the intense focus of the therapist on the client, makes possible the moment-to-moment contact necessary for accurate empathic understanding.

The intensity and intimacy of the therapist's focus on the client is theoretically viewed as a separable aspect of the therapeutic process. That intimate therapeutic discussion is significant in outcome was suggested by the work of Talland and Clark (1954), in which they studied responses from 43 patients in psychoanalytic group psychotherapy involving seven separate groups. The research investigated the topics of group discussion in respect to their judged "helpfulness"; it indicated relatively good agreement as to the topics' relative value carrying over from one group to another ($p < .01$). Two findings were of significance: first was a higher relationship between the disturbing qualities of a topic and the patients' judgment of its helpfulness ($r = .78$); the second was the correlation between the patients' rating of a topic's helpfulness and the ratings by 35 psychologists on its degree of "intimacy" (correlation $= .69$).

It seems quite significant that when accurate empathy, nonpossessive warmth, and genuineness are conceptually abstracted from the interpersonal transaction of therapy, the vital sense of intensity and personal intimacy that seems characteristic of successful therapy is somehow left out of the final abstraction. A tentative attempt at conceptualizing and measuring the intensity and intimacy of the therapist's relationship with the client seems to have borne some fruit. A tentative five-point scale has been developed attempting to specify stages along the dimension of therapist intensity and intimacy, ranging from a low point of aloof remoteness to a high point of intense absorption (Truax, 1962b).

At the lower end of the intensity and intimacy scale, the therapist is subdued and distant in voice and manner; there is an aloofness from feelings and a formal, conventional, or reserved atmosphere, a remoteness or detachment which makes the therapist appear as an "outsider" or a stranger, an inattentiveness or indifference which makes him appear unconcerned. The total interaction gives a "cool" or intellectual flavor. By contrast, at the higher ranges of the intensity and intimacy scale, the therapist communicates an intensity in voice and manner which has a compellingly personal note; there is an accentuated feeling tone communicated by a voice and manner that are both deeply concerned and confidential; a heightened atmosphere is achieved by the therapist's close, almost suspended attentiveness; his voice combines both depth and solicitous closeness, communicating an accentuated feeling tone and a fervid concentration.

In using the research scale on the small population of hospitalized schizophrenics in intensive individual psychotherapy, several findings have emerged (Truax, 1962g, 1962h, 1962i) from ratings by psychotherapeutically naive college students. They were minimally trained and then asked to rate the coded samples from every fifth interview from each of thirteen schizophrenic cases with relatively complete outcome data. The findings indicated a significant positive relationship between the level of the therapist's intensity and intimacy in psychotherapy and the patient's improvement as measured by the final outcome criteria (which included changes in evaluations on psychological test data before and after therapy, diagnostic evaluations of change, and objective hospitalization rate data). Further, in the measures of therapist intensity and intimacy for each of the sixteen cases where measures of the patient's depth of self-exploration were available, a significant positive relationship was found between intensity and depth of exploration and between intensity and outcome. These findings and those reported in Chapter 3, tended to suggest that the therapist's intensity and intimacy were somewhat related to both therapeutic outcome and the patient's engagement in the process of therapy.

The findings relevant to the question "Is it the patient or the therapist who primarily determines the level of intensity and intimacy?" have not been entirely clear-cut. One study (Truax, 1962i) suggested that both the therapist ($p < .01$) and the patient ($p < .05$) had significant effects upon the level of intensity and intimacy achieved. A second study (Truax, 1963), however, suggested that the therapist, not the patient, was the primary influence on the level of intensity and intimacy achieved by the therapist in psychotherapy. The basis for the different findings is not clear, but it *is* clear that the therapist is a significant source of effect on the level of intimacy achieved.

Because the tentative theoretical expectation was that the therapist's intensity and intimacy would contribute primarily to achieving a high level of accurate empathy, but would also increase therapist genuineness and unconditional regard or warmth, the interrelationships between the research scales measuring the central therapeutic ingredients and the intensity and intimacy scale were also of interest. The obtained correlations for therapist intensity and intimacy on the sample of sixteen long-term cases were .68 with the accurate empathy scale; .38 with the nonpossessive warmth scale; and .65 with the genuineness scale. These findings, then, suggest that the level of therapist intensity and intimacy contributes quite heavily to the achievement of both empathy and genuineness, and to a lesser significant degree to the communication of nonpossessive warmth; that is, the intensity and intimacy scale is measuring something quite similar to what is measured as "empathy, genuineness, and warmth"—a good therapeutic relationship.

The Content Aspect of Accurate Empathy

To achieve a high level of accurate empathy, the counselor or therapist must make an endless series of moment-by-moment decisions. He must decide not only how to phrase the empathic communication, when to give it, what constitutes "one step further than the patient," and what the appropriate tonal quality is, but he must also decide first upon the core feelings or meanings of the patient's communications. From all the things that the patient tells him, he must be able to separate the wheat from the chaff. In this "winnowing" process the therapist must separate the therapeutically meaningful client statements from those arising from a social facade or a defensive screen. How does he begin to do this? What cues does he use? Where are the "handles" on this jellyfish of psychotherapy?

As the term *empathy* implies, many of the cues used for deciding when and to what he will respond comes from the therapist's own experience with human existence. He can recognize from his awareness of his own feelings, reactions, and experiences the outward signs that relate to inner feelings. In part, he will also rely on the body of clinical and theoretical writings dealing with human behavior, human emotions and motivation, and the sometimes superficial, sometimes profound, insights gained from the writings of therapists and counselors. Even the best of insights, however, must be applied tentatively and conservatively to the "person" of any individual client or patient. The most reliable guideline, as most therapists since Freud have noted, will come from the client himself. He will "point" to what is therapeutically meaningful by his outward signs of upsetness, anxiety, defensiveness, or resistance as he begins to approach his troubling experiences or feelings. This cue function of the patient's own reaction not only guides the therapist to what is most therapeutically meaningful, but also alerts him to his clumsiness, when intended empathic responses are misperceived as insults, slights, or deprecations. Such defensive or anxiety reactions from the patient in the moment-to-moment process of the counseling or therapy can also warn the theapist that his intended empathic responses are moving too quickly or too deeply into the troubled aspects of the client's world. Hurried and empty laughter can communicate as deeply as moist eyes; the overly strong denial tells as much as the halting and strained "confession." Many of these cues are given directly, but they are also expressed in what has been described as *patient resistance*.

A patient's resistance to psychotherapy or counseling derives from both a natural reluctance or learned avoidance of verbalizing or even experiencing the troubled aspects of his self, and from a predictable human reaction to the therapist who has moved too rapidly or too deeply into troubled feelings, or who wittingly or unwittingly communicates a lack of regard or respect. The term *resistance* was initially introduced by Freud to mean the patient's unconscious opposition to exploring or recognizing unconscious or even preconscious material. As Freud noted, the client's ambivalent attitudes toward self-exploration, in which he both approaches and avoids coming into contact with troubling experiences or feelings, is a natural and normal state of affairs in therapy. Further, it seems to be a normal state of affairs for all human beings, including the therapist, and not a special characteristic of the patient or client. Although Freud's contribution to the understanding of resistance was of great theoretic significance, the term as used by naive or ineffective therapists has often been merely a label which obscures meaning and retards rather than facilitates the therapeutic process. Unfortunately it is not uncommon for an ill-trained counselor or therapist to say, "You seem to be showing a lot of resistance today to. . . ," and leave it there, thinking he has "understood" the patient. If the patient himself had enough ego strength and self-confidence at such a moment, he might well reply, "Of course, stupid. Try standing in my shoes and then see how you do. Your job as a therapist is to *help* me explore and understand myself, not to simply criticize me or point out when I'm obviously unable at the moment to. . . ." At such moments the therapist might be more helpful if he were to express what he senses the client's feeling to be, whether that is "You seem to be struggling with yourself at this moment, wanting to . . . and yet at the same moment very much *not* wanting to. . . ," or "Your feeling is 'no, I'm not going to . . . at least not now.'" In the hands of naive or ill-trained counselors or therapists, the label *resistance* has too often become just a synonym for "bad patient behavior," which they think they can eliminate by labeling.

Internally motivated resistance is a great asset to counseling and psychotherapy, for without it the therapist might be able to move too deeply or too rapidly and have a less clear basis for separating the therapeutically meaningful content from the therapeutically irrelevant. Similarly, without the cues provided by externally motivated resistance, the therapist would be less able to tell when he has unintentionally insulted, rejected, criticized, or in other ways hurt the patient; he would be less alert to the times when he is offering a "psychonoxious" or damaging relationship. Finally, it is both trite and profound to note that a human being devoid of "resistance" would be a person so fully self-congruent, so mature, integrated, and genuine that we mortals might feel uncomfortable in his presence; a person who experiences no internally motivated forms of resistance would certainly not need a counselor or therapist.

INITIAL STEPS IN EMPATHY TRAINING

Although specific didactic training seems to be of considerable value in training therapists to perceive and communicate accurate empathic understanding, experiential learning seems most basic. A therapist or counselor who has himself experienced the therapeutic process as a client is likely to gain important insight into both the meaning of the patient's verbal and nonverbal communications, and the effects of different therapist behaviors. One piece of research evidence reported by Strupp (1958) found, for example, that therapists who themselves had experienced psychotherapy or analysis tended to be much more active or responsive and to resort to silence less often. Apparently they had learned experientially in their own therapy the frustrating and often stressful effects of therapist silence.

We might hope that professional training in human behavior and learning would contribute heavily to a therapist's empathic ability; that such training would enable him to make judgments about other people and how they might feel or behave. However, the available evidence seems to refute this fond hope. For example, a review by Taft (1955) of 81 different studies dealing with success in judging others indicates a consistent lack of relationship between ability to judge others and amount of training in psychology. Similarly Arnhoff (1954), in studying reliability of behavioral ratings, found a consistent decrease in judgment reliabilities as amount of training and experience in clinical psychology increased. Such data, which are consistent with similar findings from other "helping" professions, would suggest that the current heavily theoretic training is either incorrect in itself, or inappropriate for changing the actual behavior of the trainee. We suspect there is truth in both explanations.

In developing the present training program, the early emphasis was on shaping behavior directly, by introducing the trainee to the research scale developed to measure accurate empathy, giving him practice in rating samples taken from a variety of tape recordings or actual counseling and psychotherapy, and thus directly teaching him to discriminate operationally between relative levels of empathic responses. After the trainee had achieved relatively good reliability as a rater, he was exposed to a situation in which he was required to make actual "empathic responses" to tape-recorded client statements. Using the research scale as the criterion for success, the trainees were given several sessions of practice in which they competed with each other to make such empathic responses. In such a situation they were motivated by both their own personal satisfactions and the approval of their peers and supervisors. After attaining minimally adequate levels of this "canned" empathy, the students paired off outside of class for role-playing. The tape recordings from these role-playings of therapist and patient were then brought to class where samples were randomly played and rated on the degree of empathy. Again, the trainees' motivation for changing their actual behavior toward more empathic responding derived from both their personal satisfaction and the status and approval given by their fellow trainees and the supervisors. Finally, a similar procedure was carried out with a series of single interviews with actual clients. Throughout this highly structured and didactic aspect of the training program, broader cognitive and experiential learnings occurred both in the classroom and in the quasi-group therapy sessions.

The following excerpt is taken from course discussions focusing upon the perceptive aspects of empathy involving the therapist's accurate and sensitive grasp of the client's internal frame of reference:

To Be a Tree . . . : The Perceptive Aspects of Empathy

Jim: I don't know whether we disagree or whether we really haven't talked about this bit. One of my feelings is that dramatic training, particularly, although I don't care for it—in some cases what I understand is method acting—is invaluable training for a therapist. Since as I understand it, what you're taught to do is, literally, get inside and walk around in the part whether it'd be—somebody told me, they said, "Be a tree." I don't know how you walk around inside a tree and think like a tree thinks, but the notion is of being so in tune with whatever character you're to play that you can actually feel and experience what he is supposed to have experienced. I think my own feeling is that this is really a very valuable training for therapy.

Dr. T: Sort of an empathy training?

Jim: Yes, very much so. You have to become aware and sensitive and it's much more difficult to do it with someone, with some words on a page than it is to do it with a human being. You can see how he's reacting. You have to . . . as the little girl in *To Kill a Mockingbird* says, "You have to get in and walk around in his shoes," and this I think is really good training for therapists because probably the most difficult task you have—is to actually get inside.

Dr. T: Yeah, I guess this does a lot of things for us when we're able to do that in addition to helping us be sensitive to what the other person is feeling and experiencing as opposed to how they're acting. Any clod can see how they're acting, but it takes much more to sense what they are feeling in that moment, what they are experiencing. It does more than that though. It has a lot of bonus features; that it allows us as therapists to step out of our own complex of needs. When we step into another person's shoes and walk around, we're so busy standing there and walking around, sort of stretching our arms and seeing what it feels like, that we're not focusing on our own needs. In a very real sense our needs don't exist. Sort of like when we're engrossed in painting or almost anything that takes up our attention. Our needs, our own usual needs, recede far in the background because we're so busy being with the patients, stepping into their shoes and seeing what they're feeling.

Sam: Can one do this, can one step in? Well, I have Lindner's jet-propelled couch on my mind. Can one step into the patient's experience and experience it as he does and still stay apart and keep rooted in your own . . . role as a therapist?

Dr. T: I think that when I do it, when I am empathic, I am not that person and I'm not bound up in their needs system. I'm not tied to their viscera, so that I can recognize that it's anxiety-arousing . . . but I'm obviously not anxious, but can recognize this is anxiety-arousing for them. And it's this, I don't know, this "disembodied nature" of the empathy may be helpful to another person to help them see how it fits *without* the intensity of the emotion confusing the picture.

Sam: How can you disembody empathy?

Dr. T: Well, for example, a patient gets upset, is concerned about death, thinking of suicide. They're a bundle of intense anxiety when they're thinking about suicide and all the pressures on them that force them in this direction, as they see it. I can, in a sense, reflect this but in a much "cooler" fashion. I might say something like "God, it's just impossible to live." Even if I say it with the hallmarks of feeling or the hallmarks of active feeling, the person can see me talking about it and recognizing the intense feelings associated with it without having those feelings. He can also see that I'm not viscerally anxious as I'm saying it.

Sam: You've also changed your type of reflection, you will, or you've changed it from the third to the first person here, which is different, too, haven't you? Instead of reflecting back how he feels or rephrasing what he's saying, you're actually saying what he might be thinking.

Dr. T: Yeah.

Sam: And this is quite a change.

Dr. T: This is often a useful technique.

Sam: Um hmm.

Dr. T: It's a faster way of communicating. Most often in therapy, after you get into it, you'd drop out all these phrases that you use to start with. Maybe the first time you start interacting with a patient, you'll preface what you have to say with "Is it as though you were saying, blah, blah?" After a while you just say "blah!" It pops out without all of the verbal bridging that usually goes on.

Jim: There is this notion of becoming empathic, of walking around in the other persons' shoes in dramatics. It falls in line with the notion of phoniness and incongruence. The danger which most method actors succumb to, and a good many therapists, is that the phoniness comes through when you've seen somebody that's "living the part." You know, you've seen, on every college campus there's about 10 girls walking around with their . . . "living the part" expressions on their faces and the phoniness, the intense phoniness that comes through. It's not simply enough to get around and walk inside somebody else which is better than saying, "This is the way I would have done this," . . . there is a difference between being able to walk around in somebody else's shoes, to experience what they experience and still be yourself. This doesn't mean that you surrender.

Dr. C: This is an "as if" condition.

Dr. T: Yes, as if. And it should always be stated that way because I think where sometimes, beginning therapists really get in trouble, is when they communicate to the patient that *they* are the judge of what things are, you know . . .

Jim: Um hmm.

Dr. T: It's almost like "I'm walking around inside of you and I feel so good at this that *I'm going to tell you how you feel*" and I lose sight of the fact that it's always "as if" and I have to always check every movement with you to see if that's really the right movement, if that really rings true. I may use the word, for anxiety, I may use the word panicky. But maybe that isn't quite the right word. Maybe it's more a feeling of having to move or a feeling of being unable to move. It could be so many different things and the only way you can tell is by constantly checking back with the person, and this is almost . . .

Jim: (Interrupting) If you become so engrossed in the other person, and lose your own bearings . . .

Sam: Lose your roots . . .

Jim: Of what you are. You're supposed to be the stable influence in the relationship and all of a sudden you've walked so far inside of this fellow that you are no longer there . . .

Dr. T: Maybe that's all right but maybe you shouldn't be there. Maybe you just confuse things by being there—most of the time.

Jim: Does he want you in his world, first of all?

Dr. T: You know, I can feel at times where I've wanted to explore something . . . where I really wanted to explore it. I can remember one example where I used Dr. O. for about an hour and a half as my therapist. It didn't really matter to me whether he was with me. It was nice if he was with me, but his real value was that I couldn't just walk around in a loop within myself, you know, rehearsing the end of this, and that led to this. This kind of "mickey mouse" that you do when you're talking to yourself. I had to pull it out and look at it well enough to be able to communicate to him. There were moments, however, where he started to focus on something irrelevant and about all I could feel was "Shut up, dammit, you're slowing me down, I don't want to explain that to you!" That is, the less intrusive the therapist is, the better, but we always have to tie it to what the patient is doing. If he's not "working" he needs help but if he is working along well, then maybe we should stay out of his way.

Understanding the feelings of the client involves, for the moment, becoming the client in all of his experiences. In the "trial identification" of empathy the balance which the therapist must effect is "being inside and outside at the same time." This balance is not unlike the relationship to the tree which has gone long without water; you may grasp its urgent thirst yet you are not truly thirsty yourself.

In "empathy training," where a recording of counseling or psychotherapy is played to the trainees and then periodically stopped after a client's statement to allow the trainees to formulate their own "empathy responses," this actual process is often interspersed with discussion. The following excerpt illustrates this and underscores the potential richness of the communicative aspect of empathy:

A Variety of Responses . . . : The Communicative Aspects of Empathy

Dr. T: And I think it's plain from the last tape that we do bring to bear all of our experiences with people; that this wasn't the first person we had met with a paranoid element in his life. We have paranoid elements in our lives. All the people around us do and almost every patient we've ever talked to does, so that we can bring to bear a whole host of experiences. We know that there is a very high probability that a number of other feelings will occur simultaneously with the one expressed, and we can bring to bear this experience. It's not certain. We want to put it tentatively when we push further, but we can bring to bear all of our actual experience within our own lives and in our lives with patients that we've already seen. Let's try another tape with a different therapist.

(Tape example played to the trainees)

T: It would make you feel worse to actually not live up to someone's expectations.

C: Yeah, it would make me feel worse not to do it, even though it cost me money and time, maybe valuable time to do it.

T: Um hmm.

C: But before I'd let people know I couldn't do it I would lose the time and maybe money too if it became necesary, which I have done a few times.

T: Well, how would it make you feel worse, say uh, to try and live up to your wife's expectations?

C: Well, I just don't know about her, I mean it seems kind of different to, toward her, the way, about not living up to what she expects does kinda have a different feeling and I don't know the difference, in uh, not doing what she expects me to do and not doing what other people expect out of me, or what they believe I can do. I don't feel the same, kinda the same in one sense, but maybe another not.

T: I wonder how it seems different to you.

C: Well, it would seem that above anyone else she should understand more about the things that I could do or couldn't do, and she should understand what she could expect of me more than someone else would, but it seemed that she would give me a harder time from things that she expected out of me that I didn't do than other people would. Maybe other people wouldn't say anything to me. That, what would worry most about that is what they might think of me or what they might say to someone else about me making believe I could do something, then it turned out that I couldn't do it.

But as far as my wife, she, she would you know, say maybe, embarrass me with words about maybe something that I didn't do or couldn't do that she expected me to do. ANYONE *else wouldn't say a word, not to me, but they might say it to my back. She would say what she had to say to my face where in other cases someone else might, if they have anything to say, they wouldn't say it to my face to hurt me or anything, but I always had a feeling that they might, you, know, talk to, talk about me to my back about things like that. I don't know if I explained it . . . I'm not, I really don't know what I mean myself.*

T: Sort of like all these feelings are very strong.

C: Well they are, always have strong feeling toward things like that. Maybe other people wouldn't pay any attention. (Pause) That's the one thing that hurt me the worse, when my wife left me. Just wondering what people thought, what they think of me or what they thought of her, and later I, you know I got where I would, you know, go out with this, this lady I met, this girl, and I was always ashamed to be seen with her, you know where, I mean not on her account but she was nice and she was nice-looking, but I was ashamed to go down the street with her and I told her it was because of what people might think or say, and some people that seen me didn't know I wasn't living with my wife. It might have started gossip. But it, it took me about a year before I'd ever go anywhere with her that I thought someone would see me that knew me. Then finally that kind of wore off. (Long pause) That's one thing people will talk about, if they don't know you're not living with your wife, or any man or any woman down the street a man with some other woman, that'd be the first thing, lots of people would tell their friends, some of my friends maybe, say "I saw him down there with a woman" or something like that. Before I would be seen anywhere with another woman, I wanted to be sure that anyone who knew me had plenty of time to find out that we wasn't living together without me having to tell them.

T: It's all still a very painful area for you.

C: Yeah . . . I don't know if I should get where I wouldn't care what people thought about me or, or try to be like I've always been. I've always tried to make people think well of me, everywhere I go, on anything I do. When I walk down the street, instead of people criticizing me I always thought I would like to hear, or hear of someone saying, "There goes a good man" or something like that instead of maybe saying "There goes a man or a rough man" or something like that.

T: You would like to be well thought of.

C: That's what I've tried to do all my life and I did pretty well with it, 'cept for the past couple years. And there's, oh, a lot of doubt in mind how, how people feel about me now, or back home people that I knew, I knew thought well of me before and I'm not sure if they still think well of me . . . because I haven't been living the life the past two and a half years that I lived up to before. (Pause) And that's the way I want to get back to doing when I leave here, is try to live up to what I've lived up to before! (Long pause)

T: Even the thought of all this is enough to make you angry, hurt.

C: Well, it makes you feel different or funny some way. Mad or angry or hurt or disappointed or somethin', I don't know what you might call it.

T: It sort of opens up those feelings you must have had all along.

C: Well that makes me think of the past a lot and wonder how it had to change so quick.

T: Makes you sort of wonder why your marriage didn't really . . .

C: Didn't work out like I wanted it to. I wanted it to be one of the best in the world and ah, got along pretty good making people believe it was up until the time that me and my wife separated. Then she gave me a hard time and ah, we had a lot of disagreements and she didn't understand me and all that stuff but I'd say this much for her, she never let anyone ever know it and neither did I. Far as all our other friends and neighbors knew, they thought we was he ideal family because she would always be good to me when someone was around. One man, or at least one man works for the highway patrol said he told his wife one day if ah, if he had to pattern his family and their family life by any one family that he'd like for it to be . . . like me.

T: So whenever you realized, at this point what everyone thought, even you thought, that something happened to go wrong, sort of shakes your confidence in most anything.

C: Well, I guess I guess something like that hurts worse than it would if, if the whole neighborhood and your friends knew you was, fussin' and fightin' and drinkin' all the time like some people do and then separate, there wouldn't be much said about it, no more than someone would say, "well, it didn't end no further than I thought it would" or something like that. But mine, my place was that there wasn't anyone that I ever knew of that ever thought that we wouldn't, we wouldn't live together many more years and then it shocked people, the neighbors and friends and as bad as it did me.

T: And you wonder why that happens . . .

C: Well, I guess anyone would wonder. Like I say, she was pretty mean to me at times but I enjoyed living and people believing that, that we had a fine family which we did have, a fine family. I had two nicer girls as anyone would ever have and they still are nice. But I sacrifice . . . being pushed around by my wife and being treated mean by her, I'd sacrifice all of that just to have kept my home like it was.

T: In the same way that you tried very, very hard to meet your father's expectations you tried very hard to meet your wife's expectations and to hide any sort of evidence of discord or agony from anybody else.

C: Yeah. Didn't anyone ever know. Course, far as I know I lived up to, to what I know my father expected out of me.

T: Um hmm.

C: But I never could do it with my wife.

T: She seemed to . . . never be satisfied with what she expected of you.

C: No she was never satisfied. She always wanted something new or something different, and then for the past several years, well, we, we built a brand new home and we hadn't lived in it two or three years before she started telling that that wasn't the kind of a home she wanted. She, we'd go and look at other homes, she'd want, it didn't cost but five thousand dollars to build that house that I had to start with see, cause I remodeled it several times and I had about eight thousand in it. But that still wasn't good enough for her, she worried me every month about "Let's trade it for a better house." She wanted a $25 or $30,000 house and, and I just didn't, couldn't see how I could make the payments on it. Then she tried to show me where we could, but I know we couldn't have. And if she couldn't get that then she'd want something else. She never quit wanting. If she didn't get one thing she wanted she'd say "Well, I have something else." And then she would curse at me for not being rich enough to get her the things she wanted and always reminded me that someday she would get what she wanted and it wouldn't be from me.

T: I wonder if she knew what she wanted.

C: No, she don't know what she wanted. I don't think she does.

T: The more things you gave her, that didn't seem to help satisfy her.

C: That didn't seem to satisfy her.

T: I wonder if she wanted you to give her something else, something different . . . so, new homes, new furniture, new cars . . .

C: Well I gave her all, all of my time, and I gave her you might say all the love I had for her which was a great deal, and I tried to show her I loved her by giving her the things she wanted, the best that I could do, the best that I could give her.

T: Your way of showing your love was in working in even double shifts . . .

C: I worked two shifts ever since we been married, most all the time, to get the things that she wanted.

T: Your way of showing your love and your desire to make her happy was in terms of giving her a lot of things as well as your time.

C: That's right. And then she didn't, then she would raise that at me for ah taking so much time for me to make a living. I spent too much time working. I worked 12, 15 hours a day all the time. Then she would even curse me about it. She wanted me to make enough money in a seven or eight hours a day to live in mansions instead of having to spend 12 or 15 hours a day and have to live in a eight thousand dollar house. She couldn't understand. Then like I said, she always reminded me that someday she will have it and it won't be from me. She told me I was no good. She never had seen anyone in my family that was any good. And there never would be one would be any good.

T :I just wonder how this must have made you feel toward her.

C: Well, I don't ever know myself. But, it, it hurts, *to be talked to like that. When you think you're doing your best and someone says, "You're no good, never have been and never will be."*

T: She was hurting you in what she was saying to you.

C: Yeah, it hurt bad. It hurt real bad. And if I tried to explain to her about it, tried to make her understand, she would still get madder. Then she stated several times that one of these days someone's going to kill me. Said my days are coming, said somebody'll shoot you down. Just because I didn't get her the things she wanted and tried to show where I couldn't get 'em and tried to get her to not be selfish and live happy with what we had, that we had a whole lots more than a lots of people have. But she wanted more than the richest people have. She didn't want to be down in the middle class. I would say maybe we were in the middle class people . . . But she didn't want it there. (Long pause)

T: She seems, ah, to be even angrier with you when, you would try to explain to her that . . .

C: Yeah . . .

T: How she was hurting you . . .

C: You couldn't explain anything to her. Every time I'd attempt a try I would get hurt more by things she would say to me.

T: Sort of like she was trying to provoke you to be angry with her.

C: Yeah, I believe she would've, I believe sometimes she would enjoy seeing me mad enough really to, to try to beat up on her. 'Cause . . .

(Trainee reactions and discussions)

Dr. T: Let's just go around the room with some of the feelings that you might expect to be associated with this kind of experience. Feelings that you might expect to also occur in this person.

Sam: Guilt.

Dr. T: Guilt? Do you feel guilty? Feel it to some degree? How would that come out? How would you express the guilt? How would it really feel?

Sam: It would be guilt knowing that other people would be judging you in a sense—your actions which you, that you have done wrong?

Dr. T: All right, then. You felt you were doing something wrong so you might, even, in pushing this, you might say to the patient, "I wonder, from what you're saying, if maybe you didn't feel some moments that you were being wronged." Huh?

Ted: Do you think he'd be wrong himself?

Dr. T: Yes, but it's the first interview. But if it were the fifteenth interview and if it were put tentatively enough, he might open up and admit that not only did others "wrong" him, but he himself was also "wrong." I think if you put it as a road block in front of him or as a challenge or as a threat, then of course, he would have to deny it. What else, what other ways . . .

Tod: I think he might experience some disappointment of breaking up with his first wife.

Dr. T: Okay. How might that feel? Concretely, in terms of a response, how might that feel?

Tod: Well, I think he's already brought it out . . . in that one long statement he made. When he got engrossed after a while. He first started talking about feeling hurt.

Dr. T: Um hmm.

Tod: I don't think he actually said it quite that way but he pretty much implied that he was hurt . . . he was separated from his wife . . .

Dr. C: Then he swiched over and he was hurt by what people thought about him . . .

Dr. T: What might you say as a therapist in that moment?

Tod: Weli, my response to the whole business was that it really hurt and I was going to let him take which side of it hurt most.

Dr. T: Yeah.

Tod: The fact that his wife left or that other people would think ill of him for running around with another woman.

Dr. T: So, make your response, right now.

Tod: "You still love her . . . don't you?"

Dr. T: If we put ourselves in that patient's shoes, or if we put any human being in that patient's shoes we would expect that at some moment he felt sorry to lose his first wife; he felt hurt, he felt some sense of, well, "I'm doing wrong going out with somebody else because I really am still married." What other kinds of feelings would he very likely have?

Ben: I think he was ashamed, socially ashamed. This ties up with the guilt.

Dr. T: So that he would feel, "If I saw somebody doing that, I'd sure think they weren't doing right." So he expects other people to (not) act that way. What else?

Jim: He might feel a failure. That all of his friends have gotten along with their wives and here he comes along . . .

Dr. T: Um hmm. You might express this at one moment in therapy by saying something like what?

Jim: You kind of get a feeling of having failed in your life.

Dr. T: Um hmm. You might preface it perhaps by saying, "I sort of sense that one thing you're saying," or, "One thing from what you're saying is that you felt sort of like a failure . . . separated from your wife." What else?

Jack: I think he also might feel insecure and inadequate as a male, having failed one woman and being afraid to be seen with another.

Dr. T: Right!

Jane: Somehow I get the feeling, too, that he blames his wife for not maybe trying harder.

Dr. T: All right. How would you say that?

Jane: Just that way—"You feel your wife didn't really try to hold up her end."

Dr. T: Yeah. On something that doesn't follow so directly from what the patient says you might put some kind of tentative beginning on to it so that it's clear that you're not accusing him. So that he can easily say "no" without making it a big deal and has to develop all kinds of resistance to you as a therapist. Whenever we take a chance and try to go a little below the surface we have to put some kind of tentative beginning on it. Otherwise, if he doesn't want to admit to it at this moment, he has to fight it. What kind of thing might you say to allow him to say "No" if he wanted to?

Jane: "Try to explain why you feel" . . . without . . .

Dr. T: Or, "I wonder if you don't feel . . ." and then say . . .

Jane: "Or I wonder if you don't feel that your wife may have tried a little harder."

Dr. T: Yeah. Something like that. That would allow him to say "No" without having to fight with you. Without making him feel that you're against him. After all, these are just suggestions. It may very well be that we would expect, probably ten per cent anyway, of our guesses would be wrong. All we're doing is going on the basis of what people in the past that we have known have felt. We expect to be wrong sometimes. This is the kind of thing that allows a very rich variety of responses to almost anything. It allows us, even more importantly, to take responses that we might dismiss as trivial on the part of the patient, that is, things he says that don't seem to have real meat to them, and pull some meat out of them. Because after the tenth time he says, and he's probably been saying a thousand times during therapy, that he's worried about what other people think, you obviously can't make a hundred responses that "you're wondering whether people think" (laughter) or "you're worried about what other people think . . ." But there is a variety, a richness that we can draw upon because we've had experiences similar to that through our lives and in the lives of other people.

Tod: Might there also be some anxiety as a result of, . . . comes from these conflicting feelings—"I love my wife but I'm angry with her? It's my failure but yet she could have tried harder," some of these things?

Dr. T: Yeah, right.

Tod: "This kind of confusion."

Dr. T: Must be really upsetting to have so many conflicting feelings." Something like this—"to feel so many ways at once,"—"to love her and hate her"—"want her and hate her." You can often throw out a couple of them to give the person a feel of what you're getting from him.

Sam: He also in a very real sense, is constricting his whole life. There are vast changes, whereupon all his old friends and neighbors who used to see him and his wife together, don't really want to, now. Now he's not only ashamed, he's wholly afraid to go out.

Dr. T: Yeah.

Sam: His whole life is changed radically. He's more or less moving into his room . . .

Dr. T: This is another elaboration that we can move out into, keeping in mind that there's always the small probability that we could be wrong. Allow him to have room to say "No" to us without having to feel that he has to call an expert wrong. Because in the field of therapy we *are* . . . the patient does look up to the therapist, and it is almost like the feeling of telling your internist, "No, no it isn't my kidneys!" (Laugher) How could you sensibly do that? He's the expert! So, we have to take great pains to get the patient willing to disagree with us, to say, "No, that isn't the way I feel."

Ben: Would it be inappropriate to sort of recap for the patient this point . . . something along "I know you're going to ask me so I thought I might as well tell you?" (Laughter)

Dr. T: That's real empathy! (Laughter) Next.

Ben: "You've pointed out that it's very difficult to live up to the expectations of others and it's even harder to live with the criticisms of your wife, but after she leaves you, it sort of gives you some freedom. You find out that it's still very difficult and perhaps this difficulty is as much inside you as it is outside"—okay?

Dr. T: Yeah. How do we make this more personal now?

Ben: I don't know.

Dr. T: Well, let's try to make this a more personal response. The ideas are there but they're in an intellectual mode that would call him away from his experience into an intellectual formulation, so let's think of how can we put that in a form that will not make it intellectual. How do we make that more personal?

Ben: "When you come right down to it, your problem is as much the way you feel as it is the way other people act toward you."

Jim: I think here that it might be appropriate at times to bring out or to suggest or reflect his tremendous feelings of inadequacy and inferiority, to say something like, "I sort of sense that you just think so little of yourself, hate yourself. You feel that you are just so, worthless." Something like this.

Dr. T: Um hmm. And then again, you start it off with a tentative approach there because it would allow him to say, "No, I don't really think that's true. I don't think I'm so worthless." He could back off from that. To respond more to him, perhaps one way of making it more personal would be to say it something like, "In part, you're sort of saying 'I can't stand taking the insults she throws at me, and yet I don't know whether I can really live apart from her either. Maybe it's in me . . .' "

Tod: I think this is the value of this sort of probing in that throughout the whole entire interview, the person is always placing responsibility on someone outside himself.

Dr. T: That's right.

Tod: And it's . . . if he would at least be aware that he is possibly one of the causing factors.

Dr. T: Right. The only way we're going to do it effectively, communicate this message, is not to make it intellectual. He might agree or he might disagree, but it's something to argue about, not something you experience. We can make our response a more continuing part of the flow rather than make it sound like, "Okay, for the last five minutes."

Dr. C: I'd like to make a further point on that. I do think that something like this could be premature, too.

Dr. T: Yeah.

Dr. C: Give some sort of consideration . . . I think you might want to show him that you're really with him against the outside world for a long period of time before you start telling him to take a look at himself.

Sam: Won't he feel this way, by your continuing to have these sessions with him? While all the other people on the outside are more or less shying away from him and talking about him—you're talking with him, not about him.

Dr. T: I think where you could really get away with this is if you say it in a fairly personal and fairly tentative way, so that he can say, "No, you've misunderstood me," which is very different than, "I think your professional evaluation is wrong." If you ever put the patient in the position where he has to, say, "No, your professional evaluation is wrong," this is just an impossible thing for him. But it's very easy for him to say, "I didn't make myself clear."

Dr. C: I think part of this . . . his message is that, "They don't understand me out there."

Dr. T: Yeah.

Dr. C: And . . . I would probably want to be with this message a long time and if I push too soon, then I don't understand, either. Then I'm with *them*, and I think this is what I'm saying.

Dr. T: We really can't bank on the fact that we're willing to see him as of itself, communicating any positive regard because his wife continued to see him, too, and she continued with the purpose of insulting him. We've all had experience with people who like to goad us. That's really why they're seeing us: they like to tease us. I think you can't really, therefore, depend upon the format to communicate much.

Dr. C: I do want to hammer it home because I think that . . . sure, we all know that it's not just in the outside world, that he's not there, and what I'm saying is if the therapist's set is to exercise this insight to his dynamics too soon, he can really hurt.

The example gives some flavor of the early interactions involved in attempts to shape the trainee's response through empathy training. At a later stage, when the trainees are rating on the accurate empathy scale a sample from a tape by one of the class, discussion is interspersed with the rating as issues arise spontaneously. The following class excerpt illustrates this, as the ratings are the spontaneous starting point for considering how much information is provided a patient and what implications this has for the role of the therapist:

To Commit or Not . . .

Dr. T: Did everybody get a chance to write down their ratings? Okay, lets start with Al.
Al: 4
Ted: I had 3.5
Jane: 4
Sam: 4
Dot: 4
Paul: 4
Jack: 4
Ray 4:
Tod: 3.5
John: 3
Hank: 4
Dr. T: I guess this would be almost exactly 4, about 3.8. Want to go on to another tape? Okay.

(Sample from a trainee's tape recording is played)

C: Well, I feel awful nervous and sick now. I didn't feel so bad when I first came in here but, I got to thinking maybe my husband didn't want me and he ah, we had a little bit of trouble and ah, I just got so nervous and weak and rundown and seemed like I couldn't . . . and I thought it would help me to see a doctor and see if something helps.
T: Um hmm.
C: My nerves and my legs.
T: Um hmm.
C: And all that. And so he put me on a diet . . .
T: You were feeling pretty bad.
C: Um hmm.
T: How do you feel about your husband . . .
C: Well he came in to see me . . . I got a letter from him yesterday which was a very sweet letter from him, and he's done the best he can with the children, I know he's done all he can do without help, but he can't . . . he ain't got no way of coming in to see me unless he . . . a car or something to come in to see me and it worries me about not coming in, getting to come in to see me.

T: You feel better about him since you got the letter, you feel better about how he feels about you.

C: Yah, I feel better toward him. Ah, I've always really loved him and cared for him and uh, therefore I want to get well to go back home to him if I can at all. But I don't know what is the matter with me, I'm just burned out, and my hands and this feeling in my legs.

T: Must be pretty hard to understand what you can do to help yourself.

C: Well, I don't know what I can do now, cause there for a while I helped myself pretty good till Sunday night. It just seemed like it took me all at once, this nervousness and weakness and feeling I got.

T: How long have you been here?

C: I've been here about 10 or 15 days.

T: Um hmm.

C: See, I came in here about the 26th of September, I think, late in September. . . . on the day that my mother passed away too. (Client is weeping)

(Trainee reactions and discussions)

Bill: 8

Tod: 4

Al: 6

Frank: 6

Jim: 6

Ray: 4

Dr. T: There's quite a bit of spread there.

John: Was she crying there?

Hank: Yes.

Sam: I couldn't hear well, but what I heard I was impressed with.

Dr. T: So this would average about 6 or something close to that.

Dr. C: Um hmm.

Paul: I think the tears gave it a halo effect.

Bill: That's good concrete evidence of emotion.

Ben: I think the tears gave it a halo. (Long pause)

(Before another example is played, one of the trainees raises an issue about the case to be played next.)

Sam: I think it was important, but this person saw the result of her intelligence test, she saw the result of her Rorschach, she knows how she's classified and everything else, and the doctor just let her see everything . . . the whole works, right down the line. I didn't react to it there but afterwards I was really teed-off at the doctor who would do something like that. He just let her see. She knows she's a paranoid schizophrenic and she knows all these other things about herself.

Dr. T: He really shouldn't have let her see that?

Sam: I didn't think it was ethical to let her see it.

Dr. T: In what sense? You felt it was damaging to her?

Sam: In the sense that I felt it would be damaging to her because this is the way I felt after talking with her. She knows this is what she is, she's a paranoid schizophrenic. "It must be. The tests said so. I'm not intelligent, the tests say 90-88, therefore I'm not intelligent. If they were high I'd be intelligent." And she takes these things to heart. So I thought this was damaging.

Dr. T: I don't know, what do other people think?

Ben: I don't know, I mean you said yourself, she had a lot of insight about herself. Maybe this was helpful to her to get a more realistic picture of herself.

Sam: But her whole outlook, she doesn't say she has intelligence, she has common sense. She berates herself as far as intelligence and other things and reduces this all to just common sense.

Ben: Does she really? The 90-88?

Sam: Well, according to what she says and what I consider a little understanding of it, she berates herself.

Dr. T: And that's because of the tests?

Sam: I think that she has berated herself for a long, long time and I think that she can focus it on one specific thing now and say, "Because of this it must be so." I think this is the problem.

Dr. T: I don't know, I'd like to get . . .

Jim: I just wonder if she's really seen the tests, I mean probably; people often think different things, probably it isn't actually true, they think they're true I mean they see somebody else's test and say "Well, that's mine."

Sam: I can't say for sure that she's seen the tests. I believe that she's seen the tests. She described them sufficiently. She described the doctor at his situation on the ward. She says she saw the tests and to me that seemed realistic. I didn't think she was making it up . . . Cause she's able to focus on her delusions and hallucinations, at least on the intellectual level—"Yeah, they're hallucinations, delusions." She's able to do this . . . (Pause)

Dr. T: Yeah.

Sam: Like another me.

Dr. T: Yeah, I've thought about this many times and I'm not sure I'd be willing to take any position . . . totally generally, or total strongly, but I have felt that all information, particularly psychologicals and case writeups and so on, should be freely available to the patient. I would certainly fire my internist very quickly if he didn't let me have access to the various reports. That's a matter of information that I want to have. I want to take into consideration his advice and his information and I may sometimes decide that on some issues . . . like advice about what to do in case of colds—I know that my "wives' tales" are just as good as his. In the area of personality I feel it still holds. A patient probably won't become any more paranoid if he knows what the hospital really thinks of him. In a basic sense I feel that he has a right to know. A patient, or anyone, could have access to any diagnostic writeup that I have done and I would probably be willing to stand by it. I'd say "Well, yes, I could be wrong here or here but basically this is my best opinion." And in some ways I feel a patient is entitled to that. I have done this on a number of occasions where I've simply said, "Well, here's what I and other people think of you. You may not seem dangerous to yourself, but I wonder what it is about you that leads people with lots of experience to decide that you're dangerous. Is there something you're doing that makes it look this way if it's not true?"

Sam: How can you determine beforehand, about having the person see something, at least whether it will be facilitating or inhibiting? I think this to me is the criteria that I would use.

Dr. T: There would be occasions where I'd want to withhold information. I'm not convinced that that would ever be wise, however. It might very well be my own fears and prejudices operating. I guess basically what it amounts to is that the more reality that is available to even a paranoid, the less he has to project and imagine. I can think of a number of examples, particularly, one old fellow, who was a hospitalized schizophrenic. He was under the impression that once he got his social security, he could go home. The physician didn't ever argue with him about this. He just said "Uh huh, uh huh," and the ward people didn't argue with him either on this, so he kept believing this and he was convinced that the staff had told him this. You couldn't really argue with that because they had clearly, *by implication,* told him yes. They had refused to say "No," because they didn't want to argue, and yet the real fact was that people at home were afraid he was some kind of dangerous person because he shot at the neighbor's dog. This was really the reality that he was facing. I felt he should know what he's up against. He doesn't have to sit back and invent imaginary reasons why he's here. There are several reasons why he's here and if he doesn't agree that he's dangerous, which he probably won't, he has to at least be forced to look at what the heck it is about him that makes other people think he's dangerous. I don't know, I guess what it basically boils down to is a conviction I have that basically most people who are neurotic, psychotic, etc., have been misinformed and uninformed. So, the more reality you can communicate to them the better. I'm not emotionally able to carry this out always. I sometimes feel, no, I might upset the patient by letting him know the truth. And yet, intellectually, I can't help but feel that I'm encouraging projection and distortion . . . because if I were in that person's place where something very disturbing was happening in my life, I would certainly be compelled to imagine reasons why. Sometimes it has turned out that case histories and so forth were in error, as a matter of fact. The patient then has an opportunity to correct it or at least state his view.

Jane: I have no, you know, commitment one way or the other. But I've felt the same way. It was just that I reacted with them against . . . they didn't show the case. They didn't know what it was they had coming . . .

Dr. T: Um hmm.

Jane: And also reacted against . . . that we were setting up ourselves as some kind of . . . father symbol: "Well, no, you can't; you don't have the right. You're sick and so you can't see it. You can't know . . ."

Sam: Say, lets get back to the tapes, I want to hear some reaction to the one that's on the tape recorder ready to go.

(The supervisors and trainees agree, and the following tape sample is played)

T: Well, could you tell me just a little bit about it?

C: Well, I think just vaguely, it was about six years ago.

T: Um hmm.

C: I had Dr. S's . . . inkblot . . .

T: Inkblot

C: I read the results of it.

T: What did you think of it? After you, after you read it?

C: Some of it was flattering and some was rather derogatory.

T: Was it interesting?

C: Oh, I don't know, it took about three hours.

T: Quite a long time, isn't it.

C: Um hmm.

T: You came in here about twelve days ago, you said.

C: I guess, um hmm. The 30th. What is today?

T: Today I think is around the 12th or 13th. I think I've lost track of the time.

C: (Laughs) You do in a place like this. I know my husband brought the paper Sunday, I caught up on the Sunday news.

T: Since you first came in here, I mean, what, what's happened since you first came in here?

C: You mean the first day?

T: Well, since you came here to E—?

C: Hmm?

T: What happened when you came here to E—?

C: Well, ah, they gave me a shot, I went to snooze.

T: Um hmm.

C: And . . . gave me a shot and brought me down in a car, I didn't even . . .

T: You didn't even remember.

C: Oh yes. I remember because I answered a lot of questions at the main building, but I was rather groggy.

T: Um hmm. Yah, it's probably a funny feeling to come in here pretty groggy.

C: Hmm, rather humiliating.

T: Humiliating?

C: Um hmm.

T: Just didn't like that at all.

C: Um—well, really, after 12 days of thinking about it I couldn't give you one opinion or another.

T: (Chuckles) Doesn't make any difference any more.

C: No, you get used to it. It's routine.

T: Well, tell me a little about . . . what happened at home or what happened. Just tell me a little about yourself, just pick anything. Just sit and talk for awhile.

C: Well . . . (Clears throat) What do you want to know, of my early childhood or my married life. (Laughs)

T: (Talking together) No reason, something that you just would like to talk about. I'll let you pick out whatever you'd like.

C: Well, I'm all talked out. (Laughs)

T: You're all talked out. (Talking together and laughing.)

C: Yeah.

T: Everybody's been talking to you, just keeping you pretty busy talking.

C: Well, not here especially, although I talked to the minister. I think I'm no different than anyone else. I have to be in the mood to talk. I mean, really it seems useless to go over the same things over and over again. I've come to the conclusion that I was having hallucinations, I guess. Although fundamentally there was something to it and I guess if I were a more stable person I would have dis-dis-dismissed it from my mind but it just became an obsession.

T: You, you're not sure though, that you were just . . . to you they're real, they're very real, aren't they?

C: Not any more.

T: Not any more?

C: Although the move . . . I guess that's what you're getting at, what started it all, I mean started all the pressure . . . well, I moved about a year and a half ago.

T: Um hmm.

C: And I didn't particularly like the house. It was terribly rundown, terribly shabby and ah, surroundings that weren't . . . and I have absolutely no gift except homemaking and I must say, I made a doll house out of it.

T: That's a pretty big gift.

C: I papered and painted and sanded the stairs myself and stained them. One day I did thirteen windows.

T: Boy, that's quite a lot.

C: Painting and . . . don't be condescending. (Laughs)

T: I'm not condescending. I couldn't do that. I couldn't do that. I can hardly keep a home myself.

C: And really, ah, it's really a nice excuse. I, this isn't of interest to you, but give you an idea . . .

T: This takes a certain amount of talent, I think this is . . .

C: I think so . . .

T: Many people cannot do this and . . .

C: In a way . . . like in the living room they had ah, green walls and green woodwork and I painted the woodwork white and I painted the walls white and got white curtains and then I got everything in gold and brown and I couldn't afford wall-to-wall carpeting so I bought two 9 x 12 rugs and divided them up . . .

T: Um hmm.

C: It's really pretty. It's beautiful.

T: You're a little bit of an interior decorator.

C: . . . did the living room. Well I took a little bit, a course in it and I did the kitchen in turquoise and yellow. I painted woodwork and windows and that. I enjoy things like that. Any-anyway it's real cute now, real cute, darling. And I tore out a patio that was on the side and put it in the back.

T: Certainly a lot of improvements.

C: Anyway, it doesn't improve the value of the property fundamentally, but it, the appearance is a whole lot better.

T: You can live in it a lot better.

C: But, I just didn't like the neighborhood too well. I'm ah, more or less a recluse and when I lived here, this one woman she's a very nice person, but she came to visit me one evening, her and another one and they stayed about two hours. I had worked until I was exhausted, I'd been there about two weeks, and ah, she frightened me to death. She was too aggressive, and I had been told that she was in your house constantly drinking coffee and she has a son at Duke University and ah, she has a maid and nothing to do.

T: . . . have coffee.

C: Well, she didn't at my house anyway, and it's, I can't explain it but the thought of someone coming, feeling free to come in my house a dozen times a day just, it just makes me frantic. I like my privacy too well.

T: Privacy is pretty damn important.

C: And I couldn't, I couldn't, I just couldn't stand it, naturally I never did anything halfway, I went to the other extreme and I just didn't speak or anything. I, I think 90 per cent of it was shyness. I think maybe I feel inferior to her plus *I didn't want my privacy invaded and ah, she stayed about two hours and she's a lovely person and everyone liked her, but I just cut her dead and then the man next door called the police on our dog . . .*

T: On your dog?

C: Our dog. And ah, he's blind, he's old, he doesn't bother anyone and we adore him as if he were a human being and a few days after we moved there, the school had given my little girl a tree and I had planted it and it was two inches on his property and he made us move it. Then he got a . . . he's just a cantankerous man, I found out later he does it to everybody, but I took it personal like I do everything else. And well, he made us move the tree and then he called the police on our dog and then he got ah, a surveyor and surveyed his property which to me, I, you know, seemed terrible.

T: What does he do this for?

C: Well, I guess to give us an understanding what was his. We were padding the grass two inches on his property . . .

T: (Laughs)

C: Well, it just snowballed, you know.

T: Yeah.

C: And then the woman in back, she called four times, in a lovely voice, she had a very lovely voice, she herself is rather homely but she called and in a charming way told me that the tree in my back yard was unsightly and she would like for me to cut it down. I felt rather sorry for her because she spent nine-tenths of the time telling me about her ancestors and her mother belonged to the D.A.R. and everything and I was, well, I got tired of the pressure so we paid $35 to have the tree cut down.

T: Um hmm.

C: And the, the people that had owned the house before us, had lived there four years and two and a half of it they had the house up for sale. The neighbors decided they didn't want them and diplomatically shut them out. Well, I made, I'm just stubborn and nobody, I just, even though the, the, the net result is this I thought.

T: . . . a hell of a lot of pressure living, living right there in that neighborhood. Neighbors really just put, put pressures on you, it's . . .

C: Well I guess nothing tangible, nothing you can say, just little things.

T: You can feel it though.

C: Um hmm.

T: And you know it's there.

C: Um hmm.

T: You know listening to you talk now for the last few minutes I, I was just thinking that you seem to have a great deal of knowledge about yourself. You're able to well, explain some of these things that you do feel inside . . . hallucinations aren't real. That seems as if you've gotten well, inside, so to speak, that you're able to . . .

C: Yes, I . . .

T: You realize these things.

C: You sound like my husband. He thinks I'm a genius.

T: Well, there's a, there's a certain amount of . . .

C: Yeah, my, my, I.Q. is very norm, in fact I think its below normal. I'm not very intelligent. I've got a lot of common sense but I'm not very intelligent.

T: You don't, just don't think you're intelligent.

C: Um hmm.

T: How, how do you know these things?

C: Well for one thing, I made terrible grades in school and I saw the results on my, ah, psychological tests.

T: Um hmm.

C: And it averaged, they had three grades, is that the way you do? I remember there was three grades, I don't know how they were because I just ran through it once. I wasn't supposed to see the results, but . . .

T: That's what I was wondering.

C: Insisted on it. I insisted on it and I guess he thought I would, I'm pretty obnoxious when I want to be. (Laughs) Anyway, he let me see it. Not the psychologist, but my doctor.

T: Right, hmm.

C: He sent it to my doctor. And my I.Q. hovers between 89 and 98 and that isn't very good.

T: Well, this is pretty close, it's normal.

C: Normal. Little bit below.

T: Not very much, just a little tiny bit. It's a, I think maybe 100 is . . . about average.

C: I don't grasp things very easily.

T: Well . . .

C: The only thing that interests me is people. (Laughs)

T: Sometimes this is even better than grasping school subjects. After all you, when you do leave school you've got all the people to deal with, not, not school subjects any more.

C: Well, my mother and I lived together. My father was killed when I was real young.

T: Um hmm.

C: And ah, she never made me study. I know my daughter, ah mother, worked and I had an awful lot to do at home. I think that's why at home, I know when I was twelve, my little girl was here visiting me Sunday and I got after her because I thought she was doing too many school activities although I encourage it, and not helping her father enough and I told her, I said, "When I was twelve I played hooky from school one day and made curtains for the whole house and I'd never run a sewing machine in my life. And I made curtains then out of unbleached muslin. And this was what, twenty some odd years ago, the very same thing that I just paid $32 for (both laugh) twenty years later, they're all in rags now.

T: Oh boy. That's quite a difference, isn't it.

C: But I didn't know anything about it. I remember there was blue thread in the bobbin and white thread at the top but I, we needed curtains and I didn't like school, so I stayed home and made curtains.

T: There are many people who go to school and maybe make top grades in the class but can't do half the things that you do.

C: No, I can't sew. I can't sew. I've never sewed a seam.

(Discussion)

Dr. T: Shall we rate this one?

Sam: (The therapist on the tape) I think it was terrible . . . let's rate it on warmth.

Ben: It was my impression that Sam exhibited a real warmth and perhaps equaled or exceeded most of the ingredients that we've judged so far.

Sam: How much money would you like? (Laughter)

Tod: I think you reacted to something the same way I did. Sam's voice was Sam. It wasn't any therapist. He didn't go . . . I've caught myself doing this in these tapes . . . going into the therapist voice: you didn't do that. You were just plain old Sam and it comes across a hundred times better. It really does.

Sam: It's a funny thing. I like my other ones better than this one.

Tod: I mean just that segment.

Sam: I know what you mean, Tod.

Dr. T: Yeah, I think this . . . this has a warmth and sincerity as well as empathy.

Sam: Well, I couldn't say anything. I couldn't show that I was empathic. Whether I was or not, that's another question, but I couldn't show it so directly with this patient.

Dr. T: Yeah, that's really what part of the scale is in aiming at: being successful and moving the person from talking about external events to talking more personal by going beneath the surface and trying to catch some things. I have seen you more sensitively attuned to their feeling state but I would agree that I don't think I've seen you more congruently warm.

Tod: I get the feeling that Sam was 100 per cent on the side of the patient. Here the patient was going on and on, telling all about the neighbor's persecuting her and somebody may say, well, this therapist was completely sucked in by the patient's delusions of persecution. But here Sam was 100 per cent on the side of the patient. He was not being a diagnostician, he was not thinking, at least he was not giving evidence of thinking, "Well, I'll have to weigh what she says and it probably is somewhat delusional." He was strictly on the side of the patient.

Dr. T: Um hmm. O.K. Let's go over our ratings.

(Class proceeds to read off their individual ratings of empathy.)

In ending this discussion of empathic understanding, a good example of a nonempathic therapist should perhaps be given. Almost any set of tape recordings, even with a highly empathic therapist, will contain many examples of low accurate empathy. The following example of a beginning therapist who happened to see a disturbed psychotic patient provides an extreme example of a lack of understanding. In part, as the reader will note, the patient *is* extremely difficult to understand. But as the reader gets through the first client statement and on to the first therapist statement, the sense of confusion grows rather than subsides. Probably for this reason, it may become the reader's favorite example of a therapist who doesn't understand.

Sharing and Togetherness Without Understanding . . .

C: It seems that recently, uh, we, uh, set up our program for the next year, and uh, outlined it, and concurred it by phone and all of this stuff, and I sent him a letter, a concurring letter, a letter to concur his phone call. I want him to send me a concurring letter to the letter that I concurred from to make more triply sure that I didn't—what's going on. So, I don't know what, uh, what's going on, what's going on in this guy's head.

T: (Mhm)

C: 'Cause, uh, I assume at the outset then that this is a

T: (Mhm)

C: . . . guy that reacts normally to acts, normally. Then when a person does have something that is supposed to, or that he was going to be especially secretive about . . .

(T: Mhm)

C: . . . that does have a definite meaning. Not a type that just promotes himself to . . . out of proportion like . . . let's say, uh, say a certain general. Perhaps, uh, this fellow likes servants.

T: Maybe you're saying that . . . I mean, what I see you doing is, uh escaping, considering . . . letting a, a justification . . . for . . . your feeling of anxiety in this situation.

C: (Interrupting) Yeah, well, uh, I'm trying to figure out just how . . . well, just kind of what the outcome would be, what day do you think

(Therapist attempts to interject some comment, but client does not yield) . . . I could go on with the delusions, of trying to be a fortune teller, which I can't . . .

(T: Mhm)

C: . . . I can't stand that.

T: Then, I heard you say something else, uh, right at the beginning, I suppose this way, that, uh, there it was a hot day, and you didn't think there was, you know, there was any calls coming downstairs.

C: Well, I . . . I would like to try to figure that out for myself, the feeling I . . . I sort of get the feeling, you know, of . . . of getting to be triply sure, you know. Perhaps this is what I meant to convey here.

T: Well, uh . . . I don't know whether you really said this, but it's . . . you conveyed it to me, anyhow. And, I perceived the notion that, uh . . . you were feeling this way and, uh, sore and so on, and along comes this phone call and this situation . . .

C: Mhm.

T: . . . to which, immediately, you respond with anxiety . . .

C: Yah.

T: . . . which, umh, you then felt was, uh, an indication of the insecurity of your level of confidence . . .

C: Yah

T: . . . in yourself . . . I'm very frank!

The ingredient most often pointed to in theory and most often related to constructive client outcome in research is the level of accurate empathy: the sensitive and accurate grasp of the other person's deeper and surface feelings, meanings and experience. The focus is on the perceptive and communicative aspect of empathy, in which the therapist experiences the client's feelings as if they were his own, and communicates this perception in a way that the client can understand and work with. Initial steps in the training of prospective therapists in the perceptive and communicative aspects of empathy were described and illustrated with transcripts of the actual process.

It is a most difficult undertaking indeed to attempt to train persons in the perceptive and communicative aspects of empathy. The present approach testifies to an on-going attempt to systematize in training one of the most critical of therapeutic dimensions.

CHAPTER 11 TOWARD THE COMMUNICATION OF NONPOSSESSIVE WARMTH IN THE THERAPIST

NONPOSSESSIVE warmth or unconditional positive regard, though separable from the other basic ingredients of effective interpersonal skills, inevitably overlaps and intertwines with the communication of accurate empathy and genuineness. Thus, Rausch and Bordin (1957), in an excellent theoretical analysis of the components of warmth, specify the commitment of the therapist, his effort to understand, and his spontaneity. As noted in the preceding chapter, the intensity and intimacy offered by the therapist also overlap with and contribute to his communication of warmth. Another overlapping aspect of warmth involves the concept of "psychological distance"; the more distant the relationship, or the more aloof the therapist, the less warmth communicated. The degree of active personal participation and the use of client-oriented focus (as defined by Whitehorn and Betz, 1954) to discriminate successful from unsuccessful therapists represent a modality of communicating warmth.

A careful cataloging of the kinds of behaviors and verbalizations that people use to communicate warmth or positive regard could easily fill a number of books. Even in the more limited relationship of counseling or psychotherapy, warmth and respect can be communicated or not communicated by the therapist in a variety of ways: by sitting silently for a full session with a client who is weeping, struggling, and experiencing a deep "aloneness"; by genuine laughter as the patient recounts an incident in his life; by being willing to accept the patient's choosing *not* to share an experience; by agreeing to extend the therapeutic session for two hours or more when that is possible and appropriate; by the apologizing for unintentionally hurting the client by act, gesture, or word; and, by being open enough to voice his own feelings when he has been hurt or angered by the client.

Because of the many different ways in which individuals communicate and interpret the communications of nonpossessive warmth, the therapist must inevitably rely heavily upon his accurate, empathic understanding of the client to sense the mode and the content that will communicate his positive caring or warmth most effectively.

In our everyday life, unfortunately, we often have not only too little practice in communicating warmth, but also too little practice in experiencing a meaningful nonpossessive warmth for others. The beginning therapist is likely to transfer his feelings about the actions and behaviors of others, including evaluation with implicit praise or condemnation, to the therapeutic relationship. Such a prospective therapist usually asks: "But how can you feel warmth for someone who is actually bad, who is destructive to others, who is just plain mean, petty, and selfish?" In everyday life we don't. Moreover, if we did it would probably encourage such destructive, cruel, etc., behavior. In the unique encounter of counseling or psychotherapy, however, such actions can be viewed correctly as merely defensive behaviors that will change as the client becomes less threatened by aspects of himself and others; therefore, the social convention of condemning them is no longer useful or appropriate. The communication of nonpossessive warmth to the client and the acceptance of even antisocial or destructive behavior does not demand accepting his behavior as desirable, but only as natural, normal and expected *given his circumstances and perceptions*. It involves taking the attitude that "if I had had the same background, the same circumstances, the same experiences, it would be inevitable in me, as it is in him, that I would act in this fashion" (Rogers and Truax, 1966). Acceptance of *what is,* rather than a demand for *what ought to be,* implies neither approval nor disapproval. To return to the analogy of the reader who identifies with the hero of a novel, as readers we become engrossed in following the actions and feelings of the hero without having to personally agree or disagree, approve or disapprove of his feelings and actions. In much the same way, when we are engrossed in reading or understanding the client, we would have to stop and disengage ourselves from him to feel or voice our agreement or disagreement, approval or disapproval of what is in him. As we come to know the client, his experiences, his achievements and failures, the important people in his life and their relationship to him as *he construes or perceives them,* we tend through the process of "trial identification" to both respect and like him (as we do the sometimes inadequate, sometimes weak, sometimes selfish and petty hero of the novel).

We have briefly discussed, earlier in this book, the Principle of Reciprocal Affect (Truax, 1966) which simply says: It is a rare human being who does not respond to warmth with warmth and to hostility with hostility. It is probaly the most important principle for the beginning therapist to understand if he is to be successful in the therapeutic relationship.

Although theoretic psychology has largely ignored this basic fact of human relationships, there is considerable evidence to show its importance. It is so ubiquitous and so commonplace that even a moment's reflection will show that even our own lives are governed by it. How do we ourselves respond to warmth in others? We respond positively, with something closely akin to warmth. How do we respond to rejection or hostility from others? We react defensively, with reciprocal defensiveness or something closely akin to rejection and hostility.

From another viewpoint, it may be that our ability to experience nonpossessive warmth for the feelings and person of the client depends on our ability to feel an unconditional positive regard for our own self—an acceptance of both the good and the bad that lives in us. Clinically, there appears to be a direct relationship between one's self-regard and the regard felt for others. Two pieces of research evidence tend to confirm this. Fey (1955) found strong positive correlations between research measures of self-acceptance and measures of acceptance of others. Even more striking, recent research by Kanfer and Marston (1963a), on externally induced changes in the rate of self-reinforcement, indicated that when the rate of self-reinforcement was changed, there was a consequent parallel change in the rate of reinforcement that the subject gave to others. Thus, there is at least meager clinical and research evidence suggesting this conclusion: the greater the degree to which we are acceptant of the sometimes petty, selfish, destructive, or "bad" feelings and experiences in ourselves, the more able will we be to experience unconditional positive regard and acceptance of the wide range and depth of feelings and experiences in the client. This may be a partial explanation for the recurrent findings that the more healthy, mature, integrated, and nonanxious person makes the best counselor or therapist (Arbuckle, 1956; Bandura, 1956; Bergin and Solomon, 1963).

The communication of warmth can be greatly enhanced by training, but to be effective it must be a distinctly human communication completely congruent with the personality of the therapist. In this context, May (1958) notes that "The therapist is assumedly an expert; but, if he is not first of all a human being, his expertness will be irrelevant and quite possibly harmful" (p. 82).

This personal nature of the communication of warmth and respect is emphasized by Rogers (1955b) who describes his own experience as follows:

> I launch myself into the therapeutic relationship having a hypothesis or a faith that my liking, my confidence, and my understanding of the other persons' inner world will lead to to a significant process of becoming. I enter the relationship not as a scientist, not as a physician who can accurately diagnose and cure, but as a person, entering into a personal relationship. Insofar as I see him only as an object, the client will tend to become only an object.

WARMTH, TRANSFERENCE AND REPRESSION

Transference, as a grouping of phenomena, has several meanings but, since Freud's early descriptions, has referred to the client's positive and negative feelings toward the therapist. The word *transference* was used to specify the similarity of these feelings to those occurring in childhood toward the parent; in a sense the feelings could be thought of as being "transferred" from the basic family model relationships to the relationship with the therapist. In recent years, existentially oriented psychoanalysts have shifted the emphasis in understanding the process of transference. Thus May (1958) interprets Boss's (1955) reformulation as follows:

What really happens is not that the neurotic patient "transfers" feelings he had toward mother or father to wife or therapist. Rather, the neurotic is one who in certain areas never developed beyond the limited and restricted forms of experience characteristic of the infant. In later years he perceived wife or therapist through the same restrictive distorted "spectacles" as he perceived father or mother. (p. 79)

May then goes on to delineate the meaning in counseling and therapy of this reformulation:

Almost everything the patient does vis-a-vis the therapist in a given hour has an element of transference in it. But nothing is ever "transference" to be explained to the patient as one would an arithmetic problem. The concept of "transference" has often been used as a convenient protective screen behind which both therapist and patient hide in order to avoid the more anxiety-creating situation of direct confrontation. For me to tell myself, say when especially fatigued, that the patient-is-so-demanding-because-she-wants-to-prove she-can-make-her-father-love-her may be a relief and may also be in fact true. But the real point is that she is doing this to me in this given moment, and the reasons it occurs at this instant . . . are not exhausted by what she did with her father. Beyond all considerations of unconscious determinism—which are true in their partial context—she is at some point choosing to do this at this specific moment. Furthermore, the only thing that will grasp the patient, and in the long run make it possible for her to *change,* is to experience fully and deeply that she is doing precisely this to a real person, myself, in this real moment. (p. 83)

May also quotes from Binswanger in discussing the failure of the resolution of transference:

If such a treatment fails, the analyst inclines to assume that the patient is not capable of overcoming his resistance to the physician, for example, as a "father image." Whether an analysis can have success or not is often, however, not decided by whether a patient is capable *at all* of overcoming such a transferred father image but by the opportunity *this particular physician* accords him to do so; it may, in other words, be the rejection of the therapist as a person the impossibility of entering into a genuine communicative rapport with him, that may form the obstacle against breaking through the "eternal" repetition of the father resistance. (p. 81)

Binswanger goes on to point out that in his view the therapist's inability to overcome negative transference hinges upon the therapist's inability to adequately communicate human warmth in a true person-to-person encounter. From this viewpoint, the therapist's inability to adequately communicate nonpossessive warmth serves to heighten rather than resolve negative transference.

As noted earlier, nearly all theorists since Freud have dealt with the importance of the therapist's communication of warmth for the establishment of positive transference. This positive transference, born in part from the patient's response of warmth, through the principle of reciprocal affect as a response to the therapist's communicated warmth, provides the context for the work of psychotherapy or counseling.

It is perhaps quite useful to distinguish between feelings of dependency and actual positive transference. When warmth is communicated in a possessive or conditional manner, it is likely to engender, elicit, or foster feelings of dependency. Actually, when the therapist communicates warmth in a conditional manner he is defining the locus of evaluation within himself rather than within the client, and thereby also defining the relationship as one of dependency for the client. It is difficult to think of any situation in which fostering dependency in the client can be construed as therapeutic. Normally, of course, the patient will come to counseling or therapy with the expectation, drawn from the analogy of physical medicine, that the doctor will somehow cure him; but such learned expectations should not be confused with the patient's internal dependency.

To deal successfully with dependency or negative transference, the therapist must not only attempt to communicate an accurate empathic understanding of the specific real feeling, but also make greater efforts to ensure unambiguous communication of warmth, unconditional regard, and respect for the client. Since reciprocal affect is a two-way street, the danger in negative transference is that the patient's anger, displaced on the therapist, will elicit anger or resentment and thus effectively destroy for the moment his therapeutic value. At such moments the counselor or therapist is most tempted to become defensive and simply label the client's behavior as "negative transference," telling the patient that it is inappropriate or irrational. However, a more effective response to such feelings might be to treat them as genuine and attempt to explore them. The therapist might initially respond by saying something like "I sense you're feeling almost a real anger toward me" or, "In part, you seem to be feeling very disappointed with me, with our relationship, and with the possibility of getting a real help here."

Similarly, expressions of dependency, whether internally or externally motivated (by cultural expectations for counseling or therapy or by conditional or possessive warmth from the therapist), can probably also be most directly handled by treating them as real feelings. If a client attempts to get the counselor to make decisions for him, or asks for tests to tell him what to do, the counselor may respond by saying "You expect *me* to sort of take the responsibility for your life right now. Perhaps in part because I'm *supposed* to have all of the answers, which of course I don't, and in part, perhaps you're not sure that you want to take the risk of deciding for yourself," or "It's almost as if you had said, 'Won't somebody *please* tell me what to do.'" As in all the therapist's responses, he will have to be guided by his understanding of the client at that moment.

Repression is perhaps even more closely related to the therapist's communication of warmth. Repression, as Freud and others since have noted, is a specific aspect of self-acceptance; it is withholding from oneself unacceptable faults, desires, etc., in order to defend an acceptable view of oneself. In order for the patient to experience or verbalize these unacceptable or repressed feelings or experiences, he must come to share the therapist's unconditional positive regard for all experiences and all feelings. To the extent, therefore, that the therapist himself is conditional in his warm acceptance of expressed feelings, the patient will continue to perceive "bad feelings or thoughts" as unacceptable and thus retain the repression.

LEARNING TO COMMUNICATE NONPOSSESSIVE WARMTH

At the outset, the training group's discussion of warmth and respect for the client was based upon the cognitive learnings from practice in the use of the research scale (presented in Chapter 2) and theoretic writings. Vicarious experiential learnings were derived from the trainees' listening to recordings of counseling and therapy available in the tape library. The following excerpt from class discussion focuses upon the personal meaning for the trainee of the basic concept:

Of Love and Anxiety . . .

Dr. T: I suppose today we were planning on focusing on nonpossessive warmth. Who would like to start off the . . . discussion?

Sam: At least to me, this concept doesn't set well yet. I can't visualize it and I can't pick it out of the tapes, and uh, I just don't know really what it is yet.

Dr. T: Um hmm.

Sam: Except, ah, to compare a textbook definition of it . . .

Dr. T: Not easy to see on the therapy tape?

Sam: Besides that, I don't *feel* anything about it yet.

Dr. T: "It's not easy to see on the tapes" . . . did you listen to Dr. P's tape last?

Sam: Yeah.

Dr. T: I guess for me it came through very clearly that he liked this person, and that he respected . . . this person's feelings.

Sam: I think he difinitely cared about him.

Dr. T: Do you think, did you get any sense of his having a respect for feelings? For that patient's feelings?

Sam: Yeah, but he didn't mince words with him; he knocked him around a little bit. But I think he did *care* for him.

Dr. T: What did other people think?

Sam: It seemed like it was easier to pick out . . . genuineness and empathy rather than . . . unconditional warmth.

Dr. T: There are fewer instances of where only warmth is going to be demanded in therapy, except when a patient attacks a therapist. Last week we were talking about congruence and one way of rephrasing congruence would be that the therapist . . . has a respect for his own feelings, that he has a positive valuing of them. That means that he can accept negative feelings in himself. He can accept pettiness, cruelty, all kinds of feelings with the sort of implicit assumption that they're not a central and eternal part of his makeup. They don't define him. Sort of, that, as a therapist, I can experience things that I feel that are bad, or damaging, that I shouldn't experience, you know, but I accept these as transient and not a basic part of me, or only as a part of me, perhaps . . . as a transient part of me. And in this same sense, unconditional warmth would be holding these kinds of feelings toward the patient . . . Congruence would be holding these feelings toward oneself; and holding these same feelings toward the patient would be unconditional positive regard. Dr. C. and I were talking this morning about this, talking about how this occurred throughout the process of therapy. Part of our feeling was that initially, the focus was on the unconditionality in therapy to allow the patient to open up, to get to know the patient . . . but that once the relationship was formed, the focus really shifted from the unconditionality to the positiveness of the regard as we invested ourselves in the patients.

Tod: Doesn't this unconditionality have a lot to do with just simple relaxation?

Dr. T: And by relaxation, genuineness?

Tod: Just being, sort of completely at ease . . .

Sam: Can a patient be at ease in a relationship?

Tod: I think if the therapist can, in turn it will let him. Even a therapist, doesn't he get a little bit anxious during the relationship? He's usually very anxious but I think that there comes a time when he is not being anxious.

Dr. T: Do you think the therapist really has to . . . that the therapist who is experienced gets anxious? It's one thing to be anxious initially as people often are in anything they do that's new, because of their uncertainty about themselves and their adequacy, and their uncertainty about the process . . .

Sam: The differences may lie in levels of anxiety, in this case. I think one may operate under low levels of anxiety and still have the anxiety, as opposed to the higher levels. I guess it's positively correlated with experience.

Dr. T: Do you think they ever have . . . do you think that a therapist could be nonanxious?

Sam: I think, well, I have the feeling that there always has to be a certain amount of anxiety aroused in any relationship. First of all, you're dealing with another human being and you have, well, a great deal at stake, both for this human being and for you. I think one can't get away with the idea that the therapist is not really involved in this relationship, and to the degree of his involvement, then I think this is also correlated with his degree of anxiety . . . When this degree of involvement gets too great, his anxiety gets too great. When he has a moderate degree of involvement, I think it's . . .

Dr. T: (Interrupting) So that the generalization of this is that any human relationship, you feel, would provoke anxiety in the people involved?

Sam: Right, I think so.

Dr. C: You're, you mean, that . . .

Sam: No, it isn't a provoking anxiety.

Dr. C: With your girlfriend, or with your best buddy, that the deeper the involvement, the more anxious it gets?

Sam: Now, I'm not quite sure. Where we have the idea of a human relationship with the idea of therapy in mind first of all, as opposed to a human relationship with some other idea in mind, I think there is a degree of involvement anxiety in these other relationships. But I think . . . in other words, I think anxiety is necessarily there and it's prevalent in all types of relationships, that it may be concentrated in therapy. Well, the outlets may be different in a therapeutic relationship.

Dr. T: That it wouldn't seem likely that a person could feel . . . so secure in a relationship that he would be able to *not* focus on the loss aspect, or the potential loss, and instead be able to focus on the potential rewards?

Sam: I think that the anxiety may arise from the sessions, well in looking, in dealing with each session, not the eventual outcome . . .

Dr. T: Um hmm, um hmm.

Sam: In the long term, whether he will help his patient or he will lose his patient.

Dr. T: Right.

Sam: I think this is where we're getting to now.

Dr. T: I have the feeling, for example, that Dr. P. feels fairly secure in what he's doing; with him, he doesn't feel anxious, or, he rarely feels anxious in his relationships with patients. It doesn't seem to occur to him that he's likely to lose from the encounter. It just doesn't cross his conscious or even preconscious to feel that he could potentially lose from this encounter. With him it seemed that he had a certain degree of faith in what he was doing; he felt secure that what he was doing had the potential of being helpful and he didn't focus on the possibility of loss for him personally in the encounter. Perhaps, he was not, in any clear sense, anxious in the relationship.

Sam: I think he did have a hell of a lot of power in the relationship first of all. I think I had the feeling of anxiety in a few cases early in the tape rather than later on. After the first 60 feet or so—it was real fine, but up to that point, it seemed he was pretty anxious, for example, when he more or less made the interpretation that when he said something, the patient didn't hear him.

Dr. T: Yeah.

Sam: He said "sometimes people don't hear what I say." I mean, he may have been a little bit anxious there.

Tod: I couldn't understand him either. (Laughter) I thought he rode his patient a little hard at this point.

Dr. T: Yeah.

Sam: I feel it was really his fault, in that therapy.

Dr. C: Is the implication of what you're saying that anxiety tended to decrease in the therapist as therapy went on?

Sam: Right, after this went on . . .

Dr. C: Right, and how about personal involvement?

Sam: Personal involvement? Well, like the others have said, I felt that this person knew that Dr. P. did have a high degree of involvement, or I'm not sure whether involvement means positive regard in this case, and I think he felt *very much* toward the patient. But now I can't, well I have a hard time trying to . . . specifically define the degree of investment. It doesn't sit well with the concept of . . . positive regard, but he did seem to become more involved in the patient.

Dr. C: And yet the anxiety did seem to increase.

Sam: Right. I thought he had a high level when he got into this argument with the patient, really early, and I couldn't understand why he wanted to argue with the patient. I just couldn't understand that point, to get into this heated argument . . . it's about 30 or 40 feet into the tape.

Tod: Strangely enough though, that had a sort of freeing effect upon the patient. The patient was much more free to disagree with him.

Dr. C: I don't agree with you. I feel; live and learn. You know oftentimes you think that you're very cagey.

Dr. T: The therapist who plays the role so as not to get caught in an argument can't be defeated (laughter), huh?

Sam: Dr. P.'s pretty powerful early in the relationship. This makes it not so much to free the patient, but to make it more difficult for him to do anything a little later on. It may serve to inhibit the patient. How could you argue with a guy who's so powerful, so strong, knows so much? He was very forceful early in the relationship.

Tod: The patient did though.

Sam: Did he? He did a little bit, but the argument was cut off, I thought, real fast.

Tod: I think the patient did argue a little. Toward the end of the tape he had dropped the problem back on the therapist. He said, "Now, look, I've expressed hostility to my father and have it worked out and I still don't feel better. Now what are you going to do?" I think this is where . . .

Sam: Argumentation with the patient is a double-edged sword, it seems to me. On the one hand, it says in a way something of what nonpossessive warmth tries to do. It sets up the patient to . . . be himself and appreciate his own position. By the same token it sets it up a contest between you and the patient. As soon as you structure a contest, that's what you get until you change the thing around, and so, most people I think, and I think this is my feeling, that when you're in an argument with the patient, that's the way it stays until you do something to get both of you out of it and working together.

Dr. T: You have to shift it from an arena of competition to one of cooperation—we're both in this together, to work on what may be troubling you?

Dr. C: I wonder if we could just go back just a little. I wonder if we can't say that anxiety decreases with personal involvement in therapy where the therapist focuses on gains, such as the experienced therapist who has come to know gain in therapy and comes to expect it. He has respect for it. Dr. P. even makes this explicit; he expected a gain-type therapy relationship. Whereas, anxiety increases with personal involvement when it focuses on loss, which is a beginner, you know; the more involved he gets the more he has at stake about this case and everything else, and then he becomes more anxious.

Dr. T: This is why I feel very strongly that the beginning therapist should never start off, first of all, in therapy and, second of all, should never start off with just one case when he finally starts therapy because not only do you have, you know, a lot of random conditioning of superstitious behavior (laughs) on the part of the therapist, but even more than that, whenever you have one case, it's going to go up and down. You're going to have good days and bad days and unless you have some perspective, some experiential mass . . . against which you can weigh the momentary downs, this can be very threatening to beginning therapists; whereas if you had, say, three patients to start off with, at least it's not likely that they would all have sour days coinciding. You can afford to have a patient regress, simply because you know that "Well, heck, one of my patients who is an outstanding success regressed, and you see it didn't really make . . ." so you can feel more free to allow a patient to regress at moments and at periods.

Sam: I think we also come to the idea that the patient in early relationships or with the gaining of experience is more an object than a human being. I think once this is overcome then there may be room for the dissipation of his feelings and anxieties.

Dr. T: And this whole question of anxiety is a central one. It has always seemed to me that whenever I have done something out of anxiety this has never been something I've been proud of. I have never done something creative. The creative things that I have felt and done came out of involvement. In the same sense, if I work with a patient after I get involved and I'm doing things for the positive gain involved . . . I get involved and I'm doing things because I have a real caring and concern for this person. I think that is totally different than the kinds of ways I would act if I were motivated out of anxiety to *not* foul up on this patient. The kinds of behavior would be different . . . that in the one case I'd be very cautious because my concern is on losses, and I would play a very cautious role, and to that extent, be forced into being incongruent—be forced into being opaque, perhaps remote. I think this is what frequently happens in beginning therapy, that because we are concerned about the losses we inhibit ourselves from otherwise doing things that would make just good sense. It might seem, on reflection, to be a very sensible way of acting, but because at that moment we're afraid of losing, we play an overconservative game. And then what does this look like to the patient? What does he get out of this protective-armored therapist who is really afraid to reach out, afraid to extend himself?

Tod: I used to think I knew, or so I was told by someone who was certainly one of the most respected therapists in the state, that the therapist *shouldn't* become involved with the patient.

Dr. T: What do you mean by "involvement"?

Sam: You mean *in* the relationship or *outside* of the relationship. In other words you can treat the patient as a friend outside the relationship without having any of these involvement problems.

Tod: I think what they mean when they say you shouldn't become involved . . . I don't know, it seems that the whole therapy, the way I understood it was . . . you shouldn't take it personally if the patient doesn't work out as you hoped.

Dr. T: This is something we were talking about this morning, Dr. C. and I. The way I can conceptualize it best or feel it best, is in relation to children—say to my daughter . . . I want very much for her to be say, a generous, giving person. And I value her of course, very highly. I love her and I respect her and I have a great deal of belief in her potential and not only her potential, but her ability to actualize herself. I have a great deal of faith in this. So at times, and I can feel this so strongly, I can afford for her to be jealous and ungiving, so that she can take little Tammy and *not* give her some toys. Or, say, she'll pick up one of her books and she has 20 books on the floor and each one Tammy picks up, Terri will grab. I can feel so strongly in her potential that I don't have to stop her and say, "No, dammit, be generous. . . ." (Laughter) I don't have to jump in because I have the belief that she will find out for herself that she can afford to be generous and still get things. She'll still have things, she won't lose by being generous. In the same sense, this kind of involvement with a patient might mean that I have such positive regard for him, in his potential and his capacity to actualize that he can get behaviorally worse and I won't jump in. I'm not tied to his momentary ups and downs. I can see his behavior as transient and not some eternal part of him—so that he can regress behaviorally, without upsetting me.

For warmth to be effectively communicated it must be authentic or genuine. It is not difficult for the beginning counselor to learn the "form" of warmth, the kinds of words to say, etc.—the danger, of course, is that he will wind up with an imitation warmth that is clearly not part of him. Such a "warmth" fools few patients; they recognize it for what it is, a professional facade. The following excerpt from the course experience focused on the genuineness of communicated warmth as the class was engaged in rating samples of tapes of role-playing. The vital nature of feedback in providing the trainee with an understanding of "how he sounds to others" is illustrated.

A Role Is a Role Is Not a Role . . .

Dr. T: It seems that on genuineness it ranges between two and three; it's 2.2 or something like that. On warmth, I guess the real question was some people felt some conditionality . . . other people felt very little conditionality. Anybody? Can you think of any cues that made you feel a conditionality?

Ben: As the "therapist" on the tape I'm surprised that it's that high, because I'm still mad at Jim [who role-played the patient] because he'd just done another real long 20-minute segment that we thought was real good . . .

Jim: This we did this morning. That was this morning.

Ben: Yeah, but I'm still mad at you. (Laughter) You forgot to push the button and start the recorder.

Dr. T: Did you say it with anger?

Sam: I rate it one more now! (Laughter)

Dr. T: You thought he was warm and liked you?

Jim: No, as the "patient" I didn't sense anything back, so I thought it was a pretty straightforward "four" on warmth.

Dr. T: He concealed it well.

Jim: Yes, he did. It came over to me as warmth.

Dr. T: I think this does say something: that *it's what gets across.* You could be, in one sense, internally annoyed and at least for this 15- or 20-minute period you could have kept it under wraps.

Tod: It did get across in his interpretation that Jim was somewhat angry [as the "patient"]. He really hit Jim hard a couple of times, I thought.

Jim: He rated on some other scales, he missed it on empathy.

Tod: Yeah.

Jim: On that particular time. It's unfortunate because we did miss the 20-minute segment that was really top flight. (Laughter) It was really good, that's why I don't blame him for getting aggravated but (laughter), as to his congruence, well, I didn't have much feeling one way or the other about that. But he was with me and cared about what I was saying.

Dr. T: So it's very clear that there was no evidence of ingenuineness at all, and there was clear warmth, and the only question was really to what degree was this conditional. Can't somebody who thought of it as a clear "three" on warmth think of what cues they were using for conditionality?

Tod: I think I was probably influenced by the empathy content, that it was clear that the empathy wasn't there and I think this sort of tended to bias my rating.

Jim: I think, rated overall, it was a "three." But there was one point when the idea came to mind he was kind of feeling like, if you agree with me, I'll like you.

Dr. T: Um hmm.

Jim: If you agree with my interpretation of what you're saying.

Dr. C: I also had the feeling, in relation to genuineness, that Jim [the patient] gave him a wider range of responses than on the previous one. I had the feeling that the tone of the therapist is 20 per cent of what the client says. The feeling tone of the therapist is almost independent of the feeling tone of the client, that is, he's always going to talk this way no matter what feeling the client could be expressing. This is what we were talking about when talking about slipping into the therapeutic role . . .

Tod: Sometimes I know that I react to this and I'm sure that you do very much. The soft voice all of a sudden, where you're normally not soft at all.

Dr. T: Right.

Tod: I do the same thing. I play the same game.

Dr. T: Yeah, I think it's . . . but I wouldn't knock it.

Dr. C: That's right, I want to hear what you have to say. I think this is important.

Dr. T: I think even when people know me in other situations, where clearly my voice qualities and all kinds of things change, I think it still does communicate something. The irritation that people (as clients) might feel, I think they would only feel for the first moments, and that for the patient who is not a therapist himself and who doesn't know you in other roles, I think it is a very effective way of communicating warmth. This ability to communicate, the concern, the warmth . . .

Dr. C. I think the point I'm making is that when this kind of attitude is independent of the client, then I think that it is not an effective therapeutic means. That is, when the client feels some of the things like you felt, only strongly, stronger in that excerpt than previously, and he's still giving you the pain and the warmth, then I don't think this is meaningful to you. I think this is what you're reacting to.

Tod: I think it would be more effective if almost you could get the agitation—it's almost like the therapist is on tranquilizers. I put the same tone into it; I sound the same way with patients.

Dr. C: I think that this pain and warmth have to be related to what the client is doing, and if pain and warmth comes over when the client is happy or loving or angry, then I think it's an ineffective therapeutic mechanism.

Dr. T: This is probably more true as time goes on, so that we keep to the warmth of therapeutic voice in initial interviews. You will probably vary your tonal qualities less than you will later in therapy.

Dr. C: Right.

Dr. T: I agree with you wholeheartedly. I can think of a therapist, an experienced person, a very experienced person who is very ineffective with schizophrenics, very ineffective. And I think this is the reason—he's *always* a nice warm guy. After a while it just seems phony.

Dr. C: This isn't what people are used to experiencing all the time.

Dr. T: You wouldn't catch it in a four-minute excerpt, but after a while, as a patient, you would decide he's operating down here at stage one on genuineness because no matter what you do, he gives you this syrupy business.

Tod: In a way, here, we're being taught to act, and yet the more we act the less effective we are in therapy.

Dr. T: I suppose if it turns out that you are just acting, then it won't be effective. When you're advised to be just genuine yourself, this is not enough either.

Tod: Yeah.

Dr. T: We have to know when we are being most effectively ourselves so that, for example, when we're really intending warmth and it comes across as *not* warmth, or when we're really being sincerely ourselves and it comes across as phony, then we have to know this and if we know this, we will probably develop better modes of expressing ourselves.

Tod: I think this is where the group therapy and individual therapy for us comes in . . . I think that it would eventually give you a much better understanding . . . what the patient is feeling, as well as how it feels to get warmth, etc., if you are a patient yourself.

Dr. T: It's a matter of communicating. If we were just acting I don't think we could carry it off. If I really didn't like this other person and I pretended that I did, I just don't think I could keep this up very long without him knowing it. On the other hand, it would seem to me almost as tragic if I really did care, but somehow had developed ineffective modes of communicating this.

Tod: You have to learn responses, which bar to press!

Dr. T: Yeah. There are really more bars than one. In that way, one's individuality, being oneself has real meaning. The idea that it seems almost "machinelike" to talk about training therapists to be empathic, in the behavior of being empathic or in the behavior of being warm. I can see the reason for taking that tack, but I think it's even more complicated than that because it is a matter of learning one's social stimulus value and learning more effective ways of communicating feelings.

Dr. C: Should I play this tape over?

Dr. T: O. K. Why don't you play it.

(The following tape excerpt from role-playing is played).

C: One thing, I hope my mother stays in good health.

T: Um hmm.

C: So she can be with me. I like to do things for her . . .

T: Uh huh.

C: Because she's been good to me.

T: Your mother's been very good to you.

C: Yes.

T: You've been very close to her.

C: Yes.

T: Very close.

C: And so I'd like to do something for her.

T: Um hmm.

C: And then I have these three nephews and a niece that I, they just worship me.

T: Um hmh.

C: I'm not bragging about it because, they, they all call me sister, they don't call me by my name. And so I, I when I was working four or five years ago here in town.

T: Um hmm.

C: When my little nephew was growing up, the oldest one, I took care of him. I bought him things, and those children are part of my life.

T: Um hmm. They're a very important part of your life.

C: Yes, yes, and I like to do things for them. I try to do things for my mother and I like to do things for the children cause they're very close to me.

T: Makes you feel real good inside, doesn't it?

C: Yes, it does.

T: To do things for other people.

C: Yes, it does. I know I've had to, and I know it does.

T: Feels real good inside.

C: Yes, it does.

T: You don't feel quite as tense then, do you?

C: No. No, when you're working you have your mind on your job.

T: Uh huh. Uh huh.

C: And you're not hurting anyplace.

T: Yah.

C: Why, you really build up a . . . I don't know.

T: Uh huh.

C: It takes, takes care of you.

T: Yeah, yah. It helps you take your mind off your problems.

C: Yes.

T: If only you could get your mind off your problems, if only you could get your mind off, off all this, this is . . .

C: Yes.

T: On your mind.

C: Yes.

T: This stuff goes over and over in your mind and you wish you could get it out.

C: Yes.

T: Doesn't it?

C: Yeah, uh huh.

T: That pain in the chest and so forth.

C: Yeah.

T: Pretty disturbing.

C: It is.

T: Who else have you been close to in life besides your mother?

C: Well, my brother—his family come in there. And then I have friends and relatives and neighbors that, that are still, they're close to me, too.

T: Um hmm. Ever been married?

C: No. I could've been but I just didn't because the one time, this man drinks so, that I didn't want to, I was afraid he wouldn't stop drinking.

T: Uh huh.

C: Though he said he would, and so, that's why I didn't want to marry him.

T: When was that?

C: It's been about twelve years ago.

T: About twelve years ago.

C: Yes.

T: Tell me how you felt about him.

C: Well he was a . . . he was nice to me and he was good and thoughtful to me, and uh, I went with him for two years. And so he asked me to marry him and so I told him, said that he hadn't been drinking for a year but I knew that he had because his sister had told me about it, that he had, even though he didn't know it.

T: Yah.

C: So when he asked me to marry him, why I didn't say anything and he said, well, that I didn't care anything about him and I said "No, it's not that. You've got to let me think awhile about it." And so, he as, I reckon he just, I told him to show me another year. If he'd been good one year to be good one more year and I'd consider it. And he just couldn't, went to drinking again. And he, he's still drinking. Then he did marry about two years ago. He waited about eight years on me but I just couldn't marry a drunkard.

T: . . . you in love with him?

C: Well, I don't know.

T: Don't know if you were or not.

C: No. I liked him a lot.

T: Liked him a lot though. Do you feel bad about not, not, not marrying him?

C: Well, I don't know. I was hurt in a way.

T: Uh huh. You were hurt.

C: Yeah.

T: Uh huh. That hurt down deep again.

C: Yes.

T: Feel lonely afterwards?

C: Yes, the doctors say that was lot of my trouble.

T: Uh huh.

C: That I, that was, they called it loneliness.

T: Uh huh. That was a lot of your trouble, loneliness.

C: Yes.

T: Think that still is a lot of your trouble, loneliness?

C: Well I don't know. I never could pin it down, on loneliness. The doctor said it was.

T: Uh huh.

Discussion

Dr. T: Okay, did everyone get their rating written down? Okay, read them off. (Round-robin rating by the class)

Dr. T: We seem to have a fairly clear consensus of warmth, but also some conditionality. On congruence we found some evidence of a lack of congruence . . . What kind of cues did people use in feeling there was some degree of ungenuineness?

Ben: I felt that Tod was saying what he ought to say but not really what he felt. That's why I gave it a "two" on genuineness.

Dr. T: There's some degree of a professional front?

The discussion of ratings turned quickly to a discussion of "slipping into the therapeutic role" and a consideration of some of the activities of the therapist, such as the traditional warm and pained expression, which are often really independent of the client before him.

The warmth communicated by the therapist to the client, and his regard for the client's worth as a person and his rights as a separate individual, constitute the contextual basis of all effective therapeutic encounters. Only within a human encounter offering nonpossessive warmth can the severely distressed person come to trust not only the "other" and the relationship, but ultimately himself as well. The degree to which the therapist can communicate this warm concern for his client will be reflected in the degree to which the client feels free to experience all aspects of himself, comes to value these experiences, and, finally comes to value the experiences of others.

The construct of nonpossessive warmth is in many ways intangible. It is not communicated by warm modulated voice tones alone, although the voice qualities are centrally important. Genuine warmth takes many forms. To the degree that it reflects only a set of techniques, it will be ineffective. Effective training relies heavily on "shaping" of the trainee's spontaneous responses through ratings by supervisor and peers toward the communication of a higher level of nonpossessive warmth.

CHAPTER 12 TOWARD AUTHENTICITY OR GENUINENESS

THAT the therapist, within the relationship, be himself integrated, genuine, and authentic seems most basic to therapeutic outcome. Without such genuineness, a trusting relationship could scarcely exist. The counselor or therapist must be a real person in the encounter, presenting himself without defensive phoniness, without hiding behind the facade of the professional role. The current conceptualization of genuineness (or authenticity or congruence) requires the therapist's personal involvement; he is not simply "doing his job" as a technician. The therapist's capacity for openness and personal freedom in the therapeutic encounter offers, in part, a model for the client to follow in moving toward openness and freedom to be oneself.

Stating this negatively, it could be asked "Can the counselor expect openness, self-acceptance, and personal freedom in the client if he himself lacks these qualities in the relationship?" It also seems more than doubtful that a client could value the counselor's communication of warmth if it seemed "ingenuine," unauthentic, artificial, or rehearsed.

To be genuine, self-congruent, and authentic in the relationship does not imply that the counselor will act or behave as he does with his family at home, with the barber, or with colleagues at a professional convention or meeting. As he focuses on the client, he inevitably puts aside much of his own need system and many of his everyday ways of relating to others.

Perhaps the major contribution of existential psychotherapy has been its emphasis on the therapist's being a "real person, in a real encounter." Although for more than forty years, most therapists have recognized this and put it into practice (particularly such theoretician-practitioners as Freida Fromm-Reichmann and Rogers), the existentialists have given even more importance to this central aspect of effective interpersonal skills. Thus May (1958) has suggested: ". . . the relationship of the therapist and patient is taken as a real one, the therapist being not merely a shadowy reflector but an alive human being who happens, at that hour, to be concerned not with his own problems but with understanding and experiencing, so far as possible the being of the patient" (p. 80); and ". . . the therapist is assumedly an expert; but, if he is not first of all a human being, his expertness will be irrelevant and quite possibly harmful" (p. 82). Further, May says, "the therapist is what Socrates named the 'midwife'—completely real in 'being there,' but being there with the specific purpose of helping the other person to bring to birth something from within himself" (p. 82).

For the therapist to be genuine or authentic as a therapist and as a person means, above all, that he cannot be simply an imitation, a carbon copy, of even the most idealized therapist. In an important sense he will be *himself,* with the inner-directed spontaneity and flexibility that that implies. If he uses the approach of behavior therapy, he will not be a Wolpian; if he follows the approach of Adler, he will not be an Adlerian; if he follows the work of Rogers, he will not be a Rogerian, and so on. In all of these possible roles, he will first and foremost be himself.

Although the therapist's genuineness seems basic to his interpersonal skills, genuineness alone and of itself is not maximally therapeutic; rather the absence of genuineness is antitherapeutic. May (1958) puts the role of genuineness into its proper perspective when he says: "The therapist's situation is like that of an artist who has spent many years of disciplined study learning technique; but he knows that if specific thoughts of technique preoccupy him when he actually is in the process of painting, he has at the moment lost his vision" (p. 85).

It seems likely that the therapist, as a person, can become more genuinely himself within the therapeutic hour than he can in other everyday relationships. In this sense it is possible for a person to be somewhat defensive in everyday relationships and yet during the therapy hour, in the security of the counselor's role, be genuinely his therapeutic self. The counseling situation itself provides maximum security for the counselor: there are no peers with whom to compete; if the patient comes not to respect him or like him, he may feel hurt, but it will not disrupt the fabric of his life; he, not another, is the "presumed authority or expert"; and his own needs are in the background because of his focus upon the client. He is *relatively* invulnerable to frustration. The evidence cited earlier suggests that defensive or unauthentic people (who are not genuine in daily life) make poor counselors or therapists; still, the nature of the therapeutic situation may enhance genuineness in the therapist. The available evidence also suggests that trainees who show gains in their therapeutic skills also show concomitant lessening of defensiveness in their daily lives. Indeed, the concept of genuineness assumes free self-exploration by the therapist so as to lessen the gap between his actual experience and his awareness.

Some specific indication of the clinical meaning of genuineness for the practice of counseling is given in a discussion by Rogers and Truax (1966) when they say:

> So if I sense that I am feeling bored by my contacts with this client and this feeling persists, I think I owe it to him and to our relationship to share this feeling with him. The same would hold if my feeling is one of being afraid of this client, or if my attention is so focused on my own problems that I can scarcely listen to him. But as I attempt to share these feelings I also want to be constantly in touch with what is going on in me. If I am, I will recognize that it is *my* feeling of being bored which I am expressing, and not some

supposed fact about him as a boring person. If I voice it as my *own* reaction, it has the potentiality of leading to a deep relationship. But this feeling exists in the context of a complex and changing flow, and this needs to be communicated too. I would like to share with him my distress at feeling bored and the discomfort I feel in expressing this aspect of me. As I share these attitudes I find that my feeling of boredom arises from my sense of remoteness from him and that I would like to be more in touch with him and even as I try to express these feelings, they change. I am certainly not bored as I await with eagerness and perhaps a bit of apprehension for his response. I also feel a new sensitivity to him now that I have shared this feeling which has been a barrier between us. I am very much more able to hear the surprise or perhaps the hurt in his voice as he now finds himself speaking more genuinely because I have dared to be real with him. I have let myself be a person—real, imperfect—in my relationship with him. (p. 8)

TOWARD "GENUINENESS TRAINING"

Direct "shaping" of the trainee's responses (using the research scale, presented in Chapter 2), aimed at making them more authentically an expression of his own person is carried out in the course in much the same fashion as "empathy training." Perhaps an even greater source of learning comes from spontaneous discussions throughout the course and from the rating and discussion of samples from the trainee's own attempts to carry out counseling or therapy. (Illustrative excerpts dealing with genuineness in the communication of both accurate empathy and warmth have been given in the previous chapters in relation to learning to communicate "genuine nonpossessive warmth" or "genuine accurate empathic understanding.")

The classroom discussions of the meaning of genuineness ordinarily lead into spontaneous questioning. A brief excerpt from one of the early class periods with one group of students is given to suggest an attempt, using discussion and exploration, to incorporate the construct in a fashion which is most meaningful and effective for the individual:

No Alternatives . . .

Dr. T: You don't have any alternative, any real alternative to congruence because the alternative is obvious phoniness that everybody can see anyway. Why not be open, and say, "Yes, I'm threatened." What is the alternative to that? Me to pretend that I am not threatened when you know darn good and well that I am? Where does that leave me? What is my real alternative? You know I'm threatened anyway if you're astute at all, and so is there really an alternative? When you see Dr. K get flustered in therapy, it's no secret he's flustered. Everybody knows it and the alternative to him being congruent and saying "that touches me in a sensitive area" and maybe opening up a little—is to be obviously defensive. The problem is that it's obvious and everybody knows it. So you're really not getting away with fooling anybody, probably not even yourself.

Jim: Well how can these patients that can't see their nose in front of their faces see phoniness in you—when they can't see it in themselves?

Dr. T: Well, how can we see it in others, people around you?

Jim: Suppose I'm putting on an act and they think I'm being congruent?

Dr. T: You're in!

Dr. C: You're in!

Jim: Yeah.

Dr. C: *You* know. (Laughter)

Dr. T: A person can say, I'm being very genuine. I'm really a very frightened, withdrawn, aloof, cold—that's me. But that's not really congruence. That's perhaps an awareness of incongruence. For me to stop there and not go on to find that I am afraid of people (or whatever the reason for my shyness or whatever you want to call it might be)—for me to stop before exploring, is not really congruence. It's surface awareness.

Tod: I think that's a paradox, isn't it—as soon as you admit to being frightened, you stop being frightened, and the other person will . . . you know. This has happened to me many times—I'll admit my anxiety and the other person will laugh and say "You're not anxious at all," and, hell, I am anxious.

Dr. T: See, I hide it well.

Dr. C: Maybe you're not anxious when you start admitting it . . .

Tod: I guess that that's true.

Perhaps an extremely important training device in contributing to the development of genuineness or authenticity in the trainee derives from effective use of role-playing. When the students were paired off for role-playing outside class, they were encouraged to make use of the experience of "being a client" by exploring their own feelings, goals, and experiences. Ordinarily, in role-playing the focus is only on the student who is learning to be a therapist. In the present training program, trainees were strongly encouraged to learn more about themselves, their feelings about their professional development, their role as a therapist, and the meaning this had for their life goals. This encouragement of self-exploration during the time they were role-playing as the "client" seemed to result in significant self-explorations productive of movement toward genuineness as counselors. Some of the examples were too personal to be presented publicly, but the following excerpt from a role-playing tape gives some indication of this "quasi-individual therapy" which can be a planned part of the role-playing aspect of the total training.

Just Who Am I?

C: Well, it's just the aspect that, everything I do, I would like to, you know, I guess in one way . . . I'd sort of like to be pretty good at it. You know, to be "tops" at it, but yet I don't really know, really know, if I can cut it that well. I don't really know if I'm that capable and I sort of think way down deep inside that maybe I'm not. Yet I keep trying when I'm pushing myself to show that I am. Not necessarily just to show, but I think it's a bit of . . . just to prove to myself that I can do it.

T: You want to be better than everybody else, but you're not really sure that you are.

C: Yeah, I guess, well, it's not really better than everybody else. It's that, well, a name for it; "approval" I guess . . . would sort of fit in, an, I guess this goes way back to the way my parents raised me, and my relationship with them. I think I had a real fine home life and most of the time the things that I've had, had as goals; that I've had since I've come in to school are things that my parents initially set up for me, but gradually they, they were wise enough to step aside with their goals and let me make them, make goals of my own. But yet I sort of feel like everything that I do, somehow, *is* for their approval, and in a very real sense, I just can't get away from the effect of wondering sometimes, "Am I really doing this because this is what I want, or am I doing it because ah, I'm just rationalizing and these are the goals my parents set up, that they wanted me to be somebody?" Ah, do I really want to be what I'm trying to be. I guess that's the real question I'm asking.

T: Am I working for my parents or just who am I working for?

C: Um hmm. It sort of gets down to . . . who, who's really important now that I'm no longer a child and I'm a man on my own. Am I going to work for things that really satisfy myself or am I going to try to satisfy others. But really, somehow really it's all intermingled because to satisfy myself I really want to please them in some way. That's definitely a part of it.

T: The two of them just go right together, so you can't get away from one side or the other.

C: That's right.

T: If you don't satisfy them, you don't satisfy yourself.

C: That seems to be pretty much the way it is. Course I know that when it comes down to basic differences, I couldn't really satisfy myself and them too. If it was something that they didn't fully understand all the implications of, I think I'd try to be true to myself. But yet there's this kind of constant gnawing about it. Am I really, am I really cut out to be what I'm trying to be? And back of it all I guess: "Is my mode of action strictly my own or has it been so, sort of ingrown into me just by the life I've led that, that I can't really make a . . . can't really separate it." It's really sort of confusing . . . to put into words what I really feel about it.

T: It's sort of a feeling of, as I *think* this is what I want to be but perhaps it would be better if I were something else."

C: Yeah, but, I don't know *what* else. I think I'd be satisfied, I think I'd be a good psychologist, but I don't really *know*. I, I . . . guess everyone questions their motivation for going into something and its constant questioning of "are you sure." Maybe this is kind of late in the game to be questioning that . . . ah, the dye is cast: I can't really change at this stage of the game, so this makes it all the more stressing really. Knowing that you can't really afford to get *out* now . . . even if you suddenly came to some big realization about yourself.

T: It's sort of a hopeless question then isn't it.

C: Yeah. I don't know why I spend any time worrying about it but I do.

T: Even though you know there's not much way out now, it still nags at you, you're still not really satisfied with what you've chosen.

C: Well, I think I would be more satisfied in it if I was sure of, well . . . I'm not really sure. I guess no one can ever be sure of anything like that, but if I had some sort of a feeling within myself that eventually I was going to make it through, that things were going to go pretty much the way I've envisioned them but . . .

T: If you could *know* that you were going to be successful, be satisfied, it would be different then, wouldn't it?

C: Um hmm. Then I don't think I'd have to worry so much about it. That, ah, . . . why am I really doing all this, because I think just that aspect of being successful in it, as, is a pretty big part of the reward. I think that there are little parts of the reward that come along the way . . . of doing something that's helpful to someone else . . . and, uh, feeling as though you're useful to other people perhaps, and being more than just being a parasite in life. And, I really wonder, ah . . . I guess there just isn't any answer to the question till I, until I wait and see, but . . . Well, why does it sort of *nag* at you, why does it stay with you all the time?

T: The payoff just seems like an awful far distance off.

C: Yeah, that's right. There's just no way that . . . it seems just as soon as you get over one hurdle, then another one jumps right up in front just lurking about. Oh like so, suddenly it becomes . . . insurmountable then, or it looks so. By . . . the things you know you have to do to get by it, and by the things that you don't know you have to do. How can anyone really ever know enough to say this man's competent in the field of psychology because he's passed these exams? Nothing in the exams really discovers that.

T: So maybe there really isn't a way to tell whether, to get the kind of thing, the information, you want.

C: Well, that's that's true enough but it still doesn't take away the . . . the sort of vague anxiety about it of knowing you have to live with this. It's a part of everyday life, my knowing that I've got to get up and do something today that'll reduce the ah . . . probability of failure here and increase the probability of success. I mean I've got to do something that's constructive toward getting over these hurdles because many of them have seemed to me to be that: just simply hurdles that are put up in front of me, like two language examinations. I see that as *nothing* but hurdles. And it . . . there's just so, so many things you have to do to prove to, that, that you're competent in something that no one can really be competent in. I guess that's it. How can anyone set himself up and say that he is really a competent psychologist? And the task of knowing all that I think I should know just looks so hopeless, that I guess this is what comes back to the, to the other point of making me wonder about. Is this really what I want something like this, I feel that I can't really completely master because no one can, I know that. I know that *positively* and yet . . . somehow . . . I want to know it all, if that's what a good psychologist should know. I want to be the best psychologist I know how to be.

T: You want, you want something you can take hold of. You can say, I'm good, I am, this is how much good I am. I know that nobody can take it away from me, nobody else can say I'm not this good.

C: Yeah. That's important to me. It's as though really ah . . . really . . . getting approval from somewhere else other than my parents, other than people who, who love me of course, and have to approve many things I do because they love me, but getting some kind of outside measure of this . . .

T: This would mean something to you.

C: Oh yeah. Very much. I guess it means something to everybody to get it.

T: You'd like, perhaps to know, perhaps I could put it this way, that you'd like to know that what other people judged as right, is right, so that you would feel better about what they've . . . about their judgment on you.

C: Yeah, yeah, I guess that's true. I, I guess I'm as prone, or maybe more so, than the other people to be conscious of other people's evaluations of me. And it's important. I have as much as . . . need for approval as most other people, more so maybe. And this is why . . . ah . . . being good at my chosen field is important I think. Anyway all the things which come up before me as barriers somehow, I . . . well, they just seem to go all out of proportion to what they really are because I see the people who passed the other examinations and I think I have some reasonable estimate of their ability and they've made it through. I think, well, surely if I really apply myself, I could maybe squeak by if they've done it, but it doesn't make it more comfortable.

T: You sort, sort of said three things there, I think. One, you see the standards that are applied to others, and other people get by these things don't mean much and they're called psychologists, quote good psychologists . . .

C: Um hmm.

T: And yet, by your opinion it doesn't mean much, and then you say, "Well, they apply that same standard to me, will it not mean much then?"

C: Yeah. I, I never thought of it, I guess that's true though. Why before, before I pass them they seem so important . . . like this is some sort of ultimate criterion if I'm going to be a good psychologist: if, if these other Ph.D., psychologists have judged me in a sense on the basis of examinations, will say this person is competent, and then after I pass them is it not going to mean that? Is it going to be that this was just another hurdle put up?

T: Is there going to be somebody out there looking at you like you look at some of these others?

C: Yeah. Is somebody going to say, "Hell, he got by on a fluke or they just asked him easy questions." So I guess it comes down to how much do I really value myself as a person. I think I value myself and naturally want other people to value me as a person too. So I guess this is part of my concern . . . course, I may be over-concerned.

T: Really, what they say does have meaning to you.

C: Yeah, yeah. I believe in a real sense it does, although I think many times when . . . I think I play a role sometimes of pretending not to care what other people say. I say that being true to myself is more important . . .

T: In fact, you'd like to be that way, more so than you are.

C: Yeah. I guess. I can't conceive of myself ever getting so upset at someone, even though they'd be pretty devastating to one of my principles perhaps, ah, of my doing something to jeopardize my position in graduate school. And that's something, that . . . that . . . worries me a little. Because I have, as, so much, well, I guess . . . most of, all of my life up to this point is invested in graduate school. If I don't make it . . .

T: Everything's summed up in getting through, these sometimes meaningless hurdles.

C: Yeah. That's right. I, ah, can't even make any plans as to ultimate, far-off goals as to what you want to accomplish in life until you get this really important intermediate goal behind, so . . .

Authenticity—the ability to be freely and deeply oneself in nonexploitative relationships with others—constitutes in a very real sense the goal of counseling and therapy. That is, it is hoped that the outcome of therapeutic endeavors will find the client a more authentic, genuine, and congruent person. The issue to which the helping professions must address themselves is this: How can we expect authenticity in our clients if we as counselors are not authentic in therapy? Thus, in therapy the therapist is the model for genuineness in the client. In training, the supervisor becomes both the model and the facilitator for genuineness in the trainee.

As with warmth training, genuineness is a most elusive entity. It is simply something that we experience; we know when it happens, but there are no clear-cut rules for training beyond the attempt to "shape" the trainee's communication by feedback from his peers. Still, just as one of the goals of therapy is a more authentic client, so must one of the goals of training be more authentic therapists. Therefore, much as we provide therapy experiences for our clients, so must we also provide extensive therapy experiences for the unauthentic trainee.

CHAPTER 13 AN APPLICATION OF LEARNING FROM THE TRAINING PROGRAM TO GROUP COUNSELING

by Walter Dickenson, Ph.D.[11]

INTRODUCTION

ANY ATTEMPTED training program in counseling or psychotherapy can be best judged by its effects. As indicated in the earlier chapters on research and training, the present approach seems on the basis of empirical research to be useful in producing beginning counselors and therapists, both lay and professional. The evidence suggests that the trainees who have completed the program showed significant gains in these areas: an ability to communicate accurate empathy, nonpossessive warmth and genuineness; significant personality change along dimensions that have previously been shown to be correlates of interpersonal skills; an ability to communicate levels of the therapeutic conditions as well as produce levels of patient self-exploration only slightly below that of highly experienced and effective therapists; and consequent effectiveness in producing significant personality and behavioral change in patients beyond that observed in control groups. In part, the positive results of the training program shown in the research findings could be attributed to the enthusiasm surrounding what was a new venture for the authors. Still, since the evidence of positive effects was obtained on different groups of trainees trained over a period of years, the attempt to integrate a specific didactic approach with a broader experiential approach does seem to be a useful one, which may well be worth the effort of further development and refinement by others.

Student evaluations obtained at the end of each training program were almost unanimous in evaluating the three most useful aspects of the training program as (1) the quasi-group therapy experience, (2) the ratings on their own tapes, and (3) the "empathy training."

There was considerable variation in the student's evaluation of role-playing, the opportunity to listen to tapes of experienced therapists, and the required reading list. Trainees with some previous background seemed to find these aspects of the training program minimally useful, whereas students who were completely naive found them relatively more useful.

A solid evaluation of the value of the present approach to training

11. Participated in training program in September-December, 1963, received Ph.D., July 1965.

in counseling and psychotherapy will depend on its usefulness to other supervisors in other settings—the present evidence, though, suggests that such might be fruitful.

Chapter 13, written by a participating traineee, is one illustration of an application of the learnings from the present training program. The group counseling experience that Dickenson discusses occurred immediately after his participation in the three-and-a-half month training program. It represents a trainee's beginning attempts to apply both the didactic and experiential learnings to actual practice.

It does seem evident in the examples that the particular client, Joyce, actually responds differently when the beginning therapist's mistakes are corrected. It cannot be argued that Dickenson's interpretations are the best ones, but they are the ones used at the time.

The following verbatim excerpts were taken from Dickenson's interactions with one member of a college counseling group [12] during one session. These examples were not chosen for their excellence, but simply as illustrations of an attempt to translate the theoretic concepts and ideals of the training program into practice. They thus include mistakes other beginning therapists might avoid. And, of course, no one knows the degrees of truth or error included in the present discussion and interpretation of that interaction.

AS background information, it might be helpful to know that Joyce had talked about her father in a rather defensive way in previous group sessions. She had said he would be gone from home for days at a time, usually on gambling binges. When she said he was gone on the day she graduated from high school, there were tears in her eyes which she seemed to be striving to suppress. The counselor concluded that she was not conscious, or was trying to avoid becoming aware, of any deeper feelings of disappointment that seemed apparent on a nonverbal level.

I

In the beginning of the sixteenth session, from which these excerpts were taken, the therapist noticed that Joyce's eyes had begun to look watery even though she had ben participating as usual in the group exchange concerning money problems. After a lull, he turned to Joyce and asked her a question. (Therapist responses have been numbered for referral in the text discussion.)

Counselor: How is everything with you, Joyce? (*1*)

Joyce: Well, I thought I was fine but now I've gotten here I'm so depressed I can't stand it! (Laughs as if to shrug it off) . . . I don't know why

12. The research from which these excerpts were taken provided evidence that an experimental group of twenty-four college freshmen underachievers receiving group counseling showed significantly greater improvement in grade-point averages than a matched, no-counseling control group (for further details see Dickenson and Truax, 1966).

(quick half-laugh as if in disbelief) . . . I don't know (barely audible).

Counselor: You feel sort of sad? (*2*)

Joyce: Yeah.

Betty: Do you get depressed with another (person) when you do?

Joyce: No, but I usually don't, I'm usually in such a terrific mood when I get in here, but today I just feel like crying. (Half-hearted laugh)

John: Well, go ahead and cry if it would make you feel better.

Joyce: If you all don't stop talking, I'll start crying any minute!

Counselor: I sort of felt that you needed to cry. (*3*)

Joyce: (Half-laugh as she starts to cry)

Counselor: What do you think that is related to? (*4*)

Joyce: I don't know (quick laugh). It's just so . . . *silly,* crying for no reason at all (half-laugh).

Counselor: You feel like it's . . . (*5*)

Joyce: It's as bad as crying about the chain letter.*

Betty: Did you have any good luck?

Joyce: No, I didn't get my package.

Counselor: (Gently) You don't want to let yourself cry; you mustn't cry. (*6*)

Joyce: (Barely audible) I don't have a Kleenex.

Counselor: Even if you need to cry, you mustn't let . . . (7)

Joyce: (Breaks in quickly and loudly) If you don't shut up, I'll *start!* (Burst of laughter from group)

Betty: You're going to talk her into it! (Tension-releasing laughter in group continues)

Jack: Like digging up dead bodies! (More tense laughter)

Betty: Leave them buried! (Tense laughter continues)

Counselor: Hm. (As laughter subsides). I wonder if you couldn't get it buried better by just crying? . . . and also finding out what it is about? . . . and getting it out? . . . instead of running away from it all the time? (Longer silence). I have a feeling that's why you feel sadness now in here, because this is feeling in you that needs to come out and is pushing up. (*8*)

Joyce: I know but I'm not unhappy about anything (sniffles). I feel like a stupid idiot just sitting here crying for no reason at all (sniffles).

Counselor: Do people ever cry for no reason at all? (*9*)

Betty: I do! (Group laughter)

Jack: You've got a friend down there. (Laughter continues)

Jack: That kind of killed off that!

Counselor: In other words you're crying and don't know really why you're crying. (*10*)

Betty: No!

John: I don't think, uh, there *must* be a reason!

Betty: No, there's *not,* you just cry.

Jack: Oh, you know Harold Jackson? I think he had a . . . (Group attention is quickly diverted to Jack's interesting story about Harold, and only returns to preceding topic later)

Joyce's first response shows the accuracy of the therapist's perception of her nonverbal communication. The context of her speech up to this point in the session would have given no clues to the feelings of depression that were communicated by her watery eyes. The therapist's alertness to

* Two weeks before, Joyce had said she had been puzzled because she had started crying "for no reason at all" when she received a chain letter saying she would receive a package or would have some good luck if she would send five more letters like the one she had received within six hours after receiving it.

this unspoken message enabled him to ask Joyce how she was feeling, and thus give her an opportunity to tell the group what was wrong without her having to change the subject of discussion herself, and perhaps give the impression of wanting to monopolize attention.

The therapist's question, delivered in a soft personal tone of voice, served to deepen the level of communication in the group. From an ordinary conversation that could have gone in any direction, the tone quickly changed to that of a therapy session in which one group member voices her puzzlement about the feelings of depression that she has suddenly and somewhat mysteriously begun to feel as soon as she walked into the group meeting. She almost seems to welcome the therapist's question because it gives her an opportunity to be congruent—to talk about the actual feelings of sadness that she does not understand but that she still feels at that moment. Of course, she would not have been able to talk about these genuine feelings of sadness so readily unless a trusting relationship had already been established to some degree.

Joyce, the group member, seems to recognize that her depressed feelings are somehow inappropriate, because she does not usually feel this way and can think of no reason why she should. She does not realize that these feelings *are* appropriate to some past interpersonal relationship, and that the present group relationship stimulates them.

The therapist, of course, is not surprised that she feels this way because, in a sense, he has seen these feelings coming or developing over the past few sessions. He had noted that she defensively avoided expressing deeper feelings about her father's absence at her graduation, though her red eyes and suppressed tears communicated nonverbally what she was unable to admit to awareness. He had also noted, in a later session, her surprise that she had just started crying "for no reason at all" when she received the letter promising good luck. As a result of this knowledge, the therapist is in a position to formulate a number of hypotheses concerning Joyce's deeper denied feelings.

The obvious hypothesis would have to do with the presence of unacknowledged and unexpressed *sadness.* This sadness could come from her father's actions (in which case it could have many ramifications) or from some other source. Her reaction to the letter, then, might mean that this sadness is getting closer to the surface of her awareness, for the tears actually broke through even though she did not experience any conscious reasons for her emotion. Having thought along these channels, as the therapist in fact did, there would be little element of surprise in Joyce's strange feelings of depression, which now occur in an interpersonal context in which the affect is present minus its original and present cognitive connections.

The therapist's task is to nurture these feelings and bring them to fruition, so to speak, so that the gaps in Joyce's awareness can be filled by restoring the genuine feelings that she is now denying. In this manner Joyce will become more fully herself and thus more truly human.

The therapist's delicate task now is to accomplish this without violating the realities of her feelings. In other words, he has only a more or less valid hypothesis concerning Joyce's real feelings; for all he knows, Joyce may be feeling something completely different. He must, therefore, be ready to change gears and follow any new clues to what she really feels. In this respect, he is like a detective on a criminal's trail or a bloodhound following a scent. Unlike the detective or the bloodhound, however, he must not violate certain other ethical and technical principles in this pursuit.

The therapist's second response, while accurate, does not invite further exploration or lead Joyce on to further self-discovery. It is too much of a rehash of what she has already said so much more richly, and so gets only a brief "yeah."

The group is sympathetic, and their encouragement leads her to warn the others that she may not be able to hold back her tears unless they stop encouraging her. The therapist's third response then pushes her over the brink, probably because what he says is true and because the warmth in it communicates on a nonverbal level that it is all right for her to cry—that this is appropriate.

At this point, instead of staying with the tears and trying to understand her feelings empathically (with, for example, a response of silence or "You're almost bursting with sadness") the therapist asks Joyce what she thinks her tears are related to. This response calls for cognition from Joyce, and she quickly stops crying as she tries to figure out *what* is making her cry. The therapist has actually just abnegated his responsibility, asking the client to do his job for him. *By asking* gently what she thinks her tears are related to, he has switched from an empathic response to one that calls for a complex intellectual process which prohibits the very activity he is trying to encourage. He admittedly has fewer cues because she is not verbalizing them, but this is no excuse to discontinue empathic responses.

The therapist gets back on the track in his next response (his fifth) as he searches out loud for her feelings. This response does invite further exploration, and she relates her crying in the group to her identical crying "for no reason at all" in response to the letter. However, it might have been more empathic for the therapist to have focused on her embarrassment about crying. He could have done this, for example, by just repeating the one word "Silly?" This one word, said with the right inflection, might well have given her more opportunity to express her feelings about crying in the group instead of going on, too quickly perhaps, to the similarity between her reaction in the group and her response to the letter.

The therapist in his sixth response brings the discussion squarely back to Joyce's efforts to prevent herself from crying, almost as if he doesn't want to "let her off the hook." The conditionality present is conveyed by his seventh response, which makes it all too apparent that he is trying to push her over the brink whether or not she chooses this for herself. This brings him a good-natured rebuke, which is not unexpected in clients as relatively healthy as these. (The same mistake with a really sick individual might have had much more serious consequences.)

Having made known his desires and having been told by the group to let sleeping dogs lie, the therapist has put himself on the defensive and now seeks to justify his efforts to help Joyce cry. He seems to be saying that he knows what is best for Joyce, thus making himself the locus of evaluation. He tells her clearly what he thinks she should do with his response that she is "running away" from her sad feelings.

Although the warmth of his response seems to take away any negative impact on the client, it nevertheless fails because Joyce is quite naturally unaware of having the sad feelings she is *unaware of having*. By the very nature of her denial to awareness, she can only answer that she does not have anything to be unhappy about, even though tears are rolling down her cheeks at that moment. The therapist has, in effect, forced his client to be incongruent by more or less accusing her of hiding feelings that she is unaware of having in the first place. Regardless of whether the therapist is dynamically correct, he is clearly in error in a technical sense because he has lapsed into what amounts to be a kind of debate about whether or not Joyce is running away from her real feelings and whether or not she should stop doing this. The therapist is clearly defending one side of the debate instead of responding empathically. It is thus not surprising that this interaction does not bear fruit and deteriorates into group debate. The therapist has lost Round 1.

II

The next sequence in interaction with Joyce takes place after the group has heard a graphic description of the painful discrepancy between a person's deeper feelings about himself, which were revealed while he was drunk, and the facade or front he usually assumed. Unfortunately, the therapist uses the opportunity presented by this description to continue the argument with Joyce about crying and to reinforce his position.

Counselor: I kind of wonder, Joyce, if it wouldn't help you to talk about the things you are feeling? (*11*)

Joyce: I know, but I don't know what I'm feeling.

Betty: It's just a feeling you get sometimes when you feel like you're just going to scream! So you cry. (Group laughter)

Counselor: Well, I wonder if, uh, it wouldn't be possible, if you let yourself, to, to kind of talk about that and find out what it is about, huh? (*12*)

Joyce: I don't even know what it is. I mean there's nothing really that has happened to me (half-laugh), as far as that goes.

(Discussion drifts to another topic)

This excerpt underlines even more clearly the mistakes made in the first excerpt—telling Joyce what she *should* do instead of employing therapeutic principles to help her actually *do* it. Instead of getting to the reasons why Joyce feels like crying by being genuine, empathic, and warm, the therapist has again lapsed into telling Joyce she should talk about her feelings and let herself cry because she would then feel better. Joyce does not respond to this advice, and all it produces is an argument from Betty to the effect that Joyce's feelings are quite normal and natural because she herself cries without any reason.

In this excerpt, the therapist reaps the argument he sowed in the first excerpt when he lapsed into conditionality. It takes two people to have an argument, and the advice-giver creates the advice-refuser. In this instance, Joyce may even have wanted to take the therapist's advice. But in complete honesty, she can say only that she does not know what she feels that makes her want to cry. She is completely unaware at that moment of any possible reason for her depressed feelings. She does not even feel depressed at that moment, and so the therapist's eleventh response is inappropriate. It does not deal with her *current* feelings.

The therapist has lost Round 2 because the client is still incongruent—she has depressed feelings but is unaware of their source and is still trying to prevent full expression and discharge of them.

III

Before this excerpt, the group members had been discussing their feelings during the present session and after the last session the previous week. Following the previous session, some had felt great and some had felt depressed. Joyce was one of those who had felt depressed after laughing so hard. The excerpt begins at the point where the therapist has turned to Joyce to suggest a possible reason for her feelings in hopes that she would explore these further.

Counselor: . . . but I remember we sort of, uh, we didn't really get to the talk about your feelings, Joyce, last time here. (*13*)

Joyce: Oh, I don't know, I don't think that was it, just not talking about me. You know, just because we laughed so much.

John: Yeah.

Joyce: I don't know why that would make you unhappy but I was really in a rotten mood all day and all night.

Counselor: It is sort of like, uh, maybe the laughter is sort of like whistling in the dark? And it's sort of like, uh, this isn't, soon as this is sort of out then, gee, the real feelings come bursting forth and it's really very sad, kind of, depressed . . . (*14*)

Joyce: The whole thing was sad and I really don't even know why. I don't know too much today at all (half-laugh).

Betty: I feel great.

Joyce: I'm afraid I won't be very helpful today (half-hearted laugh with suggestion of returning sadness).

Counselor: Maybe this is really more helpful what we are doing today, than the laughing and joking that we oftentimes do. Maybe this will bring up more of your real feelings. Maybe that's just, it's sort of making you uncomfortable because you don't want to let your real feelings come out maybe, I don't know . . . Is it sort of like if you started crying you would feel ashamed of yourself? . . . That you don't really want to cry in front of anybody else here? (*15*)

Joyce: Well, I don't, well I just, well it's just so silly for me to sit here and cry for no reason (laughs). You know.

Counselor: Well, is it that . . . (*16*)

Joyce: People just feel, I don't know, oh, if *I* were here and *she* started crying, I'd really feel, oh, I don't think I'd feel so bad but they all would feel funny, because they wouldn't know what to do.

Betty: Nobody likes to see anybody cry.

Joyce: Yeah.

Counselor: Is that right? Would you all feel funny if Joyce cried? (*17*)

Jack: (Quickly) She can cry! (Group laughter)

Joyce: I know but you all would just sit there with your heads down just ignoring me.

Jack: (Joking) No, I'd start laughing. (Group laughter) I'd get this big smile on my face.

John: (Seriously) I'd wonder what was wrong, I'd want to know *why* she was crying.

Counselor: You'd want to know . . . (*18*)

John: (Breaks in) I'd want to know why.

Counselor: (Continuing) A little bit more about it . . . (*19*)

John: Yeah, so if there's something you could do, you know.

Counselor: In other words, if Joyce would talk about what she was crying about or whatever she could, or whatever she was thinking (Joyce laughs) in her mind at that time, you would feel better, you'd feel more "Gee, I'm understanding a little bit about why she *is* sad right now!" (*20*)

Don: Exactly.

John: Yeah.

Counselor: Maybe Joyce will . . . (*21*)

Joyce: (Breaks in laughing) Skip it, skip it. (Laughs)

Jack: Slug her! (Joyce laughing above group laughter) Come on cry, my God . . . (Group laughter)

Betty: Can't you cooperate? (Further group laughter)

Jack: You're ruining the whole group . . . Now we're starting to laugh again. (Group continues with Jack's feelings)

The *tentative nature* of the therapist's first response (#13), suggesting a possible connection between Joyce's depressed feelings and the fact that the group did not focus on her that hour, creates the right atmosphere for further exploration. This atmosphere is apparent from the complete freedom Joyce seems to feel to dismiss this connection without further thought simply because it doesn't fit in her mind. The hypothesis is rejected (or in other instances would be accepted) *on its own merit,* not because it was or was not offered by a professional or because of any other extraneous reason.

Since this first tentative approximation has missed the mark, Joyce is stimulated to offer her own hypothesis. To her it seems that she felt so depressed simply because she had laughed so hard. But the therapist does not say, "Yes, I think that's right," indicating that he thinks that the final explanation has been reached. Instead, he takes this further, as if he does not feel the client has gotten to the bottom of the matter yet. He wonders out loud if there was some kind of falseness (which he likens to whistling in the dark) in the excessive laughter during the group session, since completely opposite feelings followed it. This encourages Joyce to look again at her feelings from a different perspective. She seems to realize then, for the first time, that even the laughter in the group was sad. She realizes further that she does not know why this was so.

This reaction may show that the therapist's hypotheses, or approximations, or tentative formulations of connections are *having an effect* on Joyce's perception of her feelings even though she has not accepted any of his offerings. At the very least, they have succeeded in stimulating Joyce to think of new possibilities beyond those suggested by the therapist —possibilities which Joyce would probably not have even thought about unless encouraged by the therapist to explore further. What had been merely a sterile fact has now become a kind of new mystery of her own being—a mystery she is aware of being unable to fathom at that moment. Some theorists might view this in terms of a change in her identity in which she finds herself a little more complex than she had at first thought, or a little more suggestive of rich potentialities that had remained dormant and unknown heretofore.

Whether or not Joyce's identity is changing somewhat, the way the therapist sums up and redefines her feelings and the group interaction (#15) *has an effect to the extent that it is correct.* If the therapist were completely wrong, his words would fall on deaf ears, so to speak, or be completely brushed off by the group. To the extent that they are correct, however, they will hit home because they do fit appropriately. This is the primary function of accurate empathy. It enables the therapist to help the client narrow the gap between his awareness and his deepest, most genuine feelings. Each accurate response strikes another blow for truth, honesty and integrity.

In this excerpt, the therapist makes a gradual transition from empathically inaccurate responses to responses of higher and higher accuracy. The first response suggesting a connection between her depressed feelings, however true or untrue it may have been in reality, was clearly inaccurate in an empathic sense. It was rejected. But because it was genuine and warmly unconditional, it did not offend Joyce and inhibit further exploration. If anything, it encouraged Joyce to take up the pursuit of the truth of the matter herself. She could do this freely because of the safe therapy atmosphere that was present.

By the end of the 15th response, the therapist's accuracy level is high as he brings up the feelings she had expressed earlier concerning crying in the group. The transition has finally been made from telling Joyce she should let herself cry to using empathy to find out what is stopping her from crying. As soon as one of the barriers that prevents her from expressing her feelings has been understood, it is relatively easy to remove that barrier by simply asking the other group members if they would really feel the way Joyce is afraid they would feel if she cried.

The group members can now express their own individual reactions, which tell Joyce what to expect. Since the group clearly agree that they would not feel uncomfortable if Joyce would just express something of her reasons for crying, she has been told now *by the group as well as by the therapist* that it is all right for her to cry. She sees clearly what is making others uncomfortable when she cries without expressing her feelings. She, thus, understands what she can do differently to prevent others from feeling this way in the future. Her laughter at several points shows the extent to which the group feeling toward her has hit home, providing support, acceptance and understanding. The impact of these human qualities will be evident in the excerpts to follow, so perhaps Round 3 was a draw.

IV

Betty: (After a momentary lull) Can't you ever just be happy?

John: Yeah.

Joyce: Uh huh.

Don: Yeah.

Counselor: I wonder if you're not that way whenever you just face all your feelings as they come, the good ones and the sad ones? (*22*)

Betty: Yeah, but can't you just be happy? I mean, you don't have to be hiding anything do you? Just not facing something or ignoring something?

Counselor: Well, I would think that if that were the case you wouldn't be crying at times without knowing why you were crying. (*23*)

Betty: Yeah, but you're not like that all the time.

Joyce: You go through spells, like I started crying the other day . . .

Betty: (Interrupts) Yeah, just occasionally.

Joyce: (Continues) When I was talking, uh, you know my three best friends were home, Becky, she's at Williams, and Cathy goes to Midwestern, and we all went over to Judy's house, she's at Southwestern, and, you know, we were all just talking just about, you know, thoughts and things like that, not about people or places, but, you know, just about thoughts, and Becky had to go and I just started crying, I mean, you know, I like Becky so much, but I'm not going to, I mean I don't miss her that much that I cry every time she leaves. I was just, I just couldn't explain why.

Counselor: You didn't understand why you started to cry there. (*24*)

Joyce: Yeah, just all of a sudden.

Counselor: You really liked talking with her? (*25*)

Joyce: Yeah! I really do like Becky, she's got a lot on the ball!

Counselor: Then to have this break off, her walk away was sort of like . . . (*26*) (Therapist pauses as if searching for the right words)

Joyce: Oh, she, oh, you know, she didn't just get up and leave. I guess she had to have the car home, but then, I don't know, she, you know, we all just talked and Cathy and I went for a ride and, you know, went up to the park and climbed all over the big cliffs and climbed over the big rocks in

Jackson Park and we just talked some more, and then I got home and I just felt so good!

Counselor: In a way you had, uh, talked and expressed feelings you felt and . . . (*27*)

Joyce: Yeah.

Counselor: Close feelings. (*28*)

Joyce: Yeah, I had accomplished something.

Counselor: I wonder if . . . (*29*)

Joyce: (Interrupts) Or *started* to accomplish something!

Counselor: Have you ever wished that this were true at home? That you felt this way with your parents, sisters, and so forth. (*30*)

Joyce: Like how.

Counselor: Like talking this way, uh, don't let so many problems and feelings pushing one way or other . . . (*31*)

Joyce: I don't know, I haven't talked to my parents in such a *long time.*

John: It's hard, it's so hard to talk to your parents without letting . . .

Joyce: (Breaks in) Oh, I can *talk* to them!

John: Without letting other, I mean other things enter in, cause, just like we talk here.

Joyce: Yeah, well sometimes I did but not, particularly with my father because I could tell him practically *anything,* you know, I mean, he'd, he'd take it and wouldn't say anything at all.

John: Gosh, it's, I don't . . .

Joyce: (Breaks in) I was going to talk, talk to my parents when I went home, but . . . (Ends with sigh that sounds as if she were shrugging her shoulders)

Counselor: It was just a real good feeling to share feelings with her? (*32*)

Joyce: Yeah.

Counselor: Could it be that it was sort of sad to have this stop? (*33*)

Joyce: It might have been, it might have been that, yeah . . .

Counselor: In a way it's sort of like . . . (*34*)

Joyce: (Breaks in) But she *thinks* so much more than people down here do! I mean, it's it's . . . it's *sickening* to think that they get so much done and we don't get anything done!

Counselor: In a way, you sort of wish then, that . . . (*35*)

Joyce: (Breaks in) I, I wish I were there (shrugging half-laugh) . . . I *really do!*

Counselor: That does kind of make it sad . . . (*36*)

Joyce: Yeah.

Counselor: . . . to think that you wish you were not here, you wish you were there. (*37*)

Joyce: Yeah, you know you can think with people, you know, just *think* with people instead of just talking with them . . . well, you talk but you think at the same time. And you don't talk just about the parties you went to or the people you saw, you know, just about the things you think.

Counselor: That's something you really enjoyed doing with her then? (*38*)

Joyce: Uh huh.

Counselor: You had a sense of really making some kind of progress? (*39*) (Sounds of Joyce starting to cry again)

Betty: I feel the way Joyce does. (Tearful laugh from Joyce) So many times nobody says anything. All, oh, "What are you going to wear?" or "Who are you going with?" or "What party, what did you do at the party?" That's all anybody talks about; they never talk about anything.

John: Yeah.

Counselor: You know, Joyce was really feeling something here . . . (Tearful laugh from Joyce as she starts to cry again) In a way you're sort of realizing how much you miss a good relationship like that . . . Is it sort of like that? (*40*)

Joyce: (Crying, but still fighting to hold back her tears) Yeah, I guess it is.

Counselor: You miss that here. (Short silence as Joyce begins to win the struggle to suppress the feelings that had started again in her) And you don't want to let yourself cry about it . . . You know, it's a funny thing how we fight letting ourselves feel what we really feel—all of us do this, we do it over, over and over . . . it seems like Joyce really wants to cry right now (sounds of Joyce starting to cry again) and yet doesn't want to let herself cry . . . You, you feel like saying, "I wish he'd shut up." (*41*)

Joyce: (Laughs again with sense of release, then short silence)

Counselor: You feel this too, Jack? (*42*)

The way Betty returns to the unfortunate debate started by the counselor again demonstrates the futility of telling someone there is a reason for his behavior when he is unaware of that reason. Betty does not try to explore her own reactions to see if there possibly *was* some reason for her to "start bawling" when she was looking out a window while studying. Not knowing any such reason, she concluded logically that there does not always have to be a reason. As a result, the therapist finds himself defensively talking about *hypothetical* instances and what such-and-such behavior might mean in those instances instead of responding empathically to Betty and Joyce's *present feelings.*

Joyce then offers her second hypothesis concerning the reason she was crying without reason. She explains it on the basis of "spells." At certain times you just behave this way as, for example, when she talked with her girl friends and just started crying when Becky left. Even though she knew she did not miss Becky that much, she still started to cry and she does not understand why.

The counselor begins to respond empathically, and the productivity of this excerpt should be contrasted with the first two (in which empathy was low) in order to gain some idea of the effects that higher levels of accurate empathy, unconditional positive regard, and therapist congruence have on intrapersonal exploration.

The 24th and 25th responses help Joyce to focus on the significant elements—her puzzlement about suddenly starting to cry and her genuine feeling for Becky. The 26th response leads in the wrong direction, and Joyce corrects what she seems to feel may be a misimpression about the suddenness of Becky's departure. Then the therapist again helps (#27 and #28) Joyce to focus on the particular element that was important—the close feelings shared.

At this point the therapist fails to respond to the key word "accomplished," because the close feeling element reminded him of his earlier hypothesis concerning sadness possibly related to Joyce's father. Responses #30 and #31 thus go awry, and Joyce goes down a side alley until in response #32 the therapist brings her back to the feelings she was sharing with her friends. Response #33 gets closer, and then Joyce breaks in with further insight into the reasons for her sadness—her realization of how little she was accomplishing in comparison with her friends.

As exploration deepens, it takes very few tentative words from the counselor to help her come to the next realization that she wishes she were there instead of where she is. She realizes further what it is that she valued there so much more highly than the superficial relationships she has where she is at present.

The counselor's 39th response strikes home, and Joyce begins to really *experience* the reasons for her sad feelings. When she starts to cry, almost in spite of herself, Betty picks up the conversation much as many people would do in an ordinary conversation to avoid confronting deeper emotions directly. But the therapist will not permit the group to continue the discussion as if Joyce were not emotional; he responds to her feelings empathically (#40).

Nevertheless, Joyce again finally succeeded in fighting back the tears that threatened to overpower her, although it seemed to be getting increasingly more difficult for her to do this. The therapist eventually turned to John because Joyce seemed to want this and John's expressive face seemed to warrant it. Round 4 felt like a winner.

V

John: . . . Sometimes a bunch of us would just get together, go out and go to some place where we could just sit and talk. We sat one evening, we started talking about 9 o'clock and we were all going to stay over that night, and we didn't knock off until about 3:30 in the morning. We just sat and talked the whole time, just sat there and talked. We all felt better for it, with a little sleep, we all felt better.

Counselor: Sort of a feeling of sharing feelings and thoughts with other people, and this really is satisfying in here, something you need. (*43*)

John: Uh huh.

Counselor: Sort of something like Joyce had, I guess, and then when she realized she had to leave this, it was sad. I guess it really hit her. (*44*)

John: Uh huh, two of my best buddies are going to East Southern and boy, I wish they were going here. I know if they had been here, I would never have been on academic probation, 'cause, call them a good influence, or call them what you want, but I know I started fooling around here and I fooled around 'til I got to fooling around too much with another one of my buddies. He can either be serious or likeable, and it's much easier for him to be liked so I just kind of went along with him, but it seems like the only times I really got something done was the weekends when these other guys would come back and we'd sit and talk . . .

Counselor: Uh huh.

John: . . . and say for the week after that here I would be feeling great and I could, knock everything off. If they had been here, or if I had gone to East Southern, I wouldn't have had any trouble at all.

Counselor: Uh huh.

John: I know what she means about, you know, you just (turns to Joyce) kind of . . . about . . . makes you, you feel kind of . . . *lonely*. (Joyce obviously reacting strongly to this, rest of group silent and serious)

Counselor: (To Joyce, gently) I imagine that is a very strong feeling . . . Something you don't even want to talk about right now . . . (25-second pause) . . . I guess in a way I have the feeling that when you fight the feeling that you have that it sort of, it doesn't get out, and it'll just kind of be pushing out again later . . . (*45*)

Joyce: I don't know, maybe I'm just sick of being lonely! (Starts sobbing with her head in her arms on the table as at last she gives in to her feelings)

Counselor: . . . I'm sure you *are* sick of being lonely (sounds of Joyce really letting loose) . . . it's extremely difficult to live without loving and being loved by someone . . . (more sounds of crying) . . . You know, you really can't live that way, you can't live without loving and being loved . . . I think that's as strong as the need for water and food . . . (more sounds) . . . I think Joyce really feels her need to love someone and to be loved by someone . . . Is that what you're feeling mostly right now, Joyce? (*46*)

Joyce: (Still crying) I don't know, I just feel like, out of all these people, I mean there's so many people here and yet I'm, it's so, it's so easy to be so, so *alone* with all these people. I mean I've got so many friends, but they're not really my *friends*, I mean, well, they are, but they're not really because they know *nothing* about me and I know nothing really about them except who they go out with and all that stuff (blows nose).

Betty: That's true. (Counselor hands Joyce handkerchief)

Joyce: (Laughs) Thank you. Now I'll be all messed up and ugly the rest of the day.

Counselor: I think you look very charming. (*47*)

Joyce: (Laughs) Thank you, but it's a lie. (Tension-releasing laughter in group)

Counselor: I think that's really true; I think you really have a feeling, when you have a good relationship, and you can look back at all the other relationships you have had and say, "Gee, these were pretty superficial, weren't they!" (*48*)

John: Yeah. (John, Betty and Don continue talking about their friendships and the value of open communication)

This excerpt is a good illustration of the manner in which genuine emotion in one group member has a strong impact on the others present. In this instance John gets a higher rating on empathy than the therapist because he introduced the key word "lonely" to Joyce. This word so aptly fits Joyce's feelings at that moment that the torrent of sadness that has built up in her can no longer be denied. Joyce then seems actually to *experience* the sadness that goes with being alone. She also seems to experience at least one of the reasons for her sadness. She can no longer think she cries for no reason at all (and as a matter of record, she never did say this again during the remainder of the group meetings).

Her perception of herself also seems to change as she seems to realize that she is really alone despite the fact that she has so many friends. She focuses on the superficiality of their knowledge of each other as evidence that she has no real friendships at school. She allows herself to become aware of these feelings and to react with full emotion in a manner that should be integrating, unifying and therapeutic.

Theoretically, Joyce can now behave differently in real life because she is more aware of her deeper feelings and needs. Instead of feeling depressed without knowing why, she will now experience a variety of new reasons for her sad feelings when they recur. Probably she will continue to experience these feelings until she has taken sufficient action in real life to remove their causes. This action, it could be noted, was not very likely to occur before she had experienced her loneliness and depression.

No evidence exists to show whether Joyce was able to establish deeper friendships in real life, but in that hour there *was* further evidence of the change in her self-perception or self concept. In the last excerpt to be presented, Joyce attacked John's view that it doesn't help to find out what your problems are. She recognizes the similarity between this way of coping with *his* problems and the way she had been coping with hers.

VI

John has just said he doesn't think people can live together happily, and that all he cares about is his dog, his car and his little sister.

John: (Continuing) It doesn't bother me most of the time, I mean, God, you can and there's no use thinking about something that bothers you. All right, what good's it going to do, how is it going to solve my problems thinking about it now? I was perfectly happy, I could just . . .

Counselor: In a way, I guess, it sort of, it's sort of irritating to find yourself feeling this way. (*49*)

John: Yeah, it isn't going to do me any good, it isn't going to help me at all, not one bit!

Joyce: Well, you've got to think about it because that's what I've been doing. I've been putting everything off. *Everything!*

John: I do my homework!

Joyce: (Vehemently) No, I don't mean just homework!

John: Well, that's all, I mean, there isn't anything else, I mean what *else* is there to do?

Betty: What do you want to study?

John: I don't want to study anything. I'm just doing stuff to do it. I wish that, I don't have to, I couldn't, there isn't any place that I want to be, and I don't even want to be here. I mean, everything is just, I mean, my God, there's not *anything anywhere!*

SUMMARY

Before summarizing this discussion, it may be necessary to stress again the fact that this view of the interaction just presented is *merely* an interpretation based on my present tentative understanding of these variables and their operation. It seems to me that this kind of interaction sets forces in motion that facilitate positive changes in personality functioning.

Joyce at first thought there was no reason for her to feel so depressed because she did not think she was unhappy about anything. At the end of that hour, however, I think she was aware of her loneliness among all the people and friends around her. I believe she had experienced some of the sadness this loneliness produced in her and realized that she wanted more than superficial friendships. She seemed to realize that she even wished she could be with her girl friends at other schools who were accomplishing things now and making the kind of progress she had been unable to make. She no longer wanted to put everything out of her mind as she had been doing before.

Joyce thus changed from a girl who thought she was perfectly happy, even though buffeted by mysterious, contradictory, depressive episodes, to a girl who realized to some extent what was causing these depressed feelings. This change in her awareness and self-perception could presumably lead to further positive changes in her real-life behavior.

This does not, of course, mean that Joyce is now integrated. For all we know, Joyce may have much deeper feelings related to her father, family, etc., which would have to be resolved before she could establish deeper friendships and make better progress in school. In fact, this is what experience with other clients in similar circumstances would strongly suggest. The point is not that all her problems are now solved, but that high therapeutic conditions helped Joyce take constructive steps toward their solution. Each step forward can make the next step that much easier. High levels of therapeutic conditions can thus provide the impetus which gets clients moving toward the goals they themselves affirm for themselves.

In summary, then, an attempt was made to focus especially on different levels of accurate empathy and unconditional positive regard to show how these levels seemed either to facilitate or retard Joyce's intrapersonal exploration. More specifically, it seems to me that this interaction supports the following points:

(1) The verbal and nonverbal cues (and *verbal inflection* in particular) provide a continuous *stimulus* that in turn provides a continuous *challenge* to the counselor's sensitivity, timing, and capacity for relationship.

(2) The client's reactions provide constant feedback to the therapist as he continually modifies, sharpens and reformulates hypotheses concerning the most genuine and the most deeply denied feelings present. In this respect, he is an integrating center, an emotional computer, or a bloodhound or detective in pursuit of the genuine (and he is, of course, also many *other* things—a source of genuine reaction, a participant observer, a patient teacher who cares without coercing, and above all, a truly *human* person).

(3) The therapist continually translates this understanding and acceptance into facilitative action. He does this by responding in such a way as

to throw further light on existing problems. He does this by trying to listen and respond to the unspoken as well as the spoken. He tries to catch the finer nuances of *inter-* and *intra*personal functioning so that he can help both to a deeper level of understanding.

(4) He tries to be open to any feedback that contradicts his present verbal models, hypotheses, or representations of the human being in front of him. If it were possible, he would do away with all models and theoretical formulations or abstractions that prevent him from reacting fully, genuinely, and sensitively to the person before him.

(5) He tries to stay with the client's current feelings so that he will not get too far ahead of the client or misdirect him down side alleys, but he also does not just lag behind, rehashing what the client has already discarded.

(6) He does not push onto the client what the client is unaware of at that moment and cannot handle. He lets the client proceed at his own pace without trying to make extra progress through "forced marches."

(7) He does sometimes redefine and sum up his perceptual realities, even when they are somewhat in advance of the client, because these may fall on fertile ground and bear fruit later.

(8) He does not generally call for cognition and intellectual effort from the client because these processes generally inhibit relaxation of defenses and expression of feelings. He will take it upon himself to do a great part of the thinking so that the client can be free to *experience fully* the deeper emotion he has previously been unable to discharge or integrate.

(9) He facilitates the transition from ordinary conversation back and forth to the therapy level, where feelings that are *inappropriate* in the everyday, logical, work-a-day world can be explored *appropriately* in the safe therapy atmosphere. Although he recognizes the fact that these feelings are oftentimes inappropriate to the external environment in which they are experienced, he seeks to understand the original conditions and situations in which they are appropriate, so that the client can be freed of the tendency to make the same old mistakes over and over again.

(10) He tries to get at the *realities* regardless of evaluative, judgmental standards. "Just the facts, ma'am, just the facts" might well be his motto as he strives to deal with what *is* rather than what should be. In other words, he tries to accept his clients as they are in all their humanness, just as he accepts himself as he is in all his own humanness.

(11) He does not talk in the abstract about "doing therapy" or what would be therapeutic—he simply tries to *be therapeutic.*

(12) He is sensitive to and can use group reaction and interstimulation for therapeutic aims, because he is aware of the extent to which group feeling can build up and have an impact on the individual stronger than that of the therapist alone.

(13) He recognizes the fact that his efforts to understand and accept, even when he misses the mark, will encourage the client to offer his own hypotheses and explore further when the therapy atmosphere is safe.

(14) And finally, he knows that real problems, denied feelings, etc., persist and recur until they are worked through adequately. Even if he fails over and over, he can get progressively better in time as he understands more and continues trying to be empathic, unconditional and genuine. Just as the counselor lost the early rounds in the examples presented, the therapist knows that he must try and try again until he succeeds.

There are many other principles and examples that could be extracted from this material. This is simply my present working model in brief and provides a sample of the kind of stimulation the training program provided for me.

Perhaps less has been said about therapist congruence than would be desirable, but this was not because genuineness is that much less important. It was because it seems easier to "see" accurate empathy in printed material. The reader knows whether the client says, "Yes, that's exactly it. . . ," but the reader cannot know how the therapist said what he said. It is this "how" of inflection, speed, and facial expression which is the primary cue to congruence. For this reason, it is far more difficult to tell from a printed page whether a response rings true than to tell whether it is empathic.

Even this minimum of interpretation, discussion and principles would require much further explication and elaboration to resolve many of the points raised to the satisfaction of many of those working in this area. Rather than to stir up controversy, however, my purpose was to show how I have learned to learn in this area so that these working hypotheses can be applied and extended.

SECTION III TOWARD THE MATURE THERAPIST AND COUNSELOR

EXPERIENCE is not synonymous with maturity. Most of us become experienced, but few of us will truly mature as therapists or counselors. Maturity implies a continuing perfection of our abilities to induce or facilitate constructive change in the client who comes to us for help. The evidence reviewed in Chapters 1 and 3 suggested strongly that, on the average, highly experienced therapists show no greater ability to induce or facilitate constructive change in the patient. We suspect that this lack of correlation between experience and maturity grows out of a tendency for the experienced therapist to offset this growing ability by an increased acceptance of professional prejudices, and a consequent unconcern with feedback from the client he seeks to help.

Chapter 14 specifies some ancillary therapeutic ingredients: other therapeutic factors that have been shown by research to affect patient outcome—for better or for worse. It is a brief chapter which, in its brevity, reflects the current lack of validated knowledge. Undoubtedly many other factors not discussed will be found to affect therapeutic outcome. Although we ourselves believe others to be important and act on these beliefs in practice (as will you), we know of no solid research evidence suggesting their validity, and so have not discussed them.

Chapter 15 suggests guidelines for the continuing growth of the counselor or therapist. In specifying such guidelines, the focus is on using (1) *direct feedback* from clients in terms of moment-by-moment changes in the level of patient depth of self-exploration (with the research scale presented in Chapter 5) and in measures of behaviorial improvement outside therapy; and (2) *indirect feedback* from clients in terms of learnings from research findings and the clinical innovations and experiences of other therapists.

CHAPTER 14 ANCILLARY THERAPEUTIC INGREDIENTS

MUCH of what goes into becoming an effective therapist is the day-by-day experiential learning of *what works best* with particular kinds of patients. Through his concentration on constructive change in his own clients, day by day and year by year, the therapist learns more about what he can borrow from others and successfully use with his own personality in dealing with the type of clients he meets. In this way he learns that while "friendly confrontation" may work well with a college counseling client or a well-integrated vocational rehabilitation client, it may bring on withdrawal or even panic in the fearful hospitalized mental patient. In this very crucial sense, training provides the basic substrata but there is no substitute for experience.

It is vitally important for both the beginning and the experienced counselor or therapist to recognize that what he most strongly believes, whether based on clear-cut research findings or solid experiential learnings, must inevitably be wrong in many respects when dealing with an individual client. Thus he must be both personally committed and skeptical in whatever he does. Counselors and therapists who are *only* committed cannot easily discover when they are ineffective. But those who are *only* skeptical cannot act with the confidence and assurance necessary for any approach to have positive effect. In a broad sense this is an essential part of the meaning of "expert knowledge": knowledge of *what seems likely to be helpful,* alongside an even more certain knowledge that in the complex field of interpersonal relations and human motivation, nothing will prove effectively helpful 100 per cent of the time. This calls for an attitude of *conservative experimentation,* a willingness to try other approaches and techniques that seem potentially helpful when the current approach seems ineffective at a given time with a given client.

At times this may even mean referring a given patient to another counselor or therapist whose specialization and knowledge are more likely to be helpful; one therapist cannot be all things to all people. For example, a psychotherapist or counselor who has only minimal knowledge of the world of work may discover that his patient has chosen a job and career ill-matched to his abilities. In such a case making use of the expert knowledge of a vocational counselor might be the most helpful move for the therapist to make. In another case, a vocational rehabilitation counselor may discover, from an opinion rendered by a physician-consultant, that his physically handicapped client is, without physiological cause, sexually impotent in his marriage. The counselor or physician might be most helpful in such a case by calling on the skills of a behavior therapist specializing in such problems. In dealing with any particular client, then, a given therapist might do a grave disservice by not calling upon the social worker's knowledge of community resources, a child psychologist or psychiatrist's knowledge of child development and treatment, a marriage counselor's skill in marital problems, a vocational counselor's knowledge of the world of work and vocational choice, an educational counselor's knowledge of the requirements and differential opportunities in educational career planning, and so on.

Similarly, it is at times in the interest of the client for the therapist to suggest other professional services: a medical specialist, a legal specialist, a religious specialist, or a labor or economic consultant. This is not to say that the counselor or therapist should become an overburdened juggler of schedules for the client, balancing contacts with eight different consultation services from his reference point at one time. However, he is committed to accomplishing all that he can for the client, and this "all" does not end at the intrapsychic or limited interpersonal level. There are other areas in the environment that impinge upon the client's effective functioning, and the therapist can call upon necessary resources both in himself and others.

Not only is the effective therapist or counselor an expert in interpersonal skills that facilitate the client's resolution of emotional, motivational, and interpersonal problems, but to be maximally effective the therapist must also have expert knowledge across the wide range of human functioning. In this expert knowledge of human and social functioning, the professional therapist or counselor differs from even the warmest, most understanding, and most spontaneously genuine nonprofessional. His expert knowledge, when it actually exists, not only contributes heavily to accurate empathic understanding of the client in the moment-to-moment encounter of the relationship, but also provides a basis for providing the client with both information and advice.

Much has been written condemning the therapist who engages in advice or information-giving. This criticism of the counselor as a source of information and advice is quite valid when applied to the rank beginner (or to the clumsy and ineffectual "experienced" professional) who tries to tell the patient how he *ought* to live his life. Such persuasive advice and information has probably already been given by a friend, a neighbor, a spouse, or a parent—without benefit. There are times, however, where only a rigid (and foolish) counselor would fail to use his expert knowledge in giving information or advice.

Just as problems arising from the client's defensive distortions of self and others cannot be resolved by information or advice, those arising from his lack of information, misinformation, or deficit in behavioral learning clearly cannot be resolved by deep emotional or cognitive self-exploration and experiencing. The chief dangers and pitfalls of giving advice or information arise from two sources: (1) the manner in which it is given; and (2) the frequency with which it is given. Providing information or advice should never shift the responsibility for decision-making from the client to the counselor. In this sense, the way the advice or information is given is more important than its content. The effective therapist avoids any implication that he is attempting to lead the patient's life for him. Instead, he will usually give advice of this kind: "Some people have tried . . . do you think it might be worth trying for you?", or, "There are no sure ways of dealing with that: some people have tried . . . while others have tried. . . , what do you think?" The intent is to provide possible alternatives that seem in the therapist's experience to be feasible as he understands the patient, letting the patient in turn explore their potential value for himself. The therapist can then focus his skills on facilitating the client's exploration of the advantages and disadvantages, and the meaning and implications, as he sees them, of the potential alternatives.

The second great danger in giving advice and information revolves around the temptation to overuse such an approach and become a "helpful Henry" with a barrage of solutions. To use advice and information-giving effectively, the therapist must have an accurately empathic grasp of the patient's inner world and give advice only when it is soundly based on his expert knowledge and when it is clear that the patient cannot discover from his own experience the possible alternatives or the informational facts.

With these two restrictions in mind, there appear to be no valid reasons for failing to provide information or advice when it is appropriate. The research evidence does, in fact, suggest that providing information and advice is one way of producing observable and measurable change in the client. The study of Krumboltz (1965) discussed in Chapter 4 produced findings indicating a significant degree of behavior change occurring outside of therapy as a result of information and advice giving during counseling sessions. Other studies provide similar evidence.

One way in which the therapist's expert knowledge can be put to use economically is in providing clients and patients with selected reading materials. Having the patient read selected books, chapters, articles, or pamphlets does present the potential danger (particularly with psychotic patients) that they will grossly misinterpret what they read, but with most client and patient populations the advantages far outweigh the disadvantages.

A few examples may clarify this aspect of the expert role in practice. In the course of therapy, a hospitalized 23-year-old male schizophrenic patient was greatly upset by his own masturbation. He had been told by his parents and others that it was extremely sinful and "dirty" and caused insanity, he had developed strong feelings of guilt, fear and anxiety. He was even more upset because of his sporadic attempts to eliminate this behavior. In the process of helping this patient explore his feelings and experiences surrounding the "masturbation problem," the therapist gave him the factual information that more than nine out of every ten American males had masturbated at one time or another. The therapist also indicated that even when the average young male decided that he wanted to stop masturbating before he had developed a heterosexual outlet, it was usually difficult since the behavior itself was physiologically pleasurable. Over the course of several interviews, the therapist introduced this new (to the patient) information; after the patient had decided for himself that he would like to stop such behavior (primarily as a way of testing himself to see if he were actually in control of himself), the therapist suggested possible alternative and incompatible behaviors to be tried in situations where masturbation had normally occurred. The information- and advice-giving occurred as an inseparable part of the transactions of therapy rather than as interjected "lectures" or "professional opinions." In this case the suggestions and information were not only helpful in the patient's resolution of his problems about masturbation, but also had important repercussions on his self concept and his evaluation of other damaging parental teachings.

A second example of information- and advice-giving occurred in the marital counseling of a middle-aged graduate student and his wife. Both had sought counseling in "one last try" before seeking formal divorce action. They had been married three years, were without children, and had a continuous history of bickering, arguing, and well-practiced recriminations. During a session in which the couple discussed the events and feelings that typically led up to intense marital discord as well as their genuine positive feelings toward each other, the therapist gave advice from his knowledge of human learning, operant conditioning and the nature of stimulus control. His suggestion was that they might want to try changing the "background" stimulus complex that made up at least part of the conditioned stimuli eliciting their anger and mutual recriminations. The couple together decided that such changes might help them in learning to express to each other their positive feelings and might even help in breaking up what they described as a "habit" of getting into an argument after supper. Consequently, they rearranged the furniture in their apartment, purchased several new shirts, blouses, etc. for evening wear, changed the hour of the evening meal, and in other ways radically altered the total stimulus complex of their routine daily life. Improvement in their marriage was marked and rapid. Although they continued to explore their mutual relationship in further counseling sessions, they attributed much of their improvement to the changes in the stimulus complex. (The therapist, for his part, has found the suggestion useful for a number of subsequent cases.) Whether the marked improvement following the therapist's suggestion was due to the novelty, the mutual commitment involved in the actions, or the total therapy sessions, the information and advice contained in the therapist's suggestions did seem to play an important role. The husband later reported to the counselor that he had applied the same basic idea to problems he had had in using his study time effectively. That is, he decided on his own that he could improve his study habits by changing the "background stimulus complex" that was associated with his habit of "sitting at the desk and looking at a book, turning pages, but not really reading what it said."

A third example of advice-giving occurred during psychotherapy with another graduate student who had developed an anxiety neurosis and become incapable of taking examinations. Among his many feelings of inadequacy and insecurity, he expressed a persistent fear that he "was not really very bright" and had somehow "tricked his way" even through college. At one point during a session in which the patient was exploring this specific fear in the context of his general feelings of inadequacy, the therapist suggested that he might want to arrange for an intelligence test to check for himself his relative intellectual capacity. It seemed clear that this particular student had no other good way of assessing his relative ability. As it turned out, the client decided to see a psychologist for testing (which for him was a major risk). From the results of the testing, he learned that he ranked in the lower ten per cent for students entering that particular professional school. The client then had several sessions with a vocational counselor and transferred his training to another area where his abilities were more competitive. Although the original therapist might have helped the client without the services of a vocational counselor, neither the client nor the original therapist was in a position to assess accurately a student's ability and appropriate educational opportunities through self-exploration alone. There was the further danger in therapy: they might focus too heavily on the client's *feelings* of inadequacy at the expense of recognizing his real-life situational inadequacy.

In the three case examples just given, the advice- and information-giving occurred spontaneously within the process of therapy. They made available to the client alternatives or information that were unknown to him but within the counselor's fund of expert knowledge. Thus, advice-giving depends for its effectiveness not only upon providing new alternatives to the client, but also upon the context of an effective interpersonal relationship.

THE USE OF REINFORCEMENT, OPERANT PRINCIPLES, AND THE ISSUE OF CONTROL BY THE THERAPIST

Many counselors and therapists have been greatly concerned about the issue of control in therapeutic practice: to what extent should they attempt to control the client's behavior, manipulate his behavior, or otherwise seek to influence him? The thousands of printed pages in books and journal articles devoted to this question is in itself an amazing phenomenon, and the writings on the subject are at least faintly reminiscent of the medieval controversy about how many angels could be placed on the head of a pin. In large part, the issue seems to be one of semantic differences. Clearly, the counselor or therapist is devoting his time, talent, personal involvement and energies to influencing the patient toward positive behavioral change or personality growth. Just as clearly, most human beings, and this certainly includes clients, may welcome "help" but strongly resent and resist "control."

It should be emphasized that in the successful operant approaches to inducing behavior change, the therapist himself does not convince the patient that he is attempting to "control" him, "manipulate" him, or "mastermind" him. Instead, such behavior therapists as Goldiamond are very careful to leave decision-making to the client and to describe their role as that of a consultant. There is, in short, no factual basis for claiming that they are any more "manipulators" and any less "helpers" than an effective nondirective therapist. While it is true that there are instances in which the patient is "influenced" without his awareness, there is no basis for claiming that any single approach to psychotherapy or treatment is more guilty of this than others. If anything, it would be easiest to argue that traditional conversation psychotherapy offers more opportunity for the therapist to influence the patient covertly.

The evidence, as noted in Chapter 4, suggests that reinforcement and operant principles have been useful to some degree in specific cases. The careful use of rewards or reinforcement in slowly shaping verbal behavior in a catatonic schizophrenic patient who had been mute for 19 years was illustrated in a clinical report by Isaacs, Thomas, and Goldiamond (1960). Even the most ardent humanistic counselor, for whom such terms as "reinforcement" and "stimulus control" are anathema, would have difficulty in arguing that the procedures involved were unethical or destructive. It would be harder still to argue that it would be better for that patient to have remained mute simply because the therapist was not open to experimental techniques for influencing client behavior.

It should be reemphasized that, in spite of the cold and mechanistic language used to describe such techniques, the actual practice often involves a warm, authentic, and deeply understanding therapist. As this becomes more generally recognized, we might look forward to increasing clinical applications of such techniques.

THE INFLUENCE OF SITUATIONAL INGREDIENTS

In addition to the attitude of cautious experimentation which the therapist maintains in coming to utilize all human resources necessary to the growth of both client and therapist, there is in the therapy situation a whole area of nonhuman dimensions that potentially influence its outcome. Indeed, a number of situational or contextual factors that are relatively under the direct control of the counselor appear to be significant for constructive therapeutic outcome. In order to be most effective, the counselor or therapist must continually strive to understand the contextual effects of the therapeutic encounter. In doing so, he not only learns new ways of influencing client behavior, but also develops more effective ways of using himself in the therapeutic interaction.

For example, the placing of time limits as an aspect of structuring the relationship appears to be of therapeutic value. Thus, Phillips and Johnson (1954) report results indicating that in family therapy a limit of ten interviews, established at the outset, leads to fewer premature terminations than conventional methods. Of the sixteen time-limited cases studied, all proved successful. A more thorough study of individual therapy by Shlien, Mosak and Dreikurs (1960) tends to confirm the positive effects of placing time limits upon the conduct of counseling or therapy. They studied a sample of client-centered therapy and cross-validated the findings on a sample of Adlerian therapy. Possibly, when the therapist tells the patient in advance the limits of time commitment, the patient himself will be motivated earlier for constructive change. Whether it would be valuable to structure the time limits for long-term therapy appears to be a separate question. For relatively brief counseling or psychotherapy (up to 30 sessions), however, the evidence is clear and consistent in showing positive effects upon therapeutic outcome. Those findings, in general, confirm the clinical thesis held by many theorists, such as French, that the factor of a specific goal or subgoal in the therapeutic situation tends to accelerate the process.

Another aspect of the structure of therapy usually defined by the therapist is the frequency of therapeutic contact. The evidence to date suggests that more frequent therapy sessions have a moderate therapeutic advantage compared with relatively infrequent ones. Such findings are shown by the Lorr et al. (1962)[13] and the Frank et al. (1963) research studies. Although these are general findings, studies comparing daily versus twice-weekly versus once-weekly sessions have yet to be done. If we extrapolate the present data, it would seem that sessions held daily or at least three times per week might prove maximally therapeutic. In light of such data it is interesting to note that the current trend in psychotherapy and counseling is to have less frequent sessions than ten or twenty years ago.

In a great many institutional settings for psychotherapy and counseling, a desk is interposed between patient and therapist; in private practice the therapist more often conducts sessions without a desk separating them. There is no direct evidence for one setting or another, but a report by White (1953) did study a quite large population of medical patients during case-history interviewing. Using an objective system for classifying postures, the data indicated that 55 per cent initially sat at ease without

13. Lorr et al. conclude otherwise, but on inspection their *data* actually support the hypotheses that frequent sessions yield greater therapeutic outcome than infrequent (biweekly) sessions—after 4 months, 8 months and 12 months.

the desk, but only 10 per cent were at ease when the desk separated them from the doctor. This is quite consistent with clinical impressions that the interposition of a desk between therapists and client serves to "separate" the two and thus create a psychological distance and depersonalization of the relationship.

Since the very early development of the "talking-cure," theorists and practitioners have debated the merits of structuring the role of the patient at the outset of therapy. Some therapists or counselors begin the relationship by telling the client what to expect, what he is to do, and what he can expect from the therapist. Others have argued that this is a waste of time or even harmful. Several recent studies provide some solid information.

Using a "role-induction interview," the research group at Johns Hopkins (Hoehn-Saric, Frank, Imber, Nash, Stone and Battle, 1963) attempted to give the patient appropriate expectations about psychotherapy which would facilitate the process of therapy and its outcome. The interview (which was based upon the anticipatory socialization interview developed by Orne) tried to develop realistic expectations of improvement, explain the therapist's anticipated behavior, tell the patient how he was expected to behave and instruct him how to recognize and overcome superficial manifestations of resistance. In a very well-designed study, with twenty patients assigned to the role-induction interview and twenty control patients, the findings indicated significantly greater improvement for patients who went through the role-induction interview. That study seems to suggest clearly that a systematic attempt to prepare the patient for his role in psychotherapy contributes positively to outcome.

A separate attempt has been made to provide both cognitive and experiential structuring using "vicarious therapy pretraining" (VTP). In a study of time-limited group therapy with 40 hospitalized mental patients, Truax and Carkhuff (1965a) borrowed from studies of verbal and motor learning the idea that vicarious experiencing of a task would improve performance. To try vicarious therapy pretraining, they developed a 30-minute tape recording of excerpts of "good" patient therapy behavior. The tape was designed to illustrate very concretely how clients often explore themselves and their feelings; it allowed patients to experience therapy vicariously prior to the first session. The findings from that study gave uniform but modest support to the therapeutic value of VTP; the patients receiving such structuring showed greater improvement on all subscales of the MMPI and significantly greater improvement on four of the psychotic subscales.

In the extension of that study to 160 hospitalized patients in group psychotherapy (Truax and Wargo, 1966c), modest support for the beneficial effects of vicarious therapy pretraining was also reported. In particular, patients receiving this training showed significantly greater improvement over controls on measures of anxiety, the measures of schizophrenic symptomatology and depression obtained from the MMPI, and improvement in maturity of interpersonal relationships as measured by the Palo Alto Group Psychotherapy Scale.

When VTP was used in a study of 80 juvenile delinquents, Truax and Wargo (1966b) obtained findings suggesting no positive effects. Those delinquents receiving vicarious therapy pretraining and those serving as controls showed equivalent changes during group psychotherapy.

When the vicarious therapy pretraining tapes were used with outpatient group therapy populations, the findings were relatively clear in suggesting beneficial effects (Truax, Wargo and Carkhuff, 1966). Thus, on the 23 measures of outcome, patients receiving VTP showed above-average improvement on 21 measures; patients serving as controls showed above-average improvement during psychotherapy on only two measures ($p < .001$). VTP had significant beneficial effects on depressive, psychasthenic, and hysteric symptomatology in particular.

These studies, taken together, suggest no negative effects and relatively consistent positive therapeutic effects of both cognitive and experiential structuring of the patient's role in counseling and psychotherapy. One exception is the lack of positive effects with juvenile delinquents. The lack of effectiveness with juvenile delinquents may derive from their feeling that to imitate the VTP patient behavior would amount to accepting a "sick" role. If that is the case, then positive benefits from structuring might occur if "nonpatients" were used in the examples used for the VTP tape.

That structuring tends to facilitate the therapeutic process and to enhance outcome is further suggested by several studies dealing with "goal directedness." For example, Vernallis and Reinert (1961) reported a study suggesting that specifying the goal of treatment and retaining this as a major focus was significantly helpful in group therapy in an inpatient setting.

In a sense, the converging evidence on the value of experiential and cognitive structuring fits well with what is known about human learning. If psychotherapy or counseling is indeed a process of learning and relearning, then the therapeutic process should allow for structuring what is to be learned, rather than depending on what amounts to "incidental learning," where the client does not have clearly in mind from the outset what it is he is supposed to learn.

In recent years the use of "alternate sessions" in counseling or psychotherapy, particularly group therapy, has become more frequent. That is, the therapist meets with the patients on a regular basis but then has them hold in-between sessions in which he is absent. Wolf (1961) and Wolf and Schwartz (1962) suggested, especially in regard to group therapy, that sessions without the therapist, if alternated with regular meetings, would prove therapeutic and thus contribute to outcome. However, in a study of 40 hospitalized patients, Truax and Carkhuff (1965a) reported findings indicating that patients receiving alternate sessions (even with the same number of regular sessions as the control group) not only derived no additional benefit, but actually showed less improvement than the control group on all measures of the MMPI. Those findings support the position taken by Slavson (1963). In a further evaluation of the effect of alternate sessions on time-limited group therapy with the population of 160 hospitalized patients, 80 juvenile delinquents and 80 outpatients, Truax and Wargo obtained findings for the hospital patients that confirmed the earlier (1966c) study. Moreover, the juvenile delinquents also showed therapeutic loss. However, with the outpatient population (Truax, Wargo and Carkhuff, 1966) the findings were quite different. Evidence on a variety of measures suggested that with an outpatient population, alternate sessions had moderately positive effects upon outcome. Thus, taken together, the evidence (if the findings of this latter study can be cross-validated) suggests that alternate sessions are desirable with outpatients, but inadvisable in dealing with institutionalized clients or patients.

A recent and exciting line of research initiated by Betty Berzon (1964) has focused upon the self-directed therapeutic group. Her first tentative findings from the program of research and clinical application perhaps shed further light on the use of alternate sessions in group psychotherapy. The basic notion is to provide conditions under which a therapeutic group experience will take place without the presence of a therapist. The use of leaderless "discussion" groups is an old one, but the therapeutic potential for such leaderless groups has been relatively ignored. The work of Berzon (1964) and Berzon and Solomon (1962) carefully compared self-directed and professionally directed groups; and simultaneously evaluated the influence of clients' previous therapeutic experiences on their response to the two types of groups.

In their major study of twelve eight-person groups, half the groups were composed entirely of clients with prior therapeutic experience, while half were composed of clients with no previous therapeutic experience; of these groups half participated in self-directed groups and half in professionally led groups. Additionally, all twelve groups were given vicarious therapy pretraining at the beginning of the first meeting, providing them all with the same cognitive and experiential structuring that was the same for all groups. The findings suggested that significant positive personality change (a reduction in neurotic and withdrawal behavior) occurred primarily with professionally directed groups composed of therapeutically inexperienced clients.

Using the Constructive Personality Change Index for the MMPI, there was a tendency for self-directed groups composed of therapeutically inexperienced clients to show negative change, while professionally directed groups tended to show positive change. Thus, only 22 per cent of the therapeutically inexperienced clients in self-directed groups showed positive change, compared with 78 per cent of the therapeutically inexperienced clients under professionally directed groups. When the Depth of Self-exploration Scale (Truax, 1962c) was used, the findings indicated that group members who had had prior therapeutic experience showed significantly greater self-exploration than did inexperienced group members ($p < .01$). Also, there was a significant interaction ($p < .01$) indicating that experienced group members engaged in greater self-exploration than did inexperienced group members, and that this difference was increased by the absence of a professional group leader. That is, in professionally-led groups, the effects of group members' prior therapeutic experiences were less important; but in the absence of a leader, the prior therapeutic experience of group members had major effects.

Another quite important finding from their research program concerns the levels of accurate empathy, nonpossessive warmth and genuineness communicated by group members to each other. Using the Facilitative Behavior Scale developed by Berzon, which was based upon the three specific scales developed previously by Truax, analysis of the data indicated that experienced subjects were significantly more facilitative in their behavior than therapeutically inexperienced subjects ($p < .01$). Thus, clients with prior therapeutic experience offered each other higher levels of empathy, warmth and genuineness than did inexperienced clients. This difference was significantly accentuated by the presence or absence of professional leadership—the lowest levels of empathy, warmth and genuineness occurred in the self-directed groups with inexperienced clients.

These research findings, then, seem to strongly suggest the central importance of the prior therapeutic experience of patients in determining the outcome of either professionally directed or self-directed groups. Self-directed groups may be harmful when clients have had no prior therapeutic experience, while professionally directed group experience may be most valuable for clients in therapy for the first time. In terms of the implications for the use of alternate sessions, the findings of Berzon and Solomon suggest that alternate sessions will be most therapeutically valuable for outpatients who have had considerable prior experience in counseling or psychotherapy.

SOME QUALIFICATIONS

Psychotherapy, in all of its varieties, is not a panacea. There are times when persuasion, suggestion and encouragement are indeed more therapeutic than psychotherapy or counseling that emphasizes self-exploration. Although specific evidence is lacking concerning the types of human problems in which psychotherapy may do definite harm, Glass (1954) has made an important contribution by pointing to some of the evidence concerning effective and harmful treatments of "combat fatigue" or "war neurosis." He notes that in World War I the experience was that evacuation for long-term treatment to rear area hospitals worked markedly against the patient's improvement. By the end of the war the technique of a week of rest, encouragement and persuasion in or near the combat zone was effective in producing 60 to 75 per cent "return to duty" rates. In World War II, cathartic-abreactive techniques of interviewing were used initially, with only a 15 per cent salvage rate. Later revival of the rest-and-encouragement method yielded a 50 per cent "return to combat" rate by 1943. Glass' comments are worth noting:

Indeed, any therapy including usual interview methods, that sought to uncover basic emotional conflicts or attempted to relate current behavior and symptoms with past personality patterns seemingly provided patients with logical reasons for their combat fatigue. The insights achieved by even such mild depth therapy readily convinced the patient, and often his therapist, that the limits of combat endurance had been reached as proved by vulnerable personality traits. Patients were obligingly cooperative in supplying details of their neurotic childhood, previous emotional difficulties, lack of aggressiveness and other traits." (p. 727)

The report by Glass, which deals with a particular kind of stress reaction in otherwise normal and adequate individuals, might very well suggest extreme caution on the part of the counselor or therapist in dealing with any client undergoing a "crisis" or "severe-stress" reaction. There seems to be a very real possibility that the therapist may succeed only in convincing the patient of his "sickness" or inadequacy. It may be that postpartum depression, and depression or disorganization following family upheaval, death, physical trauma, or loss of long-term employment can be aggravated rather than helped by the usual psychotherapeutic or counseling approach.

Where psychotherapy is contraindicated, the use of various psychoactive drugs or electric-stimulation therapy is often the chosen treatment. One of the main values of these procedures is that they allow a person undergoing a "crisis" or "severe-stress" reaction to weather the temporary storm. With particularly disturbed patients, such treatments have also been reported to facilitate the effectiveness of psychotherapy.

In summary, then, the attitude of conservative experimentation dominates the growth of the professional counselor or therapist. He is knowledgeable about the great variety of potential techniques and services available to the client. His personalized cosmology of therapy and life is not closed to attempts to provide whatever course of treatment will prove most effective for the client, and if he cannot provide the necessary treatment he will call upon other resources that can. In his role as an expert, he will continually seek new forms of therapeutic experience in order to develop more fully his own helping role based upon a deep and comprehensive understanding of himself, a wide range of client populations and potential treatment situations. The present viewpoint includes the use of appropriate information-giving and operant learning procedures within the context of an effective interpersonal relationship. The available research evidence suggests the therapeutic value of: (1) time limits in the relationship; (2) frequent sessions; (3) physical factors (such as the absence of desks interposed between therapist and patient); (4) both cognitive and experiential structuring of client role expectations; and (5) alternate sessions with therapist absent for outpatients, particularly therapeutically experienced ones, but not with institutionalized clients.

The evidence also suggests that with some types of psychological upset —such as "crisis" or "severe-stress" reactions—traditional psychotherapy or counseling may be contraindicated. Finally, it should be stressed that other nonpsychotherapeutic approaches to helping—such as chemotherapy or electrostimulation therapy—may be in some cases the most effective means of helping the client.

CHAPTER 15 TOWARD GUIDELINES FOR THERAPIST GROWTH IN THE THERAPEUTIC ENCOUNTER

WHEN the counselor or therapist has developed his interpersonal skills to the point where he can effectively communicate high levels of nonpossessive warmth, genuineness and accurate empathic understanding, the process of becoming an effective catalyst for constructive change in the client reaches a relatively uncharted path. He is now forced to draw heavily upon his own experiential learnings in trying out approaches and techniques advocated by the many "schools" of psychotherapy and counseling. One hopes that all these existing techniques and approaches will someday be evaluated by research aimed at determining which ones produce what changes in what kinds of clients. At the present, unfortunately, such evidence is lacking. The counselor or therapist, then, must engage in a never-ending personal attempt to try out and evaluate the therapeutic effectiveness of various techniques. He must fall back upon himself, learning to modify his own therapeutic behavior and approach by attending to what seems to produce results in his clients. Perhaps a part of the challenge and excitement of counseling and psychotherapy lies in its current stage of embryonic development which forces even the experienced therapist to be forever a student of human behavior change. From this viewpoint, a client-centered therapist who has never tried some of the specialized techniques of behavior therapy, or the Freudian analyst who has never attempted to use a client-centered approach, is a very poor student.

It has often been suggested that the therapist use his own comfort (or emotional feeling of well-being) in working with a particular technique or approach as a basic criterion for accepting or rejecting it. This assumes that if a therapist is uncomfortable or anxious in using any particular method, he will automatically be ineffective. It is probably unnecessary to point out again that the self-consciousness, the unnaturalness, and the uncomfortableness of behaving *in any new way* is itself a transient reaction which disappears with practice and reinforcement from the environment. If that criterion were used in ordinary affairs, few people would be driving automobiles, using typewriters, or even dressing themselves in the morning.

There is only one criterion for accepting or rejecting any proposed therapeutic procedure, although it has many aspects. The only possible criterion to be used is whether it actually produces positive behavioral and personality changes in a particular type of client in a given setting. Since the practicing counselor or therapist is not likely to be able to rely on solid research evidence in the immediate future, it is vitally important that he keep his own permanent records of his effectiveness with each client, with a general description of the approach and methods used. Unfortunately, this is all too rare. As Freud, and more recently a series of research studies, have shown, retrospective guesses five or ten years from now are not likely to be reliable or useful in guiding the individual practitioner. Keeping records and making strong attempts to assess effectiveness with each client does involve the risk that the therapist will discover that, on the average, he is not helpful, or, even worse, is actually harmful. However difficult such a discovery might be to accept personally, it would still be better to discover it early.

The therapist might also gain important guidelines for his own development by writing down a brief statement about the client's goals and his own goals for each case, and then mailing it to the client one month after therapy termination for an assessment of outcome. Such a procedure would give him a crude guideline by which to judge his own effectiveness and plan his own professional learning and growth. Although one goal of counselors and therapists is to make the client more satisfied with his current existence, and to ease his anxiety or depression, it must be remembered that these kinds of changes are demonstrably induced by placebos—inert substances. Placebos can be quite helpful, but few therapists or counselors would choose a life-long career as one—even as an *effective* one. In view of the available evidence suggesting that on the average psychotherapy and counseling is not superior to no-treatment controls (see Chapter 1), it must be suspected that a number of "experienced" counselors and therapists could not be described as being even as helpful as a placebo; instead they might more aptly be described as psychonoxious or destructive in spite of their professed intention to be helpful. The important point for counselors and therapists is recognizing that those "experienced" counselors and therapists who are in fact damaging do not know it: they think they are helpful.

To repeat, one fairly certain way of ensuring that we ourselves are neither professional placebos nor psychonoxious, is to collect information on outcome for each and every client we see. If we aim toward becoming effective counselors or therapists then we will want to know at each point in our own development the behavioral effects that we have on our all too human clients.

That we cannot depend on our own clinical impressions to assess our effectiveness is indicated not only by the evidence, but also by several lines of argument. Meehl (1955) says in considering the question of effectiveness of psychotherapy or counseling:

I cannot agree with those who consider this a foolish question or who feel little need to meet such challenges as Eysenck's. The history of the healing arts furnishes ample grounds for skepticism as to our non-systematic "clinical observations." Most of our older relatives had their teeth extracted because it was "known" in the 1920's that the clearing up of occult focal infections improved arthritis and other disorders. No doubt the physicians who treated our ancestors by venesection had "observed" many "cures" in longitudinal study of their patients. Like all therapists, we personally experience an utter inability not to believe we effect results in individual cases; but as a psychologist we know it is foolish to take this conviction at face value. In order to bring about the needed research, it will probably be necessary for therapists and administrators to get really clear on this point: our daily therapeutic experiences, which (on good days!) make it hard for us to take Eysenck seriously, can be explained within a crude statistical model of the patient-therapist population that assigns very little specific "power" to therapeutic intervention. If the majority of neurotics are in "unstable equilibrium" and hence tend to improve under moderately favorable regimes, those who are in therapy while improving will be talking about their current actions and feelings in the sessions. Client and therapist will naturally attribute changes to the therapy. Furthermore, neurosis often shows cyclical fluctuations, and upswing terminators will be perceived as "successful," since therapists do not automatically find out when cases relapse or enter therapy with someone else. How will such a statistical system be experienced by therapists? Very much as therapy admittedly appears to its candid practitioners. The best cases are types which seem most likely to improve anyhow. Sometimes there are temporal associations between improvement and interview events of the kind considered important, at other times such co-variation is disconcertedly lacking. The therapist gradually conceptualizes the client, but there seems to be no clear cut connection between the client's learning of this conceptualization and outcome. (pp. 373-374)

Add to this the placebo effect of simply "getting attention" and the natural reluctance of clients to admit that their time and their money have been wasted, and it becomes difficult indeed to use clinical impressions as guidelines for our own effectiveness.

A TENTATIVE MOMENT-BY-MOMENT GUIDELINE FOR THERAPIST GROWTH

The only certain guideline for the therapist's personal growth lies in his differential effectiveness with clients—but in terms of *observable client changes* the beginning trainee will be seeing so few patients that such a criterion would be not immediately useful. Further, in long-term treatment involving many therapist behaviors, client changes cannot be connected with any degree of certainty to specific therapist actions. A relatively large body of evidence, reviewed in an earlier chapter, has suggested that the client's degree or depth of self-exploration is positively associated with therapeutic outcome or behavior change, and so the moment-by-moment level of self-exploration engaged in by the client can be used as a crude intermediary guideline for the counselor's assessment of his effectiveness (see Self-Exploration Scale in Chapter 5). That is, the beginning therapist can "shape" his own behavior by attending to the depth of the client's self-exploration: those responses that enhance client self-exploration can be practiced and refined, and those that lead to less client self-exploration can be dropped from his therapeutic repertoire.

For this purpose, the depth of self-exploration scale was used in the training program in much the same way as the research scales dealing with the therapeutic conditions. The beginning counselors or therapists were trained in the use of the self-exploration scale; after learning to discriminate scale values they practiced applying them to tape-recorded excerpts of clients with experienced therapists; they then practiced rating on the scale using samples taken from their own role-playing and from individual counseling interviews.

After achieving relatively high skill in identifying levels of patient self-exploration, the beginning trainee can use the scale as a guideline to his own development as a counselor. Depth of self-exploration in the client, then, becomes a momentary subgoal throughout the process of psychotherapy.

Considerable caution, however, should be used in making the client's depth of self-exploration a major subgoal. First, although it is the only patient in-therapy behavior shown clearly by research to relate to outcome at all, its relationship to outcome is only moderate. There is no one-to-one relationship between outcome and level of client self-exploration. It is a *rough* guide. Second, we know that in some instances the efficacy of client depth of self-exploration may be qualified—as, for example, by the client populations involved in interaction with particular therapists and environments, as in some studies of therapy with juvenile delinquents (Truax and Wargo, 1966b). A third caution derives from the possibility that the beginning trainee might become so concerned with wanting the patient to engage in a high level of self-exploration, that he is less able to be therapeutically effective.

This possibility of becoming overconcerned with the client's depth of self-exploration is illustrated in the following excerpt taken from a discussion late in the training course:

The More I Want It the Less I Get It . . .

Tod: You've *got* to see members of your counseling group getting better. And if you don't see this; something happens, well, this is what I'm experiencing now. That sort of bothers me.

Dot: What's that?

Tod: It bothers me.

Dot: What do you mean?

Tod: Well, ah . . . you have an image of yourself as *competent*, being able to help, and you should be able to see some improvement.

Dr. T: So that in patients, you're saying you want to see some growth.

Tod: Yeah. Some sort, that I really, ah, I really have a sense of failure . . . And I really can't see the unconditionality about the way I feel toward them because I don't, I have an investment in how deep their self-exploration is.

Dr. T: Um hmm.

Tod: I want lots of deep self-exploration. Whenever there's resistance too strong there, I get angry. The more I get angry, the less . . .

Dr. T: The less the patient is able to deeply explore himself.

Tod: The less *possibility* for this.

Dot: Hard to wait isn't it?

Tod: Pardon?

Dot: Kind of hard to wait. You have faith that this will come about, but . . .

Al: This depth of self-exploration in the client.

Tod: Here's the thing that really scares me. Like, one of the patients, Joe for example; there have been times in the past where I'll work for a good solid 45 minutes almost exclusively feeling this guy out and so, in that 45 minutes he's talking and I really am giving forth, but, the next hour, seems like nothing ever happened! After going through that a number of times, I do still like him, but . . . I sort of wonder, I was talking to John about such a thing. You can't let them be sick! That's their choice! They can be sick if they want to. They, they don't see themselves as being in any way, being in any way better off than they are right now. They just ah, they come in and then go to sleep. We talk to one, four go to sleep. We talk to one of those and the other four go to sleep. Some *group* counseling.

Dr. T: That's probably the most comforting rationalization.

Tod: What's that?

Dr. T: They have a right to be sick.

Sam: Well, I think what he's saying is that if you don't try so hard you, yourself, will feel better toward them, and they themselves will then have the choice to make, which they can make themselves. You can't make the choice for them. I think that's what he's saying.

Jim: This is what Dr. L. always says, he says don't become involved. And I know what he means by becoming involved. You kind of, like, he *assumes* he's always doing the best he knows how and ah, if nothing happens, it's not *his* fault, *he's done his part.*

Dr. T: You could also assume that he's stupid. I guess my feeling is this, I hope I am never willing to say that the fault is in the client, because that's how he came to me and I could have said that without ever seeing him. I do have some kind of obligation to try to search out why I am not as facilitative as I am trying to be.

Tod: I can see, you know, tightening up, you know the switch-over from "you can be the way you want to be" to "God damn," you know, "what a poor spot to be in."

Dr. T: You're feeling one of those feelings?

Tod: Both, I guess. Though, it's not in the context of that. It's anger building up in me, frustration.

Dot: How do you feel toward the rest of the clients in the counseling group, ah, if they don't care any more about their problems than to just sit there?

Tod: Well, this is about three-fourths of the groups, always exactly the same ones. See, we've got, right now we've got, two have gone, so there are six. But there are only two that will really talk, without, without you know, just *pulling* it out of them.

Dr. T: I guess then the question is, you know, "What kinds of things could I do to make these people more able to talk in this setting?"

Tod: Yeah.

Dr. T: This is part of why the counselor is there. If they were energetically exploring and doing all of these wonderful things, why would they need a counselor in the first place?

Tod: Right.

Dr. T: I guess I react terribly strongly to therapists who say "it's a 'bad' patient" when they're supposed to be helping "bad" patients. That's why they were there. If the clients were helping, and were fully functioning, they'd probably be helping the therapist. (Laughter)

Sam: There's another aspect to this though, that ah, when the therapist assumes that he's doing the best job he can that doesn't mean . . . he's effective. That means he's certainly aware of his limitations and that probably he'll never be a perfect therapist. He's facing reality that there is a maximum level which he can attain.

Dr. T: Um hmm.

Sam: Like there's a maximum level at which he can operate right now.

Dr. T: Perhaps when that happens you're . . .

Sam: No, I mean as an effective therapist. I think . . .

Dr. T: I think I have almost never done the best I could. This isn't upsetting to me. I can probably accept what I *do* do, but it strikes me as a real rationalization, an outright forgery, that it's better for me to say that "I'm doing the best that I could do."

The internal and external conflicts are apparent; the guidelines are provisional at best. However, they offer us the potential means to organize and integrate our current experience, and in a very real sense will guide the search for more conclusive evidence.

One puzzling concomitant of increasing experience is the frequency with which experienced therapists become less sensitive (rather than more sensitive) to feedback from patients. The finding by Strupp and his coworkers (1963) that more experienced therapists are more likely to have and express negative attitudes toward patients is indeed sobering. It might prove useful for the client (and it would certainly be useful for the therapist) if he were encouraged to express his reactions to the therapist in each and every session. In such an atmosphere, the client and the therapist could provide mutual feedback focusing on those moments when the client himself felt most deeply understood or misunderstood, most deeply accepted or unaccepted, and most deeply in or out of contact with the therapist.

Such feedback for both client and therapist is perhaps most dramatic in group therapy where consensual validation or invalidation can occur routinely.

Most therapists have heard themselves on audiotape recordings and have had a chance to learn something about how they sound to others; all too few have had an opportunity to find out how they look to others in therapy. For those experienced counselors and beginning therapists who have never seen themselves on videotape or film, placing a full-length mirror in the room might prove quite revealing. Since part of the therapist's effectiveness depends on nonverbal communications, visual feedback of behavioral communication patterns in either of these ways should be a part of every therapist's learning experience. All too often, the therapist will discover that while his feelings and even his voice are genuine, the mirror reflects posing, a stilted posturing that makes him seem to be a mannequin rather than a helping person.

Another potentially useful approach for the therapist's understanding the consequences of his own therapeutic behavior is routinely requesting all clients or patients to analyze their subjective reactions after the termination of the relationship. The client can be asked to mail to the therapist his own brief subjective account of those moments that were most meaningful—both the helpful and hurtful moments. Such posttherapy subjective accounts by the client, though perhaps somewhat distorted, offer a meaningful learning experience to any therapist or counselor. The authors, in reading such accounts from their own clients, have learned something new about themselves from almost every patient. As we might expect, such accounts by the client himself rarely focus on those occasional moments of important insight (which therapists tend to value so highly) but instead, upon the more intensely personal moments where deep caring or love is expressed or rejection is communicated by a silence that was intended to be helpful.

RESEARCH FINDINGS AS GUIDELINES

Although this book has used many research findings as guidelines, the research findings on therapeutic ingredients themselves still require further questions. Several major research projects now underway at the Arkansas Rehabilitation Research and Training Center, University of Arkansas (Fayetteville), are aimed not only at further cross-validating the present findings on larger populations of experienced counselors, therapists, and trainees, but also at refining measurements of the therapeutic conditions and determining their most effective use. Beyond this, other studies are aimed at analyses from behavioristic, learning theory, and reinforcement viewpoints. Answers breed further questions in research, in training, and in practice. Just as with the researcher, the counselor or therapist who is not guided by the evidence toward further questioning moves toward a closed and immature existence.

To be most useful, research must now become more specific—and be related to indices of patient outcome. It must focus on the kinds of things that a therapist can do that are helpful, that are irrelevant, that are harmful.

Unfortunately, research findings to date have had relatively little impact upon the practice of counseling and psychotherapy. In part this is due to the slowness with which research results find their way into clinical writings. Probably more important, it is due to the language barriers that separate the researcher from the clinician. The researcher seems to talk about numbers, levels of statistical significance, procedures and, *occasionally,* concepts; the practitioner is concerned about people. Given this state of affairs, the practitioner must learn to translate the researcher's dry and often artificial reports into the general meanings that can be applied to the therapeutic encounter. The researcher also bears some responsibility for his lack of impact, for too often his questions are irrelevant and his answers given in terms of measures of client change that are not meaningful even for the therapist, much less the client.

A large part of the lack of impact of past research arises from the fundamental characteristics of the whole field of psychotherapy and counseling research.

The subject matter or substance of the majority of research is highly idiosyncratic. The chaos of labels and concepts that are used even in only one or two studies is striking. With the exception of the main lines of evidence traced in this book, the outcome and even process studies of the therapeutic encounter are seldom, if ever, replicated. Each investigator has his own favorite variable which is studied in one or a few contexts and then dropped. Beyond this, the same label may be used with radically different meanings in studies of operationally different concepts. Thus, "empathy" has been used to label the diagnostic skill with which a therapist can predict a patient's answers on a personality test. The reverse side of this is that we might not use the findings of such studies in attempting to understand the "accuracy of diagnostic skill" phenomena.

The result is that there is very little real accumulation of systematic knowledge. When thirty or one hundred or more concepts are studied in attempts to predict what kind of patients lead to what kind of therapeutic outcome, with few systematic replications and extensions of positive findings, we cannot claim that scientific knowledge has been accumulated. This has been true of counseling and psychotherapy research too often in the past. The future, however, gives promise of more systematic programs of research that will lead to the development of a scientific body of knowledge rather than the mere accumulation of unrelated bits and scraps of ungeneralizable "facts."

Research can provide the therapist with objective, if indirect, feedback that allows him to evaluate his effects on clients. Research can provide a corrective tool for guiding the therapist's growth.

THE ROLE OF CLINICAL WRITINGS AND RESEARCH FINDINGS IN FORMULATING PERSONAL HYPOTHESES

Although the therapist or counselor must inevitably fall back upon his own learnings and evaluation of what works most successfully for him, he will also draw heavily upon both clinical writings and research findings to form personal hypotheses about what might be effective with his clients and his own personality. In recognition of this fact, good training programs require the beginning student to read, both broadly and intensively, in the many divergent theoretic views currently in existence. This probably becomes even more important after the beginning therapist has acquired clinical experience.

As the therapist matures in experience and capacity, probably the greatest obstacle to continued broad reading is the semantic problems that arise from the specialized jargon associated with most viewpoints in counseling and psychotherapy. Unfortunately, a therapist has little chance of understanding the ideas unless he, to some degree, speaks the language. To make use of divergent clinical writings he must first learn to "translate" the language of a writer with a different viewpoint into the language he speaks and understands. The rational-emotive therapist talks of a client's "beliefs,"; the client-centered therapist speaks of his "feelings" or "personal growth"; the Jungian therapist speaks of "ego-consciousness"; the Freudian speaks of the client's "libidinal cathexis"; the behavior therapist speaks of the client's "avoidance response"; and the Wolpian therapist speaks of the client's "anxiety response"—yet all their statements are meaningless unless the therapist can first translate those words into his experience of the very human client with whom he shares the therapeutic enterprise. Only by such crucial translation can hypotheses be gained from readings for personal testing in therapeutic contacts. And only by such personal translations can the therapist hope to avoid the built-in prejudices that are apt to lead him to reject ideas and therapeutic approaches simply because he dislikes the writer's language.

Another important source or resource for personal growth is the short (three- or five-day) "workshop" or "conference." Large conferences or professional association meetings provide a stimulation of ideas, but the human encounters in small group workshops or conferences provide the stimulation both of ideas and of the experiences which can translate ideas into personal practices.

CONCLUDING REMARKS

The single thread of thought and feeling that binds this book into a whole is this: *counseling and psychotherapy as commonly practiced are not highly effective, but can be extremely powerful in reshaping the existence of troubled man.* Some therapists are helpful, others are not.

As practitioners, teachers and researchers dedicated to our fellow man's individual welfare—his happiness, productiveness, and joy in "being"—we have often not been helpful. In part, this is because we have been enamored of the process and not looked closely at the product. We have often been fascinated with the client's internal dynamics and deservedly pleased with our own ability to conceptualize them, but have sometimes been sidetracked by dynamics fiom the goal of the therapeutic enterprise—constructive, observable, measurable, and significant positive changes in the client.

We are approaching the point in the development of our field where we will no longer tolerate—even in ourselves, much less in clinics, hospitals and agencies—a failure to keep objective and adequate detailed records of each therapist's effects on patients. We are approaching the point where the laissez-faire attitude that allows many nontherapeutic practices under the name of therapy will no longer be tolerated. We are approaching the point where mere *theoretic* reasons for a given therapeutic practice will no longer be acceptable—it will have to do more than "sound" effective before it is incorporated into practice. We are at the point where clinical testimonials or case reports are no longer acceptable bases for adopting new approaches to counseling and psychotherapy. In short, as a field we are growing up. As we focus more upon outcome, we require evidence of *better outcome* before we adopt new techniques or approaches.

We are rapidly approaching the time when the counselor's and therapist's attempts to help will be based upon solid research knowledge—remaining at the same time objective and deeply personal—rather than merely upon theory or clinical experience. Today the available research evidence of "what works" is only a small beginning—tomorrow will be busy and exciting.

REFERENCES

ADAMS, S. Interaction between individual interview therapy and treatment amenability in older youth authority wards. In *Monograph No. 2,* Board of Corrections, State of California, 1961, 27-44.

ADAMS, W. R. The psychiatrist in an ambulatory clerkship for comprehensive medical care in a new curriculum. *J. med. Educ.,* 1958, *33,* 211-220.

———, HAM, T. H., MAWARDI, BETTY H., SCALI, H. A., and WEISMAN, R. A naturalistic study of teaching in a clinical clerkship. *J. med. Educ.,* 1964, *39,* 164-174.

ALBRONDA, H. F., DEAN, R. L. and STARKWEATHER, J. A. Social class and psychotherapy. *A.M.A. Arch. gen. Psychiat.,* 1964, *10,* 276-283.

ANKER, J. M. and WALSH, R. P. Group psychotherapy, a special activity program, and group structure in the treatment of chronic schizophrenia. *J. consult. Psychol.,* 1961, *25,* 476-481.

APPLEBY, L. Evaluation of treatment methods for chronic schizophrenia. *Arch. gen. Psychiat.,* 1963, *8,* 8-21.

ARBUCKLE, D. S. Client perception of counselor personality. *J. counsel Psychol.,* 1956, *3,* 93-96.

———. The learning of counseling: Process not product. *J. Counsel. Psychol.,* 1963, *10,* 163-168.

ARIETI, S. Introductory notes on the psychoanalytic therapy of schizophrenics. A. Burton (Ed.), *In Psychotherapy of the psychoses.* New York: Basic Books, 1961.

ARING, C. D. Neurological precepts. *Arch. of Neurology,* 1961, *4,* 587-589.

ARNHOFF, F. N. Some factors influencing the unreliability of clinical judgments. *J. Clin. Psychol.,* 1954, *10,* 272-275.

ASHBY, J. D., FORD, D. H., GUERNEY, B. G., and GUERNEY, LOUISE F. Effects on clients of a reflective and a leading type of psychotherapy. *Psychol. Monogr.,* 1957, *71,* 24 (Whole No. 453).

ASPY, D. N. A study of three facilitative conditions and their relationships to the achievement of third grade students. Unpublished doctoral dissertation, University of Kentucky, 1965.

——— and HADLOCK, W. The effect of empathy warmth and genuineness on elementary students' reading achievement. Unpublished thesis, University of Florida, 1966.

AYLLON, T. Some behavioral problems associated with eating in chronic schizophrenic patients. Paper read at Amer. Psychol. Assoc., Chicago, September 1960.

——— and HAUGTON, E. Control of the behavior of schizophrenic patients by food. *J. exp. anal. Behav.,* 1962, *5,* 343-352.

——— and MICHAEL J. The psychiatric nurse as a behavioral engineer. *J. exp. anal. Behav.,* 1959, *2,* 323-334.

Baldwin, T. and Lee, Joan. Evaluation of programmed instruction in human relations. *Amer. Psychologist,* 1965, *20,* 489. (Abstract)

Bandura, A. Psychotherapists' anxiety level, self-insight, and psychotherapeutic competence. *J. abnorm. soc. Psychol.,* 1956, *52,* 333-337.

———. Psychotherapy as a learning process. *Psychol. Bull.,* 1961, *58,* 143-159.

———. Social learning through imitation. In M. R. Jones (Ed.), *Nebraska symposium on motivation.* Lincoln, Neb.: University of Nebraska Press, 1962. Pp. 211-269.

———. Psychotherapy conceptualized as a social learing process. Centennial Psychotherapy Symposium and Workshop, University of Kentucky, April 1965. (a)

———. Behavioral modification through modeling procedures. In L. Krasner and L. P. Ullmann (Eds.), *Research in behavior modification.* New York: Holt, Rinehart and Winston, 1965. (b)

———. Influence of models' reinforcement contingencies on the acquisition of imitative responses. *J. pers. soc. Psychol.,* 1965, *1,* 589-595. (c)

——— and Kupers, J. Transmission of patterns of self-reinforcement through modeling. *J. abnorm. soc. Psychol.,* 1964, *69,* 1-9.

——— and McDonald, F. J. The influence of social reinforcement and the behavior of models in shaping children's moral judgments. *J. abnorm. soc. Psychol.,* 1963, *67,* 274-281.

Banks, G., Berenson, B. G. and Carkhuff, R. R. The effects of counselor race and training upon counseling process with Negro clients in initial interviews. *J. clin. Psychol.,* in press, 1966.

Barendregt, J. T. A psychological investigation of the effects of psychoanalysis and psychotherapy. In Barendregt, J. T. (Ed.), *Research in psychodiagnostics.* Paris: Mouton, 1961.

Barrett-Lennnard, G. T. Dimensions of the client's experience of his therapist associated with personality change. *Genet. Psychol. Monogr.,* 1962, *76,* No. 43.

Barron, F. An ego-strength scale which predicts response to psychotherapy. *J. consult. Psychol.,* 1953, *17,* 327-333.

——— and Leary, T. Changes in psychoneurotic patients with and without psychotherapy, *J. consult. Psychol.,* 1955, *19,* 239-245.

Bateson, G., Jackson, D. H., Jr., and Weakland, J. H. Toward a theory of schizophrenia. *Behavioral Science,* 1956, *1,* 251-264.

Baumeister, A. Application of reinforcement principles to toilet training of the severely retarded. Psychotherapy Symposium, Midwest. Psychol. Assoc., Chicago, April 1965.

Baymurr, F. B. and Patterson, C. H. A comparison of three methods of assisting underachieving high school students. *J. counsel. Psychol.,* 1960, *7,* 83-89.

Baxter, J. C., Becker, J., and Hooks, W. Defensive style in the families of schizophrenics and controls. *J. abnorm. soc. Psychol.,* 1963, *66,* 512-518.

Berenson, B. G., Carkhuff, R. R. and Myrus, Pamela. The interpersonal functions and training of college students. *J. counsel. Psychol.,* 1966, *13,* 4.

Bergin, A. E. The effects of psychotherapy: Negative results revisited. *J. counsel. Psychol.,* 1963, *10,* 244-250.

——— and Solomon, Sandra. Personality and performance correlates of empathic understanding in psychotherapy. Paper read at Amer. Psychol. Assoc., Philadelphia, September 1963.

BERKOWITZ, L. Group standards, cohesiveness, and productivity. HUMAN RELATIONS, 1954, 7, 509-519.

———. *Aggression: A social psychological analysis.* New York: McGraw-Hill, 1962.

———. Aggressive cues in aggressive behavior and hostility catharsis. *Psychol. Rev.*, 1964, *71*, 104-122.

BERLIN, J. I. and WYCKOFF, L. B. Human relations training through dyadic programmed instruction. Paper read at Amer. Pers. and Guidance Assoc., 1964.

BERZON, BETTY. The self-directed therapeutic group: An evaluative study. Paper read at Amer. Psychol. Assoc., Chicago, 1964.

——— and SOLOMON, L. N. The self-directed therapeutic group: An exploratory study. In *Western Behavioral Sciences Institute Report,* 1962. *Int. J. Group Psychother.*, 1964, *14*, 366-369.

BETZ, BARBARA J. Bases of therapeutic leadership in psychotherapy with the schizophrenic patient. *Amer. J. Psychother.*, 1963, *17*, 196-212. (a)

———. Differential success rates of psychotherapists with "process" and "non-process" schizophrenic patients. *Amer. J. Psychiat.*, 1963, *11*, 1090-1091. (b)

BISHOP, B. M. Mother-child interaction and the social behavior of children. *Psychol. Monogr.*, 1951, *65*, 328.

BLACK, J. D. Common factors of the patient-therapist relationship in diverse psychotherapy. *J. clin. Psychol.*, 1952, *8*, 302-306.

BLAU, B. A. A comparison of more improved with less improved clients treated by client-centered methods. In W. U. Snyder (Ed.), *Group report of a program of research in psychotherapy.* State College, Pa.: Pennsylvania State College, Psychotherapy Research Group, 1953.

BLOCKSMA, D. D. and PORTER, E. H. JR. A short-term training program in client-centered counseling. *J. consult. Psychol.*, 1947, *11*, 55-60.

BOARD, F. A. Patients' and physicians' judgments of outcome of psychotherapy in an outpatient clinic. *AMA Arch. gen. Psychiat.*, 1959, *1*, 185-196.

BOEHM, W. Social work: Science and art. *Social serv. Rev.*, 1961, *35*, 144-151.

BORDIN, E. S. *Psychological counseling.* New York: Appleton-Century-Crofts, 1955.

BOSS, M. *Psychoanalyse and Daseinsanalytik,* 1955, *11*, 5.

BOWEN, M. A family concept of schizophrenia. In D. Jackson (Ed.), *The etiology of schizophrenics.* New York: Basic Books, 1960. Pp. 346-372.

BRAATEN, L. J. The movement from non-self to self in client-centered psychotherapy. Unpublished doctoral dissertation, University of Chicago, 1958.

BRAMMER, L. M. and SHOSTROM, E. L. *Therapeutic psychology: Fundamentals of counseling and psychotherapy.* Englewood Cliffs, N.J.: Prentice-Hall, 1964.

BREGER, L. and MCGAUGH, J. L. Critique and reformulation of "learning theory" approaches to psychotherapy and neurosis. *Psychol. Bull.*, 1965, *63*, 338-357.

BRILL, N. Q. and BEEBE, G. W. A follow-up study of war neuroses. *V. A. medical Monogr.*, Washington, D. C.: Veterans Administration, 1955.

BROEDEL, J., OHLSEN, M., PROFF, F., and SOUTHARD, C. The effects of group counseling on gifted underachieving adolescents. *J. counsel Psychol.*, 1960, *7*, 163-170.

BUBER, M. Distance and relation. *Psychiatry*, 1953, *16*, 104.

———. *I and thou.* New York: Charles Scribner's Sons, 1958.

BURNHAM, D. Autonomy and activity—passivity in the psychotherapy of a schizophrenic. In A. Burton (Ed.), *Psychotherapy of the psychoses.* New York: Basic Books, 1961.

BUTLER, J. M. Self-concept change in psychotherapy. *Counseling Center Discussion Papers,* Univer. of Chicago, 1960, *6* (13), 1-27.

CABEEN, C. W. and COLEMAN, J. C. The selection of sex offender patients for group psychotherapy. *Int. J. Group Psychother.*, 1962, *12*, 326-334.

CAMERON, N. *Personality development and psychotherapy: A dynamic approach.* Boston: Houghton Mifflin Co., 1963.

CAMPBELL, D. P. Achievements of counseled and non-counseled students twenty-five years after counseling. *J. counsel. Psychol.*, 1965, *12*, 287-293.

CARKHUFF, R. R. and DEBURGER, R. Gross ratings of patient behavior. Unpublished manuscript, University of Kentucky, 1964.

———, FELDMAN, M. J., and TRUAX, C. B. Age and role reversal in therapy. *J. clin. Psychol.*, 1964, *20*, 398-402.

——— and TRUAX, C. B. Training in counseling and psychotherapy: An evaluation of an integrated didactic and experiential approach. *J. consult. Psychol.*, 1965, *29*, 333-336. (a)

——— ———. Lay mental health counseling: the effects of lay group counseling. *J. consult. Psychol.*, 1965, *29*, 426-431. (b)

——— ———. Toward explaining success or failure in interpersonal learning experiences. *Personnel guid. J.*, 1966, *44*, 7, 723-728.

CARTWRIGHT, ROSALIND D. The effects of psychotherapy: A replication and extension. *J. consult. Psychol.*, 1961, *25*, 376-382.

——— and LERNER, BARBARA. Empathy: Need to change and improvement with psychotherapy. *J. consult. Psychol.*, 1963, *27*, 138-144.

——— and VOGEL, J. L. A comparison of changes in psychoneurotic patients during matched periods of therapy and no therapy. *J. consult. Psychol.*, 1960, *24*, 121-127.

CASS, L. K. Parent-child relationships and delinquency. *J. abnorm. soc. Psychol.*, 1952, *47*, 101-104.

CHOROST, S. B. Parental child-rearing attitudes and their correlates in adolescent hostility. *Genet. Psychol. Monogr.*, 1962, *66* (1), 49-90.

CHRISTENSEN, C. M. Relationships between pupil achievement, pupil affect-need, teacher warmth and teacher permissiveness. *J. educ. Psychol.*, 1960, *51*, 169-174.

COLEMAN, J. V. The teaching of basic psychotherapy. *Amer. J. Orthopsychiat.*, 1947, *17*, 622-627.

COMBS, A. W. and SOPER, D. W. The perceptual organization of effective counselors. *J. counsel. Psychol.*, 1963, *10*, 222-226.

CRIDER, B. Psychotherapy in a case of obesity. *J. clin. Psychol.*, 1946, *2*, 50-58.

DARLEY, J. G., et al. Studies of group behavior. *J. abnorm. soc. Psychol.*, 1951, *46*, 564-576.

DEMOS, G. D. The application of certain principles of client-centered therapy to short-term vocational-educational counseling. *J. counsel. Psychol.*, 1964, *11*, 280-294.

——— and ZUWAYLIF, F. H. Counselor movement as a result of an intensive six-week training program in counseling. *Personnel guid. J.*, 1963, *42*, 125-128.

DESHARMES, R. LEVY, J., and WERTHEIMER, M. A note on attempted evaluations of psychotherapy. *J. clin. Psychol.*, 1954, *10*, 233-235.

DICKENSON, W. A. Therapist self-disclosure as a variable in psychotherapeutic process and outcome. Unpublished doctoral dissertation, University of Kentucky, 1965.

——— and TRUAX, C. B. Group counseling with college underachievers: Comparisons with a control group and relationship to empathy, warmth and genuineness. *Personnel guid. J.*, in press, 1966.

DINOFF, M., RICKARD, H. C., SALZBERG, H. and SIPPRELLE, C. N. An experimental analogue of three psychotherapeutic approaches. *J. clin. Psychol.*, 1960, *16*, 70-73.

DISKIN, P. A study of predictive empathy and the ability of student teachers to maintain harmonious interpersonal relations in selected elementary classrooms. *Dissertation abstracts*, 1956, *16*, 1399.

DITTES, J. E. Extinction during psychotherapy of GSR accompanying "embarrassing" statements. *J. abnorm. soc. Psychol.*, 1957, *55*, 187-191. (a)

———. Galvanic skin responses as a measure of patient's reaction to therapist permissiveness. *J. abnorm. soc. Psychol.*, 1957, *55*, 295-303. (b)

DOLLARD, J. and MILLER, N. E. *Personality and psychotherapy*. New York: McGraw-Hill, 1950.

DRASPA, L. J., Psychological factors in muscular pain. *Brit. J. Psychiat.*, 1959, *32*, 106-116.

DUGAN, W. E. The impact of N.D.E.A. upon counselor preparation. *Personnel guid. J.*, 1960, *39*, 37-40.

DULANY, D. E. Hypotheses and habits in verbal "operant conditioning." *J. abnorm. soc. Psychol.*, 1961, *63*, 251-263.

EISENBERG, L. and KANNER, L. Early infantile autism: 1943-1955. *Amer. J. Ortho-psychiat.*, 1956, *26*, 556-566.

EKSTEIN, R. and WALLERSTEIN, R. S. *The teaching and learning of psychotherapy*. New York: Basic Books, 1958.

ELLIS, A. Comment on Rogers' necessary and sufficient conditions. *J. consult. Psychol.*, 1957, *21*, 104.

ELLIS, N. R., BARNETT, C. D., and PRYOR, M. W. Operant behavior in mental defectives: Exploratory studies. *J. exp. anal. Behav.*, 1960, *3*, 63-69.

ENDS, E. J. and PAGE, C. W. A study of three types of group psychotherapy with hospitalized inebriates. *Quart. J. stud. Alcohol.*, 1957, *18*, 263-277.

ENELOW, A. J., ADLER, L. M., and MANNING, P. R. A supervised psychotherapy course for practicing physicians. *J. med. Educ.*, 1964, *39*, 140-146.

ENGLISH, O. S. *Emotional problems of living*. New York: W. W. Norton, 1945.

ERIKSON, C. W. (Ed.) *Behavior and awareness: A symposium of research and interpretation*. Durham, N. C.: Duke University Press, 1962.

EYSENCK, H. J. The effects of psychotherapy: An evaluation. *J. consult. Psychol.*, 1952, *16*, 319-324.

———. The effects of psychotherapy: A reply. *J. abnorm. soc. Psychol.*, 1955, *50*, 147-148.

———. (Ed.) *Behavior therapy and the neuroses.* New York: Pergamon Press, 1960.

———. (Ed.) The effects of psychotherapy. In H. J. Eysenck *Handbook of abnormal psychology.* New York: Basic Books, 1961.

FARBER, I. E. The things people say to themselves. *Amer. Psychologist,* 1963, *18,* 185-197.

FEIFEL, H. and EELLS, JANET. Patients and therapists assess the same psychotherapy. *J. consult. Psychol.,* 1963, *27,* 310-318.

FELDMAN, M. J. and CARKHUFF, R. R. *Role conflicts of beginning therapists.* Buffalo, N. Y.: Psychol. Educ. Tapes, 1963.

FERENCZI, S. Further contributions to the theory and technique of psychoanalysis. (Translated by J. Suttie and others.) *Int. Psychoanal. Libr., 11.* London: Hogarth Press, 1927.

FEY, W. F. Acceptance by others and its relation to acceptance of self and others: A reeavluation. *J. abnorm. soc. Psychol.,* 1955, *50,* 274-276.

———. Doctrine and experience: Their influence upon the psychotherapist. *J. consult. Psychol.,* 1958, *22,* 403-409.

FIEDLER, F. E. The concept of an ideal therapeutic relationship. *J. consult. Psychol.,* 1950, *14,* 339-345.

———. Comparison of therapeutic relationships in psychoanalytic, non-directive and Adlerian therapy. *J. consult. Psychol.,* 1951, *14,* 436-445.

——— and SENIOR, KATE. An exploratory study of unconscious feeling reactions in 15 patient-therapist pairs. *J. abnorm. soc. Psychol.,* 1952, *47,* 446-453.

FLEMING, JOAN. The role of supervision in psychiatric training. *Bull. Menninger Clin.,* 1953, *17,* 157-169.

——— and BENEDEK, THERESE. Supervision: A method of teaching psychoanalysis. *Psychoanalyt. Quart.,* 1964, *33,* 71-96.

——— and HAMBURG, D. A. An analysis of methods for teaching psychotherapy with description of a new approach. *A.M.A. Arch. Neurol. Psychiat.,* 1958, *79,* 179-200.

FLEISS, R. The metapsychology of the analyst. *Psychol. Quart., 11,* 1942.

FLINT, A. A. and RIOCH, MARGARET, J. An experiment in teaching family dynamics. *Amer. J. Psychiat.,* 1963, *119,* 940-944.

FOSSETT, KATHRINE. Guidance institutes—N.D.E.A. *Personnel guid. J.,* 1960, *39,* 207-209.

FRANK, J. D. *Persuasion and healing.* Baltimore: Johns Hopkins Press, 1961.

———. The role of hope in psychotherapy. Paper read at Kentucky Centennial Psychotherapy Symposium, University of Kentucky, 1965.

———, GLIEDMAN, L. H., IMBER, S. D., STONE, A. R., and NASH, E. H., JR. Patient's expectancies and relearning as factors determining improvement in psychotherapy. *Amer. J. Psychiat.,* 1959, *115,* 961-968.

———, NASH, E. H., STONE, A. R., and IMBER, S. D. Immediate and long-term symptomatic course of psychiatric outpatients. *Amer. J. Psychiat.,* 1963, *120,* 429-439.

FRAZEE, H E. Children who later become schizophrenic. *Smith College Stud. Social Work,* 1953, *23,* 125-149.

FREEMAN, R. V. and GRAYSON, H. M. Maternal attitudes in schizophrenia. *J. abnorm. soc. Psychol.,* 1955, *50,* 45-52.

FREEMAN, T., CAMERON, J. L. and MCGHIE, A. *Chronic schizophrenia.* New York: Int. Univ. Press, 1958.

FRENCH, J. R. P. and SNYDER, R. Leadership in interpersonal power. In D. Cartwright (Ed.), *Studies in Social Power.* Ann Arbor: University of Michigan Press, 1959.

FREUD, S. *Selected papers on hysteria and other psychoneuroses.* (Translated by A. A. Brill) New York: *J. Nerv. Ment. Dis. Publ. Co.,* 1912.

———. *The dynamics of the transference. In Collected papers of Sigmund Freud,* Vol. 2. London: Hogarth Press, 1959.

FROMM-REICHMANN, FREIDA. Note on the personal and professional requirements of a psychotherapist. *Psychiatry,* 1949, *12,* 361-378.

———. Some aspects of psychoanalytic psychotherapy with schizophrenics. In E. Brody and F. C. Redlich (Eds.), *Psychotherapy with schizophrenics.* New York: International Universities Press, 1952.

———. *Principle of intensive psychotherapy.* Chicago: University of Chicago Press, 1958.

GENDLIN, E. T. and GEIST, MARILYN. The relationship of therapist congruence to psychological test evaluations of personality change. Wisconsin Psychiatric Institute, University of Wisconsin, *Brief Research Reports,* 1962, *24.*

——— and TOMIINSON, T. M. Experiencing scale. Mimeographed paper, Wisconsin Psychiatric Institute, University of Wisconsin, 1962.

GERARD, D. L., SAENGER, G. and WILE, R. The abstinent alcoholic. *Arch. gen. Psychol.,* 1962, *6,* 83-95.

GINOTT, HAIM, G. *Between parent and child.* New York: Macmillan, 1965.

GLASS, A. J. Psychotherapy in the combat zone. *Amer. J. Psychiat.,* 1954, *110.* 725-731.

GLIEDMAN, L. H., NASH, E. H, IMBER, S. D., STONE, A. R., and FRANK, J. D. Reduction of symptoms by pharmacologically inert substances and by short-term psychotherapy *A.M.A. Arch. Neurol. Psychiat,* 1957, *79,* 345-351.

GOLANN, S. E., WURN, C. A., and MAGOON, T. M. Community mental health content of graduate programs in departments of psychology. *J. clin. Psychol.,* 1964, *20,* 518-522.

GOLDFARB, W. Infant rearing as a factor in foster home placement. *Amer. J. Orthopsychiat.,* 1944, *14,* 162-167.

GOLDSTEIN, A. P. and SHIPMAN, W. G. Patients' expectancies, symptom reduction, and aspects of the initial psychotherapeutic interview. *J. clin. Psychol.,* 1961, *17,* 129-133.

GOLDSTEIN, F. J. Guidelines and obstacles in training for the profession of clinical psychologists. *J. clin. Psychol.,* 1962, *18,* 248-251.

GOMPERTZ, K. The relation of empathy to effective communication. *Journ. Quart.,* 1960, *37,* 533-546.

GOODSTEIN, L. D. Behavior theoretical views of counseling. In B. Stefflre (Ed.), *Theories of counseling.* New York: McGraw Hill, 1965.

——— and CRITES, J. O. Brief counseling with poor college risks. *J. counsel. Psychol.,* 1961, *8,* 318-321.

GOTTSCHALK, L. A. *Arch. Neurol. Psychiat.* 1953, *70,* 361-384.

GRAHAM, F. R. The effects of psychoanalytically-oriented psychotherapy on levels of frequency and satisfaction in sexual activity. *J. clin. Psychol.*, 1960, *16*, 94-95.

GRANT, J. D. and GRANT, M. Q. A group dynamic approach to the treatment of nonconformists in the Navy. *Annals of the American Academy of Political and Social Science*, 1959, *322*, 126-130.

GROSSBERG, J. M. Behavior therapy: A review. *Psychol. Bull.*, 1964, *62*, 73-88.

GUTHRIE, E. R. *Psychology of human conflict*. New York: Harper, 1938.

HALKIDES, GALATIA. An investigation of therapeutic success as a function of four variables. Unpublished doctoral dissertation, University of Chicago, 1958.

HANSEN, J. C. and BARKER, E. N. Experiencing and the supervisory relationship. *J. counsel. Psychol.*, 1964, *11*, 107-111.

HART, J. T. A replication of the Halkides study. Unpublished manuscript, University of Wisconsin, 1960.

HARVEY, L. V. The use of non-professional auxiliary counselors in staffing a counseling service. *J. counsel. Psychol.*, 1964, *11*, 348-357.

HAWKES, G. R. and EGBERT, R. L. Personal values and the empathic response: Their interrelationships. *J. educ. Psychol.*, 1954, *45*, 469-476.

HEALY, V., BRONNER, G. F., BAYLOR, E. G., and MURPHY, J. P. *Reconstructing behavior in youth: A study of problem children in foster families.* New York: Knopf, 1929.

HEINE, R. W., and TROSMAN, H. Initial expectations of the doctor-patient interaction as a factor in continuous psychotherapy. *Psychiatry*, 1960, *23*, 275-278.

HELLER, K., MYERS, R. A., and KLINE, LINDA, V. Interviewer behavior as a function of standardized client roles. *J. consult. Psychol.*, 1963, *27*, 117-122.

HERZBERG, F., INKLEY, S., and ADAMS, W. R. Some effects on the clinical faculty of a critical incident study of performance of students. *J. med. Educ.*, 1960, *35*, 666-674.

HIELBRUN, A. B. Psychoanalysis of yesterday, today and tomorrow. *Arch. gen. Psychiat.*, 1961, *4*, 321-330.

HIRSHBERG, F., CARKHUFF, R. R. and BERENSON, B. G. The differential effectiveness of counselors and therapists with in-patient schizophrenics and counseling center clients. *Discussion Papers*, Arkansas Rehabilitation Research and Training Center, University of Arkansas, 1966, *1* (Whole No. 6).

HOBBS, N. Client-centered therapy. In *Six approaches to psychotherapy*. New York: Dryden Press, 1955. Pp. 11-60.

HOEHN-SARIC, R., FRANK, J. D., IMBER, S. D., NASH, E. H., STONE, A. R., and BATTLE, CAROLYN C. Systematic preparation of patients for psychotherapy. I. Effects on therapy behavior and outcome. *J. Psychiat. Res.*, 1963, *Z*, 267-281.

HOLLENBECK, G. P. Conditions and outcomes in the student-parent relationship. *J. consult. Psychol.*, 1965, *29*(3), 237-241.

HOLT, R. R., and LUBORSKY, L. *Personality patterns of psychiatrists*. New York: Basic Books, 1958.

Institute for Human Adjustment. *Training of psychological counselors*. Ann Arbor: University of Michigan Press, 1950.

IRGENS, E. M. Must parents' attitudes become modified in order to bring about adjustment in problem children? *Smith College Stud. Social Work,* 1936 *7,* 17-45.

ISAACS, K. S. and HAGGARD, E. A. Some methods used in the study of affect in psychotherapy. In L. A. Gottschalk and A. H. Auerbach (Eds.), *Methods of research in psychotherapy.* New York: Appleton-Century Crofts, 1966.

ISAACS, W., THOMAS, J., and GOLDIAMOND, I. Application of operant conditioning to reinstate verbal behavior in psychotics. *J. Speech hearing Disord.,* 1960, *25,* 8-12.

ISAACSON, R. L., MCKEACHIE, W. J., and MILHOLLAND, J. E. A correlation of teacher personality variables and student ratings. *J. educ. Psychol,* 1963, *54,* 110-117

JAMES, N. E. By-products of a motivational and surveillance program for talented college students. *Personnel guid. J.,* 1962, *40,* 723-727.

JONES, V. Attitude changes in an N.D.E.A. institute. *Personnel guid. J.,* 1963, *42,* 709-710.

KAMIN, I. and CAUGHLAN, JEANNE. Patients report the subjective experience of outpatient psychotherapy: A follow-up study. *Amer. J. Psychother.,* 1963, *17,* 660-668.

KANFER, F. H. and MARSTON, A. R. Conditioning of self-reinforcement responses: An analogue to self-confidence training. *Psychol. Rep.,* 1963, *13,* 63-70. (a)

———, ———. Determinants of self-reinforcement in human learning. *J. eper. Psychol.,* 1963, *66,* 245-254. (b)

KNIGHT, R. P. Evaluation of the results of psychoanalytic therapy. *Amer. J. Psychiat.,* 1941, *98,* 434-446.

KORNER, I. N. and BROWN, W. H. The mechanical third ear. *J. consult. Psychol.,* 1952, *16,* 81-84.

KRASNER, L. Behavior control, values and training. In Symposium on predoctoral training, Western Psychol. Assoc., Seattle, 1961.

———. The therapist as a social reinforcement machine. In H. H. Strupp and L. Luborsky (Eds.), *Research in psychotherapy,* Vol. 2. Washington, D. C.: American Psychological Assoc., 1962.

KRUMBOLTZ, J. D. Counseling for behavior change. Paper read at American Pers. and Guidance Assoc., Boston, 1963. Also *J. consult. Psychol.,* 1965.

——— and THORESON, C. E. The effects of behavioral counseling in group and individual settings on information-seeking behavior. *J. counsel. Psychol.,* 1964, *11,* 325-333.

LAKIN, M. and LEBOVITS, B. Bias in psychotherapists of different orientations. *Amer. J. Psychother.,* 1958, *12,* 79-86.

LANG, P. J. Psychotherapy, pseudotherapy and behavior therapy. Symposium: The implications of conditioning techniques for interview therapy. Midwest. Psychol. Assoc., Chicago, 1965.

——— and LAZOVIK, A. D. The experimental desensitization of a phobia. *J. abnorm. soc. Psychol.,* 1963, *66,* 519-525.

———, ——— and REYNOLDS, D. J. Desensitization, suggestability, and pseudotherapy. *J. abnorm. Psychol.,* 1965, *6,* 395-402.

LAZARUS, A. A. Group therapy of phobic disorders by systematic desensitization. *J. abnorm. soc. Psychol.,* 1961, *63,* 504-510.

LAZOVIK, A. D. and LANG, P. J. A laboratory demonstration of systematic desensitization psychotherapy. *J. Psychological Studies,* 1960, *11,* 238-247.

LESSER, W. M. The relationship between counseling progress and empathic understanding. *J. counsel. Psychol.,* 1961, *8,* 330-336.

LESTER, B. K., GUSSEN, J., YAMAMOTO, J., and WEST, L. J. Teaching psychotherapy in a longitudinal curriculum. *J. med. Educ.,* 1962, *37,* 28-32.

LEVITT, B. E. The results of psychotherapy with children: An evaluation. *J. consult. Psychol.,* 1957, *21,* 189-196.

LEVITT, E. E., BEISER, H. R., and ROBERTSON, R. E. A follow-up evaluation of cases treated at a community child guidance clinic. *Amer. J Orthopsychiat.,* 1959, *29,* 337-349.

LIDZ, RUTH W. and LIDZ, T. The family environment of schizophrenic patients. *J. Amer. Psychiat.,* 1949, *106,* 332-345.

LIDZ, T., CORNELISON, ALICE, FLECK, S., and TERRY, DOROTHY. The intrafamilial environment of schizophrenic patients: II. Marital schism and marital skew. *Amer. J. Psychiat.,* 1957, *114,* 241-248.

LINDSLEY, O. R. Characteristics of the behavior of chronic psychotics as revealed by free-operant conditioning methods. *Dis. Nerv. Syst.* (Monograph supplement), 1960, *21,* 66-78.

———. Operant conditioning and therapy: A discussion. Presented at symposium: Implications of conditioning techniques for interview therapy. Midwest, Psychol. Assoc., Chicago, 1965.

LIPKIN, S. Clients' feelings and attitudes in relation to the outcome of client-centered therapy. *Psychol. Monogr.,* 1954, *68,* (1).

———. In Brammer, L. M. and Shostrom, E. L. (Eds.), *Therapeutic psychology: Fundamentals of counseling and psychotherapy.* Englewood Cliffs, N. J.: Prentice-Hall, 1964.

LORR, M. and MCNAIR, D. M. Methods relating to evaluation of therapeutic outcome. In Gottschalk, L. A. and Auerbach, A. H. (Eds.), *Methods of research in psychotherapy.* New York: Appleton-Century-Crofts, 1966.

———, ———, MICHAUX, W. W., and RASKIN, A. Frequency of treatment and change in psychotherapy. *J. abnorm. soc. Psychol.* 1962, *64,* 281-292.

LOTT, G. M. The training of non-medical cooperative psychotherapists by multiple psychotherapy. *Amer. J. Psychother.,* 1952, *6,* 440-448.

———. Multiple psychotherapy: The efficient use of psychiatric treatment and training time. *Psychiat. Quart.,* 1957, *2,* 1-19.

LUBIN, B. Survey of psychotherapy training and activities of psychologists. *J. clin. Psychol.* 1962, *18,* 252-255.

LUBORSKY, L. A note on Eysenck's article "The effects of psychotherapy: An evaluation." *Brit. J. Psychol.,* 1954, *45,* 129-131.

MAAS, H. S., KAHN, A. J., STEIN, H. D., and SUMMER, D. Socio-cultural factors in psychiatric clinic services for children. *Smith College Stud. Social Work,* 1955, *25,* 1-90.

MARK, J. C. The attitudes of the mothers of male schizophrenics toward child behavior. *J. abnorm. soc. Psychol.,* 1953, *48,* 485-489.

MARKS, I. M. and GRELDER, M. G. Deconditioning (desensitization) in phobic disorders: Indications and limitations. Paper in Symposium on higher nervous activity, IV World Psychiatry Congress, Madrid, Spain, September, 1966.

MARSTON, A. R. Response strength and self-reinforcement. *J. exp. Psychol.*, 1964, *68*, 537-540. (a)

———. Variables affecting incidence of self-reinforcement. *Psychol. Rep.*, 1964, *14*, 879-884. (b)

———. Imitation, self-reinforcement, and reinforcement of another person. *J. pers. soc. Psychol.*, 1965, *2*, 255-261. (a)

———. Self-reinforcement research: Analogue to psychotherapy. Unpublished manuscript, University of Wisconsin, 1965. (b)

MARTIN, J. C., CARKUFF, R. R., and BERENSON, G. B. A study of counseling and friendship. Unpublished manuscript, University of Massachusetts, 1965.

MATARAZZO, J. D. A postdoctoral residency program in clinical psychology. *Amer. Psychologist*, 1965, *20*(6), 432-439. (a)

———. Psychotherapeutic processes. Chapter in *Annu. Rev. Psychol.*, 1965, *16*, 181-224. (b)

MATARAZZO, RUTH G., PHILLIPS, JEANNE S., WIENS, A. N. and SASLOW, G. Learning the art of interviewing. A study of what beginning students do and their pattern of change. In *Psychotherapy: theory, research and practic.* In press (1966).

MATZ, P. B. Outcome of hospital treatment of ex-service patients with nervous and mental disease in the U. S. Veterans Bureau. *U. S. Veterans Bureau Med. Bull.*, 1929, *5*, 829-842.

MAY, P. R. A. and TUMA, A. H. The effects of psychotherapy and stelazine on length of hospital stay, release rate and supplemental treatment of schizophrenic patients. *J. nerv. ment. Dis.*, 1964, *139*, 362-369.

MAY, R. Historical and philosophical presuppositions for understanding therapy. Chapter in O. H. Mowrer (Ed.), *Psychotherapy theory and research.* New York: Ronald Press, 1953.

———. Contributions of existential psychotherapy. In May, R., Angle, E., and Ellenburger, H. (Eds.), *Existence*. New York: Basic Books, 1958.

MCGOWEN, J. F. and SCHMIDT, L. D. *Counseling: Readings in theory and practice*. New York: Holt, Rinehart and Winston, 1962.

MCMITCHELL, J. The conference on psychiatric education. *J. med. Educ.* 1952 *27*, 166-181.

MCNAIR, D. M., CALLAHAN, D. M., and LORR, M. Therapist "type" and patient response to psychotherapy. *J. consult. Psychol.*, 1962, *26*, 425-442.

———, LORR, M., YOUNG, H. H., ROTH, I., and BOYD, R. W. A three-year followup of psychotherapy patients, *J. clin. Psychol.*, 1964, *20*, 258-263.

MEEHL, P. E. Psychotherapy. *Annu. Rev. Psychol.*, 1955, *6*, 357-378.

MEEKER, F. A. An exploratory study of specific and general personality dimension related to length of hospitalization among psychiatric patients. Unpublished master's thesis, University of California, Berkeley, 1958.

MELLOH, R. A. Accurate empathy and counselor effectiveness. Unpublished doctoral dissertation, University of Florida, 1964.

MENDEL, W. M. and RAPPORT, S. Outpatient treatment for chronic schizophrenic patients: Therapeutic consequences of an existential view. *Arch. Psychiat.*, 1963, *8*, 190-196.

MENNINGER, C. *Theories of psychoanalytic technique.* New York: Basic Books, 1958.

MILLER, MAURINE R., and LUBIN, B. Rehabilitation counselor training in the U. S. *Personnel guid. J.*, 1963, *41*, 606-608.

MINK, O. G. and ISAACSON, H. L. A comparison of effectiveness of non-directive therapy and clinical counseling in the junior high school. *School Counselor,* 1959, *6,* 12-14.

MITCHELL, K. M. An evaluation of the schizophrenogenic mother concept by means of the TAT. Unpublished doctoral dissertation, Michigan State University, 1965.

MONTALTO, F. D. Maternal behavior and child personality: A Rorschach study. *J. project Tech.,* 1952, *16,* 151-178.

MORRIS, D. P., SOROKER, E., and BURRESS, G. Followup studies of shy, withdrawn children: I. Evaluation of later adjustment. *Amer. J. Orthopsychiat.,* 1954, *24,* 743-754.

MOUSTAKAS, C. E. Psychotherapy with children—the living relationship. New York: Harper and Bros., 1959.

MOWRER, O. H. A stimulus-response analysis of anxiety and its role as a reinforcing agent. *Psychol. Rev.,* 1939, *46,* 553-565.

MUNGER, P. F. and JOHNSON, C. A. Changes in attitudes associated with an N.D.E.A. counseling and guidance institute. *Personnel guid. J.,* 1960, *38,* 751-753.

MUNROE, RUTH L. *Schools of psychoanalytic thought.* New York: Dryden Press, 1955.

NORRIS, WILLA. More than a decade of training guidance and personnel workers. *Personnel guid. J.,* 1960, *39,* 287-291.

NOYES, A. P. and KOLB, LAWRENCE C. *Modern clinical Psychiatry.* Philadelphia: W. B. Saunders Co., 1964.

NUNBERG, M. D. *Principles of psychoanalysis: Application to the neurosis.* New York: International Universities Press, 1955.

O'CONNOR, J. F., DANIELS, G., FLOOD, C., KARUSH, A., MOSES, L., and STERN, L. O. Evaluation of the effectiveness of psychotherapy in the treatment of ulcerative colitis. *Annals of Internal Med.,* 1964, *60,* 587-601.

PALMER, T. Types of treators and types of juvenile offenders. *Youth Authority Quarterly,* 1965, *18,* No. 3, Fall.

PATTERSON, C. H., Supervising students in the counseling practicum. *J. counsel. Psychol.,* 1964, *11,* 47-53.

PAUL, G. L. *Insight versus desensitization in psychotherapy: An experiment in anxiety reduction.* Stanford: Stanford University Press, 1965.

——— and SHANNON, D. T. Anxiety and group desensitization. *J. abnorm. Psychol.,* 1966, *2,* 124-135.

PERES, H. An investigation of non-directive group therapy. *J. consult. Psychol.,* 1947, *11,* 159-172.

PHILLIPS, E. L. and JOHNSON, M. S. H. Theoretical and clinical aspects of short-term parent-child psychotherapy. *Psychiatry,* 1954, *17,* 267-275.

PILOWSKY, I. and SPEAR, F. G. The psychiatrist's role in the interview situation. *Amer. J. Psychother.,* 1964, *18,* sup. 1, 174-183.

POSER, E. G. The effect of therapist training on group therapeutic outcome. *J. consult. Psychol.,* 1966, *30*(4), 283-289.

POWERS, E. and WITMER, HELEN. *An experiment in the prevention of delinquency*. New York: Columbia University Press, 1961.

RACHMAN, S. The treatment of anxiety and phobic reactions by systematic desensitization psychotherapy. *J. abnorm. soc. Psychol.*, 1959, *58*, 259-263.

RAUSCH, H. L. and BORDIN, E. S. Warmth in personality development and in psychotherapy. *Psychiatry*, 1957, *20*, 351-363.

READ, H. H. Parents' expressed attitudes and children's behavior. *J. consult. Psychol.*, 1945, *9*, 95-100.

RICHARDSON, L. H. Counseling the ambitious mediocre student. *J. counsel. Psychol.*, 1960, *7*, 265-268.

RICKS, D., UMBARGER, C., and MACK, R. A measure of increased temporal perspective in successfully treated adolescent delinquent boys. *J. abnorm. soc. Psychol.*, 1964, *96*, 685-689.

RIOCH, MARGARET J., ELKES, C., FLINT, A. A., UDANSKY, BLANCHE S., NEWMAN, RUTH G., and SILBER, E. National Institute of Mental Health pilot study in training mental health counselors. *Amer. J. Orthopsychiat.*, 1963, *33*, 678-689.

ROBINSON, F. P. The dynamics of communication in counseling. *J. counsel. Psychol.*, 1955, II, *3*, 163-169.

ROGERS, C. R. *Counseling and psychotherapy*. Boston: Houghton Mifflin, 1942.

———. Divergent trends in methods of improving adjustment. *Pastoral Psychol.*, 1950, *1*, 11-18.

———. *Client-centered therapy*. Boston: Houghton Mifflin Co., 1951.

———. Persons or science? A philosophical question. *Amer. Psychologist*, 1955, *10*, 267-278. (a)

———. The concept of the fully functioning person. Unpublished manuscript. Chicago Counseling Center, University of Chicago, 1955. (b)

———. The necessary and sufficient conditions of therapeutic personality change. *J. consult. Psychol.*, 1957, *21*, 95-103. (a)

———. Training individuals to engage in the therapeutic process. In C. R. Strother (Ed.), *Psychology and mental health*. Washington, D. C.: Amer. Psychol. Assoc., 1957. (b)

———. The interpersonal relationship: The core of guidance. *Harvard educ. Rev.*, 1962, *32*, 416-429.

——— and DYMOND, ROSALIND F. *Psychotherapy and personality change*. Chicago: University of Chicago Press, 1954.

———, GENDLIN, E. T., KIESLER, D., and TRUAX, C. B. *The therapeutic relationship and its impact: A study of psychotherapy with schizophrenics*. Madison: University of Wisconsin Press, in press, 1966.

——— and SKINNER, B. F. Some issues concerning the control of human behavior. *Science*, 1956, *124*, 1057-1066.

——— and TRUAX, C. B. The relationship between patient intrapersonal exploration in the first sampling interview and the final outcome criterion. *Brief Research Reports*, Wisconsin Psychiatric Institute, University of Wisconsin, 1962, *73*.

——— ———. The therapeutic conditions antecedent to change: A theoretical view. In C. R. Rogers, E. T. Gendlin, D. Kiesler, and C. B. Truax (Eds.), *The therapeutic relationship and its impact: A study of psychotherapy with schizophrenics*. 1966, in press.

———, Walker, A., and Rablen, R. Development of a scale to measure process changes in psychotherapy. *J. clin. Psychol.*, 1960, *16*, 79-85.

Romano, J. Basic orientation and education of the medical student. *J. Amer. med. Assoc.*, 1950, *143*, 409-412.

———. The conference on psychiatric education. *J. med. Educ.*, 1952, *27*, 116-181.

———. Teaching of psychiatry to medical students. *Lancet*, July, 1961, 93-95. (a)

———. Basic contributions to medicine by research in psychiatry. *J. Amer. med. Assoc.*, 1961, *178*, 1147-1150. (b)

———. Comparative observations in the teaching of psychiatry to undergraduate students. *Perspect. Biol.*, 1962, *5*, 519-526.

———. The new humanism. *Lancet*, 1963, November, 1046-1047. (a)

———. Requiem or reveille: The clinician's choice. *J. med. Educ.*, 1963, *38*, 584-590. (b)

Rosen, J. N. The treatment of schizophrenic psychoses by direct analytic therapy. *Psychiat. Quart.*, 1947, *21*, 3-38.

Rosenzweig, S. A transvaluation of psychotherapy: A reply to Hans Eysenck. *J. abnorm. soc. Psychol.*, 1954, *49*, 298-304.

Ross, T. A. *An enquiry into prognosis in the neuroses.* London: Cambridge University Press, 1936.

Rotter, J. B. *Clinical psychology: Foundations of modern psychology series.* Englewood Cliffs, N. J.: Prentice Hall, 1964.

Salzman, L. F. and Romano, J. Grading clinical performance in psychiatry. *J. med. Educ.*, 1963, *38*, 746-751.

Sanford, N. Clinical methods: Psychotherapy. *Annu. Rev. Psychol.*, 1954, *5*, 311-336.

Sapolsky, A. Effect of interpersonal relationships upon verbal conditioning. *J. abnorm. soc. Psychol.*, 1960, *60*, 241-246.

Sargent, L. W. Communicator image and news reception. *Journ. Quart.* 1965, *42*, 35-42.

Schachter, S., Ellertson, T., and Gregory, D. An experimental study of cohesiveness and productivity. *Human Relations*, 1951, *4*, 229-238.

———, ——— and McBride, D. Deviation, rejection and communication. *J. abnorm. soc. Psychol.*, 1951, *46*, 190-207.

Schofield, W. *Psychotherapy: The purchase of friendship.* Englewood Cliffs, N. J.: Prentice-Hall, 1964.

Schulman, R. F., Shoemaker, D. J., and Moelis, I. Laboratory measurements of parental behavior. *J. consult. Psychol.*, 1962, *26*, 109-114.

Schwartz, E. K. and Abel, Theodora M. The professional education of the psychoanalytic psychotherapist. *Amer. J. Psychother.*, 1955, *9*, 253-261.

Searles, A., Jr. The effectiveness of limited counseling in improving the academic achievement of superior college freshmen. *Personnel guid. J.*, 1962, *40*, 630-633.

Seeman, J. A study of the process of non-directive therapy. *J. consult. Psychol.*, 1949, *13*, 157-168.

———, Barry, E., and Ellinwood, C. Interpersonal assessment of play therapy outcome. *Psychotherapy theory, research and practice*, 1964, *1*, 64-66.

SHAPIRO, J. G. Consistency in the expression of emotion. Unpublished doctoral dissertation, Pennsylvania State University, 1965.

———. Agreement between channels of communication in interviews. *J. Consult. Psychol.,* in press, 1966.

SHLIEN, J. M. A client-centered approach to schizophrenia: First approximation. In A. Burton (Ed.), *Psychotherapy of the psychoses.* New York: Basic Books, 1961.

———, MOSAK, H. H. and DREIKURS, R. Effect of time limits: A comparison of client-centered and Adlerian psychotherapy. *Amer. Psychologist,* 1960, *15,* 415. (Abstract)

———, ——— and ———. Effect of time limits: A comparison of two psychotherapies. *J. counsel. Psychol.,* 1962, *9,* 31-34.

SHOBEN, E. J. A learning theory interpretation of psychotherapy. *Harvard educ. Rev.,* 1948, *18,* 129-145.

———. Psychotherapy as a problem in learning theory. *Psychol. Bull.,* 1949, *46,* 366-392.

———. Some observations on psychotherapy and the learning process. In O. H. Mowrer (Ed.), *Psychotherapy: Theory and research.* New York: Ronald Press, 1953.

———. Counseling. *Annu. Rev. Psychol.,* 1956, *7,* 147-172.

SHOUKSMITH, G. and TAYLOR, J. W. The effects of counseling on the achievement of high ability pupils. *Brit. J. of Educ. Psychol.,* 1964, *1,* 51-57.

SKEELS, H. M., and DYE, H. B. A study of the effects of differential stimulation on mentally retarded children. *Proc. Amer. Assoc. ment. Defects,* 1939, *44,* 114-136.

SLAVSON, S. R. *The fields of group psychotherapy.* New York: International Universities Press, 1956.

———. *Textbook in analytic group psychotherapy.* New York: International Universities Press, 1963.

SNYDER, W. U. Professional training for clinical psychologists. *J. clin. Psychol.,* 1962, *18,* 243-247.

SPIELBERGER, C. D., WEITZ, H., and DENNY, J. P. Group counseling and the academic performance of anxious freshmen. *J. counsel. Psychol.,* 1962, *9,* 195-204.

SPITZ, R. A. Hospitalism: An enquiry into the genesis of psychiatric conditions in early childhood. In O. Fenichel (Ed.), *The psychoanalytic study of the child.* Vol. 1. New York: International Press, 1945.

———. Hospitalism: A followup report on investigation described in volume 1. In O. Fenichel (Ed.), *The psychoanalytic study of the child.* Vol. 2. New York: International Press, 1946.

SPITZER, R., LEE, JOAN, CARNAHAN, W., and FLEISS, J. A comparison of rural and urban schizophrenics in differing state institutions. Paper read at Amer. Psychiat. Assoc., Los Angeles, 1964.

SPOTTS, J. The perception of positive regard by relatively successful and relatively unsuccessful clients. *Brief Research Reports,* Wisconsin Psychiatric Institute, Univer. of Wisconsin, 1962, *15.*

——— and WHARTON, W. P. Spotts-Wharton scale of positive regard. *Brief Research Reports,* Wisconsin Psychiatric Institute, Univer. of Wisconsin, 1962, *9.*

STEELE, B. L. The amount of exploration into causes, means, goals and agent: A comparison of successful and unsuccessful cases in client-centered therapy. Unpublished master's thesis, University of Chicago, 1948.

STEPHENS, J. H. and ASTRUP, C. Treatment outcome in "process" and "non-process" schizophrenics treated by "A" and "B" types of therapists. *J. nerv. ment. Dis.*, 1965, 140 (6), 449-456.

STEVENSON, I. The challenge in psychotherapy. In J. Wolpe, A. Salter, and L. J. Reyna (Eds.), *The conditioning therapies.* New York: Holt, Rinehart & Winston, 1964.

STIEPER, D. R. and WIENER, D. N. *Dimensions of psychotherapy: An experimental and clinical approach* (J. D. Matarazzo and J. S. Brown, Eds.), Chicago: Aldine Publishing Co., 1965.

STOLER, N. The analysis of the initial test battery and the sampling interview procedure. *Psychiatric Institute Bull.*, Wisconsin Psychiatric Institute, 1961, 1, *10.*

———. Client likeability: A variable in the study of psychotherapy. *J. consult. Psychol.*, 1963, *27*, 138-144.

STONE, A. R., FRANK, J. D., NASH, E. H., and IMBER, S. D. An intensive five-year follow-up study of treated psychiatric outpatients. *J. nerv. ment. Dis.*, 1961, *133*, 410-422.

STRAUSS. B. V. Teaching psychotherapy to medical students. *J. Assoc. Amer. med. Coll.*, 1950, July, 1-6.

STRUPP, H. H. The effect of the psychotherapist's personal analysis upon his techniques. *J. consult. Psychol.* 1955, *19*, 197-204. (a)

———. Psychotherapeutic technique, professional affiliation and experience level. *J. consult. Psychol.*, 1955, *19*, 97-102. (b)

———. The performance of psychiatrists and psychologists in a therapeutic interview. *J. clin. Psychol.* 1958, *14*, 219-226.

———. Nature of psychotherapists' contribution to the treatment process. *Arch. gen. Psychiat.*, 1960, *3*, 219-231. (a)

———. *Psychotherapists in action.* New York: Grune and Stratton, 1960. (b)

———, WALLACH, M. S., and WOGAN, M. Psychotherapy experience in retrospect: Questionnaire survey of former patients and their therapists. *Psychol. Monogr.*, 1964, *78*, No. 11 (Whole No. 588).

———, ———, ———, and JENKINS, JOAN W. Psychotherapists' assessments of former patients. *J. nerv. ment. Dis.*, 1963, *137*, 222-230.

SULLIVAN, H. S. *The psychiatric interview.* New York: W. W. Norton, 1954.

TAFT, J. *The dynamics of therapy in a controlled relationship.* New York: Dover Publications, 1962.

TAFT, R. The ability to judge people. *Psychol. Bull.*, 1955, *52*, 1-23.

TALLAND, G. A. and CLARK, D. H. Evaluation of topics in therapy group discussion. *J. clin. Psychol.*, 1954, *10*, 131-137.

TEUBER, H. L. and POWERS, E. Evaluating therapy in a delinquency prevention program. *Proceedings of the Assoc. Res. nerv. ment. Dis.*, *31*, 138-147. Baltimore: Williams and Wilkins, 1953.

THETFORD, W. N. The measurement of physiological responses to frustration before and after non-directive psychotherapy. *Amer. Psychologist*, 1948, *3*, 278. (Abstract)

THOMPSON, CLARA. *Psychoanalysis: Evolution and development.* New York: Hermitage House, 1950.

THORNE, F. C. *The principles of personal counseling.* Brandon, Vt.: J. Clin. Psychol. Press, 1950.

TOMLINSON, T. M. The process of personality change in schizophrenics and neurotics. *Brief Research Reports,* Wisconsin Psychiatric Institute, Univer. of Wisconsin, 1962, *17.*

——— and HART, J. T. A validation study of the process scale. *J. consult. Psychol.,* 1962, *26,* 74-78.

TOWLES, CHARLOTTE. Roles of the supervisor in the union of cause and function in social work. *Social serv. Rev.,* 1961, *35,* 144-151.

TRUAX, C. B. The process of group psychotherapy: Relationships between hypothesized therapeutic conditions and intrapersonal exploration. *Psychol. Monogr.,* 1961, *75,* 7 (Whole No. 511). (a)

———. A scale for the measurement of accurate empathy. *Psychiatric Institute Bull.,* Wisconsin Psychiatric Institute, Univer. of Wisconsin, 1961, *1,* 12. (b)

———. Symposium: A program of psychotherapy with hospitalized schizophrenics. Amer. Psychol. Assoc. convention, New York, 1961. (c)

———. Therapeutic conditions. *Psychiat. Inst. Bull.,* Wisconsin Psychiatric Institute, Univer. of Wisconsin, 1961, *1,* 10. (d)

———. A tentative scale for the measurement of unconditional positive regard. *Psychiatric Institute Bull.,* Wisconsin Psychiatric Institute, Univer. of Wisconsin, 1962, *2,* 1. (a)

———. A tentative approach to the conceptualization and measurement of intensity and intimacy of interpersonal contact as a variable in psychotherapy. *Discussion Papers,* Wisconsin Psychiatric Institute, Univer. of Wisconsin, 1962, *25,* (b)

———. A tentative scale for the measurement of depth of intrapersonal exploration (DX). *Discussion Papers,* Wisconsin Psychiatric Institute, Univer. of Wisconsin, 1962, *29.* (c)

———. A tentative scale for the measurement of therapist genuineness or self-congruence. *Discussion Papers,* Wisconsin Psychiatric Institute, Univer. of Wisconsin, 1962, *35.* (d)

———. The therapeutic process in group psychotherapy: A research investigation. Mimeographed paper, Wisconsin Psychiatric Institute, Univer. of Wisconsin, January 1962. (e)

———. The sampling interview: A method of assessment of psychotherapeutic personality change. *Brief Research Reports,* Wisconsin Psychiatric Institute, Univer. of Wisconsin, 1962, *18.* (f)

———. Intensity and intimacy of interpersonal contact: Relationships between the level of intensity and intimacy of interpersonal contact offered by the therapist throughout the course of psychotherapy and the degree of positive personality change occurring in the patient. *Brief Research Reports,* Wisconsin Psychiatric Institute, Univer. of Wisconsin, 1962, *55.* (g)

———. Intensity and intimacy of interpersonal contact: Relationships between the level of IC offered by the therapist and the level of patient intrapersonal exploration throughout the course of psychotherapy. *Brief Research Reports,* Wisconsin Psychiatric Institute, Univer. of Wisconsin, 1962, *56.* (h)

———. Intensity and intimacy of interpersonal contact: Effects of therapists and effects of patients upon the level of intensity and intimacy of interpersonal contact offered by the therapist. *Brief Research Reports,* Wisconsin Psychiatric Institute, Univer. of Wisconsin, 1962, *65.* (i)

———. Personal constructs: Relationships between conditions offered in psychotherapy and personal constructs and between constructive personality change and personal constructs. *Brief Research Reports,* Wisconsin Psychiatric Institute, Univer. of Wisconsin, 1962, *80.* (j)

———. Immediacy of feeling: Relationship between conditions offered in psychotherapy and immediacy of feeling. *Brief Research Reports,* Wisconsin Psychiatric Institute, Univer. of Wisconsin, 1962, *81.* (k)

———. Degree of defensiveness: Relationship between conditions offered in psychotherapy and degree of defensiveness and between constructive personality change and degree of defensiveness. *Brief Research Reports,* Wisconsin Psychiatric Institute, Univer. of Wisconsin, 1962, *82.* (l)

———. Relationship quality: Relationship between conditions offered in psychotherapy and relationship quality and between constructive personality change and relationship quality. *Brief Research Reports,* Wisconsin Psychiatric Institute, Univer. of Wisconsin, 1962, *83.* (m)

———. Relationships to problem elements of the self: Relationship between conditions offered in psychotherapy and relationship to problem elements of the self and between constructive personality change and relationship to problem elements of the self. *Brief Research Reports,* Wisconsin Psychiatric Institute, Univer. of Wisconsin, 1962, *84.* (n)

———. Variations in levels of accurate empathy offered in the psychotherapy relationship and case outcome. *Brief Research Reports,* Wisconsin Psychiatric Institute, Univer. of Wisconsin, 1962, *38.* (o)

———. Comparisons between control patients, therapy patients pereceiving high conditions, and therapy patients perceiving low conditions on measures of constructive personality change. *Brief Research Reports,* Wisconsin Psychiatric Institute, Univer. of Wisconsin, 1962, *31.* (p)

———. The relationship between the patient's perception of the level of therapeutic conditions offered in psychotherapy and constructive personality change. *Brief Research Reports,* Wisconsin Psychiatric Institute, Univer. of Wisconsin, 1962, *1.* (q)

———. Effective ingredients in psychotherapy: An approach to unraveling the patient-therapist interaction. Symposium: The empirical emphasis in psychotherapy. Amer. Psychol. Assoc., St. Louis, 1962. *J. counsel. Psychol.,* 1963, 10, *3,* 256-263.

———. Therapist empathy, warmth, and genuineness and patient personality change in group psychotherapy: A comparison between interaction unit measures, time sample measures, and patient perception measures. *J. clin. Psychol.,* 1966, 22, *2,* 225-229. (a)

———. Influence of patient statements on judgments of therapist statements during psychotherapy. *J. clin. Psychol.,* 1966, 22, *3,* 335-337.

———. Reinforcement and non-reinforcement in Rogerian psychotherapy. *J. abnorm. soc. Psychol.,* 1966, 71, *1,* 1-9. (c)

———. Therapist reinforcement of patient self-exploration and therapeutic outcome. Manuscript in preparation, Arkansas Rehabilitation Research and Training Center and University of Arkansas, 1966. (d)

——— and CARKHUFF, R. R. For better or for worse: The process of psychotherapeutic personality change. Chapter in *Recent advances in the study of behavior change.* Montreal, Canada: McGill University Press, 1963.

——— ———. Concreteness: A neglected variable in the psychotherapeutic process. *J. clin. Psychol.*, 1964, 20, *2*, 264-267. (a)

——— ———. Significant developments in psychotherapy research. In Abt and Riess (Eds.), *Progress in clinical psychology*. New York: Grune and Stratton, 1964. (b)

——— ———. The effects of vicarious therapy pretraining and alternate sessions upon depth of patient self-exploration. Unpublished manuscript, University of Kentucky and Kentucky Mental Health Institute, 1964. (c)

——— ———. The old and the new: Theory and research in counseling and psychotherapy. *Personnel guid. J.*, 1964, *42*, 860-866. (d)

——— ———. Personality change in hospitalized mental patients during group psychotherapy as a function of alternate sessions and vicarious therapy pretraining. *J. clin. Psychol.*, 1965, *21*, 225-228. (a)

——— ———. The experimental manipulation of therapeutic conditions. *J. consult. Psychol.*, 1965, *29*, 119-124. (b)

——— ———. Client and therapist transparency in the psychotherapeutic encounter. *J. counsel. Psychol.*, 1965, *12*, 3-9. (c)

——— ———, and Douds, J. Toward an integration of the didactic and experiential approaches to training in counseling and psychotherapy. *J. counsel. Psychol.*, 1964, *11*, 240-247.

——— ———, and Kodman, F., Jr. Relationships between therapist-offered conditions and patient change in group psychotherapy. *J. clin. Psychol.*, 1965, *21*, 327-329.

———, Leslie, G. R., Smith, F. W., Glenn, A. W. and Fisher, G. H. Empathy warmth, and genuineness and progress in vocational rehabilitation. Unpublished manuscript, Arkansas Rehabilitation Research and Training Center, University of Arkansas, 1966.

———, Liccione, J., and Rosenberg, M. Psychological test evaluations of personality change in high conditions therapy, low conditions therapy and control patients. *Brief Research Reports,* Wisconsin Psychiatric Institute, Univer. of Wisconsin, 1962, *10*.

———, and Silber, L. D. Personality and psychotherapeutic skills. Unpublished manuscript, University of Arkansas, 1966.

——— ———, and Carkhuff, R. R. Accurate empathy, non-possessive warmth, genuineness and therapeutic outcome in lay group counseling. Unpublished manuscript, University of Arkansas, 1966.

———, ———, and Wargo, D. G. Training and change in psychotherapeutic skills. Unpublished manuscript, University of Arkansas, 1966. (a)

———, ———, ———. Personality change and achievement in therapeutic training. Unpublished manuscript, Arkansas Rehabilitation Research and Training Center, Univ. of Arkansas, 1966. (b)

——— and Tatum, C. R. An extension from the effective psychotherapeutic model to constructive personality change in preschool children. *Childhood Education, 42,* 456-462. 1966.

———, Tunnell, B. T., Jr., Fine, H. L., and Wargo, D. G. The prediction of client outcome during group pshychotherapy from measures of initial status. Manuscript in preparation. Arkansas Rehabilitation Research and Training Center, University of Arkansas, 1966.

———, ———, and GLENN, A. W. Accurate empathy, non-possessive warmth, genuineness and patient outcome in silent and verbal outpatients. Unpublished manuscript, Arkansas Rehabilitation Research and Training Center, University of Arkansas, 1966. (a)

———, ———, ———. Accurate empathy, non-possessive warmth and genuineness of the therapist and patient outcome in most and least adjusted patients, Unpublished manuscript, Arkansas Rehabilitation Research and Training Center, University of Arkansas, 1966. (b)

———, ———, and WARGO, D. G. Prediction of group psychotherapeutic outcome. Unpublished manuscript, Arkansas Rehabilitation Research and Training Center and University of Arkansas, 1966.

———, and WARGO, D. G. Psychotherapeutic encounters that change behavior: For better or for worse. *Amer. J. Psychother.,* 1966, *22,* 499-520. (a)

———, ———. Antecedents to outcome in group psychotherapy with juvenile delinquents: Effects of therapeutic conditions, alternate sessions, vicarious therapy pretraining, and patient self-exploration. Unpublished manuscript. University of Arkansas, 1966. (b)

———, ———. Antecedents to outcome in group psychotherapy with hospitalized mental patients: Effects of therapeutic conditions, alternate sessions, vicarious therapy pretraining, and patient self exploration. Unpublished manuscript, University of Arkansas, 1966. (c)

——— ———. Comment on Van der Veen's study "Effects of the therapist and the patient on each other's therapeutic behavior." Unpublished manuscript, Univer. of Kentucky, 1966. (d)

———, ———, and CARKHUFF, R. R. Antecedents to outcome in group psychotherapy with outpatients: Effects of therapeutic conditions, alternate sessions, vicarious therapy pretraining and patient self-exploration. Unpublished manuscript. University of Arkansas, 1966.

———, ———, ———, TUNNELL, B. T., JR. and GLENN, A. W. Client perception of therapist empathy, warmth, and genuineness and therapeutic outcome in group counseling with juvenile delinquents. Unpublished manuscript, Arkansas Rehabilitation Research and Training Center, University of Arkansas, 1966.

———, ———, FRANK, J. D., IMBER, S. D., BATTLE, CAROLYN C., HOEHN-SARIC, R., NASH, E. H., and STONE, A. R. Therapist empathy, genuineness, and warmth and patient therapeutic outcome. *J. consult. Psychol.,* in press, 1966 (a)

———, ———, ———, ———, ———, ———, ———, ———. Therapist's contribution to accurate empathy, non-possessive warmth and genuineness in psychotherapy, *J. clin. Psychol.,* 1966, 22, *3,* 331-334. (b)

———, ———, and SILBER, L. D. Effects of high accurate empathy and non-possessive warmth during group psychotherapy upon female institutionalized delinquents. *J. abnorm. Psychol.,* 1966, *71,* 267-274.

———, ———, TUNNEL, B. T., JR. and GLENN, A. W. Patient perception of therapist empathy, warmth, and genuineness and therapeutic outcome in outpatient group therapy. Unpublished manuscript, Arkansas Rehabilitation Research and Training Center, University of Arkansas, 1966.

TUDOR, GWENN. A socio-psychiatric nursing approach to intervention in problem of mutual withdrawal on a mental hospital ward. *Psychiatry,* 1952, *15,* 193-217.

VAN DER VEEN, F. Effects of the therapist and the patient on each other's therapeutic behavior. *J. consult. Psychol.*, 1965, *29*, 19-26.

———, and TOMINSON, T. M. Problem expression scale. Mimeographed paper, Wisconsin Psychiatric Institute, University of Wisconsin, 1962.

VAN KAAM, A. L. The feeling of being understood. *J. individ Psychol.*, 1959, *15*, 69.

VAN ZELST, R. H. Worker popularity and job satisfaction. *Personnel Psychology*, 1951, *4*, 405-412.

VERNALLIS, F. F. and REINERT, R. E. An evaluation of a goal-directed group psychotherapy with hospitalized patients. *Group Psychotherapy*, 1961, *14*, 5-12.

WAGSTAFF, A. K., RICE, L. N., and BUTLER, J. M. Factors of client verbal participation in therapy. *Counseling Center discussion papers*, University of Chicago, 1960, *6*, 1-14.

WALKER, R. G. and KELLEY, F. E. Short-term psychotherapy with hospitalized schizophrenic patients. *Acta Psychiat. Neurol. Scand.*, 1960, *35*, 34-56.

WARD, C. H. An electronic aid for teaching interviewing techniques. *Arch. gen. Psychiat.*, 1961, *49*, 357-358.

———. Electronic preceptering in teaching beginning psychotherapy. *J. med. educ.*, 1962, *37*, 1128-1129.

WARGO, D. G. The Barron Ego Strength and LH^4 scales as predictors and indicators of change in psychotherapy. *Brief Research Reports*. Wisconsin Psychiatric Institute, Univer. of Wisconsin, 1962, *21*.

WEBB, A. P. and HARRIS, J. T. A semantic differential study of counselors in an N.D.E.A. institute. *Personnel guid. J.*, 1963, *42*, 260-263.

WEINER, M. The effects of two experimental counseling techniques on performances impaired by induced stress. *J. abnorm. soc. Psychol*, 1955, *51*, 565-572.

WEISS, R. L., KRASNER, L., and ULLMANN, L. P. Responsivity to verbal conditioning as a function of emotional atmosphere and patterning of reinforcement. *Psychol. Rep.*, 1960, *6*, 415-426.

WESSEL, ROSA. Social work education and practice. *Social serv. Rev.*, 1961, *35*, 151-160.

WHARTON, W. P. Positive regard in therapy with schizophrenic patients. *Brief Research Reports*, Wisconsin Psychiatric Institute, Univer. of Wisconsin, 1962, *9*.

WHITAKER, C. A. Teaching the practicing physician to do psychotherapy. *Southern med. J.*, 1949, *42*, 899-903.

——— and MALONE, T. P. *The roots of psychotherapy*. New York: Blakiston, 1953.

WHITE, A. G. The patient sits down: A clinical note. *Psychosom. Med.*, 1953, *15*, 256-257.

WHITE, A. N., FICHTENBAUM, L., and DOLLARD, J. Measure for predicting dropping out of psychotherapy. *J. consult. Psychol.*, 1964, *28*, 326-332.

WHITE, R. W. *The abnormal personality*. New York: Ronald Press, 1948.

WHITEHORN, J. C. Human factors in psychiatry. *Bull. of N. Y. Acad of Med.*, 1964, *40*, 451-466.

——— and BETZ, BARBARA J. A study of psychotherapeutic relationships between physicians and schizophrenic patients. *Amer. J. Psychiat.*, 1954, *3*, 321-331.

WILLIAMSON, E. G. and BORDIN, E. S. Evaluating counseling by means of a control-group experiment. *School and Society*, 1940, *52*, 434-440.

WILLIS, MARGARET. *The guinea pigs after 20 years*. Columbus: Ohio State University Press, 1961.

WINOKUR, G. Brainwashing: A social phenomenon of our time. *Hum. Organization*, 1955, *13*, 16-18.

WINTHROP, H. Relation between appeal value and highbrow status on some radio and television programs. *Psychol. Reports*, 1958, *4*, 53-54.

WOLBERG, L. R. *The technique of psychotherapy*. New York: Grune and Stratton, 1954.

WOLF, A. Group psychotherapy with adults: The alternate meeting. Paper read at APGA conference, New York, January 1961.

——— and SCHWARTZ, E. K. *Psychoanalysis in groups*. New York: Grune and Stratton, 1962.

WOLFSON, K. S. Clients' exploration of their problems during client-centered therapy. Unpublished master's thesis, University of Chicago, 1949.

WOLPE, J. *Psychotherapy by reciprocal inhibition*. Palo Alto, Calif.: Stanford Univer. Press, 1958.

———. Reciprocal inhibition as the main basis of psychotherapeutic effects. In H. J. Eysenck (Ed.), *Behavior therapy and the neuroses*. New York: Pergamon Press, 1960. Pp. 88-113.

———. Behavior therapy in complex neurotic states. *Brit. J. Psychiat.*, 1964, *110*, 28-34.

———. Behavior therapy: Its origins and achievements. Centennial Psychotherapy Symposium and Workshop, Univer. of Kentucky, April 1965.

WOOD, E. C., RAKUSIN, J. M., MORSE, E., and SINGER, R. Interpersonal aspects of psychiatric hospitalization: II. Some correlations between admission circumstances and the treatment experience. *Arch. gen. Psychiat.*, 1962, *6*, 39-45. (a)

———, ———, ——— and ———. Interpersonal aspects of psychiatric hospitalization: III. The follow-up survey. *Arch gen. Psychiat.*, 1962, *6*, 46-55. (b)

WORKMAN, S. L. Teaching the interpretive process to medical students. *Amer. J. Psychiat.*, 1961, *117*, 897-902.

WYATT, F. The self experience of the psychotherapist. *J. consult. Psychol.*, 1948, *12*, 83-87.

WYNNE, L. C., RYCKOFF, J. M., DAY, JULIANA, and HIRSCH, S. J. Pseudomutuality in the family relations of schizophrenics. *Psychiatry*, 1958, *21*, 205-220.

ZIMBARDO, P. G. Involvement and communication discrepancy as determinants of opinion conformity. *J. abnorm. soc. Psychol.*, 1960, *60*, 86-94.

ACKNOWLEDGMENTS

We wish to express our appreciation for the consideration shown us by the following publishers and journals in allowing us to reproduce excerpts from their articles and books.

American Journal of Orthopsychiatry for: J. V. Coleman, "The Teaching of Basic Psychotherapy," 1947, *17*, 622-627, and D. P. Morris *et al.*, "Follow-up Studies of Shy, Withdrawn Children: I. Evaluation of Later Adjustment," 1954, *24*, 743-754.

American Journal of Psychiatry for: A. J. Glass, "Psychotherapy in the Combat Zone," 1964, *110*, 725-731.

American Journal of Psychotherapy for: E. K. Schwartz and T. N. Abel, "The Professional Education of the Psychoanalytic Psychotherapist," 1955, *9*, 253-261.

American Medical Association for: C. D. Aring, "Neurological Precepts," *Archives of Neurology*, 1961, *4*, 587-589, and *Journal of the American Medical Association*, 1950, *143*, 409-412.

American Psychological Association for: D. Rick *et al.*, "A Measure of Increased Temporal Perspective in Successfully Treated Adolescent Delinquent Boys," *Journal of Abnormal Social Psychology*, 1964, *69*, 685-689; S. Rachman, "The Treatment of Anxiety and Phobic Reactions by Systematic Desensitization Psychotherapy," *Journal of Abnormal Social Psychology*, 1959, *58*, 259-263; L. Breger and J. L. McGaugh, "Critique and Reformulation of 'Learning Theory' Approaches to Psychotherapy and Neurosis," *Psychological Bulletin*, 1965, *63*, 338-357; H. H. Strupp *et al.*, "Psychotherapy Experience in Retrospect: Questionnaire Survey of Former Patients and Their Therapists," *Psychological Monograph*, 1964, *78*, No. 11 (Whole No. 588); F. Wyatt, "The Self-Experience of the Psychotherapist," *Journal of Consulting Psychology*, 1948, *12*, 83-87; and C. Rogers, "Psychology and Mental Health," *American Psychologist*, 1955.

Annual Reviews, Inc., for: J. D. Matarazzo, "Psychotherapeutic Processes," *Annual Review of Psychology*, 1965, *16*, 181-224, and P. E. Meehl, "Psychotherapy," *Annual Review of Psychology*, 1955, *6*, 357-378.

Appleton-Century-Crofts for: E. S. Bordin, *Psychological Counseling*, New York, 1955.

Archives of Psychiatry for: W. M. Mendel and S. Rapport's "Outpatient Treatment for Chronic Schizophrenic Patients: Therapeutic Consequences of an Existential View," 1963, *8*, 190-196.

Basic Books, Inc., for: S. Arieti, "Introductory Notes on the Psychoanalytic Therapy of Schizophrenics," in A. Burton (Ed.), *Psychotherapy of the Psychoses*, New York, 1961; D. Burnham, Autonomy and Activity—Passivity in the Psychotherapy of a Schizophrenic," *Psychotherapy of the Psychoses*, New York, 1961; R. May, "Contribution of Existential Psychotherapy," in R. May, E. Angle, and H. Ellenburger (Eds.), *Existence*, New York, 1958; K. Menninger, *Theories of Psychoanalytic Technique*, New York, 1958; and J. Shlien, "A Client-Centered Approach to Schizophrenia: First Approximation," *Psychotherapy of the Psychoses,* New York, 1961.

Blakiston Press for: C. A. Whitaker and T. P. Malone, *The Roots of Psychotherapy,* New York, 1953.

British Journal of Psychiatry for: J. Wolpe, "Behavior Therapy in Complex Neurotic States," 1964, *110,* 28-34.

Dryden Press for: Ruth L. Munroe, *Schools of Psychoanalytic Thought,* New York, 1955.

Grune and Stratton for: H. H. Strupp, *Psychotherapists in Action,* New York, 1960.

Harper and Brothers for: C. E. Moustakas, *Psychotherapy with Children—The Living Relationship,* New York, 1959.

Hibbert Journal for: Martin Buber, "Distance and Relation," 1951, *49,* 105-113.

Holt, Rinehart and Winston for: J. F. McGowen and L. D. Schmidt, *Counseling: Readings in Theory and Practice,* New York, 1962.

Houghton-Mifflin Company for: N. Cameron, *Personality Development and* Psychopathology, *A Dynamic Approach,* Boston, 1963.

International Universities Press for: Freida Fromm-Reichmann, "Some Aspects of Psychoanalytic Psychotherapy with Schizophrenics," in E. Brady and F. C. Redlich (Eds.), *Psychotherapy with Schizophrenics,* New York, 1962; M. D. Nunberg, *Principles of Psychoanalysis: Application to the Neurosis,* New York, 1955; and S. R. Slavson, *The Fields of Group Psychotherapy,* New York, 1956.

Johns Hopkins Press for: J. D. Frank, *Persuasion and Healing,* Baltimore, 1961.

Journal of Clinical Psychology for: J. D. Black, "Common Factors of the Patient-Therapist Relationship in Diverse Psychotherapy," 1952, *8,* 302-306, and F. C. Thorne, *The Principles of Personal Counseling,* The Journal of Clinical Psychology Press, Brandon, Vermont, 1950.

Journal of Counseling Psychology for: F. P. Robinson, "The Dynamics of Communication in Counseling," 1955, *3,* 163-169.

Journal of Medical Education for: Herzberg *et al.,* "Some Effects on the Clinical Faculty of a Critical Incident Study of Performance of Students," 1960, *35,* 666-674, and B. K. Lester *et al.,* "Teaching Psychotherapy in a Longitudinal Curriculum," 1962, *37,* 28-32.

Journal of Nervous Mental Diseases for: S. Freud, *Selected Papers on Hysteria and Other Psychoneuroses,* New York, 1912.

Lancet for: J. Romano, "Teaching of Psychiatry to Medical Students, 1961, July, 93-95.

Macmillan Company for: Haim Ginott, *Between Parent and Child,* New York, 1965.

W. W. Norton Company for: O. S. English, *Emotional Problems of Living,* New York, 1954, and H. S. Sullivan, *The Psychiatric Interview,* 1954.

Pergamon Press for: H. J. Eysenck, *Behavior Therapy and the Neuroses,* New York, 1960.

Prentice-Hall Publishing Company for: L. M. Brammer and H. L. Shostrom, *Therapeutic Psychology: Fundamentals of Counseling and Psychotherapy,* Englewood Cliffs, New Jersey, 1964, and J. B. Rotter, *Clinical Psychology: Foundations of Modern Psychology Series,* 1964.

Psychiatry for: Freida Fromm-Reichmann, "Note on the Personal and Professional Requirements of a Psychotherapist," 1949, *12*, 361-378.

Psychoanalytic Quarterly for: J. Fleming and T. Benedek, "Supervision—A Method for Teaching Psychoanalysis," 1964, *33*, 71-96.

Ronald Press for: E. J. Shoben, "Some Observations of Psychotherapy and the Learning Process," in O. H. Mowrer (Ed.), *Psychotherapy: Theory and Research*, New York, 1953, and R. W. White, "*The Abnormal Personality*," 1948.

W. B. Saunders Company for: A. P. Noyes and L. C. Kolb, *Modern Clinical Psychology*, Philadelphia, 1964.

Southern Medical Journal for: C. A. Whitaker, "Teaching the Practicing Physician to Do Psychotherapy," 1949, *42*, 899-903.

Stanford University Press for: J. Wolpe, *Psychotherapy by Reciprocal Inhibition*, Palo Alto, California: 1958.

We also wish to thank Dr. Peter J. Lang for his article, "Psychotherapy, Pseudotherapy and Behavior Therapy," presented at the symposium on the Implications of Conditioning Techniques for Interview Therapy, at the Midwestern Psychological Association in Chicago, 1965, and Dr. Carl R. Rogers for his unpublished manuscript, "The Concept of the Fully Functioning Person," from the University of Chicago Counseling Center, 1955.

The authors wish to express their appreciation to the following journals and publishers for their cooperation in allowing the reprinting of data from their own articles.

Grune and Stratton for: C. B. Truax and R. R. Carkhuff, "Significant developments in psychotherapy research," in Abt and Reiss, (Eds.), *Progress in Clinical Psychology*, New York: 1964.

Journal of Clinical Psychology for: C. B. Truax and R. R. Carkhuff, "Concreteness: A neglected variable in the psychotherapeutic process," 1964, 20, *2*, 264-267; C. B. Truax and R. R. Carkhuff, "Personality change in hospitalized mental patients during group psychotherapy as a function of alternate sessions and vicarious therapy pre-training," 1965, *21*, 225-228; and C. B. Truax, R. R. Carkhuff, and F. Kodman, Jr., "Relationships between therapist-offered conditions and patient change in group psychotherapy," 1965, *21*, 327-329.

Journal of Consulting Psychology for: R. R. Carkhuff and C. B. Truax, "Training in counseling and psychotherapy: An evaluation of an integrated didactic and experiential approach," 1965, *29*, 333-336; R. R. Carkhuff and C. B. Truax, "Lay mental health counseling: The effects of lay group counseling," 1965, *29*, 426-431; and C. B. Truax and R. R. Carkhuff, "The experimental manipulation of therapeutic conditions," 1965, *29*, 119-124.

Journal of Counseling Psychology for: C. B. Truax and R. R. Carkhuff, "Client and therapist transparency in the psychotherapeutic encounter," 1965, *12*, 3-9; C. B. Truax, R. R. Carkhuff and J. Douds, "Toward an integration of the didactic and experiential approaches to training in counseling and psychotherapy," 1964, *11*, 240-247; and C. B. Truax, "Effective ingredients in psychotherapy: An approach to unraveling the patient-therapist interaction," 1963, *3*, 256-263.

AUTHOR INDEX

SUBJECT INDEX